The Palgrave Handbook of Occupational Stress

"This book is an impressive multidisciplinary compilation of chapters, written by esteemed international scholars, on the rapidly expanding field of stress research psychobiology. The book's unique strength is a strong focus on aspects of occupational stress, and so the readers are expected to benefit markedly from both conceptual (biological) and practical (workplace stress) sides of this publication."

—Prof. Allan V. Kalueff, PhD, DrSci, *President of the International Stress and Behavior Society (ISBS)*

"Despite technology being developed and adopted to make our life easier, we are constantly pressed to achieve more. Whether it is in a personal or professional context, this burden causes stress which eventually affects all aspects of our life, including our performance. This comprehensive book covers all aspects of stress at work, including how it can be managed, and more importantly, prevented, and recognized! Based on collective expertise, it is highly relevant to both employees and managers from all industry sectors."

—Guillaume Alinier, PhD, *Director of Research, Hamad Medical Corporation Ambulance Service, Doha Qatar*

Philippe Fauquet-Alekhine • James Erskine
Editors

The Palgrave Handbook of Occupational Stress

palgrave
macmillan

Editors
Philippe Fauquet-Alekhine
SEBE-Lab, Department of Psychological and
Behavioural Science
London School of Economics and
Political Science
London, UK

James Erskine
London Hertfordshire Therapy Centre
St George's University of London
London, UK

Laboratory for Research in Science of Energy
Montagret, France

Groupe INTRA Robotics
Avoine, France

ISBN 978-3-031-27348-3   ISBN 978-3-031-27349-0   (eBook)
https://doi.org/10.1007/978-3-031-27349-0

© The Editor(s) (if applicable) and The Author(s), under exclusive licence to Springer Nature Switzerland AG 2023
This work is subject to copyright. All rights are solely and exclusively licensed by the Publisher, whether the whole or part of the material is concerned, specifically the rights of translation, reprinting, reuse of illustrations, recitation, broadcasting, reproduction on microfilms or in any other physical way, and transmission or information storage and retrieval, electronic adaptation, computer software, or by similar or dissimilar methodology now known or hereafter developed.
The use of general descriptive names, registered names, trademarks, service marks, etc. in this publication does not imply, even in the absence of a specific statement, that such names are exempt from the relevant protective laws and regulations and therefore free for general use.
The publisher, the authors, and the editors are safe to assume that the advice and information in this book are believed to be true and accurate at the date of publication. Neither the publisher nor the authors or the editors give a warranty, expressed or implied, with respect to the material contained herein or for any errors or omissions that may have been made. The publisher remains neutral with regard to jurisdictional claims in published maps and institutional affiliations.

Cover illustration © Hayri Er / Getty Images

This Palgrave Macmillan imprint is published by the registered company Springer Nature Switzerland AG.
The registered company address is: Gewerbestrasse 11, 6330 Cham, Switzerland

Foreword[1]

The book you are about to start reading will no doubt prove to be a profitable investment in reading time and money.

That stress has significant individual, organisational, and macroeconomic costs is now widely accepted. Individuals bear human costs such as death and grief, emotional strain, reduced quality of life, or reduced relational quality with family. Work organisations bear costs related to absenteeism, presenteeism, staff turnover, loss of quality, and poor social cooperation. Public health systems bear financial costs of psychosocial risk-related diseases and disorders, be they mental (depression, anxiety, sleep disorders, etc.) or somatic (in particular, cardiovascular diseases and musculoskeletal disorders, not to mention diabetes or cancer). All in all, the estimated costs of stress are tremendous: €617 billion each year in the European Union in a EU-funded survey (Matrix, 2013), or $200–300 billion in the United States (Blanding, 2015).

Such amounts probably explain why the literature on stress is pervasive and ubiquitous. As a scholar in burnout, exhaustion, and organisational health, I would say popular books usually suggest lists of recipes and tips to overcome stress on an everyday basis. Consulting books offer intervention strategies for organisational life. Academic books try to define, to circumscribe, or, on the contrary, to expand the concept, or to understand how stress impacts decision-making, organisational climate, and quality. Those destined for posterity emit compelling theoretical propositions or models, such as Seyle's *The Stress of Life* (1956), Siegrist and Wahrendorf's *Work*

---

[1] Co-editor of the French Psychosocial Risks dictionary (Zawieja, P., & Guarnieri, F. (2014). *Dictionnaire des risques psychosociaux* (pp. 882-pages). Paris: Le Seuil.)

Stress and Health in a Globalized Economy: The Model of Effort-Reward Imbalance (2018), Karasek's *Healthy Work: Stress, Productivity, and the Reconstruction of Working Life*, or Hobfoll's *Stress, Culture, and Community: The Psychology and Philosophy of Stress* (1998).

The Palgrave Handbook of Occupational Stress is one of these promising reference books, in my view. This book distinguishes itself by several strengths.

First, it is *exhaustive and up-to-date*, which may seem the least that can be done when editing a book but proves particularly difficult and touchy when using such a multifaceted, ever evolving, and interdisciplinary material as stress.

Second, it is *innovative*, and will help its readers be innovative too in their analyses and interventions: chapters dedicated to simulation, to diary techniques while assessing stress, and to coping skills when hiring are particularly insightful.

Last, it raises in passing crucial questions. Among the most relevant, I would mention ethics in evaluative approaches and psychological assessment; sex variability in stress response, even in animal models, which advocate for further research and probably for sex- or gender-differentiated interventions; and cultural variability in stress perceptions and responses, which is of particular importance in a globalised economy, with a culturally diverse workforce.

These are the reasons why this book will be beneficial reading for stress scholars in organisational and business psychology and sociology, for professionals in human resources, and, more generally, managers in public and private organisations, and for consultants, who will find fertile ideas to renew their intervention strategies.

AlterNego Consulting, Paris, France   Philippe Zawieja
Observatory on Health and
Wellbeing at Work, University of Montreal
Montreal, QC, Canada
Research Centre Psychoanalysis,
Medicine, and Society
Université Paris-Cité, Paris, France
Literature, Science & Medicine
University of Florence, Florence, Italy
Project in Medical Humanities
University of Lisbon, Lisbon, Portugal

References

Blanding, M. (2015). Workplace stress responsible for up to $190B in annual U.S. healthcare costs. *Forbes*, January 26.

Matrix. (2013). *Economic analysis of workplace mental health promotion and mental disorder prevention programmes and of their potential contribution to EU health, social and economic policy objectives.* Executive Agency for Health and Consumers, Specific Request EAHC/2011/Health/19 for the Implementation of Framework Contract EAHC/2010/Health/01 Lot 2, 2013. http://ec.europa.eu/health/mental_health/docs/matrix_economic_analysis_mh_promotion_en.pdf

Contents

1	**Introduction**	1
	Philippe Fauquet-Alekhine and James Erskine	

Part I   Stress Description   5

2	**Conceptualization of Stress**	7
	Vsevolod Rozanov	
3	**The Cycle of Stress**	25
	Philippe Fauquet-Alekhine and Laetitia Rouillac	
4	**Animal Models in Neuroscience: A Focus on Stress**	47
	Victoria Luine	

Part II   Stress Assessment   63

5	**Physiological Assessment of the State of Mental Stress at Work**	65
	Philippe Fauquet-Alekhine and Jean-Claude Granry	
6	**Psychological Assessment of the State of Mental Stress at Work**	97
	Philippe Fauquet-Alekhine and Anne Boucherand	

x   Contents

7   Stress Assessment in Daily Life Using the Experience Sampling Method   117
Thomas Vaessen, Ulrich Reininghaus, and Inez Myin-Germeys

8   Psychosocial Risks at Work: Fundamentals and Stakes   137
Philippe Fauquet-Alekhine

9   Psychosocial Risks at Work: Outlines of the Evaluation Approach   151
Philippe Fauquet-Alekhine and Nicolas Roudevitch

10   Assessment of Psychosocial Risks: Methods   167
Philippe Fauquet-Alekhine

11   Assessment of Psychosocial Risks: Questionnaire Review   197
Philippe Fauquet-Alekhine

12   Visualising Results of a Psychosocial Risks Assessment through Questionnaires   207
Philippe Fauquet-Alekhine

Part III   Using Stress at Work   219

13   Leadership Styles: Work Stress, Related Outcomes and Health   221
James Erskine and George Georgiou

14   Leadership Styles, Related Outcomes and Practical Suggestions   257
James Erskine and George Georgiou

15   Occupational Training, Competencies, and Stress   269
Philippe Fauquet-Alekhine, Marion Buchet, Julien Bleuze, and Charlotte Lenoir

16   Stress Adjustment as a Criterion for Hiring in High-Risk Jobs   299
Frédéric Choisay, Solange Duvillard-Monternier, Vanessa Fournier, Ghislain Champeaux, Alexandre Rey, and Jean-Louis Dubert

Contents   xi

Part IV   Macro Description of Stress   319

17   Cross-cultural Ideas on Stress   321
Philippe Fauquet-Alekhine and James Erskine

18   Stress in Different Professional Sectors   337
Philippe Fauquet-Alekhine and James Erskine

19   The Impact of Stress Among Undergraduate Students: Supporting Resilience and Wellbeing Early in Career Progression   347
Linda Perkins-Porras

Part V   Dealing with Stress   373

20   Stress Prevention Measures in the Workplace   375
James Erskine and Philippe Fauquet-Alekhine

21   Stress Management   437
Bruno Guion de Meritens and Philippe Fauquet-Alekhine

22   Stress and Resilience in the Workplace   455
James Erskine and George Georgiou

23   Pharmacology for Stress   485
Philippe Fauquet-Alekhine and Jean-Claude Granry

24   Conclusion   499
James Erskine and Philippe Fauquet-Alekhine

Index   503

Notes on Contributors

Julien Bleuze received a Masters of Nuclear Engineering from the University of Valence-Grenoble (France), with a speciality addressing Radioactive Waste Management. He also has a Bachelor's in Environment, Analytical Chemistry and Ecosystems, and is Radioprotection Officer (level III) specialized in nuclear reactors.

Bleuze began his professional career as Project Engineer at ORANO, working on the facilities of ORANO and CEA (Commissariat à l'Energie Atomique et aux énérgies renouvelables), with a special focus on teleoperated decommissioning. He was a member of the national intervention force of ORANO (Force d'Intervention NAtionale). He was then Chargé d'Affaires on decommissioning and joined Groupe INTRA robotics in 2015 as Project Engineer. He took the position of Scientific and Technical Director in 2019 and then Director of Operations in 2020.

Bleuze's competencies cover the field of intervention in hostile environments, with versatility in interventions in nuclear environments (interventional robotics, emergency response, operation of nuclear installations at ORANO and CEA, radiation protection, decommissioning).

Bleuze is Senior Expert Engineer in Robotics of Groupe INTRA robotics and was awarded first prize at the AREVA Innovation Challenge in 2010. He is author and co-author of several papers and book chapters addressing interventional robotics.

Anne Boucherand Work Psychologist from Grenoble University (France), Boucherand works at the Operation Engineering Offices (EDF-UNIE, Paris) as an expert on Operational and Conservative Decision Making and Safety Culture. Previously, she worked at the 900 MWe Nuclear Power Plant (NPP)

xiv **Notes on Contributors**

of Chinon and the 1400 MWe NPP of Civaux (France) after a short period at the World Health Organization (Geneva, Switzerland). She is specialized in the ergonomy of work stations, involved in analysis of work organization, safety, and security management, and also in experimental psychology research regarding work activity, occupational stress, and training. She has contributed to several scientific communications on these topics.

Marion Buchet was a fighter pilot in the Armée de l'Air et de l'Espace for more than 20 years. She has nearly 3000 hours of flight time on the Mirage 2000, the Mirage F1, and the Alphajet. Passionate about cognitive psychology, she holds a Bachelor's degree in Psychology and develops, in her lectures, topics related to decision-making, performance determinants, and emotion management.

She transitioned to the private sector as a top executive for a cybersecurity publisher. She serves on the board of directors at CARAC and is a member to the risk committee.

Ghislain Champeaux is a work psychologist engaged in leading psychological interviews for the French Air Force as part of selection processes for new recruits and militaries.

In parallel, he is an educator in Tactics to Optimize the Potential. He helped health professionals during the COVID crisis to manage their emotions and stress, and to maintain their motivation. Throughout his course, he trained him in stress, in post-traumatic stress disorder and complicated mourning.

During his Masters degree, he worked on social psychology (LPNC CNRS—UMR 5105; CeRCA CNRS—UMR 7295), social cognition, implicit cognition, group stereotypes, discrimination, legal psychology, and occupational settings. His Masters thesis deals with national symbols as triggers of nationalism, antisemitism, and Islamophobia.

Frédéric Choisay is a senior officer in the French Air and Space Force (FASF). He was a transport pilot and flight instructor for 15 years. He has been working in an executive position at the FASF Centre for Psychological Studies and Researches since 2014. He is in charge of multiple projects dealing with personnel selection (e.g., fighter pilots, special forces) and flight instructor training. More precisely, he has managed major updates for the selection processes for air traffic controllers and pilots, including improvement of predictive validity for these jobs.

A doctor in Work and Organizational Psychology (Université de Tours, France), Choisay is an associate member of the EE 1901 QualiPsy research team in the psychology department of the University of Tours, whose main purpose is to conduct research dealing with life quality and psychological health at work. His main research subject involves examining the role of personal resources (e.g., psychological capital, hardiness) in stressful environments such as the armed forces. He is the author of several scientific articles for peer-reviewed journals and popularization literature. He is also a lecturer for graduate students in Work and Organizational Psychology.

Jean-Louis Dubert is a recruiting officer at the CERP'Air, a communications teacher, a psychopedagogical trainer for pilot instructors, and a math teacher.

Dubert has been a pilot for high-ranking civil and military personalities. Trainer in techniques for optimizing potential and stress management, he created a unit to take charge of student pilots suffering from stress in training. He has been a transport pilot trainer, instructor trainer, and pilot examiner trainer. He worked at the Directorate General for Civil Aviation, the Directorate of Security Control, and the Office of Training and Schools. Former director of the CERP'Air, he conducts recruitment sessions and pursues research activities in applied psychology for the development of selection processes of candidates for recruitment in the French Air Force. In particular, he developed a spatial orientation test adapted to the recruitment of air traffic controllers. Dubert is working on an inventory of motivations and professional interests and participating in the development of an attention management test adapted to the recruitment of fighter pilots.

Solange Duvillard-Monternier is a senior officer in the French Air and Space Force (FASF).

After five years as a non-commissioned officer engineer in a fighter squadron, she passed an internal competitive exam and became an officer in 1995. She practiced as an Information/Communication System's engineer until 2004, and then began the second part of her career in the field of social sciences and humanities. She obtained the title of psychologist in 2007 and received her PhD in 2014. Her studies and research focus on the abilities of Remotely Piloted Aircraft operators. In 2013, she joined the CERP'Air and implemented these selection process: Sensor Operator in 2014, RPA's pilots in 2018, Tactical Coordinator in 2020 in the French Air and Space Force (FASF). From 2017 to December 2020, she co-supervised the thesis work of Mr Ferrandez, in partnership with the CerCA/CNRS (Research Centre on Cognition and Learning/French National Centre for Scientific Research) of Tours/Poitiers. From 2019 to July 2022, she assumed command of the CERP'Air as director. Since August 2022, she has been responsible for the team Crew Resource Management at the French Armed Forces Biomedical Research Insititute.

James Erskine (BSc Psychology, MSc Research Methods and Statistics, PhD Psychology, DCounsPsy) is Senior Lecturer at St George's University of London, UK. He is involved in teaching the psychological and psychiatric components of the MBBS medical degrees and Biomedical Sciences BScs. In addition to academic research and teaching, Erskine is also a qualified clinician with a second doctorate in Counselling Psychology, and continues to see patients in clinical practice.

Erskines' research interests focus on methods of coping with difficult life events such as poverty, divorce, death, and job loss, among others. He has authored numerous academic papers, as well as book chapters on different methods of coping and their effects. His research interests and clinical interests focus on building resilience in individuals and companies. Toward that end he is starting a new venture with the express aim of building individuals' capacity to be resilient across a range of situations.Erskine is a chartered member of the British Psychological Society (BPS—chartered in counselling psychology), and Member of the Health and Care Professions Council.

Philippe Fauquet-Alekhine is Scientific Director at INTRA robotics, in charge of international projects addressing training and performance of pilots in operational situations. He is also former Human Factors Consultant and& Researcher at Chinon nuclear power plant (Electricité de France). He is a member of the Laboratory for Research in Science of Energy (France: www.hayka-kultura.org) and of the SEBE-Lab at the London School of Economics and Political Science (UK: www.SEBE-Lab.net).

Doctor in Physics Science (Pierre and Marie Curie University, Paris, France), Work Psychologist (MSc from the Conservatoire national des arts et métiers, Paris, France), Doctor in Behavioural Psychology (London School of Economics and Political Science, UK), Fauquet-Alekhine is author of numerous scientific articles and books. He has more than 20 years' experience in work activity analysis and research applied to human performance within high-risk industries. He contributes to research and interventions in firms regarding the study of humans in work situations, work organization, and management, with a special focus on the effect of stress on performance. He collaborated on research in psychosociology at the Institute of Social Psychology and in the Department of Psychological and Behavioural Science (LSE, London, UK), and also at the Hospital of Paris, Angers and Toulouse (France). In the industrial field, he investigates aerospace, aeronautics (civil and military), navy, nuclear industry, and medicine. He has received several awards mainly related to his work addressing stress at work.

Fauquet-Alekhine (co)edited the following publications:

- *Améliorer la pratique professionnelle par la simulation*, Fauquet-Alekhine, Ph., & Pehuet, N. (2011)
- *Simulation Training: Fundamentals and Applications*, Fauquet-Alekhine, Ph., & Pehuet, N. (2015) Springer Verlag,
- *Knowledge Management in High-Risk Industries: Coping with Skills Drain*, Fauquet-Alekhine, Ph. (2020) Palgrave Macmillan,

Fauquet-Alekhine is Member of the American Psychological Association, Chartered Member of the British Psychological Society, Life Member of the International Stress and Behavior Society, Member of IAENG Society of Mechanical Engineering, and Member of the American Association for Science and Technology.

Vanessa Fournier Work Psychologist, participates in the selection process of applicants or personnel from the Armed Forces Ministry (CERP'Air, Air-Base 705, Tours, France). In this context, Fournier drives training courses on interview techniques and acts as Gender Equality Referent, through the implementation of prevention, awareness-campaign, and listening actions with people who are victims of harassment, discrimination, and sexual violence, as well as providing advice to the Base Commander.

Since obtaining a PhD in Social Psychology (Lille University, PSITEC EA 4072 laboratory) on gender socialization, Fournier has been an associate member of CRTD EA 4132 Laboratory, "gender and guidance" axis (INETOP, Paris, France). Her studies rely on guidance behavior, for example her participation in the French Ministry of Higher Education, Research and Innovation-financed project entitled "The emotional impact of ParcourSup on guidance guidelines" (CRTD-CNAM, 2020) and its latest publication:

- Fournier, V., De Bosscher, S., & Durand-Delvigne, A. Professional aspirations of young adults in female vs male vocational training: a gendered educational guidance maintained ? (Dunod, 2020)

Associate Member of the Cognitive and Behavioral Techniques French Association, Fournier conducts a three-year training course in Cognitive and Behavioral Techniques. The aim of this training is to support people in work distress, using cognitive and behavioral techniques, by considering both individual and work organization, under the prism of social and work psychology.

xviii Notes on Contributors

George Georgiou is a senior lecturer in Psychology at the University of Hertfordshire, teaching in the areas of cyberpsychology and statistics, and is the Deputy Head of the Centre for Research in Psychology and Sport Sciences at the university. Georgiou is a Chartered Psychologist (CPsychol) and Associate Fellow of the British Psychological Society (BPS), and a Chartered Scientist with the Science Council, UK. He has previously served on the committees of the BPS Cyberpsychology Section and the Cognitive Psychology Section. Georgiou has published impactful peer-reviewed papers, organized conference symposia, and presented at national and international conferences. His research interests span the areas of cognition, cyberpsychology, health, and occupational psychology, in particular cognition and health, leadership and resilience, problem-solving and creativity, and the impact of digital technologies on thinking, behavior, and wellbeing.

Jean-Claude Granry Is Professor Emeritus at the University of Angers, France, certified with Habilitation à diriger des Recherches (empowerment to conduct and supervise research). He is also former Head Manager of the Anesthesiology and Intensive Care Department at University Hospital of Angers, expert at the French national health regulator (Haute Autorité de Santé), and President-Founder of the French language society of medical simulation (Société Francophone de Simulation en Santé).

Bruno Guion de Meritens graduated from the Special Military School of Saint-Cyr, Technical Patent Higher Military Studies (CSEM 111th Promotion) and Superior Military Studies Patent (Joint Defence College 6th Promotion). He was Platoon Leader, Deputy Officer to the Company Commander and Commander of the 141st engineering company of the 9th Marine Infantry Division. Officer Editor on the Army Staff for four years, he became Head of the Regiment's Operations Office of the 1st Civil Security Training and Intervention Regiment in Nogent-le-Rotrou in 2002. He was Commander of the 7th Civil Security Training and Intervention Regiment in Brignoles between 2004 and 2006. From 2006 to 2011 he was Deputy Colonel to the General commanding the Military Civil Security regiments. Since retiring, he has been a civil security expert on the Nuclear Rapid Action Force staff (EDF) since 2013.

Auditor of the Centre for Higher Armament Studies (45th national session) and auditor of the National Institute of Higher Security Studies (19th promotion,) he has more than 35 years' experience in mine-clearance, combat of engineers, aid to the population, crisis management in a national crisis cell (earthquakes, storms, cyclones, floods, shortages, management of NRBC incidents, counter-terrorism, technological accidents, securing multinational summits or gatherings). He also has solid experience in operational crisis leadership: detachment leader in military operations, civil-military and humanitarian actions (repatriation of French nationals from Lebanon), storms, floods or cyclones, maritime and land pollution, forest fires, searches for mass graves, and neutralizing explosive charges.

Charlotte Lenoir prepares a PhD in Psychology at the Conservatoire National des Arts & Métiers, France. She has worked in several organizations opening various fields of psychology such as IFF Europe (youth support) in Belgium or Groupe INTRA robotics (robotic intervention in accident) in France. Lenoir was a member of the scientific committee of the 11th edition of the International Workshop INTRA (IWIN2021) in 2021. She has several publications to her credit in the field of psychology.

Victoria Luine received her PhD in Pharmacology at the State University of New York at Buffalo. Before joining Hunter College, she was Associate Professor of Neuroendocrinology at Rockefeller University in NYC. Luine has a worldwide reputation presenting lectures in the USA, Europe, and Asia, and is the recipient of numerous government and private grants and awards. Her research utilizes rodents to understand the biological underpinnings of how hormones, both adrenal and gonadal, alter neural function, which leads to impairments or enhancements, respectively, of cognition and also alters affect/mood. Her studies were among the first to highlight important sex differences in neural responses to hormones and long-term alterations of brain functioning especially following chronic stressors. Luine directed several National Institutes of Health programs at Hunter College which supported research for undergraduate and graduate students (RISE), and improved the research environment and enhanced the ability of the faculty to conduct biomedical research (SCORE). She was the first recipient of the Bernice Grafstein Award for mentoring (2009) from the Society for Neuroscience, and has received many CUNY Chancellor's Awards for Scholarship and Public Service, as well as the Association for Women in Science's Outstanding Woman Scientist, NYC Chapter award. She maintains collaborative research at Hunter College and other universities, as well as serving on government review panels and writing and editing for the scientific community. She serves as a Grant Writing Coach for the National Resource Mentoring Network, the Leadership Alliance, and Society for Neuroscience.

Notes on Contributors

Inez Myin-Germeys is a psychologist and professor of Contextual Psychiatry at KU Leuven, Belgium. She is the head of the Center for Contextual Psychiatry (CCP), a research lab with over 25 researchers, that she founded in 2015. Myin-Germeys is a world-renowned expert in the field of Experience Sampling Methodology (ESM) and mobile Health (mHealth) in relation to psychopathology in general, and psychosis in particular. The CCP is focusing on the study of stress-sensitivity and altered social interactions in the development of psychopathology, on the clinical implementation of ESM as a tool for self-management and shared decision-making, on the development of new Ecological Momentary Interventions, and on research from a first-person perspective. Myin-Germeys received an European Research Council (ERC) consolidator grant in 2012 and an ERC proof-of-concept grant in 2019, and she is the principal investigator of IMMERSE, a Horizon2020 implementation grant. She also received a highly prestigious 5.2 m euro brain gain Odysseus grant from the Flemish Research Council. She has published over 400 papers and supervised over 30 PhD projects.

Linda Perkins-Porras is a senior lecturer in Behavioural Medicine and Psychology at St George's University of London. She completed her undergraduate degree at Bristol University and a PhD in Psychology at University College London. This was followed by a research fellowship at University College London jointly funded by the Medical Research Council and Economic and Social Research Council. Prior to this she had 20 years of clinical experience working as a critical care nurse and was awarded the Royal College of Nursing Research Society New Researcher's Award. She trained in cognitive behavior therapy at Goldsmiths,, University of London. As well as teaching the psychology and behavioral medicine curriculum on the undergraduate medical and biomedical science courses, she leads the pastoral support and personal tutoring program for over 1500 medical students at St George's, and has recently introduced a range of measures aimed at improving engagement. She supervises research students and has over 40 publications in peer-reviewed journals. Her research interests include investigating stress, wellbeing, resilience, and burnout in staff, patients, and students, and developing psychological interventions to support wellbeing.

Recent publications:

- Perkins-Porras L; Riaz M; Okekunle A; Zhelezna S; Chakravorty I; Ussher M (2018) Feasibility study to assess the effect of a brief mindfulness intervention for patients with chronic obstructive pulmonary disease: A Randomized Controlled Trial. Chronic Respiratory Disease 15 (4): 400–410.

- Colville G, Dawson D, Rabinthiran S, Chaudry-Daley Z, Perkins-Porras L. A survey of moral distress in staff working in intensive care in the UK. Journal of the Intensive Care Society. 2019;20(3): 196–203.
- Howarth A, Riaz M, Perkins-Porras L, Smith JG, Subramaniam J, Copland C, Hurley M, Beith I, Ussher M. Pilot randomised controlled trial of a brief mindfulness-based intervention for those with persistent pain. J Behav Med. 2019 Dec;42(6): 999–1014.
- Colville GA, Smith JG, Brierley J, Citron K, Nguru NM, Shaunak PD, Tam O, Perkins-Porras L. Coping With Staff Burnout and Work-Related Posttraumatic Stress in Intensive Care. Pediatr Crit Care Med. 2017 Jul;18(7): e267–e273.

Ulrich Reininghaus is a lecturer in the Health and Population Research Department, Institute of Psychiatry, King's College London, and a Postdoctoral Research Fellow in the Department of Psychiatry and Psychology, School for Mental Health and Neuroscience, Maastricht University.

His scientific career to date has been that of a psychologist with a strong interest in social psychiatry and psychiatric epidemiology, focusing on the onset, course, and outcome of psychosis. Reininghaus was awarded a PhD in Social and Community Psychiatry by Queen Mary University of London in 2011, having previously obtained an MSc in Mental Health Studies at the Institute of Psychiatry, Kings College London in 2005, and a Diploma in Psychology (Dipl.-Psych.) at the University of Hamburg in 2006. His studies were funded by a scholarship grant by the Evangelisches Studienwerk, Villigst, Germany. Reininghaus was formerly a research associate at the Department of Psychiatry, University of Cambridge, working on the 10-year Medical Research Council-funded follow-up of the Aetiology and Ethnicity in Schizophrenia and Other Psychoses study, and a Research Fellow at Queen Mary University of London, funded through a doctoral Research Training Fellowship by the National Institute for Health Research (NIHR), UK. The research he conducts as part of his NIHR Postdoctoral Research Fellowship at the Institute of Psychiatry, King's College London, uses the Experience Sampling Method to investigate stress sensitivity, aberrant salience, and threat anticipation as potential candidate mechanisms through which exposure to social adversity, particularly in childhood, may increase risk for psychosis. His work at Maastricht University is funded by a Veni grant from the Nederlandse Organisatie voor Wetenschappelijk Onderzoek to investigate whether reasoning biases are a causal mechanism in the development of delusions in daily life, combining a real-life temporal association with an interventionist causal-model approach. Reininghaus is also a co-investigator at the South London site of the HTA-funded NEgative

Symptoms of Schizophrenia trial and is involved in the analysis of experience sampling data of the European Network of National Networks studying Gene-Environment Interactions in Schizophrenia.

Alexandre Rey is Senior Officer at the CERP'Air, and is in charge of developing and updating the selection process concerning 20 different specialties for the French Air and Space Force (FASF) and more specifically for pilots.

A fighter pilot for 18 years, Rey took part in several operations in Chad and Central African Republic. FASF took advantage of his experience as an instructor at the fighter pilot school for nine years.

A work psychologist since 2016, he is now an expert in analyzing cognitive tests to predict potential formation success of candidates for pilot selection. In his work interpreting personality tests, he is used to identifying stress coping strategies used by candidates and balancing these with job demand.

As a researcher, he is working on creating a test to detect during the selection process the ability for candidates to efficiently prioritize information. This ability is increasingly in force on last generation aircraft.

Rey also develops formation courses on the psychological process involved in instruction flights in order to certify and improve instructor formation.

Nicolas Roudevitch is an ergonomist. He was the manager of a risk center in an occupational health service in France (SIST79) and his job involved intervening in client companies between 2003 and 2010. Since 2010, he is Human Factor Consultant at Chinon nuclear power plant in France and is mainly involved in organization and work analyses.

Laetitia Rouillac is a clinical and work psychologist. She has opened her own private practice in Munich, mainly for the French-speaking population. As an integrative clinical psychologist, she sees patients of all ages. She has an additional interest in play therapy with children and biodecoding for helping sick people.

Rouillac also has significant experience in pediatric hospitals working with sick children, in nurseries, in psychiatry, and in geriatrics. Previously as work psychologist, she has worked in recruitment and human resources at several major international firms. Author and co-author of several articles on work psychology, she is pursuing her studies in these domains, through research. In parallel, she also accompanies othersin their skills assessments.

Vsevolod Rozanov received his MD from Odessa Pirogov Medical Institute and a PhD in Clinical Biochemistry from Kiev Bogomolets Medical Institute. In addition, he received his Doctor of Medical Science degree in Neurochemistry and Neuropharmacology from the People's Friendship University of Russia,

Moscow. Later he specialized in Suicidology and Mental Health Promotion at Karolinska Institute, Stockholm.

Rozanov is a full professor of Suicidology and Medical Psychology in the Department of Psychology of Saint Petersburg State University, a Chief Scientist at V.M. Bekhterev Psychiatry and Neurology Center, and an affiliated professor at NASP, Karolinska Institute (Stockholm, Sweden). He has been a leader of several international projects dedicated to suicide genetics and mental health promotion in the young and elderly, and is the author of more than 360 published articles, chapters, and books. His main scientific contribution addresses biological aspects of suicidal behavior, especially in relation to stress-vulnerability. Rozanov has extensive experience in analysis of the role of psychosocial stress in modern trends in mental health and suicide. He is a well-known lecturer and speaker at public events, and organized of a series of training seminars for suicide prevention in different settings, including schools and for the military.

Rozanov is a member of the suicidology sections of the World Psychiatric Association and of the European Psychiatric Association, and is an active member of the International Association of Suicide Prevention. In 2016, he was inducted as International Stress and Behavior Society Fellow and Life Member. He is the author of *Stress and Epigenetics in Suicide* published by Elsevier in 2017.

Thomas Vaessen PhD, from the Department of Psychiatry and Psychology, School for Mental Health and Neuroscience, Maastricht University, acquired a Bachelor's degree in Biological Psychology and a research Masters degree in Clinical and Cognitive Neuroscience at Maastricht University. His interests lie in experimental psychopathology and neuroscience with a focus on biobehavioral mechanisms of psychopathological symptomatology. Vaessen gained hands-on experience in this field working at the Department of Clinical Psychological Science, Maastricht University, the Oxford Centre for Functional Magnetic Resonance Imaging of the Brain, Oxford University, and the International Research Training Group Brain-behavior relationship of emotion and social cognition in schizophrenia and autism, Rheinisch-Westfälische Technische Hochschule Aachen University. In addition, he has gathered experience as a psychological therapist working at the Regionale Instelling voor Ambulante Geestelijke Gezondheidszorg and at Mondriaan, in Maastricht. His research focuses on the neurobiological and biobehavioral stress response in psychosis and the effectiveness of intervention strategies that focus on stress reduction.

List of Figures

Fig. 3.1	The two 3-D space model for short-term occupational stress	27
Fig. 3.2	Human Functional States divided into three main parts: (i) central part: transient state for the subject in terms of stress effects, (ii) left part: positive state of stress, (iii) right part: potential cognitive deficit state (Source: Fauquet-Alekhine et al., 2014)	29
Fig. 3.3	The nervous system of humans	30
Fig. 3.4	Structure of the human brain	32
Fig. 3.5	The adrenergic axis of the autonomous nervous system	33
Fig. 3.6	The corticotropic axis of the autonomous nervous system	34
Figs. 3.7a and b	Variations of adrenaline and cortisol during an acute stress episode for heathy human adults (from Kuebler et al., 2013)	36
Figs. 3.8a and b	Extrapolation of variations of adrenaline and cortisol during repeated acute stress episodes (extrapolated from Kuebler et al., 2013)	37
Fig. 4.1	Schematic of hippocampal CA3 pyramidal neuron pre and post chronic stress	55
Fig. 5.1	HR variation with stress for healthy adult subjects submitted to acute mental stress	67
Fig. 5.2	Example of signal monitored when measuring heart rate	68
Fig. 5.3	Chest strap equipped with sensors. Signal transmitted to a memory buffer of a smartphone. Treatment on computer	69
Fig. 5.4	Example of comparison of mean HR for a sample of heathy male young adults (data from Kudielka et al., 2004) under two different experimental conditions: at rest and under stress	69

xxvi   **List of Figures**

Fig. 5.5   On the left, a sample of HR, and on the right, a spectrum of frequencies (or probability density function (PDF) of frequencies) showing two main components associated with LF and HF of HR   71

Fig. 5.6   Example of comparison of mean HR mean HRV for a sample of heathy young adults (data from McDuff et al., 2014) under two different experimental conditions: at rest and under stress   71

Fig. 5.7   Blood pressure with time during cardiac cycles: systolic blood pressure (SBP) and diastolic blood pressure (DBP)   73

Fig. 5.8   Breathing rate (BR) and HRV under rest and stress conditions (data from McDuff et al., 2014)   76

Fig. 5.9   Power density function (PDF) of ventilation under rest and stress conditions (data from Gutierrez et al., 2011)   77

Fig. 5.10   Measuring principle of skin conductance: an electric tension is applied between two probes pasted on the hand and the electrical intensity is measured to access the conductance G_s 78

Fig. 6.1   Factors of stress at work   98

Fig. 7.1   (**a**–**c**) Subject filling out an ESM questionnaire on a smartphone application in different daily situations   122

Fig. 8.1   Representation of a risk of constant value depending on the intensity of the hazard (or potential severity) and the probability of being confronted with that hazard   141

Fig. 8.2   The risk depends on the likelihood of being confronted with the hazard. The hazard is the fall into the void, which is more important than the height. In (**a**), the risk is low because the distance from the hazard is great and reduces the likelihood of exposure to hazard. In (**b**), the risk is significant because the distance from the hazard is small and increases the likelihood of exposure to hazard   142

Fig. 9.1   Model of quality improvement illustrated by the Deming wheel   161

Fig. 9.2   Continuous improvement model for the intervention process for the evaluation of PSRs   162

Fig. 9.3   Scheme of the categorisation of PSR factors according to Gollac and Bodier (2010)   164

Fig. 9.4   Scheme of the categorisation of PSR factors according to Leka et al. (2003)   165

Fig. 10.1   Time is a factor of stress for all participants in the PSR evaluation, including the analyst   175

Fig. 10.2   Scheme of the categorisation of PSR factors according to Gollac and Bodier (2010)   194

Fig. 10.3   Scheme of the categorisation of PSR factors according to Leka et al. (2003)   195

Fig. 12.1   Distribution of Loevinger's H coefficient values for the pairs of categories presented in Table 12.2 (N is the number of values per range)   215

Fig. 12.2	Example of results obtained with the JSS. Distribution of items according to their index as a function of intensity	216
Fig. 12.3	Average JSS index per Gollac group category	216
Fig. 12.4	Average indexes obtained with the JSS by category of the Gollac group. Example of possible evolution between two assessments of psychosocial risks, the first assessment being visualised in Fig. 12.3	217
Fig. 15.1	Example of simulation training for the piloting of nuclear reactors (hour-based simulation)—control room in the 900MW reactor	272
Fig. 15.2	Example of simulation training context for the Nuclear Rapid Action Force (FARN, France; day-based simulation)—exercise at a nuclear site	272
Fig. 15.3	Analysis by the "three-level qualitative scale" for the passage of an exam by a student: evaluation of the stressor of the situation before (**a**) and after (**b**) corrective actions is materialised by the change in shape of the stress trigon at the centre of the graph	276
Fig. 15.4	Simulator for the training of anaesthesiologists at the University of Angers (France)	283
Fig. 15.5	(**a**) Example of an indoor robot (unmanned ground vehicle); (**b**) example of a drone (unmanned aerial vehicle); (**c**) example of an outdoor robot	290
Fig. 15.6	Pilot in CBRN outfit	292
Fig. 15.7	Drivers in CBRN outfit travelling by car	293
Fig. 15.8	Pilots in CBRN outfit piloting the robot	294
Fig. 16.1	General articulation of the different predictive and evaluative tools of candidates' adaptation skills employed at the FAF Psychological Studies & Researches Center	309
Fig. 17.1	Intercomparison of the top-10 SRRS studies categorised according to seven families of concerns for the US population	322
Fig. 17.2	Intercomparison of the top-10 SRRS studies categorised according to seven families of concerns for the US population (Scully et al., 2000), Danish (Berntsen & Rubin, 2004), and Caribbean (Haque et al., 2020)	328
Fig. 17.3	The relaxing French aperitif	333
Fig. 18.1	Percentage of workers worldwide experiencing daily stress at work according to a survey conducted in 160 countries with at least 1000 respondents per country in 2021 (Gallup, 2022)	338
Fig. 18.2	Distribution of employee's perceived daily stress at work by major areas worldwide expressed as a percentage of surveyed populations in 2021 (number of respondents: more than 160,000 employees) (Gallup, 2022)	339

xxviii   List of Figures

Fig. 18.3	The 65 most work-stressed countries in the world: employee's perceived daily stress at work expressed as a percentage of surveyed populations in 2021 (number of respondents: more than 160,000 employees) (Gallup, 2022)	340
Fig. 18.4	The 65 least work-stressed countries in the world: employee's perceived daily stress at work expressed as a percentage of surveyed populations in 2021 (number of respondents: more than 160,000 employees) (Gallup, 2022)	341
Fig. 18.5	Global professional sectors most affected by burnout in 2019: proportion per sectors (Statista, 2019)	342
Fig. 18.6	Estimated prevalence and rates of self-reported stress, depression, or anxiety caused or made worse by current or most recent job, by occupation, for people working in the last 12 months in the UK, values being the number of persons concerned per 100,000 employees (Labour Force Survey: https://www.hse.gov.uk/statistics/lfs/index.htm: lfsillocc.xlsx)	343
Fig. 21.1	The two 3-D space model for short-term occupational stress	441
Fig. 23.1	Stress induced by work	486
Fig. 23.2	Drugs and stress	487
Fig. 23.3	Rate of variation of antidepressant consumption compared to 2010 based on defined daily dosage per 1000 inhabitants per day (available data for OECD countries) from 2010 to 2020. (Source: https://stats.oecd.org/; Files in: health/Pharmaceutical Market/Pharmaceutical consumption)	493
Fig. 23.4	Variation of the rate of antidepressant consumption based on defined daily dosage per 1000 inhabitants per day (available data for OECD countries) from 2018 to 2021. (Source: https://stats.oecd.org/; Files in: health/Pharmaceutical Market/Pharmaceutical consumption)	494
Fig. 23.5	Variation of the rate of anxiolytic consumption based on defined daily dosage per 1000 inhabitants per day (available data for OECD countries) from 2018 to 2021. (Source: https://stats.oecd.org/; Files in: health/Pharmaceutical Market/Pharmaceutical consumption)	494
Fig. 23.6	Antidepressant consumption—defined daily dosage per 1000 inhabitants per day for OECD countries (2010–2015–2021). (Source: https://stats.oecd.org/; Files in: health/Pharmaceutical Market/Pharmaceutical consumption)	495
Fig. 23.7	Anxiolytic consumption—defined daily dosage per 1000 inhabitants per day for OECD countries (2010–2015–2021). (Source: https://stats.oecd.org/; Files in: health/Pharmaceutical Market/Pharmaceutical consumption)	495

List of Tables

Table 4.1	Types of stresses utilized in rodent studies	50
Table 4.2	Sex differences in chronic stress effects on monoamine metabolites in brain areas of male and female rats	56
Table 5.1	Blood pressure classification for adults	74
Table 6.1	Overview of questionnaires and characteristics	101
Table 6.2	Overview of applicability of questionnaires and characteristics (JS: Job Stress)	102
Table 10.1	Summary of the steps associated with the interview group method	180
Table 10.2	Example of a grid containing the history of an evaluation	187
Table 11.1	Overview of questionnaires and characteristics, showing which categories are explored in Gollac's categorisation (Gollac & Bodier, 2010)	203
Table 12.1	Categorisation of JSS items according to the authors (Spielberger & Reheiser, 1994) and according to the Gollac group (Gollac & Bodier, 2010)	212
Table 12.2	Binary coding of the six categories of the Gollac group according to the assignment of items by category: the value 1 means that the item is assigned to this category, otherwise 0	213
Table 12.3	Loevinger's H coefficient values for the pairs of categories presented in Table 12.2	214
Table 15.1	Examples of stressors for the categorisation of Leka et al. (2003) and Leka and Jain (2010)	279
Table 16.1	Example of acute stressors of military and/or dangerous trades	303
Table 16.2	Example of environmental stressors for military and/or dangerous trades	304
Table 16.3	Example of chronic stressors of military and/or dangerous trades	305

xxx   List of Tables

Table 17.1	Top-10 items of the Social Readjustment Rating Scale (SRRS) in different studies	326
Table 17.2	List of work-related items in each of the studies using the SRRS	331
Table 20.1	Examples of the focus of interventions by the type of strategy (non-exhaustive)	386
Table 23.1	Main side effects of antidepressants (HUG, 2015)	489
Table 23.2	Main adverse reactions of benzodiazepines	490
Table 23.3	Main adverse reactions of antispychotics	491
Table 23.4	Ranking of countries regarding their consumption of antidepressants and anxiolytics, from highest to lowest values	496

1

Introduction

Philippe Fauquet-Alekhine and James Erskine

The literature on stress in general is vast, yet literature on occupational stress is a little less frequent. Most of the books are popular works for a wide audience to help people manage their stress in everyday life or at work. When considering the content of these books as a whole, none of them offers a comprehensive and exhaustive approach to the problem in terms of understanding, analysing, evaluating and managing occupational stress.

This book aims to meet this need and is addressed to the health professional as a priority, but also to workers in general since everyone is concerned by stress at work. Among the many chapters addressing occupational stress from different angles, everyone will be able to find answers corresponding to their questions, expectations or needs.

P. Fauquet-Alekhine (✉)
SEBE-Lab, Department of Psychological and Behavioural Science,
London School of Economics and Political Science, London, UK

Laboratory for Research in Science of Energy, Montagret, France

Groupe INTRA Robotics, Avoine, France
e-mail: p.fauquet-alekhine@lse.ac.uk; philippe.fauquet-alekhine@groupe-intra.com

J. Erskine
Institute for Medical and Biomedical Sciences, St George's University of London,
London, UK
e-mail: jerskine@sgul.ac.uk

© The Author(s), under exclusive license to Springer Nature Switzerland AG 2023
P. Fauquet-Alekhine, J. Erskine (eds.), *The Palgrave Handbook of Occupational Stress*,
https://doi.org/10.1007/978-3-031-27349-0_1

This book has been developed to become a valuable aid for people wishing to manage stress at work, whether before or after the onset of symptoms associated with it, whether personally or professionally.

The book is divided into five parts:

1. Stress description
2. Stress assessment
3. Using stress at work
4. Macro description of stress
5. Dealing with stress

Part I, Stress description, provides, in an approach punctuated by historical reminders, the different conceptualisations of stress and the associated models. This allows readers to gain an understanding of these different models and to make the link from one model to another or from one approach to another. The psychological and physiological mechanisms associated with different types of stress are also presented, and the concept of the stress cycle is developed for a better understanding of the links between acute and chronic stress. Finally, a discussion is proposed on the contribution of the animal model for the understanding of stress phenomena in the field of neuroscience. Our experience has shown that a good knowledge of the mechanisms of onset and manifestations of stress is necessary to understand correctly the difficulties related to stress encountered by people.

Part II, Stress assessment, presents the different techniques for assessing the state of mental stress at work, both physiologically and psychologically. In the first case, these are techniques for measuring physiological parameters varying with stress, and therefore quantified and objective data. In the second case, it is the use of scientifically validated self-positioning questionnaires that the subject will complete in order to allow the analyst to access an assessment of the stress perceived by the subject. In Part II, a chapter is specially devoted to a technique of continuous analysis of the stress perceived by the subject. Finally, five chapters are devoted to the assessment of psychosocial risks in companies. This is indeed an important point since this type of assessment aims to reduce the effects of stress at work. This is probably the main concern of most readers of the present book. These chapters present the fundamentals and stakes associated with psychosocial risks and the broad outlines of psychosocial risk assessment, and propose methods for the assessment, data analysis and evaluation report writing.

Part III, Using stress at work, whose title may seem surprising, highlights the different benefits of a better knowledge of stress at work. This section presents how managers can adjust their management methods to improve working conditions in the company, and advice is offered to achieve this objective. A chapter is devoted to training for work under stress and another is devoted to the use of stress as a criterion for hiring in companies. These chapters illustrate how stress may be seen as a resource rather than a disadvantage that should absolutely be discarded.

Part IV, Macro description of stress, presents broader considerations for understanding workplace stress. Cross-cultural ideas are first presented, followed by the link between stress and different professions, to finish with a chapter that deals with stress before entering professional life: that of students. Indeed, occupational stress does not begin with the entry into working life of individuals, but rather from academic or vocational training, the aim of this training being to integrate and transition the individual into the world of work.

Part V, Dealing with stress, the last part of this book, presents collective or individual techniques where the objective is to manage occupational stress and thus to increase performance at work or improve health at work. A special chapter is dedicated to resilience to stress in the workplace because, too often, people forget what personal resources they possess during or after episodes of stress. Finally, a chapter addressing stress pharmacology provides a portrait of the state of stress in the world population based on drug consumption data.

Our corollary objective is to make it clear to decision-makers in companies, as well as to all those who plan to intervene in the field of psychosocial risk analysis in companies, that this is a matter for specialists and not amateurs. Indeed, experience has shown the damage that ill advised and/or incompetent people can do in the field: the main negative consequences observed in practice have been the aggravation of psychosocial disorders, the appearance of new psychosocial risk factors, or, less severe, the discrediting of the psychosocial risk assessment approach in companies. Therefore, the present book is a combination of theoretical contributions and practical examples concerning stress at work and intervention in companies.

All skills being a set of know-how taking their source in a set of knowledge, theoretical contributions are proposed to form the basis of know-how already existing in the reader or to come. The practical contributions are suggestions: indeed, they are the result of academic training, professional experience and possibly scientific research that has proven its worth. It is up to the readers to grasp it and transform it so that it can meet their own needs according to their own skills. The important thing is not to derogate the fundamental principles proposed in the present book, which are neither more nor less than the principles developed by the various professions of the human sciences and interventions in companies.

Part I

Stress Description

2

Conceptualization of Stress

Vsevolod Rozanov

1 Introduction

Work, occupation, employment—all are the source of human development, self-esteem and self-actualization, and meaningful activity on the one hand, but are also a frequent cause of disease, frustration and exhaustion on the other. Scientific discussions and studies regarding how to enhance positive and attenuate the negative sides of daily labor started more than a century ago, when the Industrial Age entered its heyday. The first ideas centred around how to select the best man for the specific working conditions, how to enhance human productivity, and how to avoid sick leave. These ideas were introduced in the domain of working hygiene at the beginning of the twentieth century by a German-American psychologist Hugo Munsterberg (1863–1916), and were further developed in the USA and Europe within the International Association of Applied Psychology, and in Soviet Russia by famous psychiatrist and neurologist Vladimir Bechterev (1857–1927). The last concentrated on the concept of "collective reflexes" and labor collectivism, which was one

V. Rozanov (✉)
Department of Psychology, Saint-Petersburg State University, Saint Petersburg, Russia

Department of Borderline Disorders and Psychotherapy, V.M. Bekhterev National Medical Research Center for Psychiatry and Neurology, Saint Petersburg, Russia
e-mail: v.rozanov@spbu.ru

© The Author(s), under exclusive license to Springer Nature Switzerland AG 2023
P. Fauquet-Alekhine, J. Erskine (eds.), *The Palgrave Handbook of Occupational Stress*,
https://doi.org/10.1007/978-3-031-27349-0_2

of the central ideas of the socialist system. Thus, for a period of time psychologists and even psychiatrists were dominating in the sphere of labor safety. On the other hand, the focus was more on work intensification and workers' motivation than on the health consequences of workload, except cases of the so-called professional hazards, which were supposed to be eliminated as working conditions were improved and wide automatization could be introduced. The main question today is: What makes the modern labor market so different that the problem of occupational stress and negative health effects of work has become so acute?

2   Selye and His Concept: The Beginning

Understanding the negative side of work was suggested with the emergence of the concept of stress elaborated by Hans Selye (1907–1982). His theory has added a biological dimension to previous environmental (working conditions) and psychological (personal perceptions and attitudes) dimensions of the problem. Initially the *generalized adaptation syndrome* developed by Selye in 1936 was presented as a non-specific and universal biological mechanism of adaptation to different types of noxious agents, focusing on the endocrinological processes. Three stages of the stress reaction were identified: initial stage (alarm), stage of growing resistance and stage of exhaustion (Selye, 1936, 1937). In a broad context these stages resembled the working day process (workability, stable performance, declined performance) and even the whole human life cycle (youth, maturity, ageing). As to the immediate consequences of stress Selye has identified three main components: (1) adrenal glands hypertrophy; (2) thymus degeneration; and (3) stomach and duodenal mucosa ulceration (later called "Selye's Triad") (Selye, 1936).

It should be noted that Selye's concept was based on the earlier and wider concept of *homeostasis* (designating the steady state of internal conditions) developed by French proponent of vivisection Claude Bernard (1813–1878) and the American physiologist Walter Cannon (1871–1945). Cannon also described in detail the "fight-flight response" as an acute reaction to hazardous situations in animals and humans (Cannon, 1963). Both were discussing nerve and endocrine regulation of physiological and chemical processes in organisms, concentrating mostly on the quick reactions of the sympathetic part of the autonomous nervous system and chromaffin cells of the adrenal gland producing adrenaline. Cannon was the first to notice that different emotions (anger, aggression, fear, extreme joy) were associated with the same internal reaction—rise of blood adrenaline. Selye integrated functions of the sympatho-adrenal system (SAS) in his theory as a mechanism of immediate response, but concentrated on the role of the hypothalamic-pituitary-adrenal system (HPA) as a more protracted and potentially damaging mechanism (see Chap. 3). Today we know how these systems interact: basal cortisol inhibits SAS function, while stress-induced high cortisol activates it (Kvetnanský et al., 1995). In Selye's initial theory the central point was that these biological reactions were non-specific, so far as they were more or less uniformly represented when the organism was exposed to different noxious agents, from heat and cold to toxic substances, physical fatigue and surgical trauma (Selye, 1936).

Several observations with animals came to confirm the associated physiological process, but the concept was then nuanced when distinguishing "good and bad stress"—eustress and distress—thus starting a process of diversification of the concept initially so uniformly described (Selye, 1974). Indeed, studies undertaken by other researchers demonstrated that the stress reaction could not be non-specific (e.g. Mason, 1971) and that Selye's pioneering work, which was based on animal models, when applied to humans had overlooked the role of the stressors' perceptions as well as individual variability of the psychological processes involved in stress-reactivity (e.g. Sukiasyan et al., 2003). Moreover, soon it became clear that extreme novelty and necessity to adapt are the main factors of the uniform systemic reaction of the organism, while the nature of the stressor may be associated with some specific features of the physiological and psychological response (Zhukov, 2007). In other words, unspecific and specific components in the organism coexist, so we should talk about combination of stress (as Selye understood it) and the reaction to a specific stimulus—heat, cold, irradiation, social conflict, and so on.

3 Further Developments: Biological and Psychological Dimension

With time, further studies addressing the physiology of stress provided two revolutionary developments (Sapolsky, 2015). The first was that the hypothalamus as the main central midbrain part of the HPA acts as an endocrine gland, secreting releasing and inhibiting hormones, like corticotropin-releasing hormone, in the pituitary portal system. With this development the HPA was thus fully delineated as a functional and structural system (Schally & Guillemin, 1963). The second development was the establishment of the link between different mental states and the neuroendocrine stress system, pointing out that purely cognitive states may evolve the same physiological mechanisms as physical stressors (Campbell & Ehlert, 2011). This was the start of a new stage of involvement of psychologists in stress studies, which led to understanding that emotions, perceptions and even thoughts are important factors influencing the level of stress experienced by an individual.

Mason already in the 1970s has pointed out that HPA responses in humans might be strongly influenced by novelty, uncontrollability, unpredictability and their interactions with personality traits (Mason, 1975). Several structured models and concepts of stress from the psychological perspective have emerged with time, but the most widely accepted model to date is the transactional model of stress, developed by Richard Lazarus. It foresees that an individual's cognitive appraisal of a situation determines whether the situation is perceived as a stressor, and this is what actually evokes the stress response. More precisely, the individual's interpretation of the situation as stressful or not results from a balance between the "primary appraisal" of the situation as irrelevant, challenging or threatening and the "secondary appraisal" assessing the individual's perceived coping resources such as the competences to manage or control the situation (Lazarus & Folkman, 1984). Thus, understanding of the role of coping, and adaptation resources (especially those subjectively evaluated), became an integral part of the modern concept of stress.

This understanding of stress promoted the importance of perceptions and led to conceptualizing *perceived stress.* This is defined as a "global and comprehensive stress construct that is based on the concept that individuals actively interact with their environment, appraising potentially threatening or challenging events in the light of available coping resources" (Katsarou et al., 2013). Therefore, a situation is perceived as stressful when the individual feels that the demands posed by the challenges are exceeding his/her behavioural and emotional resources. It relates to the individual's perception of inability to cope with a problem, which may be reinforced by emerging fear, anxiety and hesitations. While general life stress was usually measured as accumulation of negative life events, perceived stress in a modern society is assessed by summarizing uncontrollability and unpredictability of one's life and assessment of one's ability to deal with problems and difficulties, as obtained through the well-known Perceived Stress Scale of Cohen et al. (1983). From this perspective stress is the result of the imbalance between the demands placed on us and our ability to cope with them (Danielson et al., 2012), not only the necessity to adapt to any harmful novelty as was initially conceptualized by Selye. This partly explains how routine working activity (e.g. of a sales manager) influenced by unpredictable changing demands and tasks in a situation of constant anticipation of the difficulties due to general economic instability may cause what is called workplace stress.

This is connected to developments of stress theory such as distinguishing short-term from long-term stress. This finding was in part provided by studies with animal models well described by Sapolsky (2004), highlighting that stress in animals is usually a short-term event (although potentially deadly, e.g. the attack of a predator), while the overwhelming majority of the lifetime of animals is devoted to nutrition, reproduction and relaxation (Sapolsky, 2004). In other words, after each stressful situation, animals do not ruminate on what would happen if they could not escape from a predator and they are never anxious in advance, expecting new misfortunes. Conversely, humans ruminate on stressful experiences and are often emotionally disturbed about the future. However, the intensity of these negative feelings and perceptions is the subject of great variability due to personality traits, values, self-regulation abilities and individual predispositions (Sapolsky, 2004).

Human beings are the most social creature, and further studies led logically to a consideration of the influence of social factors contributing to stress and to the emergence of the notion of *psychosocial stress*. Despite the fact that psychosocial stress must be considered as a general concept, embracing a variety of social determinants, it is often reduced to stress at work, which is not surprising as humans usually experience about 30% of everyday life events at work (Ababkov, 2017). However, other kinds of psychosocial stress may be considered, such as routine life stress, academic stress, or marital stress.

4   Occupational Stress: Modern Understanding

Regarding the "world of work" side of psychosocial stress, it is now widely accepted that stress mainly results from an imbalance between the demands (high-output requirements and multiple responsibilities) and the self-perceived capacity to influence or control the experienced situation (low task variety and rigid system to control how the work is done) or from a perceived injustice due to the ratio of reward/effort and commitment (Theorell & Karasek, 1996; Siegrist, 1996; Mohajan, 2012) or from a negative self-perception of competencies at work (Fauquet-Alekhine & Rouillac, 2016). In addition, fast changes in the economy, restructuring of businesses and changes in markets induce new challenges and tasks that require employees' permanent adaptation in a context of a high level of competitiveness and increasing job demands (Lundberg, 2006). It might be speculated that in the near future due to robotization of many working spheres the competition for jobs will be enhanced and other factors will be involved, like unemployment, depression, anxiety and addictions.

Within societies based on a liberal economy, this combination generates stress factors such as inequalities, high pace of life, information overload, high stakes for decision-making, instability and uncertainty, all threatening the well-being of the personality. In general, each short-term stressful situation, if successfully resolved, must induce positive outcomes such as higher self-esteem and better memories regarding how we have managed to cope, so far as stress hormones promote vigilance, energy supply and memory enhancement in the hippocampus (Sapolsky, 2015). In contrast, when psychosocial stress remains prolonged, negative effects may be observed on employees' health (e.g. chronic fatigue, memory and sleep disturbances, muscle pain, diffuse syndromes or cardiovascular diseases) and their productivity at work (e.g. poor performance, disinterest) (Danielson et al., 2012). In general, each stressor, being administered many times, loses its novelty and the stress reaction must fade, but when stressors are variable, unpredictable and of varying intensity, as is the case in the modern competitive and changing world, the results often worsen.

Recent years are also characterized by the gradual but permanent increase of workload, which is associated with informatization, being constantly online, high demands in different sectors of industry (e.g. transport operators, IT, management, logistics, etc.), and shifts from physical activity to mental tasks, based on attention, cognition, competence and experience, all with high responsibility and high costs of mistakes. Such increases of psychosocial stress should be considered in a general context of hypodynamia, designating the sedentary lifestyle inevitably imposed by the office environment and restricted physical operations. Combining hypodynamia with hectic and mentally taxing work is a high-risk factor for cardiovascular disorders (Kamarck et al., 2004) and paradoxically leads to constant muscle strain resulting in pain, which in the long run causes joint and bone problems (Danielson et al., 2012). One of the factors that make external signals of the working environment particularly stressful is the factor of time—the situation may be especially damaging when many signals come at once and there is not enough time to manage them (Danielson et al., 2012).

One more factor must be also taken into consideration: knowledge about stress and its deleterious effects has become common among people, so that "stress became a stressor itself". Worries about the fact that stress affects health are associated with worse health and mental health outcomes, and those who believed that stress affected their health had an increased risk of premature death (Keller et al., 2012). Negative stress beliefs, that is, being convinced that "stress is bad for you", predict many somatic symptoms in young adults (Fischer et al., 2016). Even talking about stress (the word "stress" is now part of common discourse) may have some influence, though with mixed effects. For instance, complaining about one's stressful life, if it helps individuals to explain their own state, can possibly help individuals to cope with it due to the evoked social support (Pietilä & Rytkönen, 2008). On the other hand, constantly feeling stressed and the anxious expectation of some unpredictable news on your smartphone, together with beliefs about stress and perceived stress due to unpredictability, may become a stressor itself (Rozanov, 2017a).

The term occupational stress (work-related stress, job stress, stress at a workplace) being Googled or entered into the PubMed search engine yields hundreds of popular resources and thousands of professional original articles and reviews. It is one of the central concepts that explain both beneficial and adverse effects of occupation and working activity. The psychosocial stress of modern life in civilized societies is possibly the most common type of stress of modernity, which is quite different from the sort of stress that could be experienced by humans in primary societies. On the other hand, the physiological process induced in the body is based on the same conservative biological mechanisms inherent to all mammals (Sapolsky, 2015; Charmandari et al., 2005). This, in our opinion, is a key point of the pathogenesis of stress-induced pathologies, the reason for both somatic and mental health problems, which have been growing recently and which are usually explained by stress. When studied using standard psychosocial stress (like Trier Social Stress Test), the emotional and cognitive experiences (anger, anxiety, helplessness, hopelessness) may be slightly dissociated with the neuro-humoral activation, but in general the biological consequences of common social stressful situations are confirmed by many studies (Campbell & Ehlert, 2011; Sapolsky, 2015).

5 From Homeostasis to Allostasis

In recent decades many authors have discussed the mechanisms that underlie the health consequences of stress and poor adaptation in the long run and chronic exposure. The most productive explanation is the concept of *allostasis*, which supplements a classical understanding of homeostasis. Allostasis was introduced by Sterling and Eyer (1988) as "the operational range, the ability of the body to increase or decrease vital functions to a new stage or challenge" and was further developed by McEwen (2012). This concept was initially called upon to explain the negative outcomes of constant arousal and appeared relevant to understanding the health-damaging effects of chronic psychosocial stress, including those induced by working environments (McEwen, 2012, 2017).

Such long-term and cyclic stress (i.e. associated with working hours), which is unavoidable and repeated, leads to "wear and tear" of the biological systems of the organism, resulting in emotional, cognitive, behavioural and physiological consequences. It is associated with complex interactions that occur within the regulatory neuroendocrine counterbalancing systems. As an example, each stressful event associated with cortisol level spikes leads to hyperglycemia. Hyperglycemia induces a rise of insulin resulting in hypoglycemia, which in turn promotes craving for carbohydrates. In the long run (stress chronicity) it may lead to disturbances in the insular and other contra-insular factor dynamics, autoimmune reactions, and type 2 diabetes (McEwen, 2012). In fact, this vicious cycle involves even more factors that counteract; we are simplifying the situation.

Such pathological adaptation processes may be described in terms of the energy required to reach a balanced state: a given operating situation with stressful conditions leads to higher tension in the counterbalancing systems of the organism, thus increasing the contribution of the regulatory system. After several repeated situations of this sort, the energy required from the regulatory system to reach the balance may become massive, and if one of the counterbalancing systems is compromised or suddenly breaks, serious negative effects may follow. The energy required for establishing the balance and for going on is conceptualized as the "allostatic load" (Fava et al., 2019).

The allostatic load reflects the cumulative effects of stressful experiences in daily life and may lead to disease over time. When the allostatic load exceeds a threshold (the value of which is specific to each individual), the principle of a working week being well balanced by weekends or holidays may no longer apply. It now becomes common that periods of serious strain and long-awaited resolving are followed by an unexpected health problem. As an example, colds and other infections, as well as traumas, often manifest themselves on weekends or on vacations after a prolonged period of intense demand. Furthermore, depression can become most evident shortly after holidays, and chronic disease exacerbation often comes a couple of weeks or a month after a serious stressful period of life has finally been resolved (Kamarck et al., 2004; McEwen, 2017; Fava et al., 2019).

When the cost of chronic exposure to fluctuating or heightened neural, psychological and systemic physiologic responses exceeds the coping resources of an individual, this is referred to as "toxic stress" and "allostatic overload" (Fava et al., 2019). One should keep in mind that the brain with its cognitive processes is the central organ of adaptation to stress because it perceives and determines what is threatening, as well as organizing and regulating behavioural and physiological responses to the stressor through neuroendocrine mechanisms. Thus, the state of the brain (perceptions, fears, anxiety, depressive thoughts, negative anticipations, ruminations, etc.) promotes prolonged and strained adaptation ("allostasis") but also contributes to pathophysiology ("allostatic load/overload") when overused and dysregulated (McEwen, 2017).

The most common consequences of allostatic overload are somatic disturbances (cardiovascular and cerebrovascular diseases, hypertension, immune system dysfunctions, chronic inflammation, metabolic syndrome) and mental health problems (depressive symptoms, anxiety, addictions, eating behavior disturbances, adjustment disorders, acute and chronic posttraumatic stress disorders) (Schneiderman et al., 2005). One of the major problems associated with chronic stress and occupational stress in particular is sleep disturbances (Danielson et al., 2012). Sleep disorders are thought to be signs of serious strain and chronic stress, very often leading to self-medication (alcohol, free sale hypnotics, etc.), which can further lead to the necessity to use psychostimulants and may result in addictions and other negative consequences (Danielson et al., 2012). The consequences of chronic work-related stress (for instance in patients diagnosed with adjustment disorder after working 60 to 70 hours per week continuously over several years prior to the onset of symptoms) can be seen on the structural level. Stressed subjects exhibited significant reductions in the gray matter volumes of the anterior cingulate cortex and the dorsolateral prefrontal cortex. Furthermore, their caudate and putamen volumes were reduced, and the volumes correlated inversely to the degree of perceived stress (Blix et al., 2013).

6 Common Effects of Chronic Psychosocial Stress

The variety of health effects of chronic stress can be explained by the systemic character of stress, while existing predispositions may contribute to interindividual variability of diseases. Nevertheless, there are two conditions that are thought to be directly caused by chronic stress: *burnout syndrome* and *chronic fatigue syndrome*. We will briefly discuss these conditions in the context of occupation.

In 1974 Herbert Freudenberger used the term "burnout" for the exhaustion, sleep disturbances and depression-like symptoms that he noticed among volunteer staff in a clinic for addicts (*Freudenberger,* 1974*)*. Burnout syndrome is usually found in medical and nursing personnel, and sometimes in other professions that are based on interactions between the person seeking aid and the caregiver (teachers, social workers, medical students, etc.). It is considered a "disease of modern societies" (Weber & Jaekel-Reinhard, 2000). Christina Maslach and colleagues further developed the Burnout Inventory that has become widely used, and has identified three main symptoms of burnout: emotional exhaustion, depersonalization and reduced professional accomplishment (Maslach et al., 1996). Burnout is often associated with other mental health problems. For instance, estimated prevalence rates for burnout among physicians in Germany vary between 4% and 20%, and for depression between 6% and 13%, with high comorbidity (Beschoner et al., 2019). After a vivid discussion about possible acceptance of burnout as an occupational disease in different countries (Lastovkova et al., 2018), the World Health Organization in the latest version of International Classification of Diseases (ICD-11) have included burnout as a syndrome with a detailed definition, which means that such diagnoses will be taken much more seriously by medical doctors and insurance companies (WHO, 2019). Burnout is defined in ICD-11 as a "syndrome … resulting from chronic workplace stress that has not been successfully managed. It is characterized by three dimensions: 1) feelings of energy depletion or exhaustion; 2) increased mental distance from one's job, or feelings of negativism or cynicism related to one's job; and 3) reduced professional efficacy". As stated by ICD, burnout refers specifically to phenomena in the occupational context and should not be applied to describe experiences in other areas of life (WHO, 2019).

The chronic fatigue syndrome seems to be a more complex phenomenon associated both with work stress and with chronic inflammation, possibly of infectious or autoimmune origin. Fatigue is a normal subjective feeling after the working day or week, but if fatigue persists for six months or more, it is considered chronic fatigue. Such chronic and severe unexplained fatigue (in the absence of any diseases or reasonable cause) is referred to as chronic fatigue syndrome/myalgic encephalomyelitis (CFS/ME) (Morris & Maes, 2013). The etiology of this condition is not known and diagnostic criteria are not well defined; nevertheless, genetic background is suspected, and stress seems to be involved. In general, the condition is considered a neuro-immune disorder in which stress plays an important role (Morris & Maes, 2013). In the Norwegian population (aged 19–80) substantial fatigue lasting six months or longer was reported by 11.4% of respondents (Loge et al., 1998). It is remarkable that chronic fatigue is associated with disabilities and somatic and psychiatric disorders: people with these conditions are more fatigued than subjects at work or in good health (Loge et al., 1998). Among the biomarkers of chronic fatigue there are signs of inflammation, immune system activation, autonomic system dysfunction, impaired functioning in the hypothalamic-pituitary-adrenal axis, and general neuroendocrine dysregulation, which resembles chronic psychosocial stress with depressive symptoms (Klimas et al., 2012).

7 Stress-Vulnerability and the Concept of Epigenetics

The brain is the central organ of stress, and individual reactions to stress depend on personality traits and such features as stress-reactivity (or stress-vulnerability), which have a mixed psycho-biological nature (McVikar et al., 2014). Studies of stress-reactivity suggested that it is a genetically based trait, depending on the process of early development of the individual, especially early adverse effects, including exposure to stress in utero (Brent & Silverstein, 2013, Sapolsky, 2015; King, 2016). Recently, *epigenetic events* that happen during early development have been suspected as an important mechanism underlying stress-vulnerability (Herbison et al., 2015).

The main sphere of action of epigenetics according to the initial concept of British embryologist Konrad Waddington (1905–1975) was the period of embryogenesis, but modern epigenetic science has extended the period of high probability of these events to early postnatal life periods, and with regard to the cell biology of the brain that accumulates experiences, to the whole life span of the individual (Roth, 2013; Rozanov, 2017b). Today it becomes clear that on the basis of the same genome the human body develops not only hundreds of epigenomes, which determine stable cellular diversity, but also possibly myriads of epigenomes inside such organs as the brain, where neurons are constantly reacting to positive and negative stimuli and where structural and functional relations between neurons are adjusted by existing challenges and rewards, or in the immune system, which reacts to all external and internal perturbations. As a result, the concept of *epigenome* has emerged, understood (using modern terms) as a dynamic interface between nature and nurture, between stressful stimuli and the changing brain (Szyf, 2009; Tammen et al., 2013). Moreover, epigenetics and epigenome are linked today to the concept of "soft inheritance"—a set of molecular mechanisms that allow environmental signals to establish reversible imprints (marks) on the genetic material and to transmit these marks further in several generations, both in cell generations and progeny. This inheritance is not rigid and does not act in a strictly determined way, that is, these imprints can either be conserved or reversed, if the environment matches or counteracts them. Changes in the environment (environmental cues) are perceived as important signals for survival and reproduction; these signals "impose prints" on the genome starting from the very early stages of development (especially within the prenatal period, but also postnatally during further development) and shape the pattern of gene expression for the further life of the individual. This provides conformity of activities of biological systems to the expected environmental conditions within the entire period of existence of the organism. This process is called ontogenetic programming. At the same time, if future environmental conditions in a broad ecological context do not match the expectations of the genome, the programmed functions can acquire a maladaptive pattern (Gluckman & Hanson, 2004; Hochberg et al., 2011).

The first facts came from animal studies, when newborn rats and mice were subjected to different types of stress induced by mother–pup interaction breaks. For instance, pups that were separated from their mothers for a short period of time (15–30 min) were more stress-resilient as adults, while those that were separated for longer time periods (2–4 h) demonstrated high stress-reactivity as measured by blood cortisol in response to standard low-temperature exposure (Meaney, 2001). This was associated with methylation of promoter regions of the genes related to the stress system of the organism in a way that corresponds to stress-reactivity, and some data give an impression that progeny of stressed mothers bore signs of high stress-reactivity though were not stressed themselves (Curley et al., 2008). Similarly, female pups that were nurtured by high-licking/grooming mothers (a typical pattern of mother-pup interaction in rodents) were more likely to become good mothers themselves, and this pattern can be seen in the second generation, while those that were brought up by neglectful mothers demonstrated opposite behavioural patterns (Champagne, 2008).

Of course, these data could not be directly translated to humans, but they have directed future research. Very soon studies provided evidence that different types of programming associated with epigenetic events (DNA methylation, histones transformation of non-coding micro-RNA synthesis) take place in situations when the mother experiences stress during pregnancy (alimentary restrictions, steroids administration, depressive symptoms, exposure to toxicants, etc.). This is associated with changes in the health profile of their children, and in many cases causes direct changes in the stress system of the child organism (Oberlander et al., 2008). Recently, a vast body of evidence has accumulated that many environmental and behavioural factors, including drug and alcohol overdose, environmental pollutants, food components, smoking, depression, being overweight may produce long-lasting programming effects in different systems of the organism of progeny (Vaiserman,

2013, 2015). They can manifest themselves after decades of life as different health problems, from diabetes to depression and addictive behaviour (Hochberg et al., 2011; Lupien et al., 2009). Some of the programming effects may influence longevity and promote early ageing along with early dementias and other age-related problems (Vaiserman, 2013, 2015; Vaiserman et al., 2011).

What is most important in the context of psychosocial stress is that epigenetic events have been identified as a potent mechanism of programming long-lasting changes of the biological systems of stress-reactivity, thus designing them for living in low-stress or high-stress conditions, building either vulnerability or resilience (King, 2016; Herbison et al., 2015; Rozanov, 2017a; see Chap. 22 of the present book). This is due to the effects of stress hormones in early life periods when neuroplasticity is high and when biological systems of stress-reactivity are under development (Hochberg et al., 2011). Such programming effects were well known for sex steroids (regarding development of sexual dimorphism), while the role of stress hormones (regarding stress system) was not so evident for a long period of time. These effects actually mean that early social conditions (and even economic, so far as stress in children is associated with the risk caused by poverty and deprivation) may have long-lasting consequences for the personality in terms of ability to cope with further challenges. This is proposed as a mechanism of *biological embedding* whereby social environment "gets under the skin" (Hertzman, 2012; Sasaki et al., 2013). Epigenetic programming of stress-reactivity also provides a plausible explanation of the increase of mental health problems and suicides in a comparatively short period of time (several decades) in the populations of economically developed countries subjected to modern types of psychosocial stress (Rozanov, 2017b).

8 Conclusion

In conclusion, taking into consideration the changing socio-economic context of work life, with the development of stress-vulnerability and evolution of the concept of stress, new forms of stress have been highlighted, widespread enough and with life consequences significant enough to be mentioned and discussed in the present chapter. Recent conceptualizations of stress turn back from purely cognitive theories to views which are placing intracellular homeostasis at the core of cognitive and biological responses, supporting the concept of stress as a genuinely psycho-biological phenomenon (McVikar et al., 2014). It is clear that the concept of stress has evolved with time and has been greatly influenced by changes in socio-economic contexts that led to the identification of new forms of stress at work and also pushed scientists and practitioners to find new ways to describe stress and the ways to cope with it. One of the illustrations of such evolution is the way well-being is now taken into account in companies, far from the Taylorism approach to life at work at the beginning of the twentieth century. No doubt the concept of occupational stress will be further developed and will be filled with new content, especially taking into consideration global shift to teleworking, jobs instability, time pressure and work overload in a rapidly changing world.

References

Ababkov, V. A. (2017). Assessment of psychological and endocrine human reactions in experimental microstress at work. *Understanding Stress at Work*, 45–51.

Beschoner, P., Limbrecht-Ecklundt, K., & Jerg-Bretzke, L. (2019). Mental health among physicians: Burnout, depression, anxiety and substance abuse in the occupational context. *Nervenarzt*. June 6.

Blix, E., Perski, A., Berglund, H., & Savic, I. (2013). Long-term occupational stress is associated with regional reductions in brain tissue volumes. *PLoS One, 8*(6), e64065. https://doi.org/10.1371/journal.pone.0064065

Brent, D. A., & Silverstein, M. (2013). Shedding light on the long shadow of childhood adversity. *JAMA, 309*, 177–1778.

Campbell, J., & Ehlert, U. (2011). Acute psychosocial stress: Does the emotional stress response correspond with physiological responses? *Psychoneuroendocrinology, 37*, 1111–1344.

Cannon, W. B. (1963). *The wisdom of the body*. W.W. Norton & Company; Rev.

Champagne, F. A. (2008). Epigenetic mechanisms and the transgenerational effects of maternal care. *Frontiers in Neuroendocrinology, 29*, 386–397.

Charmandari, E., Tsigos, C., & Chrousos, G. P. (2005). Endocrinology of the stress response. *Annual Reviews in Physiology, 67*, 259–284.

Cohen, S., Kamarck, T., & Mermelstein, R. (1983). A global measure of perceived stress. *Journal of Health and Social Behavior, 24*, 385–396.

Curley, J. P., Champagne, F. A., Bateson, P., & Keverne, E. B. (2008). Transgenerational effects of impaired maternal care on behavior of offspring and grand offspring. *Animal Behavior, 75*(4), 1551–1561.

Danielson, M., Heimerson, I., Lundberg, U., et al. (2012). Psychosocial stress and health problems. *Scandinavian Journal of Public Health, 40*(Suppl.9), 121–134.

Fauquet-Alekhine, P., & Rouillac, L. (2016). The square of perceived action model as a tool for identification, prevention and treatment of factors deteriorating mental health at work. *Journal of Mental Disorder & Treatment, 2*(3), 1–13.

Fava, G. A., McEwen, B. S., Guidi, J., et al. (2019). Clinical characterization of allostatic overload. *Psychoneuroendocrinology, 108*, 94–101.

Fischer, S., Nater, U. M., & Laferton, J. A. (2016). Negative stress beliefs predict somatic symptoms in students under academic stress. *International Journal of Behavioral Medicine*, April 18.

Freudenberger, H. J. (1974). Staff burnout. *Journal of Social Issues, 30*, 159–165.

Gluckman, P. D., & Hanson, M. A. (2004). Living in the past: Evolution, development, and patterns of disease. *Science, 305*, 1733–1736.

Herbison, C., Allen, K., Robinson, M., & Pennell, C. (2015). Trajectories of stress events from early life to adolescence predict depression, anxiety and stress in young adults. *Psychoneuroendocrinology, 61*, 16–17.

Hertzman, C. (2012). Putting the concept of biological embedding in historical perspective. *PNAS, 109*, 1750–1757.

Hochberg, Z., Feil, R., Constancia, M., et al. (2011). Child health, developmental plasticity, and epigenetic programming. *Endocrine Reviews, 32*, 159–224.

Kamarck, T. W., Muldoon, M., Shiffman, S., et al. (2004). Experiences of demand and control in daily life as correlates of subclinical carotid atherosclerosis in a healthy older sample: The Pittsburg healthy heart project. *Health Psychology, 23*, 24–32.

Katsarou, A. L., Triposkiadis, F., & Panagiotakos, D. (2013). Perceived stress and vascular disease: Where are we now? *Angiology, 64*, 529–534.

Keller, A., Litzelman, K., Wisk, L. E., et al. (2012). Does the perception of stress affects health matter? The association with health and mortality. *Health Psychology, 31*, 677–684.

King, A. (2016). Rise of resilience. *Nature, 531*, S18–S19.

Klimas, N. G., Broderick, G., & Fletcher, M. A. (2012). Biomarkers for chronic fatigue. *Brain, Behavior, and Immunity, 26*(8), 1202–1210.

Kvetnanský, R., Pacák, K., Fukuhara, K., et al. (1995). Sympathoadrenal system in stress. Interaction with the hypothalamic-pituitary-adrenocortical system. *Annals of the New York Academy of Sciences, 771*, 131–158.

Lastovkova, A., Carder, M., Rasmussen, H. M., et al. (2018). Burnout syndrome as an occupational disease in the European Union: An exploratory study. *Industrial Health, 56*(2), 160–165.

Lazarus, R. S., & Folkman, S. (1984). *Stress, appraisal, and coping*. Springer Publishing Company.

Loge, J., Ekeberg, O., & Kaasa, S. (1998). Fatigue in the general Norwegian population: Normative data and associations. *Journal of Psychosomatic Research, 45*, 53–65.

Lundberg, U. (2006). Stress, subjective and objective health. *International Journal of Social Welfare, 15*, S41–S48.

Lupien, S. J., McEwen, B. S., Gunnar, M. R., & Heim, C. (2009). Effects of stress throughout the lifespan on the brain, behavior and cognition. *Nature Reviews. Neuroscience, 10*, 434–445.

Maslach, C., Jackson, S. E., & Leiter, M. P. (1996). *MBI: The Maslach burnout inventory: Manual*. Consulting Psychologists Press.

Mason, J. W. (1971). A re-evaluation of the concept of "non-specificity" in stress theory. *Journal of Psychiatric Research, 1971*(8), 323–333.

Mason, J. W. (1975). Emotions as reflected as patterns of endocrine integration. In L. Levi (Ed.), *Emotions: Their parameters and measurements*. Raven Press.

McEwen, B. S. (2012). Brain on stress: How the social environment gets under the skin. *Proceedings of the National Academy of Sciences, 109*(Suppl.2), 17180–17185.

McEwen, B. S. (2017). Neurobiological and systemic effects of chronic stress. *Chronic Stress (Thousand Oaks)*. January–December;1.

McVikar, A., Ravallier, J. M., & Greenwodd, C. (2014). Biology of stress revisited: Intracellular mechanisms and the conceptualization of stress. *Stress and Health, 30*, 272–279.

Meaney, M. J. (2001). Maternal care, gene expression, and the transmission of individual differences in stress reactivity across generations. *Annual Reviews in Neurosciences, 24*, 1161–1192.

Mohajan, H. K. (2012). The occupational stress and risk of it among the employees. *International Journal of Mainstream Social Science, 2*(2), 17–34.

Morris, G., & Maes, M. (2013). Case definitions and diagnostic criteria for Myalgic encephalomyelitis and chronic fatigue syndrome: From clinical-consensus to evidence-based case definitions. *Neuro Endocrinology Letters, 34*(3), 185–199.

Oberlander, T., Weinberg, J., Papsdorf, M., Grunau, R., Misri, S., & Devlin, A. M. (2008). Prenatal exposure to maternal depression and methylation of human glucocorticoid receptor gene (*NR3C1*) in newborns. *Epigenetics, 3*, 97–106.

Pietilä, I., & Rytkönen, M. (2008). Coping with stress and by stress: Russian men and women talking about transition, stress and health. *Social Science and Medicine, 66*, 327–338.

Roth, T. L. (2013). Epigenetic mechanisms in the development of behavior: Advances, challenges, and future promises of a new field. *Development and Psychopathology, 402*, 1279–1291.

Rozanov, V. (2017a). *Stress and epigenetics in suicide*. Academic Press.

Rozanov, V. A. (2017b). Evolution of the concept of stress, *Understanding Stress at Work*, 17–21.

Sapolsky, R. (2004). *Why zebras don't get ulcer. The acclaimed guide to stress, stress-related disease and coping* (3rd ed.). Henry Holt and.

Sapolsky, R. (2015). Stress and the brain: Individual variability and inverted U-curve. *Nature Neuroscience, 18*, 1344–1346.

Sasaki, A., de Vega, W. C., & McGowan, P. O. (2013). Biological embedding in mental health: An epigenomic perspective. *Biochemistry and Cell Biology, 91*, 14–21.

Schally, A. V., & Guillemin, R. (1963). Isolation and chemical characterization of a β-CRF from pig posterior pituitary glands. *Proceedings of the Society for Experimental Biology and Medicine, N.Y., 112*, 1014–1017.

Schneiderman, N., Ironson, G., & Siegel, S. D. (2005). Stress and health: Psychological, behavioral, and biological determinants. *Annual Review of Clinical Psychology, 1*, 607–628.

Selye, H. A. (1936). Syndrome produced by diverse nocuous agents. *Nature, 138*, 32.

Selye, H. (1937). *The stress of life*. McGraw Hill.

Selye, H. (1974). *Stress without distress*. J.B. Lippincott.

Siegrist, J. (1996). Adverse health effects of high effort/low reward conditions. *Journal of Occupational Health Psychology, 1*, 27–41.

Sterling, P. & Eyer, J. (1988). Allostasis: A new paradigm to explain arousal pathology. In S. Fisher & J. Reason (Eds.), Handbook of life stress, cognition and health (pp. 629–649). John Wiley & Sons.

Sukiasyan, S. H., Tadevosyan, A. S., Jeshmaridian, S. S., et al. (2003). *Stress and post-stress disorders: Personality and society*. Asogik.

Szyf, M. (2009). The early life environment and the epigenome. *Biochimica et Biophysica Acta, 1790*, 878–885.

Tammen, S. A., Friso, S., & Choi, S.-W. (2013). Epigenetics: The link between nature and nurture. *Molecular Aspects of Medicine, 34*, 753–764.

Theorell, T., & Karasek, R. A. (1996). Current issues relating to psychosocial job strain and cardiovascular disease research. *Journal of Occupational Health Psychology, 1*, 9–26.

Vaiserman, A. M. (2013). Long-term health consequences of early life exposure to substance abuse: An epigenetic perspective. *Journal of Developmental Origins of Health and Disease, 4*, 269–279.

Vaiserman, A. M. (2015). Epigenetic programming by early life stress: Evidence from human populations. *Developmental Dynamics, 244*, 254–265.

Vaiserman, A. M., Voitenko, V. P., & Mekhova, L. V. (2011). Epigeneticheskaya epidemiologiya vozrast-zavisimyh zabolevaniy (Epigenetic epidemiology of age-dependent diseases). *Ontogenes (Ontogenesis), 42*, 1–21.

Weber, A., & Jaekel-Reinhard, A. (2000). Burnout syndrome: A disease of modern societies? *Occupational Medicine, 50*(7), 512–517.

WHO. (2019). *Burn-out an 'occupational phenomenon':* International classification of diseases. Retrieved August 2019, from https://www.who.int/mental_health/evidence/burn-out/en/

Zhukov, D. A. (2007). Biologiya Povedeniya. Gumoralniye mechanysmy. *[Biology of behavior. Humoral mechanisms]*. Rech.

3

The Cycle of Stress

Philippe Fauquet-Alekhine and Laetitia Rouillac

1   Introduction

The notion of stress was popularized after the work of Hans Selye introduced the general adaptation syndrome. Selye first defined "stress" as "the non-specific response of the body to any demand for change" (Selye, 1936, p. 32) and later as "a state manifested by a specific syndrome which consists of all the nonspecifically induced changes within the biological system" (Selye, 1976, p. 64). This first approach thus considered stress without aspects such as cognition and perception, which were later introduced within a dynamic approach (see, e.g., French, 1973; French et al., 1982; Lazarus & Folkman, 1984; Folkman et al., 1986) leading to the transactional model (see Rozanov, 2017, p. 17; see also Chap. 2 of the present book). The transactional model considers stress as a transaction between an individual and the context (transactional model) associated to one's perception that external demands are exceeding one's capacity of response, thus endangering well-being.

P. Fauquet-Alekhine (✉)
SEBE-Lab, Department of Psychological and Behavioural Science,
London School of Economics and Political Science, London, UK

Laboratory for Research in Science of Energy, Montagret, France

Group INTRA Robotics, Avoine, France
e-mail: p.fauquet-alekhine@lse.ac.uk; philippe.fauquet-alekhine@groupe-intra.com

L. Rouillac
Psychotherapy Office, Ottobrunn, Germany

© The Author(s), under exclusive license to Springer Nature Switzerland AG 2023
P. Fauquet-Alekhine, J. Erskine (eds.), *The Palgrave Handbook of Occupational Stress*,
https://doi.org/10.1007/978-3-031-27349-0_3

Considering stress according to the transactional model, any external demand on someone is potentially stressful, or potentially is stressful with an intensity that varies from very low (not perceived) to very high (may traumatize). Experiments undertaken during a stress-test based on psychotechnical questions showed that the simple act of reading a question could be characterized as a stress factor of low intensity: a subject with a baseline heart rate of 65 bpm showed an increase to 75 to 85 bpm every time the subject began to read a new question; the heart rate decreased to an average of 70 bpm when answering the question (Fauquet-Alekhine et al., 2012). Heart rate increase is an indicator of stress increase as demonstrated in many experiments (see, e.g., Kudielka et al., 2004; Spierer et al., 2009; Petrowski et al., 2010; Cinaz et al., 2010; Fauquet-Alekhine et al., 2016). Thus, we can invoke the proposal of Maniam and Morris (2012, p. 97) claiming that exposure to stress is clearly "inevitable, and it may occur, to varying degrees, at different phases throughout the lifespan."

When demand is perceived by a subject in a given context, the physiological and psychological dimensions of stress are engaged: a physiological response is triggered through the production of specific hormones (see following sections) and external signs may be increase in heart rate, respiration rate, excessive sweating, and muscular tension. At the same time, an emotional response occurs (part of the psychological dimension) with features such as discomfort, dread, or fear; this can have an impact on the physiological response as emotions change the production of specific hormones. All types of mental stress can impact on the psychological and physiological changes (McLean, 1974; Beehr & Newman, 1978; Karasek & Theorell, 1990; Palmer et al., 2003). Both the physiological and psychological dimensions influence the subject's behavior (e.g., agitation or uncoordinated movements may be observed). All these factors influence the subject's physiological characteristics and modify social interactions and thus the context. This produces new effects as illustrated by the two 3-D space model for short-term occupational stress (see Fig. 3.1, Fauquet-Alekhine, 2012).

However, the individual possesses resources that may attenuate the effects of stressors. This is well explained by the Psychosocial Stress Model (PSM; Taylor & Aspinwall, 1996). The PSM joined the transactional theory of stress and combines personal resources in an integrative model. Derived from research in social cognition, it identifies resources associated with individual characteristics of personality (e.g., social support perceptions, mastery, optimism) and social characteristics of the individual (e.g., gender, social status, income) that might influence perception of stressors; it also provides insights

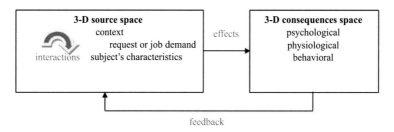

Fig. 3.1 The two 3-D space model for short-term occupational stress

into psychological and health outcomes. These characteristics are considered key moderators of stress, as well as resistance to and coping capacity for stress.

The following sections depict each dimension (psychological, psychological, and behavioral), introducing the different types of stress and the associated neurophysiological processes, as well as the possible resulting behaviors. They also examine how the interacting 3-D space may lead to a pathological cycle that becomes inevitable under certain conditions.

2 Stress Types/Psychological Dimension

The four main types of mental stress recognized to date are acute stress, episodic acute stress, chronic stress, and traumatic stress (Fauquet-Alekhine & Boucherand, 2017). They were described in detail by Taylor (1995). Each of them gave rise to numerous and specific studies.

Acute stress, also referred to as "short-term stress" or "microstress," relates to a specific event that does not last long (several milliseconds to a few hours) and that, most of the time, is identified as the source of stress by the subject (i.e., the stress is perceived as such). Examples are taking an exam, having a minor accident, or feeling frightened when facing a dangerous animal. The stress disappears with the event.

Episodic acute stress is associated with multiple stressful events or situations occurring repeatedly, while subjects are not necessarily aware of it, thus creating periodic episodes of acute stress.

Chronic stress relates to long-term stress. Usually, it is due to sustained and continuous pressures over long periods (several months or years).

Traumatic stress is a particular type in that it may be considered as a combination of an acute stress of very high intensity (e.g., sexual assault, violent accident, earthquake) prolonged by a long-term stress resulting from the experienced traumatic situation sometimes involving post traumatic disorders.

The frequency and duration of stress may be two relevant parameters that help to define the type of stress, but the intensity of the effects produced on the subject must be taken into account too. For example, episodic/acute stresses might be perceived as more intense than chronic stress.

Another way to categorize stress is to consider the context. For example, pregnancy may induce specific stress for the mother (see, e.g., Cole-Lewis et al., 2014) or for the fetus (Abbott et al., 2018). Stress may relate to social interactions (Lehman & Conley, 2010), or the workplace may induce stress, referred to as occupational stress (see Frideman et al., 1958), as the work environment may provide stressful contexts where the four aforementioned types of stress may be observed.

2.1 Stress at Work

Stress at work is a problematic issue: in Western Europe, the cost of work-related depression was estimated to be 617 billion euros per year (Hassard et al., 2014, p. 7). This combination of health and economic concerns makes stress at work an issue that requires intervention.

In the introduction to his article, Milbourn (2012) reviewed different proposals to define occupational stress (also known as job stress). Milbourn (2012, p. 1) summarized that "Sager (1991) defined job stress as a psychological state perceived by individuals when faced with demands, constraints, and opportunities that have important but uncertain outcomes; Chen and Silverthorne (2008) conclude that job stress is an individual reaction that differs from general stress as it is also organizational-and-job related; Wu and Shih (2010, p. 74) state that job stress is associated with adverse consequences for both the individual and the firm 'since it has the effect of lowering motivation levels and performance, and increases turnover intentions'. Likewise, Conway et al. (2008) concluded that job stress is one of the most important issues in health care because it has a negative effect on the safety and health of personnel."

If the pathological aspect of stress at work is most often emphasized, the stress response must not only be systematically considered in this way but also as an indispensable process of adaptation (both biological and psychological) for subjects to their environment when facing constraints (Légeron, 2008, p. 811). In some cases of acute stress with low intensity, stress may even be beneficial provided that it does not exceed a given intensity threshold that would put the subject in a state of cognitive deficit (Fig. 3.2) (see, e.g., Yerkes & Dodson, 1908; Staal, 2004; Fauquet-Alekhine et al., 2014).

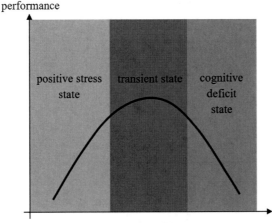

Fig. 3.2 Human Functional States divided into three main parts: (i) central part: transient state for the subject in terms of stress effects, (ii) left part: positive state of stress, (iii) right part: potential cognitive deficit state (Source: Fauquet-Alekhine et al., 2014)

These considerations explain why so many studies address stress at work and why psychosocial risks (PSR) are now taken into account as professional risks (see also Chap. 8 of the present book). For some countries, analyzing and preventing PSR at work has become mandatory.

3 The Neurophysiological Process/ Physiological Dimension

3.1 The Nervous System

Stress is perceived through and managed by the nervous system. The nervous system is made up of two main systems: the central nervous system and peripheral nervous system that includes the somatic nervous system and the autonomous system.

The central nervous system includes most of the brain as well as the spinal cord, the latter leading information from the brain to the body. The central nervous system is responsible, via the somatic nervous system, for all voluntary actions, including those of skeletal muscles (grasp, walk, run).

The autonomous nervous system, "autonomous" as in not under voluntary control, is responsible for vegetative actions (breathing, heart rate) and

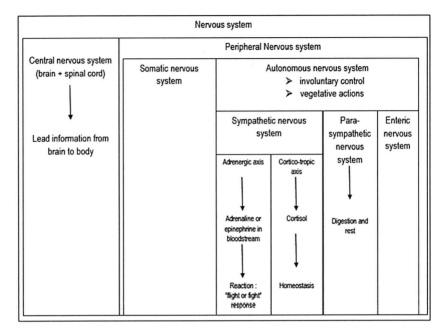

Fig. 3.3 The nervous system of humans

emotions. It is made up of two systems, the sympathetic and parasympathetic nervous systems (Fig. 3.3). The latter is called parasympathetic because it was first thought to be antagonist to the former (prefix "para") but studies showed that they are independent although interactive; only their main functions oppose the two systems: the sympathetic nervous system comes into play in the case of threat and boosts the organism, while the parasympathetic nervous system mainly promotes digestion and rest. The sympathetic nervous system prepares for fast actions through nerves in the spinal cord to muscles by releasing adrenaline (or epinephrine) into the bloodstream; this is accomplished through the adrenergic axis of the sympathetic nervous system in a few seconds that helps to prepare to fight or escape in case of danger. The sympathetic nervous system includes another axis, the corticotropic axis or HPA axis (as it involves linear interactions between hypothalamus, pituitary gland, and adrenal gland (HPA axis)). The HPA axis is slower (by several minutes) than the adrenergic axis as the information transmission is only based on the production of hormones that move through the bloodstream (slower than nerve impulses through the spinal cord). The HPA axis makes possible the recovery of homeostasis[1] through the process of allostasis[2] (McEwen & Wingfield, 2010; see also Chap. 2 of the present book) after the fast actions triggered by the adrenergic axis (Kemeny, 2003).

Some researchers include the enteric nervous system within the autonomous nervous system as being responsible for the digestive system (associated with gut, pancreas, and gallbladder), while others consider it alongside the autonomous nervous system (Sasselli et al., 2012; Laight, 2013).

3.2 The Physiological Response to Stress/ Physiological Dimension

When an individual is submitted to mental stress (psychological pressure) or certain physical stress (e.g., road accident, hemorrhage), the autonomic nervous system (ANS) is called upon, involving the sympathetic nervous system, resulting in:

- a fast response (a few seconds) through the adrenergic axis
- a slow response (a few tens of minutes) through the corticotropic axis

The first one must be immediate and boosting to provide the "fight or flight" response when facing a danger. The second one is slower because it must intervene later, after the "fight or flight" response, in the aim to bring the organism back to a normal state: the effect is to calm the organism, which cannot remain too long in an excited state, otherwise it would become exhausted.

These two axes are mainly located in the brain (Fig. 3.4) and are driven by the thalamus, hippocampus, amygdala, hypothalamus, pituitary gland (or hypophysis), and locus coeruleus.

3.3 The Adrenergic Axis

The adrenergic axis has short-term effects, mainly concerning a rise in blood glucose and, heart and ventilation rate, that is, involuntary processes driving the "fight or flight" response, by releasing norepinephrine (or noradrenaline) at various organs (e.g., see Gordan et al. (2015) for the heart) along with the

---

[1] Homeostasis is the state of steady physiological conditions of an individual.

[2] Allostasis designates the process of achieving homeostasis through psychological and physiological changes.

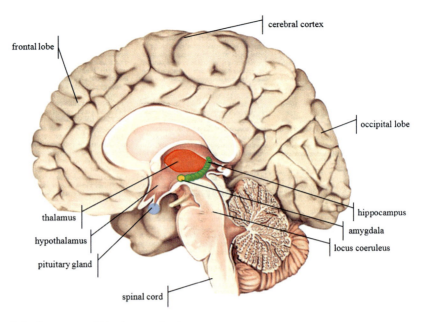

Fig. 3.4 Structure of the human brain

adrenal glands. The adrenal glands then release epinephrine (or adrenaline) into the bloodstream, which permits the stimulation of non-innervated organs by circulating epinephrine.

All of this starts with stimuli. Sensory inputs come to the thalamus; information then goes to the amygdala to provide an endocrine response ([1] in Fig. 3.5): the ANS fibers transmit information to the locus coeruleus and to various organs including the adrenal glands (or "suprenal glands" located above each kidney) through the spinal cord [2] releasing norepinephrine (or noradrenaline). Sympathetic nerves are constituted of a short preganglionic neuron connected to a long postganglionic neuron; preganglionic neurons leave the spinal nerves to enter sympathetic ganglia where, when activated, acetylcholine is secreted; this neurotransmitter triggers the release of norepinephrine at the ending of the postganglionic neuron to the target organ.

Figure 3.5 gives the example of heart and adrenal glands. For the heart, preganglionic nerves emerge from the upper thoracic segments of the spinal cord to enter sympathetic ganglia [3a] where postganglionic nerves take over and extend to the heart where norepinephrine is released. The adrenal glands receive norepinephrine [3b] through a similar process and release epinephrine (or adrenaline) into the bloodstream [4] from the adrenal medulla (the core of the adrenal glands), thus boosting the organism [5]. This process is fast because it is partly based on nerve impulses [2]: this makes it effective in a few

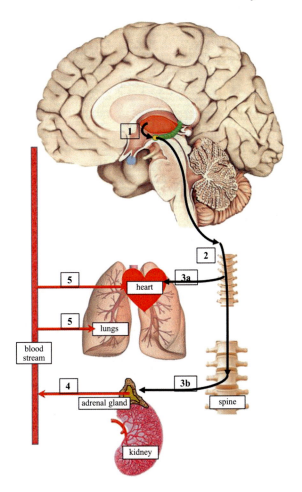

Fig. 3.5 The adrenergic axis of the autonomous nervous system

seconds. It was recently discovered that this mechanism was favored under stress by "a rapid and selective surge of circulating bioactive osteocalcin [a protein hormone in bones] […]. Osteocalcin permits manifestations of the acute stress response to unfold by signaling post-synaptic parasympathetic neurons to inhibit their activity, thereby leaving the sympathetic tone unopposed" (Berger et al., 2019, p. 890).

3.4 The Corticotropic Axis

The corticotropic axis is triggered at the same time but has a long-term effect (at least tens of minutes to several hours), mainly related to the increase of corticotropes and cortisol into blood, saliva, and urine, having a moderating effect as opposed to adrenaline. This is thus a return process maintaining body homeostasis (Kemeny, 2003).

Sensory inputs come to the thalamus and information then goes to the amygdala ([1] in Fig. 3.6). The ANS fibers transmit information from the amygdala to the hypothalamus, which releases CRH (corticotropin release hormones, also called corticotropin release factor (CRF)) from its paraventricular nucleus toward the pituitary gland (or hypophysis) [3]. CRH induces the release of ACTH (adreno-corticotropic hormones, or adrenocorticotrophine) from the pituitary gland into the bloodstream [4]. When reaching the adrenal glands [5], ACTH trigger the release of cortisol from the adrenal cortex, that is, the outer layer of the adrenal glands, into the bloodstream [6]

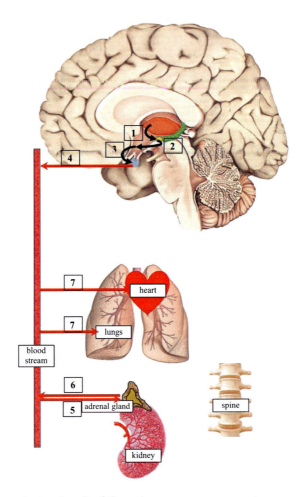

Fig. 3.6 The corticotropic axis of the autonomous nervous system

distributed to the organs [7] in order to return to a quiet state (see, e.g., Carrasco & Van de Kar, 2003; Dickerson & Kemeny, 2004). This process is slow because it is mainly based on blood circulation [4-5-6-7]: this makes it effective in a few minutes.

This increase of cortisol hormone resulting from the hypothalamic-pituitary-adrenal axis activation, the corticotropic axis is also called the HPA axis.

This description depicts the biological response of the ANS to stressors and how it comes back to a non-stressed state. It is an adaptive and transient process. The sympathetic nervous system is thus mainly concerned with short-term stress or acute stress and its effects (see, e.g., Kemeny, 2003; Davezies, 2008; Montano et al., 2009; Keitel et al., 2011).

3.5 Adrenergic and Corticotropic Interactions

When physiologically mobilizing resources for the "flight or fight" response through the sympathetic axis and HPA axis, during the time it is effective, the organism chemically blocks the capacity of the brain to have an analytical approach to the experienced situation. Arnsten (2009), while reiterating that prefrontal cortex regions are interconnected and regulate decision-making capacities (Fuster, 2008; Modirrousta & Fellows, 2008; Simons et al., 2008), emphasized that when stress pathways are activated, prefrontal cortex regulation is impaired (attention and working memory capacities are reduced) whereas amygdala function (detecting fear and preparing for emergency events) is strengthened. Knowing this may rationalize approaches to situations and may help to decrease fear and stress perception. It is clear that stress systematically engenders a short period during which it is physiologically (chemically) impossible to summon analytical capacities.

Kuebler et al. (2013) provided measures of adrenaline and cortisol release in the human body experiencing an acute stress episode. Figures 3.7a and b give an insight into the variation of adrenaline and cortisol with time and Figs. 3.7a and b shows how adrenaline changes with cortisol for healthy adults during a normal process of acute stress.

The problem arises when the exposure to stressors is repeated at a high frequency or when the stressor has a high intensity (case of traumatic stress type). One of the problematic factors comes from cortisol that inhibits the production of certain chemical mediators called cytokines involved in the regulation of immune cells. Another one comes from the fact that cortisol (and other cortico-steroids produced at the same time) provides energy to the body

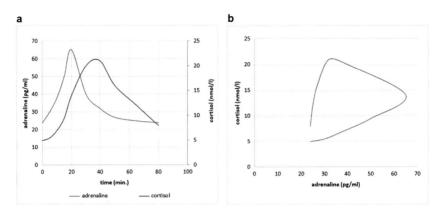

Figs. 3.7a and b Variations of adrenaline and cortisol during an acute stress episode for heathy human adults (from Kuebler et al., 2013)

(glucose) from the proteins of the muscles and of the bones, and from the lymphoid tissue involved in the immune system. This reduces some immune functions but, at the same time, this may result in an increased circulating level of cytokines promoting inflammation (Miller et al., 2002). The impact on the immune system is not without consequences for the brain (sensitive to chemical imbalance) and subsequently for the psychological state, sometimes in a sustainable way. A dangerous pathological cycle may be engaged with repeated exposure to acute stress, while the level of cortisol, following the previous stress episode, has not yet returned to its baseline. The level of cortisol may be reduced by the action of the hippocampus which slows down the hypothalamus: secretion of CRH decreases and cortisol secretion follows. But a high level of cortisol is toxic for the hippocampus, reducing its effect on the hypothalamus. Figures 3.8a and b provide an illustration of what may happen in terms of adrenaline/cortisol cycle. The increasing level of cortisol inevitably leads to chronic stress if there is no treatment. This state is self-sustaining from a physiological standpoint (cortisol favors depression) and a psychological standpoint (depression favors the increase of cortisol in favoring the negative perception of situations).

At the same time, the food cycle is disrupted, making the subject even more vulnerable to stress: HPA axis reactivity to pharmacological stimulation predicts subsequent food intake with a major role of cortisol that stimulates food consumption (George et al., 2010). However, the effect of stress on the food cycle is bidirectional: both increase and decrease of food intake may be observed (see, e.g., Maniam & Morris, 2012; Razzoli & Bartolomucci, 2016).

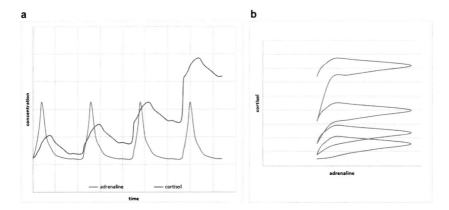

Figs. 3.8a and b Extrapolation of variations of adrenaline and cortisol during repeated acute stress episodes (extrapolated from Kuebler et al., 2013)

It is therefore clear that stress stimuli generate psychological and physiological reactions, and both have an influence on behavior. The behavioral dimension is discussed in the next section.

4 Influence of the Psychological and Physiological Dimensions/Behavioral Dimension

Behavior can be considered as part of the allostatic process aiming at maintaining or recovering homeostasis. In the "fight or flight" model, the subject exposed to a threat is expected to adapt their behavior in an optimal way to reduce or to escape from the threat. For example, when a mouse faces a cobra, running away from the predator appears the optimal option, and when the mouse is far enough from the snake, homeostasis may be recovered. Another possible behavior is freezing: the mouse is paralyzed and cannot move, thus becoming easy prey for the predator. This second behavioral option does not save the mouse and may be considered as an irrational behavioral choice. It also calls into question the way it may contribute to recovering homeostasis. Rational behavior under stress is often impossible due to physiological concerns, as noted in Sect. 3.3. This also applies to humans. This may lead subjects to reach a cognitive deficit state impairing their performance (see, e.g., Fauquet-alekhine et al., 2014). Fauquet-Alekhine (2012, p. 49) reported several cases of working situations where individuals adopted inappropriate behaviors in stressful contexts. For example, he reported the case of a technician who had to handle valves in a high-pressure room of an industrial plant resulting in unexpected and incomprehensible actions from the technician, leading to a loss of production. While the situation could not be explained either by the technician himself or by his colleagues, a work psychologist in charge of the event analysis discovered the stress mechanism when interviewing the technician, asking him to tell the story of the event: "The work analyst was astonished by one detail: during the first half part of the story, the field worker appeared to work as a good professional, but during the second part, he appeared to work as a man who did not know the job at all. During the interview, the analyst noticed several details which showed that in the work situation during the second part of the story, the field worker was frightened. Step by step, the analyst brought to light that the worker was able to work as a good professional until the time he had entered a room containing valves and ducts with high steam pressure. Then he discovered that the worker had known, several years ago, some colleagues being injured by steam loss in such a room, and that entering the high steam pressure room was frightening him. Scared by the place probably induced by the remembrance of the colleagues' accident, the field worker could not work anymore correctly" (p.49). The author concluded that the technician had reached a cognitive deficit state while entering the high-steam pressure room associated with an increased level of stress due to fear. Following the event, the technician entered another episode of stress, that of having to assume the consequences of his behavior while being responsible for a significant loss of production. As illustrated in Fig. 3.1, the behavior had an influence on the context and on the job demand that generated a new state of stress.

The literature reports cases of fear which do not seem to disturb the subjects as they have unconsciously elaborated defense mechanisms (e.g., Cramer, 2012; DeWolfe & Governale, 1964; Thobaben, 2005; Witte, 1992). "Defense mechanisms are automatic psychological responses to internal and external stressors and conflicts" (Perry, 2014, p. 407). The purpose of these mechanisms is mental inhibition of stressors and conflicts in order to reduce the level of stress. From the description of the physiological dimension of stress in Sect. 3.3, it is clear that defense mechanisms may cause a reduction of cortisol level. However, it would be wrong to consider this as a positive effect. This phenomenon was particularly emphasized by studies carried out with American soldiers returning from the Vietnam War (Davezies, 2008): it was found that some of them could present a low level of cortisol while experiencing or having experienced particularly difficult situations that had led to post-traumatic stress disorder in others. Analyses showed that the former had developed defense mechanisms such as disengagement, helping them to break the committed relationship with the situation, characterized by non-emotional behavior regarding the situation. This sort of emotional control was responsible for the low level of cortisol, but, at the same time, the CRH level was high. While cortisol has an anti-inflammatory role, CRH stimulates inflammatory processes (Lariviere & Melzack, 2000). For these subjects, the stress state was not manifest and, on the contrary, the imbalance of low cortisol/ high CRH led to diseases (e.g., chronic pain). This process is not a singularity; it is not necessary to be a soldier tackling dangerous situations to be concerned by this process: workers performing a physically constraining activity (line workers) or highly solicitous jobs (care givers) summon such mechanisms to inhibit what could cause subsequent suffering (e.g., de Souza França & Figueiredo De Martino, 2014).

The example above relates a technician affected by fear who performed inappropriate actions. This shows that action may be an important component of the behavioral dimension shaping stress. However, actions influence stress differently depending on whether they are conscious or not, possible or inhibited, effective or impaired. The following paragraphs illustrate this.

With the help of the Square of PErceived ACtion model describing how to successfully put competencies into action (SPEAC model; Fauquet-Alekhine, 2016, 2020), Fauquet-Alekhine and Rouillac (2016) demonstrated and theorized how stress at work may arise when:

- Workers are requested to do something (by management or the prescriptions) they do not want to do because it is in conflict with their own values, leading to ethical suffering, a source of stress contributing to burnout. Example: a manager is requested by the director to fire someone who works well and has a family to feed while keeping a lazy colleague on the staff.
- Workers have acquired knowledge and developed know-how to perform a task but the management or the procedures require them to not do what their competencies would permit them to do: the underuse of competencies (usually giving rise to frustration) produces stress. Example: a mechanic must repair a pump but not deal with the leaks because it takes time and increases the cost of the repair.
- Workers are requested to perform tasks for which they have not been trained. Example: someone has to drive a truck in a convoy when he knows nothing about this and has never done it before.
- Workers suffer regarding how their job changes due to quality norms that make them spend more time filling in documents rather than repairing the equipment. Example: before repairing the pump, a 100-page folder is needed, and after repairing, a high level of paperwork involving numerous signatures for traceability is required.

Fauquet-Alekhine and Rouillac (2016) showed how action is a key point in well-being at work, and that action, when inhibited or impaired, may generate stress for workers. On the basis of the SPEAC model, and to briefly summarize their work, they promoted the analysis of conflicts between the four poles of the SPEAC model, that is, between what is asked of workers, what they know, what they can do, and what they want to do in order to detect possible factors of stress that might degenerate into individual or collective deterioration of mental health.

It is worth mentioning another study regarding action in the behavioral dimension of stress. Weiss (1971) undertook interesting experiments with rats trained to avoid electric shocks when turning a wheel. Each shock was preceded by a warning audio signal. He compared the stress induced in pairs of rats placed in cages side by side. They were both given an electrical shock at the same time, one having the possibility to avoid the electric shock for all the rats by acting on the wheel, the other being in a cage without a wheel and therefore with no possibility of action. Thus, the difference was that one rat had control of the avoidance action while the other did not and was subordinate to the action of the former. After the experiment, while the former was in the same state as a third control rat which had not received any electric shocks, the latter displayed gastric ulcers and a series of behavioral manifestations related to anxiety and depression. A later analysis conducted by Lefcourt (1973) concluded that the perception of control seemed to be a common predictor of the resulting behaviors in response to stressors, and that control decreased the level of perceived stress because this contributed to forecasting a reduction of the potential future threat (Miller, 1979). Neuroscience has recently showed and explained how the experience of behavioral control over adverse events produced sustainable changes reducing not only the effects of subsequent negative events of the same sort but also those that were uncontrollable or different from the original events (Maier, 2015).

All of this illustrates how the behavioral dimension may influence the source space of the two 3-D space model for short-term occupational stress presented in Fig. 3.1.

5   Additional Considerations: Genetics and Epigenetics

Statistical data have suggested heritability of the stress response: "abnormal properties of the personality, behavioral disorders, and mental pathologies, such as depression, pathological anxiety, disorders of adaptation, antisocial manifestations, aggression, risky behavior, propensity to suicide, propensity to addictions, and many others result, to a considerable extent, from gene-determined influences" (Rozanov, 2012, p. 332). However, there are few significant relationships between genetics and stress (Fauquet-Alekhine & Boucherand, 2017)

In addition, stress exposure generates epigenetic phenomena (McEwen et al., 2015; Waddington, 1942; Tronick & Hunter, 2016) that favor stress sensitivity through phenotypes. "The phenotype in a psychological/psychiatric meaning is the result of development of a genetic program preset as a unique combination of the parents' genes, but under the influence of the environment [...], namely, conditions of prenatal development" (Rozanov, 2012, p. 333). Phenotypes may result in making some genes silent or active for a period of time or permanently, thus influencing psychological and physiological life.

Therefore, as for many other fields (e.g., intellectual, athletic, or artistic activities), humans are not equal regarding stress exposure and some characteristics are predefined.

6 Conclusion

Stress, whatever its type, is both a psychological and physiological process influencing and influenced by behavioral dimensions which are interconnected, and thus the stress response may not be reduced to a matter of mental strength or a complex combination of chemical reactions. This interconnection implies, to some extent, medical care for stressed people that involves, at the same time, psychological support (e.g., to identify coping strategies and thus lessen the effect of associated chemical reactions) and pharmacotherapy (to control chemical reactions and thus allow the brain to return to a normal chemical balance). Without such care, the risk for the individual is to fall within the pathological cycle of stress that will likely lead to undesirable outcomes. This advocates for the necessity of dealing with stress early and avoiding the establishment of a prolonged and pathogenic chemical imbalance, that is, to help the individual to maintain the homeostasis necessary for optimal functioning of the organism. Otherwise, it may create psychological disorders and autoimmune disorders. Techniques and strategies have been developed to help individuals to cope with emerging states of stress (see also Chap. 21 of the present book).

The world of work presents the reality of the world never being completely safe. It is not a family cocoon where everyone might expect help and attention from others. Intentionally or not, others may be sources of stressors: the manager asks for more production, colleagues do not complete their part of the job, the organization blocks the process, and every worker is expected by the management to do their best to make the system work. In other words, many work contexts are dysfunctional systems and workers are expected to compensate for dysfunctions. From the outset it is necessary to limit this compensatory commitment; this is the first task to preserve health at work. In parallel, it is important to identify occupational sources of stress, frequency exposure, and stress intensity in order to break any emerging potential pathogenic cycle. A periodic assessment of psychosocial risks at work may help to achieve this (see also Chap. 8 of the present book).

References

Abbott, P. W., Gumusoglu, S. B., Bittle, J., Beversdorf, D. Q., & Stevens, H. E. (2018). Prenatal stress and genetic risk: How prenatal stress interacts with genetics to alter risk for psychiatric illness. *Psychoneuroendocrinology, 90,* 9–21.

Arnsten, A. F. (2009). Stress signalling pathways that impair prefrontal cortex structure and function. *Nature Reviews Neuroscience, 10*(6), 410–422.

Beehr, T., & Newman, J. (1978). Job stress, employee health and organizational effectiveness: A facet analysis, model, and literature review. *Personnel Psychology, 31,* 665–699.

Berger, J. M., Singh, P., Khrimian, L., Morgan, D. A., Chowdhury, S., Arteaga-Solis, E., ... & Karsenty, G. (2019). Mediation of the acute stress response by the skeleton. *Cell metabolism*, 30(5), 890–902.

Carrasco, G. A., & Van de Kar, L. D. (2003). Neuroendocrine pharmacology of stress. *European Journal of Pharmacology, 463*(1–3), 235–272.

Chen, J. C., & Silverthorne, C. (2008). The impact of locus of control on job stress, job performance and job satisfaction in Taiwan. *Leadership & Organization Development Journal, 29*(7), 572–582.

Cinaz, B., La Marca, R., Arnrich, B., & Tröster, G. (2010). Monitoring of mental workload levels. *Proceedings of IADIS eHealth conference*, 189–193.

Cole-Lewis, H., Kershaw, T., Earnshaw, V., Yonkers, K., Lin, H., Ickovics, J., & Kazak, A. E. (2014). Pregnancy-Specific Stress, Preterm Birth, and Gestational Age Among High-Risk Young Women. *Health Psychology, 33*(9), 1033–1045.

Conway, P., Campanini, P., Sarori, S., Dotti, R., & Costa, G. (2008). Main and interactive effects of shift work, age, and work stress on health in an Italian sample of health care workers. *Applied Ergonomics, 39*(5), 630–639.

Cramer, P. (2012). *The development of defense mechanisms: Theory, research, and assessment.* Springer Science & Business Media.

Davezies, P. (2008). Stress et pouvoir d'agir: données biologiques. *Santé & Travail,* 64. http://philippe.davezies.free.fr/download/down/Stress_action_/biologie_2008l.pdf

3 The Cycle of Stress 43

de Souza França, S. P., & Figueiredo De Martino, M. M. (2014). Correlation between stress and burnout in mobile pre-hospital nursing care. *Journal of Nursing Uffe Online, Recife, 8*(12), 4221–4229.

DeWolfe, A. S., & Governale, C. N. (1964). Fear and attitude change. *The Journal of Abnormal and Social Psychology, 69*(1), 119.

Dickerson, S. S., & Kemeny, M. E. (2004). Acute stressors and cortisol responses: A theoretical integration and synthesis of laboratory research. *Psychological Bulletin, 130*(3), 355.

Fauquet-Alekhine, P. (2012). Causes and consequences: Two dimensional spaces to fully describe short term occupational stress. *Socio-Organizational Factors for Safe Nuclear Operation, 1*, 45–52. http://hayka-kultura.org/larsen.html

Fauquet-Alekhine, Ph. (2016). Subjective ethnographic protocol for work activity analysis and occupational training improvement. *British Journal of Applied Science & Technology, 12*(5), 1–16. Article no.BJAST.21632

Fauquet-Alekhine, P. (2020). *Knowledge management in high-risk industries—Coping with skills drain*. Palgrave Macmillan.

Fauquet-Alekhine, Ph., & Boucherand, A. (2017). The pathological cycle of stress: Insights of psychological, biological and genetic aspects, understanding stress at work, pp. 22–27.

Fauquet-Alekhine, Ph., Geeraerts, Th., & Rouillac, L. (2012). Improving simulation training: Anesthetists vs nuclear reactor pilots. *Socio-Organizational Factors for Safe Nuclear Operation, 1*, 32–44. http://hayka-kultura.org/larsen.html

Fauquet-Alekhine, P., Geeraerts, T., & Rouillac, L. (2014). Characterization of anesthetists' behavior during simulation training: Performance versus stress achieving medical tasks with or without physical effort. *Psychology and Social Behavior Research, 2*(2), 20–28.

Fauquet-Alekhine, P., & Rouillac, L. (2016). The square of perceived action model as a tool for identification, prevention and treatment of factors deteriorating mental health at work. *Journal of Mental Disorders and Treatment, 2*(3), 1–13.

Fauquet-Alekhine, Ph.; Rouillac, L.; Berton, J., & Granry, J. C. (2016). Heart rate vs stress indicator for short term mental stress. *British Journal of Medicine and Medical Research, 17*(7), 1–11, Article no.BJMMR.27593.

Folkman, S., Lazarus, R. S., Gruen, R. J., & DeLongis, A. (1986). Appraisal, coping, health status, and psychological symptoms. *Journal of Personality and Social Psychology, 50*(3), 571.

French, J. R. P., Jr. (1973). Person-role fit. *Occupational Mental Health, 3*, 15–20.

French, J. R. P., Jr., Caplan, R. D., & Harrison, R. V. (1982). *The mechanisms of job stress and strain*. Wiley.

Frideman, M., Rosenman, R. H., & Carroll, V. (1958). Changes in the serum cholesterol and blood clotting time in men subjected to cyclic variation of occupational stress. *Circulation, 17*(5), 852.

Fuster, J. M. (2008). *The prefrontal cortex*. Academic Press.

George, S. A., Khan, S., Briggs, H., & Abelson, J. L. (2010). CRH-stimulated cortisol release and food intake in healthy, non-obese adults. *Psychoneuroendocrinology, 35*(4), 607–612.

Gordan, R., Gwathmey, J. K., & Xie, L. H. (2015). Autonomic and endocrine control of cardiovascular function. *World journal of cardiology*, 7(4), 204–214.

Hassard, J., Teoh, K., Cox, T., Dewe, P., Cosmar, M., Gründler, R., Flemming, D., Cosemans, B., & Van den Broek, K. (2014). *Calculating the cost of work-related stress and psychosocial risks*. http://irep.ntu.ac.uk/id/eprint/31143/1/PubSub8693_Hassard.pdf

Karasek, R. A., & Theorell, R. (1990). *Healthy work, stress, productivity and the reconstruction of working life*. The Free Press and Basic books.

Keitel, A., Ringle, M., Schwartges, I., Weik, U., Picker, O., Stockhorst, U., & Deinzer, R. (2011). Endocrine and psychological stress responses in a simulated emergency situation. *Psychoneuroendocrinology, 36*, 98–108.

Kemeny, M. E. (2003). The psychobiology of stress. *Current Directions in Psychological Science, 12*(4), 124–129.

Kudielka, B. M., Buske-Kirschbaum, A., Hellhammer, D. H., & Kirschbaum, C. (2004). Differential heart rate reactivity and recovery after psychosocial stress (TSST) in healthy children, younger adults, and elderly adults: The impact of age and gender. *International Journal of Behavioral Medicine, 11*(2), 116–121.

Kuebler, U., Wirtz, P. H., Sakai, M., Stemmer, A., & Ehlert, U. (2013). Acute stress reduces wound-induced activation of microbicidal potential of ex vivo isolated human monocyte-derived macrophages. *PLoS One, 8*(2), e55875, 1–9.

Laight, D. (2013). Overview of peripheral nervous system pharmacology. *Nurse Prescribing, 11*(9), 448–454.

Lariviere, W. R., & Melzack, R. (2000). The role of corticotropin-releasing factor in pain and analgesia. *Pain, 84*(1), 1–12.

Lazarus, R. S., & Folkman, S. (1984). *Stress, appraisal, and coping*. Springer.

Lefcourt, H. M. (1973). The function of the illusions of control and freedom. *American Psychologist, 28*(5), 417–425.

Légeron, P. (2008). Le stress professionnel. *L'information psychiatrique, 84*(9), 809–820.

Lehman, B. J., & Conley, K. M. (2010). Momentary reports of social-evaluative threat predict ambulatory blood pressure. *Social Psychological and Personality Science, 1*(1), 51–56.

Maier, S. F. (2015). Behavioral control blunts reactions to contemporaneous and future adverse events: Medial prefrontal cortex plasticity and a corticostriatal network. *Neurobiology of Stress, 1*, 12–22.

Maniam, J., & Morris, M. J. (2012). The link between stress and feeding behaviour. *Neuropharmacology, 63*(1), 97–110.

McEwen, B. S., Bowles, N. P., Gray, J. D., Hill, M. N., Hunter, R. G., Karatsoreos, I. N., & Nasca, C. (2015). Mechanisms of stress in the brain. *Nature Neuroscience, 18*(10), 1353–1363.

McEwen, B. S., & Wingfield, J. C. (2010). What's in a name? Integrating homeostasis, allostasis and stress. *Hormones and Behavior, 57*(2), 105.

McLean, A. (1974). Concepts of occupational stress. In A. McLean (Ed.), *Occupational Stress* (pp. 3–14). Thomas.

Milbourn, G. (2012). Job stress and job dissatisfaction: Meaning, measurement and reduction–a teaching note. *The Journal of American Academy of Business, 18*(1), 1–9.

Miller, G. E., Cohen, S., & Ritchey, A. K. (2002). Chronic psychological stress and the regulation of pro-inflammatory cytokines: A glucocorticoid resistance model. *Health Psychology, 21*, 531–541.

Miller, S. M. (1979). Controllability and human stress: Method, evidence and theory. *Behaviour Research and Therapy, 17*(4), 287–304.

Modirrousta, M., & Fellows, L. K. (2008). Dorsal medial prefrontal cortex plays a necessary role in rapid error prediction in humans. *Journal of Neuroscience, 28*(51), 14000–14005.

Montano, N., Porta, A., Cogliati, C., Costantino, G., Tobaldini, E., Rabello Casali, K., & Iellamo, F. (2009). Heart rate variability explored in the frequency domain: A tool to investigate the link between heart and behavior. *Neuroscience and Biobehavioral Reviews, 33*, 71–80.

Palmer, S., Cooper, C., & Thomas, K. (2003). Revised model of organisational stress for use within stress prevention/management and wellbeing programmes—Brief update. *International Journal of Health Promotion and Education, 41*(2), 57–58.

Perry, J. C. (2014). Anomalies and specific functions in the clinical identification of defense mechanisms. *Journal of Clinical Psychology, 70*(5), 406–418.

Petrowski, K., Herold, U., Joraschky, P., Mück-Weymann, M., & Siepmann, M. (2010). The effects of psychosocial stress on heart rate variability in panic disorder. *German Journal of Psychiatry, 13*(2), 66–73.

Razzoli, M., & Bartolomucci, A. (2016). The dichotomous effect of chronic stress on obesity. *Trends in Endocrinology & Metabolism, 27*(7), 504–515.

Rozanov, V. (2017). Conceptualizing different types of stress. In *Understanding stress at work* (pp. 17–21). http://hayka-kultura.org/larsen.html

Rozanov, V. A. (2012). Epigenetics: Stress and behavior. *Neurophysiology, 44*(4), 332–350.

Sager, J. K. (1991). Type A behavior pattern among salespeople and its relationship to job stress. *The Journal of Personal Selling & Sales Management, 12*(2), 1–14.

Sasselli, V., Pachnis, V., & Burns, A. J. (2012). The enteric nervous system. *Developmental Biology, 366*(1), 64–73.

Selye, H. (1936). A syndrome produced by diverse nocuous agents. *Nature, 138*, 32.

Selye, H. (1976). *The stress of life* (Rev. ed.). McGraw-Hill.

Simons, J. S., Henson, R. N., Gilbert, S. J., & Fletcher, P. C. (2008). Separable forms of reality monitoring supported by anterior prefrontal cortex. *Journal of Cognitive Neuroscience, 20*(3), 447–457.

Spierer, D., Griffiths, E., & Sterland, T. (2009). Fight or flight: Measuring and understanding human stress response in tactical situations. *The Tactical Edge, Summer*, 30–40.

Staal, M. (2004). Stress, cognition, and human performance: A literature review and conceptual framework. *NASA report, reference*: NASA/TM—2004–212824.

Taylor, S. (1995). *Managing people at work*. Reed Educational and Professional, Publishing Ltd.

Taylor, S. E., & Aspinwall, L. G. (1996). Mediating and moderating processes in psychosocial stress: Appraisal, coping, resistance, and vulnerability. In H. B. Kaplan (Ed.), *Psychosocial stress: Perspectives on structure, theory, life-course, and methods* (pp. 71–110). Academic Press.

Thobaben, M. (2005). Defense mechanisms and defense levels. *Home Health Care Management & Practice, 17*(4), 330–332.

Tronick, E., & Hunter, R. G. (2016). Waddington, dynamic systems, and epigenetics. *Frontiers in Behavioral Neuroscience, 10*, article 107, 1–6.

Waddington, C. H. (1942). The epigenotype. *Endeavour, 1*, 18–20.

Weiss, J. M. (1971). Effects of coping behavior in different warning signal conditions on stress pathology in rats. *Journal of Comparative and Physiological Psychology, 77*(1), 1.

Witte, K. (1992). Putting the fear back into fear appeals: The extended parallel process model. *Communications Monographs, 59*(4), 329–349.

Wu, Y. C., & Shih, K. Y. (2010). The effects of gender role on perceived job stress. *The Journal of Human Resource and Adult Learning, 6*(2), 74–79.

Yerkes, R. M., & Dodson, J. D. (1908). The relation of strength of stimulus to rapidity of habit-formation. *Journal of Comparative Neurology and Psychology, 18*, 459–482.

4

Animal Models in Neuroscience: A Focus on Stress

Victoria Luine

1   Introduction

The first decades of the twenty-first century have been associated with a rise in stresses experienced at home, in the workplace, and in public areas as a result of technological advances, an escalation of social violence, more frequent and intense natural disasters, and the outbreak of warfare and genocide around the globe. Thus, the incidence of stress-related disorders such as anxiety, depression, post-traumatic stress disorder, conduct disorders, and drug use/abuse has dramatically increased, and the World Health Organization (WHO) has dubbed stress the health epidemic of the twenty-first century (Meyers, 2018). It is therefore incumbent on neuroscientists and clinicians to better understand and more effectively treat these problems.

An important issue for studying stress in humans is that prospective research on chronic stress cannot be done because of its deleterious effects, but retrospective studies have examined stress effects in Holocaust survivors (Yehuda et al., 2007), victims of childhood abuse (Chapman et al., 2004), and war veterans (Aschbacher et al., 2018), for example. Effects of mild, acute stresses can be studied in humans (Wolf et al., 2016). However, the heterogeneity of human populations, due to both nature and nurture, complicates such studies, and it is difficult to determine the biological bases of the effects. Thus,

---

V. Luine (✉)
Department of Psychology, Hunter College, New York, NY, USA
e-mail: vluine@hunter.cuny.edu

© The Author(s), under exclusive license to Springer Nature Switzerland AG 2023   **47**
P. Fauquet-Alekhine, J. Erskine (eds.), *The Palgrave Handbook of Occupational Stress*,
https://doi.org/10.1007/978-3-031-27349-0_4

48   V. Luine

animal models have been developed in order to assess physiological effects of stress and to understand its biological underpinnings. Animal models consist primarily of rodents, rats or mice, or small primates like tree shrews that are subjected to stressful experiences and then analyzed during and after the stressful experience. This chapter provides a review of previously and currently applied animal models for analyzing stress and how they may be utilized to develop novel and, hopefully, more effective therapies for disorders that are precipitated by or related to stress.

2   The Stress Response

2.1   Temporal Aspects of Stress

Stress, depending on its intensity and duration, results in adaptive or maladaptive physiological changes in systems ranging from neural cells in culture to laboratory rodents and subhuman primates to humans, a concept put forward by Selye (1976). For example, short periods of mild stress are associated with enhanced availability of energy and oxygen, inhibition of digestion, growth and immune function, and enhanced cognitive processing and analgesia in CNS[1] responses which help to cope with the stressor. However, when the duration of the same stress is increased, these responses become maladaptive to the organism and result in fatigue, myopathy, gastro-duodenal ulcers, impaired immune function, and, ultimately, death (for further discussion, see Nelson, 2000; also see Chap. 3 of the present book). More recently, McEwen and colleagues introduced the concept of allostasis/allostatic load to describe the stress response. Allostasis refers to adaptive processes by which the body responds to stressors in order to maintain homeostasis, which is defined as maintenance of equilibrium in physiological processes. When stress is chronic or repeated, allostatic load ("wear and tear on the body") accumulates, and the individual is no longer able to maintain homeostasis (McEwen & Stellar, 1993). As long as allostatic processes maintain homeostasis, effective coping occurs, but when stress imparts too large an allostatic load, stress becomes debilitating to both peripheral and central nervous systems (see McEwen, 2016 for further information).

Recent studies show that some brain functions, including learning and memory, are also subject to the same adaptive/maladaptive pattern (Luine & Gomez, 2015). This outcome has major implications for maintaining the

---

[1] CNS: central nervous system.

4 Animal Models in Neuroscience: A Focus on Stress   49

safety and effectiveness of workplaces, especially those involving teams piloting complex technical systems such as aircraft, space shuttles, or nuclear reactors, and for dealing with the aftermath of disasters and war (Fauquet-Alekhine & Rouillac, 2016). Thus, it is important to develop animal models for understanding and coping with job-related stresses.

2.2   Types of Stressors

In experimental animals, two major categories of stressors are acknowledged: systemic and processive stressors (Anisman et al., 2001). Systemic stressors, which constitute an immediate physiological threat to homeostasis, include immunologic challenge, hemorrhage, excess alcohol, and hypoglycemia. These stresses are relayed directly to the paraventericular nucleus (PVN) via brain stem monoaminergic projections to influence hormone release (Herman & Cullinan, 1997). These stressors are not common in relation to stresses that humans usually experience, and, thus, their use as animal models to study stress has waned. Processive stressors, on the other hand, require integration and interpretation at higher brain centers before relay to the PVN through limbic forebrain circuits in the prefrontal cortex, hippocampus, and amygdala (Herman & Cullinan, 1997) and are experienced by humans. There are two types of processive stressors, psychogenic and neurogenic. Psychogenic stressors are mainly psychological such as exposure to a predator or a novel open field for animals, and anxiety over an upcoming event or exam for humans, while neurogenic stressors are mainly physical such as foot shock, pedestal, cold swim, immobilization, social defeat, and isolation for animals. For humans, neurogenic stressors include overcrowding in subways or buses, exposure to natural disasters like hurricanes, earthquakes, and so on, and traffic accidents. Some processive stressors used in animal research have both psychogenic and neurogenic elements such as overcrowding, restraint stress (subject is placed in a plastic tube or wire mesh container where they have limited movement), and resident intruder or social defeat stress. Restraint and overcrowding have psychogenic elements in that subjects cannot escape and they are not physically painful, but unlike a purely psychogenic stressor, they involve physical components that limit the response/defensive style of the subject (McIntyre, et al., 1999). Thus, a variety of stress paradigms are available for analyses which to some degree model the human experience.

It needs to be acknowledged that animal models do not replicate human stress situations as accurately as, for example, models for breast cancer or diabetes. However, it should be noted that, as described here, various kinds of

50   V. Luine

Table 4.1 Types of stresses utilized in rodent studies

Stress method	Description	Comments	References
Restraint	Commercially available plastic tubes keep rats or mice unable to escape but not immobilized	Acute or chronic use; mesh restrainers are not allowed by some regulatory agencies	Watanabe et al., 1992; Conrad et al., 2003; Bowman et al., 2009
Resident intruder	Aggressive mouse introduced to home cage	Not usable for females or young animals	Nasca et al., 2019
Social isolation	Removed from cagemates daily	None	Carnevali et al., 2012; Rowson et al., 2019
Social instability/ isolation	Change cagemates or groups daily 2x/week Removed from cagemates each day	None	Rowson et al., 2019
Pedestal	30-inch-high platform, 30 min –1 h	Some protocols put the platform in water pool	Zanca et al., 2018; Avital et al., 2005
Forced swim	Put in water pool for various periods of time	Monitoring health is important	Avital & Richter-Levin, 2005
Tail or foot shock	Brief shocks given intermittently	Need to carefully monitor health	Wood et al., 2001
Chronic variable or unpredictable stress (CVS or UCS)	Different stressors applied daily for days or weeks	Various investigators combine different types of stress	Hodes et al., 2015

stressors lead to the same final, common outcome: elevations in stress hormones, cortisol (humans), or corticosterone (animals). Further, animal models provide the advantage of being able to examine internal organs, circulating hormones and other factors, and the brain of subjects before, during, and after stress (see Table 4.1 for a list and short description of commonly used stressors in rodent research and studies that have utilized these stressors).

The hallmark of stress is enhanced synthesis and release of cortisol or corticosterone which occurs within minutes following the initiation of stress and is sustained for hours. It is notable that major differences in amount of release between various stresses are not apparent. However, it is difficult to compare the intensity of the stimulus between stressor types. Rivier (1999) assessed the effects of the neurogenic stressor, foot shock, and the systemic stressor, alcohol, and found similar levels of circulating corticosterone following their application. Likewise, Anisman et al. (2001) compared corticosterone levels in mice exposed to the psychogenic stressors—a rat or fox odor—and the neurogenic stressors—restraint, foot shock, cold swim, acoustic startle, or open field—and found more similarities than differences in circulating corticosterone. Thus, a variety of stressors are effective in causing release of generally high and similar levels of circulating corticosterone.

2.3 Sex as a Biological Variable

While there is general agreement on the debilitating effects of chronic stress, it is remarkable to note that the vast majority of studies were conducted in only males of these species. Thus, it is only quite recently that the response of females to stress has been investigated. Surprising to some researchers, but not to most neuro-endocrinologists, responses in females can be different than in males (Luine et al., 2017b, 2018). The importance of determining possible sex differences in stress responses is firstly that a model derived solely in a male may not pertain to a female and vice versa, and thus the model does not provide translational value. Furthermore, determining the extent and nature of sex differences in responses may provide information for understanding why some stress-related diseases have different incidence rates between the sexes. For example, women have a higher incidence of anxiety disorders, posttraumatic stress disorder, and major depression than men, while they have a lower incidence of alcohol and drug abuse and behavior disorders than men (Bangasser & Valentino, 2014). A better understanding of sex differences in stress responding and their bases may inform the development of novel and more effective therapies for these disorders, which are often precipitated by or related to stress and which pose an enormous burden on society. Examples of sex differences in stress responses are detailed below.

3 Stress Alters Anxiety, Depression, and Cognitive Function

3.1 Effects in Adult Rodents

The assessment of complex interactions between stress, gender, hormones, mood, and neural plasticity requires study in a vertebrate where physiological and behavioral indices can be assessed. Thus, rodents are ideal for study since they display mood characteristics, and cognition can also be measured. Changes in mood and behavior have been measured following numerous stress paradigms, and tissue sizes are sufficient such that multiple analyses can be conducted from a single subject, thus reducing the total number of animals needed. In addition, there is a large database of literature on rats and mice on which to base studies. Finally, the relatively low cost of large numbers of rodents needed for stress studies makes rats or mice the species of choice.

In the last 20 years, more research has focused on higher-order neural functions, and results show a more complex picture than with other physiological systems, with several factors influencing outcomes including the sex of the subject as well as the specific domain assessed. The vast majority of experiments have been conducted in males, but recent studies have included females and bring fresh insight into the nature of stress effects. In male rodents, acute stress enhances some forms of learning including classical conditioning (Wood et al., 2001), and generally enhances consolidation of memory but impairs retrieval and working memory (Green & McCormick, 2013). In contrast, chronic stress, one–three weeks of stress elicited by daily restraint or different daily stressors (unpredictable chronic stress, UCS), results in impaired learning and memory in spatial tasks such as radial arm maze (RAM), Morris water maze, Y-Maze, and recognition memory tasks such as object and place recognition (Luine et al., 2017b, 2018; Conrad et al., 2003; Ortiz & Conrad, 2018). Remarkably, female rodent cognitive responses to stress are often different: acute stress impairs classical conditioning (Wood et al., 2001) and does not affect object placement (Luine et al., 2017a), while chronic stress enhances performance of spatial memory tasks (Bowman et al., 2001; Conrad et al., 2003), but does not alter object recognition (Gomez & Luine, 2014). Our lab was the first to show that chronic stress impairs RAM performance in males (Luine et al., 1994) and enhances it in females (Bowman et al., 2001), and we continue to consider sex as a variable in our studies.

While less investigated than cognition, anxiety increases following chronic stress in both male and female rats as assessed by either the elevated plus maze or the open field. It appears that males show stress-dependent increase in anxiety before females (seven days; Bowman et al., 2009) but by 21 days females are also affected (Noschang et al., 2009). However, few studies include females, and further study is required. Depression in rodents is assessed by preference for sucrose-containing vs plain water wherein less consumption of sucrose indicates anhedonia (loss of pleasure) and therefore depression. In males, exposure to a variety of stressors (one–four weeks) including predator stress, social defeat coupled with chronic isolation, and variable stressors increases male depression in the sucrose preference test (Dalla et al., 2010; Carnevali et al., 2012; Gronli et al., 2005; Burgado et al., 2014). Few studies have utilized females but we found that both sexes exhibited decreased sucrose preference at seven, 14, and 21 days of restraint stress (Buenaventure et al., unpublished) and seven days of unpredictable stress decreased preference in female but not male mice (Hodes et al., 2015). Thus, stress appears to alter anxiety and depression, but the parameters may be somewhat different between the sexes and require further investigation.

Thus, current studies have shown that stress deleteriously impacts the higher-order neural functions of cognition and mood in rodents. Importantly, if stress is not severe or maintained for extended periods, the changes are generally reversible (Ortiz & Conrad, 2018). For example, we found that if RAM training and testing begins immediately after chronic stress, males are impaired, but if training and testing begins 14 days following stress cessation, impairments are not present (Luine et al., 1994). This pattern follows anatomical results which show retraction of hippocampal pyramidal neuron dendrites following chronic stress and re-growth of the tree by 10 days following cessation of stress (McEwen, 2001) (see Sect. 4 for further discussion of neural changes).

3.2 Stress during Developmental Periods Causes Long Lasting Behavioral and Cognitive Changes

As indicated above, when stress is experienced during adulthood, effects are generally reversible and transitory in nature, but during the pre- and post-natal stage, chronic stress can result in long-lasting effects (reviewed in Weinstock, 2016). The long-lasting effects of environmental agents, food restriction, or toxic chemicals at this time period are also well documented and long known. In regard to stress in rats, we restrained pregnant dams and found that at adulthood, anxiety was increased in female but not male offspring, and RAM performance was impaired in males and enhanced in females (Bowman et al., 2004). Other research shows similar stress effects in males, but females are not often assessed (Weinstock, 2016). Stress during the post-natal period (up to weaning at 21 days) is also associated with permanent alterations in neural and behavioral function (Hodes & Epperson, 2019).

In recent years, the developmental period for the exerting of long-lasting effects has been lengthened to include periadolescent/adolescent and pubertal effects of drugs, environmental factors, and hormones at adulthood (Green & McCormick, 2013). Adult performance on mazes is impaired in rats given stress at 28 days of age (Isgor et al., 2004). Adolescent stress increases anxiety in both sexes at adulthood (Holder & Blaustein, 2014). Adult males show depressive-like behavior and cognitive impairment following adolescent stress but females do not (Gomes & Grace, 2017; Klinger et al., 2019). Further research in females is clearly warranted in order to determine the extent of sex differences at adulthood following adolescent stresses.

Thus, acute and chronic stress given across the rodent lifespan is associated with alterations in higher-order brain functions like cognition and mood. Therefore, animal models of stress can provide important translational information for developing new treatments for stress-related diseases.

4   Neural Effects of Stress

The main advantage of conducting stress experiments in animals, as in most pre-clinical research, is that post-mortem examinations can be made to determine which neural systems are affected and how. Such results can inform the design of clinical studies and treatment paradigms. Chronic stress is associated with sex-specific alterations in areas important for learning and memory like the prefrontal cortex and hippocampus and for mood and anxiety in areas like the amygdala and prefrontal cortex. However, the vast majority of neural studies, like the behavioral studies, fail to include females. A brief synopsis of important changes follows, and the pattern of results suggests that stress often downregulates neural activity or expression in males but either does not alter activity or causes different changes in females.

Chronic stress differentially affects neuronal survival; in males short-term survival of new dentate gyrus neurons is decreased whereas survival is increased in females (Westenbroek et al., 2004). Retraction/pruning of dendrites in CA3 pyramidal neurons of the hippocampus following stress has been well described in male subjects (Watanabe et al., 1992; Ortiz & Conrad, 2018). As shown in Fig. 4.1, three weeks of daily restraint stress causes loss of tertiary dendrites (most distal dendrites) from the apical dendritic tree, but basal dendrites remain unaffected. The density of dendritic spines (small protrusions from the dendrites which are the site of synapses) is not changed following stress. Galea et al. (1997) confirmed retraction of CA3 apical dendrites following 21 days of restraint stress in males and found that females do not show changes in these dendrites but that basal CA3 dendrites retract. McLaughlin et al. (2009) also showed that estradiol treatment of female rats without circulating estradiol because of ovariectomy prevents CA3 dendritic retractions and increases CA1 spine density (number of spines/segment of dendrite). These results provide some morphological evidence for the idea that the female hormone, estradiol, may confer cognitive resilience to stress in females.

Chronic stress leads to retraction or loss of tertiary apical dendrites (most distal dendrites) in hippocampal CA3 pyramidal neurons in male rats. The

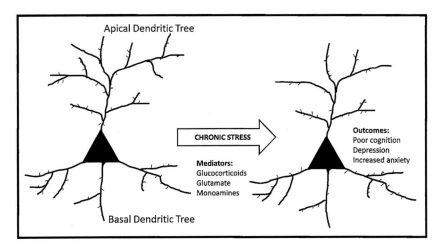

Fig. 4.1 Schematic of hippocampal CA3 pyramidal neuron pre and post chronic stress

basal dendrites are not affected, but other sub-regions are impacted when chronic stress is sufficiently robust or long-lasting. Density of dendritic spines is not altered in CA3 apical or basal spines. Retraction of apical dendrites underlies impaired hippocampal function and contributes to decrements in learning and memory and alterations in mood. Mediators of dendritic retraction are prolonged exposure to the stress hormones glucocorticoids, increases in glutamatergic activity, and changes in monoaminergic activity (adapted from the studies of Watanabe et al., 1992; Galea et al., 1997; and Ortiz & Conrad, 2018).

Several neurotransmitters show sexually dimorphic responses to stress. Glutamate activity is critical in learning and memory, and 21 days of restraint stress decreased glutamatergic neurotransmission and surface expression of glutamate receptors in the PFC[2] of male, but not female, rats (Wei et al., 2014). Chronic unpredictable mild stress for 21 days caused a 50% decrease in the endocannabinoid receptor, CB1, in the dorsal hippocampus of male rats, whereas an approximately 150% increase was found in females (Reich et al., 2009).

Monoaminergic systems are among rapid and important stress responders/mediators, and following 21 days of restraint decreased levels of norepinephrine, dopamine, and serotonin (5-hydroxytryptamine, or 5-HT) levels are found in the hippocampus of males (Beck & Luine, 1999; Sunanda et al., 2000), but opposite changes in these monoamines are found in females (Beck & Luine, 2002). We examined effects of restraint for a shorter period,

---

[2] PFC: prefrontal cortex.

56   V. Luine

Table 4.2 Sex differences in chronic stress effects on monoamine metabolites in brain areas of male and female rats

AREA	MHPG		HVA		5-HIAA	
	MALE	FEMALE	MALE	FEMALE	MALE	FEMALE
CA1	↑ 153%	↑ 122%	↓ 63%	↑ 18%	↓ 45%	↑ 30%
CA3	↓ 41%	↑ 105%	↑ 46%	↓ 11%	↓ 22%	↑ 24%
MP-CORTEX	↓ 18%	↑ 21%	=	=	=	=
BL-AMYGDALA	↓ 18%	↑ 21%	↓ 24%	4%	↓ 25%	=

Entries show significant increases (↑) or decreases (↓) in metabolites for norepinehrine (MHPG, 3-methoxy-4-hydroxyphenolglycol), dopamine (HVA, homovanillic acid), and serotonin (5-HIAA, 5-hydroxyindole acetic acid). An arrow of the same color but a lighter hue indicates a significant difference. Significant differences range from $p < 0.05$ to 0.001. Adult male and female rats served as controls or received seven days of 6 h/day restraint stress. Data from Bowman et al. (2009)

one week, and like the behavioral responses, monoaminergic systems showed robust sex differences (Bowman et al., 2009, Table 2). Changes in metabolites of the major amines, 3-methoxy-4-hydroxyphololglycol (MHPG) for norepinephrine, homovanillic acid (HVA) for dopamine, and 5-hydroxyindole acetic acid (5-HIAA) for serotonin, are shown by arrows in CA1, CA3, medial prefrontal cortex, and baso-lateral amygdala in Table 4.2. Metabolites provide a measure of activity, but other assessments like in vivo release of transmitters need to be made. In the majority of cases, metabolites decreased in males and increased in females following stress.

The cortex showed the fewest changes, with only MHPG affected: an 18% decrease in males and a 21% increase in females. The largest changes were found in CA1 where both sexes showed an increase in the NE metabolite, MHPG, but males showed a significantly larger increase, 153%, than females, 122%, and both HVA and 5-HIAA decreased 45–63% in males and increased 18–30% in females. However, the largest difference between the sexes occurred in CA3 where MHPG decreased 41% in males and increased 105% in females. These remarkably different patterns in monoaminergic activity in the sexes following stress may be critically important in mediating memory and mood changes. However, further experiments are necessary to link the changes in activity to behavior and to determine their translatability.

5   Ethical Considerations

Stress procedures, like all research in animals, must be approved by a committee which oversees animal care and protection at the institution where the research is carried out. Researchers must insure welfare of the animals and demonstrate that procedures do not cause undue harm or morbidity/mortality. Examples include daily weighing of subjects to insure against excessive weight loss because chronic stress causes weight loss. All researchers need to be trained in proper implementation of the stressors and to monitor untoward effects, in which case the stress must be stopped. Such symptoms can include porphyrin discharge from the eyes and excessive weight loss. Stress experiments have been conducted for many years, and thus if researchers follow standard protocols and are attentive to animal well-being, problems should not arise. In the United States, researchers adhere to guidelines from the National Institutes of Health (*Guide for the Care and Use of Laboratory Animals*, Eighth Edition, n.d.). Many European researchers also follow these guidelines, but many countries issue their own. Researchers should check with their home institution's research office for the guidelines which they should follow.

6   Conclusions

An array of acute and chronic stress models is available in rodents to model stress in humans. Proper implementation can lead to critical information for understanding the mechanisms underlying stress effects and for developing new treatments. Since stress is a growing issue for our society, obtaining such information is ever more critical.

Acknowledgments Experimental work from the author's laboratory discussed in this review was supported by The City University of New York, PSC-CUNY, NIH grant RR003037 from the National Center for Research Resources (HC); and Training Grants GM060665 (VL) and NS080686 (HC). Dr. Maya Frankfurt assisted in drawing Fig. 4.1.

References

Anisman, H., Hayley, S., Kelly, O., Borowski, T., & Merali, Z. (2001). Pshchogenic, neurogenic and system stressor effects on plasma corticosterone and behavior: Mouse strain-dependent outcomes. *Behavioral Neuroscience, 115*, 443–454.

Aschbacher, K., Mellon, S. H., Wolkowitz, O. M., Henn-Haase, C., Yehuda, R., Flory, J. D., Bierer, L. M., Abu-Amara, D., Marmar, C. R., & Mueller, S. G. (2018). Posttraumatic stress disorder, symptoms, and white matter abnormalities among combat-exposed veterans. *Brain Imaging and Behavior, 12*, 989–999.

Avital, A., & Richter-Levin, G. (2005). Exposure to juvenile stress exacerbates the behavioural consequences of exposure to stress in the adult rat. *The International Journal of Neuropsychopharmacology, 8*, 163–173.

Avital, A., Ram, E., Maayan, R., Weizman, A., & Richter-Levin, G. (2005). Effects of early-life stress on behavior and neurosteroid levels in the rat hypothalamus and entorhinal cortex. *Brain Research Bulletin, 68*, 419–424.

Bangasser, D. A., & Valentino, R. J. (2014). Sex differences in stress-related psychiatric disorders: Neurobiological perspectives. *Frontiers in Neuroendocrinology, 35*, 303–319.

Beck, K. D., & Luine, V. N. (1999). Food deprivation modulates chronic stress effects on object recognition in male rats: Role of monoamines and amino acids. *Brain Research, 830*, 56–71.

Beck, K. D., & Luine, V. N. (2002). Sex differences in behavioral and neurochemical profiles after chronic stress: Role of housing conditions. *Physiology and Behavior, 75*, 661–73.

Bowman, R. E., Zrull, M. C., & Luine, V. N. (2001). Chronic restraint stress enhances radial arm maze performance in female rats. *Brain Research, 904*, 279–289.

Bowman, R., MacLusky, N. J., Sarmiento, Y., Frankfurt, M., Gordon, M., & Luine, V. N. (2004). Sexually dimorphic effects of prenatal stress on cognition, hormonal responses and central neurotransmitters. *Endocrinology, 145*, 3778–3787.

Bowman, R. E., Micik, R., Gautreaux, C., Fernandez, L., & Luine, V. N. (2009). Sex dependent changes in anxiety, memory, and monoamines following one week of stress. *Physiology & Behavior, 97*, 21–29.

Buenaventure, J, Khanddaker, H., & Luine, V. (Unpublished) Chronic stress effects on anxiety, depression and cognition in male and female rats.

Burgado, L., Harrell, C. S., Eacret, D., Reddy, R., Barnum, C. J., Tansey, M. G., Miller, A. H., Wang, H., & Neigh, G. N. (2014). Two weeks of predatory stress induces anxiety like behavior with co-morbid depressive-like behavior in adult male mice. *Behavioural Brain Research, 275*, 120–125.

Carnevali, L., Mastorci, F., Graiani, G., Razzoli, M., Trombini, M., Pico-Alfonso, M. A., Arban, R., Grippo, A. J., Quaini, F., & Sgoifo, A. (2012). Social defeat and isolation induce clear signs of a depression-like state, but modest cardiac alterations in wild-type rats. *Physiology & Behavior, 106*, 142–150.

Chapman, D. P., Whitfield, C. L., Felitti, V. J., Dube, S. R., Edwards, V. J., & Anda, R. F. (2004). Adverse childhood experiences and the risk of depressive disorders in adulthood. *Journal of Affective Disorders, 82*(2), 217–225.

Conrad, C. D., Grote, K. D., Hobbs, R. J., & Ferayorni, A. (2003). Sex differences in spatial and non-spatial Y-maze performance after chronic stress. *Neurobiology of Learning and Memory, 79*, 32–40.

Dalla, C., Pitychoutis, M., Kokras, N., & Papadopoulou-Daifoti, Z. (2010). Sex differences in animal models of depression and antidepressant response. *Basic & Clinical Pharmacology & Toxicology, 106*, 226–233.

Fauquet-Alekhine, Ph., & Rouillac, L. (2016). The square of perceived action model as a tool for identification, prevention and treatment of factors deteriorating mental health at work. *Journal of Mental Disorders and Treatment, 2*(3), 1–13, paper #1000126.

Galea, L. A., McEwen, B. S., Tanapat, P., Deak, T., Spencer, R. L., & Dhabhar, F. S. (1997). Sex differences in dendritic atrophy of CA3 pyramidal neurons in response to chronic restraint stress. *Neuroscience, 81*, 689–697.

Gomes, F. V., & Grace, A. A. (2017). Prefrontal cortex dysfunction increases susceptibility of schizophrenia-like changes induced by adolescent stress exposure. *Schizophrenia Bulletin, 43*, 592–600.

Gomez, J. L., & Luine, V. (2014). Female rats exposed to stress and alcohol show impaired memory and increased depressive-like behaviors. *Physiology and Behavior, 123*, 47–54.

Green, M. R., & McCormick, C. M. (2013). Effects of stressors in adolescence on learning and memory in rodent models. *Hormones and Behavior, 64*, 364–379.

Gronli, J., Murison, R., Fiske, E., Bjorvatn, B., Sorensen, E., Portas, M., & Ursin, R. (2005). Effects of chronic mild stress on sexual behavior, locomotor activity and consumption of sucrose and saccharine solutions. *Physiology & Behavior, 84*, 571–577.

Guide for The Care and Use of Laboratory Animals, Eighth Edition. (n.d.). Institute for Laboratory Animal Research, Division on Earth and Life Studies, National Academies of Science, USA. National Research Council of the National Academies, The National Academies Press, Washington, D.C., USA. www.nap.edu or National Institutions of Health Publication 80–23, www.nih.gov.

Herman, J. P., & Cullinan, W. E. (1997). Neurocircuitry of stress: Central control of the hypothalamo-pituitary-adrenocortical axis. *Trends in Neurosciences, 20*, 78–84.

Hodes, G. E., & Epperson, C. N. (2019). Sex differences in vulnerability and resilience to stress across the life span. *Biological Psychiatry, 86*, 421–432.

Hodes, G. E., Pfau, M. L., Purushothaman, I., Cahn, H. F., Golden, S. A., Histoffel, D. J., & Russo, S. J. (2015). Sex differences in nucleus accumbens transriptome profiles associated with susceptibility versus resilience to subchronic variable stress. *The Journal of Neuroscience, 35*, 16362–16376.

Holder, M. K., & Blaustein, J. D. (2014). Puberty and adolescence as a time of vulnerability to stressors that alter neurobehavioral processes. *Frontiers in Neuroendocrinology, 35*, 89–110.

Isgor, C., Kabbaj, M., Akil, H., & Watson, S. J. (2004). Delayed effects of chronic variable stress during peripubertal-juvenile period on hippocampal morphology and on cognitive and stress axis functions in rats. *Hippocampus, 14*, 636–648.

Klinger, K., Gomes, F. V., Rincon-Cortes, M., & Grace, A. A. (2019). Female rats are resistant to the long-last neurobehavioral changes induced by adolescent stress exposure. *European Neuropsychopharmacology, 10*, 1127–1137.

Luine, V. N., & Gomez, J. L. (2015). Sex differences in rodent cognitive processing and responses to chronic stress. In R. Shansky (Ed.), *Sex differences in the central nervous system* (pp. 365–404). Elsevier.

Luine, V., Villegas, M., Martinez, C., & McEwen, B. S. (1994). Repeated stress causes reversible impairments of spatial memory performance. *Brain Research, 639*, 167–170.

Luine, V., Gomez, J., Beck, K. D., & Bowman, R. E. (2017a). Sex differences in chronic stress effects on cognition in rodents. *Pharmacology, Biochemistry and Behavior, 152*, 13–19.

Luine, V. N., Bowman, R. E., & Serrano, P. A. (2017b). Sex differences in acute stress effects on spatial memory and hippocampal synaptic neurochemicals. In P. Fauquet-Alekine (Ed.), *Understanding stress at work* (pp. 52–56). http://hayka-kultura.org/larsen.html

Luine, V., Bowman, R., & Serrano, P. (2018). Sex differences in cognitive responses to stress in rodents. In A. Ennaceur & M. A. de Souza Silva (Eds.), *Handbook of research on object novelty recognition* (pp. 531–540). Elsevier/Academic Press.

McEwen, B. S. (2001). Plasticity of the hippocampus: Adaptation to chronic stress and allostatic load. *Annals of the New York Academy of Sciences, 933*, 265–277.

McEwen, B. S. (2016). In pursuit of resilience: stress, epigenetics, and brain plasticity. *Annals of the New York Academy of Sciences, 1373*, 56–64.

McEwen, B. S., & Stellar, E. (1993). Stress and the individual. Mechanisms leading to disease. *Archives of Internal Medicine, 153*, 2093–2101.

McIntyre, D. A., Kent, P., Hayley, S., Merali, Z., & Anisman, H. (1999). Influence of psychogenic and neurogenic stressors on neuroendocrine and central monoamine activity in fast and slow kindling rats. *Brain Research, 840*, 63–74.

McLaughlin, K. J., Wilson, J. O., Harman, J., Wright, R. L., Wieczorek, L., Gomez, J., Korol, D. L., & Conrad, D. (2009). Chronic 17β-estradiol or cholesterol prevents stress-induced hippocampal CA3 dendritic retraction in ovariectomized female rats: Possible correspondence between CA1 spine properties and spatial acquisition. *Hippocampus, 20*, 768–786.

Meyers, T. (2018). Stress: The health epidemic of the 21st century. https://thriveglobal.com/stories/stress-the-health-epidemic-of-the-21st-century/

Nasca, C., Menard, C., Hodes, G., Bigio, B., Pena, C., Lorsch, Z., Zelli, D., Ferris, A., Kana, V., Purushothaman, I., Dobbin, J., Nassim, M., DeAngelis, P., Merad, M., Rasgon, N., Meaney, M., Nestler, E. J., McEwen, B. S., & Russo, S. J. (2019). Multidimensional predictors of susceptibility and resilience to social defeat stress. *Biological Psychiatry, 86*, 483–491.

Nelson, R. (2000). *An introduction to behavioral endocrinology, chapter on stress.* (pp. 557–592). Sinauer Associates.

Noschang, C. G., Pettenuzzo, L. F., von Pozzer, T. E., Andreazza, A. C., Krolow, R., Fachin, A., Avila, M. C., Arcego, D., Crema, L. M., Diehl, L. A., Gonçalvez, C. A., Vendite, D., & Dalmaz, C. (2009). Sex-specific differences on caffeine consumption and chronic stress-induced anxiety-like behavior and DNA breaks in the hippocampus. *Pharmacology, Biochemistry, and Behavior, 94*, 63–69.

Ortiz, J. B., & Conrad, C. D. (2018). The impact from the aftermath of chronic stress on hippocampal structure and function: Is there a recovery? *Frontiers in Neuroendocrinology, 49*, 114–123.

Reich, C. G., Taylor, M. E., & McCarthy, M. M. (2009). Differential effects of chronic unpredictable stress on hippocampal CB1 receptors in male and female rats. *Behavioural Brain Research, 203*, 264–269.

Rivier, C. (1999). Gender, sex steroids, corticotropin-releasing factor, nitric oxide, and the HPA response to stress. *Pharmacology, Biochemistry, and Behavior, 64*, 739–751.

Rowson, S. A., Bekhbat, M., Kelly, S. D., Binder, E. B., Hyer, M. M., Shaw, G., Bent, M. A., Hodes, G., Tharp, G., Weinshenker, D., Qin, Z., & Neigh, G. N. (2019). Chronic adolescent stress sex-specifically alters the hippocampal transcriptome in adulthood. *Neuropsychopharmacology, 44*, 1207–1215.

Selye, H. (1976). *The stress of life*. McGraw Hill.

Sunanda, R., Rao, B. S., & Raju, T. R. (2000). Restraint stress-induced alterations in the levels of biogenic amines, amino acids and AchE activity in the hippocampus. *Neurochemical Research, 25*, 1547–1552.

Watanabe, Y., Gould, E., & McEwen, B. S. (1992). Stress induces atrophy of apical dendrites of hippocampal CA3 pyramidal neurons. *Brain Research, 588*, 341–345.

Wei, J., Yuen, E. Y., Liu, W., Li, X., Zhong, P., Karatsoreos, I. N., McEwen, B. S., & Yan, Z. (2014). Estrogen protects against the detrimental effects of repeated stress on glutamatergic transmission and cognition. *Molecular Psychiatry, 19*, 588–598.

Weinstock, M. (2016). Prenatal stressors in rodents: Effects on behavior. *Neurobiol Stress, 6*, 3–13.

Westenbroek, C., Den Boer, J. A., Veenhuis, M., & Ter Horst, G. J. (2004). Chronic stress and social housing differentially affect neurogenesis in male and female rats. *Brain Research Bulletin, 64*, 303–308.

Wolf, O. T., Atsak, P., de Quervain, D. J., Roozendaal, B., & Wingenfeld, K. (2016). Stress and memory: A selective review on recent developments in the understanding of stress hormone effects on memory and their clinical relevance. *Journal of Neuroendocrinology, 28*. https://doi.org/10.1111/jne.12353. Review.

Wood, G. E., Beylin, A. V., & Shors, T. (2001). The contribution of adrenal and reproductive hormones to the opposing effects of stress on trace conditioning in males versus females. *Behavioral Neuroscience, 115*, 175–187.

Yehuda, R., Morris, A., Labinsky, E., Zemelman, S., & Schmeidler, J. (2007). Ten-year follow-up study of cortisol levels in aging Holocaust survivors with and without PTSD. *Journal of Traumatic Stress, 20*, 757–761.

Zanca, R. M., Sanay, S., Avila, J. A., Rodriguez, E., Shair, H. N., & Serrano, P. A. (2018). Contextual fear memory modulates PSD95 phosphorylation, AMPAr subunits, PKMζ and PI3K differentially between adult and juvenile rats. *Neurobiol Stress, 10*, 100139. https://doi.org/10.1016/j.ynstr.2018.11.002. eCollection 2019 Feb.

Part II

Stress Assessment

5

Physiological Assessment of the State of Mental Stress at Work

Philippe Fauquet-Alekhine and Jean-Claude Granry

1   Introduction

The transactional model of Lazarus and Folkman (1984) considers mental stress as a transaction between an individual and the context associated with one's perception that external demands are exceeding one's capacity for response (Folkman et al., 1986; Rozanov, 2017, p. 17; see also Chap. 2 of the present book). The perception of the stress factors by the subject is related to emotions combined with physiological responses of the body to these factors. Therefore, subjects' stress state may be assessed through physiological measurements, providing an objective evaluation. The advantage of such methods is that they are not submitted to the subjective bias that might occur when assessing the stress state through questionnaires, for example (see Chap. 6 of the present book). Responses to questionnaires may sometimes be systematically biased (Fauquet-Alekhine et al., 2020).

P. Fauquet-Alekhine (✉)
SEBE-Lab, Department of Psychological and Behavioural Science,
London School of Economics and Political Science, London, UK

Laboratory for Research in Science of Energy, Montagret, France

Groupe INTRA Robotics, Avoine, France
e-mail: p.fauquet-alekhine@lse.ac.uk; philippe.fauquet-alekhine@groupe-intra.com

J.-C. Granry
University Hospital, Angers, France

© The Author(s), under exclusive license to Springer Nature Switzerland AG 2023
P. Fauquet-Alekhine, J. Erskine (eds.), *The Palgrave Handbook of Occupational Stress*,
https://doi.org/10.1007/978-3-031-27349-0_5

The purpose of this chapter is to present and comment on a selection of methods aiming at characterizing subjects' state of acute mental stress through physiological measurements. The chapter does not address assessment of chronic stress. The methods were chosen because their reliability has been proven in many studies and they are now widespread in the scientific community, and they present a low level of disturbance for the subjects when applied. Each method presented addresses only one physiological factor (e.g., heart rate or ventilation variation) but they may be combined in order to consolidate the conclusions regarding the subjects' state of stress.

1.1 General Considerations Regarding Reliability and Limitations

As for any physiological measures, the equipment necessary to perform the measurement may disturb the subjects relatively more or less and thus be a factor of stress that must be taken into account by the analysts. Physiological measures are also impacted by subjects' physical efforts. Therefore, assessing a mental state through physiological measurements must exclude physical efforts or, at least, their contribution to the measures must be quantified. Furthermore, measurements may be distorted by diseases affecting the subjects' organ providing data (e.g., pulmonary oedema disturbs ventilation) or by mental troubles. This means that the analysts need to bear in mind that the equipment must be chosen to create as little discomfort as possible for the subjects, and that they must consider the subjects' medical and physiological history.

1.2 Methods Presented

The methods chosen for characterizing subjects' state of stress are based on the following physiological parameters:

- heart rate variation
- heart rate variability
- blood pressure
- respiratory frequency
- skin resistivity or conductance
- salivary alpha-amylase
- cortisol
- cytokine

5 Physiological Assessment of the State of Mental Stress at Work

The way these parameters are linked to acute mental stress is depicted in detail in Chap. 3 of this book and will not be reconsidered in the present chapter.

As a conclusion, the chapter ends with comment regarding ethics and advice.

2 Heart Rate Variation

Heart rate (HR) increase is an indicator for acute mental stress escalation, as demonstrated in many experiments (see, e.g., Kudielka et al., 2004; Spierer et al., 2009; Choi & Gutierrez-Osuna, 2009; Petrowski et al., 2010; Cinaz et al., 2010; Fauquet-Alekhine et al., 2016).

Heart rate (HR) increase with mental stress is not linear. It follows a power-type curve (Fig. 5.1) as emphasized by Fauquet-Alekhine et al. (2016) starting at the rest value to a maximum corresponding to high levels of stress.

Heart rate is the frequency of heartbeat. It is usually measured in beats per minute (bpm) by considering the lapse in time between two maxima of the signal (Fig. 5.2). The typical signal shows a periodical wave depicted by several points among which are the Q-R-S points associated with the main wave, the maximum being R. This is why it is common to read results presented in terms of RR intervals (in ms).

Heart rate is usually measured through a monitor connected to electrodes distributed on the subject's chest. However, during stress studies, it is better to opt for a wearable device allowing subjects to perform their activity without being disturbed by the measuring system. The more realiable systems are based on a chest strap equipped with sensors that provide a signal transmitted to a memory buffer often located inside a dedicated watch worn on the wrist of the subject or, more recently, to a smartphone (Giles et al., 2016; Baker et al., 2017; Gilgen-Ammann et al., 2019; Climstein et al., 2020; Speer et al.,

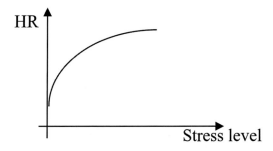

Fig. 5.1 HR variation with stress for healthy adult subjects submitted to acute mental stress

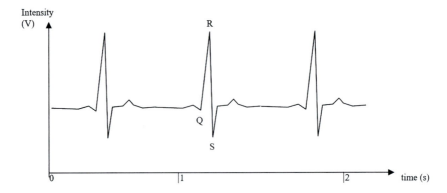

Fig. 5.2 Example of signal monitored when measuring heart rate

2020). Systems involving a measurement located at the wrist using a watch are not recommended because they lack reliability (Fig. 5.3).

The signal being acquired continuously, the measure of HR is actually obtained during the stress episode for which the variations of the state of stress may be recorded. Data may be analyzed per individuals or per cohorts of similar subjects (see, e.g., Fig. 5.4). The quantity taken to characterize the state of stress is thus an averaged heart rate over the period of time during which the subject was submitted to stress. Fauquet-Alekhine et al. (2014) suggested a variation of the stress indicator HR by considering the product of the mean HR (HR_{mean}) by the difference between the maximun HR (HR_{max}) and the mean HR; they introduced the coefficient of stress K_s:

$$K_{sr} = HR_{mean} \times (HR_{max} - HR_{mean})$$

This gave interesting results.

2.1 Expected Averaged Values for Samples of Healthy Adults

Usually, HR at rest ranges from 45 to 65 bpm.
Subjects reading a question on a test (Fauquet-Alekhine et al., 2012) may rise over 75 bpm.
Experienced air traffic controllers (Fallahi et al., 2016) performing their job in normal conditions may have a mean HR at 75–80 bpm.
Experienced airplane pilots (Lehrer et al., 2010) performing their job in normal conditions on simulator may have a mean HR up to 93 bpm.

5 Physiological Assessment of the State of Mental Stress at Work

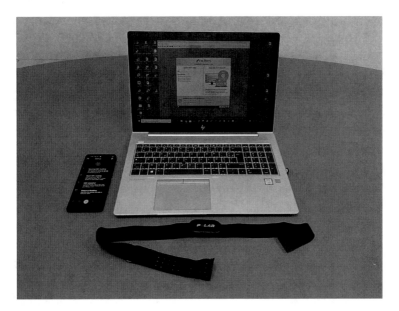

Fig. 5.3 Chest strap equipped with sensors. Signal transmitted to a memory buffer of a smartphone. Treatment on computer

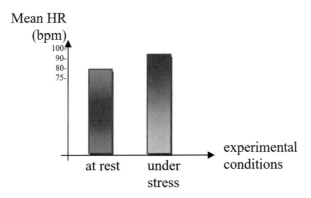

Fig. 5.4 Example of comparison of mean HR for a sample of heathy male young adults (data from Kudielka et al., 2004) under two different experimental conditions: at rest and under stress

When carrying out an oral presentation in front of a group, subjects' HR may rise to 95 bpm (Berger et al., 2016).

Subjects being interviewed may have a mean HR from 75 bpm (Stedmon et al., 2015) to 100 bpm (Petrowski et al., 2010).

Physicians managing a critical situation in the operating theater may increase their HR to between 100 and 105 bpm (Berton et al., 2015).

When comparing data between cohorts of different subjects (e.g., a group of healthy adults and a group of adults suffering from schizophrenia; Reinertsen et al., 2017), data may be normalized by a baseline. The baseline is typically the data obtained from the signal measured at rest.

2.2 Reliability and Limitations

While the studies have shown a satisfactory acceptability of the data when averaged over samples, the use of data to compare the stress state between two individuals is more delicate even when using baselines to normalize data. For example, if subject A gives 120 bpm under stress and 60 bpm at rest, and subject B gives respectiveley 130 and 65 in the same conditions as for subject A, the conclusion might be that subject B was more stressed than A, but the ratio (HR under stress)/(HR at rest) gives the value 2 for both. Factors specific to the subjects such as gender, weight, genetics, and regularity of physical activity may influence HR.

In addition, certain stress conditions may superimpose physical stress (associated with physical efforts) onto mental stress; this is the case of anesthetists managing cardiac distress with cardiac massage, for example. In such cases, the results are different when comparing subjects submitted to physical stress with those not submitted to this stress (Fauquet-Alekhine et al., 2014).

3 Heart Rate Variability

Many studies have promoted the ratio of power frequencies for low vs high values of heart rate variability (ratio LF/HF of HRV) as a relevant and confident parameter to differentiate levels of stress state.

Since it is derived from HR measurement, the calulation of HRV is considered as obtained during the stress episode but it requires sampling HR over a lapse in time in order to acquire enough data to perform a satisfactory treatment of the signal. The ratio HRV is obtained by analyzing fluctuations in beat-to-beat periods, to consider the ratio of the probability density function of the low frequencies of HR by the probability density function of the high frequencies of HR. HRV being deduced from HR, the measurement systems are the same.

5 Physiological Assessment of the State of Mental Stress at Work

In other words, a spectral analysis of HRV (see, e.g., Camm et al., 1996; Kim et al., 2018) highlights several frequency bands among which are a low-frequency component reflecting sympathetic activity (usually referred to as LF: 0.04–0.15Hz) and a high-frequency component reflecting parasympathetic activity (usually referred to as HF: 0.15–0.4Hz). The ratio of LF to HF densities illustrates the autonomic parasympathetic and sympathetic balance and is used as an indicator of stress (e.g., Camm et al., 1996; McDuff et al., 2014; Fallahi et al., 2016; Kim et al., 2018). The spectral analysis is usually carried out using a Fast Fourier Transformation. An illustration of the HRV spectrum is given in Fig. 5.5.

When compared with HR measurements, HRV presents the advantages of being more discriminant, as illustrated in Fig. 5.6. It also does not require baseline measurements, thus offering a higher reliability when comparing two individuals.

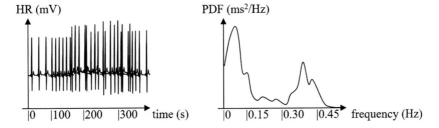

Fig. 5.5 On the left, a sample of HR, and on the right, a spectrum of frequencies (or probability density function (PDF) of frequencies) showing two main components associated with LF and HF of HR

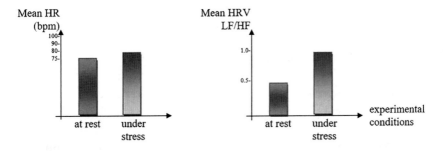

Fig. 5.6 Example of comparison of mean HR mean HRV for a sample of heathy young adults (data from McDuff et al., 2014) under two different experimental conditions: at rest and under stress

3.1 Expected Averaged Values for Samples of Healthy Adults

The ratio HRV LF/HF increases with stress.

At rest, LF/HF is expected to be between 0.5 and 1.5 (McDuff et al., 2014; Pereira et al., 2017).

When reading, LF/HF is about 2.5, and for an oral presentation, it is about 3 (Pereira et al., 2017).

Experienced pilots of ground robots performing an easy task give LF/HF between 1 and 4 (unpublished data from INTRA robotics, France).

During an interview, LF/HF may rise to 6 (Petrowski et al., 2010).

Experienced airplane pilots performing their job in normal conditions on a simulator may have a ratio LF/HF up to 6.3 (Lehrer et al., 2010; Cao et al., 2019).

Anesthetists managing critical situations in real operating conditions may have a mean ratio LF/HF up to 7.5 (Baker et al., 2017).

3.2 Reliability and Limitations

Among all the methods available to date for assessment of the stress state through physiological measures, HRV appears to be the most reliable. However, a sensitivity to ventilation disturbance was pointed out by Choi and Gutierrez-Osuna (2011). Decreased HRV was observed with aging and obesity (Cao et al., 2019).

In addition, as for HR, certain stress conditions may superimpose physical stress (associated with physical efforts) onto mental stress, inducing a bias in the results.

4 Blood Pressure

Two values are measured corresponding to particular phases of the cardiac cycle: systolic blood pressure (SBP) and diastolic blood pressure (DBP), associated with peaks of pressure when compared to lowest pressure in the arteries (Fig. 5.7). The unit for blood pressure measurement is mmHg (millimeters of mercury).

During stressful episodes, increases in SBP magnitude compared to that of DBP have been observed. They are considered as a reliable indicator of the

5 Physiological Assessment of the State of Mental Stress at Work

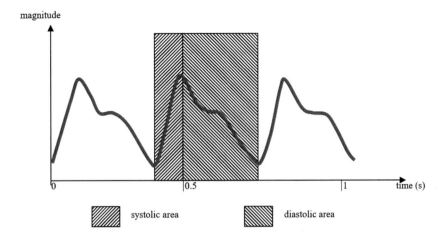

Fig. 5.7 Blood pressure with time during cardiac cycles: systolic blood pressure (SBP) and diastolic blood pressure (DBP)

stress state (see Brownley et al., 2000). Blood pressure wave may be analyzed in terms of variation (Hjortskov et al., 2004).

The most reliable system to measure blood pressure is based on a device stopping blood flow usually by placing a sensor on the upper arm at the brachial artery or on the wrist at the radial artery. This is usually done on the non-dominant side. The principle is thus to occlude the artery for each measurement, thus not providing a sampled wave but a succession of instant measures of blood pressure. It is clear that the higher the number of measurements, the higher the probability to disturb the subject.

It is possible to obtain a continuous sampling of the blood pressure signal in an indirect way. The signal being acquired continuously, the measure is actually obtained during the stress episode. The variations thus account for the state of stress and may be recorded. For example, the Finometer is a continuous hemodynamic monitor using a volume-clamp method based on photoelectric measurement (photophethysmography) through a cuff worn on the finger (Penaz, 1973). The recorded signal makes it possible to reconstruct the blood pressure signal (Guelen et al., 2003; Schutte et al., 2003; Lyu et al., 2015; O'Súilleabháin et al., 2018; Cho et al., 2019). However, to avoid artifacts, movement of the hand must be maintained at a minimum and the system requires individual calibration for each subject.

Tonometric-based systems consist in measuring blood pressure from the radial artery, a device applying a varying force on the artery (Parati et al., 2003). This technology is not recommended because it is sensitive to subjects' movements and to the positioning relative to the heart.

More recently, researchers have developed a watch-type sensor with an automatic oscillometric device for the measurement of blood pressure at the wrist (Tomitani et al., 2020; Kuwabara et al., 2019; Kario et al., 2020). However, this development is too recent to provide sufficient feedback regarding reliability and application to the assessment of emotional states.

4.1 Expected Averaged Values for Samples of Healthy Adults

The World Health Organization has provided a classification of expected values for adult blood pressure (WHO, 1999; see Table 5.1). The normal values for healthy adults are <130 mmHg for systolic blood pressure and <85 mmHg for diastolic blood pressure.

The relevant indicator for stress is the increase in blood pressure between rest and the stress episodes.

During a mathematical task, the variation for SBP was measured from rest to stress 129–131 and for DBP 78–81 (O'Súilleabháin et al., 2018), thus giving an increase of 2 for SBP and 3 for DBP; for a similar task, it was found to vary from rest to stress 115–134 for SBP and 70–82 for DBP (Edwards and Morris, 2018), thus giving an increase of 19 for SBP and 12 for DBP.

For cold pressure task (putting the hand in cold water), the variation for SBP was measured from rest to stress 115–128 and for DBP 70–81 (Edwards and Morris, 2018), thus giving an increase of 13 for SBP and 11 for DBP.

During an oral presentation, SBP may vary from rest to stress 112–127 and DBP 70–85 (Shilton et al., 2017), thus giving an increase of 15 for SBP and 15 for DBP.

It is therefore clear that values for blood pressure under different stress conditions may remain in the normal range. The criterion to detect a state of stress is the increase of the values between a rest condition and a stress

Table 5.1 Blood pressure classification for adults

Classification	Systolic blood pressure (mmHg)	Diastolic blood pressure (mmHg)
Optimal	<120	<80
Normal	<130	<85
High-normal	130–139	85–89
Hypertension (mild)	140–159	or 90–99
Hypertension (moderate)	160–179	100–109
Hypertension (severe)	≥180	≥110

Source: WHO (1999)

5 Physiological Assessment of the State of Mental Stress at Work

condition, and it is not certain that values associated with a stress state in a given experiment would be similar to those obtained in another experiment.

4.2 Reliability and Limitations

In addition to drawbacks due to calibrations and inaccuracy related to the subjects' movements, other factors may affect the accuracy of blood pressure measurement.

The accuracy of the blood pressure measure can be modified as the level between the heart and the sensor is changing (hydrostatic effect).

Repeated assessments of blood pressure with techniques that temporally and periodically squeeze the arm or the wrist might physiologically elevate blood pressure (in addition to the elevation due to stressors) and psychologically distract subjects from the experienced situation, thus creating a bias in subjects' response to the experimental condition.

Some authors complain that blood pressure measurements to characterize the state of stress have given diverging results (Koudela-Hamila et al., 2020); the preceding description of the expected values does not refute this.

This may explain why the characterization of a state of stress through blood pressure measurement is less used than those based on HR or HRV in the scientific literature. Very often, it is complementary to another physiological parameter measured to characterize the state of stress.

5 Respiratory Frequency

In resuscitation departments at hospitals, respiratory frequency is accurately measured through monitoring of the respiration flow collected in a mask worn on the face linked through a duct to a monitor which also displays moisture in the exhaled breath and O2 saturation in the blood. Since the gases may be flammable (e.g., O2 input), caution is required to ensure that the safety features are active and electrical hazards are removed. It is obvious that such a system is not suitable for stress analysis.

Researchers have thus developped wearable systems, most of them based on sensors distributed on a chest strap connected to a monitor that samples the signals at a chosen frequency. The signal being acquired continuously, the measure is actually obtained during the stress episode for which the variations of the state of stress may be recorded subject to some limitations (see below). The principle for the measurement is based on the chest movements.

Choi and Gutierrez-Osuna (2011) have used a piezoelectric respiratory effort sensor and a pressure-based respiration sensor. They pointed out that "the piezo sensor has a very low profile but is sensitive to motion artifacts, whereas the pressure-based sensor works well in the presence of body movements though at the expense of a larger package" (p. 2651). McDuff et al. (2014) and Hernando et al. (2016) used a similar system. Liu et al. (2019) used a chest strap combining accelerometers and gyroscopes used to capture signals modulated by respiration. However, this requires being correctly positioned over the diaphragm. Recently, a wearable sensor was developed (Chu et al., 2019), integrating low-powered piezo-resistive sensors that can be integrated with wireless Bluetooth units, allowing the simultaneous measurement of both respiration volume and rate with a satisfactory accuracy, especially under various ambulatory conditions.

Interestingly, Hernando et al. (2016) promoted the joint analysis of respiration and HRV in order to obtain a more reliable characterization of stress. However, limitations are noteworthy (see below).

5.1 Expected Averaged Values for Samples of Healthy Adults

As for the heart, ventilation may be analyzed in terms of rate or variability. Figure 5.8 gives an example of results for breathing rate compared to HRV in the same two conditions (rest and stress), and Fig. 5.9 shows the power density function of ventilation in two conditions (relax and stress).

However, the literature does not provide an estimation of expected values under different conditions of stress. Values depend on the principle and the device used for measurement. The state of stress is thus determined from the difference of values obtained at rest and in stressful conditions.

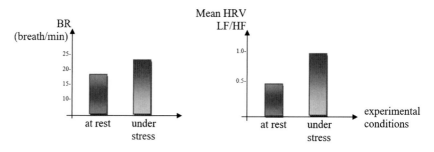

Fig. 5.8 Breathing rate (BR) and HRV under rest and stress conditions (data from McDuff et al., 2014)

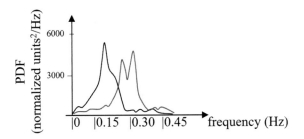

Fig. 5.9 Power density function (PDF) of ventilation under rest and stress conditions (data from Gutierrez et al., 2011)

5.2 Reliability and Limitations

The main drawback of this approach is that the measure is significantly disturbed when subjects are speaking and it is very sensitive to the physical efforts of the subjects.

6 Skin Conductance or Resistivity

The relation to stress of skin conductance G_s (or skin resistivity $R_s=1/G_s$) is well described by Sun et al. (2010, p. 4): when measuring the electrical conductance of the skin, "a transient increase in skin conductance is proportional to sweat secretion. When an individual is under mental stress, sweat gland activity is activated and increases skin conductance. Since the sweat glands are also controlled by the sympathetic nervous system, skin conductance acts as an indicator for sympathetic activation due to the stress reaction. The hands and feet, where the density of sweat glands is highest, are usually used to measure [skin conductance]. There are two major components [...]. Skin conductance level (SCL) is a slowly changing part of the signal, and it can be computed as the mean value of skin conductance over a window of data. A fast-changing part of the signal is called skin conductance response (SCR), which occurs in relation to a single stimulus." In a recent paper, Posada-Quintero et al. (2018) mentioned "Electrodermal activity" instead of skin conductance to define the phenomenon analyzed using this method.

The measurement involves two probes pasted on the hand (e.g., on two fingers: Sun et al., 2010) connected to a watch worn on the wrist which provides signals via Bluetooth to a computer for sampling and treatment. The signal being acquired continuously, the measure is actually obtained during the stress episode subject to some limitations (see below). An electric tension

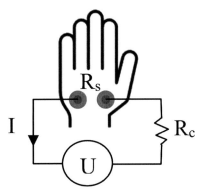

Fig. 5.10 Measuring principle of skin conductance: an electric tension is applied between two probes pasted on the hand and the electrical intensity is measured to access the conductance G_s

U being applied between the probes (direct current), the electrical intensity I is measured to access the conductance (Fig. 5.10) through the galvanic skin response (GSR).

$$As\ U = (R_s + R_c) \times I$$

The conductance is:

$$G_s = (U/I - R_c)^{-1}$$

6.1 Expected Averaged Values for Samples of Healthy Adults

The values expected for GSR depend mainly on the place where the probes are pasted, the electrical circuit used, and the subject's capacity to sweat. In any case, the electrical values are not interesting as the relevant quantities are those associated with the fast-changing part of the signal, that is, the skin conductance response (SCR). The changes of the subject's state (relax or stress) are thus detected. However, the intensity of the stress is difficult to assess.

6.2 Reliability and Limitations

Subjects may sweat due to the environment temperature, thus contributing to biasing the measurements.

Moreover, successive stress stimuli may induce a cumulative production of sweat while there may be no actual accumulative perception of stress by the subject; Posada-Quintero et al. (2018: see Fig. 1 of the article) provided a sample of signals suggesting this process. In other words, a high SCL may not reflect a high stress episode but rather a succession of low stress episodes. It seems difficult to differentiate the two possibilities only on the basis of the skin conductance measure: the approach is not self-sufficient conversely to HR or HRV, for example.

In addition, when someone sweats, there are two latent times. The first is the delay following the stress stimulus until the actual presence of sweat on the hands, and the second is the delay for the skin to recover a "normal" wetness. Shimmer (2015: see Fig. 5 of the article) gives samples of GSC and HR simultaneously sampled for a subject submitted to successive stress episodes. While the trigger of each episode seems to be correctly correlated between the two signals, GSC does not give any reliable information regarding the intensity of the perceived stress conversely to HR, and the second latent time is clearly illustrated.

7 Salivary Alpha-amylase

Salivary alpha-amylase (sAA) has emerged as a valid and reliable biomarker of Autonomous Nervous System (ANS) activity and as a relevant contributor to behavioral analysis (Ali & Nater, 2020).

Salivary alpha-amylase concentration is an indirect marker for sympathoadrenal medullary activity (SAM, see Chap. 3 of the present book) (Granger et al., 2007; Nater et al., 2005; Filaire et al., 2010) with significant variations in response to stressful experiences (Chatterton et al., 1997; Bosch et al., 2003; Geeraerts et al., 2017). Correlations between sAA variations and heart rate variability (HRV) have long been demonstrated (Bosch et al., 2003; Nater et al., 2006). The concentration decreases just after the stress episode during several minutes.

The approach is based on the fact that the salivary glands are innervated by the sympathetic and parasympathetic branches of the ANS (Kawano et al., 2013), the former increasing salivary protein secretion, the latter increasing salivary flow rate (Baum, 1993). Both innervate the salivary glands which produce sAA: in response to neurotransmitter activation, salivary secretions arise, reflecting ANS activity (Garrett, 1999; Nater et al., 2005).

The procedure to collect and analyze sAA samples is not simple and any mistake during the conservation process of the samples may spoil them. The following is an example depicting the procedure by Thoma et al. (2012) similar to that of Chu et al. (2013):

> Participants were instructed in the saliva sampling method, which included placing cotton swabs (Salivettes, Sarstedt, Nümbrecht, Germany) in their mouth and circulating it for 2 min, as recommended by Harmon et al. (2008) [...]. Saliva samples were immediately stored at -20 °C. For batch analysis at the end of data collection, salivettes were thawed and centrifuged at 2000×g for 5min. This procedure resulted in a clear supernatant of low viscosity. Salivary alpha-amylase measurement was completed using an enzyme kinetic method as described previously (Bosch et al., 2003; Rohleder & Nater, 2009). Saliva was processed on Genesis RSP8/150 liquid handling system (Tecan, Crailsheim, Germany). Saliva was diluted at 1:625 with ultrapure water by the liquid handling system. Twenty microliters of diluted saliva and standard were then transferred into standard transparent 96-well microplates (Roth, Karlsruhe, Germany). Standard was prepared from 'Calibrator f.a.s.' solution (Roche Diagnostics, Mannheim, Germany) with concentrations of 326, 163, 81.5, 40.75, 20.38, 10.19, and 5.01 U/L alpha-amylase, respectively, and ultrapure water as zero standard. Afterwards, 80µl of substrate reagent (alphaamylase EPS Sys; Roche Diagnostics, Mannheim, Germany) were pipetted into each well using a multichannel pipette. The microplate containing sample and substrate was then heated to 37 °C by incubation in a waterbath for 90s. Immediately afterwards, a first interference measurement was obtained at a wavelength of 405 nm using a standard ELISA reader (Anthos, Labtech HT2, Anthos, Krefeld, Germany). The plate was then incubated for another 5min at 37 °C in the waterbath, before a second measurement at 405 nm was taken. Increases of absorbance in samples were transformed to alpha-amylase concentrations using a linear regression computed against the standard curve on each microplate (Graphpad Prism 4.0c for Mac OS X, Graphpad Software, San Diego, CA). Inter- and intraassay variation was below 10%.

Geeraerts et al. (2017) made the procedure simpler:

> Just before and after the session (before debriefing), saliva was collected from each participant. Samples were stored at 4°C and then centrifuged at 3000 rounds per min before storage at 4°C. Salivary amylase concentration was then measured by enzymatic method.

Chu et al. (2013) made it even more simpler:

> sAA activity and cortisol concentrations were measured according to the manufacturer's recommendations (Salimetrics Salivary alpha-amylase Assay Kit and Salimetrics Salivary Cortisol immunoassay kit, Salimetrics, USA).

While researchers often present sampling by absorbing the saliva with salivette or a cotton swab at the salivary gland area under the tongue, others prefer applying a spitting method that "prevents the noise associated with absorbent materials, such as incomplete recovery of sAA, inducing flow rate by accidental chewing, and poor quantification of saliva production [...]. There is also evidence that the use of absorbent materials may attenuate stress effects" (Nagy et al., 2015, p. 118).

The measure is not obtained during the stress episode. The resulting data is based on the variation of sAA between the two samples obtained just before and just after the stress episode. Therefore, the variations of the state of stress during the episode cannot be recorded except if intermediate samples are collected. The issue is that it may induce a disturbance of the subjects' state.

7.1 Expected Averaged Values for Samples of Healthy Adults

The values below must be considered bearing in mind the limitations exposed in the next section.

For all following examples, the first sample of saliva was obtained just before the test. The second sample was obtained just after the stress episode.

Students in a flight simulator for F16 fighter pilots showed no significant sAA variation (Chu et al., 2013).

Experienced military personnel during a simulated nuclear-biological-chemical mission on an AH-64 Apache helicopter exhibited an sAA increase of +4% (Waugh et al., 1999).

Subjects exposed to infants crying showed an sAA increase of about +18% (Out et al., 2011).

The cold pressure task led to an increase of +60% (Nagy et al., 2015).

Oral presentation induced increases ranging from +40% to about 122%: +40% (Petrakova et al., 2015), +50% (Filaire et al., 2010), +66% (Rohleder & Nater, 2009) +73%, (Thoma et al., 2012), and +122% (Degroote et al., 2020).

Anesthesiologists in critical situations in the operating theater reached an average increase of +220% (Geeraerts et al., 2017).

Soldiers involved in parachute jumps increased to +300% (Waugh et al., 1999).

7.2   Reliability and Limitations

Although sAA secretion begins in a few seconds when glands are stimulated, sAA needs several minutes to develop, implying that the impact of very short-term stress tests might be underestimated. The dynamic of the process also differs along the circadian cycle.

The approach is sensitive to the method adopted to sample the saliva (i.e., the collection material and sampling such as salivette, spitting method, duration of sampling), which may create a bias that is difficult to evaluate in the results. The conservation protocol with low temperature is also a key point: it must be carefully and strictly respected, otherwise it spoils the samples.

In addition, the results may be affected by the "history of the mouth." This is why some researchers ask subjects not to drink coffee or not brush their teeth at least one hour before the experiment. Similarly, habitual smokers (more than 15 cigarettes a day) exhibit higher sAA values than non-smokers (Thoma et al., 2012).

8   Salivary Cortisol

The use of salivary cortisol as a stress indicator is based on the same arguments as sAA. Kim et al. (2014, p. 205) give a simple and clear argumentation: "cortisol hormone has been used as a reliable bioindex indicating human's stress level. When a human is exposed to stress situation, CRF (corticotropin releasing factor) is released in the hypothalamic paraventricular nucleus, and the CRF stimulates anterior pituitary gland, and adrenal cortical stimulating hormone is secreted. When stress continues, cortisol hormone is secreted, because hypothalamus-pituitary gland-adrenal axis is stimulated. The cortisol hormone can be sampled through saliva, blood and urine, and the method to sample the hormone through urine or saliva than the one through blood is used more in research." However, while sAA begins to decrease when the stress stimulus is removed, the concentration of cortisol continues to increase for several tens of minutes after the stress episode and then decreases during several minutes. The physiological process is detailed in Chap. 3 of the present book.

5 Physiological Assessment of the State of Mental Stress at Work   83

Researchers provide succinct descriptions of the protocol applied for sampling cortisol from saliva. Kim et al. (2014) suggested the following:

> The measurement of cortisol level was analyzed through enzyme-linked immunoassay (EIA). The saliva was sampled by locating a cotton swab at the salivary gland area under the tongue by absorbing saliva for 2min. The saliva absorbed on the cotton swab was centrifugated, kept frozen at −20°C and was analyzed following the procedure offered by Salimetrics.

Schönfeld et al. (2014) were more concise:

> From saliva, we analyzed concentrations of the stress hormone cortisol by means of an immunoassay (IBL, Hamburg).

8.1 Expected Averaged Values for Samples of Healthy Adults

The values below must be considered bearing in mind the limitations exposed in the next section.

For all following examples, the first sample of saliva was obtained just before the test.

Subjects involved in a two-minute oral presentation showed an increase in cortisol concentration by +7% just after the test and +70% nine minutes later (Singer et al., 2017).

Subjects undertaking a memory test with negative items exhibited an increase of +12% after a four-minute test and +25% 20 minutes later (Schönfeld et al., 2014).

Experienced military personnel in a Fighter flight simulator, thus trained for the activity used as a stress experience, showed an increase by +16% to +38% (Kim et al., 2014).

The same military personnel on a real Fighter flight showed an increase by +51% (Kim et al., 2014).

Firemen during a fire simulation for strategic and tactical operation, thus trained for the activity used as a stress experience, showed an increase by +50% just after the 27-minute activity and +70% 15 minutes later (Webb et al., 2011).

Subjects involved in a five-minute oral presentation showed an increase in cortisol concentration by +67% just after the test (Degroote et al., 2020).

Subjects involved in a 15-minute oral presentation showed an increase by +73% just after the test and +93% 15 minutes later (Petrakova et al., 2015).

Subjects involved in a 20-minute oral presentation showed an increase by +140% just after the test and +171% 10 minutes later (Von Dawans et al., 2011).

Subjects involved in a 20-minute oral presentation showed an increase by +160% just after the test and +280% 20 minutes later (Kuebler et al., 2013).

8.2   Reliability and Limitations

The limitations for cortisol as a stress biomarker are the same as those for sAA. We must add that it was also detected as sensitive to gender (Singer et al., 2017). The fact that cortisol concentration in saliva continues to increase even after the end of the stress episode may call into question the relevancy of the measuring point after experiencing stress: Is it just after the stress episode (i.e., as soon as the stress situation is over) or is it at the maximum of cortisol concentration? Moreover, this leads to the conclusion that cortisol concentration depends more on the time than on the stress intensity.

We can conclude that cortisol concentration is more suitable for the study of chronic stress, and in this case other possibilities exist that may be more easily adapted than salivary cortisol such as cortisol in hair, fingernails, or plasma (see, e.g., Wu, Zhou, et al. 2018; Izawa et al., 2017; Wolf et al., 2008; Kunz-Ebrecht et al., 2003).

9   Cytokine

Inflammatory biomarkers mobilized as part of the immune response must be considered as a promising method to assess stress reactivity. Inflammation is measured by assessing cytokines (e.g., C-reactive protein [CRP], factor alpha [TNF-α]), interleukin-1beta [IL-1β], interleukin-10 [IL-10]) using serum or plasma-based blood intravenous samples (see, e.g., Kunz-Ebrecht et al., 2003; Koelsch et al., 2016; Prather et al., 2009; Kamezaki et al., 2012; Yamakawa et al., 2009; Davis et al., 2020). Several studies have shown an increase in the concentration of these biomarkers in response to acute stress (see Sect. 3.5 in Chap. 3 of the present book).

As blood sampling may be troublesome for both subjects and experimenters, the protocol and results expected with this method are not presented here because it is less used. However, researchers have explored the possibility of detecting cytokines variations in saliva, as done for sAA and cortisol. Slavish and Szabo (2019) pointed out that the correlations between salivary cytokines variations and acute stress were modest in view of current publications. They presented the schema of a review addressing the effect of acute stress on inflammatory biomarkers, the results of which are not yet published. They predicted that "salivary markers of inflammation will increase in response to acute stress, though we anticipate there will be variation across the studies. Although we expect results to vary by biomarker, we expect most inflammatory biomarkers to peak 0–60 min after completion of the stressor based on initial findings from Slavish and colleagues (2015)."

10   Ethics

Like any contribution of individuals in scientific experiments, physiological measurements must be based on volunteering. The results must be confidential and must remain between the analyst and the subject. When the questionnaires are used within a research framework or an organizational analysis involving several participants, subjects must know that the results will be used in an anonymous way through statistical analysis. It is also expected that participants will be given the freedom to withdraw from the study at any time if they feel uncomfortable with the experiment. Usually, all of this is written in an informed consent form co-signed by the subject and the analyst (see Appendix).

11   Conclusions

We have presented methods to assess humans' state of stress from physiological measurements. The methods were chosen because they provide a low level of disturbance for the subjects, have been studied for a long time by the scientific community, and their reliability has now been demonstrated. Some of them provide an assessment of stress from a difference between two values acquired at two time-points (just before and just after the stress episode): salivary alpha-amylase, blood or salivary cortisol, and cytokines. Others are based on averaged values over a period of time or on the analysis of recordings; the latter allows the researchers to access the evaluation of stress over different periods of the stress episode. These methods are heart rate variation, heart rate variability, blood pressure, respiratory frequency, and skin conductance (or resistivity).

From our standpoint, methods based on heart rhythm are more reliable than the others. However, the study of stress may gain benefits when other methods complement the heart rhythm-based measure (e.g., Wu, Pirbhulal, et al., 2018).

Appendix: Example of Informed Consent Form Co-signed by the Subject and the Analyst

Study: Calibration of "stress tests" for the recruitment of pilots in robotics

Informed Consent

A 1: Purpose of the Study

To assess the ability of tests to measure participants' performance under acute stress and resilience.

A 2: Profile of Participants

Any adult person able to control a robot with a joystick and having no medical contraindication (hereinafter referred to as "participant").

A 3: Procedure

The calibration of the tests, hereinafter referred to as the "activity," is conducted by the supervisor (see article A9). After carrying out a risk analysis specific to the equipment used for the activity, the participant is equipped with a chest strap with heart rate monitor electrodes connected to a smartphone. The supervisor may optionally place a camcorder with or without a tripod to record the progress of the activity.

The activity requires the participant to individually sequence the following sequences: … [to be developed]

At the end of the activity, the supervisor offers participants the opportunity to be debriefed on what has just happened.

All this data is stored anonymously by the supervisor. They are then used statistically without any of the participants being identifiable in all the data collected and analyzed during the calibration of the tests.

A 4: Duration

Taking into account the preparation and travel times between sequences, as well as the debriefing time, the activity lasts about one hour.

A 5: Recordings

Data from tests and questionnaires are stored in paper format in an anonymized manner. Measurements, like the data mentioned above, are entered into a spreadsheet for processing and analysis. All processes respect the anonymity of the participants. In the event that recordings are made by camera during the realization of the activity with the agreement of the participant, they are kept by the supervisor: they can be used to complete the analysis of the activity carried out by the participant.

A 6: Benefits/Risks for the Participant

Participants can gain insight into their resistance to acute stress during work activities and thus identify their margins for improvement if necessary.

All participants contribute to the improvement of operational performance in robotics intervention in general by helping to calibrate high-performance recruitment tests.

The first risk for the participants in this study is medical: the exposure of some people to activity under acute stress can lead to certain complications. To avoid this risk, the participant is invited to fill in and sign the health questionnaire annexed to this informed consent or to meet with the occupational physician.

The second risk for participants in this study is the malicious use of acquired data. In order to reduce this risk, records and data are stored by the supervisor anonymously and are used by him according to the code of ethics of his trade.

A 7: Voluntary Nature of the Study/Confidentiality

In this study, participation is entirely voluntary; participants may decline the study at any time or refuse to answer questions they are uncomfortable with. They can also ask any questions they want to the supervisor.

A 8: Cost, Reimbursement, and Compensation

Contribution to this study is voluntary as part of the participant's job. No additional remuneration will be received.

A 9: Questions and Contacts—Supervision of the Study

The study is supervised by the supervisor (custodian of the data for archiving):
Dr. Philippe Fauquet-Alekhine
Occupational Psychologist, Behavioral Psychologist, code ADELI: 37 93 0490 0
Email: p.fauquet-alekhine@lse.ac.uk ou philippe.fauquet-alekhine@groupe-intra.com
Address: Groupe INTRA-BP61-F37420 Avoine
Telephone: +33247986505
During and after the study, participants can ask any questions they may have about the study. If participants have questions later, they can also contact the supervisor again.

A 10: Declaration of Consent

The above content is read, approved, and good for agreement.
Name of participant:_____ Name of analyst:_____
Date/Signature: Date/Signature:

References

Ali, N., & Nater, U. M. (2020). Salivary alpha-amylase as a biomarker of stress in behavioral medicine. *International Journal of Behavioral Medicine, 27*, 337–342.

5 Physiological Assessment of the State of Mental Stress at Work 89

Baker, B. G., Bhalla, A., Doleman, B., Yarnold, E., Simons, S., Lund, J. N., & Williams, J. P. (2017). Simulation fails to replicate stress in trainees performing a technical procedure in the clinical environment. *Medical Teacher, 39*(1), 53–57.

Baum, B. J. (1993). Principles of saliva secretion. *Annals of the New York Academy of Sciences, 20*, 17–23.

Berger, J., Heinrichs, M., von Dawans, B., Way, B. M., & Chen, F. S. (2016). Cortisol modulates men's affiliative responses to acute social stress. *Psychoneuroendocrinology, 63*, 1–9.

Berton, J., Rineau, E., & Conte, M. (2015). Appraisal of Life Event Scale (ALES) to differentiate mental stress perceived by Physicians and Nurses involved in the same simulation training situation of anesthesiology. Stress self-assessment & questionnaires: Choice, application, limits, 39–43.

Bosch, J. A., de Geus, E. J., Veerman, E. C., Hoogstraten, J., & Nieuw Amerongen, A. V. (2003). Innate secretory immunity in response to laboratory stressors that evoke distinct patterns of cardiac autonomic activity. *Psychosomatic Medicine, 58*, 374–382.

Brownley, K. A., Hurwitz, B. E., & Schneiderman, N. (2000). Cardiovascular psychophysiology. In J. T. Cacioppo, L. G. Tassinary, & G. G. Berntson (Eds.), *Handbook of psychophysiology* (2nd ed., pp. 224–264). Cambridge University Press.

Camm, A. J., Malik, M., Bigger, J. T., Breithardt, G., Cerutti, S., Cohen, R. J., et al. (1996). Heart rate variability standards of measurement, physiological interpretation, and clinical use. *European Heart Journal, 17*, 354–381.

Cao, X., MacNaughton, P., Cadet, L. R., Cedeno-Laurent, J. G., Flanigan, S., Vallarino, J., et al. (2019). Heart rate variability and performance of commercial airline pilots during flight simulations. *International Journal of Environmental Research and Public Health, 16*(2), 237.

Chatterton, R. T., Jr., Vogelsong, K. M., Lu, Y. C., & Hudgens, G. A. (1997). Hormonal responses to psychological stress in men preparing for skydiving. *The Journal of Clinical Endocrinology & Metabolism, 82*(8), 2503–2509.

Cho, Y., Julier, S. J., & Bianchi-Berthouze, N. (2019). Instant stress: Detection of perceived mental stress through smartphone photoplethysmography and thermal imaging. *JMIR Mental Health, 6*(4), e10140.

Choi, J., & Gutierrez-Osuna, R. (2009, June). Using heart rate monitors to detect mental stress. In *2009 Sixth International Workshop on Wearable and Implantable Body Sensor Networks* (pp. 219–223). IEEE.

Choi, J., & Gutierrez-Osuna, R. (2011). Removal of respiratory influences from heart rate variability in stress monitoring. *IEEE Sensors Journal, 11*(11), 2649–2656.

Chu, H., Li, M. H., Huang, Y. C., & Lee, S. Y. (2013). Simultaneous transcutaneous electrical nerve stimulation mitigates simulator sickness symptoms in healthy adults: A crossover study. *BMC Complementary and Alternative Medicine, 13*(1), 84.

Chu, M., Nguyen, T., Pandey, V., Zhou, Y., Pham, H. N., Bar-Yoseph, R., et al. (2019). Respiration rate and volume measurements using wearable strain sensors. *NPJ Digital Medicine, 2*(1), 1–9.

Cinaz, B., La Marca, R., Arnrich, B., & Tröster, G. (2010). Monitoring of mental workload levels. *Proceedings of IADIS eHealth Conference*, 189–193.

Climstein, M., Alder, J. L., Brooker, A. M., Cartwright, E. J., Kemp-Smith, K., Simas, V., & Furness, J. (2020). Reliability of the Polar Vantage M Sports Watch when measuring heart rate at different treadmill exercise intensities. *Sports, 8*(9), 117.

Davis, K. M., Engeland, C. G., & Murdock, K. W. (2020). Ex vivo LPS-stimulated cytokine production is associated with cortisol curves in response to acute psychosocial stress. *Psychoneuroendocrinology, 121*, 104863.

Degroote, C., Schwaninger, A., Heimgartner, N., Hedinger, P., Ehlert, U., & Wirtz, P. H. (2020). Acute stress improves concentration performance: Opposite effects of anxiety and cortisol. *Experimental Psychology, 67*(2), 88–98.

Edwards, K. M., & Morris, N. B. (2018). Who's the boss: determining the control pathways of cardiovascular and cellular immune responses to acute stress. *Advances in Physiology Education, 42*(2), 374–379.

Fallahi, M., Motamedzade, M., Heidarimoghadam, R., Soltanian, A. R., & Miyake, S. (2016). Effects of mental workload on physiological and subjective responses during traffic density monitoring: A field study. *Applied Ergonomics, 52*, 95–103.

Fauquet-Alekhine, P., Geeraerts, T., & Rouillac, L. (2012). Improving simulation training: Anesthetists vs nuclear reactor pilots. *Socio-Organizational Factors for Safe Nuclear Operation, 1*, 32–44.

Fauquet-Alekhine, P., Geeraerts, T., & Rouillac, L. (2014). Characterization of anesthetists' behavior during simulation training: Performance versus stress achieving medical tasks with or without physical effort. *Psychology and Social Behavior Research, 2*(2), 20–28.

Fauquet-Alekhine, P., Rouillac, L., Berton, J., & Granry, J. C. (2016). Heart rate vs stress indicator for short term mental stress. *British Journal of Medicine and Medical Research, 17*(7), 1–11. Article no. BJMMR.27593.

Fauquet-Alekhine, P., Rouillac, L., & Granry, J. C. (2020). Subjective versus objective assessment of short term occupational stress: Bias and analysis of self-assessment of high stress levels. *Journal of Advances in Medicine and Medical Research, 32*, 50–64.

Filaire, E., Portier, H., Massart, A., Ramat, L., & Teixeira, A. (2010). Effect of lecturing to 200 students on heart rate variability and alpha-amylase activity. *European Journal of Applied Physiology, 108*(5), 1035–1043.

Folkman, S., Lazarus, R. S., Gruen, R. J., & DeLongis, A. (1986). Appraisal, coping, health status, and psychological symptoms. *Journal of Personality and Social Psychology, 50*(3), 571.

Garrett, J. R. (1999). Effects of autonomic nerve stimulations on salivary parenchyma and protein secretion. In J. R. Garrett, J. Ekstrfm, & L. C. Anderson (Eds.), *Oral biology. Neural mechanisms of salivary gland secretion* (pp. 59–79). Karger.

Geeraerts, T., Roulleau, P., Cheisson, G., Marhar, F., Aidan, K., Lallali, K., Leguen, M., Schnell, D., Trabold, F., Fauquet-Alekhine, P., Duranteau, J., & Benhamou, D. (2017). Physiological and self-assessed psychological stress induced by a high fidelity simulation course among third year anesthesia and critical care residents: An observational study. *Anaesthesia Critical Care & Pain Medicine, 36*(6), 403–406.

Giles, D., Draper, N., & Neil, W. (2016). Validity of the Polar V800 heart rate monitor to measure RR intervals at rest. *European Journal of Applied Physiology, 116*(3), 563–571.

Gilgen-Ammann, R., Schweizer, T., & Wyss, T. (2019). RR interval signal quality of a heart rate monitor and an ECG Holter at rest and during exercise. *European Journal of Applied Physiology, 119*(7), 1525–1532.

Granger, D. A., Kivlighan, K. T., El-Sheikh, M. O. N. A., Gordis, E. B., & Stroud, L. R. (2007). Salivary α-amylase in biobehavioral research: recent developments and applications. *Annals of the New York Academy of sciences, 1098*(1), 122–144.

Guelen, I., Westerhof, B. E., Van Der Sar, G. L., van Montfrans, G. A., Kiemeneij, F., Wesseling, K. H., & Bos, W. J. W. (2003). Finometer, finger pressure measurements with the possibility to reconstruct brachial pressure. *Blood Pressure Monitoring, 8*(1), 27–30.

Harmon, A. G., Towe-Goodman, N. R., Fortunato, C. K., Granger, D. A. (2008). Differences in saliva collection location and disparities in baseline and diurnal rhythms of alpha-amylase: a preliminary note of caution. *Hormones and Behavior, 54*(5), 592–596.

Hernando, A., Lázaro, J., Gil, E., Arza, A., Garzón, J. M., López-Antón, R., et al. (2016). Inclusion of respiratory frequency information in heart rate variability analysis for stress assessment. *IEEE Journal of Biomedical and Health Informatics, 20*(4), 1016–1025.

Hjortskov, N., Rissén, D., Blangsted, A. K., Fallentin, N., Lundberg, U., & Søgaard, K. (2004). The effect of mental stress on heart rate variability and blood pressure during computer work. *European Journal of Applied Physiology, 92*(1–2), 84–89.

Izawa, S., Matsudaira, K., Miki, K., Arisaka, M., & Tsuchiya, M. (2017). Psychosocial correlates of cortisol levels in fingernails among middle-aged workers. *Stress, 20*(4), 386–389.

Kamezaki, Y., Katsuura, S., Kuwano, Y., Tanahashi, T., & Rokutan, K. (2012). Circulating cytokine signatures in healthy medical students exposed to academic examination stress. *Psychophysiology, 49*(7), 991–997.

Kario, K., Shimbo, D., Tomitani, N., Kanegae, H., Schwartz, J. E., & Williams, B. (2020). The first study comparing a wearable watch-type blood pressure monitor with a conventional ambulatory blood pressure monitor on in-office and out-of-office settings. *The Journal of Clinical Hypertension, 22*(2), 135–141.

Kawano, A., Tanaka, Y., Ishitobi, Y., Maruyama, Y., Ando, T., Inoue, A., et al. (2013). Salivary alpha-amylase and cortisol responsiveness following electrical stimulation stress in obsessive–compulsive disorder patients. *Psychiatry Research, 209*(1), 85–90.

Kim, H. G., Cheon, E. J., Bai, D. S., Lee, Y. H., & Koo, B. H. (2018). Stress and heart rate variability: A meta-analysis and review of the literature. *Psychiatry Investigation, 15*(3), 235.

Kim, J., Lim, Y., Seol, H., Jee, C., & Hong, Y. (2014). A study of psychological effects of pilots depending on the different environments between actual and simulated flights. 대한인간공학회지, *33*(3), 203–214.

Koelsch, S., Boehlig, A., Hohenadel, M., Nitsche, I., Bauer, K., & Sack, U. (2016). The impact of acute stress on hormones and cytokines, and how their recovery is affected by music-evoked positive mood. *Scientific Reports, 6*, 23008.

Koudela-Hamila, S., Smyth, J., Santangelo, P., & Ebner-Priemer, U. (2020). Examination stress in academic students: A multimodal, real-time, real-life investigation of reported stress, social contact, blood pressure, and cortisol. *Journal of American College Health, 70*(4), 1047–1058.

Kudielka, B. M., Buske-Kirschbaum, A., Hellhammer, D. H., & Kirschbaum, C. (2004). Differential heart rate reactivity and recovery after psychosocial stress (TSST) in healthy children, younger adults, and elderly adults: The impact of age and gender. *International Journal of Behavioral Medicine, 11*(2), 116–121.

Kuebler, U., Wirtz, P. H., Sakai, M., Stemmer, A., & Ehlert, U. (2013). Acute stress reduces wound-induced activation of microbicidal potential of ex vivo isolated human monocyte-derived macrophages. *PLoS One, 8*(2), e55875.

Kunz-Ebrecht, S. R., Mohamed-Ali, V., Feldman, P. J., Kirschbaum, C., & Steptoe, A. (2003). Cortisol responses to mild psychological stress are inversely associated with proinflammatory cytokines. *Brain, Behavior, and Immunity, 17*(5), 373–383.

Kuwabara, M., Harada, K., Hishiki, Y., & Kario, K. (2019). Validation of two watch-type wearable blood pressure monitors according to the ANSI/AAMI/ISO81060-2: 2013 guidelines: Omron HEM-6410T-ZM and HEM-6410T-ZL. *The Journal of Clinical Hypertension, 21*(6), 853–858.

Lazarus, R. S., & Folkman, S. (1984). *Stress, appraisal, and coping*. Springer.

Lehrer, P., Karavidas, M., Lu, S. E., Vaschillo, E., Vaschillo, B., & Cheng, A. (2010). Cardiac data increase association between self-report and both expert ratings of task load and task performance in flight simulator tasks: An exploratory study. *International Journal of Psychophysiology, 76*(2), 80–87.

Liu, H., Allen, J., Zheng, D., & Chen, F. (2019). Recent development of respiratory rate measurement technologies. *Physiological Measurement, 40*(7), 07TR01.

Lyu, Y., Luo, X., Zhou, J., Yu, C., Miao, C., Wang, T., … Kameyama, K. I. (2015, April). Measuring photoplethysmogram-based stress-induced vascular response index to assess cognitive load and stress. In *Proceedings of the 33rd annual ACM conference on human factors in computing systems* (pp. 857–866).

McDuff, D., Gontarek, S., & Picard, R. (2014, August). Remote measurement of cognitive stress via heart rate variability. In *2014 36th Annual International*

5 Physiological Assessment of the State of Mental Stress at Work 93

Conference of the IEEE Engineering in Medicine and Biology Society (pp. 2957–2960). IEEE.

Nagy, T., Van Lién, R., Willemsen, G., Proctor, G., Efting, M., Fülöp, M., et al. (2015). A fluid response: Alpha-amylase reactions to acute laboratory stress are related to sample timing and saliva flow rate. *Biological Psychology, 109*, 111–119.

Nater, U. M., La Marca, R., Florin, L., Moses, A., Langhans, W., Koller, M. M., & Ehlert, U. (2006). Stress-induced changes in human salivary alpha-amylase activity—Associations with adrenergic activity. *Psychoneuroendocrinology, 31*(1), 49–58.

Nater, U. M., Rohleder, N., Gaab, J., Berger, S., Jud, A., Kirschbaum, C., & Ehlert, U. (2005). Human salivary alpha-amylase reactivity in a psychosocial stress paradigm. *International Journal of Psychophysiology, 55*(3), 333–342.

O'Súilleabháin, P. S., Howard, S., & Hughes, B. M. (2018). Openness to experience and stress responsivity: An examination of cardiovascular and underlying hemodynamic trajectories within an acute stress exposure. *PLoS One, 13*(6), e0199221.

Out, D., Bakermans-Kranenburg, M. J., Granger, D. A., Cobbaert, C. M., & van IJzendoorn, M. H. (2011). State and trait variance in salivary α-amylase: A behavioral genetic study. *Biological Psychology, 88*(1), 147–154.

Parati, G., Ongaro, G., Bilo, G., Glavina, F., Castiglioni, P., Di Rienzo, M., & Mancia, G. (2003). Non-invasive beat-to-beat blood pressure monitoring: New developments. *Blood Pressure Monitoring, 8*(1), 31–36.

Penaz, J. (1973). Photoelectric measurement of blood pressure, volume and flow in the finger'In: Digest of the 10th International Conference on Medical and Biological Engineering. *Dresden, 104.* International Federation for Medical and Biological Engineering, Publishers New York.

Pereira, T., Almeida, P. R., Cunha, J. P., & Aguiar, A. (2017). Heart rate variability metrics for fine-grained stress level assessment. *Computer Methods and Programs in Biomedicine, 148*, 71–80.

Petrakova, L., Doering, B. K., Vits, S., Engler, H., Rief, W., Schedlowski, M., & Grigoleit, J. S. (2015). Psychosocial stress increases salivary alpha-amylase activity independently from plasma noradrenaline levels. *PLoS One, 10*(8), e0134561.

Petrowski, K., Herold, U., Joraschky, P., Mück-Weymann, M., & Siepmann, M. (2010). The effects of psychosocial stress on heart rate variability in panic disorder. *German Journal of Psychiatry, 13*(2), 66–73.

Posada-Quintero, H. F., Reljin, N., Mills, C., Mills, I., Florian, J. P., VanHeest, J. L., & Chon, K. H. (2018). Timevarying analysis of electrodermal activity during exercise. *PloS one, 13*(6), e0198328.

Prather, A. A., Carroll, J. E., Fury, J. M., McDade, K. K., Ross, D., & Marsland, A. L. (2009). Gender differences in stimulated cytokine production following acute psychological stress. *Brain, Behavior, and Immunity, 23*(5), 622–628.

Reinertsen, E., Osipov, M., Liu, C., Kane, J. M., Petrides, G., & Clifford, G. D. (2017). Continuous assessment of schizophrenia using heart rate and accelerometer data. *Physiological Measurement, 38*(7), 1456.

Rohleder, N., & Nater, U. M. (2009). Determinants of salivary α-amylase in humans and methodological considerations. *Psychoneuroendocrinology, 34*(4), 469–485.

Rozanov, V. A. (2017). Evolution of the Concept of Stress. *Understanding Stress at Work*, 17–21. http//haykakultura.org/larsen.html

Schönfeld, P., Ackermann, K., & Schwabe, L. (2014). Remembering under stress: Different roles of autonomic arousal and glucocorticoids in memory retrieval. *Psychoneuroendocrinology, 39*, 249–256.

Schutte, A. E., Huisman, H. W., van Rooyen, J. M., Oosthuizen, W., & Jerling, J. C. (2003). Sensitivity of the Finometer device in detecting acute and medium-term changes in cardiovascular function. *Blood Pressure Monitoring, 8*(5), 195–201.

Shilton, A. L., Laycock, R., & Crewther, S. G. (2017). The Maastricht Acute Stress Test (MAST): Physiological and subjective responses in anticipation, and post-stress. *Frontiers in Psychology, 8*, 567.

SHIMMER. (2015). Measuring emotion: Reaction to media. https://www.shimmer-sensing.com/assets/images/content/case-study-files/Emotional_Response_27July2015.pdf

Singer, N., Sommer, M., Döhnel, K., Zänkert, S., Wüst, S., & Kudielka, B. M. (2017). Acute psychosocial stress and everyday moral decision-making in young healthy men: The impact of cortisol. *Hormones and Behavior, 93*, 72–81.

Slavish, D. C., Graham-Engeland, J. E., Smyth, J. M., & Engeland, C. G. (2015). Salivary markers of inflammation in response to acute stress. *Brain, Behavior, and Immunity, 44*, 253–269.

Slavish, D. C., & Szabo, Y. Z. (2019). The effect of acute stress on salivary markers of inflammation: A systematic review protocol. *Systematic Reviews, 8*(1), 1–8.

Speer, K. E., Semple, S., Naumovski, N., & McKune, A. J. (2020). Measuring heart rate variability using commercially available devices in healthy children: A validity and reliability study. *European Journal of Investigation in Health, Psychology and Education, 10*(1), 390–404.

Spierer, D., Griffiths, E., & Sterland, T. (2009). Fight or flight: Measuring and understanding human stress response in tactical situations. *The Tactical Edge, Summer*, 30–40.

Stedmon, A. W., Eachus, P., Baillie, L., Tallis, H., Donkor, R., Edlin-White, R., & Bracewell, R. (2015). Scalable interrogation: Eliciting human pheromone responses to deception in a security interview setting. *Applied Ergonomics, 47*, 26–33.

Sun, F. T., Kuo, C., Cheng, H. T., Buthpitiya, S., Collins, P., & Griss, M. (2012). Activity-aware mental stress detection using physiological sensors. In Mobile Computing, Applications, and Services: Second International ICST Conference, MobiCASE 2010, Santa Clara, CA, USA, October 25–28, 2010, Revised Selected Papers 2 (pp. 282–301). Springer Berlin Heidelberg.

5 Physiological Assessment of the State of Mental Stress at Work

Thoma, M. V., Kirschbaum, C., Wolf, J. M., & Rohleder, N. (2012). Acute stress responses in salivary alpha-amylase predict increases of plasma norepinephrine. *Biological Psychology, 91*(3), 342–348.

Tomitani, N., Kanegae, H., Suzuki, Y., Kuwabara, M., & Kario, K. (2020). Stress-induced blood pressure elevation self-measured by a wearable watch-type device. *American Journal of Hypertension, 34*(4), 377–382.

Von Dawans, B., Kirschbaum, C., & Heinrichs, M. (2011). The Trier Social Stress Test for Groups (TSST-G): A new research tool for controlled simultaneous social stress exposure in a group format. *Psychoneuroendocrinology, 36*(4), 514–522.

Waugh, J. D., Fatkin, L. T., Patton, D. J., Mullins, L. L., Burton, P. A., Barker, D. J., & Mitchell, D. A. (1999). *Aviator behavior and performance as affected by aircrew life support and protective equipment* (No. ARL-MR-440). Army Research Lab Aberdeen Proving Ground Md Human Research and Engineering Directorate.

Webb, H. E., Garten, R. S., McMinn, D. R., Beckman, J. L., Kamimori, G. H., & Acevedo, E. O. (2011). Stress hormones and vascular function in firefighters during concurrent challenges. *Biological Psychology, 87*(1), 152–160.

WHO-World Health Organization. (1999). 1999 World Health Organization--International Society of Hypertension Guidelines for the management of hypertension. Guidelines sub-committee of the World Health Organization. *Journal of Hypertension, 17*, 151–183.

Wolf, J. M., Nicholls, E., & Chen, E. (2008). Chronic stress, salivary cortisol, and α-amylase in children with asthma and healthy children. *Biological Psychology, 78*(1), 20–28.

Wu, H., Zhou, K., Xu, P., Xue, J., Xu, X., & Liu, L. (2018). Associations of perceived stress with the present and subsequent cortisol levels in fingernails among medical students: A prospective pilot study. *Psychology Research and Behavior Management, 11*, 439.

Wu, W., Pirbhulal, S., Zhang, H., & Mukhopadhyay, S. C. (2018). Quantitative assessment for self-tracking of acute stress based on triangulation principle in a wearable sensor system. *IEEE Journal of Biomedical and Health Informatics, 23*(2), 703–713.

Yamakawa, K., Matsunaga, M., Isowa, T., Kimura, K., Kasugai, K., Yoneda, M., et al. (2009). Transient responses of inflammatory cytokines in acute stress. *Biological Psychology, 82*(1), 25–32.

6

Psychological Assessment of the State of Mental Stress at Work

Philippe Fauquet-Alekhine and Anne Boucherand

1 Introduction

Within a dynamic approach, stress is considered as a transaction between an individual and the context (transactional model) associated with one's perception that external demands are exceeding one's capacity for response (Lazarus & Folkman, 1984; Folkman et al., 1986; Rozanov, 2017, p. 17; see also Chap. 2 of the present book). From this perspective, the perception of stress factors and related subsequent emotions is as important as the physiological response of the body to these factors in determining the state of stress. Therefore, the two main approaches to stress state assessment are "subjective," addressing perceptions and emotions (Fig. 6.1), and "objective," through physiological measurements (see also Chap. 5 of the present book). The former provides an "image" of the stress perceived by the subjects (subjective state) during stress exposure. This may be obtained through an Experience Sampling Method (ESM; see also Chap. 7 of the present book) or subsequently using

---

P. Fauquet-Alekhine (✉)
SEBE-Lab, Department of Psychological and Behavioural Science,
London School of Economics and Political Science, London, UK

Laboratory for Research in Science of Energy, Montagret, France

Groupe INTRA Robotics, Avoine, France
e-mail: p.fauquet-alekhine@lse.ac.uk; philippe.fauquet-alekhine@groupe-intra.com

A. Boucherand
Operation Engineering Offices-EDF-UNIE, Paris, France

© The Author(s), under exclusive license to Springer Nature Switzerland AG 2023
P. Fauquet-Alekhine, J. Erskine (eds.), *The Palgrave Handbook of Occupational Stress*,
https://doi.org/10.1007/978-3-031-27349-0_6

Fig. 6.1 Factors of stress at work

questionnaires or interviews. Questionnaires may be individual or collective and may be combined with interviews by an analyst (e.g., psychologist). Although these methods are biased by the fact that the stress assessment is based on recall (Zawadzki et al., 2019), and they do not give access to the "in-the-moment" response to stress as can be provided by physiological measurements, questionnaires or interviews are the only method that may give access to the identification of stress factors.

The purpose of this chapter is to present and comment on a selection of questionnaires used for the self-assessment of stress.

Questionnaires may address a situational exposure to a past stressful event (e.g., taking an exam or a certification) or an exposure to stressors over a period (e.g., being exposed to the manager's bad mood every day, being overwhelmed).

Questionnaires may aim to provide an assessment of the perceived impact of stressors for the subject (e.g., Did you experience a crisis situation?) or an assessment of the subject's perceived stress (e.g., Do you feel nervous and restless?), or a combination of both, depending on the questions asked. Addressing the effectiveness of stressors means that the questions help evaluate the extent to which some factors contribute to the state of stress of the respondents from their standpoint. Stressors, or factors of stress, are also called determinants of stress or causes of stress. Addressing the subject's perceived stress usually means asking respondents to assess the emotional or physiological consequences of the state of stress. Therefore, depending on the questions asked, questionnaires may also address emotional aspects (e.g., Do you feel nervous and restless?) and/or may address perceived physiological aspects of stress (e.g., Do you sweat?) or a combination of both.

Some of these questionnaires are not dedicated to stress assessment at work but nevertheless may be relevant for this purpose.

Questionnaires addressing major life events are not considered here. The first renowned scale was designed by Holmes and Rahe (1967). On the basis of the available studies, they elaborated a list of 43 life events which would usually change life in a major way, requiring adaptation. Events could be desirable (e.g., job promotion) or undesirable (e.g., death of a child). The events were weighted by more than 300 subjects, resulting in the Social Readjustment Rating Scale: each item of the scale was assigned a score and the total life stress score was obtained by summing the score of all the events being experienced by the subject during a recent time interval (e.g., 6 to 24 months). Although some studies demonstrated that the resulting score could be correlated to the occurrence of serious illness, and despite several following adjustments of the scale or modifications giving rise to new major life events scales (Dohrenwend et al., 1978) considering mainly undesirable events (Lewinsohn et al., 1985), the predictive nature of the scale remained unsatisfactory and the reliability of weighted items was not fully demonstrated (Lei & Skinner, 1980; Zimmerman, 1983). Following the work of Lazarus (1984), it was admitted that minor life events would constitute a more important source of stress than major events. Several scales were elaborated and showed a significant correlation with stress symptoms while not correlated with major life event scales (Chamberlain & Zika, 1990; Hahn & Smith, 1999). It was also shown that the individual perception of the stressors (thus its subjective evaluation) was more important than the effectiveness of the stressors, when approximating an accurate evaluation of the subject's state of stress (Lindsay & Norman, 1980).

This chapter presents a selection of questionnaires that may be used for self-assessment of the state of stress applicable to the world of work. It presents their characteristics, validation, and reliability and discusses advantages and limitations from the standpoint of the users (researchers, practitioners). Other questionnaires than those presented in this chapter exist (see, e.g., the World Health Organization review in Leka & Jain, 2010); the selection appearing here was made among the most widely used questionnaires within the scientific community and among practitioners with good psychometric properties. Table 6.1 gives an overview of the selected questionnaires and Table 6.2 suggests the fields of application. This may help readers to choose which questionnaire(s) may be adapted to their studies.

All these questionnaires, even when available for free, must be used by specialists, that is, professional graduates in the Human Sciences and, optimally, trained in Psychometry.

2 Validity of Questionnaires for Self-Assessment of Stress

The items on a questionnaire are based on naturalistic observation and scientific studies that help the questionnaire designers to select and formulate items. An exploratory analysis is then undertaken in order to remove, adjust, or add items. A confirmative analysis follows including one or several phases of test-retest. It helps the designers to evaluate the theoretical validity (usually associated with the external validity, i.e., looking for results correlated significantly and relevantly with various criteria evaluated through other methods such as interviews), and the internal validity (usually assessed through the calculation of the Cronbach coefficient α). The discriminative sensitivity of the questionnaire must also be rated, a higher discrimination being more probable with a higher number of items in the questionnaire (to a certain extent: a large number of items may increase time to take the questionnaire without improving its reliability). Both exploratory and confirmative analyses usually involve several hundred participants.

A questionnaire must be validated in the language of the subjects it is presented to. For example, a questionnaire designed and validated in the UK in English must undergo confirmative analysis in French to be used with French subjects. Therefore, readers who might be interested in using some of the questionnaires hereafter presented are encouraged to carry out a bibliographic review to know whether they have been validated in the language they plan to use.

The questionnaires are not reproduced in this chapter because they are either available online (links provided) or because they must be purchased.

6 Psychological Assessment of the State of Mental Stress at Work 101

Table 6.1 Overview of questionnaires and characteristics

Questionnaire name	Original designer	Number of items	Measurement scale	Comments	French version
JCQ, Job Content Questionnaire	Karasek et al. (1998)	39 to 119 items	Likert Scales		www. jcqcenter. com
JSS, Job Stress Survey	Spielberger & Reheiser (1994)	30 (long term) + 30 (short term)	standardized 9-point numerical scale		Boudarene and Kellou (2005)
NASA Task Load Index	Hart & Staveland (1988)	6	numerical scale		Cegarra & Morgado (2009)
STAI-Y, State-Trait Anxiety Inventory	Spielberger (1983b)	20 (trait) + 20 (state)	4-level Likert Scale	Be aware of reversed questions for which question score must be reversed before summing into the overall score	Bruchon-Schweitzer and Paulhan (1993)
PSS, Perceived Stress Scale	Cohen et al. (1983)	14	5-level Likert Scale	Be aware of reversed questions for which question score must be reversed before summing into the overall score	Bruchon–Schweitzer (2002) Lesage et al. (2012)
ALES, Appraisal of Life Events Scale	Ferguson et al. (1999)	16	6-level Likert Scale	Assessment is done through adjectives	–
PDI, Peritraumatic Distress Inventory	Brunet et al., 2001	13	5-level Likert Scale	May help to diagnose a post-traumatic stress disorder See also DSM-IV	Jehel et al., 2005 and 2006
IES-R , Impact of Event Scale- Revised	Weiss (2007)	22	5-level Likert Scale	Assume that at least 24h elapsed between the event and taking the questionnaire; may help to diagnose an acute stress disorder	Brunet et al. (2003).

NB:
- Most of the questionnaires are available online in many languages. Please verify the validity of the foreign versions through bibliographic research
- Some questionnaires are available in short, intermediate or long versions

Table 6.2 Overview of applicability of questionnaires and characteristics (JS: Job Stress)

Questionnaire name	Event	Period	Dedicated JS	Applicable JS[a]	Addresses physiology
PSS, Perceived Stress Scale		X		X	
JCQ, Job Content Questionnaire		X	X		
JSS, Job Stress Survey	x	X	x		
STAI-Y, State-Trait Anxiety Inventory	x	X		X	
IES-R , Impact of Event Scale-Revised	x	X		X	X
NASA Task Load Index	x		x		
PDI, Peritraumatic Distress Inventory	x			X	X
ALES, Appraisal of Life Events Scale	x			X	

[a]Usually not alone but as complement to another questionnaire

3 Questionnaires for Self-Assessment of Stress State

This section presents questionnaires in three sub-sections depending on the properties of the questionnaire: dedicated to assessing occupational stress in general or with a particular focus, or developed for another purpose than that of occupational stress assessment but nevertheless applicable to assessing occupational stress in general or with a particular focus.

3.1 Questionnaires Dedicated to Assessing Occupational Stress: General Approach

The JCQ, Job Content Questionnaire, developed by Karasek et al. (1998) is likely the most translated questionnaire addressing stress at work. Several versions are available depending on the number of items to be considered. The original version consisted of 18 items covering five dimensions: decision latitude, psychological demand, social support, physical demand, and job insecurity. It has evolved over time to version 2, itself proposed in two versions: JCQ2 User Version with 39 items and JCQ2 Researcher Version with 76 items (Karasek, 2015). Leka and Jain (2010) and the JCQ Centre (www.jcq-center.com) recommended using the 49-item version JCQ1 and mentioned a long version including 119 items. They were tested with thousands of subjects through different studies, all demonstrating a good validity and reliability.

6 Psychological Assessment of the State of Mental Stress at Work

Online Access:

To be purchased: https://www.jcqcenter.com/questionnaires-jcq-jcq2/

Advantages and Limits:

All versions of the JCQ have good psychometric properties that make the questionnaire a useful tool. The limits are related to the version used; a shorter version restrains the spectrum examined.

JSS, Job Stress Survey, elaborated by Spielberger (Spielberger & Reheiser, 1994) is devoted to perceived stress in a professional context.

JSS permits obtaining three scores (intensity, frequency, overall) within three domains: job pressure and lack of support, the combination of which refers to occupational stress. The subject is asked to give his opinion regarding the amount of stress felt for each event (each item) and to assess the intensity of its impact by assigning a score on a numerical scale ranging from 1 to 9. Score 5 is the average reference score pre-assigned to item 1, "The allocation of unpleasant obligations," which is considered the standard event; this reference score reinforces the comparability of the results from one subject to another by increasing the reliability of the numerical scale (Fauquet-Alekhine & Rouillac, 2015). The job stress index is obtained by adding the item products intensity × frequency, all divided by 30 for the 60-item questionnaire. The overall index varies from 0 to 81.

The number of items for the questionnaire is 60 (2 × 30) for the original version and 40 (2 × 20) for the shortened version keeping the more stable items (Spielberger & Reheiser, 1994).

The number of participants involved in the validation process was N = 1781.

The internal consistency was good while repeatedly scoring around 0.80 for the alpha coefficient, and test-retest coefficient was reported at 0.48 to 0.75.

Online Access:

To be purchased

Items of the survey listed at https://www.creativeorgdesign.com/tests/job-stress-survey/

Advantages and Limits:

The questionnaire is well adapted for the assessment of stress at work and less for acute stress. Compared with the other questionnaires presented in this chapter, it is the only one combining intensity and frequency of the stressors and it presents the advantage of exploring a wide scope of occupational difficulties, but some are missing such as personal competencies.

3.2 Questionnaires Dedicated to Assessing Occupational stress: Focused Approach

The NASA Task Load Index is the tool most often used for subjective assessment of workload (Alpert et al., 2018). The NASA Task Load Index (TLX) was developed by Hart and Staveland (1988). Rubio et al. (2004) undertook a comparative analysis of the TLX with other methods and found a good convergence of the results. The TLX explores six dimensions (mental demand, physical demand, temporal demand, performance, effort, frustration) which are scored on a numerical scale (rating scale) and then compared by pair (weighing scale) as shown below.

The TLX was validated in a longitudinal study over three years involving more than 40 experiments. The Cronbach's coefficient was greater than 0.80 and the correlation coefficients between dimension scores and total score were more than 0.60 except for the performance dimension, demonstrating good inner consistency. The retest reliability coefficients of rating and weighing ranged from 0.51 to 0.76, showing a good retest reliability.

Administering the TLX implies two steps:

- Subjects must rate each of the six dimensions on a numerical scale, from Low to High or from Good to Poor.
- Subjects must then reflect on the task addressed by the questionnaire (such as "taking a certification exam") and assess for the 15 pairs of the six dimensions which one of the two contributes more to workload. For example, for the pair Effort & Frustration, they choose whether Effort increased workload more than frustration or vice versa. If Effort is chosen five times when compared with others, it is assigned a weight of 5.

The overall workload score for the task considered is obtained by multiplying the score of a dimension by its weight and adding the results.

Online Access:
https://humansystems.arc.nasa.gov/groups/TLX/downloads/TLXScale.pdf
Advantages and Limits:
The questionnaire is specialized and assesses only one aspect of occupational stress factors, related to workload. Therefore, the questionnaire is used to refine examination of the influence of workload on stress and must be a complement to another questionnaire if the aim is to assess perceived stress.

The questionnaire is very easy and fast to implement, and to take and analyze. The questionnaire must be taken just after experiencing the stress episode. The responses may be biased by the subject's performance during the stress episode as it may be assumed that, for identical actual workload, the perceived workload will be lower for subjects who achieved the goals than for those who failed.

3.3 Questionnaires Applicable to Assessing Occupational Stress: General Approach

STAI, State-Trait Anxiety Inventory, was elaborated by Spielberger (Spielberger, 1983b).

The number of items for the complete questionnaire is 40, 20 for trait anxiety and 20 for state anxiety. They are answered on a 4-level Likert scale and 50% of the items have a reversed score.

The STAI intends to assess subjects' conscious awareness at two extremes of anxiety, labeled state anxiety (A-State) and trait anxiety (A-Trait). The original Form X of the STAI was revised resulting in Form Y, a more popular version with improved psychometric properties. The Y version was developed to eliminate items that were more related to depression. It is one of the most widely used anxiety self-assessment tools.

The number of participants involved in the validation process was N>5000. Internal consistency coefficients are satisfactory, ranging from 0.86 to 0.95; two-month test-retest reliability coefficients have ranged from 0.65 to 0.75 (Spielberger, 1983a).

Online Access:

https://vdocuments.mx/stai-spielberger-state-trait-anxiety-inventory.html

Advantages and Limits:

The STAI items relate only to the psychological and non-somatic aspects of anxiety. However, it may be considered as adapted for the assessment of acute stress. Occupational difficulties are little addressed. For example, lack of social support and work overload are not questioned; however, one item addresses competencies. The questionnaire was developed for anxiety in general rather than for occupational stress, and its use must therefore be combined with other questionnaires to correctly explore occupational stress.

PSS, Perceived Stress Scale, was elaborated by Cohen et al. (1983). The number of items for the questionnaire is 14. They are answered on a 5-level Likert scale and 50% of the items have a reversed score.

The questions ask subjects about their feelings and thoughts during the past month and thus are adapted for long-term mental stress assessment but not for acute stress. It assesses overall stress, and is therefore not specific to work.

The number of participants involved in the validation process was N>2300 (40% male) selected as representative of the North American population (gender, age, income, ethnicity, profession).

It has good discriminative sensitivity and a good theoretical validity, with positive correlations with other objective or perceived stress scales. Internal validity is satisfactory (Cohen & Williamson, 1998) and external validity shows that PSS correlates significantly and positively with various indicators of disease, among which is the Psychosomatic Index of Derogatis et al. (1976).

Online Access:

https://www.pdffiller.com/95570588-Perceived-Stress-Scale1pdf-Perceived-Stress-Scale-Mind-Garden-Inc-

or

https://lisakenny91.wixsite.com/stressfreenurses/perceived-stress-scale

Advantages and Limits:

Dedicated to long-term stress, the questionnaire is not adapted for acute stress assessment. The items are general: they address problems and difficulties as a whole. When applied to occupational stress assessment, it provides an overall evaluation of the subject's state but an interview is necessary to identify the specificities of the problems encountered by the subject.

ALES, Appraisal of Life Events Scale, was elaborated by Ferguson et al. (1999) for primary appraisal of stress.

The number of items for the questionnaire is 16, selected with reference to the primary evaluation forms described by Folkman and Lazarus (1985). It consists of adjectives that must be rated to describe an event. Six adjectives are associated with a perception of threat or constraint, four with loss, and six with the perception of challenge or excitement. Usually, the three scores are calculated separately.

The number of participants involved in the validation process was N=260 for exploratory analysis and N=344 for confirmative analysis, giving the total of N=604.

It has good discriminative sensitivity and good theoretical validity. The internal validity of each factor is satisfactory (α=0.94 to 0.99), as well as the reproduction through one month test-retest (r=0.77 to 0.90, p<0.01) as well as three-month test-retest (r=0.49 to 0.59, p<0.01). Regarding external validity, ALES factors are correlated significantly and relevantly with various criteria when jointly evaluated (Ferguson et al., 1999).

Online Access: https://www.psyc.nott.ac.uk/research/rasph/downloads/ALE%20Scale%20PC.pdf

6 Psychological Assessment of the State of Mental Stress at Work

Advantages and Limits:

The adjectives selected address stress due to constraint (10) or to excitement (6). Another classification may be considered in terms of threat (6), challenge (6), and loss (4). This is both an advantage (in that few questionnaires consider excitement as a source of stress) and an inconvenience (the results cannot be compared to results obtained with questionnaires only focusing on constraints). It does not give any information regarding the source of stress: if the subject is not interviewed, the data will show that the subject was frightened or perceived the event as hostile, but nothing will help the analyst to know whether it was due to a noise, a person, lack of social support, or something else. However, it is a good complementary questionnaire when used with another questionnaire made up of explicit questions and it is well adapted for the assessment of acute stress. Considering these remarks, it is adapted for both occupational and acute stress assessments.

3.4 Questionnaires Applicable to Assessing Occupational Stress: Focused Approach

PDI, Peritraumatic Distress Inventory (Brunet et al., 2001), was elaborated in order to obtain a quantitative measure of the level of distress experienced during and immediately after a traumatic event (e.g., aggression, car accident, earthquake) but, surprisingly, it does not question dissociative symptoms (see, e.g., IES-R).

The number of items for the questionnaire is 13, answered on a 5-level Likert scale.

The number of participants involved in the validation process was N=1003.

It included the subject's feelings regarding physiological parameters (sweating, shaking, pounding heart). This questionnaire was developed for the diagnosis of post-traumatic stress disorder (PTSD), which requires that subjects had experienced high levels of distress during or after a traumatic event. It is nevertheless applicable to occupational stress but this may be a drawback when subjects are exposed to a low level of stress: the questionnaire may not discriminate the stress states of different subjects experiencing the same situation or of one subject submitted to different situations (e.g., Fauquet-Alekhine et al., 2014).

Online Access (see Table 2 in Brunet et al., 2001):

https://ajp.psychiatryonline.org/doi/full/10.1176/appi.ajp.158.9.1480?
url_ver=Z39.88-2003&rfr_id=ori:rid:crossref.org&rfr_dat=cr_pub%3
dpubmed

Advantages and Limits:

Even though it was developed and tested for assessing the effect of a traumatic event (and thus not appropriate to differentiate low levels of stress), it is adapted for the assessment of acute stress at work as a complement to a dedicated occupational stress questionnaire. Although lack of social support or work overload is not questioned, the notions of frustration, guilt, and fear are addressed, while these are too often forgotten in dedicated occupational stress questionnaires. Work situations like a patient dying, a nuclear reactor with technical failure, or airplane technical defect may induce such feelings. It also includes perception of the physiologic state (e.g., sweat, heart rate). When used for possible low levels of stress, it is necessary to combine it with another questionnaire. The PDI does not question dissociative symptoms.

IES-R, Impact of Event Scale-Revised (Weiss, 2007), aims at assessing distress after stressful life events. The revised version complemented the original 15-item scale with seven additional items addressing hyperarousal. Thus, the questionnaire provides three subscales:intrusion, avoidance and hyperarousal. Dissociative symptoms are addressed. Many studies report results about the reliability and validity of the questionnaires. Creamer et al. (2003)

undertook a study involving male Vietnam War veterans (N =274). Internal consistency was high: α=0.96. Confirmatory factor analysis did not provide any factor solution corresponding to the three subscales. Exploratory factor analysis suggested that single- or two-factor solutions (avoidance or intrusion/hyperarousal) provided the best data fit. A high correlation was found between the IES-R and the PTSD Checklist (Weathers et al., 1993): r=0.84.

Two other questionnaires are similar, also addressing dissociative symptoms: the ASDS (Acute Stress Disorder Scale; Bryant et al., 2000) is similar but "event" is replaced by "trauma" in the question and may induce certain feelings by suggesting to the subject that the recalled event has to be considered as traumatic; the SASRQ (Stanford Acute Stress Reaction Questionnaire; Cardeiia et al., 1996) is similar; the event may be named. For example, if experiencing a flood, questions will address "flood" in the text.

Online Access for IES-R:

https://www.aerztenetz-grafschaft.de/download/IES-R-englisch-5-stufig.pdf

Online Access for ASDS:

see appendix in Bryant et al. (2000).

Online Access for SASRQ:

http://stresshealthcenter.stanford.edu/research/documents/StanfordAcuteStressReactionQuestionnaire-Flood.pdf (replace "flood" with "event")

Advantages and Limits:

IES-R assumes that at least 24h elapsed between the event and taking the questionnaire because it questions the subject's sleep. Like ASDS and SASRQ, it is adapted to assess acute stress following a traumatic event. It may help to diagnose an acute stress disorder. These questionnaires are adapted for events inducing a high level of stress.

4 Overall Limits of Questionnaires

4.1 Overestimation for High Level of Stress

Studies have shown that self-assessment of stress was overestimated for high levels of acute mental stress (Fauquet-Alekhine et al., 2015, 2020). The effectiveness of this gap was indisputably objectified: the analysis showed that, in a work context, professionals tended to overestimate factors of stress linked with the traits specific to their profession (Fauquet-Alekhine et al., 2020). One of the issues is that detecting this gap is not easy: it implies being able to correlate the self-assessments with physiological measures (see also Chap. 5 of the present book). Another issue is that the threshold of level of stress beyond which the gap occurs is also difficult to identify.

4.2 Delay Bias

Zawadzki et al. (2019) reported that post-assessment of stress through questionnaire was underrated by a factor of 2 when compared with an instant report during the stressful context (see also Chap. 8 of the present book). This difference varying from one subject to another adds a subjective bias to the self-assessment, which reduces the reliability of the results when comparing subjects submitted to a given stressful situation. Thus, the comparison of the scores from one subject to another may not reflect an actual difference of state of stress. This is why Berton et al. (2015) suggested using these results when averaged per cluster of subjects rather than individual data.

4.3 Major Cognitive Biases

Halo effect is a tendency to perceive a situation in a given area the same way it is perceived in another area (e.g., Holmlund-Rytkönen & Strandvik, 2005; Giovannoni, 2015). For example, students taking an oral exam with a professor whose face is stern (thus perceived as stressful) may have a tendency to perceive the exam as more stressful than with a professor with a kind face.

Primacy-recency effect (or Serial-position effect) is the tendency for subjects to better recall the first and last items in a series: recalling the last items relates to the recency effect and recalling the first items relates to the primacy effect. For example, subjects may assess a 30-minute situation as stressful because the last minute was constraining even though overall the situation was not constraining (e.g., Macdonald et al., 2009).

Recall bias relates to the fact that subjects may remember and weigh particularly emotionally impactful events better than others when recalling an experienced situation (e.g., Zawadzki et al., 2019).

4.4 Effect of the Type of Stressor

Not all the questionnaires explore the same sort of stressors. For example, the PDI explores only constraining factors while the ALES questions both constraining and exciting factors. It is thus obvious that an individual whose stress is mainly due to the exciting aspect of a situation will score low on PDI and medium on ALES. This is why some studies analyzing correlations between results of the two questionnaires consider only the constraining items of ALES (e.g., Fauquet-Alekhine et al., 2015). The positive side of this is that such questionnaires may be interestingly considered as complementary. The resulting important recommendation for researchers and practitioners is thus to always use at least two different questionnaires for self-assessment of stress carefully chosen according to what is studied.

5 Deontology and Ethics

Taking questionnaires is based on volunteering. When it concerns an individual, the results are confidential and remain between the analyst and the subject. When the questionnaires are used within a research framework or an organizational analysis involving several participants, subjects must know that the results will be used in an anonymous way. This is also expected to give participants the freedom to withdraw from the study at any time if they feel uncomfortable with the questionnaire. Usually, all of this is written in an informed consent form co-signed by the subject and the analyst.

6 Conclusion

As a conclusion, the following are suggestions of questionnaires to be used depending on the objective of the study or analysis that must be undertaken.

For the assessment of short-term mental stress at work, it is suggested to combine:

- STAI-Y, State-Trait Anxiety Inventory
- PDI, Peritraumatic Distress Inventory
- ALES, Appraisal of Life Events Scale

And additionally if a special focus is needed on the workload:

- NASA Task Load Index

For the assessment of potential traumatic event at work, it is suggested to use one of the following questionnaires or to combine them:

- PDI, Peritraumatic Distress Inventory
- IES-R , Impact of Event Scale-Revised

For the assessment of stress at work over a period, several possibilities are suggested.

If an exhaustive approach is sought, one of the following questionnaires is suggested:

- COPSOQ, the Copenhagen Psychosocial questionnaire
- NIOSH Generic Job Stress Questionnaire
- JCQ, Job Content Questionnaire

If the use of short questionnaires is sought, one of the following questionnaires is suggested:

- PSS, Perceived Stress Scale
- JSS, Job Stress Survey
- STAI-Y, State-Trait Anxiety Inventory

Whatever approach is chosen, if an additional special focus is needed:

- on the workload, use NASA Task Load Index
- on the reward, use ERI, Effort-Reward Imbalance (Chap. 11 of the present book)

It is highly recommended that these questionnaires be used by specialists, that is, professionals graduated in Human Science and, optimally, trained in Psychometry. This is a guarantee of compliance with deontology and of reduced risks of misinterpretations of the results.

References

Alpert, F. F., Harada, D. S., Bonnet, F. R., Campos, K. J. P., Gimenes, M. J. F., Sá, E. C., & Muñoz, D. R. (2018). Evaluation of subjective scales for measuring mental workload: Literature review. *Work Organisation and Psychosocial Factors*, Paper #533.

Berton, J., Rinau, E., & Conte, M. (2015). Appraisal of Life Event Scale (ALES) to differentiate mental stress perceived by Physicians and Nurses involved in the same Simulation Training situation of Anesthesiology. *Stress Self-assessment & Questionnaires-choice, application, limits*, 39–43.

Boudarene, M., & Kellou, C. (2005). Le stress professionnel: Enquête préliminaire dans une entreprise algérienne d'hydrocarbures. *Revue francophone du stress et du trauma, 5*(3), 141–151.

Bruchon-Schweitzer, M. (2002). *Psychologie de la santé. Modèles, concepts et méthodes*. Dunod.

Bruchon-Schweitzer, M., & Paulhan, I. (1993). In Y. S. T. A. I.-Y. Forme (Ed.), *Spielberger CD, adaptation française de Inventaire d'Anxiété Trait-État*. Les Éditions du Centre de Psychologie Appliquée.

Brunet, A., Weiss, D. S., Metzler, T. J., Best, S. R., Neylan, T. C., Rogers, C., et al. (2001). The Peritraumatic Distress Inventory: A proposed measure of PTSD criterion A2. *American Journal of Psychiatry, 158*(9), 1480–1485.

Brunet, A., St-Hilaire, A., Jehel, L., & King, S. (2003). Validation of a French version of the impact of event scale-revised. *The Canadian Journal of Psychiatry, 48*(1), 56–61.

Bryant, R. A., Moulds, M. L., & Guthrie, R. M. (2000). Acute Stress Disorder Scale: A self-report measure of acute stress disorder. *Psychological Assessment, 12*(1), 61–68.

Cardeiia, E., Classen, C., Koopman, C., & Spiegel, D. (1996). Review of the Stanford Acute Stress Reaction Questionnaire (SASRQ). In B. H. Stamm (Ed.), *Measurement of stress, trauma and adaptation* (pp. 293–297). Sidran Press.

Cegarra, J., & Morgado, N. (2009, September). Étude des propriétés de la version francophone du NASATLX. In *EPIQUE 2009: 5ème Colloque de Psychologie Ergonomique* (pp. 233–239). France: Nice.

Chamberlain, K., & Zika, S. (1990). The minor events approach to stress: Support for the use of daily hassles. *British Journal of Psychology, 81*, 469–481.

Cohen, S., Kamarck, T., & Mermelstein, R. (1983). A global measure of perceived stress. *Journal of Health and Social Behavior, 24*, 385–396.

6 Psychological Assessment of the State of Mental Stress at Work 113

Cohen, S., & Williamson, G. (1998). Perceived stress in a probability sample of the US. In S. Spacapam, & S. Oskamp (Eds.), *The social psychology of health: claremont symposium on applied social psychology*. Newbury Park: Sage.

Creamer, M., Bell, R., & Failla, S. (2003). Psychometric properties of the impact of event scale—revised. *Behaviour Research and Therapy, 41*(12), 1489–1496.

Derogatis, L. R., Rickels, K., & Rock, A. (1976). The SCL-90 and the MMPI: A step in the validation of a new selfreport scale. *British Journal of Psychiatry, 128*, 280–289.

Dohrenwend, B. S., Krasnoff, L., Askenasy, A. R., & Dohrenwend, B. P. (1978). Exemplification of a method for scaling life events: The PERI life events scale. *Journal of Health and Social Behavior, 19*, 205–229.

Fauquet-Alekhine, Ph., Geeraerts, Th., & Rouillac, L. (2014). Characterization of anesthetists' behavior during simulation training: performance versus stress achieving medical tasks with or without physical effort. *Psychology and Social Behavior Research, 2*(2), 20–28.

Fauquet-Alekhine, Ph, & Rouillac, L. (2015). Arbitrary Self-Assessment Scale of Stress: Analysis and Discussion of the limited Relevance. *Stress Self-assessment & questionnaires: choice, application, limits*, 15–20.

Fauquet-Alekhine, Ph., Berton, J., Rouillac, L., & Granry, J. C. (2015). High stress and self-assessment: Assumption of systematic over-estimation. In *Stress self-assessment & questionnaires: Choice, application, limits* (pp. 44–50). http://hayka-kultura.org/larsen.html

Fauquet-Alekhine, Ph., Rouillac, L., & Granry, J. C. (2020). Subjective versus objective assessment of short term occupational stress: Bias and analysis of self-assessment of high stress levels. *Journal of Advances in Medicine and Medical Research, 32*(10), 50–64.

Ferguson, E., Matthews, G., & Cox, T. (1999). The appraisal of life events (ALE) scale: Reliability and validity. *British Journal of Health Psychology, 4*(2), 97–116.

Folkman, S., & Lazarus, R. S. (1985). If it changes it must be a process: A study of emotion and coping during three stages of a college examination. *Journal of Personality and Social Psychology, 48*, 150–170.

Folkman, S., Lazarus, R. S., Gruen, R. J., & DeLongis, A. (1986). Appraisal, coping, health status, and psychological symptoms. *Journal of Personality and Social Psychology, 50*(3), 571.

Giovannoni, J. (2015). Probation officers reduce their stress by cultivating the practice of loving-kindness with self and others. *International Journal of Caring Sciences, 8*(2), 325–343.

Hahn, S. E., & Smith, C. S. (1999). Daily hassles and chronic stressors: Conceptual and measurement issues. *Stress Medicine, 15*, 89–101.

Hart, S. G., & Staveland, L. E. (1988). Development of NASA-TLX (Task Load Index): Results of empirical and theoretical research. *Advances in Psychology, 52*, 139–183.

Holmes, T. H., & Rahe, R. H. (1967). The social readjustment rating scale. *Journal of Psychosomatic Research, 11*, 213–218.

Holmlund-Rytkönen, M., & Strandvik, T. (2005). Stress in business relationships. *Journal of Business & Industrial Marketing, 20*(1), 12–22.

Jehel, L., Brunet, A., Paterniti, S., & Guelfi, J. D. (2005). Validation of the peritraumatic distress inventory's French translation. *Canadian Journal of Psychiatry. Revue canadienne de psychiatrie, 50*(1), 67–71.

Jehel, L., Paterniti, S., Brunet, A., Louville, P., & Guelfi, J. D. (2006). Peritraumatic distress prospectively predicts PTDS symptoms in assault victims. *L'encéphale, 32*(6 Pt 1), 953–956.

Karasek, R. (2015, May). Job Content Questionnaire 2.0 (JCQ2): How to Use and Understand its Many New Features and Theory. *APA Work, Stress, and Health Conference*. Atlanta, Georgia.

Karasek, R., Brisson, C., Kawakami, N., Houtman, I., Bongers, P., & Amick, B. (1998). The Job Content Questionnaire (JCQ): An instrument for internationally comparative assessments of psychosocial job characteristics. *Journal of Occupational Health Psychology, 3*(4), 322–355.

Lazarus, R. S. (1984). Puzzles in the study of daily hassles. *Journal of Behavioral Medicine, 7*, 375–389.

Lazarus, R. S., & Folkman, S. (1984). *Stress, appraisal, and coping*. Springer.

Lei, H., & Skinner, H. A. (1980). A psychosomatic study of life events and social readjustment. *Journal of Psychosomatic Research, 24*, 57–65.

Leka, S., & Jain, A. (2010). *Health impact of psychosocial hazards at work: An overview*. World Health Organization.

Lesage, F., Berjot, S., & Deschamps, F. (2012). Psychometric properties of the French versions of the perceived stress scale. *International Journal of Occupational Medicine and Environmental Health, 25*(2), 178–184.

Lewinsohn, P. M., Mermelstein, R. M., Alexander, C., & Mac Phillamy, D. J. (1985). The unpleasant events schedule: A scale for the measurement of adverse events. *Journal of Clinical Psychology, 41*, 483–498.

Lindsay, P. H., & Norman, D. A. (1980). Stress et émotion. In *Comportements humains et traitement de l'information*. Sciences de la vie, Raget.

MacDonald, S., Linton, S. J., & Jansson-Fröjmark, M. (2009). Reconstructing the past on the original pain recall assessment form (OPRA). *The Journal of Pain, 10*(8), 809–817.

Rozanov, V. A. (2017). Evolution of the Concept of Stress. *Understanding Stress at Work*, 17–21. http://haykakultura.org/larsen.html

Rubio, S., Díaz, E., Martín, J., & Puente, J. M. (2004). Evaluation of subjective mental workload: A comparison of SWAT, NASA-TLX, and workload profile methods. *Applied Psychology, 53*(1), 61–86.

Spielberger, C. D. (1983a). Traduction française Schweitzer MB et Paulhan I, 1990. D'après Guelfi JD (ref 58 of the ANAES report and also ref 76).

Spielberger, C. D. (1983b). *State-Trait Anxiety Inventory for Adults (STAI-AD)* [Database record]. APA PsycTests. https://doi.org/10.1037/t06496-000

Spielberger, C. D., & Reheiser, E. C. (1994). The job stress survey: Measuring gender differences in occupational stress. *Journal of Social Behavior and Personality, 9*(2), 199.

Weathers, F. W., Litz, B. T., Herman, D. S., Huska, J. A., & Keane, T. M. (1993). *The PTSD Checklist (PCL): Reliability, validity, and diagnostic utility.* Paper presented at the 9th annual conference of the ISTSS, San Antonio.

Weiss, D. S. (2007). The impact of event scale-revised. In J. P. Wilson & T. M. Keane (Eds.), *Assessing psychological trauma and PTSD: A practitioner's handbook* (2nd ed., pp. 168–189). Guilford Press.

Zawadzki, M. J., Scott, S. B., Almeida, D. M., Lanza, S. T., Conroy, D. E., Sliwinski, M. J., et al. (2019). Understanding stress reports in daily life: A coordinated analysis of factors associated with the frequency of reporting stress. *J Behav Med, 42*(3), 545–560.

Zimmerman, M. (1983). Using scalings on life events inventories to predict dysphoria. *Journal of Human Stress, 9*, 32–38.

7

Stress Assessment in Daily Life Using the Experience Sampling Method

Thomas Vaessen, Ulrich Reininghaus, and Inez Myin-Germeys

1 Introduction

During the last century, stress has taken a central position in both preclinical and clinical research. Its implications range from an organism's most basic survival tactics to physical and mental well-being (Juster et al., 2011). Typically, it involves activation of the autonomic nervous system and the hypothalamic-pituitary-adrenal axis (see Chap. 3 of the present book). This activation results in a rapid physiological response in the form of an energy boost that prepares the organism for immediate physical action, also known as the fight-or-flight response. As such, the system is highly adaptive and promotes well-being. However, stress may have very detrimental effects as well. In humans, in addition to major stressors such as childhood adversity or stressful life events, minor stressors that occur naturally in the flow of daily life have been shown to pose a risk to those individuals who carry a vulnerability to developing somatic or mental illness (Ingram & Luxton, 2005). Especially when stress is prolonged or recurrent (i.e., chronic), the excessive

---

T. Vaessen
Department of Neurosciences, Center for Contextual Psychiatry, KU Leuven, Leuven, Belgium

Department of Psychology, Health, and Technology, University of Twente, Enschede, The Netherlands
e-mail: thomas.vaessen@kuleuven.be; T.R.Vaessen@utwente.nl

© The Author(s), under exclusive license to Springer Nature Switzerland AG 2023
P. Fauquet-Alekhine, J. Erskine (eds.), *The Palgrave Handbook of Occupational Stress*,
https://doi.org/10.1007/978-3-031-27349-0_7

118 T. Vaessen et al.

release of stress hormones may increase allostatic load. As a consequence, chronic stress can impair cardiovascular, metabolic, and immune functioning (McEwen, 1998, 2006) and is implicated in the epidemiology of a broad range of mental disorders (de Kloet et al., 2005; McEwen, 1998, 2004; Varese et al., 2012; Walker & Diforio, 1997), urging for a better understanding of stress and its dynamics. In order to identify, understand, and possibly influence this complex concept and its consequences, accurate assessment of stress is crucial.

1.1 Subjective Appraisal of Stress

Importantly, a stimulus or situation is only considered a stressor (and thus triggers a stress response) when appraised as such by an individual. According to the classical appraisal theory of Lazarus and Folkman (1984), stress occurs when a given situation is appraised as threatening or challenging while resources to cope with it are perceived as insufficient. Whether or not an individual appraises a situation as such is highly subjective. Indeed, there are large inter-individual differences in stress appraisal. Under identical circumstances, a given situation may be a stressor to one person but not to another, depending on their respective appraisals. Furthermore, these appraisals do not necessarily resemble the situation's actual threat level. In today's Western society, stress often arises from psychosocial stressors such as busy traffic, interpersonal quarrels, or a high workload. Whereas often these situations do not pose an immediate threat to one's well-being, and effective coping strategies may well be available, psychosocial factors may cause considerable problems when

---

U. Reininghaus
Health and Population Research Department, Institute of Psychiatry, King's College, London, UK

Department of Public Mental Health, Central Institute of Mental Health, Mannheim, Germany

Department of Psychiatry and Psychology, School for Mental Health and Neuroscience, Maastricht University, Maastricht, The Netherlands
e-mail: u.reininghaus@maastrichtuniversity.nl; Ulrich.reininghaus@zi-mannheim.de

I. Myin-Germeys (✉)
Department of Neurosciences, Center for Contextual Psychiatry, KU Leuven, Leuven, Belgium
e-mail: Inez.germeys@kuleuven.be

7 Stress Assessment in Daily Life Using the Experience Sampling...

a person appraises them as stressful (see Chap. 10). Moreover, subjective appraisal predicts the acute physiological stress response (Gaab et al., 2005; Harvey et al., 2010). Hence, a physiological stress response may be triggered solely by the perception of a threat, even in the absence of an objective threat. This may have important implications when considering that memories, nightmares, or flashbacks of past life events, traumatic experiences, or daily hassles may trigger again the full-blown stress response if they are appraised as threatening. Indeed, subjective appraisal contributes to the development of posttraumatic stress disorder (Dunmore et al., 1999), and constitutes one of its core symptoms (i.e., re-experiencing/reliving of traumatic events[1]). In summary, a situation is only stressful to someone if it is appraised as such by that individual. To measure stress, it is therefore important to gain information on an individual's perception of the situation.

1.2 The Concept of Momentary Stress Assessment

Although much research has been done on stress, most studies have been conducted in a laboratory setting. Retrospective questionnaires (see Chap. 7) are typically opted for when assessing recent perceived stress, work-related stress, occurrence of stressful life events, or history of childhood adversity. Administration of these questionnaires is fast and inexpensive, while their predictive value is often good. However, retrospective questionnaires suffer, to various extents, from recall bias. The memory of a past situation is arguably contaminated by its outcome and subsequent events. Also, memory can be heavily influenced by current mood (Mayer et al., 1995; Ruci et al., 2009), further restricting the usefulness of such measures. Thus, asking how one felt at a particular moment, a month or more ago, does not provide a reliable picture of the subjective experience of that moment. Since stress crucially depends on subjective appraisal in the moment, the reliability and validity of retrospective stress questionnaires remains questionable.

Alternatively, stress tasks are used to investigate how individuals respond to an experimentally induced stressor. According to the sensitization theory (Collip et al., 2008; Myin-Germeys et al., 2001; van Winkel et al., 2008), exposure to severe or chronic stressors sensitizes the stress system. As a result of this sensitization, responses to milder stressors become excessive, as evidenced by increased affective or biological reactions to less stressful situations. Standardized stress tasks aim to induce mild to moderate levels of stress and

---

[1] Re-experiencing stress in the absence of an actual threat is Criterion B of PTSD in both DSM-V and ICD-10.

can hence be used to investigate sensitization. Some of the most commonly used tasks include public speech, arithmetic problem solving, physical pain induction, or a combination of these. The benefit of such paradigms lies in their artificial nature: they allow for assessment of the stress response while the stressor itself is standardized and kept constant over participants, or time (in the case of repeated measures designs). As such, they provide an indication of an individual's stress responsivity at a given moment in time, which has been shown to be indicative for factors related to (mental) health. However, these tasks typically have low ecological validity. Some tasks use physiological stimuli to induce stress, such as pain or pharmacological agents, whereas in real life stressors are often of a psychosocial nature. Even tasks that induce psychosocial stress, such as those depending on social evaluative threat, are somewhat artificial (i.e., solving arithmetic problems) and very distinct from stressors that are encountered in everyday life. As we are interested in investigating the detrimental effects of stress in the real world, assessing responses to artificial tasks may be of limited use.

1.3   Aim of This Chapter

With the current chapter, we aim to provide an overview of some of the most important experience sampling method (ESM) stress measures that have been mentioned in scientific literature so far. Taken together, although both retrospective questionnaires and stress tasks undeniably have their benefits, they have clear limitations as well. In order to assess how real-life stress affects an individual, we therefore need to measure in daily life and from moment to moment. Experience sampling methodology (ESM; Csikszentmihalyi & Larson, 1987; Myin-Germeys et al., 2009, 2018) offers this possibility. ESM, also known as ecological momentary assessment (Shiffman et al., 2008) or ambulatory assessment (Trull & Ebner-Priemer, 2013), is a structured diary technique that enables in-the-moment assessment of subjective experience, behavior, and context. Individuals fill out short questionnaires throughout the day in their natural environments, where daily hassles and small disturbances form a natural source of stressful events and situations. ESM thus provides an excellent opportunity to study stress in real life and real time. To date, ESM has left its mark on research in the fields of psychiatry (Myin-Germeys et al., 2018), psychopharmacology (Bos et al., 2015), oncology (Kampshoff et al., 2019), and ecological momentary interventions (Myin-Germeys et al., 2011, 2016; Reininghaus, 2018; Steinhart et al., 2019). Over the past three decades, the method has also increasingly been used in stress research, in a wide range of applications, and with numerous operationalizations.

Moreover, we will briefly evaluate each measure, where applicable, based on its associations with traditional questionnaires or biological features, or on its psychometric properties and practical issues. We do not aim to give an exhaustive listing of all measures that have been used to assess stress in daily life, nor will we provide a complete overview of all studies that have used a certain measure or discuss all evaluation criteria per measure. For a more detailed account on evaluation and validation of some often used ESM items, please see our previous contribution (Vaessen et al., 2015). We will end this chapter with a short summary and conclusions based on the evaluation of the discussed measures, and ESM stress assessment in general.

2 Stress Assessment Using the Experience Sampling Method

As discussed earlier, ESM typically consists of multiple measurements over the day on a number of consecutive days. Users receive an alarm watch and a paper and pencil diary, a palm-top, or an app on their smartphone. In so-called time-contingent designs, these devices emit an auditory signal at semi-random occasions throughout the day, referred to as a *beep*. Following a beep, users are required to fill out a short questionnaire assessing stress and other variables (Fig. 7.1). Typical time-contingent designs consist of eight to 10 beeps per day over a period of five or six consecutive days (Palmier-Claus et al., 2011), although other designs have been used, such as long-term daily diary approaches with one diary entry per day, or intense 24-hour ambulatory assessment studies with up to four beeps per hour. In event-contingent designs, no beeps are pre-programmed but questionnaires are rather initiated at the occurrence of an event, in most cases by the user, for instance at the occurrence of stress. To assess subjective experiences of stress or stress appraisals (Myin-Germeys & van Os, 2007; Myin-Germeys et al., 2001), different operationalizations have been used. One distinction is that between momentary measures and retrospective measures. Momentary measures assess stress at the moment of the beep, or right before the beep, to capture the subjective experience while keeping recall bias to an absolute minimum. As stress can be transient, however, the peak moments often occur in between assessment moments. Retrospective measures, therefore, assess instances of stress since the last beep, and although they do introduce a recall bias, it is negligible compared to what standard questionnaires suffer from. Finally, stress does not

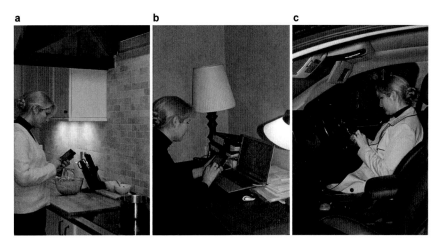

Fig. 7.1 (a–c) Subject filling out an ESM questionnaire on a smartphone application in different daily situations

exist in a vacuum, and several methods have looked at stress in relation to other momentary variables, and their dynamics. Below, we summarize the main stress measures for momentary and retrospective approaches separately, and discuss several methods of daily life stress dynamics.

2.1 Momentary Stress Measures

Perceived Stress

The most straightforward method of momentary stress assessment is asking an individual if they feel stressed. Several studies have opted for this method using a single item, although the wording of this item may vary slightly across studies. For instance, 'Do you feel stressed?' or 'How stressed are you?' have both been used (Bacon et al., 2004; Buckley et al., 2004; Kennedy et al., 2015). One-item momentary perceived stress was moderately correlated with chronic work stress assessed with a standard questionnaire in female managers (Lumley et al., 2014), which suggests that these concepts are related, but are not assessing the same phenomenon.

Instead of a single item, some studies have averaged the response to multiple items that are supposed to assess the same construct. For instance, Carels et al. (2000) combined the items 'I feel stressed,' 'I feel frustrated,' and 'I feel tense' and performed a factor analysis, which revealed that all three items loaded on the same factor. A benefit of an operationalization using multiple items is that it may provide for more variability in the scores. However, the items need to measure the same underlying construct (stress), and unless they are part of a previously validated questionnaire, a confirmatory factor analysis may be required.

Negative Affect

A broader way of looking at subjective stress is to assess general distress, often operationalized as negative affect (NA). NA is typically assessed as a composite score of several items indicative of negative mood (e.g., 'I feel down', 'I feel anxious', 'I feel lonely', 'I feel guilty', 'I feel insecure', 'I feel embarrassed', 'I feel nervous'). NA has been used as a proxy for stress by several studies (e.g., Kimhy et al., 2010; Schwerdtfeger & Gerteis, 2014; Sloan et al., 1994; van Eck & Nicolson, 1994). Daily life momentary NA has been shown to be associated with higher cortisol levels (Jacobs et al., 2007; van Eck et al., 1996), and with momentary heart rate (Schwerdtfeger & Gerteis, 2014), physiological variables indicative of the stress response (see Chap. 6). However, it is important to note that not all studies find associations between NA and autonomic arousal measured with heart rate (Kimhy et al., 2010; Lehman et al., 2015). This may have to do with the fact that many NA measures include low-arousal items, which may not directly reflect sympathetic activity characteristic for the experience of stress. In the end, particularly the low-valence and high-arousal items may more closely represent the subjective experience of stress.

Activity-Related Stress

Stress may often emerge from the momentary context. For instance, walking in a busy street, doing an important task, or an unpleasant conversation can have a significant impact on mood and stress. Inquiring about how the current context is appraised may indicate how stressful the momentary situation is. One such context relates to the activity that one is currently involved in. Participants are asked to report the activity that they are currently doing and subsequently provide an appraisal of this activity. According to the work of Lazarus and Folkman (Lazarus & Folkman, 1984), stress emerges from situations that are considered threatening, while having the feeling of not being able to cope with them. In line with this theory, the current activity can be evaluated according to the statements 'I would rather do something else,' 'This activity requires effort,' and 'I am skilled to do this activity' (reverse scored), to constitute a measure of activity-related stress (e.g., Myin-Germeys et al., 2001; van der Steen et al., 2017). Three studies have looked at the association between activity-related stress in daily life and momentary cortisol levels. They found that activity-related stress was (positively?) associated with cortisol levels (Jacobs et al., 2007), and that they are differentially related within healthy controls and individuals at risk for (van Duin et al., 2019) or with (Vaessen et al., 2018) psychosis, which resembles findings from lab studies (Pruessner et al., 2017).

Social Stress

Stress may also be related to the social context. For instance, having an argument with someone and feeling judged or threatened are commonly reported sources of daily stress. Lehman and Conley (2010) assessed social stress as social-evaluative threat, or the extent to which an individual is 'worried about others' reactions.' In an effort to establish construct validity, they found that the scores on this item correlated with those on questionnaires assessing depressive symptoms, anxiety, and neuroticism, and not with age, gender, and self-esteem. In a follow-up study, the authors adopted a momentary version of the daily social interaction anxiety measure (Kashdan & Steger, 2006) to assess subjective social evaluative threat and found that it correlated with the social worry item (Lehman et al., 2015).

Another indication of social stress can be derived from the general appraisal of the social context. In a number of studies, participants were asked about their current social context ('Whom are you with?') and, subsequently, to appraise this context. The items 'I like this company' (reverse scored) and 'I would rather be alone right now' are used to estimate the stressfulness of being in that company and constitute the social stress measure. These two items tend to correlate well over time (Gevonden et al., 2015; Myin-Germeys et al., 2001). Adding a third item ('I am enjoying myself'), social stress was correlated with the perceived stress scale (Levenstein et al., 1993), an indicator of past-month stress (Palmier-Claus et al., 2012). As individuals are not always in the company of others, however, data is lost for all situations where someone is alone. Therefore, some authors have come up with a no-company equivalent of social stress, using 'I like being alone right now' and 'I would rather be in company' (Reininghaus et al., 2016). Indeed, the study by Jacobs et al. (2007) showed that social stress was associated with salivary cortisol levels at the time of assessment, linking it to the physiological stress response.

It is important to keep in mind that a social context may not be physical but rather digital. Precise phrasing of the items or thorough briefing beforehand can clarify how social context is defined. Needless to say, this definition is of crucial importance for the interpretation of results. Furthermore, a current social context may be more of a background setting than an active environment. For instance, on a work floor, there may be very little interaction with other individuals present. Items on the appraisal of the social interaction are thus not always warranted when an individual is in a social context.

Demand and Control

Based on the model on work-related stress of Karasek (1979), there are ESM items developed to assess the perceived situational control and demand related to work (e.g., Kamarck et al., 2002). Johnston et al. (2016) assessed perceived control as the average response to two items (i.e., allowed a lot of say in what they did, allowed to make the main decisions about what they did) and demand as the average response to five items (i.e., work fast, work hard, do too much, interrupted, and enough time available). The internal consistency for both scales was good. Both scales predicted subjective arousal, suggesting they are indeed indicative of stress. However, their interaction was unrelated to subjective arousal, meaning that demand was predictive of arousal regardless of perceived control, and vice versa. Since, according to Karasek's model, stress occurs when demand is high and control is low, an interaction effect would be expected.

Others have operationalized work-related stress as the ratio between perceived demands of the current activity and ability to meet those demands, which was associated with ratings of loneliness, depression, and neuroticism (Hawkley et al., 2003).

Self-Initiated Reports

Thus far, we have described measures that are part of a questionnaire which is presented at (random) preselected moments throughout the day. Most likely, the peak of the acute stress response, which is transient, is hence not captured by these measures. A few studies have attempted to overcome this issue by adopting an event-sampling scheme—a protocol in which sampling does not occur based on time, but on preselected events. In this case, a user is instructed to fill out a report whenever they experience stress. Farmer et al. (2017) instructed their participants to indicate when a stressful event occurred, which resulted in an average of 26.5 reports over the course of 42 days. Although this method enables very timely assessment of the acute stress response, the average of 4.4 reports per week exposes its limitations for statistical purposes.

Whether this number reflects an accurate estimation of the number of stressful events an individual may encounter or these participants did not report all stressful events that occurred cannot be determined based on these data. However, a recent study indicated that occurrence of stressors may range up to 31.7% of beeps using time-sampling methods (Zawadzki et al., 2019), and, arguably, it is the milder stressors that are not reported by users in event-related designs. This taps into the issue of selection bias, where the user is left with the decision to report a situation or not, which may differ considerably across individuals and hence introduce a bias. Still, event-related sampling remains an interesting ESM approach and it may be worthwhile to further explore its use in stress research.

2.2 Retrospective Stress Measures

Perceived Stress

Similar items that have been used to assess momentary stress can be reformulated to inquire about recently perceived stress over a longer period of time. Pollard et al. (2007) asked participants to rate their level of perceived stress over the past hour. Similarly, Smets et al. (2018) have instructed their participants to rate the maximum stress level during the past hour. Both studies have found associations with physiological measures of arousal over the corresponding hour (Pollard et al., 2007; Smets et al., 2018), suggesting that potential effects of recall bias are weak for these time windows. It thus seems that retrospective ESM assessment of recent subjective stress is related to the physiological stress response. However, with longer inter-beep intervals, this association is likely to fade.

Event-Related Stress

Event-related stress is most closely related to the concept of daily hassles. Several protocols require users to first indicate if a stressful event did occur since the last beep using YES/NO response options, and only in case of a stressful event is the individual asked about the stressfulness of the event (Mogle et al., 2019; Ruiz et al., 2017; Scott et al., 2015; Smyth et al., 2014). In early approaches to assessing event-related stress, participants were asked if any stressful event had occurred since the last beep, and to subsequently rate its unpleasantness, importance, predictability, controllability, and frequency of prior occurrence (van Eck et al., 1996). Ideally, however, participants indicate an event at every beep (regardless of the event's absolute importance or stressfulness). This is to avoid biases in response style, such as only endorsing the item when an extreme event has occurred, and to gain information on less stressful events for comparison. In the approach of Myin-Germeys et al. (2001), participants are therefore instructed to think about the most important event that happened between the previous and the current beep, and are then asked to report the event's pleasantness on a bipolar Likert scale (-3 'very unpleasant' to 3 'very pleasant'). Events that are rated as unpleasant are considered stressful events. The reason for using an implicit approach (i.e., using unpleasantness as a proxy for stressfulness) is to avoid questions that may cause reactivity. Stress is a loaded concept that may trigger global self-reflections, and a more implicit approach may be better suited to assessing subjective stress without influencing responses. However, it still remains to be shown that the implicit approach is indeed preferential over an explicit approach. Using the implicit approach, Collip et al. (2011) found that event-related stress is predictive of increased free cortisol levels in individuals at familial risk for psychosis, suggesting its link to the physiological stress response. Alternatively, ESM protocols provide users with a list of potentially stressful events and require them to indicate if any of the events occurred since the last beep. The benefit of this approach is that the user does not have to decide what a stressful event entails. However, such lists are never exhaustive and may contain very general events that are not necessarily experienced as stressful by everyone.

Importantly, an individual may feel stressed for other reasons than a recent stressful event. For instance, events or situations that lie further in the past, or ruminative thoughts, may cause lasting feelings of distress. Indeed, whereas frequencies of reported recent stressful events average at about 20% of all beeps, individuals report subjective perceived stress on 46–56% of the moments (Zawadzki et al., 2019). Event-related stress therefore may underestimate an individual's momentary allostatic load. However, event-related measures have their benefits. Apart from the obvious purpose of providing an indication of the number and intensity of stressful moments an individual encounters, event-stress is often used to investigate an individual's response to those events. In some cases, the user is asked how long ago the event happened, which can be used in the statistical models. In the next paragraph, we will discuss how the association between stress and other variables can be modeled.

2.3 Stress Dynamics

Reactivity to Stress

ESM can be used to examine the subjective response to stressors. A number of studies have investigated the impact of stressful events, activities, or work- or social-related contexts on current mood or (sub)clinical symptoms. This is often referred to as reactivity to stress. Affective stress reactivity has been investigated in relation to event-related stress, activity-related stress, and social stress, both in healthy populations and in individuals suffering from psychopathological symptoms. This is not assessed explicitly (i.e., 'How does this stressor influence your mood'). Rather, users rate their current mood and symptoms, as well as the stressfulness of a current or recent situation. The association between subjective appraisal and emotional reaction is then inferred statistically, to preclude social desirability and response biases. Affective stress reactivity is thus a measure of association between stress and mood; a stronger relationship suggests a stronger effect of stress on mood (although see next paragraph for a discussion on directionality). Greater affective reactivity to event-, activity-, and social-related stress has been reported in depression (Wichers et al., 2009), anxiety (Herres et al., 2018), personality disorder (Glaser et al., 2008), and psychosis (Myin-Germeys et al., 2001, 2005; Reininghaus et al., 2016). Within psychiatric populations, a stress response can also consist of increases in psychopathology. This has often been investigated in relation to psychotic experiences, assessed with items such as 'I feel suspicious,' 'I feel unreal,' 'My thoughts are being influenced by others,' 'I can't get rid of my thoughts,' 'I see things that aren't really there,' 'I hear voices,' and 'I'm afraid I'll lose control.' These psychotic experiences have also been associated with subjective experiences of stress, especially within individuals at early stages of psychotic illness (Palmier-Claus et al., 2012; Reininghaus et al., 2016; van der Steen et al., 2017). As such, ESM stress reactivity measures have been shown to have clinical relevance and elucidate potential disease mechanisms.

Recovery from Stress

In addition to the immediate response to stress, people differ in their recovery from stress. Recovery, here, means the return to a baseline following stress and may relate to resilience (see Chap. 13). One study so far has looked at affective recovery from daily stressors using ESM (Vaessen et al., 2019). Stress recovery was operationalized as the number of beeps before NA was no longer significantly increased compared to the beep before the stressor. Indeed, in individuals at early stages of psychosis, the number of beeps to recover from stress was higher than in healthy volunteers, indicating lingering NA following a stressful event. However, considering the significant sparsity of publications on this form of stress assessment, evaluation of this method is premature.

Networks

An approach that has received much attention recently is that of network models. Network models in ESM are used to study multivariate, time-varying psychological systems (Bringmann et al., 2013, 2016). Networks based on ESM data have been applied to psychopathology. For instance, worrying has been shown to have a larger impact on momentary affect dynamics in individuals with higher neuroticism levels (Bringmann et al., 2013) and negative affect spreads, and persists especially in individuals with depressive disorder (Wigman et al., 2015). Only one study to date has specifically looked at stress from a network perspective. Using network modeling, the authors found that momentary stress occupied a central position in the dynamic interplay of psychological variables, including psychotic experiences in individuals diagnosed with psychotic illness (Klippel et al., 2018). Although their application in ESM research is still relatively recent, network approaches offer a multitude of possibilities for the modeling of stress-related dynamics in daily life.

3   Summary and Conclusions

This chapter provides an overview of measures used in ESM research to assess stress in daily life and thus at work. Various ESM measures of stress have been put forward to capture important aspects of the subjective stress experience and appraisal of context. In general, perceived stress seems to be a more efficient measure of subjective stress than overall NA. Moreover, although both control and demand were related to physiological arousal, the control–demand interaction—as operationalization of work-related stress—did not show convincing associations. Momentary and retrospective measures have their own benefits and protocols often use a combination of both. While momentary measures provide accurate snapshots of daily-life stress experiences, retrospective measures may provide a proxy for filling in the gaps and can be used for modeling stress dynamics. Although stress dynamics, such as stress reactivity, suggest an effect of stress on mood or symptoms, the direction of this association cannot be confirmed using observational methods such as ESM. Even in time-lagged designs, where stress measured at t_0 is predictive of affect at t_1, directionality cannot be proven. Therefore, although temporality does provide strong hints about the direction of the effect, claims on causality are not warranted. Still, research on these dynamics has provided much insight into the role of stress in mental and somatic health and as such can be considered to be clinically meaningful. Ultimately, which measures are the most appropriate depends on the research question and design. In general, however, a combination of several measures will provide the most complete picture.

References

Bacon, S. L., Watkins, L. L., Babyak, M., Sherwood, A., Hayano, J., Hinderliter, A. L., et al. (2004). Effects of daily stress on autonomic cardiac control in patients with coronary artery disease. *The American Journal of Cardiology, 93*(10), 1292–1294. https://doi.org/10.1016/j.amjcard.2004.02.018

Bos, F. M., Schoevers, R. A., & aan het Rot, M. (2015). Experience sampling and ecological momentary assessment studies in psychopharmacology: A systematic review. *European Neuropsychopharmacology, 25*(11), 1853–1864. https://doi.org/10.1016/j.euroneuro.2015.08.008

Bringmann, L. F., Pe, M. L., Vissers, N., Ceulemans, E., Borsboom, D., Vanpaemel, W., et al. (2016). Assessing temporal emotion dynamics using networks. *Assessment, 23*(4), 425–435. https://doi.org/10.1177/1073191116645909

Bringmann, L. F., Vissers, N., Wichers, M., Geschwind, N., Kuppens, P., Peeters, F., et al. (2013). A network approach to psychopathology: New insights into clinical longitudinal data. *PLoS One, 8*(4), e60188. https://doi.org/10.1371/journal.pone.0060188

Buckley, T. C., Holohan, D., Greif, J. L., Bedard, M., & Suvak, M. (2004). Twenty-four-hour ambulatory assessment of heart rate and blood pressure in chronic PTSD and non-PTSD veterans. *Journal of Traumatic Stress, 17*(2), 163–171. https://doi.org/10.1023/B:JOTS.0000022623.01190.f0

Carels, R. A., Blumenthal, J. A., & Sherwood, A. (2000). Emotional responsivity during daily life: Relationship to psychosocial functioning and ambulatory blood pressure. *International Journal of Psychophysiology, 36*(1), 25–33.

Collip, D., Myin-Germeys, I., & Van Os, J. (2008). Does the concept of "sensitization" provide a plausible mechanism for the putative link between the environment and schizophrenia? *Schizophrenia Bulletin, 34*(2), 220–225. https://doi.org/10.1093/schbul/sbm163

Collip, D., Nicolson, N. A., Lardinois, M., Lataster, T., van Os, J., & Myin-Germeys, I. (2011). Daily cortisol, stress reactivity and psychotic experiences in individuals at above average genetic risk for psychosis. *Psychological Medicine, 41*(11), 2305–2315. https://doi.org/10.1017/s0033291711000602

Csikszentmihalyi, M., & Larson, R. (1987). Validity and reliability of the Experience-Sampling Method. *The Journal of Nervous and Mental Disease, 175*(9), 526–536.

de Kloet, E. R., Joels, M., & Holsboer, F. (2005). Stress and the brain: From adaptation to disease. *Nature Reviews Neuroscience, 6*(6), 463–475. https://doi.org/10.1038/nrn1683

Dunmore, E., Clark, D. M., & Ehlers, A. (1999). Cognitive factors involved in the onset and maintenance of posttraumatic stress disorder (PTSD) after physical or sexual assault. *Behaviour Research and Therapy, 37*(9), 809–829.

Farmer, S., Mindry, D., Comulada, W. S., & Swendeman, D. (2017). Mobile phone ecological momentary assessment of daily stressors among people living with HIV: Elucidating factors underlying health-related challenges in daily routines. *The Journal of the Association of Nurses in AIDS Care, 28*(5), 737–751. https://doi.org/10.1016/j.jana.2017.04.001

Gaab, J., Rohleder, N., Nater, U. M., & Ehlert, U. (2005). Psychological determinants of the cortisol stress response: The role of anticipatory cognitive appraisal. *Psychoneuroendocrinology, 30*(6), 599–610. https://doi.org/10.1016/j.psyneuen.2005.02.001

Gevonden, M. J., Myin-Germeys, I., van den Brink, W., van Os, J., Selten, J. P., & Booij, J. (2015). Psychotic reactions to daily life stress and dopamine function in people with severe hearing impairment. *Psychological Medicine, 45*(8), 1665–1674. https://doi.org/10.1017/s0033291714002797

Glaser, J. P., Van Os, J., Mengelers, R., & Myin-Germeys, I. (2008). A momentary assessment study of the reputed emotional phenotype associated with borderline personality disorder. *Psychological Medicine, 38*(9), 1231–1239. https://doi.org/10.1017/s0033291707002322

Harvey, A., Nathens, A. B., Bandiera, G., & Leblanc, V. R. (2010). Threat and challenge: Cognitive appraisal and stress responses in simulated trauma resuscitations. *Medical Education, 44*(6), 587–594. https://doi.org/10.1111/j.1365-2923.2010.03634.x

Hawkley, L. C., Burleson, M. H., Berntson, G. G., & Cacioppo, J. T. (2003). Loneliness in everyday life: Cardiovascular activity, psychosocial context, and health behaviors. *Journal of Personality and Social Psychology, 85*(1), 105–120.

Herres, J., Caporino, N. E., Cummings, C. M., & Kendall, P. C. (2018). Emotional reactivity to daily events in youth with anxiety disorders. *Anxiety, Stress, and Coping, 31*(4), 387–401. https://doi.org/10.1080/10615806.2018.1472492

Ingram, R. E., & Luxton, D. D. (2005). Vulnerability-stress models. Development of psychopathology: A vulnerability-stress perspective, 32–46.

Jacobs, N., Myin-Germeys, I., Derom, C., Delespaul, P., van Os, J., & Nicolson, N. A. (2007). A momentary assessment study of the relationship between affective and adrenocortical stress responses in daily life. *Biological Psychology, 74*(1), 60–66. https://doi.org/10.1016/j.biopsycho.2006.07.002

Johnston, D., Bell, C., Jones, M., Farquharson, B., Allan, J., Schofield, P., et al. (2016). Stressors, appraisal of stressors, experienced stress and cardiac response: A real-time, real-life investigation of work stress in nurses. *Annals of Behavioral Medicine, 50*(2), 187–197. https://doi.org/10.1007/s12160-015-9746-8

Juster, R. P., Bizik, G., Picard, M., Arsenault-Lapierre, G., Sindi, S., Trepanier, L., et al. (2011). A transdisciplinary perspective of chronic stress in relation to psychopathology throughout life span development. *Development and Psychopathology, 23*(3), 725–776. https://doi.org/10.1017/s0954579411000289

Kamarck, T. W., Janicki, D. L., Shiffman, S., Polk, D. E., Muldoon, M. F., Liebenauer, L. L., & Schwartz, J. E. (2002). Psychosocial demands and ambulatory blood pressure: A field assessment approach. *Physiology & Behavior, 77*(4–5), 699–704.

Kampshoff, C. S., Verdonck-de Leeuw, I. M., van Oijen, M. G., Sprangers, M. A., & Buffart, L. M. (2019). Ecological momentary assessments among patients with cancer: A scoping review. *European Journal of Cancer Care, 28*(3), e13095. https://doi.org/10.1111/ecc.13095

Karasek, R. A., Jr. (1979). Job demands, job decision latitude, and mental strain: Implications for job redesign. *Administrative Science Quarterly, 24*, 285–308.

Kashdan, T. B., & Steger, M. F. (2006). Expanding the topography of social anxiety. An experience-sampling assessment of positive emotions, positive events, and emotion suppression. *Psychological Science, 17*(2), 120–128. https://doi.org/10.1111/j.1467-9280.2006.01674.x

Kennedy, A. P., Epstein, D. H., Jobes, M. L., Agage, D., Tyburski, M., Phillips, K. A., et al. (2015). Continuous in-the-field measurement of heart rate: Correlates of drug use, craving, stress, and mood in polydrug users. *Drug and Alcohol Dependence, 151*, 159–166. https://doi.org/10.1016/j.drugalcdep.2015.03.024

Kimhy, D., Delespaul, P., Ahn, H., Cai, S., Shikhman, M., Lieberman, J. A., et al. (2010). Concurrent measurement of "real-world" stress and arousal in individuals with psychosis: Assessing the feasibility and validity of a novel methodology. *Schizophrenia Bulletin, 36*(6), 1131–1139. https://doi.org/10.1093/schbul/sbp028

Klippel, A., Viechtbauer, W., Reininghaus, U., Wigman, J., van Borkulo, C., Myin-Germeys, I., & Wichers, M. (2018). The cascade of stress: A network approach to explore differential dynamics in populations varying in risk for psychosis. *Schizophrenia Bulletin, 44*(2), 328–337. https://doi.org/10.1093/schbul/sbx037

Lazarus, R. S., & Folkman, S. (1984). *Stress, appraisal, and coping.* Springer Publishing Company.

Lehman, B. J., Cane, A. C., Tallon, S. J., & Smith, S. F. (2015). Physiological and emotional responses to subjective social evaluative threat in daily life. *Anxiety, Stress, and Coping, 28*(3), 321–339. https://doi.org/10.1080/10615806.2014.968563

Lehman, B. J., & Conley, K. M. (2010). Momentary reports of social-evaluative threat predict ambulatory blood pressure. *Social Psychological and Personality Science, 1*(1), 51–56. https://doi.org/10.1177/1948550609354924

Levenstein, S., Prantera, C., Varvo, V., Scribano, M. L., Berto, E., Luzi, C., & Andreoli, A. (1993). Development of the perceived stress questionnaire: A new tool for psychosomatic research. *Journal of Psychosomatic Research, 37*(1), 19–32.

Lumley, M. A., Shi, W., Wiholm, C., Slatcher, R. B., Sandmark, H., Wang, S., et al. (2014). The relationship of chronic and momentary work stress to cardiac reactivity in female managers: Feasibility of a smart phone-assisted assessment system. *Psychosomatic Medicine, 76*(7), 512–518. https://doi.org/10.1097/psy.000000 0000000085

Mayer, J. D., McCormick, L. J., & Strong, S. E. (1995). Mood-congruent memory and natural mood: New evidence. *Personality and Social Psychology Bulletin, 21*(7), 736–746. https://doi.org/10.1177/0146167295217008

McEwen, B. S. (1998). Stress, adaptation, and disease. Allostasis and allostatic load. *Annals of the New York Academy of Sciences, 840,* 33–44.

McEwen, B. S. (2004). Protection and damage from acute and chronic stress: Allostasis and allostatic overload and relevance to the pathophysiology of psychiatric disorders. *Annals of the New York Academy of Sciences, 1032,* 1–7. https://doi.org/10.1196/annals.1314.001

McEwen, B. S. (2006). Protective and damaging effects of stress mediators: Central role of the brain. *Dialogues in Clinical Neuroscience, 8*(4), 367–381.

Mogle, J., Munoz, E., Hill, N. L., Smyth, J. M., & Sliwinski, M. J. (2019). Daily memory lapses in adults: Characterization and influence on affect. *The Journals of Gerontology. Series B, Psychological Sciences and Social Sciences, 74*(1), 59–68. https://doi.org/10.1093/geronb/gbx012

Myin-Germeys, I., Birchwood, M., & Kwapil, T. (2011). From environment to therapy in psychosis: A real-world momentary assessment approach. *Schizophrenia Bulletin, 37*(2), 244–247. https://doi.org/10.1093/schbul/sbq164

Myin-Germeys, I., Delespaul, P., & van Os, J. (2005). Behavioural sensitization to daily life stress in psychosis. *Psychological Medicine, 35*(5), 733–741.

Myin-Germeys, I., Kasanova, Z., Vaessen, T., Vachon, H., Kirtley, O., Viechtbauer, W., & Reininghaus, U. (2018). Experience sampling methodology in mental health research: New insights and technical developments. *World Psychiatry, 17*(2), 123–132. https://doi.org/10.1002/wps.20513

Myin-Germeys, I., Klippel, A., Steinhart, H., & Reininghaus, U. (2016). Ecological momentary interventions in psychiatry. *Current Opinion in Psychiatry, 29*(4), 258–263. https://doi.org/10.1097/yco.0000000000000255

Myin-Germeys, I., Oorschot, M., Collip, D., Lataster, J., Delespaul, P., & van Os, J. (2009). Experience sampling research in psychopathology: Opening the black box of daily life. *Psychological Medicine, 39*(9), 1533–1547. https://doi.org/10.1017/s0033291708004947

Myin-Germeys, I., & van Os, J. (2007). Stress-reactivity in psychosis: Evidence for an affective pathway to psychosis. *Clinical Psychology Review, 27*(4), 409–424. https://doi.org/10.1016/j.cpr.2006.09.005

Myin-Germeys, I., van Os, J., Schwartz, J. E., Stone, A. A., & Delespaul, P. A. (2001). Emotional reactivity to daily life stress in psychosis. *Archives of General Psychiatry, 58*(12), 1137–1144.

Palmier-Claus, J. E., Dunn, G., & Lewis, S. W. (2012). Emotional and symptomatic reactivity to stress in individuals at ultra-high risk of developing psychosis. *Psychological Medicine, 42*(5), 1003–1012. https://doi.org/10.1017/s0033291711001929

Palmier-Claus, J. E., Myin-Germeys, I., Barkus, E., Bentley, L., Udachina, A., Delespaul, P. A., et al. (2011). Experience sampling research in individuals with mental illness: Reflections and guidance. *Acta Psychiatrica Scandinavica, 123*(1), 12–20. https://doi.org/10.1111/j.1600-0447.2010.01596.x

Pollard, T. M., Pearce, K. L., Rousham, E. K., & Schwartz, J. E. (2007). Do blood pressure and heart rate responses to perceived stress vary according to endogenous estrogen level in women? *American Journal of Physical Anthropology, 132*(1), 151–157. https://doi.org/10.1002/ajpa.20468

Pruessner, M., Cullen, A. E., Aas, M., & Walker, E. F. (2017). The neural diathesis-stress model of schizophrenia revisited: An update on recent findings considering illness stage and neurobiological and methodological complexities. *Neuroscience and Biobehavioral Reviews, 73,* 191–218. https://doi.org/10.1016/j.neubiorev.2016.12.013

Reininghaus, U. (2018). Ecological momentary interventions in psychiatry: The momentum for change in daily social context. *Psychiatrische Praxis, 45*(2), 59–61. https://doi.org/10.1055/s-0044-101986

Reininghaus, U., Kempton, M. J., Valmaggia, L., Craig, T. K., Garety, P., Onyejiaka, A., et al. (2016). Stress sensitivity, aberrant salience, and threat anticipation in early psychosis: An experience sampling study. *Schizophrenia Bulletin, 42*(3), 712–722. https://doi.org/10.1093/schbul/sbv190

Ruci, L., Tomes, J. L., & Zelenski, J. M. (2009). Mood-congruent false memories in the DRM paradigm. *Cognition and Emotion, 23*(6), 1153–1165. https://doi.org/10.1080/02699930802355420

Ruiz, J. M., Taylor, D. J., Uchino, B. N., Smith, T. W., Allison, M., Ahn, C., et al. (2017). Evaluating the longitudinal risk of social vigilance on atherosclerosis: Study protocol for the North Texas Heart Study. *BMJ Open, 7*(8), e017345. https://doi.org/10.1136/bmjopen-2017-017345

Schwerdtfeger, A. R., & Gerteis, A. K. S. (2014). The manifold effects of positive affect on heart rate variability in everyday life: Distinguishing within-person and between-person associations. *Health Psychology, 33*(9), 1065–1073. https://doi.org/10.1037/hea0000079

Scott, S. B., Graham-Engeland, J. E., Engeland, C. G., Smyth, J. M., Almeida, D. M., Katz, M. J., et al. (2015). The Effects of Stress on Cognitive Aging, Physiology and Emotion (ESCAPE) project. *BMC Psychiatry, 15*(1). https://doi.org/10.1186/s12888-015-0497-7

Shiffman, S., Stone, A. A., & Hufford, M. R. (2008). Ecological momentary assessment. *Annual Review of Clinical Psychology, 4*, 1–32.

Sloan, R. P., Shapiro, P. A., Bagiella, E., Boni, S. M., Paik, M., Bigger, J. T., Jr., et al. (1994). Effect of mental stress throughout the day on cardiac autonomic control. *Biological Psychology, 37*(2), 89–99.

Smets, E., Rios Velazquez, E., Schiavone, G., Chakroun, I., D'Hondt, E., De Raedt, W., et al. (2018). Large-scale wearable data reveal digital phenotypes for daily-life stress detection. *npj Digital Medicine, 1*(1), 67. https://doi.org/10.1038/s41746-018-0074-9

Smyth, J. M., Zawadzki, M. J., Santuzzi, A. M., & Filipkowski, K. B. (2014). Examining the effects of perceived social support on momentary mood and symptom reports in asthma and arthritis patients. *Psychology & Health, 29*(7), 813–831. https://doi.org/10.1080/08870446.2014.889139

Steinhart, H., Myin-Germeys, I., & Reininghaus, U. (2019). Translating treatment of mental health problems to daily life: A guide to the development of ecological momentary interventions. In J. Palmier-Claus, G. Haddock, & F. Varese (Eds.), *Novel uses of experience sampling in mental health research*. Routledge.

Trull, T. J., & Ebner-Priemer, U. (2013). Ambulatory assessment. *Annual Review of Clinical Psychology, 9*, 151–176. https://doi.org/10.1146/annurev-clinpsy-050212-185510

Vaessen, T., Kasanova, Z., Hernaus, D., Lataster, J., Collip, D., van Nierop, M., & Myin-Germeys, I. (2018). Overall cortisol, diurnal slope, and stress reactivity in psychosis: An experience sampling approach. *Psychoneuroendocrinology, 96*, 61–68. https://doi.org/10.1016/j.psyneuen.2018.06.007

Vaessen, T., Van Nierop, M., Reininghaus, U., & Myin-Germeys, I. (2015). Stress assessment using experience sampling: Convergent validity and clinical relevance. In P. Fauquet-Alekhine (Ed.), *Stress self-assessment & questionnaires: Choice, application, limits* (pp. 21–35). LARSEN Science. http://hayka-kultura.org/larsen.html

Vaessen, T., Viechtbauer, W., van der Steen, Y., Gayer-Anderson, C., Kempton, M. J., Valmaggia, L., et al. (2019). Recovery from daily-life stressors in early and chronic psychosis. *Schizophrenia Research*. https://doi.org/10.1016/j.schres.2019.03.011

van der Steen, Y., Gimpel-Drees, J., Lataster, T., Viechtbauer, W., Simons, C. J. P., Lardinois, M., et al. (2017). Clinical high risk for psychosis: The association between momentary stress, affective and psychotic symptoms. *Acta Psychiatrica Scandinavica, 136*(1), 63–73. https://doi.org/10.1111/acps.12714

van Duin, E. D. A., Vaessen, T., Kasanova, Z., Viechtbauer, W., Reininghaus, U., Saalbrink, P., et al. (2019). Lower cortisol levels and attenuated cortisol reactivity to daily-life stressors in adults with 22q11.2 deletion syndrome. *Psychoneuroendocrinology, 106*, 85–94. https://doi.org/10.1016/j.psyneuen.2019.03.023

van Eck, M., Berkhof, H., Nicolson, N., & Sulon, J. (1996). The effects of perceived stress, traits, mood states, and stressful daily events on salivary cortisol. *Psychosomatic Medicine, 58*(5), 447–458.

Van Eck, M. M., & Nicolson, N. A. (1994). Perceived stress and salivary cortisol in daily life. *Annals of Behavioral Medicine, 16*(3), 221–227.

van Winkel, R., Stefanis, N. C., & Myin-Germeys, I. (2008). Psychosocial stress and psychosis. A review of the neurobiological mechanisms and the evidence for gene-stress interaction. *Schizophrenia Bulletin, 34*(6), 1095–1105. https://doi.org/10.1093/schbul/sbn101

Varese, F., Smeets, F., Drukker, M., Lieverse, R., Lataster, T., Viechtbauer, W., et al. (2012). Childhood adversities increase the risk of psychosis: A meta-analysis of patient-control, prospective- and cross-sectional cohort studies. *Schizophrenia Bulletin, 38*(4), 661–671. https://doi.org/10.1093/schbul/sbs050

Walker, E. F., & Diforio, D. (1997). Schizophrenia: A neural diathesis-stress model. *Psychological Review, 104*(4), 667–685.

Wichers, M., Geschwind, N., Jacobs, N., Kenis, G., Peeters, F., Derom, C., et al. (2009). Transition from stress sensitivity to a depressive state: Longitudinal twin study. *The British Journal of Psychiatry, 195*(6), 498–503. https://doi.org/10.1192/bjp.bp.108.056853

Wigman, J. T., van Os, J., Borsboom, D., Wardenaar, K. J., Epskamp, S., Klippel, A., et al. (2015). Exploring the underlying structure of mental disorders: Cross-diagnostic differences and similarities from a network perspective using both a top-down and a bottom-up approach. *Psychological Medicine, 45*(11), 2375–2387. https://doi.org/10.1017/s0033291715000331

Zawadzki, M. J., Scott, S. B., Almeida, D. M., Lanza, S. T., Conroy, D. E., Sliwinski, M. J., et al. (2019). Understanding stress reports in daily life: A coordinated analysis of factors associated with the frequency of reporting stress. *Journal of Behavioral Medicine, 42*(3), 545–560. https://doi.org/10.1007/s10865-018-00008-x

8

Psychosocial Risks at Work: Fundamentals and Stakes

Philippe Fauquet-Alekhine

1 Introduction

This chapter provides an overview of the fundamental principles and issues at stake associated with psychosocial risks (PSRs) in the world of work, but it must not be forgotten that the psychosocial dimension of work must primarily be a resource rather than a risk. For example, the psychosocial dimension will cover social support, cooperation, or recognition of work completed well. When assessing psychosocial risks, it is therefore important to look at psychosocial risks as well as psychosocial resources in the work environment.

Why should we be interested in PSRs? With regard to PSRs in business, the demonstration of this need is no longer required. Many studies and surveys emphasize the importance of identifying and dealing with psychosocial risks at work. The risk observatory report of the European Agency for Safety and Health at Work pointed out an "increasing number of workers exposed to psychosocial risks at work and affected by work-related stress" (EASHW, 2012). The possible consequences include "anxiety, fatigue, insomnia, boredom, relationship problems, emotional instability, depression, psychosomatic

---

P. Fauquet-Alekhine (✉)
SEBE-Lab, Department of Psychological and Behavioural Science,
London School of Economics and Political Science, London, UK

Laboratory for Research in Science of Energy, Montagret, France

Groupe INTRA Robotics, Avoine, France
e-mail: p.fauquet-alekhine@lse.ac.uk; philippe.fauquet-alekhine@groupe-intra.com

© The Author(s), under exclusive license to Springer Nature Switzerland AG 2023
P. Fauquet-Alekhine, J. Erskine (eds.), *The Palgrave Handbook of Occupational Stress*,
https://doi.org/10.1007/978-3-031-27349-0_8

diseases, excessive smoking, cardiovascular problems, increased alcohol consumption, drug abuse, eating disorders or even suicide" (Teasdale, 2006), therefore affecting the individual's health.

Studies show that 70 to 90% of work-related stress contributes to the cost of loss of productivity (Hassard et al., 2018).

In the context of a global pandemic, the challenges are reaching new dimensions. The World Federation for Mental Health (WFMH, 2020, p. 134) reports that "the International Labour Organisation (ILO [2020]) and Institution of Occupational Safety and Health (IOSH) position mental health promotion during the return-to-work process as being an essential part of the OSH [Occupational Safety and Health] response to the COVID-19 pandemic. A mental illness crisis is looming as millions of people worldwide are confronted by death and disease and forced into isolation, poverty and anxiety by the COVID-19 pandemic according to UN health experts". In addition, lockdowns and telework practices radically alter conflicts between the private and professional spheres. The WFMH (2020, p. 107) also recommends paying particular attention to groups at increased risk: "who were harder to reach, rural and remote communities, people in quarantine, people with chronic mental illness and their carers, those with limited capacity to access smart phones and related technology, people exposed to family and domestic violence, and those from different cultures and backgrounds". Furthermore, attention must also be paid to certain trades: the health and law enforcement professions were heavily involved during the pandemic, as were many other professions, often paying a high price in terms of health or in extreme cases their lives.

In this chapter, we first propose to clarify the concepts of "psychosocial risks" and to differentiate them from the notion of "psychosocial disorders" and "psychosocial risk factors". This prior clarification will help to illuminate what specialists can act on in the management of PSRs. The evaluation and treatment of PSRs is a specialist's business: just as one goes to a physician to treat an injury and a plumber to repair a sink, PSRs are the responsibility of people with academic training and experience in Human Sciences, Medicine or Prevention. One cannot assume that satisfactory results will be obtained without inducing new PSRs when involving incompetent people because of the clumsiness of non-specialists; unfortunately, some decision-makers still employ them. Experience also shows that, in some cases, this is not an error, but a deliberate choice associated with the intention of preventing problems from being dealt with in depth. Entrusting PSR assessment to incompetent people is sometimes a strategy of corporate management just to show that it is interested in the problem.

8 Psychosocial Risks at Work: Fundamentals and Stakes   139

The Joint German Occupational Safety and Health Strategy (GDA, 2014, p. 7) recommends the following:

> For the risk assessment of psychosocial factors to be planned and implemented successfully, the parties involved need to be aware of the importance of the topic and have basic knowledge of the fundamental correlations between the occurrence and effect of psychosocial factors at work. [...] If a large group of stakeholders will be involved in the risk assessment, as is often the case in large companies, it can be useful to hold an in-company training seminar. The risk assessment must refer to the concrete conditions and jobs in the business. Therefore, the successful planning and implementation of the risk assessment is contingent upon the parties involved having an overview of the range of jobs performed in their company and being aware of the different types of task and work requirements. Apart from this basic knowledge, more in-depth specialist knowledge is generally also needed to implement the risk assessment, specifically knowledge concerning:
>
> - psychosocial factors that can occur/are relevant in the areas/jobs under observation;
> - procedures and methods for identifying and assessing psychosocial factors;
> - specific ways to adapt wok to the individual.
>   If required, this specialist knowledge can be supplied by internal or external experts, such as the OHS expert, the company doctor, the competent accident insurance institution or the government inspection body.

However, if the evaluation of PSRs is a matter of specialists, it cannot be solely a matter of specialists: they must work collectively with other stakeholders in the PSRs paradigm. Indeed, whatever the approach chosen, each step must be constructed with stakeholders including specialists. To this end, establishing a steering committee for the evaluation of PSRs bringing together stakeholders can be an effective way to guarantee this social construction.

Furthermore, entrusting the evaluation of PSRs to specialists reduces the risk of the evaluation being misguided; in particular, the specialist is framed by a code of ethics.

2   Definitions

2.1   Definitions by Convention

By convention and to facilitate further reading, the following definitions have been adopted for this chapter:

The analyst is the person who conducts the evaluation of the PSRs. He has skills to suggest the method, manage the handing over of questionnaires and/or conduct interviews, analyse data, validate it, and draft and present evaluation reports.

The analysis designates the evaluation of PSRs in general.

Participant refers to each employee who will participate in the evaluation of the PSRs.

2.2 The Concepts of Risk, Factor, Hazard and Disorder

Psychosocial risks relate to the psychological and social risks to people at work. In the workplace, they mainly concern the mental health of people who may be affected by psychological disorders or psychosocial disorders (e.g. burnout) due to the work context or situation.

Generally, the term "risk" defines the probability of reaching a situation of hazard (psychological or psychosocial disorder), which is characterized by its intensity. The greater the intensity I of the hazard (or the severity of the hazard), the greater the risk R. Risk therefore appears as the product of probability p by intensity I:

$$R = p \times I$$

In other words, on the one hand, risk depends on the temporal distance between the individual and the hazard and, on the other hand, its potential gravity. This distance is estimated by a probability, which can be considered as a frequency of occurrence. With the above proposed expression for R, when the accepted or acceptable risk is bounded by a maximum threshold not to be exceeded, the greater the intensity, the lower the probability of occurrence, as shown in the well-known "Farmer" graph in Fig. 8.1. This maximum threshold is a threshold of acceptability according to Farmer (1967), beyond which the risk is unacceptable (upper area of the graph). This approach was developed for nuclear engineering.

Whether it is technological risks or socio-organizational or human risks, the approach remains valid. What changes are the levers of action or anticipation: the analyst must not lose sight of the view that social objects (including humans) are less predictable than technical objects. For example, the technician knows that after 10 hours of operation, the pump will have reached the right greasing oil temperature to be able to make the expected adjustment; on the other hand, no one can guarantee that a service restructuring will go

8 Psychosocial Risks at Work: Fundamentals and Stakes

smoothly after two months of preparation. This unpredictability is what makes the richness of humankind.

Another classic illustration proposes risk as the combination of a probability associated with spatial distance and hazard: probability is sized by the distance between the individual and the hazardous situation such as an individual at the edge of a cliff (Fig. 8.2). The greater the distance, the lower the probability of falling.

The risk is therefore the product of a probability (spatial or temporal distance from exposure to hazard) by the intensity of the hazard.

Engaging in PSRs work is therefore about working on the risk of reaching a psychosocially hazardous situation for one or more people. As the human is a psychosocial being in essence, there are (fortunately) non-harmful psychosocial situations for people. Humans at work are constantly in psychosocial situations. Some of these can become harmful to people's mental health and therefore pose a potential hazard that PSRs work must be able to either anticipate or treat. When the situation becomes harmful to the mental health of one or more people, the individual or collective psychosocial balance is disturbed. This consideration helps better understand the main hazard associated with PSRs, the hazard being to reach a state of Psychosocial Disorder (PSD), which is the symptoms (or symptomatic manifestations) associated with PSRs. The difficulty lies in identifying what is acceptable: the distance "risk" on Figs. 8.1 and 8.2a, b does not materialize by frank limits or stopped values,

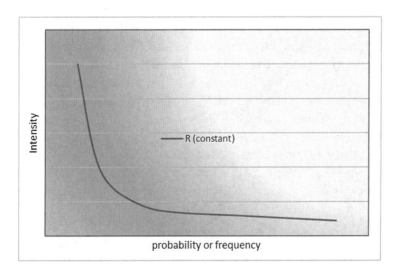

Fig. 8.1 Representation of a risk of constant value depending on the intensity of the hazard (or potential severity) and the probability of being confronted with that hazard

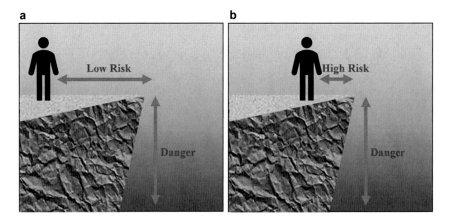

Fig. 8.2 The risk depends on the likelihood of being confronted with the hazard. The hazard is the fall into the void, which is more important than the height. In (**a**), the risk is low because the distance from the hazard is great and reduces the likelihood of exposure to hazard. In (**b**), the risk is significant because the distance from the hazard is small and increases the likelihood of exposure to hazard

but rather by emerging and subjective space. Indeed, before being disturbed, the individual or collective psychosocial state is mostly in balance or stabilized, or at least little disturbed. This balance is possible when the factors of influence are not very disruptive or when countervailing measures are put in place to manage this influence at the individual or collective level. For example, individual defence mechanisms or collective defence strategies or "multifaceted defensive processes deployed by subjects to fit into work situations" (Huez, 2003) contribute to this stabilization. Another example: the methods of recognition at work also contribute to this effect according to the forms they take; appropriate recognition has a moderating effect on the potential PSDs for the individual concerned, while under-recognition proceeds inversely, which can go beyond the PSDs, that is, to stress-related mental disorder (Van der Molen et al., 2020).

One example of a psychosocial hazard now well known to the public is burnout. This PSD was recently classified by the WHO (2019) as "an occupational phenomenon" in the 11th revision of the International Classification of Diseases (ICD-11). The WHO also completed its definition compared to the previous version (ICD-10) as follows:

> Burn-out is a syndrome conceptualized as resulting from chronic workplace stress that has not been successfully managed. It is characterized by three dimensions:

8 Psychosocial Risks at Work: Fundamentals and Stakes 143

- feelings of energy depletion or exhaustion;
- increased mental distance from one's job, or feelings of negativism or cynicism related to one's job; and
- reduced professional efficacy.

Burn-out refers specifically to phenomena in the occupational context and should not be applied to describe experiences in other areas of life. (ICD-11)

The probability of reaching the hazard (often inferred from analysis of the frequency of exposure to the hazard over a past period) depends on factors that shape the context and environment in which people live. In the case of PSRs, these are psychosocial risk factors (PSR factors) that may be more or less numerous and express themselves with more or less intensity. An example of a PSR factor is an employee who is exposed to the bad mood of his manager: the more strongly this bad mood is expressed towards the employee, the greater the influence of this factor on the increase in PSRs. The same applies if the occurrence of this expression is greater, since the more the employee is exposed to this type of situation, the greater the influence of this factor. Another example of a PSR factor is an employee who feels that he or she is not recognized by management: the lower the level of perceived recognition, the longer this perception lasts, and the greater the influence of this PSR factor.

Each factor is a potential cause of PSD. The combination of several factors in the professional context with certain factors of the private sphere and with a given mental state of the individual may lead to the PSD.

2.3 Fundamentals

Thus, three concepts must be distinguished: psychosocial risks (PSRs), which is the probability of reaching a state of psychosocial hazard, psychosocial hazards (e.g. psychosocial disorders or PSDs, chronic stress or stress-related mental disorder) that need to be avoided, and psychosocial risk factors (PSR factors, potential causes of PSD) that influence the importance of psychosocial risks (i.e. help increase or decrease risk). Of these three concepts, the only one it is possible to preventively act directly on is that of PSR factors, which indirectly reduce PSRs and thus keep people away from psychosocial hazards.

An evaluation of PSRs therefore requires the identification of PSR factors and the implementation of measures to reduce the influence of these factors in the workplace. As the world of work is a complex evolutionary system, such an assessment must be repeated periodically on the one hand to estimate the effect of the measures taken in the previous evaluation, and on the other hand to identify possible new PSR factors.

3 PSRs and Stress

The notion of PSRs is often reduced to the term "stress". In this case, "stress" is in fact just a manifestation of the risk factors in the company. PSRs actually cover occupational risks of various origins and natures (see below), which can affect the mental and physical health of employees, and have an impact on the proper functioning of companies. The term "psychosocial" refers to the interface between the individual (psychological aspect) and the work situation (social aspect).

This reduction to the term "stress" can be explained by the fact that stress and PSR factors are difficult to dissociate as these factors can lead to the perception in individuals that work-related demands and constraints exceed their capacity to respond in terms of their skills (WHO, 2003).

However, some researchers go beyond this stage and attempt to produce an exhaustive identification of the factors of influence (Gollac & Volkoff, 2000; Clot, 2010; Cartron & Guaspare, 2010; Gollac & Bodier, 2010). In the synthesis proposed by Gollac (2011), the factors characterizing the forms of organization potentially producing PSDs are also factors identified elsewhere as stress factors. They can be endogenous to the individual (personal characteristics of the individual) or exogenous (from the organization, relationships to colleagues or hierarchy, ergonomics of the situation and tools of work, etc.), they interact with each other, and they produce psychological, physiological and behavioural effects that have a retroactive effect on the source factors (Fauquet-Alekhine, 2012a). Anticipating or treating PSDs therefore (at least to a large extent) involves working on these endogenous or exogenous factors. The former can be treated by individual-specific stress management techniques (Leonova, 2009), while the latter can be treated by organizational actions and by the transformation of social relationships at work (Fauquet-Alekhine, 2012b). In addition, depending on the type of stress, anticipation, treatment and management are not the same. With regard to occupational stress, two major forms must be considered: short-term (or punctual, acute) stress and long-term (or chronic) stress. Often, the latter occurs either in relation to specific physiological predispositions or after repeated exposure to one-time stress situations that occur during life (long-term stress can occur in childhood as well as in active adulthood; see Bordet et al., 2011). Once long-term stress is established, the individual's psychological terrain becomes such that short-term stress can be difficult to manage (see Chap. 3 of the present book).

A recent literature review (Van der Molen et al., 2020), on nearly 100,000 subjects in seven different countries, showed "moderate evidence for associations between stress related mental disorder and effort reward imbalance, high job demands, organisational justice, social support, high emotional demands and decision authority, whereas no significant associations were found for job insecurity, decision latitude, skill and discretion".

Engaging in work on PSRs therefore essentially addresses stressors in a work situation. Endogenous factors are the responsibility of medicine (which will refer to the adapted specialist) because often individual "Psychic suffering of professional origin is not a suffering like any other. Decompensation processes are unique stories that require specialized care" (Huez, 2003). However, the company must organize itself to help identify such cases because "defensive procedures prevent [...] often act to transform work, but psychopathological processes themselves often exclude abused subjects from work collectives". Unfortunately, they are not sympathetic to others, do not attract compassion, and can even be experienced as a potential hazard through their unconscious ability to destabilize collective defensive procedures. These are not the only contexts of social isolation (see, e.g., Vézina et al., 2001).

The company (excluding occupational medicine) can essentially act on:

- collective endogenous factors such as interpersonal relationships with conditions to refocus or remain focused on work activity (e.g. to transform the work environment, to promote communication between people, difficult interpersonal relationships can be reconstructed collectively by refocusing on work activity)
- exogenous factors, for example intervening in work activities, as well as their organization and context.

4 PSRs and Stakes

For the company, the issues associated with PSRs can be determined primarily in three main areas: health, performance and law. While each of these areas is important, both the analyst and the instigator of the review must keep in mind that the primary stake is health. Indeed, undertaking an evaluation of PSRs to respond only to the legal stake would result in a fictitious assessment from the standpoint of health. This approach could even have a deleterious effect on the health of the participants.

4.1   Health Stake

The evaluation of PSRs requires listening to the subject in order to have access to the information that will inform this evaluation. This assumes a transmitter on the one hand and a receiver on the other. If one of the two is missing, or if the message does not express the subjective reality of the subject, then there is no possibility of accessing the PSR factors. There are therefore also no treatment options for PSRs, that is, their reduction. The possible consequence is the long-term installation of PSR factors and a psychological imbalance for people, and a deleterious imbalance for health. This psychological imbalance relates to what the subject perceives from what is asked of him in relation to his ability to meet the demand. The installation of this imbalance in a sustainable way exposes the subjects to the risk of chronic stress, the result of which can be highly consequential (e.g. suicide). Such an imbalance shifts from the psychological level to the physiological level (see Chap. 3 of the present book). It is then that PSDs may appear such as loss of sleep, decreased digestive capacity, and increased blood sugar levels with the risk of high blood pressure--associated diabetes. This can lead to burnout that needs to be prevented in advance.

PSRs can be categorized into six main categories (Gollac & Bodier, 2010):

- intensity and working time, for example the intensity of the pace of work, the complexity of tasks, adaptation to a new environment
- emotional demands, for example situations of interpersonal tension, fear of failure
- the autonomy of flexibility, for example the predictability of work, the monotony of work, the pleasure at work
- social relations at work, for example the relationship with colleagues, with hierarchy, recognition of work
- conflicts of values, for example a sense of usefulness at work
- insecurity of the work situation, for example job security, career, structural changes of the company

PSDs can be categorized into four main registries:

- emotional, for example loss of self-confidence or decreased self-esteem, aggression, anxiety, euphoria
- cognitive, for example decreased concentration, memory loss
- behavioural, for example co-worker violence or social isolation of the subject

- kinesthetics, for example sleep disorders or digestive disorders that cause abdominal pain

These categorizations are interesting in that they help analysts to structure their investigations and reduce the risk of forgetting to explore one of the possible aspects of PSRs.

4.2 Performance Stake

As noted in the introduction, the deterioration of the health of employees at work has a significant cost, which in fact has an impact on the performance of the company. The emergence of difficulties for the teams due to absenteeism, organizational dysfunctions due to difficult interpersonal relations, or the misdemeanors of collectives are only a few examples of factors leading to a decline in a company's performance. Therefore, it is in the employer's best interest to implement an evaluation of PSRs and to implement a preventive program for PSRs.

4.3 Legal Stake

In France, the evaluation of PSRs corresponds to a regulatory request expressed in the ministerial circular of April 18, 2002, complementing Article R4121-1 of the Labour Code relating to the Risk Assessment Document (Document Unique d'Evaluation des Risques, or DUER). It stipulates that the employer is required to conduct an analysis of the risks to which employees may be exposed in the course of their work, including PSRs. In particular, the law refers to two main principles to be applied:

- fighting risks at the source and adapting work to humans
- plan for prevention

Companies are accountable for compliance with two national inter--professional agreements:

- the national inter-professional agreement on workplace stress of July 2, 2008 (transposition of the 2004 European Framework Agreement), made mandatory by the ministerial decree of April 23, 2009

- the national inter-professional agreement on harassment and violence in the workplace of March 26, 2010 (transposition of the 2007 European Framework Agreement), extended by the decree of July 23, 2010.

The first provides indicators of stress at work and identifies certain stressors.

The second declares workplace harassment and violence as not tolerated and calls for appropriate measures to manage and prevent workplace harassment and violence. Both recall the employer's responsibility for identifying and treating PSRs in the company.

From the standpoint of the French legislator, three legal categories for PSRs appear: occupational stress, moral harassment and violence.

In Great Britain, in the context of the preservation of occupational health and safety, employers have the obligation to ensure the safety of their employees in accordance with the 1974 Act (Act1974). While this duty was initially interpreted as the guarantee of physical integrity, the difficulties associated with stress at work led to a change in the interpretation of the law to also include psychological aspects. Employers who do not meet their obligations under this law, that is, the obligation to assess and treat psychosocial risks in the company, are liable to legal action.

In Germany, the Occupational Health and Safety Act (Arbeitsschutzgesetz, or ArbSchG) requires the implementation of European Directive 89/391/ EEC (Framework Directive on Occupational Health and Safety). It regulates safety and health at work, including by defining the employer's obligations. The evaluation of PSRs was introduced by an amendment in 2013.

5 Conclusions

The concept of psychosocial risks in the workplace (or PSRs) and related concepts, as well as the assessment of PSRs, are clearly fundamental dimensions of work. By law, employers must take them into account in the company. This legal stake has a direct impact on the stake of workers' health, and the employer must keep in mind that many studies have shown that taking these stakes into account has a direct link with the company's performance stake. Thus, the obligation to consider and process PSRs in companies can only be beneficial for all actors in the world of work. This consideration and processing remain a matter for specialists: it would be a mistake to entrust these tasks to people who are incompetent in the field, the resulting risk being to increase existing PSRs or create new PSRs in the company.

Some Web References in French

INRS National Institute for Health Research. http://www.inrs.fr/accueil/risques/psychosociaux.html

Ministry of Labour. https://travail-emploi.gouv.fr/IMG/pdf/Note_thematique_-_Risques_psychosociaux_au_travail_-_une_problematique_europeenne.pdf

National Agency for the Improvement of Working Conditions, ANACT. http://www.anact.fr/web/dossiers/sante-au-travail/PSR

Some Web References in English

British Standard Institution, BSI. http://mtpinnacle.com/pdfs/Guidance-on-the-management-of-psychosocial-risks-in-the-workplace-1.pdf

European Agency for Safety and Health at Work, EASHW. https://osha.europa.eu/en/publications/management-psychosocial-risks-work-analysis-findings-european-survey-enterprises-new

Health and Safety Executive, HSE. https://www.who.int/occupational_health/publications/PRIMA-EF%20Guidance_9.pdf

References

Bordet, J., Pierrehumbert, B., Sanchez, S., Bénony-Viodé, C., & Bénony, H. (2011). Maternal anxiety, sensitivity and quality of mother-toddler interactions during feeding. *Proceedings of the 15th European Conference on Developmental Psychology—ECDP*, Pianoro: Medimond Srl. Ed., 159–164.

Cartron, D., & Guaspare, C. (2010). *Revue de littérature en sociologie sur les risques psycho-sociaux*, rapport remis le 13 août 2010 au collège d'expertise sur le suivi statistique des risques psycho-sociaux au travail sous la présidence de Michel Gollac (Administrateur Insee).

Clot, Y. (2010). *Le travail à cœur—pour en finir avec les RPS*. Ed. la Découverte, 190p.

EASHW (European Agency for Safety and Health at Work). (2012). Management of psychosocial risks at work: An analysis of the findings of the European Survey of Enterprises on New and Emerging Risks.

Farmer, F. R. (1967). Reactor safety and siting: A proposed risk criterion. *Nuclear Safety, 8*, 539.

Fauquet-Alekhine, P. (2012a). Behavior as a consequence to fully describe short term occupational stress. *Proceedings of the 17th Annual International "Stress and*

Behavior" Neuroscience and Biopsychiatry Conference, May 16–19, 2012, St. Petersburg, Russia, 31.

Fauquet-Alekhine, P. (2012b). Causes and consequences: Two dimensional spaces to fully describe short term occupational stress. *Socio-Organizational Factors for Safe Nuclear Operation, 1*, 45–52.

GDA. (2014). Occupational safety and health in practice—Recommendations for implementing psychosocial risk assessment. Berlin: Management of the GDA Mental Health Working Programme c/o Federal Ministry of Labour and Social Affairs.

Gollac, M. (2011). Quelques raisons de se plaindre, *In* Lallement, M., Marry, C., Loriol, M., Molinier, P., Gollac, M., Marichalar, P., & Martin, E. (2011). Maux du travail: dégradation, recomposition ou illusion? *Sociologie du travail, 53*, 3–36.

Gollac, M., & Bodier, M. (2010). *Mesurer les facteurs psychosociaux de risque au travail pour les maîtriser*, rapport du Collège d'expertise sur le suivi des risques psychosociaux au travail, faisant suite à la demande du Ministre du travail, de l'emploi et de la santé.

Gollac, M., & Volkoff, S. (2000). *Les conditions de travail*. Ed. La Découverte, 122p.

Hassard, J., Teoh, K. R., Visockaite, G., Dewe, P., & Cox, T. (2018). The cost of work-related stress to society: A systematic review. *Journal of Occupational Health Psychology, 23*(1), 1–17.

Huez, D. (2003). Psychopathologie du travail: thérapeutique, réparation, action? *Travailler, 2*(10), 7–11

ILO (International Labour Organization). (2020). Managing work-related psychosocial risks during the covid-19 pandemic. Geneva: International Labour Organization.

Leonova, A. B. (2009). The concept of human functional state in Russian applied psychology. *Psychology in Russia: State of the Art, 1*, 517–538.

Teasdale, E. L. (2006). Workplace stress. *Psychiatry, 5*(7), 251–254.

Van der Molen, H. F., Nieuwenhuijsen, K., Frings-Dresen, M. H., & de Groene, G. (2020). Work-related psychosocial risk factors for stress-related mental disorders: An updated systematic review and meta-analysis. *BMJ Open, 10*(7), e034849.

Vézina, M., Derriennic, F., & Montfort, C. (2001). L'impact de l'organisation du travail sur l'isolement social. *Travailler, 2001/1*(5), 101–117.

WFMH (World Federation for Mental Health). (2020). World Mental Health Day 2020—Mental Health for all: Greater investment-Greater access. https://wfmh.global/world-mental-health-day-2020

WHO. (2003). Authored by S. Leka, A. Griffiths, & T. Cox, Work organization and stress. Protecting Workers' Health Series, No. 3. Geneva: World Health Organization.

WHO. (2019). https://www.who.int/standards/classifications/classification-of-diseases

9

Psychosocial Risks at Work: Outlines of the Evaluation Approach

Philippe Fauquet-Alekhine and Nicolas Roudevitch

1 Introduction

This chapter offers an outline of an approach to the evaluation of psychosocial risks (PSRs) in companies based on the experience of two practitioners: the chapter's authors. One is a psychologist in charge of the evaluation of PSRs in a French intervention robotics group since 2020 and was responsible for this activity from 2012 to 2017 at the Chinon nuclear power plant (France). As such, he has always acted as an internal consultant, being an employee of these companies. The second author is an ergonomist. He was manager of a psychosocial risk centre in an occupational health service in France (SIST79) in order to intervene in client companies between 2003 and 2010. As such, he was an external consultant. The chapter is therefore written as a common testimony punctuated by complements highlighting the divergence or convergence of some essential points of view between the psychologist and the ergonomist or between the internal consultant and the external consultant.

P. Fauquet-Alekhine (✉)
SEBE-Lab, Department of Psychological and Behavioural Science,
London School of Economics and Political Science, London, UK

Laboratory for Research in Science of Energy, Montagret, France

Groupe INTRA Robotics, Avoine, France
e-mail: p.fauquet-alekhine@lse.ac.uk; philippe.fauquet-alekhine@groupe-intra.com

N. Roudevitch
Chinon Nuclear Power Plant, Avoine, France

© The Author(s), under exclusive license to Springer Nature Switzerland AG 2023
P. Fauquet-Alekhine, J. Erskine (eds.), *The Palgrave Handbook of Occupational Stress*,
https://doi.org/10.1007/978-3-031-27349-0_9

By convention, the body of the chapter is written as a testimony of the psychologist and validated by the ergonomist, and the complements are written as testimony of the ergonomist/external consultant in counterpoint to or in support of the psychologist/internal consultant.

This chapter focuses on outlining the psychosocial risk (PSR) assessment approach in the world of work: the analyst's posture according to his/her relationship to the company in which s/he operates, general principles of the PSR assessment approach, including ethical aspects, and finally, the analyst's resources in terms of collaboration.

PSRs are often seen as problems to be addressed by the company. However, it should be remembered that the psychosocial dimension of work is primarily a resource rather than a risk. For example, the psychosocial dimension will cover social support, cooperation or recognition of a job well done. When assessing PSRs, it is therefore important to focus on psychosocial risks as well as psychosocial resources in the work context.

2 The Analyst's Posture

When evaluating PSRs, the analyst's posture should ideally incorporate the following:

- Opt for a distancing empathetic attitude:
- The term "distanced" weights empathy by allowing recognition and understanding of the participants' feelings and emotions without engaging in an emotional relationship that would be harmful to the analysis.
- Take the approach of helping and supporting both teams and management:
- Experience shows that even specialists sometimes get trapped in the point of view of only one of the stakeholders in the situation to be analysed; for example, the situation is analysed only from the standpoint of technicians, forgetting the comparison of the technical and managerial points of view in the analysis.
- Develop an analytic approach that is non-judgemental and therefore divorced from the search for responsibility:
- This aspect of the analyst's posture needs to be clarified at the information meeting of the evaluation. The absence of judgement helps to free the participants' speech and more relevant information to be accessed.
- Focus the analysis on work, not people:

9 Psychosocial Risks at Work: Outlines of the Evaluation Approach

- This is a question of considering work as a source of the difficulties and issues faced by the actors in the workplace and to which the action plan will be directed. It will not be a question of adjusting people to the work but altering the work to benefit the people.

2.1 The Psychologist's Posture

In France, the psychologist's posture for an analysis is fully described in Principle 1 of the 1996 Code of Ethics for Psychologists updated in 2012:

Principle 1: Respect for human rights
The psychologist refers her/his exercise to the principles enshrined in national, European and international legislations on respect for the fundamental rights of individuals, especially their dignity, freedom and protection. S/He strives to respect the autonomy of others and in particular the possibilities of information, freedom of judgement and decision. S/He promotes direct and free access for anyone to the psychologist of their choice. Intervention occurs only with the free and informed consent of the persons concerned. S/He preserves the privacy and intimacy of individuals by guaranteeing respect for professional confidentiality. S/He respects the fundamental principle that no one is required to reveal anything about her/himself.

These provisions are also set out in the Code of Human Research Ethics published by the British Psychological Society (2014), UK:

Principle of 'Respect for the autonomy, privacy and dignity of individuals and communities': Psychologists have respect for the autonomy and dignity of persons. In the research context this means that there is a clear duty to participants. [...] [Psychologists] accept that individuals may choose not to be involved in research, or if they agree to participate, they may subsequently request that their data be destroyed. Under such circumstances, researchers will comply with any requests that any related data be destroyed, and removed from any datasets. [...] Researchers will respect the privacy of individuals, and will ensure that individuals are not personally identifiable, except in exceptional circumstances and then only with clear, unambiguous informed consent. They will respect confidentiality, and will ensure that information or data collected about individuals are appropriately anonymised and cannot be traced back to them by other parties, even if the participants themselves are not troubled by a potential loss of confidentiality. Where a participant wishes to have their voice heard and their identity linked with this, researchers will endeavour to respect such a wish. In their research, as in all other professional dealings, psychologists will seek to ensure that people's rights are respected and protected.

When applied to the evaluation of PSRs, these principles imply that:

- The analyst has a benevolent attitude towards the participants in the analysis.
- Participation in the analysis is voluntary.
- The analyst ensures that the participants have understood the purpose of the analysis.
- Participants can opt out of the analysis at any time without having to justify themselves.
- The analyst guarantees that the data will be processed anonymously and gives him/herself the means to achieve this goal.
- Eventually, these points may result in the co-signing of informed consent by the analyst and each participant.

2.2 The Ergonomist Posture

The ergonomist is also bound by a strict professional posture as part of her/his duties. In France, the framing is relatively vague in the absence of official documents. The title of ergonomist is not protected in France. Conversely, at the European level, the Association for the Recognition of the Title of European Ergonomist offers an online code of ethics (https://www.artee.com/charte-de-deontologie). To remain in the French-speaking field, in Canada, the Canadian Council for the Certification of Ergonomic Practitioners (https://www.cccpe.ca) has developed a code of ethics for ergonomists that it requires all its members to sign and respect. This code addresses confidentiality, integrity, and the duties and obligations of the ergonomist, particularly towards the profession, peers and clients.

Finally, at the international level, the International Ergonomics Association (https://iea.cc) proposes the Code of Conduct for Ergonomists (approved in 2006) which establishes the ethical principles of the profession. Overall, the ergonomist's posture is similar to the psychologist's.

2.3 The Posture of the Internal Consultant Analyst

Being an internal consultant means being an employee of the company in which the analysis is to be carried out, and therefore requires intervening with participants who are colleagues. This may be difficult when some of the colleagues have an emotional relationship with the analyst. This type of relationship can be induced by a common sports practice between colleagues, for example being part of the same basketball team and therefore leaving work

9 Psychosocial Risks at Work: Outlines of the Evaluation Approach

together in the evening to train together several times a week, having a drink together in the evening and meeting on weekends. These games may create an emotional relationship between colleagues and this could undermine the analyst's objectivity by reducing his/her ability to distance him/herself from the subject during the analysis. One potential solution is to propose that the person concerned withdraws from the participants prior to the analysis.

Being an internal consultant has the advantage of reducing the risk of loss of contract associated with the intervention since there is none in the commercial sense of the term, that is, between a client and his supplier. It is easy for the internal consultant analyst to interrupt the analysis due to problems identified by him as being contrary to his ethics. Another example: The analyst may refuse to provide interim reports to the management of the analysis (which are often requested) without fear of losing the contract associated with the current analysis.

In order to avoid the kind of disagreement mentioned above, it is recommended that the internal consultant analyst frame in writing the terms of the analyses at the time of taking up his/her position with his/her manager. This written framing is thus the reference to which each of the parties, analysts, managers and order-givers can refer in case of disagreements. This also allows the analyst to ensure that the order-giver has understood the conditions of the analysis. This document may take the form of a mission letter signed by the analyst's manager and must refer to the code of ethics of the analyst (if any). In particular, for the psychologist, the document may mean that in the event of a disagreement between the command and the Code of Deontology of psychologists, the analyst reserves the right to refuse the intervention.

2.4 The Posture of External Consultant Analyst

The posture of the external consultant analyst is more delicate. Indeed, not being an employee of the company in which the evaluation of the PSRs will be carried out, but being an employee of the firm of experts that concludes a contract with this company, the external consultant analyst is subject to stronger economic constraints than the internal consultant. It is quite easy to imagine the competition that may exist between different consulting firms and the concessions that could be made by some of them methodologically, including ethically, to obtain the contract with the company. In other words, some clients will prefer the most conciliatory consulting firm, even if this is at the expense of the quality of the results of the evaluation. The external consultant must therefore demonstrate great pedagogy to assert and make accepted ethical constraints in interventions.

3 General Principles

3.1 A Cautious Approach

Rather than accurately and exhaustively identifying the psychosocial disorders (PSD) to which employees might be exposed, the PSR assessment approach aims to identify the factors that could contribute to the emergence of PSD of any kind, without removing identification of PSD, because if they have been installed for years, they are to be identified and treated. Knowledge of psychosocial risk factors through the PSR assessment is not sustainable over time; it refers to a particular moment (i.e. valid on a given date), so it will necessarily have to be upgraded periodically.

In the process, the assessment of psychosocial risk factors should not be confused with the assessment of psychosocial factors of the risks (see definition of concepts in Chap. 8 of the present book). The scope of psychosocial risk factors is broad and not limited to the psychosocial nature of the risks. For example, the PSR evaluation focuses as much on situations of interpersonal tension (psychosocial involvement) as on the intensity of work (organisational involvement). Transforming the identification of psychosocial risk factors into identifying psychosocial factors of the risks would lead the approach to ignore important factors. One of the attitudes that leads to switching from psychosocial risk factors to psychosocial factors of the risk is denial: people, including the non-specialist analyst, may tend to think that the problems are personal or only exist in the subject's head or are a particular case. Therefore, organisational, contextual or managerial aspects would not be taken into account.

The approaches proposed in the following chapter are based on the investigative results of French working groups and the work of the World Health Organization. For the French, it is the so-called Gollac research group named after the coordinator of the French group initiated in the early 2000s, a collection of experts on the monitoring of psychosocial risks at work. This working group was created at the request of the Minister for Work, Employment and Health of the French Government. The resulting PSR categorisation is presented as an appendix in the form of a "Gollac grid" scheme and serves as a support for the proposed methods (Gollac & Bodier, 2010). For the World Health Organization (WHO), the work of Leka et al. (2003; Leka & Jain, 2010) under WHO's Program of Occupational Health aimed at developing a common global strategy in accordance with the agreement of the Fourth Network Meeting of the WHO held in Finland in 1999. Similarly, the resulting PSR categorisation is presented in an appendix as a diagram to support the proposed methods.

However, it should be kept in mind that an assessment is not without potential consequences. Depending on the method used, the analysis itself carries the risk of altering the defence mechanisms or strategies guaranteeing the psychosocial stability of the collective investigated. This situation can be achieved by leading people, through questioning, to think of potentially problematic elements at work that are deemed settled. This risk is minimised if the re-thinking approach is precisely sought by the analyst, especially when the analyst diagnoses that psychosocial stability is not sustainable. It is then a matter of deconstructing the mechanisms or strategies of defence to immediately rebuild something else. If this is not possible, it is not recommended to achieve such a situation, otherwise the analysis would itself constitute a psychosocial risk.

3.2 An Approach for Anticipation

Different methods are used to evaluate or contribute to the evaluation of PSRs in general. These methods include online surveys based on multiple-choice questionnaires or direct surveys of the staff also by questionnaire. In the field of Human Sciences, more elaborate methods are based on the analysis of work activity (Clot, 1999; Clot et al., 2000; Fauquet, 2006; Fauquet-Alekhine, 2012) or on psychodynamics (Dejours, 2000), which are also applicable in an approach for treatment. In the case of evaluation of PSRs, the evaluation cannot be reduced to a questionnaire survey, that is, the questionnaires give a necessarily restrictive view of the situation due to their limited number of questions. This also leads to thinking about how the evaluation tool (the so-called Gollac grid presented in the appendix) will be used.

It is also possible to work on a predictive approach as some analysts try to do based on longitudinal studies (see, e.g., De Jonge et al., 2012).

3.3 An Approach for Treatment

An evaluation of PSRs necessarily highlights problems and resources. If the problems identified do not give rise to action, then the participants and all those involved in the evaluation of the PSRs can be disappointed. This disappointment has a double disadvantage. The first is that the participants who contributed to the analysis will not be motivated to contribute again to such an analysis when it comes to reassessing the PSRs. In addition, the feedback they will provide will demotivate their colleagues. The second drawback is that this disappointment can itself become a psychosocial risk factor by eventually adding to other factors of deterioration at work.

The treatment of the factors enhancing PSD can be conducted in at least three ways:

- according to the group's therapeutic approach.
- according to the resource management approach, which consists mainly of dealing with peripheral elements of work activity and sometimes assuming that treating PSRs only requires involvement in QWL (Quality of Work Life) actions.
- depending on the approach of work analysis, such as psychodynamics or clinical analysis of work activity; "It is first of all the profession that is suffering", and so it is work, rather than employees, that needs to be cared for (Clot, 2010; Dejours, 2008); there is also a need to look at the strategic analysis of social relations in organisations (Sainsaulieu, 1997; Crozier & Friedberg, 1997) or at the analysis of the "tensions" and "regulations". Most of the time, they require a pair of analysts.

The therapeutic group approach (which sometimes involves psychoanalysis) is strongly discouraged because it does not refocus on the work that is the source of the problem. It has little chance of dealing with the substantive problem.

The approach to resource management that treats PSRs by getting involved in WBW (Well-Being at Work) is a decoy. Although investing in WBW is important, it does not address the fundamental problem. It tends to treat well-being without worrying about well-doing when there can be no well-being without doing well at work. This is not to say that the WBW approach is not useful; it still contributes to the reduction of PSRs.

The work analysis approach is recommended. Depending on the form of the problem, either approach (psychodynamic or activity analysis) is possible. They focus on collective deliberation over individualised coaching, action on the causes of suffering at work rather than the treatment of one's symptoms alone (Clot, 2010). These types of approaches are long term since they are all structured by an information meeting, an analysis of the application, an intervention with voluntary participants, and a restitution to these participants and then to the trade collective (including the hierarchy). This structure of PSR assessment is described in the next chapter. The intervention phase is the longest because it involves interviews and possibly observations of work situations, or a series of collective meetings spaced about one or two weeks apart. This type of analysis has the advantage of bringing out the problems, the resources and the proposals for solutions, which the management must then seize and turn into actions. These approaches can only be implemented by specialists at the risk of creating the opposite to anticipated effects. In particular, the specialist will be able to take into account that any conduct has a meaning other than physiological; for example, forgetting to distribute an important document can have an unconscious meaning of a far greater scope than being the sole result of physical or cognitive fatigue.

3.4 A Participatory Approach

The involvement of all stakeholders is fundamental to successfully achieving the goal. Therefore, the more participatory the approach, involving as many employees as possible in evaluating and developing solutions for treatment, the greater the likelihood of succeeding in reducing PSR factors. This participation also concerns the management and the order-giver; indeed, an approach that would not be continuously supported by the management and the order-giver would be doomed to failure because not only may the means necessary to succeed not be made available to analysts, but above all it is unlikely that management will seize the conclusions of the evaluation and transform them into an action plan that would deal with the PSRs. The establishment of a steering committee for the evaluation involving health actors, staff representatives and management can be an added value.

3.5 The Optimal Level of Analysis

We use the term "unit of analysis" to refer to the level at which the evaluation of PSRs in the company is to be conducted. The level of analysis can be associated with an organisational stratum of the company, such as a department, a service or a team. The level of analysis can also be considered cross-cutting, such as a project team or a trade, taking into account that a trade can involve different teams (e.g. shift teams) or different departments (e.g. managers, assistants). The level of analysis will be chosen based on what the analyst or order-giver is looking for. Depending on the level chosen, the evaluation of the PSRs will be more or less accurate. For example, it is clear that a PSR assessment to the level of the company will not be able to deal with the problems of the teams in depth.

This is why we believe that the optimal level of analysis for the PSR assessment is that of the trade. Indeed, for the analysis to be effective, groups of people whose constraints are the same, which are intimately linked to psychosocial risk factors, must be considered. This also means that these people of the same trade are on the same team. In this way, the unit of analysis is subject to the same demands, the same managerial constraints, the same organisational constraints, and the same working context. However, there are exceptions for isolated occupations such as "secretary" or "manager". For example, the work of analysis in a collective of secretaries necessarily involves grouping the secretaries of different departments of the company when possible. For the PSR assessment to be effective, this work of analysis by trade must be carried out in all occupations. For example, the analysis will have to be conducted within a collective of trade A, then in a collective of trade B, then in the collective of assistants, then in the collectives of team leaders, then in the collectives of first line managers, then in the collectives of second line managers, then in the collectives of directors, and so on. The analyst will ultimately have to make a global synthesis of the interactions from one trade to another in terms of PSRs. It is sometimes possible to consider grouping similar trades. For example, on an industrial site, it is not uncommon to see a team from a trade A dedicated to a production unit and another team of the same trade A dedicated to another production unit. Under these conditions, the formation of a unit of analysis at the trade level, regardless of the production unit, can be considered. The optimal level of analysis thus defined remains the same, regardless of the approach adopted, either by questionnaire or by interview, or the combination of the two.

3.6 Ethics

Any result of a PSR assessment can only be carried beyond the circle of evaluation participants after validation by the participants. This is fundamental to ensure that what has been said to the analyst is properly understood and transcribed by him/her. This ensures the protection of participants who may not wish to see in writing some of the things they have said, and guarantees the quality of restitution beyond the circle of participants. For example, this rule gives management the guarantee that the written data is reliable.

This principle also frees up speech during interviews. This confidentiality allows participants to provide certain information that they would not provide in the same way if there was not this principle of confidentiality. Even if, later, during the feedback/validation of what was said during the interview, the participants wish to remove certain information that they have provided, and therefore which will not be included in the PSR evaluation report, this information will nevertheless have contributed to a better understanding of the situations presented during the interviews.

3.7 Collaborations

Meetings between analysts and trade union organisations, social workers and occupational physicians are recommended. These meetings should take place, if possible, before the start of the intervention for the PSR assessment or as part of a steering committee of the analysis. Indeed, these professionals may have information that will be very useful to the analyst to better understand the situations that will be exposed to him/her by the participants during the PSR assessment. Although these professionals are bound by professional secrecy, they can nevertheless provide general and anonymous information. This is not at odds with their profession since their objective, as for the analyst, is to improve the working conditions of the employees of the company. The exchange of information is therefore the result of a collaboration between workers' health professionals.

4 Methodological Conclusions

The model for the intervention approach for PSR evaluation that we propose is simple since it is based on the model of continuous improvement illustrated by the Deming wheel represented in Fig. 9.1.

The intervention approach for the PSR evaluation is shown in Fig. 9.2. This model highlights that any evaluation must necessarily lead to an action plan, which must absolutely be implemented and subsequently reassessed. "Absolutely" is a term that is very important here. Experience shows that, all too often, the order-giver and/or the management engages in the intervention

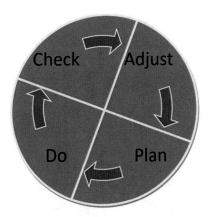

Fig. 9.1 Model of quality improvement illustrated by the Deming wheel

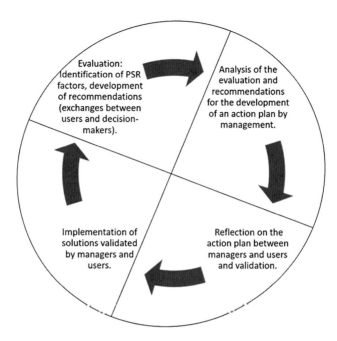

Fig. 9.2 Continuous improvement model for the intervention process for the evaluation of PSRs

without completing it; the process stops at the time of the development of the action plan or just after, that is, when something needs to be done together, that is, the management, the employees and users of the solutions envisaged (users are engineers, technicians, team members). When the analyst is an internal consultant, s/he can negotiate with the order-giver the possibility of being involved in the development of the action plan and its implementation. Some experts believe that it is not the role of the analyst to do this work; indeed, they believe that if the analyst is involved until this stage of the process, s/he does not allow the management to grasp what the PSR evaluation produces; thus, being less involved in the process, the management is more engaged in the process. However, the culmination of the intervention process, that is, the transformation into effective action of the recommendations resulting from the evaluation, contributes to the construction of the credibility of the analyst-internal consultant. Indeed, if the internal consultant does not ensure the completion of the process as defined, and then it builds for him/her a reputation of someone who engages the trades in a reflection that is supposed to improve working conditions but that produces only wind. By participating in the construction and implementation of the action plan, the analyst internal consultant participates in the construction of a reputation

9 Psychosocial Risks at Work: Outlines of the Evaluation Approach

that will allow him/her to export the approach to other departments of the company. In addition, s/he provides management with expected support, because experience shows that management often feels helpless at the time of the development of the action plan itself or its implementation. These feelings explain why the process often loses efficiency when it reaches this stage.

From the external consultant's point of view, the approach can be different if PSR evaluation is a different activity than the development and implementation of an action plan. Thus, contractually and commercially, the evaluation is the subject of an order, and the action plan is the subject of another order. There is nothing to prevent the two activities from being the subject of a single order, but it must be understood that the estimate that will be proposed in the latter case will almost double the amount to be paid. The external consultant will therefore first propose an evaluation of the PSRs, and then, during the progress meetings with the order-giver, will suggest that s/he subsequently engage the external consultant in the development and implementation of the action plan. However, too often, order-givers assume that their management teams will be able to take on this activity alone. This is probably true provided that the order-giver, who most of the time is also the manager of the managers, frees up the necessary time for the managers to carry out this activity, which is consequently added to their workload most of the time. However, another method consists in approaching the problem of the company by trying to answer the following two related questions: "What is the demand and to which issue does it respond?" The consultant's contribution is thus not a PSR evaluation but a different approach that aims to act on/with the collectives to teach them to look into the problem situation and locate the links between the apparent PSR problem and the source of this problem in the work. This first step is followed by a second one addressing the solutions emerging from multidisciplinary and multi-hierarchical work groups analysing situations at work.

Whatever the approach chosen by the analyst, there are typical stages through which many individuals have to go before they are ready to act on what will deal with the problem(s): the work. The typical first level is denial: some people (often among the management) refuse to see the suffering, the difficulties: "'There is no problem". The second level is reached when people become aware of the problems at work; unfortunately, usually, they shift the responsibility onto the people, not the work organisation: "It is a matter of individuals' behaviour". The third level is the acknowledgement that problems are linked with the work organisation; very often, it is accompanied by the decision-maker's feeling of helpless. The analyst's job is to help people to go through these stages until the last one where they will be ready to act on the work.

Appendix 1

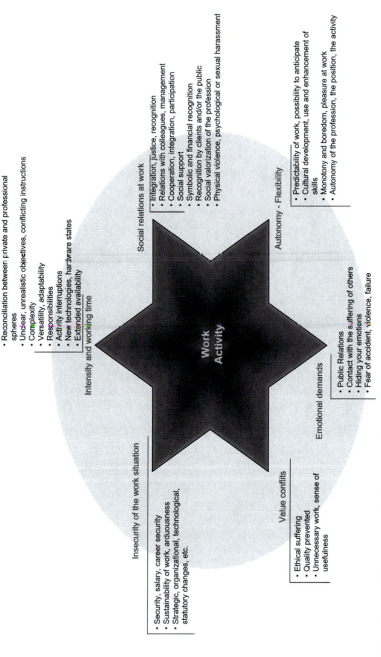

Fig. 9.3 Scheme of the categorisation of PSR factors according to Gollac and Bodier (2010)

9 Psychosocial Risks at Work: Outlines of the Evaluation Approach

Appendix 2

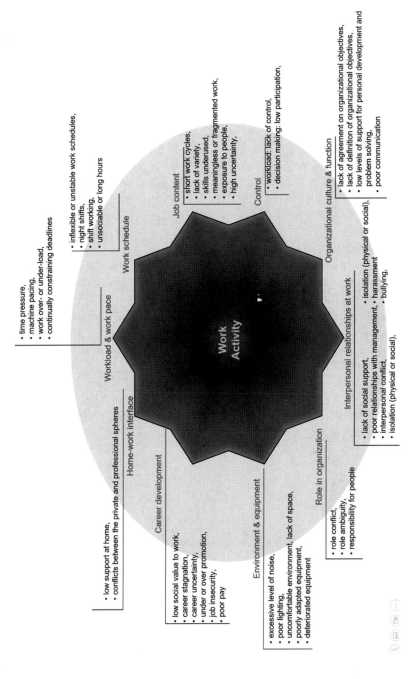

Fig. 9.4 Scheme of the categorisation of PSR factors according to Leka et al. (2003)

References

British Psychological Society. (2014). *Code of human research ethics*. British Psychological Society.

Clot, Y. (1999). *La fonction psychologique du travail*. Ed. PUF, 246p.

Clot, Y. (2010). *Le travail à cœur—pour en finir avec les RPS*, Ed. la Découverte, 190p.

Clot, Y., Faïta, D., Fernandez, G., & Scheller, L. (2000). Entretiens en autoconfrontation croisée: une méthode en clinique de l'activité. *PISTE, 2*(1).

Crozier, M., & Friedberg, E. (1997) *L'acteur et le système*, Ed. Point Seuil.

De Jonge, J., Spoor, E., Sonnentag, S., Dormann, C., & Van den Tooren, M. (2012). 'Take a break?' Off-job recovery, job demands, and job resources as predictors of health, active learning, and creativity. *European Journal of Work & Organizational Psychology, 21*(3), 321–348.

Dejours, Ch. (2000/2nd ed. 2008). *Travail, usure mentale*. Ed. Bayard, 282p.

Fauquet, P. (2006). Confrontation croisée ou analyse collective sur la base de restitutions d'entretiens individuels: deux approches pour l'analyse évènementielle. *Revue électronique @ctivités, 3*(2), 1–14.

Fauquet Alekhine, P. (2012). Training activity simulations: The complementarities of clinical approach and regulation approach. *Socio-Organizational Factors for Safe Nuclear Operation, 1*, 75–78.

Gollac, M., & Bodier, M. (2010). *Mesurer les facteurs psychosociaux de risque au travail pour les maîtriser*. rapport du Collège d'expertise sur le suivi des risques psychosociaux au travail, faisant suite à la demande du Ministre du travail, de l'emploi et de la santé.

Leka, S., & Jain, A. (2010). *Health impact of psychosocial hazards at work: An overview*. World Health Organization.

Leka, S., Griffiths, A., & Cox, T. (2003). *Work organization and stress*. World Health Organization.

Sainsaulieu, R. (1997). *L'identité au travail*. Ed. FNSP.

10

Assessment of Psychosocial Risks: Methods

Philippe Fauquet-Alekhine

1   Introduction

There are different methods for psychosocial risk assessment (PSR) in companies. Some are available online, while others have been the subject of reports or publications and criticism in the scientific literature. The methods proposed here do not claim to be better than those of the literature. They are proposals to be implemented knowing that they have already proven themselves effectively. These methods begin with the categorisation of PSRs according to considerations that have already been mentioned in Chap. 9 and that are further developed in the present chapter. They continue with the evaluation of PSRs according to two combined or non-combined approaches: one is based on group interviews and the other on the use of scientifically validated questionnaires.

These proposed methods are enriched with advice for drafting evaluation reports and feedback from practitioners.

By convention and to facilitate further reading, the following definitions have been adopted for this chapter:

P. Fauquet-Alekhine (✉)
SEBE-Lab, Department of Psychological and Behavioural Science,
London School of Economics and Political Science, London, UK

Laboratory for Research in Science of Energy, Montagret, France

Groupe INTRA Robotics, Avoine, France
e-mail: p.fauquet-alekhine@lse.ac.uk; philippe.fauquet-alekhine@groupe-intra.com

© The Author(s), under exclusive license to Springer Nature Switzerland AG 2023
P. Fauquet-Alekhine, J. Erskine (eds.), *The Palgrave Handbook of Occupational Stress*,
https://doi.org/10.1007/978-3-031-27349-0_10

The analyst is the person who conducts the evaluation of PSRs. S/He has skills to suggest the method, manage the handing over of questionnaires and/or conduct interviews. S/He has skills to analyse and validate data, and to draft and present evaluation reports.

The analysis designates the evaluation of PSRs in general.

Participant refers to each employee participating in the evaluation of the PSRs.

Unit of analysis is the level at which the evaluation of PSRs in the company is to be conducted. The level of analysis can be associated with an organisational stratum of the company, such as a department, a service or a team. The level of analysis can also be considered cross-cutting, such as a project team or a trade, taking into account that a trade can involve different teams (shift teams) or different departments (e.g. managers, assistants). The level of analysis will be chosen based on what the analyst or order-giver is looking for. Depending on the level chosen, the evaluation of PSRs will be more or less accurate. For example, it is clear that a PSR assessment to the level of the company will not be able to deal with the problems of the teams in depth.

2 Proposal of Applied Methods

2.1 The Categories of PSR Factors

There are different categorisations of PSR factors. We present two paragraphs: the first is based on the investigative results of the research group called "Gollac", named after the coordinator of the French group initiated in the early 2000s, and expertise on monitoring psychosocial risks at work (Gollac & Bodier, 2010). The second is from the work of Leka et al. (2003). One is not better than the other: the important thing is that PSR factors are covered exhaustively; indeed, during a PSR assessment, this type of categorisation will allow the analyst to verify that all possible fields of PSR factors are questioned and then will allow for structuring the rest of the evaluation. For example, the "intensity and working time" category of Gollac and Bodier (2010) corresponds to the "Workload and work pace" categories combined with "Work schedule" by Leka et al. (2003). "Conciliation of the private and professional spheres" of the category "Work Intensity and Working Time" by Gollac and Bodier corresponds to the item "conflicts between the private and professional spheres" of the category "Home-work interface" by Leka et al. Both categorisations thus take into account the factors of rhythm constraints or shift work.

10 Assessment of Psychosocial Risks: Methods — 169

Since the work that led to these categorisations, the health and economic crises associated with COVID-19 have produced new sources of PSRs. However, these sources produce PSR factors that are already included in the proposed categories. The impact of the pandemic only resizes them (ILO, 2020).

The Categorisation of the Gollac Group (Gollac & Bodier, 2010)

The Gollac Group proposed six categories of PSR factors. The figure presented in the appendix provides a synthetic view of these categories as well as items to be addressed for each of these categories. This figure is a practical medium for starting the discussion about psychosocial risks. The items discussed are succinctly described below:

- Work intensity and working time

  - Rhythm constraints, shift work, night work, extension of availability: incorporates all time constraints as well as hourly overruns.
  - Conciliation of private and professional spheres: assesses, in particular, professional constraints on privacy.
  - Blurred, unrealistic objectives, conflicting instructions: takes into account uncertainties regarding work activities as well as paradoxical injunctions.
  - Complexity: meeting the work situation or demand would exceed capacity.
  - Versatility, adaptability: is also interested in people's skill adjustments.
  - Responsibilities: is equally interested in excessive responsibilities as a lack of accountability.
  - Business interruptions: is equally interested in fragmented activities and in multi-tasking approaches.
  - New technologies, hardware states: takes into account the effect of outdated hardware as well as the difficulty of understanding the operation of new hardware.

- Emotional demands

  - Relationship to the public: concerns occupations that have a direct relationship with a clientele.
  - Contact with the suffering of others: assumes that the person may be affected by the discomfort of others.

- Hiding your emotions: often associated with interpersonal relationships when it is about containing emotions to avoid hurting the other, for example.
- Fear of accident, violence, failure: fear is constantly stressful.

- Autonomy

  - Predictability of work, possibility of anticipation: the lack of predictability or anticipation can generate anxiety.
  - Cultural development, use and skills development: challenging skills can also generate uncertainties that lead to anxiety.
  - Monotony and boredom, pleasure at work: the lack of motivation at work can be harmful.
  - Autonomy of occupation, position, activity: lack of autonomy reduces people to have a passive role at work and reduces decision-making latitude; they become hazardous when combined with high demands.

- Social relationships at work
- Integration, justice, recognition: integration into the work community depends on the quality of people-to-people ties; in particular, justice refers to the notion of a balance between all types of evaluation within the working community; recognition is to be considered from a symbolic as well as a financial point of view; justice and recognition must be considered in terms of balance of effort-reward.
- Relationships with colleagues, management, subordinates: these types of interpersonal relationships are associated with integration into the work community, on the construction of the work collective; it also contributes to the quality of cooperation and social support.
- Cooperation, participation: more than mutual aid that concerns social support, cooperation is above all the creation of a strong professional link by pooling resources in pursuit of a common goal; it also participates in integration into the work community.
- Social support: concerns the support obtained from colleagues in the broadest sense (peers, management, subordinates); it is as much about psychological support as it is about technical help; lack of social and health support.
- Symbolic, practical and financial recognition: symbolic by compliments, documents, the awarding of certificates, diplomas; practical by the average allocation and the setting of objectives; financial by promotion, salary, bonus.

10 Assessment of Psychosocial Risks: Methods   171

- Recognition by customers and/or the public: the lack of recognition on the part of the customer is all the more impactful since the customer is an individual (not a client company), that is, this multiplies the frequency of misrecognition. Indeed, the customer-individual is seen several times a day while the customer-company is seen once a day or once a week, or even less. Misrecognition is associated with the concept of justice when it is due to managerial requests that inevitably involve customer dissatisfaction.
- Social valuation of the trade: linked with recognition.
- Physical violence, moral or sexual harassment: violence ranges from insult to injury; moral stress remains of the psychological order as sexual harassment ranges from the simple remark to the sexual act itself.

- Value conflicts

    - Ethical suffering: concerns the mismatch between the person's own values and what the company or management is trying to impose on him/her.
    - Prevented quality: refers in particular to the fact that the management or the organisation may create constraints, unconsciously or not, to induce the inability to perform a good job according to the professional's criteria.
    - Unnecessary work, sense of usefulness: the sense of usefulness proceeds from the recognition of this utility judgement by others; even in the case of a lack of social recognition (e.g. by the client), the sense of usefulness can help maintain a certain degree of motivation and investment; the sense of usefulness can be damaged by the feeling of having to do unnecessary work: this feeling can be induced by a discrepancy between what the individual thinks s/he should do at work and the strategic directions of the employer, or by management giving tasks to be carried out whose results are deemed useless, or even because the way the work is organised does not allow the individual to see what the product of his/her work is used for.

- Insecurity of the work situation

    - Job, salary, career security: it is about keeping the job or being able to change it easily, maintaining the salary if not increasing it and having interesting career prospects; on the one hand, the absence of such prospects generates a feeling of insecurity that can be detrimental to health in the long run, and, on the other hand, the effectiveness of such prospects is an element of employment value and therefore pertains to recognition.

– Sustainability of work, hardship: sustainability as well as hardship work on both physical and psychological levels; their assessment provides a good synthetic indicator of the person's perception of work.

– Strategic, organisational, technological, statutory and so on: this type of exogenous change to the person often involves individual changes; it is a matter of developing new compromises to adjust the response to the demand; this may result in a different workload, such as overloading, possible change of career perspective, or the loss of a sense of work or organisational benchmarks that may generate anxiety.

The Categorisation of Leka et al. (2003).

Leka et al. (2003) proposed a 10-category approach to PSR factors.

Below is a summary presentation of these categories as well as items to be addressed for each of these categories. In the appendix, a synthetic view of this presentation is proposed as a support for the intervention. This presentation is a practical medium to start the discussion about psychosocial risks. The items discussed are succinctly described below (from WHO, 2010):

- Workload and work pace:

  - time pressure,
  - pacing machine,
  - work over- or under-load,
  - continually constraining deadlines.

- Work schedule:

  - unyielding or unstable work schedules,
  - night shifts,
  - shift working,
  - unsociable or long hours.

- Job content:

  - short work cycles,
  - lack of variety,
  - skills underused,

10 Assessment of Psychosocial Risks: Methods

- meaningless or fragmented work,
- exposure to people,
- high uncertainty.

- Control:

  - workload: lack of control,
  - decision making: low participation.

- Organisational culture and function:

  - lack of agreement on organisational objectives,
  - lack of definition of organisational objectives,
  - low levels of support for personal development and problem solving,
  - poor communication.

- Interpersonal relationships at work:

  - lack of social support,
  - poor relationships with management,
  - interpersonal conflict,
  - isolation (physical or social),
  - harassment,
  - bullying.

- Role in organisation:

  - role conflict,
  - role ambiguity,
  - responsibility for people.

- Environment and equipment:

  - excessive level of noise,
  - poor lighting,
  - uncomfortable environment, lack of space,
  - poorly adapted equipment,
  - deteriorated equipment.

- Career development:

  - low social value to work,
  - career stagnation,
  - career uncertainty,

174   P. Fauquet-Alekhine

- under or over promotion,
- job insecurity,
- poor pay.

• Home-work interface:

- low support at home,
- conflicts between the private and professional spheres.

2.2   The Proposed Methods

The work addressing PSRs consists primarily of an assessment of occupational risks concerning the psychological dimension as well as the psychosocial dimension of occupational risks. In France, this corresponds to a request for regulation integrated in the DUERP (document of occupational risk assessment). However, unlike other occupational risks, PSRs have an objectification that depends on the subjectivity of participants and analysts; the method for PSR evaluation then takes on its full importance since it will condition the quality of this objectification.

There are many writings in the scientific literature presenting various methods of evaluating PSRs and their treatment. Government health agencies or institutions associated with these organisations are using evaluation methods to help companies meet their obligations regarding PSRs. For example, in France, see Brunet (2013), and in Great Britain, see BSI (2011). The originality of this chapter lies in how it selects certain methods and justifies this selection, to propose approaches that both combine them and do not, and to discuss their respective effectiveness.

Three methods are proposed. The first is based on the use of questionnaires, the second is based on interview groups, and the third combines the first two. All of these methods require time, firstly for the collection of information, and secondly for the analysis of the collected data. Time is also needed to give feedback on the results to those concerned by the evaluation of PSRs. The least time-consuming method is the one based on the use of questionnaires. The interview group-based method is more comprehensive in terms of identifying PSR factors, provided that this analysis is conducted by a specialist. The method combining the two is ultimately the most time-consuming, but it combines the advantages: that of providing objective questionnaire indicators based on statistical analysis of scored responses, and that of being able to refine the analysis of PSR factors derived from the questionnaires. Thus, time seems to be a factor of stress for the analyst too (Fig. 10.1).

Fig. 10.1 Time is a factor of stress for all participants in the PSR evaluation, including the analyst

In the following, the "interview group" refers to a group of people doing the same job as managers or assistants, and "participants" refers to those participating in the evaluation of the PSRs.

Evaluation of PSRs Based on the Use of Questionnaires

The PSR questionnaires are usually presented in the form of proposals that the respondent must evaluate on a Likert scale in terms of agreement. Here is an example of a proposal from a questionnaire:

I have constant time pressure due to a heavy workload.

This proposal can be evaluated on a 5-point Likert scale:

Absolutely Disagree, Disagree, Neither agree nor disagree, Agree, Absolutely agree

Where the coding of responses is possible (which is almost always the case), the PSR evaluation questionnaire provides quantitative data. In the previous example, coding is relatively simple since it consists of assigning a value from 1 to 5 or from -2 to +2, for example.

The PSR evaluation questionnaire can be used individually or as part of a comprehensive approach: it then returns a statistical picture of the state of PSRs within the unit of analysis; it is filled in individually, but the processing of the responses is carried out statistically. Statistical analysis is flexible. For example, scores can be calculated by trades, teams, departments, or by categories of PSRs by gathering questions. The results are only valid after evaluation of significance by ad hoc statistical tests.

Quantitative data allow the implementation of monitoring of PSR indicators (global score by trades, teams, departments or categories). Subsequently, the use of the same questionnaire allows for re-estimating the PSRs, and comparing the quantitative data obtained with what was obtained during the previous evaluation by the participants, and for assessing trends. In addition, this is an estimate of whether assessment of PSRs per unit of analysis is necessary or not.

All of these strengths in the questionnaire are offset by significant weaknesses:

- A questionnaire that comprehensively covers all categories of PSR factors necessarily contains a large number of questions. However, the more questions there are, the more time the questionnaire takes. This leads to two difficulties: i) respondents, like their management, do not want to spend too much time answering a questionnaire as it is not their priority at work; and (ii) the more time the respondent spends answering the questionnaire, the less motivated s/he is to answer the last questions; the answers are biased.
- The completeness of the questionnaire, even with a large number of answers, is necessarily reduced compared to an interview. Indeed, the questionnaire only covers what the items suggest. For example, a stress-reward questionnaire will not evaluate the "social support" field.

To counteract the first point, some questionnaires exist in a long and short form. It is up to the analyst to choose the one best suited to the context of the intervention. On the second point, some analysts combine the use of several questionnaires. For example, the Gollac group (Gollac & Bodier, 2010) recommends the use of Karazec's Job Content Questionnaire (Karasek et al., 1998)) and Siegrist's Effort-Reward Imbalance (Siegrist et al., 2004).

Steps of the Process

Step 1: Analysis of the demand

The process begins with a meeting in the form of an interview between the analyst and the order-giver(s), usually the management representatives of the unit of analysis. The intervention area can be the company, a company department or a team in a department. The objective of this exchange is to discuss the order-giver's request, that is, the demand which is the purpose of the evaluation, to propose and agree on an approach, to choose the questionnaire(s) best suited to the unit of analysis. It should be made clear to the management that the approach is based on volunteerism and anonymity: the persons receiving the questionnaire are therefore not obliged to respond and their anonymity is guaranteed by the data collection system. If a steering committee or a follow-up committee for the PSR evaluation is formed, then the conclusions of this exchange are presented to it for discussion and possibly adjustments.

Step 2: Information

Step 2 is an information process with the unit of analysis. This consists of an information meeting by the management and the analyst(s). However, depending on the availability and if management agrees, this information meeting can be held without representation from the analyst(s). If the information process is done by email (which is not recommended), then this email is sent by the management to the persons in the unit of analysis, copying in the analysts. The purpose of this information is to present the demand (thus the purpose of the evaluation), the approach envisaged and the voluntary nature of participation.

Step 3: Distribution of the questionnaires

The PSR evaluation questionnaire is sent individually to all people working in the unit of analysis.

When participants receive the questionnaire individually, it must be accompanied by a reminder of the purpose of the evaluation, the anonymity of the approach and its voluntary nature in order to enable response to the questionnaire. An estimate of the time required to complete the questionnaire is also proposed. It is also possible to include an informed consent form to be signed by participants prior to taking part in order to keep track of the fact that the participant has been informed of the voluntary nature of participation and how the answers will be used.

Step 4: Receiving/Analysing questionnaire responses

Upon receipt of the questionnaires, an analysis is undertaken. It is recommended that answers are scored in order to obtain a quantified analysis. This allows for an overall score by category of PSR factors, as well as by trade or unit of analysis of any kind. This also helps to identify trends when the questionnaires are distributed periodically over time. The significance of the scores obtained must be assessed by applying appropriate statistical tests.

Step 5: Writing the PSR evaluation report

The report is based on the results of Step 4. It is up to the analyst to interpret these results in order to identify what is difficult or what is resourceful at work and to propose recommendations that the management might have to address in order to develop a proposed action plan (Step 6) that the management will submit to the unit of analysis.

The structure of the report may be as follows:

Glossary

Terms such as LI for Labour Inspector or PSR for Psychosocial Risks can be defined at the beginning of the report. Similarly, acronyms specific to the unit of analysis may find their place in this glossary. Also, the definitions proposed at the beginning of the present chapter may be added to the glossary if deemed useful.

The demand

The demand (the purpose of the evaluation) as formulated in writing by the order-giver at the analyst's solicitation is copied identically in this paragraph. The order-giver is clearly identified. The demand is ultimately reworded in the terms produced by the analysis of the demand.

Process, method

The method is described by mentioning the different steps. The questionnaire or questionnaires used are cited and their purpose is explained. The choice of questionnaires is debated. The limits induced by the choice of questionnaires are specified.

Evaluation of PSR factors

The presentation of PSR factors is structured by categories according to the Gollac or Leka grids. Grid categorisation can be based on the methodology presented in Chap. 12 of the present book and graphical representations can help to provide an easily readable overview of the results.

Conclusions and action plan

The "action plan" part of the section "Conclusions and action plan" is left blank until Step 7 is completed.

History of the evaluation

For each evaluation in a trade, it is strongly advised to systematically establish a history of the evaluation. For each step, the history gives the deadline that was planned and that actually reached. Each deviation is commented on, or even justified, so that the analyst is able to explain what did not respect the dynamics of the planned intervention. Indeed, the order-giver has a natural tendency to attribute the delay of the intervention to the analyst who oversees the intervention. Yet this delay is most often due to interviews that the management postpones or to returns of questionnaires that are delayed.

Step 6: Draft of an action plan

The version of the report of the PSR evaluation from Step 5 gives rise to an exchange between the analyst and management to agree about the final feedback to the unit of analysis. This is an opportunity for management to work on potential solutions (draft of an action plan) with the analyst. Actions will be presented and discussed in Step 7 with the unit of analysis. The draft of the action plan is the final chapter of the report of PSR evaluation in Step 5.

Actions may be one-off actions already under way or programmed, solutions already implemented in an existing action plan, or new actions.

Step 7: Feedback to the unit of analysis

This step of the PSR evaluation should be the springboard for solutions. The quantitative results of the questionnaires are presented and proposals for actions from Step 6 are discussed. The discussion of actions is fundamental because no one is better placed than the user to judge the relevance of a solution. For example, if an action addresses the redevelopment of a workshop, the opinion of the technicians working in this workshop will be more relevant than that of a manager; or it would be irrelevant to redesign users' workspaces without their opinion.

The feedback to the unit of analysis is done jointly by the manager and the analyst because the management would have difficulty discussing an analysis in which s/he did not participate. It is done to the unit of analysis as part of an exchange. In particular, the analyst again explains the approach and again justifies the choice of the questionnaire(s).

If there is a steering committee for the PSR evaluation, members are invited to this stage.

180 P. Fauquet-Alekhine

Step 8: Delivery of the PSR evaluation report

After Step 7, the analyst can finalise the PSR evaluation report since the content has been shared by all stakeholders. The section left blank at Step 5 may be completed.

Evaluation of PSRs Based on Group Interviews

Steps of the Process

The process is broken down into seven steps (Table 10.1). To be effective, it must be part of a sustained dynamic, that is, not spread over two years but focused on a few weeks. It must therefore be planned in its entirety from the outset according to a specific timetable.

Step 1: Analysis of the demand

The process begins with an exchange meeting in the form of an interview between the analyst and order-giver(s), usually the management representatives of the unit(s) of analysis. The unit(s) of analysis can be the company, a company department or a team in a department. Indeed, there may be one or more units of analysis. For example, the order-giver, in agreement with the analyst, may decide that the unit of analysis is an entire department or that the units of analysis in the department must be divided by profession: that of managers, that of engineers and that of technicians. The analyst must lead the choice of the order-giver towards the second option because it is preferable to conduct an assessment of psychosocial risks by profession (as argued above); the ideal unit of analysis is therefore that based on a given profession.

Table 10.1 Summary of the steps associated with the interview group method

Step	Description
Step 1	Information meeting between analysts and management
Step 2	Information meeting in the response unit
Step 3	Establishing interview groups
Step 3bis	Individual interviews if necessary
Step 4	Collective analysis meeting with each interview group on the basis of a categorisation of PSR factors
Step 5	Restitution—validation of results from each interview group
Step 6	Exchange between analysts and management: work on potential solutions (draft of an action plan)
Step 7	Return of results to the unit of analysis by analysts and management
Step 8	Writing and delivering the PSR evaluation report

The objective of the exchange is to discuss the order-giver's demand, to propose and agree on an approach, a working method in the unit of analysis, to identify the different occupations (which will increase the number of meetings of the interview groups), and to clarify to management that the approach is based on volunteerism but that management is guarantor of the representativeness of the interview groups in relation to the composition of the unit(s) of analysis. Therefore, this meeting is also a framing meeting. The management will therefore favour volunteers for the formation of interview groups by trade, but will adjust the participation. If, for example, a unit of analysis of a trade is made up of 10 experienced workers and 10 young people, the group of volunteers will be made up of close to 50% of experienced workers and 50% of young people. The interview groups set up are in principle immutable: those that come to the analysis meeting (Step 4) are the same for the restitution meeting (Step 5). Indeed, it is not advisable to set up interview groups whose size is greater than eight participants. The ideal number of people is between five and eight. Five is a minimum to have a representativeness of a trade, and eight is a maximum to allow a constructive, convergent and time-bounded discussion (Sharma & Ghosh, 2007; Wheelan, 2009; Yetton & Bottger, 1983).

During the framing meeting between the order-giver and the analyst, analysis of demand (the purpose of the evaluation) is fundamental. Transfers must be considered, that is, a possible transformation of demand. In particular, the analysis of demand should make the order-giver aware that the PSR evaluation must lead to an action plan; evaluation cannot stop at the identification of PSR factors, yet some managers imagine that this is acceptable. The result will serve as the basis for the intervention, and this should be agreed with the order-giver.

This exchange meeting is also an opportunity to state to the order-giver the general principles mentioned above, including the rules of ethics that apply.

If there is a steering committee for the PSR evaluation, members are invited to this step.

Step 2: Information meeting

Step 2 is an information meeting within the unit of analysis in the presence of management and an analyst. However, depending on availability and if management agrees, this information meeting can be held without representation from the analyst(s).

The purpose of the meeting is to present the demand (thus the purpose of the evaluation), the approach envisaged (method, pace) and the need for voluntary participation; it is aimed at potential future participants. If the unit of analysis is a department of 50 people, then it is better to carry out these information meetings at the team level in order to reduce the number of people in meetings and promote an exchange where questions could be asked.

There must be one interview group of volunteers per unit of analysis. If the best choice has been made (one unit of analysis per trade), there is one interview group per identified trade, and the number of volunteers is ideally between five and eight people. This information helps to define the number of volunteers needed per trade and therefore the number of volunteers needed in the interview group. It is important to note that the formation of the groups is expected within a month. One month is enough time to form the groups and is short enough to maintain a sustained dynamic.

Step 3: Building interview groups

This step concerns management of the unit of analysis. The aim is to set up an interview group by identified trade and to make it available for at least two meetings (Steps 4 and 5) to enable the evaluation of PSRs. As explained above, this must be done within a month to maintain the response dynamic.

As recommended above, the staff by interview group is ideally between five and eight people. However, the production requirements of the trade must be taken into account. Thus, if at the meetings the number of people announced is not respected because the participants have to respond to urgent requests for intervention because of their occupation and the collective of five is reduced to two, the meeting will be held with two. The reasons are: (i) delaying the meeting will not guarantee better participation, and (ii) delaying the meeting involves delaying the intervention over time, which will suffer from a lack of dynamism ("an end-of-the-stop intervention") and will lose credibility. In this type of situation where the analysis meeting has few participants, a waiver is possible for the restitution-validation meeting in order to involve others. To use the previous example, if the analysis meeting was held with two participants when it was scheduled to be five, the restitution meeting can be considered with the five participants although three of them did not attend the first meeting. Experience shows that this type of imperative in production units inducing the absence of certain participants is frequent. It is therefore strongly recommended to obtain the minimum of five participants per interview group.

This precision is explained to management when the interview groups are constituted.

10 Assessment of Psychosocial Risks: Methods 183

Step 3bis: Possible one-on-one interviews

Individual interviews prior to interview group meetings may be necessary. This may be the case for trades experiencing particular difficulties highlighted by management or by certain members of the unit of analysis or by the steering committee. This may be the case with individual wishes. Whether at the request of the management, the steering committee or the person him/herself, it is recommended not to refuse an individual interview if requested because it is often done for a good reason. It is refused only if the person concerned disagrees or if the request appears to stigmatise someone.

Step 4: Interview group meetings

The meetings in interview groups by trade are then initiated. Each meeting lasts between one and two hours. Experience shows that it should be planed for two hours. It must be limited in time because participants can talk for a long time about their profession, but one must know that it must end. Experience shows that the proposed time lapse allows the essentials to be discussed. If the analyst thinks this is not the case, it is possible to add meetings. They must be renegotiated with the management and the order-giver. Such a provision is quite easy for an in-house consultant. However, it becomes complicated for an external consultant, especially regarding the cost of the intervention.

These meetings of the interview groups begin with a reminder of the framing and ethics of the approach and the method is presented (meeting, analysis of meeting, restitution/validation meeting, presentation meeting to the unit of analysis to which the interview group belongs, action plan to follow). In particular, participants are reminded of the voluntary nature of participation, and the possibility for anyone to withdraw from participation as soon as they wish, without having to justify themselves.

In the meeting room, the Gollac grid (appendix) used as a support for the evaluation is projected onto the screen and kept displayed throughout the meeting. The grid is explained to the participants and serves as a support for the discussion to follow. The conduct of the meeting by the analyst(s) is semi-structured. It is advisable to start by discussing the category "intensity and working time". Indeed, this category is the easiest to put into discussion to begin, because people always have many examples illustrating time constraints. During the whole meeting, the analyst's questioning is intended to clarify certain points or to guide the discussion on categories or items that have not yet been addressed. It is important to obtain examples or verbatim quotes from participants illustrating the difficulties or resources mentioned by participants. In particular, the examples are a means of objectifying the subjective expression of the participants. This objectification is crucial because it will help to give credit to the difficulties expressed by the participants especially with the order-giver. During the discussion, the analyst takes notes that will give rise to a post-analysis. The advantage of leading the discussion with two analysts is that one is available for exchange while the other takes notes. During the group interview meeting, it is important for the analyst to be interested in the difficulties encountered, what is resourceful and also the solutions envisaged by the participants that will be used as recommendations in post-analysis.

After the interview, the analyst performs the post-analysis. Based on the notes written during the group discussion, the analyst considers the notes point by point and ranks each item by the PSR factor category. S/He concludes her/his post-analysis with recommendations from the suggestions of the interview group. It is recommended to put this post-analysis in writing in the form of PowerPoint. This presentation serves as a support for Step 5. This work is done for each interview group, that is, ideally for each trade.

The fact that the time for meeting in interview groups is limited responds to a pragmatic constraint: indeed, the analyst and the participants cannot devote all their working time to an analysis of the PSR; all have production imperatives, and it would be dishonest to want to deny this aspect. The admissibility of the analysis is therefore based on the assumption that participants express the essential and main factors of PSR from the beginning of the exchange. Experience shows that this is not always the case. For example, during an intervention, it happened that before the group interviews, some of the participants came to the analyst to express a particular problem; however, during the group interview meeting, this issue was never raised spontaneously by the participants. The analyst, being aware of this difficulty, tried to elicit some words addressing this issue by the participants using questions that were first semi-structured and then structured, to no avail; it was then clear that the group did not wish or did not know how to discuss this difficulty as a collective. Under these conditions, the analyst-psychologist, in accordance with his professional practice and ethics, cannot work on this point since it is considered not agreed by participants.

During Step 4, it is possible to convene the steering committee to make a progress point and discuss potential difficulties, including those that would compromise the response dynamic.

Step 5: Restitution/validation meetings

These meetings are set up for each interview group, that is, for each unit of analysis. Each restitution/validation meeting is conducted to validate the writings that will be incorporated into the PSR evaluation report (one report per unit of analysis) which will be presented to management in Step 7. It should be explained to participants that the recommendations of the report do not engage the management: they are the result of the interview group and the analyst for future discussion with the management. In Steps 4 and 5, it may be necessary for the analyst to consult the management in particular for the recommendations envisaged by the group, in order to avoid suggesting to participants, for example, that some of them could lead to actions when they are incompatible with the company's policy or means.

At the restitution/validation meeting, the analyst presents his PowerPoint point by point to the interview group for possible corrections, amendments or withdrawals. The final product is therefore validated by the participants and can lead to the writing of a PSR evaluation report for the unit of analysis represented by the participants.

Step 6: A draft of an action plan

Once the writings have been validated by the interview group, an exchange between the analyst and management is necessary to stall the final return to the unit of analysis. This is an opportunity for management to work on potential solutions (draft of an action plan) with the analyst that will be presented in Step 7 at the unit of analysis.

Step 7: Feedback to the unit of analysis

This stage of the PSR evaluation should be the springboard for solutions in terms of evaluation and recommendations. This is an opportunity for management to take advantage of this production with their teams.

This restitution is done jointly by the manager and the analyst because the management would have difficulty arguing an analysis in which it did not participate. It is done to the unit of analysis as part of an exchange. During this restitution, the management prepares beforehand the answers that it plans to associate with each of the recommendations produced by the interview group (Step 6). Responses may be one-off actions already under way or programmed, solutions already in place in an existing action plan, new actions, or well-argued proposals to abandon the recommendation.

This step allows discussion regarding the solutions envisaged with the users (the people for whom the solutions are implemented) who are in the best position to estimate whether the solution is suitable or not as needed.

To the extent that some individuals did not participate in the interview groups, it is necessary for the analyst to begin by recalling the method and rendering the history of the PSR assessment. History is important because it provides a better understanding of how participants in the group interview came to the conclusions and recommendations that are proposed.

Step 8: Delivery of the PSR evaluation report
Experience shows that this type of reporting is about 10 pages long for a given trade.

The work carried out from the post-analysis of Step 4 is the beginning of drafting of the PSR evaluation report. Indeed, the contents of the PowerPoint slides prepared and then adjusted during the restitution/validation (Step 5) are copy-pasted in the evaluation report. If the approach was based on the use of the Gollac grid (appendix), the structure of the report is as follows:

Glossary
Terms such as LI for Labour Inspector or PSR for Psychosocial Risks can be defined at the beginning of the report. Similarly, acronyms specific to the unit of analysis may find their place in this glossary. Also, the definitions proposed at the beginning of the present chapter may be added to the glossary if deemed useful.
The demand
The demand as formulated in writing by the order-giver is copied in this paragraph. The order-giver is clearly identified. The demand is ultimately reworded in the terms of the analysis of the demand.
Process, method
The method is described by mentioning the different stages. The tools used such as the Gollac grid are mentioned or described. In particular, it is specified that the conclusions and first recommendations proposed are from the interview group and do not engage management. It is also stated that the management is required to analyse these findings in order to consider an action plan to reduce the effect of PSR factors. The limits of the method are specified.
Evaluation per category of PSR factors

- Work intensity and working time
- Emotional demands
- Autonomy
- Social relationships at work
- Value conflicts
- Insecurity of the work situation

10 Assessment of Psychosocial Risks: Methods 187

Conclusions and recommendations

Again, it is recalled that these recommendations do not involve management but constitute support for the development of a future action plan.

History of the evaluation For each evaluation in a unit of analysis, it is strongly advised to systematically establish a history of the evaluation. The history takes the form of a grid such as Table 10.2. The purpose of this history is to reflect the dynamics of the evaluation. Sometimes the dynamics of the evaluation are compromised by repeated postponements of meetings or interviews which are not the result of the analyst, but of the people who should be involved in the participation in the PSR assessment. Experience shows that, sometimes, the PSR evaluation is not the priority of managers or of the participants in the interview groups. The history allows the order-giver to be accountable for the sources of delay in the evaluation.

For example, a manager may agree, in front of the order-giver who is his/her boss, to engage the teams in the PSR evaluation. However, the evaluation itself can only begin after an information meeting with the management. Experience shows that, in some cases, this first meeting with the management

Table 10.2 Example of a grid containing the history of an evaluation

Type of meeting	Date	Postponement #1	Postponement #2	Postponement #3	Postponement #4
Management meeting					
Information to the response unit					
Individual interviews (optional)					
Analysis meeting with interview groups					
Restitution-validation meeting with interview groups					

Note: The column "date" records the date of the meeting scheduled. The "Postponement #xxx" columns record a new scheduled date following the postponement

can be postponed up to four times and spread over a period of six months. Of course, management rarely reports these repeated postponements to the order-giver, who tends to attribute this delay naturally to the one in charge of the intervention, that is, the analyst.

PRS Evaluation Combining Questionnaires and Interview Groups

In addition to the fact that the interview group approach can refine the analysis of PSR factors produced by the use of questionnaires, the interest in combining the two approaches is as follows. The data from the questionnaire allows for comparison of the qualitative results from the interview groups with the perception of the whole occupation, and for estimation as to whether the supposed representative group of the trade reflects a perception of the PSR factors close to those of the whole occupation.

While the combination of questionnaire and interview group methods is, of course, more time-consuming than any of the methods applied separately, it does require less time than the sum of the durations of each of the methods applied separately. The results obtained with this combination of methods are much better than with the methods applied separately.

Steps in the Process

The steps in this process are the combination of steps described above. Thus, the order-giver is first met for the analysis of the demand. Then an information meeting with the unit of analysis in the presence of the management is organised. If there is a steering committee to monitor the PSR evaluation, members are invited to this step. The questionnaires are distributed to participants and the interview groups are formed. The interview group analysis does not start until the questionnaire results are analysed. The results from the questionnaires may give rise to a meeting between management and the analyst prior to the analysis in interview groups, but this is not mandatory. It is recommended that restitution/validation meetings only cover content from the interview groups; indeed, the results from the questionnaires do not concern the production of the groups but the production of the unit of analysis. It is therefore a question of getting the group discussing its own production. The final report contains two parts: one that analyses the questionnaire responses and one that reflects the categories of PSR factors from the interview groups. In the conclusion of the report, a short analysis links the results from the questionnaires and the results from the interview groups, and then the recommendations and draft action plan proposed by the management are presented to the unit of analysis.

3 Impact of the PSR Evaluation on the Management

Experience shows that when the order-giver is part of the head management, the perspective of a PSR evaluation in the departments s/he oversees raises concerns among the managers of these departments. Indeed, the head management often wonders whether the perspective of such an evaluation and its implementation will not disrupt management conditions of the teams and generate demands that the line management will not be able to manage. Similarly, with regard to the front-line management, it is common to observe a concern based on the same mistrust.

It is therefore important that analysts consider these types of possibilities from the beginning of the intervention in order to reassure the different management strata and allow them to accept the PSR evaluation intervention with relative serenity, if not at least some confidence. This assumption of possible deviation on the part of management must remain in the minds of analysts throughout the intervention, especially because management will have no view of what is going on during the exchanges in interview groups. Reassuring management beforehand is therefore fundamental. Maintaining a relatively rapid dynamic of the intervention is also important in order to prevent long-term uncertainty for management.

During an intervention based on the interview groups (as described above) undertaken in a production unit, the order-giver, and managing director, became concerned about the impact of the PSR survey on front-line management. According to them, the intervention disrupted the managers by destabilising the manager–team relations. A survey was therefore conducted with local managers in order to gauge their perception of the intervention. The results showed that none of the managers had any particular fear prior to the intervention, that they had not encountered any particular difficulty either during or after the intervention, that the results of the intervention had been communicated to them in a satisfactory time frame, and that they were ready for further intervention in the event of a necessary reassessment. This example illustrates the possible discrepancy in the perception of the PSR evaluation between the head management and front-line management. This discrepancy can be reduced by the periodic holding of progress meetings between the head management or its representative and the analyst. These meetings are not intended to disclose the subject matter of the evaluation before validation but to explain to the management the advancement of the evaluation process and how it seems to be perceived in the unit of analysis.

4 Feedback from Interventions

This section presents specific cases during interventions carried out, which we believe benefit from being brought to the attention of readers in order to warn them about certain possible difficulties and to propose a way to manage these situations.

4.1 Management's Reluctance

This specificity has already been discussed in the previous section: some managers are reluctant to see an analyst intervene in their team for a PSR evaluation. Essentially, the problem of these managers is that, in their view, the intervention could generate expectations or requests within the teams that they would have difficulty managing or meeting, and/or the intervention would involve an action plan and therefore additional workload. If the general principles presented above are applied, if stakeholders are periodically informed of the progress of the evaluation with a sufficiently short kinetic intervention, and if the management is reassured about what the intervention will produce and the support they may expect from the analyst, then these reluctances can be blurred. See above "Impact of the PSR Evaluation on the Management".

4.2 Intervention with Shift Teams

Working with interview groups from shift trades presents two challenges. The first is to be able to schedule working meetings on working time, that is, on shift time. This can be very difficult depending on the job; for example, in a hospital, health professionals are constantly in demand and have little time for meetings or working groups. Another example, in the industrial production trades, is that of the technicians in particular constantly on the production tool with very little time for meetings knowing that the limited time available is usually dedicated to training. The second challenge is to be able to keep the same interview group from one meeting to the next.

To overcome these difficulties, the PSR evaluations carried out using the method of interview groups with the operation teams in a nuclear power plant were carried out in off-shift periods but on working time, scheduling the dates and the persons concerned three months in advance, all meetings taking place in a period of one month. However, evaluation meetings and restitution/validation meetings were conducted by trade on the same day: the evaluation meeting in the morning and the restitution/validation meeting in the afternoon. This was the only way to guarantee the same population at both meetings.

This obviously requires a long meridian break to allow the analyst to write the PowerPoint support at the afternoon meeting.

4.3 Problems Identified by Participants as Pathological

When interview group participants mention what they describe as a work-related pathology, it is difficult for the analyst to write it as such in the PSR evaluation report if it is not medically recognised. Indeed, pathology is a matter of medicine. Unless the analyst is a physician, under the law, s/he is not competent to decide whether there is a pathology or not. The analyst must therefore find a formulation that does not retain the term pathology due to work. However, it should be referred as soon as possible to occupational medicine. Moreover, if this difficulty concerns only one individual among the participants, it is necessary to question the relevance of recording this difficulty in the production of collective work. In such a case, caution is required because should this point put the PSR evaluation report at fault, then discredit would be cast both on the method and on the professionalism of the analyst, as well as on all PSR evaluations in the company.

In the event that the difficulty mentioned should be medically recognised, the analyst can mention it in the intervention report only with the consent of the person concerned (which requires an interview with the person on this subject by specifying what will be written in the report and obtaining written consent). Management approval is also required, and it is recommended to consult occupational medicine. Indeed, the evaluation report of the PSR aims to improve the working conditions of everyone, and therefore putting management or the occupational physician into difficulties would contradict this objective. This must be done without giving the impression to the participants of the interview group of betrayal regarding what they may wish to see

192 P. Fauquet-Alekhine

written in the report. The management of this type of difficulty gives full meaning to the establishment of a steering committee for the PSR evaluation: it can help to deal with the problem, especially if occupational medicine is involved.

4.4 Rapidity of Action and Dynamic of Intervention

In this chapter, we emphasised a sustained dynamic of intervention as necessary for the effectiveness and credibility of the approach. Sustained dynamic requires an action plan presented to the unit of analysis within one to two months after the start of the intervention. Should we wait two months for the action plan to be validated at the unit of analysis level when the first meetings in interview groups highlight recommendations that require actions to resolve a difficult situation for workers? The answer is "no" provided the group of participants agreed at that meeting. The analyst must therefore meet the manager quickly in order to tell him/her the recommendation and the benefit that the profession and the management would derive from the implementation of immediate corrective action.

Experience has shown that the implementation of a steering committee for PSR evaluation can affect the dynamics of the evaluation. Indeed, even with early scheduling of meetings, stakeholders are rarely available at the same time and sometimes change this availability at the last minute, making reprogramming more difficult. As these meetings are a stage point of evaluation, the deprogramming of one of them generates a delay in the response dynamic. As a result, there should be few steering committee meetings.

4.5 Telescoping of Interventions

In large companies, interventions on the analysis of work by outside consulting firms may be carried out at the request of management or trade unions. In the event that teams are affected by such an intervention, it is strongly discouraged that the in-house consultant in charge of the PSR evaluation engages it with these teams at the same time. Indeed, each of the interventions produces effects and it is better for the analysts of each intervention to know well the cause of these effects to be effective. It is therefore better to delay one of the two interventions over time. This remark is not trivial because experience shows that the overlay of interventions of this type sometimes poses no problem to head management.

5 Conclusions

Three possible methods were presented in this chapter for the PSR evaluation in companies: the first was based on the use of questionnaires only, the second was based on interview group work by trade, and the last combined the first two. The recommendations for how to do this are as follows:

- In terms of quality of intervention and results produced, the method combining the use of questionnaires and interview groups is preferable to others.
- The method based on the use of questionnaires only is the one to choose last because it is less exhaustive in terms of identifying PSR factors.
- When time is limited (which is generally the case), it is better to choose the questionnaire-based method rather than engage in an interview group intervention that would be sloppy by, for example, reducing interview times, or by removing certain steps of the process. In this case, the analyst may suggest to the order-giver that questionnaires should be used to identify difficulties, and that in the event of a significant difficulty identified, a targeted PSR evaluation in certain occupations based on interview groups should be considered.

Finally, the participatory nature of the methods must be emphasised, which, as explained in the presentation of the general principles, is an important key to the success of the PSR evaluation.

Appendix 1

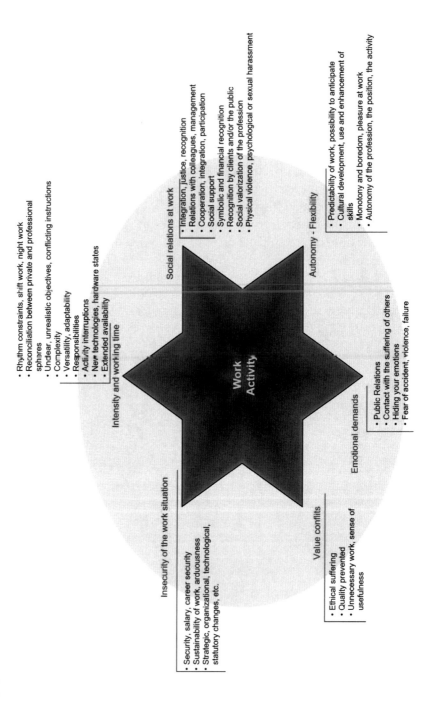

Fig. 10.2 Scheme of the categorisation of PSR factors according to Gollac and Bodier (2010)

Appendix 2

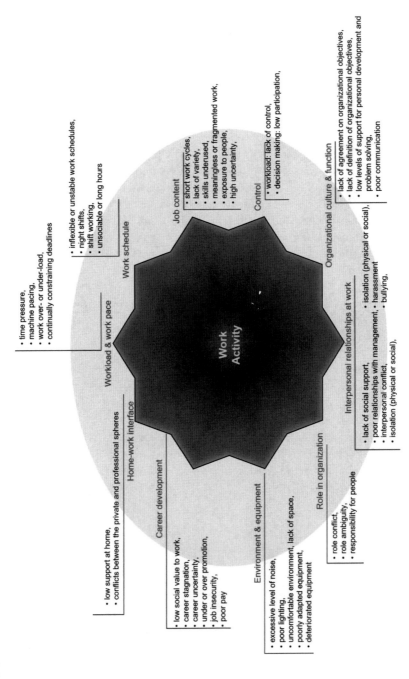

Fig. 10.3 Scheme of the categorisation of PSR factors according to Leka et al. (2003)

References

Brunet, S. (2013). La prévention des risques psychosociaux. In *Les avis du CESE*. Conseil économique, social et environnemental.

BSI—British Standards Institution. (2011). *PAS 1010: 2011 guidance on the management of psychosocial risks in the workplace*. British Standards Institution.

Gollac, M., & Bodier, M. (2010). *Mesurer les facteurs psychosociaux de risque au travail pour les maîtriser*, rapport du Collège d'expertise sur le suivi des risques psychosociaux au travail, faisant suite à la demande du Ministre du travail, de l'emploi et de la santé.

ILO—International Labour Organization. (2020). *Managing work-related psychosocial risks during the covid-19 pandemic*. International Labour Organization.

Karasek, R., Brisson, C., Kawakami, N., Houtman, I., Bongers, P., & Amick, B. (1998). The Job Content Questionnaire (JCQ): An instrument for internationally comparative assessments of psychosocial job characteristics. *Journal of Occupational Health Psychology, 3*(4), 322–355.

Leka, S., Griffiths, A., & Cox, T. (2003). *Work organization and stress*. World Health Organization.

Sharma, M., & Ghosh, A. (2007). Does team size matter? A study of the impact of team size on the transactive memory system and performance of IT sector teams. *South Asian Journal of Management, 14*(4), 96–115.

Siegrist, J., Starke, D., Chandola, T., Godin, I., Marmot, M., Niedhammer, I., & Peter, R. (2004). The measurement of effort–reward imbalance at work: European comparisons. *Social Science & Medicine, 58*(8), 1483–1499.

Wheelan, S. A. (2009). Group size, group development, and group productivity. *Small Group Research, 40*(2), 247–262.

WHO. (2010). *Authored by S. Leka, & A. Jain. World Health impact of psychosocial Hazards at work: An overview*. World Health Organization.

Yetton, P., & Bottger, P. (1983). The relationships among group size, member ability, social decision schemes, and performance. *Organizational Behavior and Human Performance, 32*(2), 145–159.

11

Assessment of Psychosocial Risks: Questionnaire Review

Philippe Fauquet-Alekhine

1 Introduction

Chapter 10 proposed methods for psychosocial risk assessment (PSR) in companies. These methods are based on analysis from interview groups or on the use of questionnaires. The purpose of the present chapter is to propose questionnaires necessary for these methods of assessing PSRs. These questionnaires should not be confused with those presented in Chap. 6; indeed, in the latter, the proposed questionnaires aim to estimate the state of stress of an individual, while this chapter proposes questionnaires whose objective is to contribute to the PSR evaluation; they thus aim to identify PSR factors, usually for a collective of workers.

The questionnaires proposed here were selected based on the following criteria:

- The number of questions is relatively small (about 30) to allow a quick handover. This criterion is essential for at least two reasons: (1) it helps to maintain good motivation of participants when answering the last questions (after answering several dozen questions), respondents sometimes

---

P. Fauquet-Alekhine (✉)
SEBE-Lab, Department of Psychological and Behavioural Science,
London School of Economics and Political Science, London, UK

Laboratory for Research in Science of Energy, Montagret, France

Groupe INTRA Robotics, Avoine, France
e-mail: p.fauquet-alekhine@lse.ac.uk; philippe.fauquet-alekhine@groupe-intra.com

© The Author(s), under exclusive license to Springer Nature Switzerland AG 2023
P. Fauquet-Alekhine, J. Erskine (eds.), *The Palgrave Handbook of Occupational Stress*,
https://doi.org/10.1007/978-3-031-27349-0_11

botch the answers to the questions in particular because they feel they have other things to do than answering such questions in the workplace, because they do not feel concerned by a certain number of questions or do not know what to answer, or because they notice the redundancy of certain questions and feel that they have already answered on the subject; (2) it guarantees management that the questionnaire will not take too much time to complete (experience shows that the negotiation of the time of availability of participants is a key point of negotiation between the analyst and the management of the teams concerned by the PSR evaluation: for some managers, the PSR evaluation is a waste of time).

- The themes covered by the questionnaire relate to the categories of PSR factors and explore them sufficiently; it is better to have a questionnaire that analyses a category with several questions but addresses few categories overall than a questionnaire that addresses many categories with only one or two questions for each.

- It is important that the tool used has been scientifically validated so that the confidence placed in the results is not questioned by stakeholders. For example, some people in charge of PSR evaluations, non-specialists, assume that the so-called Gallup or Q^{12} questionnaire, developed by the Gallup Institute in 1998 (Buckingham & Coffman, 1999; Harter et al., 2002; Schaufeli & Bakker, 2010), is suitable for such an assessment. Therefore, they recommend it for PSR evaluation although it was developed to measure commitment to work, and although it has only been partially validated, unlike those presented here. It is therefore recommended to avoid the Gallup Q^{12} questionnaire for the evaluation of PSRs. Schaufeli and Bakker (2010) write on the subject: "In the development of the instrument, practical considerations regarding the usefulness of the Q^{12} for managers in creating change in the workplace have been the leading principle. [However] [...] instead of measuring engagement in terms of an employee's involvement, satisfaction, and enthusiasm as is claimed by Harter et al. (2002), the Q^{12} taps the employee's perceived job resources". Inappropriateness is also the case for the Cognitive Appraisal Scale of Skinner and Brewer (2002) validated in its French version by Berjot and Girault-Lidvan (2009). The questionnaire resembles more a personality trait investigation than an examination of the subject's stress. In addition, among the 10 items addressing threat, more than 50% relate to what the subject perceives of what others think.

2 Questionnaires

As stated in the introduction to the present chapter, the list of questionnaires to follow is not exhaustive and meets a number of selection criteria. The World Health Organization report by Leka and Jain (2010) provides a comprehensive list of questionnaires available for the evaluation of PSRs, which are still relevant today. The Gollac Group (Gollac & Bodier, 2010) recommends the combination of Karazek's JCQ (Job Content Questionnaire) (Karasek et al., 1998) and Seigrist's ERI (Effort-Reward Imbalance) (Siegrist et al., 2004) on the grounds that their combination covers a large portion of the PSR factor categories. These questionnaires also have the advantage of having a relatively small number of questions and are therefore non-binding for respondents in terms of time. If the analyst prefers using only one short questionnaire, the JSS—Job Stress Survey (Spielberger & Reheiser, 1994) seems a good compromise and presents the advantages of (1) exploring both intensity and frequency of the stressors, and (2) standardising the scoring scale which favours comparison of the results of one subject to another.

The JCQ, Job Content Questionnaire, developed by Karasek et al. (1998) is likely the most translated questionnaire addressing stress at work. Several versions are available depending on the number of items to be considered. The original version consisted of 18 items covering five dimensions: decision latitude, psychological demand, social support, physical demand and job insecurity. It has evolved with time to version 2, itself proposed in two versions: JCQ2 User Version with 39 items and JCQ2 Researcher Version with 76 items (Karasek, 2015). Leka and Jain (2010) and the JCQ Centre (www. jcqcenter.com) recommended using the 49-item version JCQ1 and mentioned a long version including 119 items. They were tested with thousands of subjects through different studies, all demonstrating good validity and reliability.

Online Access
To be purchased: https://www.jcqcenter.com/questionnaires-jcq-jcq2/

Advantages and Limits
All the versions of the JCQ have good psychometric properties that make the questionnaire a confidant tool. The limits are related to the version used; shorter versions constrain the spectrum examined.

COPSOQ, the Copenhagen Psychosocial Questionnaire (Kristensen et al., 2005), was developed to assess stress, well-being and some personality traits at work. It was developed in three versions (long, intermediate and short) and reached its third version in 2019 (Burr et al., 2019). However, the designers validated only the intermediate version at the international level: it consists of 60 items covering 26 dimensions (the long version consists of 148 items covering 45 dimensions). The response options are not the same from one item to another (e.g. not the same Likert scale for some issues and others) and some items are reversed.

Validation of the third version (COPSOQ III) was carried out in six countries with more than 20,000 participants (Burr et al., 2019). In the international approach, 20 of the 23 scales tested had a Cronbach coefficient greater than 0.7, thus showing acceptable or good reliability. However, the coefficient was higher than 0.64 for the three dimensions Commitment to the Workplace, Demands for Hiding Emotions, and Control over Working Time. It must be noted that when looking at specific populations, the internal consistency could be slightly different; for example, Predictability, Meaning of Work and Job Insecurity for France had a coefficient less than 0.7 (probably due to local context rather than translation). The intercorrelation analysis confirmed that dimensions are measuring independent constructs.

This questionnaire is available in more than 20 languages online through the COPSOQ International Network.

Online Access

https://www.copsoq-network.org/

Advantages and Limits

According to Burr et al. (2019: 493), "it is a strength of the questionnaire that it has been developed in a joint process by different groups of practitioners and researchers from different social and national contexts". However, the international approach for validation does not reflect the specificities of the countries. The large number of items in the questionnaire might be thought of as an advantage, but it seems to increase the time to take the questionnaire and analyse the results, thus providing a minor added value when compared with shorter questionnaires. The fact that the response options are not the same from one item to another with reversed items makes the analysis of the questionnaire complex. In addition, it requires significant preparative work for the analyst. Despite this, however, the questionnaire explores a wide spectrum of possible difficulties that could be encountered at work and can be considered one of the most exhaustive approaches for the identification of stress factors. It is one of the rare questionnaires among the selection presented here that consider many resource factors versus constraining factors (e.g. dimensions "Influence at Work", "Possibilities for Development", "Control over Working time", "Social Support from Supervisor" and "from Colleagues").

JSS, Job Stress Survey, elaborated by Spielberger (Spielberger & Reheiser, 1994) is devoted to perceived stress in a professional context.

JSS allows three scores to be obtained (intensity, frequency, overall) within two domains: job pressure and lack of support, the combination of which refers to occupational stress. The subject is asked to give his opinion regarding the amount of stress felt for each event (each item) and to assess the intensity of its impact by assigning a score on a numerical scale ranging from 1 to 9. Score 5 is the average reference score pre-assigned to item 1—"The allocation of unpleasant obligations"—which is considered the standard event; this reference score reinforces the comparability of the results from one subject to another by increasing the reliability of the numerical scale (Fauquet-Alekhine & Rouillac, 2015). The job stress index is obtained by considering the item products intensity × frequency, all divided by 30 for the 60-item questionnaire. The overall index varies from 0 to 81.

The number of items for the questionnaire is 60 (2 × 30) for the original version and 40 (2 × 20) for the shortened version keeping the more stable items (Spielberger & Reheiser, 1994).

The number of participants involved in the validation process was $N = 1781$.

The internal consistency was good while repeatedly scoring around 0.80 for the alpha coefficient, and test-retest coefficient was reported at 0.48 to 0.75.

Online Access
To be purchased: Items of the survey available at https://www.creativeorgdesign.com/tests/job-stress-survey/

Advantages and Limits
The questionnaire is well adapted for the assessment of stress at work and less for the assessment of acute stress. Compared with the other questionnaires presented in the present chapter, it is the only one combining intensity and frequency of the stressors and it presents the advantage of exploring a wide scope of occupational difficulties, but some are missing, such as personal competencies.

ERI, Effort-Reward Imbalance, developed by Siegrist et al. (2004) is based on the effort-reward imbalance model. It assesses the extent to which the work context fails to provide the expected level of reward while examining effort compared with reward and (over)commitment in 22 items answered on a 4-point Likert scale. A long version is available with 28 items. Some items are reversed. The questionnaire addresses economic aspects (e.g. income) as well as symbolic aspects (e.g. respect from others) and practical aspects of the reward dimension. It also touches on what comprises resources (e.g. adequate support, adequacy training and position).

Analysis was carried out in five European countries with more than 18,000 participants.

Internal consistency of the scales was satisfactory, and the factorial structure of the scales was consistently confirmed (fit measures). More recently, a European comparison was successfully undertaken (Siegrist & Rödel, 2006).

The questionnaire is available in more than 20 languages online through the Universitätsklinikum Dusseldorf.

Online Access

https://www.uniklinik-duesseldorf.de/patienten-besucher/klinikeninstitutezentren/institut-fuer-medizinische-soziologie/forschung/the-eri-model-stress-and-health/eri-questionnaires/questionnaires-download

Advantages and Limits

The questionnaire is specialised and thus focuses on a narrow spectrum of the possible difficulties related to work. It must be used in combination with another questionnaire to assess occupational stress.

It must be noted that the issues address economic rewards to effort and not to performance or competencies (knowledge and skills). This could create a bias as individuals may make effort at work and yet be unable to achieve the task because of their capabilities: a small reward would therefore acknowledge the impossibility of reaching the goal (performance) and not the efforts.

Table 11.1 provides a synthetic view of the characteristics of the questionnaires and identifies the categories of PSR factors explored through the questions asked. The categorisation used in the table and that of Gollac (Gollac & Bodier, 2010) previously presented in Chap. 10 of the present book.

A questionnaire that was not included in the above presentation is the NIOSH. This questionnaire includes 246 items and is therefore particularly time-consuming to fill out. This is one of the most comprehensive

Table 11.1 Overview of questionnaires and characteristics, showing which categories are explored in Gollac's categorisation (Gollac & Bodier, 2010)

Name of scale	Original designer	Number of items	Measurement scale	Work intensity and working time	Emotional demands	autonomy	Social relation ships at work	Value conflicts	Insecurity of the work situation	French version
JCQ, Job Content Questionnaire*	Karasek et al. (1998)	39 to 119 items	Likert scales	×	×	×	×		×	www.jcqcenter.com
COPSOQ, the Copenhagen Psychosocial Questionnaire	Kristensen et al. (2005)	60 to 148 items	Likert scales	×	×	×	×	×	×	Dupret et al. (2012)
JSS, Job Stress Survey	Spielberger and Reheiser (1994)	30 (intensity) + 30 (frequency)	standardised 9-point numerical scale	×	×	×	×	×	×	Boudarene and Kellou (2005)
ERI, Effort-Reward Imbalance	Siegrist et al. (2004)	16 or 22 items	4-point Likert scale	×	×	×			×	Niedhammer et al. (2000)

NOTA:

–Most of the questionnaires are available online in many languages. Please verify the validity of the foreign versions through bibliographic research

–Some questionnaires are available in short*, intermediate or long versions

questionnaires for the analysis of PSR factors, which is why it is worth mentioning it even if it is not selected.

NIOSH GJSQ, Generic Job Stress Questionnaire, was developed by Hurrell and McLaney (1988) with N = 700 nurses over 50 different care facilities. They reported that "the factor-based scales had acceptable reliability (alpha) coefficients ranging from 0.65 to 0.90 (mean 0.81) and that they compared favorably with the original construction formats" (p. 27).

The National Institute for Occupational Safety and Health (NIOSH), USA, developed the GJSQ and it evolved with time (e.g. Wiegand et al., 2012), integrating advances in occupational stress and well-being research. The more recent version includes 22 dimensions (246 items) in the questionnaire and borrowed scales from earlier studies with known validity and reliability. Items are answered on a 3- to 7-point Likert scale for most of them and some of them are reversed. The questionnaire is design to be modular: practitioners may select one or several dimensions to constrain their analysis to their concerns. It is one of the rare questionnaires among the selection presented here that considers many resource factors versus the constraining factors; this is done for most of the dimensions.

Online Access
https://www.cdc.gov/niosh/topics/workorg/detail088.html

Advantages and Limits
The major limit concerns the validity and reliability of the questionnaire: developed on the basis of scales of questionnaires borrowed from studies with known validity and reliability, no study addressing specifically the validity and reliability of the GJSQ is available; moreover, the scales were reshaped when integrated into the GJSQ (some items were removed), which leads to the conclusion that, even though it is based on questionnaires with known validity and reliability, this cannot give any guarantee of validity and reliability to the GJSQ. However, the investigation of occupation offered by the questionnaire is wide.

3 Conclusions

The short list of questionnaires dedicated to the PSR evaluation presented in this chapter deliberately focused on questionnaires with a low number of items. This choice is guided by the experiences of practitioners, which show that questionnaires that are too long are difficult to apply in companies in the context of PSR evaluation: neither the order-giver nor the line management wants to see participants dedicate too much time to evaluation. In practice, a questionnaire that takes 30 minutes will be easily accepted by the management while a questionnaire that takes one hour often poses a problem. It is about the motivation of both the management and the participants. For management, it is the motivation to engage teams in the evaluation, and for participants it is the motivation to respond sincerely and seriously to the questionnaire items.

The use of these questionnaires is part of the methods presented in Chap. 10. However, there is no difficulty in choosing another questionnaire out of this list in order to implement these methods. Chapter 12 provides an example of how to use questionnaire data to graphically format the results of the PSR assessment.

References

Berjot, S., & Girault-Lidvan, N. (2009). Validation d'une version française de l'échelle d'évaluation cognitive primaire de Brewer et Skinner. *Canadian Journal of Behavioural Science/Revue canadienne des sciences du comportement, 41*(4), 252–260.

Boudarene, M., & Kellou, C. (2005). Le stress professionnel: Enquête préliminaire dans une entreprise algérienne d'hydrocarbures. *Revue francophone du stress et du trauma, 5*(3), 141–151.

Buckingham, M., & Coffman, C. (1999). *First, break all the rules: What the world's greatest managers do differently.* Simon & Schuster.

Burr, H., Berthelsen, H., Moncada, S., Nübling, M., Dupret, E., Demiral, Y., et al. (2019). The third version of the Copenhagen Psychosocial Questionnaire. *Safety and Health at Work, 10*(4), 482–503.

Dupret, É., Bocéréan, C., Teherani, M., & Feltrin, M. (2012). Le COPSOQ: un nouveau questionnaire français d'évaluation des risques psychosociaux. *Santé Publique, 24*(3), 189–207.

Fauquet-Alekhine, P., & Rouillac, L. (2015). Arbitrary self-assessment scale of stress: Analysis and discussion of the limited relevance. In *Stress Self-assessment & questionnaires: Choice, application, limits,* 15–20.

Gollac, M., & Bodier, M. (2010). *Mesurer les facteurs psychosociaux de risque au travail pour les maîtriser.* Rapport du Collège d'expertise sur le suivi des risques psychosociaux au travail, faisant suite à la demande du Ministre du travail, de l'emploi et de la santé.

Harter, J. K., Schmidt, F. L., & Hayes, T. L. (2002). Business-unit-level relationships between employee satisfaction, employee engagement, and business outcomes: A meta-analysis. *Journal of Applied Psychology, 87,* 268–279.

Hurrell, J. J., & McLaney, M. A. (1988). Exposure to job stress: A new psychometric instrument. *Scandinavian Journal of Work, Environment & Health, 14*(1), 27–28.

Karasek, R. (2015). *Job Content Questionnaire 2.0 (JCQ2): How to use and understand its many new features and theory*. APA Work, Stress, and Health Conference, May 2015, Atlanta, Georgia.

Karasek, R., Brisson, C., Kawakami, N., Houtman, I., Bongers, P., & Amick, B. (1998). The Job Content Questionnaire (JCQ): An instrument for internationally comparative assessments of psychosocial job characteristics. *Journal of Occupational Health Psychology, 3*(4), 322–355.

Kristensen, T. S., Hannerz, H., Høgh, A., & Borg, V. (2005). The Copenhagen Psychosocial Questionnaire-a tool for the assessment and improvement of the psychosocial work environment. *Scandinavian Journal of Work, Environment & Health, 31*, 438–449.

Leka, S., & Jain, A. (2010). *Health impact of psychosocial hazards at work: An overview*. World Health Organization.

Niedhammer, I., Siegrist, J., Landre, M., Goldberg, M., & Leclerc, A. (2000). Etude des qualités psychométriques de la version francaise du modèle du deséquilibre efforts/récompenses. *Revue d'Épidémiologie et de Santé Publique, 48*, 419–437.

Schaufeli, W. B., & Bakker, A. B. (2010). Defining and measuring work engagement: Bringing clarity to the concept. *Work Engagement: A Handbook of Essential Theory and Research, 12*, 10–24.

Siegrist, J., & Rödel, A. (2006). Work stress and health risk behavior. *Scandinavian Journal of Work, Environment & Health, 32*, 473–481.

Siegrist, J., Starke, D., Chandola, T., Godin, I., Marmot, M., Niedhammer, I., & Peter, R. (2004). The measurement of effort–reward imbalance at work: European comparisons. *Social Science & Medicine, 58*(8), 1483–1499.

Skinner, C., & Brewer, N. (2002). The dynamics of threat and challenge appraisals prior to stressful achievement events. *Journal of Personality and Social Psychology, 84*, 60–70.

Spielberger, C. D., & Reheiser, E. C. (1994). The job stress survey: Measuring gender differences in occupational stress. *Journal of Social Behavior and Personality, 9*(2), 199.

Wiegand, D. M., Chen, P. Y., Hurrell, J. J., Jr., Jex, S., Nakata, A., Nigam, J. A., et al. (2012). A consensus method for updating psychosocial measures used in NIOSH health hazard evaluations. *Journal of Occupational and Environmental Medicine, 54*(3), 350–355.

12

Visualising Results of a Psychosocial Risks Assessment through Questionnaires

Philippe Fauquet-Alekhine

1 Introduction

In Chap. 10 of the present book, it is proposed that the assessment of psychosocial risks at work could be carried out using questionnaires or surveys. These questionnaires are generally composed of several dozen items, which are self-assessed by the participants (i.e. the groups of employees with whom the evaluation is to be conducted). These self-reports can then result in scores, either calculated by item or calculated globally for the questionnaire. These scores lead to a quantitative evaluation. However, most of the time, managers who utilise these results like them to be synthesised in the form of graphs that provide an overview of the situation at a glance.

The purpose of this chapter is to propose a method adaptable to any questionnaire used for the assessment of psychosocial risks that allows for the results to be displayed graphically.

The method consists of categorising the questionnaire items and checking the consistency of this categorisation by a simple statistical test, and then graphing the results obtained from the scores produced by the participants.

P. Fauquet-Alekhine (✉)
SEBE-Lab, Department of Psychological and Behavioural Science,
London School of Economics and Political Science, London, UK

Laboratory for Research in Science of Energy, Montagret, France

Groupe INTRA Robotics, Avoine, France
e-mail: p.fauquet-alekhine@lse.ac.uk; philippe.fauquet-alekhine@groupe-intra.com

© The Author(s), under exclusive license to Springer Nature Switzerland AG 2023
P. Fauquet-Alekhine, J. Erskine (eds.), *The Palgrave Handbook of Occupational Stress*,
https://doi.org/10.1007/978-3-031-27349-0_12

In order to concretely present the method, a fictitious example of psychosocial risk assessment from a questionnaire will be chosen and a worked example of how the method is applied will be presented. To do this, the chapter is divided into several parts:

- The description of the case study: referring to Chaps. 10 and 11 of the present book, a questionnaire is chosen to carry out a psychosocial risk assessment for a group of N people in a company.
- Categorisation of questionnaire items: by referring to Chap. 10 of the present book, a categorisation of the questionnaire items is performed.
- Verification of categorisation consistency—adjustment: a statistical test is applied to this categorisation to verify that it is relevant.
- Visualisation of results: several proposals are analysed concerning possible graphic formatting.
- Comparative analysis of results over time: a proposal is made concerning the use of these graphic formats in order to assess the evolution of psychosocial risks over time for the group of participants.

2   Description of the Case Study

Consider that it is necessary to carry out a psychosocial risk assessment for a group of N people with the same profession in a company; this group of individuals is identified as the "unit of analysis" according to the terminology used in Chap. 10. In this case, another group of people working in that enterprise and having another occupation would constitute another unit of analysis.

Consider that the analyst in charge of the psychosocial risk assessment has chosen to carry out a questionnaire assessment and has chosen to use the Job Stress Survey (JSS) elaborated by Spielberger and Reheiser (1994) devoted to perceived stress in a professional context. This questionnaire is presented in Chap. 6 of the present book. The JSS comprises three scores (intensity, frequency, index) within two domains: job pressure and lack of support, the combination of which indexes occupational stress. The participant is asked to give an opinion regarding the amount of stress felt for each event (each item) and to assess the intensity of its impact by assigning a score on a numerical scale ranging from 1 to 9. Score 5 is the average reference score pre-assigned to item 1—"The allocation of unpleasant obligations"—which is considered as the standard event; this reference score reinforces the comparability of the results from one subject to another by increasing the reliability of the numerical scale (Fauquet-Alekhine & Rouillac, 2015). The job stress index is obtained by adding the item products (intensity x frequency), all divided by 30 for the 60-item questionnaire. The overall index varies from 0 to 81.

Items on the survey are available at https://www.creativeorgdesign.com/tests/job-stress-survey/ for the English version and in Boudarene and Kellou (2005) for the French version.

The items are evaluated twice when each participant takes the questionnaire, once to assess intensity, and a second time to assess frequency. The guidelines and associated evaluation grids are shown below.

2.1 Guidelines and Evaluation Grid to Assess the Intensity of Each JSS Item

1. For events that you feel are more stressful than the standard event (example 1: "Assignment of disagreeable duties"), grey out a number proportionally larger than [5].
2. If you experience a less stressful event than the standard event, grey out a number proportionally smaller than [5].
3. For events that you think produce approximately the same amount of stress as the standard event, grey out the number [5].

Stressful work-related events	Amount of stress		
	Low	Moderate	High
1-Assignment of disagreeable duties	1 2 3 4	**5** 6	7 8 9
2-Working overtime	1 2 3 4	5 6	7 8 9
3-Lack of opportunity for advancement	1 2 3 4	5 6	7 8 9
4-Assignment of new or unfamiliar duties	1 2 3 4	5 6	7 8 9
5-Fellow workers not doing their jobs	1 2 3 4	5 6	7 8 9
6-Inadequate support by supervisor	1 2 3 4	5 6	7 8 9
7-Dealing with crisis situations	1 2 3 4	5 6	7 8 9
8-Lack of recognition for good work	1 2 3 4	5 6	7 8 9
9-Performing tasks not in job description	1 2 3 4	5 6	7 8 9
10-Inadequate or poor-quality equipment	1 2 3 4	5 6	7 8 9
11-Assignment of increased responsibility	1 2 3 4	5 6	7 8 9
12-Periods of inactivity	1 2 3 4	5 6	7 8 9
13-Difficulty getting along with supervisor	1 2 3 4	5 6	7 8 9
14-Experiencing negative attitudes towards the organisation	1 2 3 4	5 6	7 8 9
15-Insufficient personnel to handle an assignment	1 2 3 4	5 6	7 8 9
16-Making critical on-the-spot decisions	1 2 3 4	5 6	7 8 9
17-Personal insult from customer/consumer/colleague	1 2 3 4	5 6	7 8 9
18-Lack of participation in policy-making decisions	1 2 3 4	5 6	7 8 9
19-Inadequate salary	1 2 3 4	5 6	7 8 9
20-Competition for advancement	1 2 3 4	5 6	7 8 9
21-Poor or inadequate supervision	1 2 3 4	5 6	7 8 9
22-Noisy work area	1 2 3 4	5 6	7 8 9
23-Frequent interruptions	1 2 3 4	5 6	7 8 9

(continued)

(continued)

Stressful work-related events	Amount of stress		
	Low	Moderate	High
24-Frequent changes from boring to demanding duties	1 2 3 4	5 6	7 8 9
25-Excessive paperwork	1 2 3 4	5 6	7 8 9
26-Meeting deadlines	1 2 3 4	5 6	7 8 9
27-Insufficient personal time	1 2 3 4	5 6	7 8 9
28-Covering work for another employee	1 2 3 4	5 6	7 8 9
29-Poorly motivated coworkers	1 2 3 4	5 6	7 8 9
30-Conflicts with other department	1 2 3 4	5 6	7 8 9

2.2 Guidelines and Evaluation Grid to Evaluate the Frequency of Each JSS Item

1. For each event mentioned in the first part, indicate approximately the number of days in the last six months during which you experienced the event in question.
2. Grey [0] if the event has not occurred in the last six months.
3. Grey out the number [9+] for each event you've personally experienced for nine or more days in the last six months

Stressful work-related events	Number of days the event appeared in the last six months	
1-Assignment of disagreeable duties	0	1 2 3 4 5 6 7 8 9+
2-Working overtime	0	1 2 3 4 5 6 7 8 9+
3-Lack of opportunity for advancement	0	1 2 3 4 5 6 7 8 9+
4-Assignment of new or unfamiliar duties	0	1 2 3 4 5 6 7 8 9+
5-Fellow workers not doing their jobs	0	1 2 3 4 5 6 7 8 9+
6-Inadequate support by supervisor	0	1 2 3 4 5 6 7 8 9+
7-Dealing with crisis situations	0	1 2 3 4 5 6 7 8 9+
8-Lack of recognition for good work	0	1 2 3 4 5 6 7 8 9+
9-Performing tasks not in job description	0	1 2 3 4 5 6 7 8 9+
10-Inadequate or poor-quality equipment	0	1 2 3 4 5 6 7 8 9+
11-Assignment of increased responsibility	0	1 2 3 4 5 6 7 8 9+
12-Periods of inactivity	0	1 2 3 4 5 6 7 8 9+
13-Difficulty getting along with supervisor	0	1 2 3 4 5 6 7 8 9+
14-Experiencing negative attitudes towards the organisation	0	1 2 3 4 5 6 7 8 9+
15-Insufficient personnel to handle an assignment	0	1 2 3 4 5 6 7 8 9+
16-Making critical on-the-spot decisions	0	1 2 3 4 5 6 7 8 9+
17-Personal insult from customer/consumer/ colleague	0	1 2 3 4 5 6 7 8 9+
18-Lack of participation in policy-making decisions	0	1 2 3 4 5 6 7 8 9+
19-Inadequate salary	0	1 2 3 4 5 6 7 8 9+
20-Competition for advancement	0	1 2 3 4 5 6 7 8 9+

(continued)

(continued)

Stressful work-related events	Number of days the event appeared in the last six months	
21-Poor or inadequate supervision	0	1 2 3 4 5 6 7 8 9+
22-Noisy work area	0	1 2 3 4 5 6 7 8 9+
23-Frequent interruptions	0	1 2 3 4 5 6 7 8 9+
24-Frequent changes from boring to demanding duties	0	1 2 3 4 5 6 7 8 9+
25-Excessive paperwork	0	1 2 3 4 5 6 7 8 9+
26-Meeting deadlines	0	1 2 3 4 5 6 7 8 9+
27-Insufficient personal time	0	1 2 3 4 5 6 7 8 9+
28-Covering work for another employee	0	1 2 3 4 5 6 7 8 9+
29-Poorly motivated coworkers	0	1 2 3 4 5 6 7 8 9+
30-Conflicts with other department	0	1 2 3 4 5 6 7 8 9+

The designers of the questionnaire (Spielberger & Reheiser, 1994) categorised the items according to two domains:

- Lack of support: items 1-4-6-8-9-10-11-13-14-19
- Job pressure: items 7-16-17-20-23-25-27-28-29-30

There are 10 uncategorised items left.

It is therefore interesting to proceed to another categorisation of these items in order to increase the number of domains analysed, which will allow the analysis to gain relevance and ensure that each of the items is part of a category. This allows a complete exploitation of all the items.

3   Categorisation of Questionnaire Items

In order to categorise the items in the JSS, it is proposed to use the categorisation of the Gollac group (Gollac & Bodier, 2010) as described in Chap. 10 of the present book.

The Gollac Group proposed six categories of psychosocial risks:

- Work intensity and working time
- Emotional demands
- Autonomy
- Social relationships at work
- Value conflicts
- Insecurity of the work situation

212 P. Fauquet-Alekhine

Table 12.1 Categorisation of JSS items according to the authors (Spielberger & Reheiser, 1994) and according to the Gollac group (Gollac & Bodier, 2010)

STRESSFUL WORK-RELATED EVENTS	Spielberger & Reheiser's domaines	GOLLAC group's categories	GOLLAC group's categories
1-Assignment of disagreeable duties	Lack of support	Autonomy	
2-Working overtime	Other	Work intensity and working time	
3-Lack of opportunity for advancement	Other	Social relationships at work	
4-Assignment of new or unfamiliar duties	Lack of support	Autonomy	Insecurity of the work situation
5-Fellow workers not doing their jobs	Other	Emotional demands	Work intensity and working time
6-Inadequate support by supervisor	Lack of support	Social relationships at work	
7-Dealing with crisis situations	Job pressure	Emotional demands	Insecurity of the work situation
8-Lack of recognition for good work	Lack of support	Social relationships at work	
9-Performing tasks not in job description	Lack of support	Value conflicts	Insecurity of the work situation
10-Inadequate or poor quality equipment	Lack of support	Work intensity and working time	Insecurity of the work situation
11-Assignment of increased responsibility	Lack of support	Autonomy	Emotional demands
12-Periods of inactivity	Other	Work intensity and working time	Autonomy
13-Difficulty getting along with supervisor	Lack of support	Social relationships at work	Insecurity of the work situation
14-Experiencing negative attitudes toward the organization	Lack of support	Insecurity of the work situation	Emotional demands
15-Insufficient personnel to handle an assignment	Other	Work intensity and working time	Value conflicts
16-Making critical on-the-spot decisions	Job pressure	Value conflicts	
17-Personal insult from customer/consumer/colleague	Job pressure	Insecurity of the work situation	Emotional demands
18-Lack of participation in policy-making decisions	Other	Autonomy	
19-Inadequate salary	Lack of support	Social relationships at work	
20-Competition for advancement	Job pressure	Social relationships at work	
21-Poor or inadequate supervision	Other	Social relationships at work	Work intensity and working time
22-Noisy work area	Other	Work intensity and working time	
23-Frequent interruptions	Job pressure	Work intensity and working time	
24-Frequent changes from boring to demanding duties	Other	Autonomy	
25-Excessive paperwork	Job pressure	Autonomy	Value conflicts
26-Meeting deadlines	Other	Work intensity and working time	
27-Insufficient personal time	Job pressure	Work intensity and working time	
28-Covering work for another employee	Job pressure	Social relationships at work	
29-Poorly motivated coworkers	Job pressure	Social relationships at work	
30-Conflicts with other department	Job pressure	Social relationships at work	Emotional demands

The description of each of the categories given in Chap. 10 makes it possible to associate each of the items of the JSS with one or more categories at the discretion of the analyst. The main point is not to have an exact categorisation but to maintain this categorisation throughout the various psychosocial risk assessments that will be carried out over time with the unit of analysis in order to allow an assessment of the variation in psychosocial risks in the group.

In this case, the proposed categorisation is given in Table 12.1.

4 Verification of Categorisation Consistency: Adjustment

It is then necessary to check the consistency of the categorisation. This consists of carrying out a statistical test that verifies that each of the categories is represented by items on the questionnaire in a sufficiently independent manner from each of the other categories. If this is not the case, then it is necessary to review the categorisation of certain items in order to obtain the desired independence.

To illustrate, let us assume that items 3, 5 and 7 on the questionnaire are the only ones assigned to the category *Work intensity and working time* but that they are also the only ones assigned to the category *Emotional demands*. This would mean that these two categories are represented by the same items and therefore that they are identical in terms of psychosocial risks, which is not the case. The categorisation would therefore lose consistency since it would not separate the effect of the two categories in the analysis.

The statistical test for assessing dependence between two dimensions is based on the analysis of the value of Loevinger's H coefficient (Loevinger, 1948). H is interested in accounting for similarity of relationship between two dimensions when expressed in binary mode (0 or 1) according to k given criteria.

Table 12.2 shows how each category is coded according to the items assigned to it.

The calculation of H is therefore done for each pair of categories taken two by two. Since independence between two categories is sought, it is expected that if the value of the column of the first category is 1, then the value of the column of the second category is 0, and vice versa. For each pair of categories in Table 12.2, the number of pairs of values (1, 0) or (0, 1) obtained with the number of pairs of values (1, 0) or (0, 1) expected must be compared. The number of pairs of values (1, 0) or (0, 1) expected corresponds to the number of pairs of values (1, 0) or (0, 1) obtained plus the number of pairs of values (1, 1) obtained because, to have complete independence of the two categories, these pairs of values (1, 1) should have taken the values (1, 0) or (0, 1). The pairs of values (0, 0) are not involved in the calculation since this indicates that the items associated with the row of the table do not intervene in the dimensioning of the categories considered. Mathematically, for categories i and j (where i represents one column and j another column), the coefficient H is denoted H_{ij} and is expressed as follows:

Table 12.2 Binary coding of the six categories of the Gollac group according to the assignment of items by category: the value 1 means that the item is assigned to this category, otherwise 0

STRESSFUL WORK-RELATED EVENTS	GOLLAC group's categories	GOLLAC group's categories	Work intensity and working time	Autonomy	Social relationships at work	Emotional demands	Insecurity of the work situation	Value conflicts
1-Assignment of disagreeable duties	Autonomy		0	1	0	0	0	0
2-Working overtime	Work intensity and working time		1	0	0	0	0	0
3-Lack of opportunity for advancement	Social relationships at work		0	0	1	0	0	0
4-Assignment of new or unfamiliar duties	Autonomy	Insecurity of the work situation	0	1	0	0	1	0
5-Fellow workers not doing their jobs	Emotional demands	Work intensity and working time	1	0	0	1	0	0
6-Inadequate support by supervisor	Social relationships at work		0	0	1	0	0	0
7-Dealing with crisis situations	Emotional demands	Insecurity of the work situation	0	0	0	1	1	0
8-Lack of recognition for good work	Social relationships at work		0	0	1	0	0	0
9-Performing tasks not in job description	Value conflicts	Insecurity of the work situation	0	0	0	0	1	1
10-Inadequate or poor quality equipment	Work intensity and working time	Insecurity of the work situation	1	0	0	0	1	0
11-Assignment of increased responsibility	Autonomy	Emotional demands	0	1	0	1	0	0
12-Periods of inactivity	Work intensity and working time	Autonomy	1	1	0	0	0	0
13-Difficulty getting along with supervisor	Social relationships at work	Insecurity of the work situation	0	0	1	0	1	0
14-Experiencing negative attitudes toward the organization	Insecurity of the work situation	Emotional demands	0	0	0	1	1	0
15-Insufficient personnel to handle an assignment	Work intensity and working time	Value conflicts	1	0	0	0	0	1
16-Making critical on-the-spot decisions	Value conflicts		0	0	0	0	0	1
17-Personal insult from customer/consumer/colleague	Insecurity of the work situation	Emotional demands	0	0	0	1	1	0
18-Lack of participation in policy-making decisions	Autonomy		0	1	0	0	0	0
19-Inadequate salary	Social relationships at work		0	0	1	0	0	0
20-Competition for advancement	Social relationships at work		0	0	1	0	0	0
21-Poor or inadequate supervision	Social relationships at work	Work intensity and working time	1	0	1	0	0	0
22-Noisy work area	Work intensity and working time		1	0	0	0	0	0
23-Frequent interruptions	Work intensity and working time		1	0	0	0	0	0
24-Frequent changes from boring to demanding duties	Autonomy		0	1	0	0	0	0
25-Excessive paperwork	Autonomy	Value conflicts	0	1	0	0	0	1
26-Meeting deadlines	Work intensity and working time		1	0	0	0	0	0
27-Insufficient personal time	Work intensity and working time		1	0	0	0	0	0
28-Covering work for another employee	Social relationships at work		0	0	1	0	0	0
29-Poorly motivated coworkers	Social relationships at work		0	0	1	0	0	0
30-Conflicts with other department	Social relationships at work	Emotional demands	0	0	1	1	0	0

214   P. Fauquet-Alekhine

$$H_{ij} = 1 - \frac{\text{calculated } N_{ij}(1,0)}{\text{expected } N_{ij}(1,0)}$$

where $0 \le N_{ij} \le k$, k being the number of items falling within the definition of both categories i and j considered.

The interpretation of the values of H is as follows:

- $H_{ij} = 0$: no dependency
- $H_{ij} \le 0.30$: poor dependency
- $0{,}30 < H_{ij} \le 0.40$: weak dependency
- $0{,}40 < H_{ij} \le 0.50$: medium dependency
- $H_{ij} \le 0.5$: good dependency
- $H_{ij} = 1$: full dependency

In the test that concerns us, it is important to have $H_{ij} \le 0.30$.

Table 12.3 gives the calculated values for H for the categorisation presented in Table 12.2 for each of the category pairs. Figure 12.1 shows the interval distribution of these values.

Note: H=1 when calculated for two identical categories; these values are not reported in Table 12.3 or shown in Fig. 12.1.

These results show that the categorisation adopted for the JSS according to the categories of the Gollac group is satisfactory since the categories taken two by two have a sufficiently low degree of dependence (≤ 0.30).

In the event that this degree of dependence is not low enough, the analyst must review the categorisation of the questionnaire items in order to reduce the dependence. This adjustment does not pose any difficulty in terms of scientific rigour insofar as the assignment of an item to another category is subjective and depends on the context of the company in which the psychosocial risk assessment is carried out. For example, the item "18-Lack of participation in policy-making decisions" has been assigned here to the *Autonomy* category. It is not impossible that in some work contexts, this item is also associated

Table 12.3 Loevinger's H coefficient values for the pairs of categories presented in Table 12.2

GOLLAC group's categories	Work intensity and working time	Autonomy	Social relationships at work	Emotional demands	Insecurity of the work situation	Value conflicts
Work intensity and working time	*	*	*	*	*	*
Autonomy	0.06	*	*	*	*	*
Social relationships at work	0.05	0.00	*	*	*	*
Emotional demands	0.07	0,.08	0.67	*	*	*
Insecurity of the work situation	0.06	0,.07	0.06	0.30	*	*
Value conflicts	0.07	0.10	0.00	0.01	0.10	*

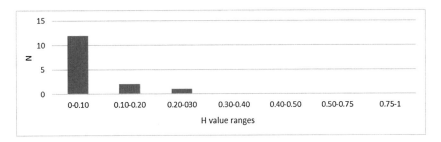

Fig. 12.1 Distribution of Loevinger's H coefficient values for the pairs of categories presented in Table 12.2 (*N* is the number of values per range)

with the category *Social relationships at work*, depending on whether the analyst appreciates whether decision-making has a dependence or an impact on social relations at work. As noted, what matters is that the categorisation remains fixed from one evaluation to another within the same company.

5   Visualisation of Results

We now present some examples of how the quantitative results obtained can be visualised. Before doing so, however, we must point out that, for each JSS item, the average score for the unit of analysis is calculated separately for intensity, frequency and index. In other words, for the data to make sense, the average intensity of each item for the unit of analysis is calculated by averaging the scores of each participant for that item, as well as for frequency and index. This precision is important because some people would be tempted to calculate the average index by making the product of the averages of the intensity and frequency. Then, for each category, the average score is calculated by averaging the scores of each of the items assigned to it; this is done independently for intensity, frequency and index.

Figure 12.2 presents an example of what can be obtained in a psychosocial risk assessment for the index values of each item as a function of intensity. This representation has the advantage of allowing the managers to focus their attention on the upper right quarter of the graph since this is where the major difficulties of the unit of analysis appear. As companies operate with limited resources, managers are interested in reducing their action plan to the most intense and frequent problems.

Figure 12.3 represents the average indexes by category of the Gollac group. This radar graph makes it possible to focus the attention of managers on the points of the curve which identify the categories that lead to major difficulties.

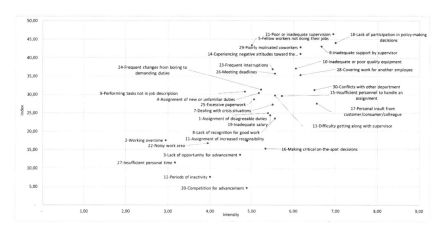

Fig. 12.2 Example of results obtained with the JSS. Distribution of items according to their index as a function of intensity

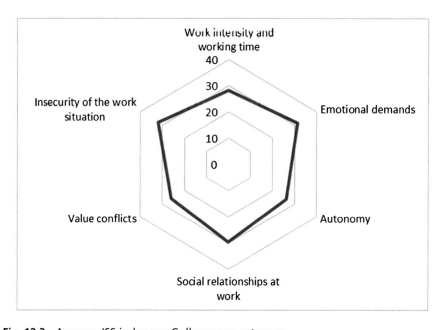

Fig. 12.3 Average JSS index per Gollac group category

6   Comparative Analysis of Results Over Time

As discussed in Chaps. 9 and 10 of the present book, it is important to periodically review the assessment of psychosocial risks in a company. For the results of the new evaluation to be comparable with the previous evaluation, it is important to rely on identical material from one evaluation to another. In particular, using the same questionnaire according to the same categorisation facilitates comparison. In the event that the analyst wishes to change the questionnaire, it is advisable to use the new questionnaire at the same time as the previous questionnaire for at least one year in order to allow a transitory comparison.

The visual representations of the quantitative data obtained during the evaluation of psychosocial risks allows a rapid assessment of psychosocial risks that have evolved favourably or unfavourably. For example, Fig. 12.4 shows what could become of Fig. 12.3 after one or two years in which an action plan has been implemented. Figure 12.4 indicates that the categories *Social relationships at work* and *Emotional demands* have evolved favourably to the extent that the index has been reduced, while the category *Insecurity of the work situation* has deteriorated.

Similarly, the representation proposed in Fig. 12.2 makes it possible to assess the evolution of the state of psychosocial risks in the enterprise by comparing the possible redistribution of data on the graph.

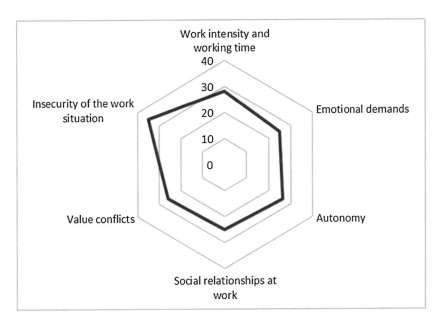

Fig. 12.4 Average indexes obtained with the JSS by category of the Gollac group. Example of possible evolution between two assessments of psychosocial risks, the first assessment being visualised in Fig. 12.3

7   Conclusions

The use of questionnaires for psychosocial risk assessment can sometimes be difficult to interpret. It is therefore important to have tools for analysing these questionnaires, which begins by scoring the results obtained in order to have quantitative data. These quantitative data have the advantage of being able to be formatted as graphs that will make it possible to quickly understand the weaknesses or strengths identified by the assessment of psychosocial risks in the company. The formatting of graphs of quantitative data is therefore of undeniable interest to managers and decision-makers because, on the one hand, it will make it possible to focus an action plan on the major difficulties identified by the evaluation, and on the other hand, it will allow a quick comparison of the company's possible progress between two psychosocial risk assessments. Although this type of treatment requires time, experience shows that the time spent represents real added value, not only in terms of facilitating the analysis of the results of the evaluation, but also in terms of valuing the work of the analyst with the collective of participants in the evaluation as well as with its management.

References

Boudarene, M., & Kellou, C. (2005). Le stress professionnel: Enquête préliminaire dans une entreprise algérienne d'hydrocarbures. *Revue francophone du stress et du trauma, 5*(3), 141–151.

Fauquet-Alekhine, P., & Rouillac, L. (2015). Arbitrary self-assessment scale of stress: Analysis and discussion of the limited relevance. In *Stress Self-assessment & questionnaires: Choice, application, limits* (pp. 15–20).

Gollac, M., & Bodier, M. (2010). *Measuring psychosocial risk factors at work to control them*, a report by the College of Expertise on monitoring psychosocial risks at work, following a request from the Minister of Labour, Employment and Health.

Loevinger, J. (1948). The technic of homogeneous tests compared with some aspects of "scale analysis" and factor analysis. *Psychological Bulletin, 45*(6), 507–529.

Spielberger, C. D., & Reheiser, E. C. (1994). The job stress survey: Measuring gender differences in occupational stress. *Journal of Social Behavior and Personality, 9*(2), 199.

Part III

Using Stress at Work

13

Leadership Styles: Work Stress, Related Outcomes and Health

James Erskine and George Georgiou

1   Introduction

The aim of this chapter is to review the evidence base for the impact of leadership style on employee health, well-being, and productivity outcomes. Practical suggestions arising from the evidence presented in this chapter will form the focus of the next chapter. In a recent review, Erskine and Georgiou (2018) highlighted the negative health and occupational outcomes associated with certain leadership styles, chiefly autocratic and laissez-faire. Also noted in the previous review, transformational and transactional leadership styles were related to a reduction of negative outcomes for employees (e.g. stress, absenteeism, staff turnover, burnout) and a simultaneous increase in their productivity. The previous review concluded that the best outcomes resulted from transformational leadership. The focus of the present work is to examine a broader array of leadership styles that have been demonstrated to have a positive impact on employee well-being and productivity. Furthermore, the

---

J. Erskine (✉)
Institute for Medical and Biomedical Sciences, St George's University of London, London, UK
e-mail: jerskine@sgu.ac.uk

G. Georgiou
Department of Psychology, Sport, and Geography, University of Hertfordshire, Hertfordshire, UK

© The Author(s), under exclusive license to Springer Nature Switzerland AG 2023
P. Fauquet-Alekhine, J. Erskine (eds.), *The Palgrave Handbook of Occupational Stress*,
https://doi.org/10.1007/978-3-031-27349-0_13

current review will examine more recent evidence. There are many studies that have already demonstrated the negative impacts of particular styles of leadership on employee well-being, for example, autocratic, authoritarian, tyrannical, laissez-faire, and so on (Francioli et al., 2018; Schyns & Schilling, 2013). Therefore, these styles will not be a central focus of this review. In simple terms the current work will look at what is best for employees, leaders, and organisations.

One outcome that will form a focus of this review and is detrimental to employees is excessive stress (Quick & Henderson, 2016). Broadly, stress can be defined as occurring when an individual appraises a situation as a threat to something that they value. During times of stress, one's ability to cope is exceeded, relative to their current resources, which in turn reduces their psychological and physical well-being (French et al., 1982; Harms et al., 2017; Lazarus & Folkman, 1984). In short, stress is experienced when the situation demands more than we feel able to give. Critically, it is necessary to realise that stress does not always harm, and original conceptualisations suggested that mild stress can act as a useful motivator leading to performance enhancements. The mild form of positive stress has been termed eustress (Selye, 1959). However, there is general agreement that past certain levels further stress is detrimental to the individual (Fauquet-Alekhine et al., 2014; Hammen, 2005; Salem, 2015).

The leadership styles and processes that will be examined in the present review have all been demonstrated to have broadly positive impacts on employee stress and well-being and are: servant, authentic, ethical, charismatic, leader-member exchange (LMX), and transformational. Each of these will be defined in the next section, under the heading of positive leadership definitions.

2   Positive Leadership Definitions

2.1   Servant Leadership

Greenleaf (1977) suggests that servant leadership transcends self-interest and focuses on fostering well-being in followers. Other researchers have suggested that servant leaders enable and encourage followers to grow as individuals, being primarily concerned with serving subordinate followers (Eva et al., 2019; Luthans & Avolio, 2003; Stone et al., 2003; van Dierendonck, 2011). Compared to transformational leadership, servant leadership prioritises the psychological needs of followers in contrast to the needs of the organisation

13 Leadership Styles: Work Stress, Related Outcomes and Health 223

(van Dierendonck et al., 2014). Andersen (2018) suggests that servant leadership is distinct from transformational because transformational leaders focus more on organisational goals than follower needs.

2.2 Authentic Leadership

Authentic leadership is typically characterised by personal attributes such as genuineness, trustworthiness, purposiveness, values, self-awareness, self-discipline, a moral perspective, relational transparency, and authentic behaviour (Avolio & Gardner, 2005; Avolio et al., 2004; Gardner et al., 2021; Harter, 2002; Luthans & Avolio, 2003; Sendjaya et al., 2016; Shirey, 2006, 2009).

One problematic issue with this conception of authentic leadership is that one can be authentic while not necessarily moral. For example, one could hold Machiavellian values and be authentic to these. Thus, leaders can be fully authentic to personal values and standards which may be malevolent and represent self-interests. The literature is often silent on these issues. Typically, authenticity is equated with a value laden ethical approach which assumes authenticity to be morally benevolent. Malevolent authenticity, while clearly possible, is largely ignored in research, although this is starting to change (see Sendjaya et al., 2016).

2.3 Ethical Leadership

Ethical leadership is seen as "the demonstration of normatively appropriate conduct through personal actions and interpersonal relationships, and the promotion of such conduct to followers through two-way communication, reinforcement, and decision-making" (Brown et al., 2005, p. 120). The literature has shown the following components to be definitional of ethical leadership: ethical awareness, character/integrity, orientation towards community and/or people, motivational, empowerment/encouragement, and navigating ethical responsibilities (Brown, & Treviño, 2006; Resick et al., 2006). However, other research goes beyond these mere traits and suggests that ethical leadership also includes relational ideas where effective communication is used to drive ethical practice (Treviño et al., 2003). Importantly research has demonstrated that ethical leadership can lead to a range of positive outcomes, including task performance increments (Mayer et al., 2012; Piccolo et al., 2010) and improvement in multiple components of well-being (Chughtai et al., 2015; Liu et al., 2010; Liu et al., 2013).

Recent evidence from Lemoine and colleagues outlines the overlap and distinctions between moral approaches to leadership said to encompass ethical, authentic, and servant leadership styles (Lemoine et al., 2019). Furthermore, they report consistent positive impacts of moral leadership on organisational outcomes.

2.4 Charismatic Leadership

Charismatic leadership is sometimes used interchangeably with transformational leadership as charisma is an integral component of transformational leadership (Babcock-Roberson & Strickland, 2010). Sy et al. (2018) have argued that charismatic leaders engender significant emotions from their followers that motivate them to action and encourage a form of devoted following (Sy et al., 2018). These strong emotions and behaviours can continue and even grow in strength following the leader's absence, for example, through death (Steffens et al., 2017).

2.5 Leader-Member Exchange (LMX)

Where other leadership theories focus on the traits and behaviours of leaders, LMX predominantly provides a theoretical framework which has at its core the quality of the relationship between the leader and the follower. Individualised attention to different staff is seen as critical (Dansereau Jr et al., 1973; Gerstner & Day, 1997; Liden et al., 1997; Martin et al., 2016). The literature suggests that LMX is not a distinct leadership style but a process that develops from leader follower interactions. As Graen and Uhl-Bien (1995) suggest: "LMX is both transactional and transformational. It is a dyadic social exchange process that begins with more limited social 'transactions' (e.g. transactional leadership), but for those who are able to generate the most effective LMX relationships, the type of leadership that results is transformational" (Graen & Uhl-Bien, 1995, p. 239).

2.6 Transformational Leadership

This was originally conceptualised by Burns (1978), and was subsequently expanded by Bass (1985) and is said to comprise of four subcomponents (Arnold & Connelly, 2013; Bass & Riggio, 2006; Ghasabeh et al., 2015), which are as follows:

I. Idealised influence—leaders possess strong consistent values, and their actions persistently reflect these values. Bass (1997) has argued this sub-component also includes consideration of ethical outcomes of decisions.
II. Inspirational motivation—leaders communicate clearly, inspirationally and charismatically, providing a sense of the way forward and convince others to follow and share in this vision. Communication effectiveness has been related to greater employee satisfaction (Madlock, 2008).
III. Intellectual stimulation—leaders encourage followers to think and act more diversely, challenging assumptions and prior beliefs, and utilising their full intellectual capacity.
IV. Individual consideration—leaders individually recognise and support employees, guiding their development in a personalised way by being responsive to their needs and competencies.

Erskine and Georgiou's (2018) review also examined transactional leadership, but studies have indicated mixed findings with respect to its efficacy in creating positive employee health outcomes (Bass, 1985; Sarros et al., 2002). Bass (1985) also found a strong positive correlation ($r = 0.72$) between transactional and transformational leadership, either suggesting they are assessing similar constructs or suggesting they are distinct but are both present in all leaders to varying degrees (Andersen, 2018).

3 Redundancy in the Concepts, Conceptual Overlap, and Issues with the More Recent Positive Forms of Leadership

The leadership styles and processes delineated above represent "positive leadership" shown to result in better employee well-being and performance outcomes. However, there are still concerns whether the leadership styles above are truly separate or represent varying degrees of similar concepts with much conceptual redundancy (Fuller et al., 2022).

Some researchers have argued that authentic leadership is a higher order construct involved in all "positive leadership" styles such as transformational, servant, and ethical (Hoch et al., 2018). Importantly Hoch et al. (2018) conducted a meta-analysis of ethical, authentic, and servant leadership to see if they explained any additional variance in critical employee outcomes relative to transformational leadership. This is vital as there is considerable conceptual overlap in some of the underlying principles. The following outcome variables were examined: job performance, employee deviance, organisational citizenship behaviour (voluntary commitment to organisation), employee engagement, job satisfaction, organisational commitment, affective commitment, supervisor trust, and leader-member exchange. Results indicated that ethical, authentic, and servant leadership explained no additional variance over transformational leadership on work performance. With organisational citizenship behaviour, transformational leadership alone explained just 8% of variance; however, servant leadership explained an additional 9% of the variance. Regarding employee deviance, transformational leadership explained the most variance; however, ethical did explain an additional 17%. Regarding job satisfaction, employee engagement, and organisational citizenship, only servant leadership explained significant variance in addition to transformational leadership. However, authentic leadership explained additional variance regarding affective commitment. Importantly ethical, servant and authentic all explained additional variance over transformational regarding supervisor trust and ethical and servant also explained additional variance regarding LMX.

The study highlights that although certain leadership forms may explain additional variance over transformational for certain follower outcomes, the majority of variance in outcomes is explained by transformational leadership, and the additional variance explained by alternate forms is often small and not consistent across outcomes. Furthermore, the study found very high correlations between transformational leadership and all three alternative forms—servant, authentic, and ethical. The most promising form of leadership that explained additional variance was servant leadership. This suggests that it may have conceptually distinct values that could be useful to incorporate with transformational leadership to obtain the best outcomes (Hoch et al., 2018). In addition to the evidence reported by Hoch et al. (2018), ethical leadership has often been subsumed within the framework of transformational and charismatic leadership models (Avolio & Bass 2004; Brown & Treviño, 2006).

Banks et al. (2016, 2018) also highlight concerns regarding conceptual proliferation within the research on leadership styles. The issue is problematic because many of the emergent leadership forms share considerable conceptual overlap with aspects of former leadership style models (Banks et al., 2016, 2018; Bormann, & Rowold 2018). Furthermore, research often demonstrates very high correlations between the supposedly different forms (Hoch et al., 2018; Shaffer et al., 2016). In addition, poor conceptual specification is common in the literature often leading to ambiguity about how certain leadership styles translate into overt behaviours (Yukl, 1999).

One further issue with the emerging positive leadership styles concerns the notion of authentic leadership. Will merely being authentic mean that actions stemming from this style always be moral. Thus, one can imagine a person that always acts in line with their principles, therefore acting authentically, but their acts are malevolent. One study to investigate this was conducted by Sendjaya et al. (2016) which examined the link between moral reasoning and moral action. They also investigated Machiavellianism (not viewing others as trustworthy and seeking status for themselves) and authentic leadership. Results indicated several unexpected findings, first there was no direct relationship between leader moral reasoning and authentic leadership. Secondly there was also no direct relationship between authentic leadership and leader moral action. In line with our former point this suggests that merely being authentic or being able to reason in moral ways does not in any way guarantee moral actions. Furthermore, the study found that when Machiavellianism was high this had an impact on the relationship between leader moral reasoning and authentic leadership, and Machiavellianism also impacted the relationship between authentic leadership and leader moral actions. Such that, individuals with high moral reasoning are more likely to be an authentic leader and display moral actions if they are also low on Machiavellianism. Thus, it is important to consider Machiavellianism when discussing leadership behaviours and styles (Eva et al., 2019; Harms & Spain, 2015; Sendjaya et al., 2016; see also Muris et al., 2017).

While this review has chosen to focus mainly on positive leadership styles that have been linked to better follower well-being and work performance outcomes, it needs to be stated that there can never be one optimal leadership style for every situation. Therefore, what is optimal will depend on the context in which it is employed (Liden & Antonakis, 2009). The last review (Erskine & Georgiou, 2018) suggested that laissez-faire leadership and autocratic/dissonant/authoritarian styles are mostly detrimental to employees and institutions; however, in certain circumstances, particular styles may be temporarily beneficial to deal with time sensitive challenges. For example, positive leadership styles where decisions are more collaborative, may not be effective in times of crisis, where rapid decisions and responses may be needed.

The following section will examine the evidence linking the positive leadership styles delineated above with better employee outcomes.

4   Review of the Evidence Base

The following review of the evidence will consider both leadership styles and leadership behaviours as these have been found to be separate and not always consistent (Yukl, 1999; Inceoglu et al., 2018). Furthermore, it has also been found that the relationship between leadership style and behaviour may be moderated by other individual differences such as Machiavellianism (Sendjaya et al., 2016).

To generate the papers used in this review a literature search was performed using PsychInfo and Google Scholar. Search terms included all of the "positive" leadership styles mentioned above and outcome terms such as stress, well-being, health, workplace engagement, job satisfaction, turnover, absenteeism, retention, burnout, performance, and productivity. The aim was to identify papers examining the effects of various leadership styles and behaviours on employee well-being and productivity outcomes where data was presented supporting their claims. In addition, the search focused on the most current published research.

When examining findings with respect to employee well-being it is important to recognise that well-being can be conceptualised as comprising of two conceptually distinct theoretical perspectives, hedonic and eudemonic. Hedonic well-being typically refers to an assessment of pleasure and happiness, whereas eudemonic refers to a sense of meaning in life attained via maximising ones' potential and a sense of autonomy (Diener, 1984; Vanhoutte & Nazroo, 2014). Modern reviews suggest eudemonic well-being may have more relevance to the modern workplace (Grant & McGhee, 2021).

From the hedonic perspective, subjective well-being is comprised of two related dimensions, cognitive well-being (global evaluation of life satisfaction/ or satisfaction in a particular life area such as relationships or work) and affective well-being—the frequency and intensity of positive and negative emotions/moods (McMahan & Estes, 2011). However, the literature on leadership and well-being does not seem to be specific about the choice of measure of well-being used, cognitive versus affective, and rarely both are used. Our recommendation for researchers would be to consistently report which type of well-being was assessed, and why this type of measurement was chosen.

The literature on leadership has focused mainly on employee productivity to the detriment of employee well-being and health. Furthermore, employee well-being has often been conflated with job satisfaction (Grant et al., 2007). The definitions above show that this conflation ignores the affective and eudemonic dimensions of well-being.

4.1 Effects on Stress/Well-being/Health

Examining the effects of leadership styles and behaviours on employee stress is vital, as previous work indicates that stress is related to seven of the ten main causes of death worldwide (Quick & Cooper, 2003). Furthermore, government intervention, policy, and standards in the UK have consistently stated that to improve management standards there must be a focus on reducing stress in the working population (MacKay et al., 2004). In addition, a meta-analysis has indicated that greater job satisfaction is related to improved mental and physical health (Faragher et al., 2005, 2013). Currently most companies view employee well-being as the responsibility of the individual employee. Although changes in how employees perceive the workplace and its potential to foster health are starting to become evidenced (Koinig, & Diehl, 2021).

One meta-analysis examining the evidence on leadership and stress reports the often-overlooked fact that leaders have the power to positively reduce or increase the work stress of employees (Harms et al., 2017). There are multiple routes through which leaders may lessen stress, but Harms and colleagues suggest that the most beneficial pathways are reducing ambiguity, providing guidance and support, encouraging followers, and promoting self-growth. Theoretically, all of these should reduce the perception of stress in followers. The results of the meta-analysis demonstrated that burnout and stress were less prevalent in environments that utilised transformational leadership. Unsurprisingly stress and burnout were enhanced under abusive leadership. Positive effects of transformational leadership and LMX were found to reduce burnout and stress. Importantly, the analysis reported greater effects for LMX and abusive leadership than transformational albeit in different directions. This suggests that avoiding abusive leadership styles is clearly one route of most promise. LMX and having positive supportive leader exchanges is related to less burnout and stress. Furthermore, reducing stress and burnout will have significant upsides to any organisation in terms of staff well-being, reduced turnover, absenteeism, and increased productivity (Harms et al., 2017).

In a further review, Inceoglu et al. (2018) examined the literature on employee well-being and leadership behaviour. The authors state that the literature has demonstrated the effects of leadership on employee productivity; however, they highlight that evidence regarding employee well-being and health has frequently been omitted. Furthermore, they lament that where employee well-being outcomes are examined these are often conflated with job satisfaction which is clearly not a representative measure of health or well-being in any true sense. Therefore, the review was designed to overcome these shortfalls and examine health and well-being and how these may be impacted by leadership styles and behaviours. In line with the literature on good psychological conceptualisations of well-being they also examined a broader conceptualisation of well-being containing cognitive (evaluative/thought based) affective (emotional) and eudemonic (meaning in life) aspects. Critically this review examined which aspects of leadership behaviours led to specific health-based employee outcomes. The results indicated that transformational and transactional leadership were significantly and negatively related to bullying. Whereas authoritarian leadership was positively related to bullying. Furthermore, passive leadership styles seemed to be related to reduced well-being, particularly hedonic. One point highlighted in the review which is often overlooked concerned the potential longer-term negative impacts of initially positive outcomes. For example, the positive leadership styles reviewed would often lead to good initial outcomes such as empowering employees to take on increased responsibilities and lead to enhanced self-efficacy. However, over time these same behaviours could lead to reduced job satisfaction and greater stress due to further work demands and increased responsibilities (Inceoglu et al., 2018).

In a review of coping and stress among nurse managers Labrague et al. (2018) examined the literature to distil key components of stress and coping in nurse managers. This is important work as previous research indicates that roughly 62% of US nurse managers, in acute care, plan on leaving their positions within two to five years primarily as a result of stress and burnout (Warshawsky & Havens, 2014). The research aimed to distil key findings and themes relating to coping. Results indicated that high workloads were a main source of stress across multiple studies. Further sources of stress were a lack of resources to tackle issues and financial pressures. The review demonstrated consistent benefits of greater autonomy for decision-making and more social support. Thus, more decision-making autonomy was associated with less stress and better well-being. Furthermore, social support was associated with reduced stress and lower likelihood of leaving employment (Labrague et al., 2018). Therefore, leadership styles and behaviours which promote decision-making autonomy, better management of workloads and social support should reduce stress, burnout, and intentions to leave their current employment.

In a study investigating potential moderators of the relationship between leadership style and stress, Abbasi (2018) distributed questionnaires measuring role stress, general health, and leadership styles to 240 medical doctors in Pakistan. Using hierarchical multiple regression, the author demonstrated that transformational leadership was related significantly to reduced role stress, better general health and less laissez-fair leadership. Furthermore, laissez-fair leadership was related significantly to poorer general health and greater role stress. Further analysis demonstrated that role ambiguity and conflict were significantly associated with poorer general health, but role overload was not. The author concluded that adopting transformational leadership will reduce negative role stressors, which should lead to improved health of workers.

Studies have also examined the potential relationship between paternalism and employee stress (e.g. Lawal & Babalola, 2017). Paternalism is reflected in practices whereby managers are personally interested in the life of employees outside work and care about their general life well-being, akin to being a parent, the manager attempts to foster a better life for employees in both their professional and personal domains. Top et al. (2015) showed that paternalism was positively correlated with servant leadership at 0.73 and that both leadership styles were predictive of organisational commitment which measures employee satisfaction and involvement (Top et al., 2015).

Using a meta-analysis, Montano et al. (2017) investigated the effects of a variety of leadership styles on the mental health and productivity of followers. Several robust findings arose, destructive leadership (abusive practices, authoritarianism, manipulation, aggressiveness, and high degrees of narcissism) was consistently related to poor mental health outcomes in followers. Therefore, in the interests of a healthy workforce, organisations must work hard to prevent or minimise destructive leadership practices. Furthermore, transformational leadership practices (shared vision, consistent values and actions which confirm these, intellectual stimulation, and encouraging individual employee consideration) were related to positive mental health, improved well-being and demonstrated positive effects on work performance. Critically, the meta-analysis shows that leadership practices can be conceptualised as both preventative and ameliorative factors, but the impact on employee health can be positive or negative depending on the leadership style present (Montano et al., 2017).

In summary, leadership styles and behaviours do have an influence on well-being, health, and stress in workers. Furthermore, a recent review of organisational best practices in supporting mental health highlights eight factors, representative of best practice. Leadership support was among the eight factors and all of the remaining factors would be heavily influenced by leaders (Wu et al., 2021). Good quality positive leadership (e.g. transformational, servant, ethical, and charismatic) is consistently related to greater staff well-being and health. In turn abusive leadership is consistently related to poor staff outcomes. However, given the intercorrelated web of factors shown to impact on employee stress, it is likely that there are multiple interacting factors involved in outcomes at the level of staff well-being. For example, studies in nurses support the notion that workload, leadership style, professional conflict, emotional cost of caring, and poor communication between staff are the main sources of stress (McVicar, 2003; Nayomi, 2016).

4.2 Effects on Workplace Engagement/Job Satisfaction

Given the impact of leadership on stress cited above, it is also important to consider how leadership styles and behaviours may impact on workplace engagement and job satisfaction.

Job demands-resources theory is often used to explain various employee outcomes such as burnout and decreased well-being (Bakker & Demerouti, 2017; Bakker et al., 2004; Demerouti et al., 2001, 2019). Job demands are defined as physical, psychological, and social effort required at work and known to have costs to the individual. Job resources are defined as physical, psychological, and social help individuals receive or have, to achieve organisational goals, often through reducing demands. The theory suggests that job demands are the most important correlate of exhaustion and job resources are the most important correlate of disengagement. This is where higher demands lead to greater exhaustion, and fewer resources lead to disengagement. Furthermore, these theories have been supported in the literature (Breevaart & Bakker, 2018). The allocation of demands and resources will typically be determined by leaders.

Charismatic leadership has often been associated with, or seen as, a component of transformational leadership (Avolio et al., 1999). A mediational analysis by Babcock-Roberson and Strickland (2010) examined the impact of charismatic leadership style on organisational citizenship behaviours (behaviours that benefit the organisation despite not necessarily being formally required) and whether this relationship was mediated by work engagement. Charismatic leadership was related to greater work engagement in followers, which was in turn related to them being more likely to display higher levels of organisational citizenship behaviours. Results showed that this was a fully mediated model. Thus, charismatic leadership benefited the organisation and the individual worker. However, the percentage of variance accounted for in organisational citizenship behaviour by the model was relatively low (17%). Furthermore, the generalisability of the results is limited due to the study using a convenience sample of university students and the data being self-report. Given the low mean age of participants who were also studying at that time, it is unlikely this sample are sufficiently committed to their jobs and saw it merely as a means to generate money while studying.

Leadership style is seen to exert an influence on follower job performance by increasing job resources, job crafting, and work engagement. In addition, leadership style is also seen to impact on well-being by influencing job demands, job strain, and self-undermining, which can also influence job performance (Breevaart & Bakker, 2018). A number of studies provide evidence that transformational leadership is most likely to provide more job resources and decrease job demands (Breevaart et al., 2014; Fernet et al., 2015). Furthermore, use of positive leadership styles can promote seeing ones work as more meaningful, which has been shown to relate to greater work engagement (Lee et al., 2017).

A further study with important findings regarding work engagement comes from Shirey (2009). The study examined 21 nurse managers in the US and using a qualitative research design. The study distilled key factors associated with positive and negative organisational cultures based on the American Association of Critical-care Nurses standards for healthy work environments—namely—"skilled communication, true collaboration, effective decision making, appropriate staffing, meaningful recognition and authentic leadership" (AACN Standards for Establishing and Sustaining Healthy Work Environments: A Journey to Excellence, 2005, 2016; Ulrich et al., 2019). Shirey (2009) concluded that nurse managers receiving support in their roles were more optimistic and engaged, and that these provided benefits at all organisational levels as the effects cascaded throughout the organisation. In contrast, nurse managers reporting negative cultures showed exhaustion, often fighting the workplace culture to promote better practices resulting in disengagement and exhaustion.

Kim et al. (2018) examined the relationship between empowering leadership (granting employees greater autonomy and providing support) and subjective well-being in a large sample ($n = 1225$) of South Korean workers. They used social exchange theory positing that workplace relationships are preserved through meaningful exchange of rewards. The variables examined were—empowering leadership, perceived organisational support, perceived co-worker support, subjective well-being and work performance. Using hierarchical linear modelling they found that empowering leadership was significantly related to an increased perception of organisational and co-worker support. Furthermore, perceived organisational support was related positively to subjective well-being. However, modelling demonstrated that the effects of empowering leadership were mediated by perceived organisational and co-worker support. Critically, while empowering leadership was related indirectly to improved subjective well-being this was not the case for work performance (Kim et al., 2018).

Effects of authentic leadership on employee job satisfaction and well-being have also been examined (Rahimnia & Sharifirad, 2015). This study investigated 212 health care workers in Iran and examined the relationship between authentic leadership and three outcomes (job satisfaction, perceived work stress and stress symptoms) and whether this relationship was mediated by attachment insecurity. Results indicated that authentic leadership had direct positive effects on job satisfaction but indirect positive effects on perceived stress and stress symptoms mediated by secure attachment.

A further study investigated the relationship between stress and leadership and job satisfaction in 1973 nurses from 65 institutions (Bratt et al., 2000). Using multiple regression, they demonstrated that job stress explained 32% of the variance in job satisfaction, leadership explained a further 11%, group cohesion 6%. The authors conclude that job stress and leadership type are the most important variables contributing towards job satisfaction. The leadership style deemed helpful was a participative and empowering towards followers, more common in positive leadership.

In two qualitative analyses, Cummings et al. (2010, 2018) examined the effects of leadership style on job satisfaction in nurses. In the first (2010) they examined 53 studies via content analysis. Importantly 24 studies indicated that positive leadership styles such as Transformational were related to greater job satisfaction. In contrast, ten studies found that task focused leadership related to less job satisfaction. They suggest that nursing environments should implement positive leadership to improve employee outcomes. The second review (2018) examined 129 studies and found that 52 studies again reported that relational leadership styles related to improved job satisfaction, and in contrast 16 reported task focused leadership to relate to less job satisfaction. Furthermore, the second study also found that 13 studies reported staff well-being and health to be higher where relational leadership styles were used by management and lower where dissonant or laissez-fair leadership styles were in use (Cummings et al., 2010, 2018).

Mauno et al. (2016) examined emotional labour (EL) and work engagement in nurses. Emotional labour refers to professional expression of appropriate emotions when interacting with patients and staff (Hochschild, 1983). This can lead to negative outcomes as the expression of certain emotions and states must be suppressed. However, the authors suggest that certain coping resources can protect workers from the negative effects of EL if present. Suggested helpful resources are supportive leadership and good emotional regulation strategies. In the study on 3466 Finnish nurses, the potentially

13 Leadership Styles: Work Stress, Related Outcomes and Health   235

buffering effects of compassion, transformational leadership and work ethic feasibility were examined. Results indicated that EL was related to lower work engagement; however, high work ethic feasibility buffered this relationship. Importantly transformational leadership did not act as a buffer and compassion seemed to increase vulnerability in the face of high EL (Mauno et al., 2016).

Sow et al. (2017) examined leadership style, organisational culture and job satisfaction in the healthcare industry. They chose the healthcare industry as it is notable that less than 20% of the employees in these industries report being satisfied with their jobs (Allen et al., 2015). The authors suggest that two factors may positively impact job satisfaction and these are—transformational leadership and improving organisational culture. Organisational culture can be defined as belonging to four quadrants of the competing values framework (Quinn & Rohrbaugh, 1983), these are: externally focused and control oriented, externally focused and flexible, internally oriented and control oriented, and internally oriented and flexible. A great deal of work suggests workers prefer and report greater satisfaction where flexible structures operate (Breevaart & Bakker, 2018; Erskine & Georgiou, 2018). Thus, Sow et al. (2017) examined 111 employees at 17 health institutions in the US. They measured transformational leadership, job satisfaction, and organisational culture. Results indicated that transformational leadership was positively related to increased job satisfaction. Furthermore, transformational leadership significantly predicted job satisfaction in regression models also including gender, race, and age, which did not significantly predict job satisfaction. Where organisational culture was examined as a predictor of job satisfaction it was found that externally focused cultures (whether flexible or not) both significantly predicted reduced job satisfaction. The final analysis examined both organisational culture and transformational leadership as predictors of job satisfaction. The main finding being that externally oriented cultures reduced job satisfaction and transformational leadership had no effect beyond that of culture. Therefore, the main message was to foster internally oriented cultures to improve healthcare workers satisfaction.

As consistently demonstrated by the literature, the impact of leadership style on workplace engagement and job satisfaction is critical to foster workplace well-being. The evidence clearly suggests that positive leadership styles (transformational, ethical, servant, and empowering) are correlated with increased workplace engagement and that in general this relationship seems to mostly hold worldwide (Kim & Beehr, 2020; Li et al., 2021). However, leadership style is not the only factor that can influence workplace engagement (Alam et al., 2022).

4.3 Effects on Staff Turnover and Absenteeism

As can be seen from the literature reviewed in the previous sections, leadership styles and behaviours have an impact on staff well-being, stress, workplace engagement and satisfaction. While the literature has often focused on outcomes significant to the individual, the following section will examine staff turnover and absenteeism which are both individually and organisationally damaging.

In a qualitative review of studies examining staff outcomes in healthcare settings, transformational leadership was found to be associated with increased staff well-being and reduced burnout. Transformational leadership was related to higher staff satisfaction than alternative leadership styles (laisse faire, and transactional) (Weberg, 2010). This qualitative review of studies examined non-randomised control trails. However, studies are now starting to manipulate variables experimentally (Lyons & Schneider, 2009) and reporting that transformational leadership benefits worker productivity and leads to perceptions of greater support. Furthermore, studies have reported that transformational leadership that is empowering is related to lower turnover (Force, 2005). In health care nursing the follower's perception of the leadership style has an impact on satisfaction with leadership. Transformative leadership demonstrates better satisfaction ratings. This is critical as leadership satisfaction is one of the elements linked to nurse retention (Andrews et al., 2012). Furthermore, Pishgooie et al. (2019) report negative relationships between transactional and transformational leadership styles and intention to leave. Importantly the opposite relationship was found for laissez-faire leadership and turnover intention.

Ram and Prabhakar (2010) investigated the effects of leadership styles on job involvement and satisfaction, turnover and job stress in 310 employees in the telecommunications industry in Jordan. They reported that transformational leadership was significantly and positively related to work involvement and job satisfaction. Furthermore, it was significantly and negatively related to turnover intentions and job stress. However, transactional leadership was significantly and positively related to increased turnover intentions and increased job stress (albeit weakly). In addition, transactional leadership was significantly negatively associated with work involvement and satisfaction, although once again the correlations were much smaller than those found for transformational leadership. This suggests further evidence of the association of transformational behaviour with outcomes of significant benefit to workers and companies. This study considered job stress and turnover intentions as separate outcomes. However, job stress is likely to impact on turnover intentions. One study to examine the effects of job stress on turnover intentions was conducted by Elçi et al. (2012). They examined the effects of ethical leadership on employee turnover intentions and whether this was mediated by stress in 1093 participants from 70 different companies. They argue that ethical leaders aim to promote ethical behaviour in their followers, which typically involves being honest, trustworthy, caring, encouraging effective and open communication and promoting ethical conduct. The results demonstrated that ethical leadership was related to reduced stress and turnover intentions. However, work stress was positively related to turnover intentions. Furthermore, the results showed that work stress mediated the relationship between positive leadership styles and effective leader behaviours (ethical) and turnover intentions. The authors conclude that ethical leadership may be a style of leadership that can simultaneously reduce follower stress and decrease turnover intentions (Elçi et al., 2012).

One important study investigated another potential factor that might increase turnover intentions. Thus, Apostel et al. (2018) suggested that being asked to undertake an illegitimate task (unreasonable or violating workplace assumptions) should increase turnover intentions. This question was investigated in 235 German information technology workers. Results indicated that turnover intentions were generally increased in response to illegitimate tasks even when controlling for job satisfaction, time pressure and level of control over work. However, they report that appreciation of staff by leaders attenuates the relationship between illegitimate tasks and turnover intention (Apostel et al., 2018). Positive leadership styles are likely to lead to workers feeling more appreciated and therefore less likely to form intentions to leave.

The positive relationship between some leadership styles (e.g. laissez faire) and intention to leave has been shown to be mediated by less employee emotional commitment to the organisation (Robert & Vandenberghe, 2022).

4.4   Effects on Burnout

Burnout has been conceptualised as occurring when an individual progressively loses the ability to care about individuals they work with and the work itself in response to consistent stress over time (Maslach, 1978; Maslach et al., 2001). There are three key dimensions of burnout: (1) emotional exhaustion—where an individual feels they do not have sufficient resources to cope with the situation, feeling tired and drained; (2) cynicism—where the individual progressively detaches from other people and their work due to their negative attitude, often treating others more as objects than people; and (3) reduced personal efficacy—lack of work-based productivity and experience of personal incompetence with commensurate loss of meaning regarding work (Lee & Ok, 2012; Maslach et al., 2001; Maslach, 2003).

Many studies examining leadership and burnout had not focused sufficiently on the dyadic relationships between leaders and followers with little appreciation of how leaders create effective groups (where identity becomes collective) and how this impacts follower well-being outcomes. Steffens et al. (2018) conducted a study designed to overcome some of the limitations of earlier studies, and therefore examined how leaders promote the development of a shared collective group identity and the extent to which this influences well-being outcomes such as engagement in work, burnout, and turnover intentions. The authors argue that shared identity should have many positive effects such as increasing the sense of belonging, and increasing the likelihood of social support and self-efficacy. Theoretically, the authors suggest this should lead to reduced burnout. This study examined this in two waves of data collection from 141 participants employed at a solar panel manufacturing company in China. Data was collected via questionnaires measuring turnover intentions, burnout, work engagement and the extent to which leaders fostered team identity. Results indicated that leaders fostering group identity at time 1 predicted less burnout and greater work engagement ten months later at time 2. Further analysis indicated that the impact of leaders fostering group identity on intentions to leave were accounted for by the degree of burnout and work engagement. The authors therefore suggest that leaders promoting a sense of shared identity can lead to improvements in a variety of employee well-being outcomes (Steffens et al., 2018).

A study by Salem (2015) investigated transformational leadership, job stress and burnout in luxury hotels in Egypt via questionnaires. Results indicated significant a negative correlation between job stress and overall transformational leadership. Furthermore, all subcomponents of transformational leadership (Idealised influence, Individualised consideration, inspirational motivation and intellectual stimulation) also correlated significantly and negatively with job stress. Correlations ranged from -0.35 to -0.39. Additional analyses on burnout demonstrated that there were significant negative correlations between overall transformational leadership (including all subcomponents) and burnout with correlations ranging from -0.51 to -0.57. Although correlational, the results are in line with a wealth of evidence indicating negative associations between transformational leadership and both stress levels and burnout.

13 Leadership Styles: Work Stress, Related Outcomes and Health

Work stress is an important antecedent of employee outcomes, for example, turnover intentions, and is also related to burnout (Smith et al., 2018). Smith et al. (2018) examined work stress, work-family conflict, safety behaviour, and burnout in US firefighters. The data indicated that both work stress and work-family conflict were antecedents of burnout. Furthermore, work stress was positively and significantly associated with work-family conflict. Of note, burnout led to reduced safety behaviour in firefighters. Although specific to firefighters it is likely the relationship between burnout and work performance with regard to safety behaviour may be generalised to other industries. In short, once burnout leads to reduced care, this may impact on the safety of self and others.

A review of burnout in prison correctional officers using 43 studies across nine countries cited evidence of higher-than-expected burnout rates (Schaufeli & Peeters, 2000). Furthermore, rates of turnover, absenteeism, psychosomatic diseases, and negative job attitudes were higher than in other occupations. Importantly some of the key stressors identified could be related to managerial style, for example, lack of autonomy, high workload, lack of variety and skill use, inadequate pay, and safety issues. The review highlights that improving the social work environment, human resource management, and professionalism would lead to reductions in negative employee outcomes. Critically these factors are all related to leadership style, and therefore, addressing leadership style should reduce burnout.

Rivers et al. (2018) collected data from UK-based student unions examining effects of ethical leadership on workplace engagement and emotional exhaustion. Using a path modelling approach, they demonstrated that trust in managers led to greater work engagement and simultaneously reduced emotional exhaustion (a subcomponent of burnout). Critically an antecedent of managerial trust was ethical leadership. Thus, ethical leadership can reduce emotional exhaustion and improve work engagement.

Jiménez et al. (2017) investigated and developed a new instrument (Health Promoting Leadership Conditions HPLC) to assess health promoting leadership conditions. Seven key areas were identified as relating to a healthy workplace, these were, health awareness, workload, control opportunities, reward, community, fairness, and value discrepancy. Using structural equation modelling the authors showed that all seven dimensions could be combined to a single higher order factor which the authors labelled health promoting leadership. In addition, this factor was shown to have validity as all areas underpinning it related significantly and negatively to stress (Jiménez et al., 2017).

In an important review of 27 studies in the literature Kelly and Hearld (2020) examine the effects of leadership on burnout and its components in behavioural healthcare. They report that generally across the sample transformational leadership was negatively associated with emotional exhaustion and depersonalisation while simultaneously being positively related to personal accomplishment (Kelly & Hearld, 2020)

In a recent study Moriano et al. (2021) reconceptualised positive forms of leadership as providing resources which could help employees to cope with demands and stresses in the workplace. They term this as security providing leadership and argue it operates through two main routes: (1) as a contributing factor enhancing the sense of psychological safety, and (2) acting to reduce organisational dehumanisation or the sense that the organisation treats people merely as tools in the service of organisational goals (Caesens et al., 2017). The study from Moriano et al. (2021) investigated how leaders' security provisions in their model acted to influence burnout. Results indicated that psychological safety and organisational dehumanisation did indeed mediate the relationship between positive leadership and burnout. Thus, positive leadership contributes to workers feeling more like humans within a psychologically safe environment this in turn reduces burnout. Furthermore, Albendin-Garcia et al. (2021) also reviewed in detail 27 studies from the literature on burnout in midwives and concluded that the factors most protective against burnout were good leadership and using continuity models of care.

In conclusion stress is an important antecedent of burnout, and supportive leadership has been reported to consistently reduce the effects of burnout. However, once burnout develops, individuals and leaders disengage from the workplace and colleagues, making corrective interventions difficult.

4.5 Effects on Performance and Productivity

In an experimental study, Lyons and Schneider (2009) compared the impact of transformational, and two types of transactional leadership styles (transactional management by exception and transactional by contingent reward) on multiple outcomes before and after a stressful task. They demonstrated that transformational leadership led to improvements in task performance compared to transactional management by exception, but no difference between transactional by contingent reward. Furthermore, participants felt more socially supported when transformationally led than either transactional style. Task-specific self-efficacy was higher in followers of transformational leaders than transactional by exception, but it is unclear whether transformational produced reliable benefits above transactional by contingent reward. None of the leadership styles had an impact on positive affect. However, transactional styles resulted in increases in negative affect although this was not found for transformational leadership.

Firth-Cozens and Mowbray (2001) presented a review of leadership style and quality of care in healthcare settings and report that leaders can influence the safety of the teams they manage. They cite evidence from the airline industry showing that friendly, confident leaders had teams that made fewer error, and teams led by dictatorial leaders demonstrated higher error rates (Chidester et al., 1991). Of more direct applicability to healthcare, studies have found that teams with authoritarian leaders reported fewer medical errors whereas well-led, more relational teams reported more errors. However, these findings could reflect an underreporting of mistakes rather than improved performance for authoritarian leadership (Edmondson, 1996, 2004; Firth-Cozens & Mowbray, 2001). What is clear is that stress in healthcare settings has been demonstrated to lower patient care and result in worse patient outcomes (Farquharson et al., 2013; Firth-Cozens, 2001). Firth-Cozens and Mowbray (2001) suggest transformational leadership may improve the situation but note that this leadership style is difficult to instigate in an industry where transactional practices are more common, because outcomes are often prescribed in guidelines, targets are rigid and imposed from above, and accountability is paramount.

Findings from a recent study in the Indian IT industry also support this overall direction where they found that transformational leadership was strongly positively related to both team performance and organisational productivity (Jaroliya & Gyanchandani, 2021). Despite being based on self-report survey data, it adds to the view that productivity can be enhanced through positive leadership. In a similar study also conducted in the IT industry Syed et al. (2021) using qualitative methods report that transformational leadership was related to significant effects on employee performance. Furthermore, the findings suggested that in the fast changing IT industry it was important that transformational leadership stimulated innovation.

In a study examining effects of leadership on several outcomes, including productivity in the education ministry in Somaliland, results indicated that autocratic leadership was detrimental to departmental efficiency, leading to higher absenteeism and poor job satisfaction and morale. Importantly transformational leadership and democratic and disruptive leadership models had opposite effects being significantly related to greater performance (Setiawan et al., 2021).

Somewhat strangely demonstrable effects on organisational or individual employee performance are less researched in the wider literature. However, as demonstrated in this brief review, where they are examined the effects are largely consistent with productivity enhancements being associated with transformational leadership and productivity being damaged by autocratic leadership styles.

4.6 Effects on Leader Health

While multiple studies reviewed above show effects of leadership on follower health, intentions to leave, absenteeism, burnout, and productivity, only a few studies have examined the effects of leadership style on health of the leader themselves. One notable exception comes from Weiss et al. (2018). They examined the impact of authentic leadership on well-being in the leaders. Results indicated that authentic leadership benefitted leader well-being by reducing stress and increasing work engagement. Importantly these effects were mediated by follower interaction, with greater follower interaction leading to decreased psychological depletion in the leaders themselves. (Weiss et al., 2018). This was not found for laissez-faire leadership where follower interactions are already minimal.

In a review focusing on leader health while in a high stress role, Lovelace et al. (2007) suggest that leaders can benefit from encouraging self-leadership in followers—thus, the authors write: "A key aspect of this process is facilitating this capacity in others in order to reduce unnecessary demands on the leader" (Lovelace et al., 2007, p. 379). They advocate an empowering leadership approach which has been shown by other studies to result in benefits (Kim et al., 2018). They further advocate principals which can help leaders to cope with the demands of a high stress role, such as, becoming physically fit and developing greater engagement with work (Lovelace et al., 2007). A more recent meta-analysis has demonstrated that managers with participative/relational leadership styles were beneficial to leader health whereas destructive and laissez-faire styles were detrimental to leader well-being (Kaluza et al., 2020). Furthermore, studies have indicated positive relationships between leader well-being and follower well-being (Skakon et al., 2010).

4.7 Detrimental Leadership Styles and Behaviours

Having reviewed the literature examining the impact of leadership styles on follower health and productivity, the following section will examine what has been shown to be detrimental and non-working. While peripheral to the main aims of this review, it is important to briefly examine which leadership styles and behaviours may specifically be detrimental to followers.

13 Leadership Styles: Work Stress, Related Outcomes and Health 243

This is important as workplace bullying has consistently been related to negative employee outcomes such as work estrangement, job dissatisfaction, exhaustion, turnover intentions, and social exclusion (Aquino & Thau, 2009; Bowling & Beehr, 2006; Nielsen & Einarsen, 2012; Glambek et al., 2015; Laschinger et al., 2012).

Kelloway et al. (2005) review evidence regarding poor leadership practices. The evidence highlights that abusive leadership practices are related to lower job satisfaction, helplessness, alienation, poorer physical and mental health and higher stress. These abusive practices include, non-contingent punishment, punitive leaders that act aggressively, asking followers to work beyond their capacity, passive leaders, and those with inadequate leadership qualities.

Another form of detrimental leader behaviour is workplace bullying. Workplace bullying has also been related to multiple negative outcomes such as exclusion from work life (Glambek et al., 2015) and job dissatisfaction (Park & Ono, 2017; Montano et al., 2017). Malik et al. (2018) define bullying as "Bullying or belittling at workplace means niggling, insulting, neglecting, negatively disturbing and manoeuvring someone's work assignments" (p. 936). They examined the effect of bullying in 320 employees in the Punjab province. The study found support for a model whereby perceived psychological contract breaches mediated the relationship between bullying and increased turnover intentions and reduced organisational commitment (Malik et al., 2018).

Workplace bullying can arise in situations where leaders are not directly abusive. In a longitudinal study Ågotnes et al. (2018) investigated the role of laissez-faire leadership on workplace bullying in a sample of 1772 Norwegian workers. Laissez-faire leadership was a precursor to co-worker conflict, and co-worker conflict was related to greater bullying two years later. Thus, laissez-faire leadership increased the risk that conflict among workers would subsequently develop into full blown workplace bullying (Ågotnes et al., 2018). Furthermore, over a two-year period, poor leadership was shown to impact on the quality of the supportive workplace community and subsequent work engagement. Where these qualities have been shown to decrease, this results in an increase in the likelihood of workplace bullying (Francioli et al., 2018). Importantly, further longitudinal work suggests that a lack of supportive leadership can have negative impacts on self-rated health at ten-year follow-up in males even when controlling for health at baseline and job strain, lifestyle, and socioeconomic status (Schmidt et al., 2018).

Hauge and colleagues examined a large sample of over 10,000 Norwegian employees across 685 departments in 65 organisations. The study was interested in how different leadership styles and role stress predicted the level of workplace bullying. Results indicated that role ambiguity was not associated with bullying, but that leadership practices and role conflict accounted for 40% of the variance in bullying. Supportive leadership reduced the incidence of bullying (Hauge et al., 2011).

Given the nature and scope of the evidence reviewed, one can conclude that it is important to train leaders to adopt a transformational approach, which has been demonstrated to result in salutogenic behaviours towards followers (Nielsen & Daniels, 2012).

5   Conclusion

The present review has examined a wide variety of studies, reviews and meta-analyses all focusing on the effects of leadership style on several aspects of staff and corporate well-being, chiefly—stress, well-being, health, workplace engagement, job satisfaction, burnout, performance, productivity, and leader health.

Several crucial conclusions can be made at this juncture. First the overall quality of the evidence is weak due to factors such as the mainly correlational nature of most of the work. Second, it is clear there are large degrees of concept redundancy in the leadership literature. Third much of the literature and research designs are overreliant on self-report data collection. Having said that there are clear effects of leadership styles on outcomes that are evident. Although peripheral to the main aim of this review the strongest evidence exists for the almost ubiquitous detrimental effects of negative leadership forms. Thus, autocratic and laissez-faire leadership or those involving harmful practices such as bullying or harassment are all demonstrably related to more stress, less staff well-being and poor health. This in turn leads to more staff turnover, absenteeism, and burnout. In conjunction negative leadership styles are associated with less workplace engagement and job satisfaction. The performance outcomes for individuals and the organisation can only be negative given the sheer amount of overall negative outcomes.

When it comes to what works the evidence although somewhat weak and plagued by conceptual redundancy is clear on many points. For example, if one accepts that the positive leadership styles discussed in Sect. 2 of this review realistically correlate at above 0.70 and encompass broadly similar forms of leadership with subtle differences, making conclusions becomes easier. The literature repeatedly finds positive leadership styles such as transformational to be related to less stress, absenteeism, burnout, and staff turnover. Simultaneously positive leadership styles are related to better staff health, well-being, productivity, and general engagement/satisfaction.

Thus, in line with previous large-scale well-conducted literature reviews (Arnold, 2017) it is certainly the case that overall transformational leadership is associated with greater well-being and negatively associated with illness. Although the evidence base for effects of positive leadership forms on direct productivity outcomes is perhaps weakest, it would be obtuse to image that a healthier, more engaged and less stressed workforce could possibly produce worse outcomes in terms of productivity.

References

AACN Standards for Establishing and Sustaining Healthy Work Environments. (2005). *A journey to excellence.* American Association of Critical-Care Nurses. (May;14(3), pp. 187–197). PMID: 15840893.

AACN Standards for Establishing and Sustaining Healthy Work Environments. (2016). *A Journey to excellence* (2nd ed., pp. 187–197). American Association of Critical-Care Nurses.

Abbasi, S. G. (2018). Leadership styles: Moderating impact on job stress and health. *Journal of Human Resources Management Research, 2018,* 1–11.

Ågotnes, K. W., Einarsen, S. V., Hetland, J., & Skogstad, A. (2018). The moderating effect of laissez-faire leadership on the relationship between co-worker conflicts and new cases of workplace bullying: A true prospective design. *Human Resource Management Journal, 28,* 555–568.

Alam, J., Mendelson, M., Boamah, M. I., & Gauthier, M. (2022). Exploring the antecedents of employee engagement. *International Journal of Organizational Analysis.*

Albendin-García, L., Suleiman-Martos, N., Cañadas-De la Fuente, G. A., Ramírez-Baena, L., Gómez-Urquiza, J. L., & De la Fuente-Solana, E. I. (2021). Prevalence, related factors, and levels of burnout among midwives: A systematic review. *Journal of Midwifery & Women's Health, 66*(1), 24–44.

Allen, B. C., Holland, P., & Reynolds, R. (2015). The effect of bullying on burnout in nurses: the moderating role of psychological detachment. *Journal of Advanced Nursing, 71,* 381–390.

Andersen, J. A. (2018). Servant leadership and transformational leadership: From comparisons to farewells. *Leadership & Organization Development Journal, 39,* 762–774.

Andrews, D. R., Richard, D. C., Robinson, P., Celano, P., & Hallaron, J. (2012). The influence of staff nurse perception of leadership style on satisfaction with leadership: A cross-sectional survey of pediatric nurses. *International journal of nursing studies, 49,* 1103–1111.

Apostel, E., Syrek, C. J., & Antoni, C. H. (2018). Turnover intention as a response to illegitimate tasks: The moderating role of appreciative leadership. *International Journal of Stress Management, 25,* 234–249.

Aquino, K., & Thau, S. (2009). Workplace victimization: Aggression from the target's perspective. *Annual Review of Psychology, 60*, 717–741.

Arnold, K. A. (2017). Transformational leadership and employee psychological well-being: A review and directions for future research. *Journal of Occupational Health Psychology, 22*(3), 381–393.

Arnold, K. A., & Connelly, C. E. (2013). Transformational leadership and psychological well-being: Effects on followers and leaders. In *The Wiley-Blackwell handbook of the psychology of leadership, change, and organizational development* (pp. 175–194). Wiley.

Avolio, B. J., & Bass, B. M. (2004). Multifactor leadership questionnaire (MLQ). *Mind Garden, 29*.

Avolio, B. J., Bass, B. M., & Jung, D. I. (1999). Re-examining the components of transformational and transactional leadership using the Multifactor Leadership. *Journal of Occupational and Organizational Psychology, 72*, 441–462.

Avolio, B. J., & Gardner, W. L. (2005). Authentic leadership development: Getting to the root of positive forms of leadership. *The Leadership Quarterly, 16*, 315–338.

Avolio, B. J., Gardner, W. L., Walumbwa, F. O., Luthans, F., & May, D. R. (2004). Unlocking the mask: A look at the process by which authentic leaders impact follower attitudes and behaviors. *The Leadership Quarterly, 15*, 801–823.

Babcock-Roberson, M. E., & Strickland, O. J. (2010). The relationship between charismatic leadership, work engagement, and organizational citizenship behaviors. *The Journal of Psychology, 144*, 313–326.

Bakker, A. B., & Demerouti, E. (2017). Job demands–resources theory: Taking stock and looking forward. *Journal of Occupational Health Psychology, 22*, 273–285.

Bakker, A. B., Demerouti, E., & Verbeke, W. (2004). Using the job demands-resources model to predict burnout and performance. *Human Resource Management: Published in Cooperation with the School of Business Administration, The University of Michigan and in alliance with the Society of Human Resources Management, 43*, 83–104.

Banks, G. C., Gooty, J., Ross, R. L., Williams, C. E., & Harrington, N. T. (2018). Construct redundancy in leader behaviors: A review and agenda for the future. *The Leadership Quarterly, 29*, 236–251.

Banks, G. C., McCauley, K. D., Gardner, W. L., & Guler, C. E. (2016). A meta-analytic review of authentic and transformational leadership: A test for redundancy. *The Leadership Quarterly, 27*, 634–652.

Bass, B. M. (1985). *Leadership and performance beyond expectations*. Free Press.

Bass, B. M. (1997). Does the transactional–transformational leadership paradigm transcend organizational and national boundaries? *American Psychologist, 52*, 130–139.

Bass, B. M., & Riggio, R. E. (2006). *Transformational leadership*. Psychology Press.

Bormann, K. C., & Rowold, J. (2018). Construct proliferation in leadership style research: Reviewing pro and contra arguments. *Organizational Psychology Review, 8*, 149–173.

13 Leadership Styles: Work Stress, Related Outcomes and Health

Bowling, N. A., & Beehr, T. A. (2006). Workplace harassment from the victim's perspective: A theoretical model and meta-analysis. *Journal of Applied Psychology, 91*, 998–1012.

Bratt, M. M., Broome, M., Kelber, S. T., & Lostocco, L. (2000). Influence of stress and nursing leadership on job satisfaction of pediatric intensive care unit nurses. *American Journal of Critical Care, 9*, 307–317.

Breevaart, K., & Bakker, A. B. (2018). Daily job demands and employee work engagement: The role of daily transformational leadership behavior. *Journal of Occupational Health Psychology, 23*, 338–349.

Breevaart, K., Bakker, A. B., Demerouti, E., Sleebos, D. M., & Maduro, V. (2014). Uncovering the underlying relationship between transformational leaders and followers' task performance. *Journal of Personnel Psychology, 13*, 194–203.

Brown, M. E., & Treviño, L. K. (2006). Ethical leadership: A review and future directions. *The Leadership Quarterly, 17*, 595–616.

Brown, M. E., Treviño, L. K., & Harrison, D. A. (2005). Ethical leadership: A social learning perspective for construct development and testing. *Organizational Behavior and Human Decision Processes, 97*, 117–134.

Burns, J. M. (1978). *Leadership*. Harper & Row.

Caesens, G., Stinglhamber, F., Demoulin, S., & De Wilde, M. (2017). Perceived organizational support and employees' well-being: The mediating role of organizational dehumanization. *European Journal of Work and Organizational Psychology, 26*, 527–540.

Chidester, T. R., Helmreich, R. L., Gregorich, S. E., & Geis, C. E. (1991). Pilot personality and crew coordination: Implications for training and selection. *The International Journal of Aviation Psychology, 1*, 25–44.

Chughtai, A., Byrne, M., & Flood, B. (2015). Linking ethical leadership to employee well-being: The role of trust in supervisor. *Journal of Business Ethics, 128*, 653–663.

Cummings, G. G., MacGregor, T., Davey, M., Lee, H., Wong, C. A., Lo, E., Muise, M., & Stafford, E. (2010). Leadership styles and outcome patterns for the nursing workforce and work environment: A systematic review. *International Journal of Nursing Studies, 47*, 363–385.

Cummings, G. G., Tate, K., Lee, S., Wong, C. A., Paananen, T., Micaroni, S. P., & Chatterjee, G. E. (2018). Leadership styles and outcome patterns for the nursing workforce and work environment: A systematic review. *International Journal of Nursing Studies, 85*, 19–60.

Dansereau, F., Jr., Cashman, J., & Graen, G. (1973). Instrumentality theory and equity theory as complementary approaches in predicting the relationship of leadership and turnover among managers. *Organizational Behavior and Human Performance, 10*, 184–200.

Demerouti, E., Bakker, A. B., Nachreiner, F., & Schaufeli, W. B. (2001). The job demands-resources model of burnout. *Journal of Applied Psychology, 86*, 499–512.

Demerouti, E., Peeters, M. C., & van den Heuvel, M. (2019). Job crafting interventions: Do they work and why? In *Positive psychological intervention design and protocols for multi-cultural contexts* (pp. 103–125). Springer.

Diener, E. (1984). Subjective well-being. *Psychological Bulletin, 95*, 542–575.

Edmondson, A. C. (1996). Learning from mistakes is easier said than done: Group and organizational influences on the detection and correction of human error. *The Journal of Applied Behavioral Science, 32*, 5–28.

Edmondson, A. C. (2004). Learning from mistakes is easier said than done: Group and organizational influences on the detection and correction of human error. *The Journal of Applied Behavioral Science, 40*, 66–90.

Elçi, M., Şener, İ., Aksoy, S., & Alpkan, L. (2012). The impact of ethical leadership and leadership effectiveness on employees' turnover intention: The mediating role of work related stress. *Procedia-Social and Behavioral Sciences, 58*, 289–297.

Erskine, J. A. K., & Georgiou, G. J. (2018). Leadership styles: Employee stress, well-being, productivity, turnover and absenteeism. In Ph. Fauquet-Alekhine (ed.) *Understanding stress at work*. Larsen editions. http://hayka-kultura.org/larsen.html

Eva, N., Robin, M., Sendjaya, S., van Dierendonck, D., & Liden, R. C. (2019). Servant leadership: A systematic review and call for future research: The leadership quarterly yearly review for 2019. *The Leadership Quarterly, 30*, 111–132.

Faragher, E. B., Cass, M., & Cooper, C. L. (2005). The relationship between job satisfaction and health: A meta-analysis. *Occupational and Environmental Medicine, 62*, 105–112.

Faragher, E. B., Cass, M., & Cooper, C. L. (2013). The relationship between job satisfaction and health: a meta-analysis. In *From stress to wellbeing volume 1* (pp. 254–271). Palgrave Macmillan.

Farquharson, B., Bell, C., Johnston, D., Jones, M., Schofield, P., Allan, J., Ricketts, I., Morrison, K., & Johnston, M. (2013). Nursing stress and patient care: Real-time investigation of the effect of nursing tasks and demands on psychological stress, physiological stress, and job performance: Study protocol. *Journal of Advanced Nursing, 69*, 2327–2335.

Fauquet-Alekhine, P., Geeraerts, T., & Rouillac, L. (2014). Characterization of anesthetists' behavior during simulation training: Performance versus stress achieving medical tasks with or without physical effort. *Psychology and Social Behavior Research, 2*(2), 20–28.

Fernet, C., Trépanier, S. G., Austin, S., Gagné, M., & Forest, J. (2015). Transformational leadership and optimal functioning at work: On the mediating role of employees' perceived job characteristics and motivation. *Work & Stress, 29*, 11–31.

Firth-Cozens, J. (2001). Interventions to improve physicians' well-being and patient care. *Social Science & Medicine, 52*, 215–222.

Firth-Cozens, J., & Mowbray, D. (2001). Leadership and the quality of care. *BMJ Quality & Safety, 10*(Suppl. 2), ii3–ii7.

Force, M. V. (2005). The relationship between effective nurse managers and nursing retention. *Journal of Nursing Administration, 35*, 336–341.

Francioli, L., Conway, P. M., Hansen, Å. M., Holten, A. L., Grynderup, M. B., Persson, R., Mikkelsen, E. G., Costa, G., & Høgh, A. (2018). Quality of leadership and workplace bullying: The mediating role of social community at work in a two-year follow-up study. *Journal of Business Ethics, 147*, 889–899.

French, J. R., Caplan, R. D., & Van Harrison, R. (1982). *The mechanisms of job stress and strain* (Vol. 7). J. Wiley.

Fuller, B., Bajaba, A., & Bajaba, S. (2022). Enhancing and extending the meta-analytic comparison of newer genre leadership forms. *Frontiers in Psychology, 13*, 872568.

Gardner, W. L., Karam, E. P., Alvesson, M., & Einola, K. (2021). Authentic leadership theory: The case for and against. *The Leadership Quarterly, 32*(6), 101495.

Gerstner, C. R., & Day, D. V. (1997). Meta-Analytic review of leader–member exchange theory: Correlates and construct issues. *Journal of Applied Psychology, 82*, 827.

Ghasabeh, M. S., Soosay, C., & Reaiche, C. (2015). The emerging role of transformational leadership. *The Journal of Developing Areas, 49*, 459–467.

Glambek, M., Skogstad, A., & Einarsen, S. (2015). Take it or leave: A five-year prospective study of workplace bullying and indicators of expulsion in working life. *Industrial Health, 53*, 160–170.

Graen, G. B., & Uhl-Bien, M. (1995). Relationship-based approach to leadership: Development of leader-member exchange (LMX) theory of leadership over 25 years: Applying a multi-level multi-domain perspective. *The Leadership Quarterly, 6*, 219–247.

Grant, A. M., Christianson, M. K., & Price, R. H. (2007). Happiness, health, or relationships? Managerial practices and employee well-being trade-offs. *Academy of Management Perspectives, 21*, 51–63.

Grant, P., & McGhee, P. (2021). Hedonic versus (true) eudaimonic well-being in organizations. In *The Palgrave Handbook of Workplace Well-being* (pp. 925–943). Palgrave Macmillan.

Greenleaf, R. K. (1977). *Servant leadership: A journey into the nature of legitimate power and greatness*. Paulist Press.

Hammen, C. (2005). Stress and depression. *Annual Review of Clinical Psychology, 1*, 293–319.

Harms, P. D., Credé, M., Tynan, M., Leon, M., & Jeung, W. (2017). Leadership and stress: A meta-analytic review. *The Leadership Quarterly, 28*, 178–194.

Harms, P. D., & Spain, S. M. (2015). Beyond the bright side: Dark personality at work. *Applied Psychology, 64*, 15–24.

Harter, S. (2002). Authenticity. In C. R. Snyder & S. J. Lopez (Eds.), *Handbook of positive psychology* (pp. 382–394). Oxford University Press.

Hauge, L. J., Einarsen, S., Knardahl, S., Lau, B., Notelaers, G., & Skogstad, A. (2011). Leadership and role stressors as departmental level predictors of workplace bullying. *International Journal of Stress Management, 18*, 305–323.

Hoch, J. E., Bommer, W. H., Dulebohn, J. H., & Wu, D. (2018). Do ethical, authentic, and servant leadership explain variance above and beyond transformational leadership? A meta-analysis. *Journal of Management, 44*, 501–529.

Hochschild, A. R. (1983). *The managed heart*. University of California Press.

Inceoglu, I., Thomas, G., Chu, C., Plans, D., & Gerbasi, A. (2018). Leadership behavior and employee well-being: An integrated review and a future research agenda. *The Leadership Quarterly, 29*, 179–202.

Jaroliya, D., & Gyanchandani, R. (2021). Transformational leadership style: A boost or hindrance to team performance in IT sector. *Vilakshan-XIMB Journal of Management*.

Jiménez, P., Winkler, B., & Bregenzer, A. (2017). Developing sustainable workplaces with leadership: Feedback about organizational working conditions to support leaders in health-promoting behavior. *Sustainability, 9*, 1944.

Kaluza, A. J., Boer, D., Buengeler, C., & van Dick, R. (2020). Leadership behaviour and leader self-reported well-being: A review, integration and meta-analytic examination. *Work & Stress, 34*(1), 34–56.

Kelloway, E. K., Sivanathan, N., Francis, L., & Barling, J. (2005). Poor leadership. In I. J. Barling, E. K. Kelloway, & M. R. Frone (Eds.), *Handbook of work stress* (pp. 89–112). Sage.

Kelly, R. J., & Hearld, L. R. (2020). Burnout and leadership style in behavioral health care: A literature review. *The Journal of Behavioral Health Services & Research, 47*(4), 581–600.

Kim, D., Moon, C. W., & Shin, J. (2018). Linkages between empowering leadership and subjective well-being and work performance via perceived organizational and co-worker support. *Leadership & Organization Development Journal, 39*, 844–858.

Kim, M., & Beehr, T. A. (2020). Empowering leadership: Leading people to be present through affective organizational commitment? *The International Journal of Human Resource Management*, 31, 1–28.

Koinig, I., & Diehl, S. (2021). Healthy leadership and workplace health promotion as a pre-requisite for organizational health. *International Journal of Environmental Research and Public Health, 18*(17), 9260.

Labrague, L. J., McEnroe-Petitte, D. M., Leocadio, M. C., Van Bogaert, P., & Cummings, G. G. (2018). Stress and ways of coping among nurse managers: An integrative review. *Journal of Clinical Nursing, 27*, 1346–1359.

Laschinger, H. K. S., Wong, C. A., & Grau, A. L. (2012). The influence of authentic leadership on newly graduated nurses' experiences of workplace bullying, burnout and retention outcomes: A cross-sectional study. *International Journal of Nursing Studies, 49*, 1266–1276.

Lawal, O. A., & Babalola, S. S. (2017). Moderating roles of leadership effectiveness and job stress on relationship between paternalism and leadership-induced stress. *International Journal of Engineering Business Management, 9*, 1–10.

Lazarus, R. S., & Folkman, S. (1984). Coping and adaptation. In W. D. Gentry (Ed.), *The Handbook of behavioral medicine* (pp. 282–325). Guilford.

Lee, J. J., & Ok, C. (2012). Reducing burnout and enhancing job satisfaction: Critical role of hotel employees' emotional intelligence and emotional labor. *International Journal of Hospitality Management, 31*, 1101–1112.

Lee, M. C. C., Idris, M. A., & Delfabbro, P. H. (2017). The linkages between hierarchical culture and empowering leadership and their effects on employees' work engagement: Work meaningfulness as a mediator. *International Journal of Stress Management, 24*, 392–415.

Lemoine, G. J., Hartnell, C. A., & Leroy, H. (2019). Taking stock of moral approaches to leadership: An integrative review of ethical, authentic, and servant leadership. *Academy of Management Annals, 13*(1), 148–187.

Li, P., Sun, J. M., Taris, T. W., Xing, L., & Peeters, M. C. (2021). Country differences in the relationship between leadership and employee engagement: A meta-analysis. *The Leadership Quarterly, 32*(1), 101458.

Liden, R. C., & Antonakis, J. (2009). Considering context in psychological leadership research. *Human Relations, 62*, 1587–1605.

Liden, R. C., Sparrowe, R. T., & Wayne, S. J. (1997). Leader-member exchange theory: The past and potential for the future. *Research in Personnel and Human Resources Management, 15*, 47–120.

Liu, J., Kwan, H. K., Fu, P. P., & Mao, Y. (2013). Ethical leadership and job performance in China: The roles of workplace friendships and traditionality. *Journal of Occupational and Organizational Psychology, 86*, 564–584.

Liu, J., Siu, O. L., & Shi, K. (2010). Transformational leadership and employee well-being: The mediating role of trust in the leader and self-efficacy. *Applied Psychology, 59*, 454–479.

Lovelace, K. J., Manz, C. C., & Alves, J. C. (2007). Work stress and leadership development: The role of self-leadership, shared leadership, physical fitness and flow in managing demands and increasing job control. *Human Resource Management Review, 17*, 374–387.

Luthans, F., & Avolio, B. J. (2003). Authentic leadership: A positive developmental approach. In K. S. Cameron, J. E. Dutton, & R. E. Quinn (Eds.), *Positive organizational scholarship* (pp. 241–261).

Lyons, J. B., & Schneider, T. R. (2009). The effects of leadership style on stress outcomes. *The Leadership Quarterly, 20*, 737–748.

MacKay, C. J., Cousins, R., Kelly, P. J., Lee, S., & McCaig, R. H. (2004). "Management Standards" and work-related stress in the UK: Policy background and science. *Work & Stress, 18*, 91–112.

Madlock, P. E. (2008). The link between leadership style, communicator competence, and employee satisfaction. *The Journal of Business Communication, 1973*(45), 61–78.

Malik, M. S., Sattar, S., & Yaqub, R. M. S. (2018). Mediating role of psychological contract breach between workplace bullying, organizational commitment & employee turnover intentions. *Pakistan Journal of Commerce and Social Sciences (PJCSS), 12*, 935–952.

Martin, R., Guillaume, Y., Thomas, G., Lee, A., & Epitropaki, O. (2016). Leader–member exchange (LMX) and performance: A meta-analytic review. *Personnel Psychology, 69*, 67–121.

Maslach, C. (1978). Job burnout: How people cope. *Public Welfare, 36*, 56–58.

Maslach, C. (2003). Job burnout: New directions in research and intervention. *Current Directions in Psychological Science, 12*, 189–192.

Maslach, C., Schaufeli, W. B., & Leiter, M. P. (2001). Job burnout. *Annual Review of Psychology, 52*, 397–422.

Mauno, S., Ruokolainen, M., Kinnunen, U., & De Bloom, J. (2016). Emotional labour and work engagement among nurses: examining perceived compassion, leadership and work ethic as stress buffers. *Journal of Advanced Nursing, 72*, 1169–1181.

Mayer, D. M., Aquino, K., Greenbaum, R. L., & Kuenzi, M. (2012). Who displays ethical leadership, and why does it matter? An examination of antecedents and consequences of ethical leadership. *Academy of Management Journal, 55*, 151–171.

McMahan, E. A., & Estes, D. (2011). Hedonic versus eudaimonic conceptions of well-being: Evidence of differential associations with self-reported well-being. *Social Indicators Research, 103*, 93–108.

McVicar, A. (2003). Workplace stress in nursing: a literature review. *Journal of Advanced Nursing, 44*, 633–642.

Montano, D., Reeske, A., Franke, F., & Hüffmeier, J. (2017). Leadership, followers' mental health and job performance in organizations: A comprehensive meta-analysis from an occupational health perspective. *Journal of Organizational Behavior, 38*, 327–350.

Moriano, J. A., Molero, F., Laguía, A., Mikulincer, M., & Shaver, P. R. (2021). Security providing leadership: A job resource to prevent employees' burnout. *International Journal of Environmental Research and Public Health, 18*(23), 12551.

Muris, P., Merckelbach, H., Otgaar, H., & Meijer, E. (2017). The malevolent side of human nature: A meta-analysis and critical review of the literature on the dark triad (narcissism, Machiavellianism, and psychopathy). *Perspectives on Psychological Science, 12*, 183–204.

Nayomi, W. V. P. N. (2016). Workplace stress in nursing: A literature review. "*Social Statistics,*". *Journal of Social Statistics, 03*, 47–53.

Nielsen, K., & Daniels, K. (2012). Does shared and differentiated transformational leadership predict followers' working conditions and well-being? *The Leadership Quarterly, 23*, 383–397.

Nielsen, M. B., & Einarsen, S. (2012). Outcomes of exposure to workplace bullying: A meta-analytic review. *Work & Stress, 26*, 309–332.

Park, J. H., & Ono, M. (2017). Effects of workplace bullying on work engagement and health: The mediating role of job insecurity. *The International Journal of Human Resource Management, 28*, 3202–3225.

Piccolo, R. F., Greenbaum, R., Hartog, D. N. D., & Folger, R. (2010). The relationship between ethical leadership and core job characteristics. *Journal of Organizational Behavior, 31*, 259–278.

Pishgooie, A. H., Atashzadeh-Shoorideh, F., Falcó-Pegueroles, A., & Lotfi, Z. (2019). Correlation between nursing managers' leadership styles and nurses' job stress and anticipated turnover. *Journal of Nursing Management, 27*(3), 527–534.

13 Leadership Styles: Work Stress, Related Outcomes and Health 253

Quick, J., & Henderson, D. (2016). Occupational stress: Preventing suffering, enhancing wellbeing. *International Journal of Environmental Research and Public Health, 13*, 459.

Quick, J. C., & Cooper, C. L. (2003). *Stress and strain.* Health Press.

Quinn, R. E., & Rohrbaugh, J. (1983). A spatial model of effectiveness criteria: Towards a competing values approach to organizational analysis. *Management Science, 29*(3), 363–377.

Rahimnia, F., & Sharifirad, M. S. (2015). Authentic leadership and employee wellbeing: The mediating role of attachment insecurity. *Journal of Business Ethics, 132*, 363–377.

Ram, P., & Prabhakar, G. V. (2010). Leadership styles and perceived organizational politics as predictors of work related outcomes. *European Journal of Social Sciences, 15*, 40–55.

Resick, C. J., Hanges, P. J., Dickson, M. W., & Mitchelson, J. K. (2006). A cross-cultural examination of the endorsement of ethical leadership. *Journal of Business Ethics, 63*, 345–359.

Rivers, J., Thompson, N., & Jeske, D. (2018). Dedicated but exhausted? The role of ethical leadership for employee wellbeing in UK student unions. *Journal of Human Resource Management, XXI*, 16–27.

Robert, V., & Vandenberghe, C. (2022, July). Laissez-faire Leadership and turnover: The role of employee's organizational identity threat. In *Academy of management proceedings*. Academy of Management.

Salem, I. E. B. (2015). Transformational leadership: Relationship to job stress and job burnout in five-star hotels. *Tourism and Hospitality Research, 15*, 240–253.

Sarros, J. C., Tanewski, G. A., Winter, R. P., Santora, J. C., & Densten, I. L. (2002). Work alienation and organizational leadership. *British Journal of Management, 13*, 285–304.

Schaufeli, W. B., & Peeters, M. C. (2000). Job stress and burnout among correctional officers: A literature review. *International Journal of Stress Management, 7*, 19–48.

Schmidt, B., Herr, R. M., Jarczok, M. N., Baumert, J., Lukaschek, K., Emeny, R. T., Landwig, K., & Investigators, K. O. R. A. (2018). Lack of supportive leadership behavior predicts suboptimal self-rated health independent of job strain after 10 years of follow-up: Findings from the population-based MONICA/KORA study. *International Archives of Occupational and Environmental Health, 91*, 623–631.

Schyns, B., & Schilling, J. (2013). How bad are the effects of bad leaders? A meta-analysis of destructive leadership and its outcomes. *The Leadership Quarterly, 24*, 138–158.

Selye, H. (1959). Perspectives in stress research. *Perspectives in Biology and Medicine, 2*, 403–416.

Sendjaya, S., Pekerti, A., Härtel, C., Hirst, G., & Butarbutar, I. (2016). Are authentic leaders always moral? The role of Machiavellianism in the relationship between authentic leadership and morality. *Journal of Business Ethics, 133*, 125–139.

Setiawan, R., Cavaliere, L. P. L., Navarro, E. R., Wisetsri, W., Jirayus, P., Chauhan, S., Tabuena, A. C., & Rajan, R. (2021). The impact of leadership styles on employees productivity in organizations: A comparative study among leadership styles. *Productivity Management, 26*(1), 382–404.

Shaffer, J. A., DeGeest, D., & Li, A. (2016). Tackling the problem of construct proliferation: A guide to assessing the discriminant validity of conceptually related constructs. *Organizational Research Methods, 19*, 80–110.

Shirey, M. R. (2006). Authentic leaders creating healthy work environments for nursing practice. *American Journal of Critical Care, 15*, 256–267.

Shirey, M. R. (2009). Authentic leadership, organizational culture, and healthy work environments. *Critical Care Nursing Quarterly, 32*, 189–198.

Skakon, J., Nielsen, K., Borg, V., & Guzman, J. (2010). Are leaders' well-being, behaviours and style associated with the affective well-being of their employees? A systematic review of three decades of research. *Work & Stress, 24*, 107–139.

Smith, T. D., Hughes, K., DeJoy, D. M., & Dyal, M. A. (2018). Assessment of relationships between work stress, work-family conflict, burnout and firefighter safety behavior outcomes. *Safety Science, 103*, 287–292.

Sow, M., Murphy, J., & Osuoha, R. (2017). The relationship between leadership style, organizational culture, and job satisfaction in the US healthcare industry. *Management and Economics Research Journal, 3*, 1–10.

Steffens, N. K., Peters, K., Haslam, S. A., & van Dick, R. (2017). Dying for charisma: Leaders' inspirational appeal increases post-mortem. *The Leadership Quarterly, 28*, 530–542.

Steffens, N. K., Yang, J., Jetten, J., Haslam, S. A., & Lipponen, J. (2018). The unfolding impact of leader identity entrepreneurship on burnout, work engagement, and turnover intentions. *Journal of Occupational Health Psychology, 23*, 373–387.

Stone, A. G., Russell, R. F., & Patterson, K. (2003). Transformational versus servant leadership—a difference in leader focus. *The Leadership & Organisational Development Journal, 25*, 349–361.

Sy, T., Horton, C., & Riggio, R. (2018). Charismatic leadership: Eliciting and channeling follower emotions. *The Leadership Quarterly, 29*, 58–69.

Syed, O. R., Gilal, A. R., Gilal, M. Y., Abro, R. A., Abbass, H., Soomro, A. W., & Yuting, Y. (2021). *Influence of leadership styles on motivation and productivity of employees: A study on Chinese it firms.* University of Sindh Journal of Information and Communication Technology.

Top, S., Öge, E., Atan, Ö., & Gümüş, S. (2015). Investigation relational levels of intensity between paternalistic and servant leadership styles and national culture, organizational commitment and subordinate responses or reactions to the leaders style. *Procedia-Social and Behavioral Sciences, 181*, 12–22.

Treviño, L. K., Brown, M., & Hartman, L. P. (2003). A qualitative investigation of perceived executive ethical leadership: Perceptions from inside and outside the executive suite. *Human Relations, 56*, 5–37.

Ulrich, B., Barden, C., Cassidy, L., & Varn-Davis, N. (2019). Critical care nurse work environments 2018: Findings and implications. *Critical Care Nurse, 39*, 67–84.

Van Dierendonck, D. (2011). Servant leadership: A review and synthesis. *Journal of Management, 37*, 1228–1261.

Van Dierendonck, D., Stam, D., Boersma, P., De Windt, N., & Alkema, J. (2014). Same difference? Exploring the differential mechanisms linking servant leadership and transformational leadership to follower outcomes. *The Leadership Quarterly, 25*, 544–562.

Vanhoutte, B., & Nazroo, J. (2014). Cognitive, affective and eudemonic well-being in later life: Measurement equivalence over gender and life stage. *Sociological Research Online, 19*, 1–14.

Warshawsky, N. E., & Havens, D. S. (2014). Nurse manager job satisfaction and intent to leave. *Nursing Economic, 32*, 32–39.

Weberg, D. (2010). Transformational leadership and staff retention: An evidence review with implications for healthcare systems. *Nursing Administration Quarterly, 34*, 246–258.

Weiss, M., Razinskas, S., Backmann, J., & Hoegl, M. (2018). Authentic leadership and leaders' mental well-being: An experience sampling study. *The Leadership Quarterly, 29*, 309–321.

Wu, A., Roemer, E. C., Kent, K. B., Ballard, D. W., & Goetzel, R. Z. (2021). Organizational best practices supporting mental health in the workplace. *Journal of Occupational and Environmental Medicine, 63*(12), e925.

Yukl, G. (1999). An evaluation of conceptual weaknesses in transformational and charismatic leadership theories. *The Leadership Quarterly, 10*, 285–305.

14

Leadership Styles, Related Outcomes and Practical Suggestions

James Erskine and George Georgiou

1 Introduction

The previous chapter reviewed the evidence regarding the effects of leadership style on multiple employee and company outcomes. The outcomes were clear, there are issues regarding the quality of study designs and operationalisation of the key constructs such as how many leadership types there are. These issues weaken some of the arguments as does the overreliance on correlational methods and self-report data. Having said that, the literature is largely in agreement that negative forms of leadership (autocratic, laissez faire, punitive) are extremely detrimental to staff health and well-being. In addition, the literature is consistent in its demonstration that positive forms of leadership such as transformational and more relational leadership forms have consistent benefits which can be demonstrated via metrics such as reduced stress, burnout, staff turnover and absenteeism while simultaneously increasing well-being, productivity and work commitment.

J. Erskine (✉)
London Hertfordshire Therapy Centre, London, UK

St George's University of London, London, UK
e-mail: jerskine@sgul.ac.uk

G. Georgiou
University of Hertfordshire, Hatfield, UK
e-mail: g.j.georgiou@herts.ac.uk

© The Author(s), under exclusive license to Springer Nature Switzerland AG 2023
P. Fauquet-Alekhine, J. Erskine (eds.), *The Palgrave Handbook of Occupational Stress*,
https://doi.org/10.1007/978-3-031-27349-0_14

The purpose of the present chapter is to take the key messages resulting from the previous chapter and to distil these into practical advice for organisations, leaders and followers.

2 Key Advice for Organisations

As a priority, organisations should seek to address detrimental leadership practices first, before subsequently trying to instil positive leadership behaviours as the negative effects of detrimental leadership are larger than the positive benefits of supportive leadership on a variety of follower outcomes (see previous chapter). These supportive leadership styles should seek to foster and value relationships (customers, staff, management), autonomy, engagement, creativity, inspiration and authenticity. In most industries greater follower satisfaction with leadership will result in a healthier workforce, which will in turn benefit the organisation.

Organisations may have positive leadership, but while this is necessary, it may be insufficient on its own to deliver optimal outcomes, if the overall ethos and culture is detrimental, toxic or resistant to new practice. Therefore, organisations need to enable systemic changes in their culture to be congruent with positive leadership. In addition, transformational leaders may not flourish in "poor-fit" environments. It is appreciated that organisational change requires time, given the temporal nature of leadership development and change of culture, there may be short-term productivity or economic losses during the period of change or development (tension of economic return vs. change). However, in the longer term, these changes will increase employee well-being, productivity and ultimately profitability. Recent evidence demonstrates that supportive leadership can lead to a more resilient workforce (see Chap. 13 of the present book; also Cooke et al., 2019).

Organisations should also take note of evidence suggesting the impact of leadership styles on different generations of workers. A study by Anderson et al. (2017) examined the effects of leadership styles on different generations of workers, comparing millennials and previous generations (Generation X, Baby boomers) in the workforce. A literature search identified several differences between millennials and previous generations such as a greater desire for supportive managers, a desire for greater work life balance and more thought regarding themselves in the workplace (Twenge, 2010; Twenge & Campbell, 2009; Ng et al., 2010). The authors review the evidence on five common leadership styles and examine how these fit with changing priorities with reference to millennial workers. They suggest that given millennials see work as less central to their self-concept than the previous two generations (Twenge & Kasser, 2013) then they may struggle with transformational leadership style of trying to motivate individuals to be concerned with organisational goals and aspirations apart from their personal goals. The authors further suggest that the LMX model will be less impactful as millennials see building social relationships at work and teamwork as less impactful given their tendency to be more individualistic. Similarly, the focus of intrinsic values in authentic leadership may be less well received because of millennials greater focus on extrinsic rewards and individualism (Anderson et al., 2017; Kupperschmidt, 2000). Organisations therefore need to consider the changing characteristics and needs of the younger workforce.

Another consideration facing both organisations and leaders represents digital transformation and technological shifts such as the move to more remote ways of working. These factors are crucial to consider as the world undergoes a digital transformation (Porfírio et al., 2021). Exactly how this transition is managed and orchestrated will have key bearings on staff well-being. Periods of transition are notorious for their disruptive potential on industry but also for their potential to destabilise well-being in the workforce. Porfírio et al. (2021) conducted a review examining digital transformation in 47 Portuguese companies using multilevel modelling. The outcomes of relevance to the current chapter concerned that they found leadership to have a crucial role in implementation chiefly in ensuring coherence to the companies' mission and communicating this effectively. The paper was largely silent on how these transformations affect employee well-being. Therefore, it is now vital research starts to investigate the effect of digital transformation on new ways of working and employee well-being outcomes.

One study to investigate how workplace digital transformation may affect staff comes from Bregenzer and Jimenez (2021). They examined data from 1412 employees in Europe via an online study looking at perceived risks in the workplace, leadership behaviours that promoted health, resources and work stress. They reported four factors of digital work to be related to higher work stress; these were: distributed teamwork, mobile work, constant availability and inefficient technical support. Importantly when examining the effects of leadership on these factors it was found that health promoting leadership could only reduce some of these stressors; thus, the authors suggest that leadership needs to adapt as the adoption of digitalisation progresses to make sure staff well-being is preserved.

At this juncture the advice for organisation could be summarised as follows: Tackle negative forms of leadership first with a view to making them a relic of the past, second instil positive leadership forms from the top down and work on the organisational ethos to make sure it is receptive to these changes and that conflict is minimised. Following this organisation should instigate staff well-being interventions in line with the latest evidence. Finally, organisation should be focused long term on changes that will alter the workplace radically and potentially permanently such as move towards more remote working and digitalisation. These must be embraced rather than fought and key systems put in place to take advantages of these shifts while considering how best to preserve staff well-being during the years of transition.

3   Key Advice for Leaders

For leaders, the outcomes are clear, abusive and laissez-faire leadership should be actively avoided and a move towards positive leadership styles should be encouraged. Transformational leadership is associated with best employee health and well-being outcomes (Skakon et al., 2010) and leader outcomes (Weiss et al., 2018). Furthermore, leaders should adopt a growth mindset as transformational leadership can be taught and developed (Barling et al., 1996; Kelloway & Barling, 2010; Kelloway et al., 2000; Tafvelin et al., 2019).

Even though leadership performance has been related to intelligence (Daly et al., 2015), Mumford et al. (2017) suggest key cognitive skills can also enhance the ability of leaders to effectively lead. Furthermore, they cite evidence that these skills can be developed in adults (Mumford et al., 2017). The following skills were identified: defining the problem, goal analysis, constraint analysis, planning, forecasting, creative thinking, idea evaluation, wisdom and sensemaking. Therefore, leaders should aim to develop these skills.

Leaders that have a genuine regard for their own and follower's well-being have been shown to maximise long-term productivity. Cared for staff perform at much higher productivity rates, take less time off and use less resources in terms of employee assistance programmes. Poor leadership practice leading to negative employee outcomes should not simply be ameliorated by employee assistance. Where possible, solutions should take the form of leaders becoming transformational and authentic as a first priority. In addition, leaders should employ resilience training as a prophylactic strategy to avoid costly employee assistance programmes once staff start to show detrimental health outcomes. This will also moderate downstream consequences for the organisation such as litigation.

Importantly where employees report that leadership supports health promotion, they are more likely to participate in wellness activities, report lower stress and show more positive health behaviours. Therefore, leaders should

14 Leadership Styles, Related Outcomes and Practical Suggestions 261

authentically implement employee well-being initiatives and show whole-heartedly support for these (Hoert et al., 2018). Indeed, modern reviews suggest leadership and resilience are related to each other such that beneficial leadership styles build workforce resilience (Jones et al., 2020). However, simply sending employees to resilience training, including stress management programmes, which place emphasis on helping employees to deal with their stress, is only part of the solution. Sending employees to stress management interventions may be shifting the problem further down the line. Therefore, leaders should focus on reducing stress in the first place. Leaders should also look to reduce stress, change unmanageable workloads and increase autonomy in their staff. What is typically within the leader's control is workload, but it is important to recognise workload per se is not the issue. The more pertinent issue is thankless work with low autonomy and little or no input from employees regarding how, where and why their work is done. Thus, leaders can control the factors that have been shown to negatively impact employees' health; these are: long work hours, work overload, lack of autonomy/control over work, non-participative decision-making, poor social support, management and role ambiguity (Michie & Williams, 2003). Improvements in these areas will also lead to significant organisational benefits.

In addition, empowering employees leads to better workplace health well-being and productivity (Kim & Beehr, 2019). Huertas-Valdivia et al. (2019) demonstrate that this empowerment can be signalled through four dimensions: "*meaning* (employees value their jobs), *competence* (employees believe they can perform job-related tasks with skill), *self-determination* (perception that one has some choice), and *impact* (belief that fulfilling the goal of a task will have positive results)" (p. 404).

One further intervention demonstrated to provide benefits to leaders concerns the practice of mindfulness in leaders themselves. Urrila (2021) reviewed the evidence and found clear consistent benefits to leaders integrating mindfulness into their daily lives. The strongest evidence was for stress reduction in the leaders themselves.

Other key considerations relate to leadership during times of crisis. This has been highlighted by the recent Covid-19 pandemic. Wu et al. (2021) present a systematic review of crisis leadership. This is important as crises (defined as unexpected events that capture attention of staff and leaders and are potentially disruptive) may require different approaches to leadership. They examine the notion of crisis leadership and define it as the process by which leaders prepare for unexpected crises, navigate through the implications and develop through turbulent times. They reviewed 168 studies using bibliometric analyses and found several conceptual clusters which were crucial to understanding crisis leadership. These were: leader psychological and behavioural responses in crisis—this examined how leaders understood the crisis and the way they acted and responded to the risks and losses potentially present in times of crisis. It is important to note that the Wu and colleagues note how emotion is completely left out with the focus being firmly on cognitive and behavioural responses and suggest that its omission may be significant.

Strategic leadership in crisis—this cluster concerned questions regarding the characteristics and behaviour of top leaders and how they influence decisions during times of crisis. The authors suggest adopting a process view of crises may be useful.

Gender in crisis leadership—this cluster was concerned with why women are more likely to be endorsed to be leaders in times of crises. Leaders being aware of the most up to date findings will prove beneficial.

Importantly research has demonstrated mixed effects with regard to leadership training; thus, Kuehnl et al. (2019) examined 25 studies in a Cochrane review examining the effects of human resource management training for supervisors and its effects on the health and well being of workers. This is a crucial endeavour as multiple sources of evidence indicate that the effects of work stress have been demonstrated to have numerous negative consequences for employee mental and physical health (Fransson et al., 2012; Marmot et al., 2012; O'Connor et al., 2021). However, the review of Kuehnl et al. (2019) found little support for the interventions through training. In the authors' own words: "we found inconsistent evidence that supervisor training may or may not improve employees' well-being when compared to no intervention" (Kuehnl et al., 2019, p. 2). It is worth noting that the interventions discussed by Kuehnl and colleagues were based on human resource managers and that there is independent evidence that training general managers to be more transformational can have health and safety benefits (von Thiele Schwarz et al., 2016).

One other key consideration concerns the recent shift to more remote working practices within most organisation both as a result of the global Covid-19 pandemic and as a result of technology and demographic shifts. At this juncture there is scarce literature regarding what optimal leadership in a remote context looks like. A review by Contreras et al. (2020) suggests that in order to remain competitive in remote work environments will require leaders to adapt by making the organisations structure less hierarchical and while maintaining concern for employee well-being. What is most certainly the case is that more research needs to be focused on the effects of leadership styles on employee health in times where more remote working practices are in effect. One important step in this direction was provided by Terkamo-Moisio et al.

(2022) who conducted a systematic review to examine evidence on remote leadership in the healthcare sphere. Outcomes demonstrated three main thematic outcomes one concerned improving the relationship between leaders and followers by maintaining trust and improving communication. A second theme concerned the importance of regular face-to-face meetings, the aim being to foster better communication and relationships. The third theme centred around the unique challenges associated with remote working. Key questions arising from the review concerned how to maintain a good working environment under remote working conditions. It is important to recognise that several dimensions of transformational/positive leadership models would be likely to enhance the ability of organisations to adapt to remote working. Chief among these would be heightened trust, better communications and a focus on maintaining quality leader-follower relationships based on authentic care.

In conclusion, any leaders can implement everyday practical adjustments in line with transformational leadership principles. These could include: providing intellectual challenge, inspiration, valuing good work, making work interesting and communicating effectively.

4   Key Advice for Followers

It is important to develop the skills to recognise toxic environments and leaders, with a view to either leaving (if no change is possible) or engaging and stimulating bottom- up change via highlighting problems authentically and potentially becoming transformational in their own right.

Followers should also consider developing personal resilience and the ability to tolerate ambiguity. O'Connor et al. (2018) examined tolerance of ambiguity (TOA) or the degree that employees are comfortable with ill-defined ambiguous situations. The authors developed a measure of tolerance of ambiguity in the context of work and found that TOA was related positively to strategic problem solving, leadership self-efficacy, creativity, participative decision-making, well-being and resilience. Furthermore, TOA correlated negatively and significantly with stress. Importantly TOA also predicted earning more. This study suggests that the ability to tolerate ambiguity is related to a multitude of positive dimensions of work functioning, making it a key variable that may exert significant effects on overall work performance. However, followers should note that by increasing personal resilience they may become susceptible to tolerating increasing workload stress or bullying which may prove detrimental. Followers should investigate whether any leadership/resilience training they embark upon is evidence based and run by trainers with relevant experience and knowledge in that domain.

Followers should attempt to actively engage with leaders around shaping and designing their role and activities, as there is evidence that allowing employees to participate in designing their own jobs and roles relate to better well-being outcomes although further study is necessary as the ability to implement one's own job design varies across roles and sectors (Bakker & Demerouti, 2017; Demerouti et al., 2019).

There can be little doubt that certain behaviours found in organisations have a detrimental effect on staff, for example—bullying, harassment and victimisation.

However, Aquino (2000) reported that an employee's conflict resolution style and their hierarchical position have an impact on their perceived victimisation. The conflict resolution styles associated with greater perceived victimisation were high on obliging style and in positions deemed to be low on the organisational hierarchy. This suggests that learning to use more effective conflict management styles (fair and just, rather than domineering or submissive) may help lower rates of perceived victimisation. Indeed, the author states "employees would be well advised to avoid being overly conciliatory in their dealings with co-workers because it might lead others to perceive them as being easy targets of exploitation or mistreatment" (Aquino, 2000, p. 189). Other studies have reported that in medical academics those with a dominating or avoidant conflict resolution style were more likely to experience increased conflict at work (Friedman et al., 2000).

The main workplace characteristic related to harassment were the presence of other stressors. However, within followers the main antecedent or workplace harassment was their level of negative affect, as higher levels of negative affect were related to greater workplace harassment, in a meta-analysis on 90 studies (Bowling & Beehr, 2006). Therefore, followers should consider addressing issues of negative affect as soon as they become aware of them.

Another concept that is useful is organisational citizenship behaviour this refers to positive behaviours of individuals that they are not contractually obliged to undertake they are not their formal responsibility, yet they benefit the organisation overall. For example, helping colleagues with questions (Organ, 1988, 2018). Importantly data shows that transformational leadership is positively associated with greater organisational citizenship behaviour, albeit often mediated through various routes (Krishnan & Arora, 2008; López-Domínguez et al., 2013; Purwanto et al., 2021).

Another recent ongoing shift in working pattern needs to be highlighted for followers. This concerns the recent large-scale shift towards greater remote

14 Leadership Styles, Related Outcomes and Practical Suggestions

working. While this shift occurred in the context of the global Covid-19 pandemic this is not the only cause. As technological improvement has made this form of working much more feasible recently. Despite these large-scale changes in the nature of work little data exists to examine the effects of these changes on employee health. One recent review highlighted one particular leadership practice that could prove detrimental to staff well-being. Thus, Magnavita et al. (2021) term this potentially detrimental leadership style as intrusive leadership, defined as overloading employees with work and information that may overspill into their domestic time, therefore intruding more into their personal lives. Furthermore, the authors present a study demonstrating that intrusive leadership and working after hours were related to more work stress, anxiety and depression (Magnavita et al., 2021). Thus, the authors suggest a need to disconnect from work is of paramount importance and one that may become clouded as greater number of staff work from home.

5 Conclusion

In line with the former review by Erskine and Georgiou (2018) the present chapter examined a broader array of positive leadership styles and found support for them being implicated in a number of beneficial employee well-being and productivity outcomes. Transformational leadership style had the strongest evidence base, but it leaves out some aspects that also benefit employees and organisation such as an orientation to authenticity and ethical considerations. Once again, the simplest way to view this data as a whole is that followers benefit from strong leaders, who act in accordance with their values, communicate clearly and inspirationally, are participative, are authentic, and think and act morally, with an orientation towards valuing people. Simply put, staff under the care of positive leaders, who feel valued, are healthier, more satisfied with work, take less time off and show greater productivity. In addition, these leaders themselves also demonstrate improved health. Where followers and leaders have better health and work-related outcomes, organisations should ultimately benefit.

References

Anderson, H. J., Baur, J. E., Griffith, J. A., & Buckley, M. R. (2017). What works for you may not work for (gen) me: Limitations of present leadership theories for the new generation. *The Leadership Quarterly, 28*, 245–260.

Aquino, K. (2000). Structural and individual determinants of workplace victimization: The effects of hierarchical status and conflict management style. *Journal of Management, 26*, 171–193.

Bakker, A. B., & Demerouti, E. (2017). Job demands–resources theory: Taking stock and looking forward. *Journal of Occupational Health Psychology, 22*, 273–285.

Barling, J., Weber, T., & Kelloway, E. K. (1996). Effects of transformational leadership training on attitudinal and financial outcomes: A field experiment. *Journal of Applied Psychology, 81*, 827.

Bowling, N. A., & Beehr, T. A. (2006). Workplace harassment from the victim's perspective: A theoretical model and meta-analysis. *Journal of Applied Psychology, 91*, 998–1012.

Bregenzer, A., & Jimenez, P. (2021). Risk factors and leadership in a digitalized working world and their effects on employees' stress and resources: Web-based questionnaire study. *Journal of Medical Internet Research, 23*(3), e24906.

Contreras, F., Baykal, E., & Abid, G. (2020). E-leadership and teleworking in times of COVID-19 and beyond: What we know and where do we go. *Frontiers in Psychology, 11*, 590271.

Cooke, F. L., Wang, J., & Bartram, T. (2019). Can a supportive workplace impact employee resilience in a high pressure performance environment? An investigation of the Chinese banking industry. *Applied Psychology, 68*(4), 695–718.

Daly, M., Egan, M., & O'Reilly, F. (2015). Childhood general cognitive ability predicts leadership role occupancy across life: Evidence from 17,000 cohort study participants. *The Leadership Quarterly, 26*, 323–341.

Demerouti, E., Peeters, M. C., & van den Heuvel, M. (2019). Job crafting interventions: Do they work and why? In *Positive psychological intervention design and protocols for multi-cultural contexts* (pp. 103–125). Springer.

Erskine, J. A. K., & Georgiou, G. J. (2018). Leadership styles: Employee stress, well-being, productivity, turnover and absenteeism. In P. Fauquet-Alekhine (Ed.), *Understanding stress at work*. Larsen editions. http://hayka-kultura.org/larsen.html

Fransson, E. I., Heikkilä, K., Nyberg, S. T., Zins, M., Westerlund, H., Westerholm, P., et al. (2012). Job strain as a risk factor for leisure-time physical inactivity: An individual-participant meta-analysis of up to 170,000 men and women: The IPD-work consortium. *American Journal of Epidemiology, 176*(12), 1078–1089.

Friedman, R. A., Tidd, S. T., Currall, S. C., & Tsai, J. C. (2000). What goes around comes around: The impact of personal conflict style on work conflict and stress. *International Journal of Conflict Management, 11*, 32–55.

Hoert, J., Herd, A. M., & Hambrick, M. (2018). The role of leadership support for health promotion in employee wellness program participation, perceived job stress, and health behaviors. *American Journal of Health Promotion, 32*, 1054–1061.

Huertas-Valdivia, I., Gallego-Burín, A. R., & Lloréns-Montes, F. J. (2019). Effects of different leadership styles on hospitality workers. *Tourism Management, 71*, 402–420.

14 Leadership Styles, Related Outcomes and Practical Suggestions 267

Jones, G., Moore, K. A., & Morgan, D. (2020). Leadership: Untapping the secret to regional wellbeing, belonging and resilience. In *Located research* (pp. 117–132). Palgrave Macmillan.

Kelloway, E. K., & Barling, J. (2010). Leadership development as an intervention in occupational health psychology. *Work & Stress, 24*, 260–279.

Kelloway, E. K., Barling, J., & Helleur, J. (2000). Enhancing transformational leadership: The roles of training and feedback. *Leadership & Organization Development Journal, 21*, 145–149.

Kim, M., & Beehr, T. A. (2019). Empowering leadership: Leading people to be present through affective organizational commitment? *The International Journal of Human Resource Management*, 1–28.

Krishnan, V. R., & Arora, P. (2008). Determinants of transformational leadership and organizational citizenship behavior. *Asia Pacific Business Review, 4*(1), 34–43.

Kuehnl, A., Seubert, C., Rehfuess, E., von Elm, E., Nowak, D., & Glaser, J. (2019). Human resource management training of supervisors for improving health and well-being of employees. *Cochrane Database of Systematic Reviews, 9*.

Kupperschmidt, B. R. (2000). Multigeneration employees: Strategies for effective management. *The Health Care Manager, 19*, 65–76.

López-Domínguez, M., Enache, M., Sallan, J. M., & Simo, P. (2013). Transformational leadership as an antecedent of change-oriented organizational citizenship behavior. *Journal of Business Research, 66*(10), 2147–2152.

Magnavita, N., Tripepi, G., & Chiorri, C. (2021). Telecommuting, off-time work, and intrusive leadership in workers' well-being. *International Journal of Environmental Research and Public Health, 18*(7), 3330.

Marmot, M., Allen, J., Bell, R., Bloomer, E., & Goldblatt, P. (2012). Consortium for the European review of social determinants of health and the health divide. WHO European review of social determinants of health and the health divide. *Lancet, 380*(9846), 1011–1029.

Michie, S., & Williams, S. (2003). Reducing work related psychological ill health and sickness absence: A systematic literature review. *Occupational and Environmental Medicine, 60*, 3–9.

Mumford, M. D., Todd, E. M., Higgs, C., & McIntosh, T. (2017). Cognitive skills and leadership performance: The nine critical skills. *The Leadership Quarterly, 28*, 24–39.

Ng, E. S., Schweitzer, L., & Lyons, S. T. (2010). New generation, great expectations: A field study of the millennial generation. *Journal of Business and Psychology, 25*, 281–292.

O'Connor, D. B., Thayer, J. F., & Vedhara, K. (2021). Stress and health: A review of psychobiological processes. *Annual Review of Psychology, 72*, 663–688.

O'Connor, P., Becker, K., & Fewster, K. (2018, July 1–5). Tolerance of ambiguity at work predicts leadership, job performance, and creativity. In *Creating uncertainty conference 2018 main content creating uncertainty: Benefits for individuals, teams, and organizations.*

Organ, D. W. (1988). *Organizational citizenship behavior: The good soldier syndrome.* Lexington books/DC heath and com.

Organ, D. W. (2018). Organizational citizenship behavior: Recent trends and developments. *Annual Review of Organizational Psychology and Organizational Behavior, 80,* 295–306.

Porfírio, J. A., Carrilho, T., Felício, J. A., & Jardim, J. (2021). Leadership characteristics and digital transformation. *Journal of Business Research, 124,* 610–619.

Purwanto, A., Purba, J. T., Bernarto, I., & Sijabat, R. (2021). Effect of transformational leadership, job satisfaction, and organizational commitments on organizational citizenship behavior. *Inovbiz: Jurnal Inovasi Bisnis, 9*(1), 61–69.

Skakon, J., Nielsen, K., Borg, V., & Guzman, J. (2010). Are leaders' well-being, behaviours and style associated with the affective well-being of their employees? A systematic review of three decades of research. *Work & stress, 24,* 107–139.

Tafvelin, S., Hasson, H., Holmström, S., & von Thiele Schwarz, U. (2019). Are formal leaders the only ones benefitting from leadership training? A shared leadership perspective. *Journal of Leadership & Organizational Studies, 26,* 32–43.

Terkamo-Moisio, A., Karki, S., Kangasniemi, M., Lammintakanen, J., & Häggman-Laitila, A. (2022). Towards remote leadership in health care: Lessons learned from an integrative review. *Journal of Advanced Nursing, 78*(3), 595–608.

Twenge, J. M. (2010). A review of the empirical evidence on generational differences in work attitudes. *Journal of Business and Psychology, 25,* 201–210.

Twenge, J. M., & Campbell, W. K. (2009). *The narcissism epidemic: Living in the age of entitlement.* Simon and Schuster.

Twenge, J. M., & Kasser, T. (2013). Generational changes in materialism and work centrality, 1976–2007: Associations with temporal changes in societal insecurity and materialistic role modeling. *Personality and Social Psychology Bulletin, 39,* 883–897.

Urrila, L. I. (2021). From personal wellbeing to relationships: A systematic review on the impact of mindfulness interventions and practices on leaders. *Human Resource Management Review, 100837.*

von Thiele Schwarz, U., Hasson, H., & Tafvelin, S. (2016). Leadership training as an occupational health intervention: Improved safety and sustained productivity. *Safety Science, 81,* 35–45.

Weiss, M., Razinskas, S., Backmann, J., & Hoegl, M. (2018). Authentic leadership and leaders' mental well-being: An experience sampling study. *The Leadership Quarterly, 29,* 309–321.

Wu, Y. L., Shao, B., Newman, A., & Schwarz, G. (2021). Crisis leadership: A review and future research agenda. *The Leadership Quarterly, 32*(6), 101518.

15

Occupational Training, Competencies, and Stress

Philippe Fauquet-Alekhine, Marion Buchet, Julien Bleuze, and Charlotte Lenoir

1 Introduction

In this chapter, we examine techniques that increase people's stress levels. In this book, where the aim is to understand how to manage stress more effectively, measure it and reduce it, why should we look at how to increase stress? The answer lies in the notion of habituation: as we shall see below, it is by getting the individual used to stressors that they will better know how to manage their stress level in real-world operating situations. Therefore, confronting the individual with stressors that mirror the operating situation in training

---

P. Fauquet-Alekhine (✉)
SEBE-Lab, Department of Psychological and Behavioural Science,
London School of Economics and Political Science, London, UK

Laboratory for Research in Science of Energy, Montagret, France

Groupe INTRA Robotics, Avoine, France
e-mail: p.fauquet-alekhine@lse.ac.uk; philippe.fauquet-alekhine@groupe-intra.com

M. Buchet
CARAC, Nice, France

J. Bleuze
Group INTRA Robotics, Avoine, France
e-mail: julien.bleuze@groupe-intra.com

C. Lenoir
Psychology at the Conservatoire National des Arts & Métiers, Angers, France

© The Author(s), under exclusive license to Springer Nature Switzerland AG 2023
P. Fauquet-Alekhine, J. Erskine (eds.), *The Palgrave Handbook of Occupational Stress*,
https://doi.org/10.1007/978-3-031-27349-0_15

programmes will allow them to reduce the stressful effect of these factors. The "real operating situation" must be understood as the professional situation that generates a high level of acute stress for the individual whilst undertaking their job. These are therefore situations specific to the particular trade, with specific stressors linked with the profession. For example, for airline pilots, this may be the landing phase of the flight; for fighter pilots, this may be the evasive phase of missile avoidance; for nuclear reactor pilots, it may be the accidental starting phase following equipment failure; for the surgeon in the operating theatre, it may be the removal phase of a specific organ; and for the anaesthesiologist, it may be a difficult intubation of a patient. As some real operating situations are predefined and known to be stressful, they can be integrated into training programmes. Sometimes, the simulated situation is a pure fiction because it has not been simulated from direct operational experience and, yet, the teams must be prepared for this sort of situation; for example, French nuclear power operations teams must be prepared to manage reactor meltdown without ever having experienced it.

This chapter is therefore interested in the simulation of stress for use in training people subjected to these types of real operating situations and in professionals facing high-intensity acute stress that they need to learn how to manage (see, e.g.: Sigwalt et al., 2020). For these types of occupation, training is generally based on the use of simulators most often referred to as "full scale" and "high fidelity." Although these expressions are decried by some experts, they give a fairly precise idea of what they are. The term "full scale" refers to a simulator representing the workstation at scale 1 and the term "high fidelity" implies a high degree of technical and functional similarity between the simulator and the actual workstation. The similarity with the real operating situation is not only the simulator but also the simulation situation: in fact, except for initial training, there is no added value in having a full-scale, high-fidelity simulator if the simulation is unable to account for the interactions between this simulator and the outside world at the workplace: in particular, the organisation, the means of communication, interpersonal interactions (see Fauquet-Alekhine & Pehuet, 2016: 2). However, as we will see in the following, it is not mandatory to have a full-scale, high-fidelity simulator in a simulation situation to help these professionals work stress management.

Simulation of stress in training situations presents two major difficulties. The first is associated with the simulation of stress at the desired level: simulating low-intensity stress does not train people to manage high-intensity stress. The scientific literature presents, in most cases, low-intensity stress situations, either because the stressors are ineffective, or because it is the focus of the research and therefore the stressors are chosen to generate this type of stress, or because the participants are not sensitive to the stressors that the researchers agree to implement. The second difficulty is related to the consequences induced by stress: the stressors of the context induce stress but the context induces specific behavioural consequences. As illustrated by Fauquet-Alekhine (2012), captains who lead a ship to shore may be as stressed on a high-fidelity simulator as in the real operating situation, but behave completely differently in both situations: this behaviour is driven by the objective of the context. In the event that the captain docks the vessel on a simulator to obtain a qualification, the objective is to carry out the activity by ensuring that each step is properly done and taking the time to check it; in this context, the quality factor is more important than the time factor; on the other hand, in a real operating situation, the longer it takes to dock the vessel, the more a queue of ships at the entrance to the harbour increases, which can lead to congestion; in this context, the time factor is more important than the quality factor as long as the safety of individuals and equipment is guaranteed. Thus, on a simulator, docking will take longer than in a real operating situation. However, the physiological manifestations of the captain may reflect the same level of stress in both situations. This shows that physiological manifestations of stress alone do not allow us to understand the consequences of acute stress (see the "two 3-D spaces model for short-term occupational stress" in Chap. 3 of the present book).

This chapter will therefore attempt to answer these two questions: how to generate acute stress of high intensity, and how to generate acute stress that can generate behaviour close to that expected in a real operating situation?

2 The Constraints of Simulation

2.1 Being in the Simulation

For learning to be effective, the simulation situation must immerse participants in a professional context with which they are part. Some trainers call it "entering the simulation." The aim is to ensure that participants experience the simulated situation by forgetting that it is a simulated situation, that they experience it as if it were a real operating situation. This is only possible if the simulated situation and the associated scenario are professionally credible for the participants. Thus, experience shows that the proliferation of disturbances or constraints to generate stressors has a counterproductive effect because it helps to extract participants from the simulated situation: an excessive number of problems discredits the simulation. The formative and pedagogical objectives are then unlikely to be achieved.

2.2 The Limited Time of the Simulation

Most simulation situations for training are limited in time from a few minutes to a few hours. This feature does not allow for long-term stressors such as fatigue.

Pilots of airliners or nuclear reactors, for example, undergo training sessions by simulating for a few hours most of the time (Fig. 15.1).

However, simulations may last several days: response teams such as army commandos, firefighters, and the Nuclear Rapid Action Force (FARN, France) can be involved in multi-day simulation exercises, which allows for examining the effects of long-term stressors, including organisational (Fig. 15.2).

Fig. 15.1 Example of simulation training for the piloting of nuclear reactors (hour-based simulation)—control room in the 900MW reactor

Fig. 15.2 Example of simulation training context for the Nuclear Rapid Action Force (FARN, France; day-based simulation)—exercise at a nuclear site

2.3 Simulation Training Principles

Simulation training meets a formative objective. The formative objective is the overall goal of the simulation training. It is broken down into pedagogical objectives, each of them related to specific skills. When the formative objective is stress management, the work activity chosen as support for the simulation situation must be an activity mastered by the participants. This helps to decouple the difficulties related to technical skills from those related to the stressors. Choosing an unmastered work activity would be counterproductive at two levels: at the stress management level because participants would focus their attention and concerns on developing the technical skills necessary to carry out the activity with little receptiveness to stress management, and at the level of the development of technical skills that would be polluted by the effect of stressors, which would be tantamount to putting the participants in a situation of failure. For example, a future anaesthesiologist working in intubation under stress on an operating theatre simulator must first know and have practised intubation in conditions that promote this learning, thus without the stressor.

3 Generating Acute Stress

In order to know how to create high-intensity acute stress, it is first necessary to understand what generates it. To do this, looking at stress factors (or stressors) is important. From this perspective, the dynamic approach to the transactional model of stress is interesting (Lazarus & Folkman, 1984; Folkman et al., 1986; see also Chap. 2 of the present book): Stress is a transaction between an individual and the context, a transaction associated with the individual's perception that external requests exceed capacities to respond, thus endangering the well-being of the individual. This leads to defining the stressor as an external factor perceived as challenging the individual's capacities. Thus, we can discern among the potential stressors:

- any factor contributing to the perception of the difficulty of a task,
- any contextual factor unknown to the individual associated with the situation,
- any factor that may disturb or distract the individual from the activity he or she must perform in a situation, and
- any physical, physiological, or psychological factor that would reduce the individual's capacities to carry out the activity in the situation.

To illustrate this, we consider the example of a person who needs to take an academic oral exam. The fact that the subject matter is difficult or that the learning has not been optimal contributes to the perception of task difficulty. If the location of the examination is not previously known by the person and the examinatory board to perform the assessment is composed of individuals who are also unknown to the person, these contextual factors are stressors. If, during the exam, visual or auditory stimuli distract the person's attention or concentration, such as students playing outside the exam room and being visible from the window or a phone repeatedly ringing, then these distractors can be stressors. Finally, if the person is tired, has slept badly, is constipated or has just had an altercation with a third party, then this helps to reduce the person's ability.

Therefore, for an individual in a given situation, by listing factors likely to be stressors or resource factors for the individual, it is possible to make a prognosis of increased or reduced stress for the individual in that situation depending on actions that can be implemented. First, factors are assessed in terms of "stressor," "neutral" or "resource," and then actions are considered to reduce the stress effect of the factors; they are then re-evaluated taking into account the effect of the actions (Fauquet-Alekhine et al., 2012). Using the simplified example of the student taking an exam, the list of factors and their characterisation before actions (in parentheses) is as follows:

- matter is difficult (stressor),
- learning is not optimal (stressor),
- the person has taken courses on this subject (resource),
- the person has the support of friends before entering the examination room (resource),
- the person has the support of his family at home (resource),
- the place of the examination is a place unknown to the person (stressor),
- exam board members are unknown to the person (stressor),
- phone rings distracting the person (stressor),
- events seen through the window can distract the person (stressor),
- the person is tired (stressor), and
- the person slept badly (stressor).

Some of the stressors may have their effect reduced by certain adjustment actions of the person—for example, resting to avoid the effect of fatigue. The following list describes possible changes resulting from actions that could be implemented for the simplified example of the student taking an oral exam with, in parentheses, the characterisation of the post-action factor:

15 Occupational Training, Competencies, and Stress 275

- matter is difficult: no action (stressor),
- learning is not optimal: work more (resource),
- the person has taken courses on this subject (resource),
- the person has the support of friends before entering the examination room (resource),
- the person has the support of his family at home (resource),
- the place of the examination is an unknown place: to make a preliminary identification by visiting the place of the examination (neutral),
- the members of the jury are unknown to the person: no possible action (stressor),
- phone ringtones can distract the person: asks for phones to be turned off (neutral),
- events seen through the window can disturb the person: position themselves with their backs to the window (neutral),
- the person is tired: pay attention to physical exertion before the exam (neutral), and
- the person slept badly: no action because difficult to manage (stressor).

Where there is no associated adjustment action, the characterisation of the factor remains the same. When an action is supposed to reduce the stressor effect of the factor, characterisation most often turns to "neutral" because it is difficult to guarantee that the action could have reversed the effect of a factor. In the simplified example of the student taking an exam, the "work more" action reverses the characterisation of the "learning is not optimal" factor provided the work is sufficient; in the example, it is assumed that the student has the ability, the will and the time to optimise learning through personal work, which allows the reversal of the characterisation.

The method then consists of calculating the proportion of stressors, neutrals, and resources for each of the two situations (before and after actions) and comparing them on a three-pole radar diagram, known as the three-level qualitative scale, as shown in Fig. 15.3.

The comparison of trigons on the graphs clearly indicates a prognosis of post-action stress reduction since the trigon on the graph, known as the "stress trigon," indicates a reduction of the "stressful" pole in favour of the "neutral" pole.

Note that there is a combined effect of stressors as well as a contextual effect. In the simplified example of the student taking an exam, the "phone ringtones can distract the person" factor, when taken out of context, is not necessarily stressful. It is only because it is combined with other factors such

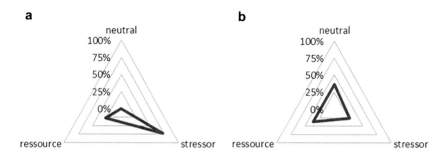

Fig. 15.3 Analysis by the "three-level qualitative scale" for the passage of an exam by a student: evaluation of the stressor of the situation before (**a**) and after (**b**) corrective actions is materialised by the change in shape of the stress trigon at the centre of the graph

as "matter is difficult" in the context of the examination that the factor "phone ringtones can distract the person" becomes a potential source of stress.

Fauquet-Alekhine et al. (2012) proceeded in the same way but with the opposite objective, that of constructing two experimental conditions involving individual psychotechnical tests: one in a low-stress condition and the other in a high-stress condition. To do this, they considered adjustment actions that convert neutral or resource factors into stressors and compared the distribution of factors from one condition to another on a "three-level qualitative scale." The results obtained in their experiments validated the "three-level qualitative scale" prognosis of increased stress from one situation to another.

The transactional model, however, has a weakness in that it does not explicitly integrate the concept of interpretation. Indeed, the "perception of a stimulus as a threat" does not explicitly mention the stage of interpretation that the individual can make of the perception of stimulus; in fact, it integrates it implicitly. However, the interpretation stage seen separately from perception is a fundamental approach because perception concerns the five senses and therefore is a physiological and cognitive process (thus partly mental), whereas interpretation is a mental process only. To illustrate the importance, let's take the example of a passenger sitting on the train tapping his tablet with his fingers. This auditory stimulus can be perceived by two persons around and interpreted differently to the point that for one, this stimulus is irritating and therefore stressful, while for the other, it is just a noise among the others and this stimulus has no stressful effect. The effect of the stimulus on the person therefore begins with perception and is extended by the person's interpretation of that perception. In the example of the train, the perception of the stimulus is the same for the two passengers, but the different interpretation makes it a stressor for one and not for the other.

Considering perception and interpretation separately also has the advantage of easier identification of potentially stressful stimuli. The identification then directs one towards what the five senses, represented by the acronym VAKOG, can perceive:

- Visual: perception is done through the eye via sight.
- Auditory: perception is done through the ear via hearing.
- Kinesthetic: perception is done throughout the body and in the body through the innervation of organs and tissues (the perception of the door handle in the hand is an external perception, i.e., on the surface of the skin; the perception of a broken tibia and an internal perception, i.e., in the body).
- Olfactive: perception is made through the nose via smell.
- Gustative: perception is done through the mouth through taste.

Similarly, this approach facilitates the construction of stressful stimuli.

Creating a stimulus that calls on VAKOG for a stressful effect does not necessarily mean creating a threat perceived as such through one of the five senses; indeed, the stress-generating stimulus may have one or more of the following characteristics:

- threatening: the stimulus is interpreted by the person as a threat to physical integrity (e.g. risk of injury by scissors),
- disturbing: the stimulus generates a situation of discomfort for the person (example: a shrill, periodic beep that irritates the person), and
- distracting, disturbing in the sense of distractor: it is a matter of distracting the person by disturbing his attention in relation to the current activity (e.g. asking questions repeatedly to the person while trying to concentrate on reading an email).

Using the simplified example of the student taking an oral exam, the list of factors relating to VAKOG and their pre-action characterisation (in parentheses) is as follows:

- phone ringtones can disturb the person (stressful because it is disturbing),
- events seen through the window can disturb the person (stressful because it is distracting),
- the person is tired (stressful because disturbing), and
- the person slept badly (stressful because disturbing).

This simplified example illustrates that the stimuli associated with VAKOG do not represent the bulk of stressors (only one third in the example), the others being psychological or psychosocial.

In order to facilitate the identification of psychological or psychosocial stressors, it is possible to rely on a categorisation that helps it to be structured. The literature proposes various categorisations (see Chap. 10 of this book); we suggest using the one developed by Leka et al. (2003) and Leka and Jain (2010), who constructed a classification of psychosocial stressors into ten categories:

- Workload and work pace
- Work schedule
- Job content
- Control
- Organisational culture and function
- Interpersonal relationships at work
- Role in organisation
- Environment and equipment
- Career development
- Home-work interface

For each category, the stressors identified by Leka et al. do not necessarily generate acute stress. As explained above, there is the combination effect of factors as well as contextualisation effects. For example, regarding the categories "Workload and work pace" and "lack of variety," the stressor associated with repetitive work is unlikely to contribute to acute stress. On the other hand, combined with "time pressure" and "poorly adapted equipment" factors, it becomes a potential contributor to acute stress.

Table 15.1 provides examples of stressors for each category and identifies the stressor effect kinetics: short term or long term. A short-term kinetic about a stressor can be implemented in training by short simulation (hour-based simulation) unlike a long-term kinetic (day-based simulation). For example, the "time pressure" stressor can be short-term and long-term because it is always possible to find a task or part of a task more or less long for which time will be constrained. Conversely, the stressor associated with working shifts is difficult to simulate on training of a few hours and can therefore only concern the simulation over several days.

Some stressors are not usable in simulation because they are irrelevant (NR) or not applicable (NA). For example, the "career stagnation" stressor does not appear to be suitable (NA) in a simulated situation because it is not simulated;

15 Occupational Training, Competencies, and Stress 279

Table 15.1 Examples of stressors for the categorisation of Leka et al. (2003) and Leka and Jain (2010)

Categories	Possible Cinetic of the Stressor		Simulation Options to Increase Stress Level
	Short Term	Long Term	
Workload and work pace			
Time pressure	×	×	Limit the time to perform the task
Machine pacing	×	×	Increase the process dynamic
Work over- or under-load	×	×	Increase the workload (adding minor side tasks)
Continually constraining deadlines		×	Set short deadlines for tasks in a chain
Work schedule			
Inflexible or unstable work schedules		×	Break down the simulation exercises during the day
Night shifts, shift working		×	Plan shift simulation sessions
Unsociable or long hours		×	Not recommended (pedogogical concerns)
Job content			
Short work cycles		×	Increase the process dynamic
Lack of variety	×	×	Increase the number of similar minor tasks (e.g. control, checklist)
Skills underused	NR	NR	Not relevant to generate stress
Meaningless or fragmented work	×	×	Switch between several activities while not yet achieved
Exposure to people	×	×	Trainers may play the role of clients, partners, or colleagues in a face-to-face interaction or by phone
High uncertainty	×	×	Create disturbance due to equipment default/failure; change the goals
Control			
Workload: lack of control	×	×	Increase the workload (adding minor side tasks)
Decision-making: low participation	×	×	Trainers may play the role of authoritarian managers
Organisational culture and function			
Lack of agreement on organisational objectives	NR	NR	Not relevant to generate stress
Lack of definition of organisational objectives	NR	NR	Not relevant to generate stress
Low levels of support for personal development and problem solving	NR	NR	Not relevant to generate stress

(continued)

Table 15.1 (continued)

| Categories | Possible Cinetic of the Stressor | | Simulation Options to Increase Stress Level |
	Short Term	Long Term	
Poor communication Interpersonal relationships at work	NR	NR	Not relevant to generate stress
Lack of social support	×	×	The trainer who plays the role of a colleague avoids providing the requested support
Poor relationships with management	×	×	The trainer who plays the role of manager deteriorates relationships
Interpersonal conflict	×	×	
Isolation (physical or social)	NR	NR	Not relevant to generate stress
Harassment	×	×	Not recommended (ethics concerns)
Bullying	×	×	Not recommended (ethics concerns)
Role in organisation			
Role conflict	×	×	The task to be performed does not correspond to the trainee's position
Role ambiguity	×	×	The task to be performed does not correspond to the trainee's position
Responsibility for people	NR	NR	Not relevant to generate stress
Environment and equipment			
Excessive level of noise	×	×	Act on environmental parameters
Poor lighting	×	×	Act on environmental parameters
Uncomfortable environment, lack of space	×	×	Act on environmental parameters
Poorly adapted equipment	×	×	Provide inadequate equipment
Deteriorated equipment	×	×	Create hardware defects

NB: The "Career development" and "Home-work interface" categories are not applicable to generate acute stress in a simulation situation

the stressor "skills underused" does not seem relevant (NR) in a simulated situation because it would generate boredom rather than stress. Some stressors are not recommended because they conflict with certain ethical or pedagogical provisions. For example, the "harassment" stressor seems difficult to implement without undermining the ethical principle that people's dignity and health should be preserved; similarly, the "unsociable or long hours" stressor resulted in prolonged simulated situations of participants; for example, it reduces their ability to learn and is educationally counterproductive.

4 Difficulty in Generating High-Intensity Acute Stress Conditions

The stress tests applied in experiments in the scientific literature to generate acute stress usually cause low-intensity stress. Fauquet-Alekhine et al. (2016) noted that most stress tests generate heart rate (HR) variability between 1 and 4. HR variability is one of the most reliable physiological measures of acute stress (see Chap. 5 of the present book); it is the ratio between low and high heart rate. In the scientific literature, stress conditions with the highest values of HR variability are generally associated with full-scale, high-fidelity simulations of professional activities. The highest values are rarely achieved in simulation, in the order of 8 for an average heart rate value around 100 bpm, while real operating situations can lead to values equal to 151 bpm (see, e.g.: Clarke et al. (2014) or Baker et al. (2017) analysing physicians managing critical situations in real operating situations).

At least two explanations can help to understand the difficulty of simulation in reproducing the acute stress of the real operating situation. The first is the design of the simulation situation for which potentially stress-generating factors have been mis-identified or misused. The second relates to the professionalism of the trainees in the simulation situation; most of the time, stress management is being worked on simulated situations associated with known professional activities; this is done to focus the training session on a reduced number of formative objectives; trainees are thus confronted with a situation for which they have been trained and many stressors have a lessened effect as the habituation process is already advanced when facing the stressful simulated situation.

There may also be confusion between "putting participants under stress" and "putting participants in difficulty." Experience shows that some trainers think that working on increasing the effect of stressors is exactly equal to working on increasing the level or the number of simulated difficulties. Observing such training sessions has shown that working on difficulties instead of stressors may put participants in a situation of failure as well as trainers.

In such conditions, trainees think that their lack of success in achieving the tasks during training is due to the accumulation of difficulties (most of the time: numerous technical problems). While trainers think that it is due to acute stress. When debriefing the training session, there is usually confrontation between trainers and trainees, the former trying to explain the effect of stress on performance, the latter denouncing "an incredible number of technical problems that would never had happen in real life." In this context, the training session has little chance to be successful.

5 Generating the Behaviour of the Actual Operating Situation

Given what is written above, it is clear that acting on the effect of stressors has multiple aspects and combinations that would be illusory to intend to fully describe here. For this reason, this chapter has chosen to illustrate using practical cases how trainers try to create a simulated situation under intense acute stress as part of training or professional training and to discuss its limitations.

Obtaining the simulated situation is based on the recommendations outlined above. As reported in the introduction, it is unlikely that the behaviour of the participants in the simulated situation would be identical to that adopted in the real operating situation. However, the use of high-fidelity, full-scale simulators and the creation of a scenario based on operational experience allows us to get as close as possible to the context of the real operating situation. While the behaviour of the participants is not that of the real operating situation, the habituation process is nevertheless effective. As a result, participants are well prepared for the management of stress in a real operating situation by reducing the effect of stressors. This contribution is supplemented during the debriefing of the simulation session by discussions between the trainer and the participants regarding the effects of stressors on their performance and on the management of the situation. This debriefing is an opportunity for participants to develop strategies or simply find solutions to manage the stress generated by the context of the situation.

5.1 Anaesthesiologist in the Operating Theatre

Description of the Simulated Situation

The residents of the hospital in Angers (France) are summoned to simulation sessions to train to manage crisis situations on a full-scale simulator (a connected manikin simulating breathing and heart rate, managed by computer and installed in an operating theatre). In the example chosen to illustrate a case of application relating to the training of physicians, each scenario involved an anaesthesiologist and one or two specialised nurses to manage a difficult situation that could be: cardiac arrest of the patient during spinal anaesthesia, difficult intubation during a general anaesthesia, an anaesthetised patient developing a laryngospasm, the coma of a patient suffering from a trauma. Each scenario could end with the loss of the patient, a situation unacceptable to the medical team (Berton et al., 2015). The simulated situation lasted about 15 minutes (Fig. 15.4).

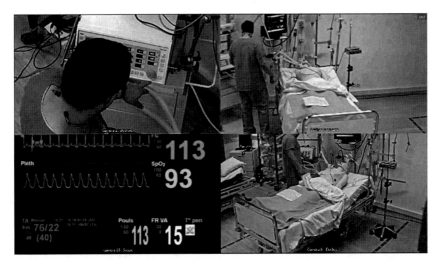

Fig. 15.4 Simulator for the training of anaesthesiologists at the University of Angers (France)

The formative objective was to enable the team and each individual in the team to identify the strengths and weaknesses associated with the stressful task and thus to improve their collective performance.

Identifying Stressors and Actions to Increase Their Effects

The "three-level qualitative scale" was applied. Two factors mainly contributed to increased physician stress:

- the fact that the medical team did not know the difficulty they were going to face, and
- uncertainty about their ability to make the right diagnosis in relation to this difficulty.

One action of the trainers helped to increase the effect of the second stressor: a slow return of the patient's physiological parameters to the normal or stabilised state.

Effect Obtained and Opinions of Participants

Psychological stress was self-assessed by means of the Appraisal of Life Event Scale (ALES) just after working with the manikin simulator (the scale was elaborated and validated by Ferguson et al. (1999)). The questionnaire consists of 16 adjectives self-rated by the participants on a six-level Likert scale coded from 0 to 5 (from "not at all" to "extremely"): ten adjectives are associated with a perception of threat, constraint, or loss; the other six are associated with the perception of challenge or excitement. Regarding the perception of threat, constraint, or loss, the average score of the physicians was $Q_{ALES}(N = 45) = 23.45$ and $Q_{ALES}(N = 45) = 23.43$ for the nurses on a scale from 0 to 50. By comparison, students taking an oral exam would have a score above 30.

During the debriefings, participants reported that they perceived intense acute stress during the simulated situation. However, the values of the ALES scores suggest that the intensity of stress was moderate. This finding was made in other medical simulation situations compared to real operating situations: Baker et al. (2017) found that the physiological measurement of stress showed very different levels for these two conditions, the simulated situation having a significantly lower level of stress than that of the real operating condition.

During the simulated situation, the trainers did not choose to act on stressors related to VAKOG in order to preserve the ecological character of the simulated situation (i.e. preserve the credibility of the simulation in relation to reality). The trainers could have acted on organisational factors but, again, excessive disorganisation would not have reflected reality.

The simulated situation and its debriefing allowed participants to work on what facilitates the management of this type of stressful situation such as operational communication with other team members, physician leadership and task distribution, the physical positioning of the physician in relation to the rest of the team in the operating room.

5.2   Nuclear Reactor Pilot

Description of the Simulated Situation

A nuclear reactor is operated from a control room and involves a team of about 15 people, three of whom are permanently assigned to the management of the control room: they pilot the nuclear reactor; one is called a "unit pilot" and the other two are called "operator." Once a year, the reactor is in outage for a period of several weeks. The outage activities in the field are numerous and generate a large amount of work for the pilots in the control room. The Chinon Nuclear Power Plant Operations Department has requested the development of a high-fidelity, full-scale control room simulation session to train pilots to manage these organisationally highly disturbed and stress-causing situations (Fig. 15.1).

In this work configuration, the unit pilot and operators are in the control room to prepare and manage field activities carried out by technicians; The unit pilot supervises these operations and distributes the tasks; the managers are likely to express requests for activities and go to the control room to do so; representatives from other departments of the nuclear power plant can also contact the control room by phone to ask for clarification where to adjust certain activities they are in charge of; sometimes they can also go to the control room. All of these activities require the consultation of many documents in the form of binders that are arranged on the desk in the middle of the control room and overlap. The simulation training session therefore replicated this organisationally disturbed context in the control room. The scenario involved five people (the three pilots and two managers), the rest of the team being simulated by the trainers. The simulated situation lasted 3 hours.

Identifying Stressors and Actions to Increase Their Effects

The "three-level qualitative scale" was applied. Five factors mainly contributed to increased pilot stress:

- a change in strategy for the operation of the reactor, involving a rescheduling of operations and an adjustment of the control room parameters;
- workload;
- the periodic solicitation of pilots by the management of the operating or maintenance departments;
- telephone solicitations from operating or maintenance engineers or technicians; and
- the appearances of alarms to be managed by the pilots in the control room.

Six actions of the trainers helped to increase the effect on the stress of the pilots:

- the increasing workload over time: activities were added to the programme presented to pilots at the beginning of the session;
- the periodic solicitations of pilots by the managers; solicitations became more pressing and inappropriate after the second third of the simulation time (this on the request of the trainers according to the scenario);

- direct solicitation of pilots by department representatives when they should have gone through pilots' management (the role of department representatives was played by trainers in accordance with the scenario);
- an actor entering the control room, playing the role of a technician in a maintenance department in order to disrupt the work of pilots by requesting permissions for specific activities, signing documents, and managing the slippage of activities to the schedule impacting his work schedules;
- the increasing frequency over time of telephone solicitations from operating or maintenance technicians; and
- the increasing frequency over time of alarms to be managed by pilots in the control room.

The formatting goal was to enable the team and each individual in the team to identify the strengths and weaknesses associated with carrying out stressful activities and to find strategies to withstand the pressure of external pressures in the control room.

Effect Obtained and Opinions of Participants

The stress level of the pilots was assessed using the ALES questionnaire as for anaesthesiologists. Three sessions were held. The overall average score was Q_{ALES} $(N = 9) = 13.44$, for the unit pilots Q_{ALES} $(N = 3) = 22$, and for operators Q_{ALES} $(N = 6) = 9.16$. It is clear that the perceived stress was not high intensity. However, the intensity of stress was managed by the trainers in order to continuously increase the effect of stressors throughout the simulation. One of the findings is reassuring because it shows that pilots are well trained to manage such stressful situations, which ensures the safety of nuclear facilities. A hypothesis associated with low stress levels leads to the assumption that the stress level of the simulated situation is probably much lower than that of the real operating situation.

Unlike anaesthesiologists, the trainers chose to act on VAKOG stressors (phones, alarms).

The simulation situation and its debriefing allowed participants to identify and anchor in their professional practices what allowed them to manage such a situation. Participants felt that the simulated situation was interesting and very close to the real operating situation.

5.3   Fighter Pilot

Description of the Simulated Situation

Simulator training is an integral part of training any airplane pilot, whether civilian or military. The simulator allows the learning of the procedures of normal situations that are repeated until they are sufficiently assimilated before the start of the progression in flight. The simulator is also used for learning and carrying out emergency procedures that are sometimes impossible to work on in a real flight such as losing the engine on a single jet -reactor or engagement by a missile, for example.

Simulator sessions are also used for competency assessment, which is regular and mandatory throughout the career. Thus, the simulator is usually associated with a rather significant intrinsic stress in relation to the professional stakes it represents, especially at the beginning of a career. However, it remains difficult to simulate the variety of stressors that exist in real operating situations.

Identifying Stressors and Actions to Increase Their Effects

For the fighter pilot, the stressors are specific and varied (see, e.g., the review of Campbell & O'Connor, 2010). The nature of the stress associated with the combat situation, and in particular the possibility of physical impairment, was detailed by Orasanu and Backer (1996). It is obviously difficult to replicate in a simulated situation. Johnston and Cannon-Bowers (1996) identify situations with low demand for attentional resources as stressful. It is quite complicated to simulate them given the cost of using the simulator and crew schedules. In any case, it is important to know and manage stress-generating situations and therefore to train the pilots: Bray et al. (2001: 397) noted that "both military women and men are exposed to a wide range of stressor events as a part of military training and work assignments. [...] The link between perceived work-related stress and impaired functioning on the job is well-documented, demonstrating the classic inverted U-shaped relationship between stress and performance. That is, employees who experience a moderate degree of job stress perform their jobs most efficiently, while those who experience either low or high work-related stress show reduced work efficiency."

First of all, the integration of stress in a simulated situation is not the main objective in military aeronautics. There are situations in crew training where stress habituation is worked on more or less directly. For example, it can occur on survival courses. One of the main objectives of the simulator is to acquire new skills. On the other hand, it is important, particularly in the context of the implementation of emergency procedures, that crews maintain some control over the impact of stressors on their work in order to avoid the deterioration of their performance in the management of the situation.

One of the factors that adjusts the pilot's stress intensity is the workload. It is possible to handle the workload via the difficulty of the assigned mission but also through breakdowns or the accumulation of failures that will be initiated in the scenario of the situation simulated by the simulator instructor. Breakdown training sessions allow this adjustment of the workload: in the scenario, the instructor has to foresee many breakdowns corresponding to a high workload, and to adjust the number of breakdowns during the training session according to the desired workload; for example, if ten breakdowns correspond to a heavy workload in 1 hour of simulation, the instructor can choose to engage only three breakdowns to generate a normal workload, or only one for a light workload. The loss of control of the situation as a result of poor management of the attentional load or the erroneous mental construction of the situation are two elements that appear in a number of incidents or accidents; working on these two aspects in the simulator not only increases crew management capabilities and works on cognitive strategies for situational analysis and control, but also allows them to recognise the feeling associated with the emergence of stress. The armies were thus interested very early in the need to offer training programmes specific to the management of stress called Stress Exposure Training or Stress Inoculation Training (Robson & Manacapilli, 2014), as evidenced by the article by Johnston and Cannon-Bowers (1996). Experiments are also being carried out to improve training (e.g. Lefrançois et al., 2009; Fornette et al., 2012).

Effect

There is little doubt regarding the benefits of training through intense stress simulation: many scientific results show that pilots improve their stress management and also their performance under stress (e.g. Fornette et al., 2012; McClernon et al., 2011; Otsuka et al., 2006). For example, pilots trained in simulator for stress management have a more flexible operation of their aircraft (McClernon et al., 2011).

However, numerous studies have shown the importance of predispositions for pilot stress management (Campbell, 2006) emphasising the importance of recruitment selection (see Chap. 16 of the present book).

5.4 Pilot of Robot on Accident Response

Description of the Simulated Situation

The INTRA robotics group is a corporate interest group created by Electricité de France (EDF), the Atomic Energy Commission (CEA) and Orano (formerly AREVA). INTRA robotics (in French: Groupe d'INtervention Robotique sur Accident, meaning Robotics INtervention Group on Accident) aims to intervene in accidents or incidents mainly nuclear with irradiation or contamination involving the intervention of robotic means in place of Human. The goal is to preserve human health. To do this, INTRA is equipped with small robots (300 kg; Fig. 15.5a) capable of intervening inside buildings as well as drones (Fig. 15.5b) and larger robots (several tons; Fig. 15.5c) capable of intervening outdoors over long distances, about several kilometres. The group acts as a priority for parent companies and can in exceptional circumstances be made available to other government agencies.

Simulation training on the performance of pilots under stress is therefore fundamental for two reasons: the first is that pilots will necessarily be subjected to acute stress of high intensity in real operating situations, the second is that the pilots have never faced this type of situation since, fortunately, there has not yet been a nuclear accident in France.

Here we present one of the many simulation situations developed at INTRA robotics (Fauquet-Alekhine et al., 2021). The aim was to carry out a visual and radiological reconnaissance mission in a nuclear power plant building believed to be contaminated as a result of a leak of radioactive products. This recognition was made with the help of a small robot equipped with crawler tracks. The robot had to advance to a water pipe connection system so that another team could intervene there with knowledge of radiological hazards and potential obstacles (the connection of the pipes was not part of the scenario as it involved teams outside INTRA robotics). The simulation scenario began when the team gathered for an intervention briefing, was extended by equipment preparation, car transfer to the intervention site, robot reconnaissance, and then ended with the return to the INTRA robotics base with the undressing and decontamination phase. The simulation lasted 1 hour to 1.5 hours. It involved a response manager, an expert engineer responsible for radiation protection, and two pilots.

The formative objective was to enable the team and each individual in the team to identify the strengths and weaknesses associated with carrying out this recognition activity under stress and implementing the necessary protocols to preserve people and equipment from irradiation and contamination.

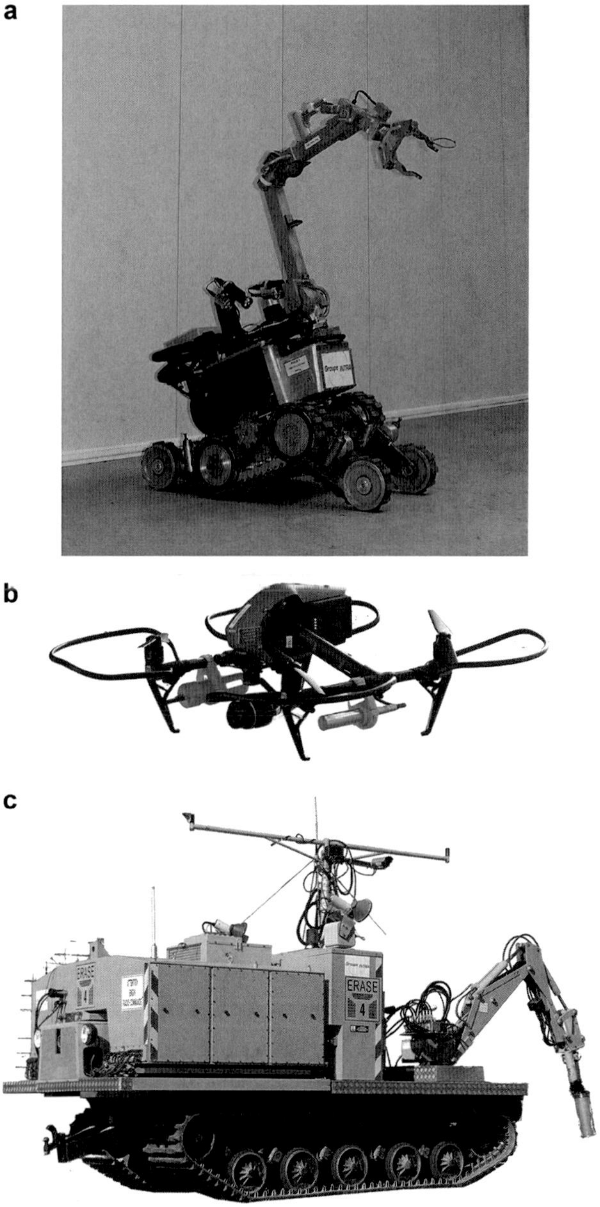

290 P. Fauquet-Alekhine et al.

Fig. 15.5 (a) Example of an indoor robot (unmanned ground vehicle); (b) example of a drone (unmanned aerial vehicle); (c) example of an outdoor robot

15 Occupational Training, Competencies, and Stress

Identifying Stressors and Actions to Increase Their Effects

The "three-level qualitative scale" was applied. Three factors contributed to the pilots' stress:

- the intervention site involved the right-angle landing climb of stairs by the tracked robot, which presented a particular difficulty of steering;
- the potentially contaminated and irradiating nature of the site required team members to wear an CBRN outfit (Fig. 15.6), which constrained their movements, reducing the ability of the pilots to drive the vehicle to the intervention site (Fig. 15.7) and to direct the robot (Fig. 15.8); and
- the simulation situation was based on an irradiation and contamination simulator, which challenged the team in terms of the radioactive dose absorbed by the team members and the surface contamination on the clothing and skin.

The actions of the trainers helped to increase the effect of the stress of the pilots:

- the intervention site was adaptable by trainers who could add obstacles to the robot's planned route,
- simulated irradiation could be adjusted remotely and could be increased or reduced by trainers,
- trainers could simulate powder-deposit contamination on the team's suits and/or equipment, and
- trainers could act as external persons who wanted information about the activity and contacted pilots by radio or telephone.

This last action was implemented sparingly because the trainers felt that this would hinder the achievement of the formatting objective.

If the main hazard cannot be simulated for this type of training (i.e. exposed personnel to real radiological hazard), a secondary hazard can be incorporated into the exercise: that associated with the loss of the robot. The loss of the robot can occur in two ways: either by the robot falling down on the stairs, for example, or because the robot has been advanced in galleries where it gets stuck mechanically or by losing the control signal where it is then impossible to get it back. This secondary danger is still being implemented in a limited way. For example, regarding the risk of the robot falling, all precautions are taken to avoid this extreme situation because the cost of a robot ranges from tens of thousands of euros to several million euros. As a result, the loss of a robot in training would raise the cost of this training in a way that is not

Fig. 15.6 Pilot in CBRN outfit

financially acceptable (Kessler & Fauquet-Alekhine, 2019; Fauquet-Alekhine et al., 2023). In addition, the loss of a robot would compromise the operational readiness of the INTRA robotics group whilst rehabilitating the equipment, which is also unacceptable.

Effect Obtained and Opinions of Participants

The stress level of the pilots was assessed only in interview during the collective debriefing of the simulated situation: according to the participants, the

15 Occupational Training, Competencies, and Stress

Fig. 15.7 Drivers in CBRN outfit travelling by car

perceived stress was low intensity. Participants explained this perception through experience with this type of situation during training exercises. Participants also stated that any exercise would never generate the stress that real contamination or irradiation could induce, such as in the Fukushima accident (Japan, 11 March 2011). This can be explained by the fact that irradiation or contamination are invisible, unlike fire flames, for example. The radiological risk is devoid of stimulus that could generate stress through the awareness of an imminent hazard.

The simulation situation and its debriefing allowed participants to identify and anchor in their professional practices what helped them to achieve their objective of visual and radiological reconnaissance while reducing exposure to irradiation and contamination. Participants felt that the simulated situation was interesting and related to the reality of their profession.

6   Ethics: Precautions

Simulation situations designed to place people under stress offer opportunities that are necessarily limited by ethics. In the context of vocational training, there is no question of undermining the physical or psychological integrity of

Fig. 15.8 Pilots in CBRN outfit piloting the robot

individuals or their dignity. This prevents participants in the simulation training from leaving the training sessions in a destabilised psychic state, or even having suffered psychological trauma. During the debriefing of the training session, the trainers must make it sure. The debriefing of the training session through the simulation should incorporate the objective of freeing participants from the stresses associated with the stressors to which they were exposed.

Beforehand, in order to prevent any such future difficulties, requiring the advice of an ethics committee can be beneficial as it allows a critical analysis of the simulation situation envisaged by people distanced from the formative objective and industrial concerns, and allows one to obtain recommendations on the sensitive points.

For the same reasons, in certain circumstances, it is recommended to practise this type of experiment with the help of specialised support. The aim is to ensure that the physical and mental integrity of the participants will not be limited. This can be done via a health questionnaire that can be developed with the help of a psychologist and/or a physician.

In addition, acting on the effect of certain stressors can be a regulatory problem. For example, increasing working hours to generate fatigue may be at odds with labour regulations that impose a maximum daily working time in some countries.

7 Conclusion

Preparing professionals through simulation to manage situations that induce acute stress of high intensity can be done by implementing intervention conditions close to the real operating situation. Indeed, with the experience and accumulation of training, professionals develop a habituation ability to stressors that, combined with the stress management techniques taught to them, allows them to act mostly serenely in a simulation situation regardless of the level of fidelity of the simulator. However, the main stressors of the real operating situation are difficult to simulate during training: this is the case of the enemy ready to kill for the fighter pilot, for example, or that of the robot pilot in the event of a nuclear accident with high level of irradiation and contamination. So, trainees are well aware that the main danger is not present during simulation training.

One way to get training closer to the real operating situation would be to generate a real stressor associated with the main hazard, which would no longer make sense because either the situation would leave the field of simulation and enter the field of the real operation, or the situation would put the response teams in physical or psychological danger. However, increasing stress by the reality of a secondary danger is possible. This is the case for fighter pilots (reality of the ground in flight exercise), paratrooper commandos (reality of the fall), pilots of intervention robots in certain exercises (reality of the loss of the robot by fall or blocking in inaccessible area).

Another way to achieve such a goal would be to make participants believe that the simulation situation is a real operating situation. For example, making INTRA robotics pilots believe that they are responding to a real major nuclear accident situation. However, there are at least two challenges to this option. The first is that a major accidental nuclear situation would give rise to information by the media that would be difficult to simulate; pilots would therefore quickly become aware of the deception. The second is ethics: it is customary to always tell accident responders whether it is an exercise or not. One reason is that, in the event of a real accident, a total commitment is expected of stakeholders, exceeding what could be done in a training situation. This provision therefore incorporates the fact that training is able to place response teams in psychological and physical conditions close to these of the real operating situation. To practise otherwise, that is, to make the response teams believe that simulation is a real operating situation, would defy their commitment to a real operating situation.

Finally, it is important to note that managing such stressful situations is not only a challenge for trainee participants but also for trainers. Fauquet-Alekhine and Pehuet (2016: 6) report how a simulation situation for the training of anaesthesiologist students had put the trainers in difficulty when they had considered pushing the simulation to the death of the simulated patient (the manikin) while this had never been done; in live, during the simulated situation, the trainers chose to modify the scenario being simulated to avoid patient death because they did not anticipate how they could handle this type of intense stress with students. Therefore, the effects of these types of simulations on participants and the importance of ensuring the preservation of their mental and physical health should be emphasised.

References

Baker, B. G., Bhalla, A., Doleman, B., Yarnold, E., Simons, S., Lund, J. N., & Williams, J. P. (2017). Simulation fails to replicate stress in trainees performing a technical procedure in the clinical environment. *Medical Teacher, 39*(1), 53–57.

Bray, R. M., Camlin, C. S., Fairbank, J. A., Dunteman, G. H., & Wheeless, S. C. (2001). The effects of stress on job functioning of military men and women. *Armed Forces & Society, 27*(3), 397–417.

Berton, J., Rineau, E., & Conte, M. (2015). Appraisal of Life Event Scale (ALES) to differentiate mental stress perceived by physicians and nurses involved in the same simulation training situation of anesthesiology. In *Stress self-assessment and questionnaires: Choice, application, limits*, 39–43.

Campbell, J., & O'Connor, P. (2010). Coping with stress in military aviation: A review of the research. In P. O. Connor & J. Cohn (Eds.), *Human performance enhancements in high-risk environments: Insights developments, and future directions from military research*. Santa Barbara, CA.

15 Occupational Training, Competencies, and Stress 297

Campbell, J. S. (2006). *Personality assessment in Naval aviation*. Proceedings of the Annual Convention of the American Psychological Association, New Orleans, LA: 258.

Clarke, S., Horeczko, T., Cotton, D., & Bair, A. (2014). Heart rate, anxiety and performance of residents during a simulated critical clinical encounter: A pilot study. *BMC Medical Education, 14*(1), 1–8.

Fauquet-Alekhine, P. (2012). Causes and consequences: Two dimensional spaces to fully describe short term occupational stress. *Socio-Organizational Factors for Safe Nuclear Operation, 1*, 45–52. http://hayka-kultura.org/larsen.html

Fauquet-Alekhine, P., Bleuze, J., Mouret, H., Frenois, S., Frenois, C., & Kessler, P. (2023). Operational return on investment of simulators regarding robotics in radioactive environments. *Advances in Research*. (submitted).

Fauquet-Alekhine, P., Bleuze, J., Mouret, H., Lenoir, C., & Kessler, P. (2021). *The usefulness of stressing people in vocational training*. Proceedings of the 28th International "Stress and Behavior" Neuroscience and Biopsychiatry Conference, May 16–19, 2021, St. Petersburg, Russia.

Fauquet-Alekhine, P., Geeraerts, T., & Rouillac, L. (2012). Improving simulation training: Anesthetists vs nuclear reactor pilots. *Socio-Organizational Factors for Safe Nuclear Operation, 1*, 32–44. http://hayka-kultura.org/larsen.html

Fauquet-Alekhine, P., & Pehuet, N. (2016). *Simulation training: Fundamentals and applications*. Springer.

Fauquet-Alekhine, P., Rouillac, L., Berton, J., & Granry, J. C. (2016). Heart rate vs stress indicator for short term mental stress. *British Journal of Medicine and Medical Research, 17*(7), 1–11.

Ferguson, E., Matthews, G., & Cox, T. (1999). The appraisal of life events (ALE) scale: reliability and validity. *The British Psychological Society, 4*, 97–116.

Folkman, S., Lazarus, R. S., Gruen, R. J., & DeLongis, A. (1986). Appraisal, coping, health status, and psychological symptoms. *Journal of Personality and Social Psychology, 50*(3), 571.

Fornette, M. P., Bardel, M. H., Lefrançois, C., Fradin, J., Massioui, F. E., & Amalberti, R. (2012). Cognitive-adaptation training for improving performance and stress management of air force pilots. *The International Journal of Aviation Psychology, 22*(3), 203–223.

Johnston, J. H., & Cannon-Bowers, J. A. (1996). Training for stress exposure. In J. E. Driskell & E. Salas (Eds.), *Series in applied psychology. Stress and human performance* (pp. 223–256). Lawrence Erlbaum Associates, Inc.

Kessler, P., & Fauquet-Alekhine, P. (2019) *Simulators, is it worth? Assessment of the "basic operational return on investment" of simulators regarding robotics in radioactive environments*. Proceedings of the 1st Int. Conf. for Multi-Area Simulation (ICMASim), 341–346.

Lazarus, R. S., & Folkman, S. (1984). *Stress, appraisal, and coping*. Springer.

Lefrançois, C., Moghaizel, C., Fornette, M., Amalberti, R., Fradin, J., & El Massioui, F. (2009). *Adaptive mental mode and performance in non-controlled situations: A study with student-pilots of the French Air Force*. In Conference Abstract: 41st European Brain and Behaviour Society Meeting (Vol. 8, No. 09.216).

Leka, S., Griffiths, A., & Cox, T. (2003). *Work organization and stress*. World Health Organization.

Leka, S., & Jain, A. (2010). *Health impact of psychosocial hazards at work: An overview*. World Health Organization.

McClernon, C. K., McCauley, M. E., O'Connor, P. E., & Warm, J. S. (2011). Stress training improves performance during a stressful flight. *Human Factors, 53*(3), 207–218.

Orasanu, J. M., & Backer, P. (1996). *Stress and military performance*. In J. E. Driskell & E. Salas (Eds.), *Series in applied psychology. Stress and human performance* (pp. 89–125). Lawrence Erlbaum Associates, Inc.

Otsuka, Y., Onozawa, A., & Miyamoto, Y. (2006). Hormonal responses of pilots to training flights: The effects of experience on apparent stress. *Aviation, Space, and Environmental Medicine, 77*, 410–414.

Robson, S., & Manacapilli, T. (2014). *Enhancing performance under stress: Stress inoculation training for battlefield airmen*. RAND Project Air Force.

Sigwalt, F., Petit, G., Evain, J. N., Claverie, D., Bui, M., Guinet-Lebreton, A., et al. (2020). Stress management training improves overall performance during critical simulated situations: A prospective randomized controlled trial. *Anesthesiology, 133*(1), 198–211.

16

Stress Adjustment as a Criterion for Hiring in High-Risk Jobs

Frédéric Choisay, Solange Duvillard-Monternier, Vanessa Fournier, Ghislain Champeaux, Alexandre Rey, and Jean-Louis Dubert

1 Stress and High-Risk Jobs

In some sensitive and critical occupations (e.g., police, firefighter, or military), exposure to danger and high risk (e.g., flight safety, vital risk for oneself and brothers in arms, the confrontation of death or the idea of death, the risk of collateral damage, life-threatening situations) requires high stress resistance. Military performance is marked by stressors, such as (1) environmental factors (noise, heat, cold, fatigue, lack of sleep), (2) workload factors (time pressure and uncertainty [Coeugnet et al., 2011], emotional and psychic, information overload), and (3) social factors (with squadron members, seniors).

F. Choisay
Centre d'études et de recherches psychologiques air (CERP'Air; French Air Force Psychological Studies & Researches Centre), Paris, France

University of Tours, Tours, France

S. Duvillard-Monternier (✉)
Crew Resource Management, The Armed Forces Biomedical Institute (Institut de Recherches Biomédicales des Armées—IRBA), Brétigny-sur-Orge, France
e-mail: solange.monternier@intradef.gouv.fr

© The Author(s), under exclusive license to Springer Nature Switzerland AG 2023
P. Fauquet-Alekhine, J. Erskine (eds.), *The Palgrave Handbook of Occupational Stress*,
https://doi.org/10.1007/978-3-031-27349-0_16

In addition, dispositional factors can mediate or moderate environmental factors because what stresses individuals is extremely variable and largely depends on the perception of the environment by individuals. Thus, these dispositional factors will interest psychologists in charge of evaluation and selection protocols (e.g., personality). For example, low self-esteem might be a vulnerability factor (Légeron, 2008), while extroverted and emotionally stable individuals might be more resistant to stress (Piedmont, 1993). Furthermore, so-called sociotropic personalities might be more vulnerable to relational stressors, unlike "autonomous" personalities, who are expected to be more subject to stressors relating to self-achievement (Légeron, 2008). An additional alternative approach is to identify protective factors, including at the individual level. Thus, when recruiting candidates, the armies seek to identify people who have good prerequisites that permits a good adjustment to a particularly constrained work environment. In this respect, the "adjustment reaction" (André et al., 1998) and the "adaptive logic" (Boisseaux, 2010, p. 30) are important for dealing with stressors of various natures.

Thus, firstly, it is necessary to identify which individual attributes are antecedents for resilience. Resilience is the ability to adapt and/or overcome stressful events (Meredith et al., 2011). Secondly, these individual qualities must be measurable in the recruitment context and show satisfactory predictive validity (Britt et al., 2016).

1.1 Adaptive Capacities of Individuals in a Professional Environment

Various studies have identified the individual attributes that confer resilience to individuals for hazardous occupations.

As part of a special report on psychological resilience in the US military, Meredith et al. (2011) conducted a literature review of 270 publications that

---

V. Fournier
Institut National d'Etudes du Travail et d'Orientation Professionnelle (INETOP; National Institute for Job Studies and Career Guidance),
Paris, France

G. Champeaux • A. Rey • J.-L. Dubert
Centre d'études et de recherches psychologiques air (CERP'Air; French Air Force Psychological Studies & Researches Centre), Paris, France
e-mail: alexandre1.rey@def.gouv.fr

identified seven key individual resilience factors: (1) positive coping (focused on problem solving), (2) positive affect (enthusiasm, optimism, flexibility), (3) positive thinking (positive reframing, positive expectations), (4) realism (realistic expectations, feeling of self-efficacy, self-confidence), (5) behavioral control (self-regulation), (6) physical fitness, and (7) altruism (intrinsic motivation, to be concerned for others). In addition, the NATO Task Force HFM-171 (2011) published a report on the psychological selection of military personnel to serve in Special Forces, one of the most dangerous jobs. In terms of personality assessment, the goal is to assess emotional stability and conscientiousness (Picano et al., 2006). Compared to the general population, elite soldiers had a lower frequency of negative affect and were more resilient, assertive, energetic, reliable, competitive, and disciplined (Picano et al., 2006). The NATO report focused on the opportunity to measure hardiness (Bartone et al., 2008) and grit (perseverance and consistency of interests; Beal, 2010; Duckworth et al., 2007), because they are specific personality traits that predict the adaptive abilities of candidates.

The adaptive capacity assessment ("adjustment" in the O*NET taxonomy, *Occupational Information Network*, by Peterson et al., 1999; Peterson et al., 2006) is operationalized differently depending on the target occupation, in terms of adaptability, self-control, emotional stability, or personal balance. These criteria come from a methodology of job analysis and are appreciated through a set of predictive and evaluative tools used by psychologists.

2 Stress Adjustment as a Criterion for Hiring?

2.1 Job Analysis Methodology

Applicant recruitment requires reaching for the best possible match between the capacities expected for the occupation and the individual skills, in the sense of an "integrated implementation of aptitudes, personality traits and also knowledge acquired to carry out a complex mission" (Lévy-Leboyer, 1996, p. 26). However, before evaluating these different characteristics when selecting candidates for so-called high-risk jobs, a job analysis is necessary. Indeed, a better understanding of the profession and its requirements makes it possible to refine the recruitment criteria, the primary aim of which is to evaluate the potential for success in specialist training. Job analysis is thus considered as "the prerequisite for any effective intervention" (Leplat, 2004, p. 207) and as a "prerequisite for developing a battery of tests designed to evaluate the likelihood for the subject to succeed in a given position "(Lévy-Leboyer, 1996, p. 24).

302   F. Choisay et al.

Concerning Air Force occupations, psychologists generally use several methods based on observation on duty, collecting experts' opinions through interviews or questionnaires based on Fleishman's approach (Job Analysis Survey; Fleishman & Chartier, 1998; Fleishman & Mumford, 1988; Fleishman & Reilly, 1998; Fleishman et al., 1993).

Post studies help to update stressful situations that require professional military adaptability. As an example, we have categorized various stressful situations of high-risk occupations according to three types of stress, following a typology adapted from Stokes and Kite (1994, p. 131): (1) acute reactive stress: generally seen as a short-term effect closely linked to the execution of operational duties and defined as a response to a threatening event or circumstance (see Table 16.1); (2) environmental stress: in aviation, generally used to refer to a rather narrow set of ambient physical conditions, including noise, temperature, and vibration (see Table 16.2); and (3) life stress with chronic effect (e.g., major life changes, turning points and crises such as death of a family member, difficulty with employers) (see Table 16.3).

Subsequently, the adaptability of the applicants is assessed through various selection tests presented in the following paragraphs.

2.2 Scenarios, Semi-structured Interviews, and Personality Inventories

According to Rivolier (1992), it is essential to consider the candidate individually and collectively, in situations close to those at the core of the intervention occupations.

Indeed, Borteyrou et al. (2006) noted the importance of evaluating both, so-called stable and decontextualized characteristics, via personality and intelligence tests and also specific and contextualized behaviors via scenarios. These scenarios are varied in nature: test-in-basket, role-play, structured interview, or group test. Structured standardized interview is a technique with good predictive validity (McDaniel et al., 1994; Borteyrou et al., 2006). If the test-in-basket, role-play, and group test scenarios are valid for correct content, good construct validity seems to be more difficult to obtain. Thus, "these different scenarios make it impossible to measure dimensions (… resistance to stress, for example) independently of the tests used to evaluate them" (Borteyrou et al., 2006, p. 3).

To conduct a selection interview, the method that seems most appropriate is the semi-structured one. It differs from the structured interview (i.e., systematic questioning related to job analysis) and the non-structured interview

16 Stress Adjustment as a Criterion for Hiring in High-Risk Jobs   303

Table 16.1 Example of acute stressors of military and/or dangerous trades

Circumstances or context	High-risk jobs concerned	Study, year (origin)	Authors
Unpredictability of unpredictable stressful events (hard landing, acceleration, stopping, loss of engine)	Steward in the FAF	2012	Chen & Chen
Experts constituting the "last safety net," "last resort to avoid the occurrence of an accident"	Flying and air control	2013	Martin, Hourlier & Cegarra
"Stress and concentration when making the laser designation via the pod (arming delivery)" (p. 4)	Fighter pilot	2011	Royal
"Sense awake, watching for the slightest signal of a critical breakdown … We clearly hear the sounds of combat on the radio … The pilot is brutally immersed in the heart of the tactical situation" (p. 42)			
"The shock of the ejection and the strong apprehensions to say that one can die certainly, but that one can also live a Calvary being made prisoner" (according to p. 34)	Fighter pilot	2016	Dubey & Moricot
"… a certainty is necessary: It is not the fear of dying that haunts me, but the one of missing a shot or remaining helpless in the face of a dramatic situation on the ground" (p. 172)	Fighter pilot (testimony)	2013	Scheffler
"Every flight lasts five to six hours. Five to six hours strapped on an ejection seat as comfortable as a metro seat …" (p. 87)	Experience feedback from fighter pilots	2009	Lert
"Ejection ejection ejection! … The canopies fly, the icy wind rushes … Exit the cockpit, climb a hundred meters while the plane continues its course … Three hundred seconds, maybe a little more, maybe a little less … Three hundred seconds descent into icy clouds without visibility, with an ambient temperature of -20 ° C or -30 ° C …" (p. 86)			

(i.e., an interview where the applicant speaks freely as in a clinical interview). The semi-structured interview is characterized as a face-to-face situation in which two people interact and exchange, where the interviewer specifically seeks to gather information through open-ended questions related to specific topics. This collection of information, of concrete and personalized facts, is

304   F. Choisay et al.

Table 16.2 Example of environmental stressors for military and/or dangerous trades

Circumstances or context	High-risk jobs concerned	Study, year (origin)	Authors
• Dynamic and complex aeronautical situations • Multitasking that can lead to excessive mental load	Flying and air control	2013	Martin, Hourlier & Cegarra
"On the flight desk, environmental stressors include excessive heat, noise, vibration, and low humidity … these stresses are mental, not physical, and are by nature cumulative" (p. 71)	Pilot	1996, reprinted in 2014	Green, Muir, James, Gradwell & Green
"The importance of not making mistakes and … The heavy responsibilities that weigh on the shoulders of certain specialists …, the responsibility for the success of the mission" (p. 114)	Drone systems operators	2015	Duvillard-Monternier, Donnot &Gilles
Work in stressful environment	Air controller	1999	Carretta
From a cognitive point of view in aeronautics, perceived stress causes certain reactions, such as a narrowing of attention or the effect of "tunnelling" as pilots say, rigid responses, inattentional deafness	Pilot	2014	Dehais, Causse, Vachon, Régis, Menant & Tremblay

done according to standardized criteria whose link with the trade was defined during previous job analyses. This last point assures the ability to evaluate the suitability of the candidate for the position as objectively as possible, particularly with regard to his capacity to adapt and manage stress.

To be effective, it is essential to establish a climate of trust with the candidate so that s/he can express her/himself. The interviewer should use a certain amount of patience so that the applicants potential faking and resistance can fade, in order that the speech becomes free. The establishment of a facilitative climate favors the emergence of incidental information that will be detected by an "active" listening, where the psychologist analyzes the information received. Let us emphasize here the importance of listening, but also of the observation of the candidate behavior in response to certain questions which will also be part of the incidental non-verbal information collected and qualified as adapted, or not, with regard to the specialty and its expectations. As Rivolier (1989, p. 230) pointed out, "it is the phenomenological appreciation

16 Stress Adjustment as a Criterion for Hiring in High-Risk Jobs   305

Table 16.3 Example of chronic stressors of military and/or dangerous trades

Circumstances or context	High-risk jobs concerned	Study, year (origin)	Authors
"Adapt to the specific conditions of the outdoor operation and the pace of succession, the management of stressful situations of the ICT type (Troup In contact) and rocket launcher" (p. 110)	Drone systems operators	2015	Duvillard-Monternier, Donnot & Gilles
Physical, emotional, and psychic fatigue (e.g., fear, frustration, remorse)	Drone systems operators	2013	Ferrari, Tronche & Sauvet
The cognitive and emotional demand of certain persistent missions (long-term) (pp. 185–188, 201)	Drone systems operators	2013	Duvillard-Monternier, Donnot & Gilles
Stress resistance	Air controller	2011	Conzelmann, Heinz & Eißfeld
Stress management	Air controller	2002	Eurocontrol
Ability to work in situations where people are stressed and tense	Air controller	1998	Siem & Carretta
The [commercial navigating personnel] is affected by the burnout syndrome because it is significantly more exposed to the emotional demands, and in particular to that of hiding its emotions, than the rest of the professional population.	Stewards	2016	Richa, Zreika, & Richa
Their study of cabin attendants demonstrates a positive relationship between the demands of employment on the one hand and emotional dissonance, emotional exhaustion and depersonalization on the other.	Stewards	2003	Heuven & Bakker
They showed that flight attendants had 2 to 5.7 times more sleep problems, depression, and fatigue than the general population.	Stewards	2014	McNeely, Gale, Tager, Kincl, Bradley, Coull & Hecker
Testimony: "I learned not to allow my face to reflect my fear and my fear … Above all, I do not want the passengers to be scared": This implies a double-mastery: of oneself and those of the others; hence, a risk of emotional exhaustion. Stewards are very subject to emotional exhaustion.	Stewards	1983	Hochschild

(continued)

Table 16.3 (continued)

Circumstances or context	High-risk jobs concerned	Study, year (origin)	Authors
This profession is one of the most demanding professions at the emotional level.	Stewards	2009	DARES study
Challenge for the biological rhythm	Stewards	2011	Avers & Johnson

of events that is important" and it is for the interviewer to "focus on recognizing how the subject has coped in certain episodes in his life, what were his defense mechanisms and what were their consequences." These elements are evaluated more specifically thanks to information collected and allow us to provide a confirmation / denial of the dimensions highlighted by the inventories of personalities and dedicated tests.

Furthermore, personality inventories constitute a support for conducting semi-structured interviews by psychologists. One of these inventories, the OCEAN (Openness to experience, Conscientiousness, Extraversion, Agreeableness, and Neuroticism; Congard et al., 2012) is a tool based on the taxonomy of the Big Five (Goldberg, 1990). The OCEAN notably includes a factor "emotional stability versus neuroticism," itself divided into two facets: (1) "serenity versus anxiety/depression" and (2) "phlegm versus anger/impulsivity."

Another inventory, the ESCAPE (a French acronym meaning coping and emotional regulation strategies assessment; SERAP, 2012a), developed by the French Navy, informs the psychologist on candidates' strategies of emotional regulation and coping (Augustine & Hemenover, 2009; Larsen & Prizmic, 2004; Delicourt et al., 2012). It permits investigation of the way the applicants' emotions influence their behaviors and how they express themselves in the face of particularly stressful situations. Composed of 150 items, this tool refers, in particular, to the transactional model of Lazarus and Folkman (1984). These authors define coping as the "set of cognitive, affective and behavioral, variable and unstable efforts that the individual deploys to manage, tolerate and diminish the specific external and internal demands made by the individual-environment relation, which exceed his personal resources and threaten his well-being." In addition, these authors highlight an important variety of coping strategies that can be filed following three areas: (1) cognitive (e.g., assessment of the stressful situation, of own resources, search for information), (2) affective (e.g., emotion expression or repression), and (3) behavioral (e.g., problem solving, seeking support). Beyond this taxonomy,

16 Stress Adjustment as a Criterion for Hiring in High-Risk Jobs 307

Carver et al. (1989) have proposed another dimension centered on "avoidance": this type of coping consists of avoiding the stressful situation (e.g., denial, wishful thinking, mental distraction). It may include a behavioral or psychological disengagement from the situation by reorienting itself to other activities. Moreover, it is considered as protective for the individual, in the case where the stressors cannot be controlled. The ESCAPE inventory consists of six dimensions: (1) problem solving-oriented regulation, (2) positive emotion regulation, (3) negative emotion regulation, (4) search for support, (5) compensation through physical activity, and (6) so-called avoidance strategies, which are all elements that reflect candidates' preferential coping strategies and the development of adaptive behaviors (Dupain, 1998).

Finally, the *Criblage* (i.e., screening) inventory (SERAP, 2012b), also developed by the French Navy, investigates various potential personality disorders (adapted/normal or maladaptive/pathological) categorized into three groups, including the C group (e.g., neurotic disorders like avoidant, dependent personality, obsessive compulsive, anxious, and depressed).

The applicants take each of these inventories individually or collectively, on a computer or manually, for French speaking people, over a period ranging from 15 to about 45 minutes. All of these personality inventories have good psychometric qualities (i.e., validity, fidelity, and sensitivity). Hence, they are relevant for use in our recruitment protocols. These inventories have predictive validity because personality traits have a lasting effect regarding their influence on behaviors (Cloninger, 1996) contextualized in an environment.

If the assessment for each facet and sub-facet of personality brings interesting specific information, the optimal use is to examine the latter altogether in a holistic approach, by comparing with applicant's behavioral and verbatim comments.

Despite their good psychometric qualities, these inventories have some limits. The first is the partial character of the measurement inherent in any psychometric tool. Indeed, during their construction, the designers of these inventories made choices of constructs to measure characteristics representing only part of the constellation of measurable personality traits. The methodological and statistical choices led to the retention of only certain items to the detriment of others to carry out the evaluation of the personality traits. Another significant limitation to all these personality inventories is the need to master the language in which they are presented to respond by ensuring the proper understanding of the titles. Moreover, it should be noted that interculturality does not lead all candidates to rely on a common frame of reference to answer certain questions, which can sometimes lead to spurious conclusions. When the psychologist analyzes the results from these tools, he must know all the limits beforehand to make the assumptions that will be checked during the semi-structured interview. Moreover, it may be necessary to ask the candidate about his/her understanding of the questions (e.g., meaning). Indeed, some applicants give sometimes wrong answers because they do not pay attention to reverse items or encounter problems with wording (e.g., unknown terms). Nevertheless, these inventories constitute true investigative tools and an adequate support for the psychologist practice.

3 Stress's Adjustment Assessment in the French Air Force (FAF)

3.1 Predictive and Evaluative Tools Used by the FAF Psychological Studies & Researches Center's Psychologists

In order to detect applicants that have the prerequisite attributes permitting them to adapt to particularly constrained environments, the FAF uses a set of predictive and evaluative tools. The aim of the latter is to get reliable evidences of the effectiveness of attributes in order to evaluate and predict the intra-individual potential to adapt to environmental, social, and professional stressors. Thus, psychologists are compelled to relate the results of personality inventories (assessing stable and decontextualized characteristics), the scenarios (evaluating specific and contextualized behaviors), as well as the semi-structured interviews used by the FAF Psychological Studies & Researches Center in order to clear a cluster of evidences.

Thus, for each targeted occupation, some predictive and evaluative tools of candidates' adaptability will be used by the FAF Psychological Studies & Researches Center's psychologists (Fig. 16.1.).

Group and Individual Scenarios

The FAF Psychological Studies & Researches Center has developed a set of individual and collective tests to place candidates in simulated situations inspired from reality, to a certain extent, in order to get ecological validity related to the targeted jobs. Some of them have been specifically designed to measure stress management capabilities (e.g., simulator instructor, flight test pilot, Special Forces pilots or weapon system officers). For the specialty of flight attendant in FAF, candidates can also be asked about the emotional reactions they would adopt a priori toward anecdotes extracted from real facts.

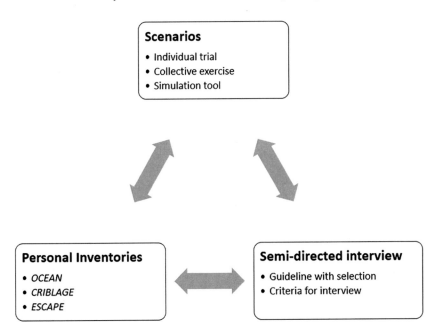

Fig. 16.1 General articulation of the different predictive and evaluative tools of candidates' adaptation skills employed at the FAF Psychological Studies & Researches Center

Most of these tests are carried out under the observation of a set of assessors composed of psychologists and professionals of the concerned specialty. All are provided with an observation grid comprising a set of criteria defined from job analysis. In order to standardize protocols as much as possible, each session or individual are presented with exactly the same instructions (e.g., time limit, return conditions of the solution to observers), the same materials (e.g., whiteboard, wall clock, written instructions, maps). Moreover, for collective scenarios, the same circular layout of the applicants' seats is used in order to facilitate interpersonal relations. Some of these tests, especially those designed to assess adaptability, include an input during the test. The latter aims to introduce a set of new data to be included in the current resolution. The input tests the capacity of adaptation and management of the stress with regard to an unexpected event leading to reconsider the solution until then developed in the remaining time to finish the exercise. In fact, the notions of evolution of the situations encountered and of time pressure are significant in occupations dealing with complex and unpredictable operations. These individual or collective scenarios provide evidence for assessing individual adaptive capacity. Indeed, the intra- and interpersonal dynamics of each candidate can be expressed, showing the strategies they implement to manage input, including coping strategies. Then, these behaviors are compared with the personality inventories results in order to find, or not, converging evidence.

The greatest difficulty lies in the construction of these tests. They must approximate the real-world that is examined (ecological validity), while being achievable by candidates who have received training neither for military nor for the job they apply for. If the ecological validity allows the greatest implication of the candidates in the resolution of the problem which is proposed to them, the level of difficulty must be carefully adapted to the level of the candidates who will present themselves to the selection (e.g., school level, prior knowledge expected).

Use of Personality Inventories in Interviews by Psychologists

All personality inventories used by the FAF Psychological Studies & Researches Center (i.e., OCEAN, CRIBLAGE, ESCAPE) are for sole and exclusive use of psychologists. They aim to assess candidates on a set of stable and decontextualized dimensions characterizing it to some extent.

In order to evaluate the candidate's ability for adaptability in relation to the position he is applying for, the psychologist will rely on the OCEAN and more particularly on the neurotic side (vs. emotional stability) presented in Sect. 2.2. Indeed, several studies have shown that people with low levels of emotional stability, enjoyment, and openness have higher levels of stress. These results argue in favor of particular attention to emotional stability, enjoyment, and openness when in order to assess stress resistance.

Then, the psychologist can explore these different areas through direct observation during the interview, but s/he can also direct some of her/his questions to remove doubts by exchanging on this subject with the candidate in an explicit and open way. This orientation allows the psychologist to assess the transferability of these traits to specific situations and characteristics of the applied occupation working conditions. Therefore, the psychologist gives his opinion pertaining to the applicant's adjustment likelihood in order to reduce potential risks for her/him or for the institution. Moreover, the psychologist determines to what extent the candidate is aware about this dimension of her/his personality. S/He also emphasizes the palliative strategies used by the applicant to cope with his potential difficulties. The psychologist relies on a set of specific and tangible facts reported by the candidate in order to establish her/his assessment regarding the criteria identified in the interviewer's handbook. A corollary constituting a real limit, especially as to the declarative aspect of speech, is the social desirability expressed through the candidate's answers. Hence, the psychologist has to take account for the inventory validity scale dealing with faking issues or social desirability. In this perspective, the psychologist will try to make the applicant think of a situation in order to get access to her/his reactions and strategies of adaptation. Thus, this practice allows to highlight the contextualization of the stable dimension which reinforce the ecology of the response.

In this perspective and in the assessment context for the evaluation of the applicants' adaptability facing a stressful situation, the psychologist will also use the CRIBLAGE inventory (group C disorders), including anxiety and depression components. The psychologist will investigate these pathologic dimensions in relation to the situations generating these states, their chronicity, their number, their intensity. The real advantage of this tool is that it warns the psychologist about certain pathological aspects that are tracks to be investigated later during the interview.

An additional transversal analysis can be found in the use of the ESCAPE inventory by the psychologist. This tool brings to light the strategies adopted by the individual to face some stressful situations. One limit is that the inventory instructions prompt the applicant to think about a specific situation before answering. Thus, the applicant profile does not characterize how s/he would deal with any stressful situation. Hence, the applicant's answers are more useful to engage a discussion with the psychologist about the situations that the candidate perceives as particularly stressful. This practice will require (1) to identify with the candidate the situation that s/he has considered to answer the inventory questions and (2) to make the candidate think about various situations during the interview to evaluate the level of transferability of each of these strategies, including the appropriate balance between problem solving and emotion regulation strategies. Besides the limit dealing with the thought situations, we could argue that young applicants may have never felt or lived stressful events. Moreover, each candidate would think about very different situations that could involve very different behaviors (e.g., bereavement, traffic accident, vexation, or a humiliating situation). Another limitation is the intra-personal aspect of stress. In fact, the same situation is not cognitively evaluated in the same way by individuals (perceived intra-personal resources and perceived situational demands) who will not use the same strategies to manage their stress and thus ensure their adaptation. This results in a real lack of homogeneity and equivalence of the subjective projections made by the candidates. Hence, the psychologists have to investigate the nature of this projection during the face-to-face interviews.

For example, we can make a connection between the ESCAPE inventory and the individual test proposed to FAF flight attendant candidates. During this individual event, the applicants are asked to think about specific anecdotes designed from real job situations. Each of these situations involves a more or less strong emotional valence. The candidates are asked to specify what they would feel in such a stressful situation and what strategy(ies) they would spontaneously implement to feel better. The objective is to access the way the applicants manage their emotions by analyzing the range of their emotional vocabulary. The assessment of the latter is essential for qualifying the identification and expression of emotions (Mikolajczak & Desseilles, 2012). The psychologist can then use the LEAS (Levels of Emotional Awareness Scale), a clinical scale developed by Lane et al. (1990) to assess the level of emotion identification. If the answer lacks precision or adaptation, the psychologist will discuss with the candidate at the end of the interview to check if there would be an issue for work in the applied occupation. Thus, a wise practice is to draw a parallel between the range of the emotional vocabulary and the used coping strategies in order to characterize them in the light of the situation.

As we have seen previously, personality inventories allow the psychologist to formulate a working hypothesis about the intrinsic behavioral resources of the subject. Thus, these results serve as a support for the psychologist to guide the questions of the semi-structured interview s/he will conduct with respect to the first hypotheses s/he has been able to formulate in correlation with these data. Indeed, the assessment of the applicants' ability to adjust to stressful situations is very complex and takes time. Hence, the psychologist should not make a decision based on a specific observation and s/he will need to perform a holistic assessment based on a body of accurate behavioral evidence.

In this respect, and among other things, the semi-structured interview aims at checking if the hypotheses are relevant, in adequacy with the convergence of collected behavioral hint bundles. Thus, the psychologist should adjust the progress of the interview according to the incidental information s/he collects to verify the suitability of the candidate for the occupation for which s/he applied.

Convergence of Different Predictive and Evaluative Tools

Finally, the entire selection process aims to collect applicants' attitudes, behaviors, and abilities to manage stress, expression of feelings and emotions or knowledge to ground an accurate assessment.

Information collected by the above-mentioned tools constitutes elements of convergence and divergence allowing us to assess if the applicant shows the basic prerequisites as well as the adequate potential of adaptation required by the applied occupation. Thus, the intrinsic capacities of the individual to cope with stressful situations, while considering operational and security requirements, are manifested by her/his ability to balance her/his perceptions (personal resources and environmental demands). These elements are used by the psychologist who will report potential issues for applicant hiring as presence of psychological weaknesses, tendencies to depression or inadequate stress resistance capacity. This allows the psychologist to make an informed opinion on the risks, for the person concerned as well as for the institution that the employer takes in case of a hiring decision. Indeed, a "soldier is more likely to trigger a traumatic pathology after a traumatic confrontation if he is depressed suffering" (Palinkas & Browner, 1995).

The main interest of this procedure is that it allows us to collect behavioral evidences of varied nature, to talk with the candidate about elements constituting the personality and the perceived behavior in order to obtain clarification if necessary. Hence, the hiring board would make its decision from a measured and well-reasoned assessment of the risks for the candidate or for the institution. With ethics and deontology, this approach ensures an assessment of the level of suitability of the candidate with the target job. Indeed, the main goal is to detect a real predisposition to resilience, while avoiding a maximum of weaknesses that could lead to any decompensation. Moreover, another goal is to protect the institution workforce from any type of harmful personality.

4   Concluding Remarks

The main objective of this chapter was to show that the evaluation of adaptability to stress is a critical criterion for the recruitment of candidates for FAF high-risk specialties (e.g., fighter pilots, Special Forces). Indeed, stress is an inherent characteristic of these occupations. However, adjustment issues should not affect the security and operational issues of missions. Hence, applicants' assessment tends to identify good intrinsic predispositions to adapt to a particularly constrained environment with regard to operational demands.

In order to deal with this issue, the FAF Psychological Studies & Researches Center's psychologists use the most complete and rigorous methodology possible in order (1) to make a discerning assessment of the individuals susceptibility to stress and (2) to provide the employer with the most sensitive and well-argued analysis possible of the potential risk of hiring a candidate in the interest of both the candidate and the institution.

The FAF Psychological Studies & Researches Center's psychologists, as well as the professionals accompanying them during the recruitment sessions, aim to converge toward a set of different types of bundles, notably to assess the candidate's ability to adapt to stress. Indeed, in the event of a favorable conclusion, the majority of the recruitment procedures result in an entry into training. This training is long and costly for the institution, but also for the candidates who will have to invest to the maximum of their capacities to validate it. Thus, the general evaluation aims to prevent failures and miscellaneous withdrawals that involve a financial cost. Moreover, candidates may consider a reorientation (within the institution or a return to the civil sector) that could lead them to lose self-esteem, self-efficacy, or a sense of competence. Indeed, this type of event can trigger a harmful personal reconsideration. Hence, the evaluation, from an ethical and deontological point of view, tends to protect the candidate from potential suffering.

However, the search for the most adaptive individual profile should not hide non-individual stressors, at the risk of falling into the "dark side of resilience" (Adler, 2013). Indeed, focus on individual abilities may lead to stigmatizing a person for failure by considering her/him as "weak." Moreover, the concentration of efforts on individual resilience can insidiously lead to a lack of interest from work organizations in optimally adapting the work environment (e.g., reducing constraints when possible, avoiding unnecessary dangers; Adler, 2013; Eidelson et al., 2011). Thus, it is necessary to identify both individual and organizational stressors in order to have a systemic approach to resilience to optimize and maintain the human potential of the armed forces.

References

Adler, A. B. (2013). Resilience in a military occupational health context: Directions for future research. In R. R. Sinclair & T. W. Britt (Eds.), *Building psychological resilience in military personnel: Theory and practice* (pp. 223–235). American Psychological Association. https://doi.org/10.1037/14190-010

André, C., Lelord, F., Légeron, P., & Etienne, J. L. (1998). *Le stress*. Editions Privat.

Augustine, A. A., & Hemenover, S. H. (2009). On the relative effectiveness of affect regulation strategies: A meta-analysis. *Cognition and Emotion, 23*(6), 1181–1220.

Avers, K., & Johnson, W. B. (2011). A review of federal aviation administration fatigue research. *Aviation Psychology and Applied Human Factors, 1*(2), 87–98.

Bartone, P. T., Roland, R. R., Picano, J. J., & Williams, T. J. (2008). Psychological hardiness predicts success in US Army Special Forces candidates. *International Journal of Selection and Assessment, 16*(1), 78–81.

16 Stress Adjustment as a Criterion for Hiring in High-Risk Jobs   315

Beal, S. A. (2010). *The roles of perseverance, cognitive ability, and physical fitness in US Army Special Forces assessment and selection* (No. ARI-RR-1927). Army Research Inst for the Behavioral and Social Sciences Fort Bragg NC Scientific Coordination Office.

Boisseaux, H. (2010). Le stress au sein de la population militaire: du stress opérationnel à l'état de stress post-traumatique. *Médecine et armées, 38*(1), 29–36.

Borteyrou, X., Rascle, N., Bruchon-Schweitzer, M., & Collomb, P. (2006). Construction et validation d'une épreuve de groupe élaborée dans le cadre d'un assessment center pour les officiers de la marine. *Orientation scolaire et professionnelle, 35*(4), 535–554. https://doi.org/10.4000/osp.1190

Britt, T. W., Shen, W., Sinclair, R. R., Grossman, M. R., & Klieger, D. M. (2016). How much do we really know about employee resilience? *Industrial and Organizational Psychology, 9*(2), 378–404.

Carretta, T. R. (1999). *Determinants of US Air Force enlisted air traffic controller success.* Air Force Research Lab Wright-Patterson Afb Oh.

Carver, C. S., Scheier, M. F., & Weintraub, J. K. (1989). Assessing coping strategies: A theoretically based approach. *Journal of Personality and Social Psychology, 56*(2), 267.

Chen, C.-F., & Chen, S.-C. (2012). Burnout and work engagement among cabin crew: Antecedents and consequences. *The International Journal of Aviation Psychology, 22*(1), 41–58. https://doi.org/10.1080/10508414.2012.635125

Cloninger, S. C. (1996). *Personality: Description, dynamics, and development.* WH Freeman/Times Books/Henry Holt & Co.

Coeugnet, S., Charron, C., Van De Weerdt, C., Anceaux, F., & Naveteur, J. (2011). La pression temporelle: un phénomène complexe qu'il est urgent d'étudier. *Le travail humain, 74*(2), 157–181.

Congard, A., Antoine, P., & Gilles, P.-Y. (2012). Assessing the structural and psychometric properties of the new personality measure for use with military personnel in the French armed forces. *Military Psychology, 24*(3), 285–307.

Conzelmann, K., Heintz, A. & Eißfeldt, H. (2011). A large scale validation study on air traffic controller selection and training-design, challenges and results. In *Proceedings of the 16th International Symposium on Aviation Psychology* (pp. 375–380). Dayton, OH, USA.

DARES–DREES. (2009). *Indicateurs provisoires de risques psychosociaux au travail,* collège d'expertise sur le suivi statistique des risques psychosociaux au travail, octobre.

Dehais, F., Causse, M., Vachon, F., Régis, N., Menant, E., & Tremblay, S. (2014). Failure to detect critical auditory alerts in the cockpit: Evidence for inattentional deafness. *Human Factors, 56*(4), 631–644.

Dejours, C. (1998). *La souffrance en France: la banalisation de l'injustice sociale.* Seuil.

Delicourt, A., Gros, F., & Congard, A. (2012). *Manuel de l'inventaire ESCAPE— Evaluation des Stratégies de Coping et d'Ajustement aux Problématiques Emotionnelles.* Etude n°12/368. Section d'Etudes et de Recherches des Applications de la Psychologie (SERAP). French Navy. Saint-Mandrier sur Mer.

Dismukes, R. K., Kochan, J. A., & Goldsmith, T. E. (2018). Flight crew errors in challenging and stressful situations. *Aviation Psychology and Applied Human Factors, 8*(1), 35–46. https://doi.org/10.1027/2192-0923/a000129

Dubey, G., & Moricot, C. (2016). *Dans la peau d'un pilote de chasse: le spleen de l'homme machine*. Presses universitaire de France.

Duckworth, A. L., Peterson, C., Matthews, M. D., & Kelly, D. R. (2007). Grit: Perseverance and passion for long-term goals. *Journal of Personality and Social Psychology, 92*(6), 1087.

Dupain, P. (1998). Le «coping»: Une revue du concept et des méthodes d'évaluation. *Journal de thérapie comportementale et cognitive, 8*(4), 131–138.

Duvillard-Monternier, S., Donnot, J., & Gilles, P.-Y. (2013). L'évaluation dynamique des opérateurs de systèmes de drones de l'armée de l'air. In S. Mazoyer, J. de Lespinois, E. Goffi, G. Boutherin, & C. Pajon (dir.), *Les drones aériens: passé, présent et avenir. Approche globale* (pp. 183–202). La documentation française.

Duvillard-Monternier, S., Donnot, J., & Gilles, P.-Y. (2015). Quelles sont les aptitudes cruciales pour les postes d'opérateurs de systèmes de drones 'Harfang'? *Le travail humain, 78*(2), 97–118.

Eidelson, R., Pilisuk, M., & Soldz, S. (2011). The dark side of comprehensive soldier fitness.

Eurocontrol. (2002). Selection tests, interviews and assessment centres for ab initio trainee controllers: Guidelines for implementation.

Ferrari, V., Tronche, C., & Sauvet, F. (2013). Persistance humaine et systèmes de drone: évaluation de la fatigue des opérateurs engagé en Afghanistan. In S. Mazoyer, J. de Lespinois, E. Goffi, G. Boutherin, & C. Pajon (dir.), *Les drones aériens: passé, présent et avenir. Approche globale* (pp. 203–213). La documentation française.

Fleishman, E. A., & Chartier, D. (1998). *Guide d'utilisation (F-JAS2). Analyse de poste de Fleishman. Compétences inter-personnelles et sociales*. ECPA.

Fleishman, E. A., & Mumford, M. D. (1988). Ability requirement scales. In S. Gael (Ed.), *The job analysis handbook for business, industry and government* (pp. 917–935). Wiley.

Fleishman, E. A., & Reilly, M. E. (1998). *Guide des aptitudes humaines. Définitions, exigences de poste de travail et évaluation* (D. Chartier, trad.). ECPA (édition originale, 1995).

Fleishman, E. A., Reilly, M. E., Chartier, D., & Lévy-Leboyer, C. (1993). *Guide d'utilisation (F-JAS). Analyse de poste de Fleishman* (D. Chartier & C. Lévy-Leboyer, trad.) ECPA (édition originale, 1992).

Goldberg, L. R. (1990). An alternative 'description of personality': The big-five factor structure. *Journal of Personality and Social Psychology, 59*(6), 1216–1229.

Green, R. G., Muir, H., James, M., Gradwell, D., & Green, R. L. (1996). *Human factors for pilots* (2nd ed.). Ashgate.

Heuven, E., & Bakker, A. (2003). Emotional dissonance and burnout among cabin attendants. *European Journal of Work and Organizational Psychology, 12*(1), 81–100.

16 Stress Adjustment as a Criterion for Hiring in High-Risk Jobs 317

Hochschild, A. (1983). *The managed heart: The commercialization of human feeling*. University of California Press.

Lane, R. D., Quinlan, D. M., Schwartz, G. E., Walker, P. A., & Zeitlin, S. B. (1990). The levels of emotional awareness scale: A cognitive-developmental measure of emotion. *Journal of Personality Assessment, 55*(1–2), 124–134.

Larsen, R. J., & Prizmic, Z. (2004). Affect regulation. In R. F. Baumeister & K. D. Vohs (Eds.), *Handbook of self-regulation research, theory, and applications* (pp. 40–61). The Guilford Press.

Lazarus, R. S., & Folkman, S. (1984). *Stress, appraisal, and coping*. Springer Publishing Company.

Légeron, P. (2008). Le stress professionnel. *L'information psychiatrique, 84*(9), 809–820. https://doi.org/10.1684/ipe.2008.0394

Leplat, J. (2004). L'analyse psychologique du travail. *Revue européenne de psychologie appliquée, 54,* 101–108.

Lert, F. (2009). *Pilotes en Afghanistan*. Editions Altipresse.

Lévy-Leboyer, C. (1996). *La gestion des compétences*. Editions d'Organisation.

Martin, C., Hourlier, S., & Cegarra, J. (2013). La charge mentale de travail: un concept qui reste indispensable, l'exemple de l'aéronautique. *Le travail humain, 76*(4), 285–308.

McDaniel, M. A., Whetzel, D. L., Schmidt, F. L., & Maurer, S. D. (1994). The validity of employment interview: A comprehensive review and meta-analysis. *Journal of Applied Psychology, 79*(4), 599–616.

McNeely, E., Gale, S., Tager, I., Kincl, L., Bradley, J., Coull, B., & Hecker, S. (2014). The self-reported health of US flight attendants compared to the general population. *Environmental Health, 13*(1), 1.

Meredith, L. S., Sherbourne, C. D., Gaillot, S. J., Hansell, L., Ritschard, H. V., Parker, A. M., & Wrenn, G. (2011). Promoting psychological resilience in the US military. *Rand Health Quarterly, 1*(2), 2.

Mikolajczak, M., & Desseilles, M. (2012). *Traité de régulation des émotions*. De Boeck Supérieur.

NATO Science and Technology Organization. (2011). *Final Report of Task Group HFM-171*. Brussels, Belgium.

Palinkas, L. A., & Browner, D. (1995). Effects of prolongea isolation in extreme environments on stress, coping, and depression. *Journal of Applied Social Psychology, 25*(7), 557–576.

Peterson, N. G., Mumford, M. D., Borman, W. C., Jeanneret, P. R., & Fleishman, E. A. (1999). *An occupational information system for the 21st century: The development of O*NET*. American Psychological Association.

Peterson, N. G., Mumford, M. D., Borman, W. C., Jeanneret, P. R., Fleishman, E. A., Levin, K. Y., & Dye, D. M. (2006). Understanding work using the occupational information network (O* NET): Implications for practice and research. *Personnel Psychology, 54*(2), 451–492.

Picano, J., & Roland, R. R. (2012). Assessing psychological suitability for high-risk military jobs. In J. H. Laurence & M. D. Matthews (Eds.), *The Oxford Handbook of Military Psychology* (pp. 148–157). Oxford University Press.

Picano, J. J., Williams, T. J., & Roland, R. R. (2006). Assessment and selection of high-risk operational personnel. In C. H. Kennedy & E. A. Zillmer (Eds.), *Military psychology: Clinical and operational applications* (pp. 353–370). The Guilford Press.

Piedmont, R. L. (1993). A longitudinal analysis of burnout in the health care setting: The role of personal dispositions. *Journal of Personality Assessment, 61*(3), 457–473.

Richa, N., Zreik, H., & Richa, S. (2016). Le syndrome d'épuisement professionnel et les facteurs de risques psychosociaux spécifiques au métier des personnels navigants commerciaux libanais, en comparaison avec un groupe témoin. *L'Encéphale, 42*(2), 144–149. https://doi.org/10.1016/j.encep.2015.12.016

Rivolier, J. (1989). *L'homme stressé.* Presses Universitaires de France.

Rivolier, J. (1992). *Facteurs humains et situations extrêmes.* Editions Masson.

Royal, B. (2011). *L'éthique du soldat français: la conviction d'humanité.* Economica. 2ᵉᵐᵉ édition.

Scheffler, M. (2013). *La guerre vue du ciel: les combats d'un pilote de Mirage 2000.* Edition Nimrod.

SERAP. (2012a). *Manuel de l'inventaire ESCAPE (Evaluation des Stratégies de Coping et d'Ajustement aux Problématiques Emotionnelles).* Psychologist report. Service de Psychologie de la Marine.

SERAP. (2012b). *Manuel de l'inventaire de personnalité Criblage.* Psychologist report. Service de Psychologie de la Marine : Toulon.

Siem, F. M., & Carretta, T. R. (1998). *Determinants of enlisted air traffic controller success.* In Air Force Research Laboratory (Ed.), ARL-HE-AZ-TR-1998-0079.

Stokes, A., & Kite, K. (1994). *Flight stress: Stress, fatigue, and performance in aviation.* University Press.

Part IV

Macro Description of Stress

17

Cross-cultural Ideas on Stress

Philippe Fauquet-Alekhine and James Erskine

1 Introduction

Beyond the spontaneous or scientific curiosity that can inspire the difference in perception of stress factors at work from one country to another, the knowledge and study of these intercultural differences takes on a practical aspect. Indeed, more and more workers are moving from one country to another, either to settle in a host country or to move temporarily for a specific mission, or because multinationals are building multicultural work contexts (see, e.g.: Lin et al., 2019). Filla et al. (2018: 229) justifies it as follows: "from an organisational behavior perspective, shared cultural characteristics in a given country are generally thought to outweigh the characteristics of any single organisation within it. This relative isomorphism is likely to result in national cultural characteristics being stronger than inherent cultural differences across

---

P. Fauquet-Alekhine (✉)
SEBE-Lab, Department of Psychological and Behavioural Science,
London School of Economics and Political Science, London, UK

Laboratory for Research in Science of Energy, Montagret, France

Groupe INTRA Robotics, Avoine, France
e-mail: p.fauquet-alekhine@lse.ac.uk; philippe.fauquet-alekhine@groupe-intra.com

J. Erskine
Institute for Medical and Biomedical Sciences, St George's University of London,
London, UK
e-mail: jerskine@sgul.ac.uk

© The Author(s), under exclusive license to Springer Nature Switzerland AG 2023
P. Fauquet-Alekhine, J. Erskine (eds.), *The Palgrave Handbook of Occupational Stress*,
https://doi.org/10.1007/978-3-031-27349-0_17

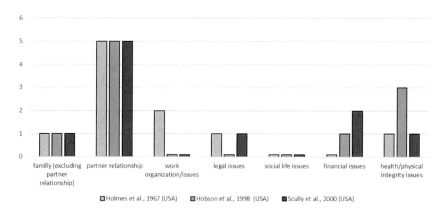

Fig. 17.1 Intercomparison of the top-10 SRRS studies categorised according to seven families of concerns for the US population

organisations within a given nation. Thus, the importance for business educators, researchers, and practitioners to understand cross-cultural differences, and the psychological mechanisms that underpin them, cannot be overstated."

Culture is usually associated with a country or region. Culture therefore has a national character which has been explored in the previous literature. Several models make it possible to theorise the culture of a country (Hofstede, 1980; Schwartz, 1994); however, this is not the subject of this chapter. The aim here is to examine the relationship between stress in general (and occupational stress in particular; Fig. 17.1) and cultural factors, and to identify the nature of these relationships.

2   Culture and Stress

Wallace (1966), a cultural anthropologist quoted by Aldwin (2004), compared "culture" to a mazeway built of values, beliefs, and resources that form a whole, influencing the collective. Differential individual impacts accrue depending on where the individual is in the mazeway.

For Hofstede (1980: 24), "culture" is "the collective programming of the human mind that distinguishes the members of one human group from those of another."

If the mazeway induces a set of stressors for all those who walk through it, the perception of these stressors by individuals differs depending on the position of individuals in the maze and therefore the reactions are different. From this analogy of culture proposed by Wallace (1966) and its link with stress, it must be understood that a cultural context generates a set of stressors that are specific to the context but that the actors of this context will not all be impacted in the same way (see also Beehr & Glazer, 2001). More specifically, cultural differences lead to different perceptions of stress at work, in particular because of the way workers perceive working conditions, knowing that these working conditions as well as their perception are influenced by the cultural context, according to the theory of culture's consequences (Hofstede, 2001). What is interesting here is the fact that a cultural context can generate a set of stressors of its own. Indeed, studies have shown how the individual is shaped to some extent by the cultural context upon which their perception of the world depends, and thus, by extension, the factors of stress (Lomas, 2018).

For example, Liu et al. (2007) have shown that lack of job control was a frequently reported stressor by North American workers, yet not by Chinese workers, and that the former reported more direct conflicts at work while the latter reported indirect conflicts. The authors concluded that this was induced by the individualistic culture of the US versus the more collective culture in China.

To illustrate this, let us take the case of a country where corruption in education is widespread, and in order to graduate, students know that they will have to work on the different disciplines and pass their exams, but also to discreetly pay the teachers responsible for academic training. Compared to another country where this type of corruption does not exist, it is clear that in the first country, the cultural context will generate a stressor on the student population that is unique to it. As a result, a comparative study between the two countries regarding graduation will likely lead students from the first country to identify the consequences of this corruption as a significant stressor while it will be absent in the second country. Similarly, if we consider a country in which crime is very high, the citizens of that country will probably identify the fear of being assaulted in the street as a significant stressor, unlike a country where crime is very low.

According to Aldwin (2004), culture can influence stress and coping strategies in four different ways. Firstly, the cultural context generates its own stressors as described above. Secondly, an individual's culture has an influence on how they perceive stressors. Thirdly, the same applies regarding the choice of coping strategy. Finally, culture has an influence on the institutional organisation of a country which can be either a resource or a constraint for the individual depending on the position of the individual in this organisation. For example, some cultures can induce stressors at specific ages on individuals; this is the case of cultures that impose a puberty ritual on their adolescents. These rituals are presented in the cultural context producing it as a normative life event. They will be perceived as stressors for the youngest population while the oldest population will have forgotten the stress induced by its rituals that are part of the distant past. Aldwin (2004) notes that, consistent with stress models (see Chap. 2 of the present book), the more restrictive a culture is, the more numerous and intense the stressors. The perception of stressors is also different depending on whether the culture is more oriented towards the Self or towards Others (Shek & Cheung, 1990). Regarding institutional resources, some cultures can produce helping professions for individuals suffering from the effects of stress: for example, psychologists or psychiatrists are supporting professions, but these professions are more or less present in the social fabric depending on the culture.

Here are some examples of studies illustrating the differential impact of sociocultural context:

- By comparing a sample of the Russian population residing in Russia with a sample of the Russian population who emigrated to Western Europe, Berezina et al. (2020) showed that the respective cultural contexts caused migrants settled in Western Europe to feel younger than their calendar age while Russians remaining in Russia felt close to their chronological age. Ageing therefore induced a stressor of different magnitude on each of the samples.
- Based on a survey conducted in 15 Western European countries on more than 10,000 adult subjects, Daniels (2004) showed that sociocultural factors reduced the perception of risk associated with occupational stress in Great Britain, Ireland, and Austria, while the opposite was true for France, Italy, and Greece. In this study, since sociocultural contexts are different, it is not surprising that they produce different effects. However, other studies show that identical stressors can cause different effects from one country to another. This is the case of Perrewé et al. (2002) who found that role conflict and ambiguity were low to moderate in both Hong Kong and the US, but while it resulted in a high self-efficacy and low levels of burnout for workers in the US, it conversely led to low self-efficacy and high levels of burnout in Hong Kong.
- Le et al. (2020: 18) have shown, from a review of the scientific literature, that "confucianism and collectivism seem to play the most influential role in explaining differences in work–life interface between employees in Asia and the West" thus differently shaping perception of stress factors in daily life.

Since the influence of cultural context is evident, and the differences from one cultural context to another can obviously induce different stressors, one would expect to find in the literature many studies identifying major specific stressors associated with different cultural contexts. Unfortunately, it is necessary to make the same observation as Aldwin (2004) several decades earlier, or more recently by Fila and Wilson (2018): there are very few practical studies on the subject in the scientific literature allowing an in-depth comparison of major specific stressors on a wide range of cultures. Scientific articles are generally limited to the intercomparison of two or three countries and do not provide a comprehensive approach to stressors but rather a categorical approach (see, e.g., the review by Van Fossen & Chang, 2020). In addition, most scientific production focuses more on coping strategies, themselves cultural dependent (as already noted more than 40 years earlier: Antonovsky, 1979).

Although practical studies addressing the diversity and specificity of stressors induced by culture are not the main core of the scientific literature, attempts were made in the mid-twentieth century in the US. In 1967, Holmes and Rahe proposed the use of the Social Readjustment Rating Scale (SRRS, Holmes & Rahe, 1967), a standardised questionnaire to identify and assess life event effects on the psychological state of people. Based on clinical experiences with American subjects, the authors drew up a list of 43 items and asked nearly 400 people to classify these items according to their degree of influence on their lives in terms of social readjustment. It is interesting to explore two axes of temporal evolution for this questionnaire. The first axis is that of its evolution with the American population, since the questionnaire was rediscussed in 1998 (Hobson et al., 1998) and then in 2000 (Scully et al., 2000). The second axis is its adjustment to other cultures: for European culture in 2004 (Berntsen & Rubin, 2004) and more recently for Caribbean culture (Haque et al., 2020).

Table 17.1 lists the top-10 items for American, Danish, and Caribbean subjects. It could be argued that this table is of limited scientific interest. Indeed, the data concerning the American population are temporally very distant from other data: 55 years separate the first study of Holmes and Rahe (1967) in the US from the last study of Haque et al. concerning the Caribbean population (2020), and even if we considered only the last study of the American population in 2000 (Scully et al., 2000), it is only four years from those for the Danish (Berntsen & Rubin, 2004) but 18 years from those for the Caribbean. It can be argued that with the effect of time, people's concerns have changed, if only by technological or economic evolution, which does not really allow to build an opinion on the influence of culture. However, it is possible to apprehend these data in another way: it would be necessary to consider a cultural context for given countries at given times and to consider that it is on this basis that the comparison is made. We will therefore focus,

326 P. Fauquet-Alekhine and J. Erskine

Table 17.1 Top-10 items of the Social Readjustment Rating Scale (SRRS) in different studies

Rank	Holmes and Rahe (1967) (US)	Hobson et al. (1998) (US)	Scully et al. (2000) (US)	Berntsen and Rubin (2004) (Danish)	Haque et al. (2020) (Caribbean)
1	Death of spouse	Death of spouse	Death of spouse	Gain of a new family member (having children)	Gain of a new family member (birth of a baby)
2	Divorce	Death of a close family member	Divorce	Marriage	Abortion
3	Marital separation	Personal injury or illness (major injury or illness)	Personal injury or illness	Begin or end school (begin school)	First job
4	Jail term	Foreclosure of mortgage or loan	Marital separation	Earn first money	Leave home
5	Death of a close family member	Divorce	Jail term	Fall in love	Parents' separation
6	Personal injury or illness	Victim of a crime (being a victim of a crime)	Marriage	Death of close friend (others' death)	Death of a close family member (close family member's death)
7	Marriage	Being the victim of police brutality	Death of a close family member	Marital reconciliation	Marriage
8	Fired from work	Infidelity	Change in financial state	Leave home	Divorce
9	Marital reconciliation	Marital separation (separation or reconciliation with spouse/mate)	Sex difficulties	Death of a close family member (parents' death)	Infidelity

(continued)

17 Cross-cultural Ideas on Stress   327

Table 17.1 (continued)

Rank	Holmes and Rahe (1967) (US)	Hobson et al. (1998) (US)	Scully et al. (2000) (US)	Berntsen and Rubin (2004) (Danish)	Haque et al. (2020) (Caribbean)
10	Retirement	Marital reconciliation (separation or reconciliation with spouse/mate)	Foreclosure of mortgage or loan	First job	Fall in love (falling in love)

Note: The countries of the studied populations are mentioned between brackets in the first row. Regarding the items, those mentioned in the columns are the ones used by the researchers in their studies; following between brackets is the correspondence with the original items of the 1967 Holmes and Rahe's scale

first, on the evolution of Americans' concerns over the three periods, 1967, 1998 and 2000, and secondly, on the comparison of the differences between Americans in 2000, Danes in 2004, and Caribbean in 2022.

To facilitate intercomparison, the top-10 items for each study were categorised into seven families. This was necessary because some items from one study do not appear in another study; for example, the item "infidelity" for the Caribbean is absent from the other studies, as well as for the item "jail term" from the study by Hobson et al. (1998) for the American population. The fact that SRRS items are present in one study and not in the other is not a handicap but an opportunity: indeed, it testifies to the willingness of researchers to adjust the items of the scale according to the cultural context considered.

The seven families are as follows:

- family (excluding partner relationship),
- partner relationship,
- work organisation/issues,
- legal issues,
- social life issues,
- financial issues, and
- health/physical integrity issues.

The comparison of the three studies concerning the American population is of double interest: first, the 1998 study attempted to recompose the items of the original 1967 study and thus modified some of the items, therefore illustrating the evolution of concerns over time; Then, the 2000 study solicited subjects to rank the items according to their concerns based on the original 1967 scale, thus allowing for appreciation of how the scale of the original study is restructured.

Figure 17.1 allows the three studies (1967, 1998, 2000) to be compared according to the seven families defined above. It seems clear that family and relationship considerations with the partner do not change, that considerations associated with social life are absent from this top-10, and that financial considerations become more and more important over time. For other families, it is quite difficult to say. The hypothesis can therefore be made that, between 1998 and 2000, stressors associated with the financial situation of Americans increased in importance. Also, the observation can be made that the most important and permanent stressors over time are those associated with romantic relationship: rapprochement (marriage, reconciliation) or separation (divorce, death) of the romantic partner.

The intercomparison of the three studies addressing Americans (Scully et al., 2000), Danish (Berntsen & Rubin, 2004), and Caribbean (Haque et al., 2020) according to the seven families categorised above is presented in Fig. 17.2.

The North American population study is based on the original SRRS by Holmes and Rahe (1967). The other two studies built on the original items but offered the possibility for participants to add items considered more important by participants than those proposed in the original version. This is why, from one study to another, the top-10 presents items that are not included in the other studies. This is also why it was necessary to categorise the top-10 into families in order to make the results comparable from one study to another.

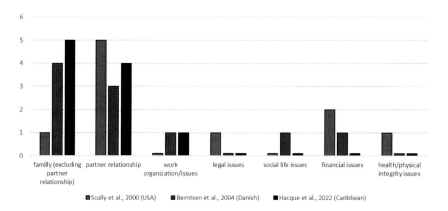

Fig. 17.2 Intercomparison of the top-10 SRRS studies categorised according to seven families of concerns for the US population (Scully et al., 2000), Danish (Berntsen & Rubin, 2004), and Caribbean (Haque et al., 2020)

The comparison indicates that the family sphere is of more concern to Danes and Caribbeans than to Americans. Financial considerations seem to be of greater concern to Americans than to others. The relationship with the romantic partner seems to produce stressors of almost identical importance for each of the populations. For other families, it is difficult to say.

This comparison clearly shows differences between the three populations in terms of types of stressors.

Studies with a wider scope, that is, covering a larger number of countries and therefore cultures, have a more macroscopic approach. One of the best known is the annual global study conducted by the Gallup Institute (Gallup, 2022). It does not focus on certain types of stress in particular but gives a global index by country and for the world. Although the stressors specific to each culture are not precisely identified, it is interesting to mention this study because the index of negative experience that is measured integrates the stress component in general. The findings for the 2022 edition (reporting results up to 2021) indicate that the negative experience index has continued to rise since 2007 with a 41% contribution of stress for 2022. The top three countries on the negative experience index are Afghanistan, Lebanon, and Iraq. At the same time, the positive experience index decreased for the first time in 2021 since 2017. Among the top five countries for this index are Panama, Paraguay, El Salvador and Honduras. The report (Gallup, 2022: 6) notes that "Latin American countries typically dominate the list of countries where adults report a lot of positive emotions each day."

The 2022 Gallup study also notes: "As people worldwide lived on a steady diet of uncertainty in the second year of the pandemic, with more people dying from the coronavirus in 2021 than the previous year despite the rollout of vaccines, people felt less well-rested and fewer derived enjoyment from the previous day" (Gallup, 2022: 4). The World Happiness Report (Helliwell et al., 2022: 28) presents an analysis of Gallup Institute data and considers stress separately from the negative experience index. The report notes that stress has steadily increased in recent years and reached its strongest growth in 2020, when the effects of the COVID-19 pandemic began worldwide. Unfortunately, it is difficult to find studies that identify the specific stressors that have evolved during this period. As with the more general studies on culture-related stress, these studies provide a macroscopic view of the stressors affected by COVID-19. This is the case, for example, of the study by Kowal et al. (2020) or Padilla (2021). Kowal et al. (2020) analysed more than 50,000 respondents from 26 different countries. The study indicates that the profile of those most affected by pandemic stress is a young single woman with children, of low academic level, living in an area with a severe pandemic situation.

The authors also indicate which countries are most affected by pandemic-related stress. There is no information regarding the stressors that have precisely evolved during the pandemic because the authors used the Perceived Stress Scale (PSS) of Cohen et al. (1983) which does not allow this type of precision. Padilla (2021) also used the PSS in their study and supplemented it with the SRRS (Social Readjustment Rating Scale), referring to American participants residing in the US. Unfortunately, the study focused only on the overall scores obtained on the questionnaires and on the correlation between the participants' income level and their stress levels. The results show that there is a more significant change in the stress levels spanning the onset and duration of the pandemic for participants with low-income levels than for those with high incomes. However, a study was published by Taylor et al. (2021) to characterise the impact of the pandemic on American families (US). The study looked at the impact of the pandemic on 30 women aged 36–56 and asked to estimate the readjustment induced by each of the SRRS items in its original version (Holmes & Rahe, 1967) before and after the pandemic. Of the items that requested pandemic induced adjustment, three items are associated with work and ten are associated with social relationships and privacy. According to the authors, more than one in two respondents had moderate-to-high risk of developing illness as a result of pandemic-induced stress, with depressive symptoms associated with the significance of stressor changes and anxiety symptoms more associated with the intensity of significant stressors before the pandemic. Unfortunately, intercultural comparison is not possible since there are no other identical studies published in English for other countries.

3   Culture, Work, and Stress

Studies based on the use of the Social Readjustment Rating Scale, SRRS (Scully et al., 2000; Berntsen & Rubin, 2004; Haque et al., 2020; Holmes & Rahe, 1967; Hobson et al., 1998) also allow a comparison of the concerns of different populations addressing the relationship to work. Table 17.2 lists the work-related items for all the studies and counts their occurrence for each of the studies. The table clearly shows a difference between the US population and the other two populations: while the number of items concerning work remains constant from 1967 to 2000 for Americans (between seven and eight), this number is much lower for the other two populations (3).

In other words, the cultural context of the Danish population in 2004 and the cultural context of the Caribbean population in 2022 produced far fewer

Table 17.2 List of work-related items in each of the studies using the SRRS

Source	Holmes and Rahe (1967)	Hobson et al. (1998)	Scully et al. (2000)	Berntsen and Rubin (2004)	Haque et al. (2020)	Changes in the Wording of the Item	
Population	US	US	US	Danish	Caribbean	for Hobson et al. (1998)	forHaque et al. (2020)
Items	Rank					Changes in the wording of the item	
Fired from work	8	12	13		11	Being fired/laid-off/ unemployed	
retirement	10		29				
business readjustment	15		40				
changed to different line of work	18		14				
change in responsibilities at work	22	45	24		25	changing work responsibilities	job promotion
		43				changing positions (transfer, promotion)	
trouble with boss	30	39	22			major disagreement with boss/co-worker	
change in work hours or conditions	31		20				
first job				10	3		
settle on career				17			
the "right" job				20			
being disciplined at work/ demoted		23					
experiencing employment discrimination/ sexual harassment		27					
employer reorganisation/ downsizing		30					
changing employers/careers		33					
Total items	7	8	7	3	3		

Note: The last columns indicate possible reformulations of the original items (Holmes & Rahe, 1967; first column) for the studies concerned requests for readjustment in the field of work than for the cultural context of the American population between 1967 and 2000. Again, this is an indication of the influence of cultural context on the stressors to which a given population may be sensitive.

Analysis of item types also indicates a difference between populations. For the Danish, readjustment refers to having a job that suits the person. For Caribbeans, readjustment is associated with being confronted with major changes in professional careers. For the US population, the items refer to being confronted with job or career changes or difficult relationships with colleagues. The result of this analysis is an additional clue illustrating the influence of cultural context on stressors.

4 Culture, Work, and Stress Coping

Bibliographic research addressing cross-cultural ideas on stress and predominant stressors across cultures confirmed Aldwin (2004): there are also cultural differences in stress-related coping strategies. The scientific literature is specific on the subject. However, this is not the purpose of this chapter, and this section will therefore be short. However, it is interesting to devote a few lines to it for at least two reasons. The first is the observation that the approaches are macroscopic and do not provide information on the cultural particularities that make up the strategies implemented. There is therefore a scientific gap that needs to be filled as for cross-cultural ideas on stress. The second is that the factors explaining cultural differences regarding coping strategies in relation to stress are similar to this one explaining cross-cultural ideas on stress, at least according to the macroscopic approach. Similarly, as with studies addressing cross-cultural aspects of stress, studies on coping strategies have a scope of investigation reduced to only a few countries.

For example, esteem-building social support was linked with greater forthcoming stress for Singaporean participants whereas less so for North American people (Pourmand et al., 2021). Han et al. (2022) have shown that European Canadians (Canadians of European descent) endorsed greater actual usage of primary control coping (control through direct influence on the external environment) while the Japanese showed greater use of secondary control coping (self-accommodation to the situational demands to deal with the emotional distress). The authors explain this difference in part by the fact that the latter have a less individualistic culture than the former. These results are in line with the conclusions proposed by Liu et al. (2007) regarding the perception of certain stressors (see above).

By extending the field of bibliographic research beyond the scientific literature, a blog appears particularly interesting on the subject. This blog provides an overview of the type of information that would make sense to produce in scientific research addressing cross-cultural ideas on stress and coping strategies. This is the blog of Susan Petang, Certified Mindful Lifestyle & Stress Management Coach (https://upjourney.com/ways-other-cultures-deal-with-stress). Although these data are not supported by any scientific research mentioned in the blog, the approach is interesting in that it specifies certain cultural particularities that make up the coping strategies implemented. This illustrates what it would have been desirable to find in the scientific literature to foster this chapter. The blog gives an example of what people in different countries are doing to reduce the effect of stress in everyday life. The French usually have an aperitif (Fig. 17.3) when s/he comes home after the working day; this consists of a glass of wine or a glass of alcohol a little stronger but in a smaller proportion. Russians prefer to spend time in the sauna regardless of whether s/he can possibly drink some tea or vodka there. Japanese favoured moments of social exchange around a tea, for example. Thailanders prefer massage. Although these indications may seem caricature, they could be

Fig. 17.3 The relaxing French aperitif

verified with samples of people living in each of these countries. It would be interesting to extend this type of consideration to a very broad cultural scope within the framework of scientific approaches that would allow statistical validation of practices implemented by culture.

5 Conclusion

The aim of this chapter was to provide an overview of how stress could be perceived from one culture to another, in particular by attempting to identify important specific stressors and their variation from one culture to another from the studies available in the scientific literature. The observation is that drawing an exhaustive picture of these specific stressors according to cultures is impossible due to lack of scientific studies on the subject. The results delivered in this chapter are, however, limited by the fact that only scientific articles published in English were analysed. The scientific literature mainly proposes macroscopic approaches to stress related to culture and it is difficult to clarify the idea of stress that people experience according to cultures. However, a few articles are available that provide insight into cultural differences using the SRRS (Social Readjustment Rating Scale). These studies have the advantage of having considered the specificities of the participating populations by allowing an adjustment of the items used in the SRRS. The number of cultures covered by these studies is very small. Nevertheless, they confirm that the specific predominant stressors differ from one culture to another. The literature review that fostered this chapter also showed that cultural differences exist in the coping strategies implemented in relation to stress. A large-scale study is needed to determine precisely what cross-cultural ideas on stress are and thus to fill this scientific gap.

References

Aldwin, C. M. (2004). *Culture, coping and resilience to stress* (pp. 563–573). Centre for Bhutan Studies.

Antonovsky. (1979). *Health, stress and coping.* Jossey-Bass.

Beehr, T. A., & Glazer, S. (2001). A cultural perspective of social support in relation to occupational stress. In *Exploring theoretical mechanisms and perspectives.* Emerald Group Publishing Limited.

Berezina, T. N., Rybtsova, N. N., & Rybtsov, S. A. (2020). Comparative dynamics of individual ageing among the investigative type of professionals living in Russia and Russian migrants to the EU countries. *European Journal of Investigation in Health, Psychology and Education, 10*(3), 749–762.

Berntsen, D., & Rubin, D. C. (2004). Cultural life scripts structure recall from autobiographical memory. *Memory & Cognition, 32*(3), 427–442.

Cohen, S., Kamarck, T., & Mermelstein, R. (1983). A global measure of perceived stress. *Journal of Health and Social Behavior, 24*, 385–396.

Daniels, K. (2004). Perceived risk from occupational stress: A survey of 15 European countries. *Occupational and Environmental Medicine, 61*(5), 467–470.

Fila, M. J., & Wilson, M. S. (2018). Understanding cross-cultural differences in the work stress process. In *Handbook of research on cross-cultural business education* (pp. 224–249). IGI Global.

Gallup. (2022). *Gallup global emotions.* Gallup Analytics. Gallup Inc.

Han, J. Y., Lee, H., Ohtsubo, Y., & Masuda, T. (2022). Culture and stress coping: Cultural variations in the endorsement of primary and secondary control coping for daily stress across European Canadians, East Asian Canadians, and the Japanese. *Japanese Psychological Research, 64*(2), 141–155.

Haque, S., Albada, N., & Rollocks, S. (2020). Cultural variances in significant life events: A focus on the English-Speaking Caribbean. *Human Arenas, 1–20.*

Helliwell, J. F., Layard, R., Sachs, J. D., De Neve, J.-E., Aknin, L. B., & Wang, S. (Eds.). (2022). *World happiness report 2022.* Sustainable Development Solutions Network.

Hobson, C. J., Kamen, J., Szostek, J., Nethercut, C. M., Tiedmann, J. W., & Wojnarowicz, S. (1998). Stressful life events: A revision and update of the social readjustment rating scale. *International Journal of Stress Management, 5*(1), 1–23.

Hofstede, G. H. (1980). Culture and organizations. *International Studies of Management and Organization, 10*(4), 15–41.

Hofstede, G. H. (2001). *Culture's consequences: Comparing values, behaviors, institutions and organizations across nations.* Sage Publications.

Holmes, T. H., & Rahe, R. H. (1967). The social readjustment rating scale. *Journal of Psychosomatic Research, 11*, 213–218.

Kowal, M., Coll-Martín, T., Ikizer, G., Rasmussen, J., Eichel, K., Studzińska, A., et al. (2020). Who is the most stressed during the COVID-19 pandemic? Data from 26 countries and areas. *Applied Psychology. Health and Well-Being, 12*(4), 946–966.

Le, H., Newman, A., Menzies, J., Zheng, C., & Fermelis, J. (2020). Work–life balance in Asia: A systematic review. *Human Resource Management Review, 30*(4), 100766.

Lin, P. C., Robbins, N., & Lin, P. K. (2019). Research of media industry's expatriates' cross-culture adjustment on the job involvement and work stress: The impact of relatedness. *Realities in a Kaleidoscope, 64*, 120–129.

Liu, C., Spector, P. E., & Shi, L. (2007). Cross-national job stress: A quantitative and qualitative study. *Journal of Organizational Behavior: The International Journal of Industrial, Occupational and Organizational Psychology and Behavior, 28*(2), 209–239.

Lomas, T. (2018). Experiential cartography and the significance of "untranslatable" words. *Theory & Psychology, 28*(4), 476–495.

Padilla, C. (2021). Greater stress level fluctuation in lower income earners since onset of coronavirus pandemic. *Journal of Student Research, 10*(1).

Perrewé, P. L., Hochwarter, W. A., Rossi, A. M., Wallace, A., Maignan, I., Castro, S. L., et al. (2002). Are work stress relationships universal? A nine-region examination of role stressors, general self-efficacy, and burnout. *Journal of International Management, 8*(2), 163–187.

Pourmand, V., Lawley, K. A., & Lehman, B. J. (2021). Cultural differences in stress and affection following social support receipt. *PLoS One, 16*(9), e0256859.

Schwartz, S. H. (1994). Are there universal aspects in the structure and contents of human values? *The Journal of Social Issues, 50*(4), 19–45.

Scully, J. A., Tosi, H., & Banning, K. (2000). Life event checklists: Revisiting the social readjustment rating scale after 30 years. *Educational and Psychological Measurement, 60*(6), 864–876.

Shek, D. T. L., & Cheung, C. K. (1990). Locus of coping in a sample of Chinese working parents: Reliance on self or seeking help from others. *Social Behavior and Personality, 18*, 327–346.

Taylor, B. K., Frenzel, M. R., Johnson, H. J., Willett, M. P., White, S. F., Badura-Brack, A. S., & Wilson, T. W. (2021). Increases in stressors prior to-versus during the COVID-19 pandemic in the United States are associated with depression among middle-aged mothers. *Frontiers in Psychology, 12*, 706120.

Van Fossen, J. A., & Chang, C. H. (2020). Occupational stress across the globe: A review of multicultural research. In *Handbuch Stress und Kultur: Interkulturelle und kulturvergleichende Perspektiven* (pp. 1–13). Springer.

Wallace, A. F. C. (1966). *Religion: An anthropological view*. Random House.

18

Stress in Different Professional Sectors

Philippe Fauquet-Alekhine and James Erskine

1 Introduction

Occupational stress mainly results from an imbalance between the demands addressed to the individual and the individual's self-perceived capacity to respond to these demands, or from a perceived injustice due to the ratio of reward to effort (Theorell & Karasek, 1996; Siegrist, 1996; Mohajan, 2012). It may also come from the individual's negative self-perception of competencies at work (Fauquet-Alekhine & Rouillac, 2016).

According to Fila et al. (2017, p. 31), "established theories such as the job characteristics model (Oldham & Hackman, 2005) suggest that perceptions of work stress are thought to differ between occupations, based on social and

---

P. Fauquet-Alekhine (✉)
SEBE-Lab, Department of Psychological and Behavioural Science,
London School of Economics and Political Science, London, UK

Laboratory for Research in Science of Energy, Montagret, France

Groupe INTRA Robotics, Avoine, France
e-mail: p.fauquet-alekhine@lse.ac.uk; philippe.fauquet-alekhine@groupe-intra.com

J. Erskine
London Hertfordshire Therapy Centre, London, UK

St George's University of London, London, UK
e-mail: jerskine@sgul.ac.uk

© The Author(s), under exclusive license to Springer Nature Switzerland AG 2023
P. Fauquet-Alekhine, J. Erskine (eds.), *The Palgrave Handbook of Occupational Stress*,
https://doi.org/10.1007/978-3-031-27349-0_18

structural differences in how jobs are designed which are thought to manifest in the stress process (Grant et al., 2011; Sulsky & Smith, 2005)."

It is therefore interesting to examine how workers, depending on their occupation, may be differently affected by stress at work. That is the purpose of this chapter.

2   Occupational Stress in the World

Chapter 16 of the present book illustrates how each country can approach stress differently depending on the respective cultural context. When the notion of stress is restricted to the world of work, similar processes may operate at a national level. The Gallup survey (2022) reporting the results of a survey about global workplace stress is a perfect example of this proposition. The survey was undertaken for 2021, in 160 countries, with roughly 1000 respondents per country, and included at least 2000 adults for larger countries (e.g. Russia, China), and all of the participants had to be at least 15 years old.

Worldwide, the percentage of employees experiencing stress had reached a plateau around 38% between 2015 and 2019; however, since then it has risen to 44% in 2021 (Fig. 18.1). This percentage has similar proportions in 2021 for women (47%) and men (42%).

The Gallup survey (2022, p. 11) notes that "overall wellbeing influences life at work. Employees who are engaged at work but not thriving have a 61% higher likelihood of ongoing burnout than those who are engaged and thriving" and adds that the factors leading to burnout are, in decreasing order of importance:

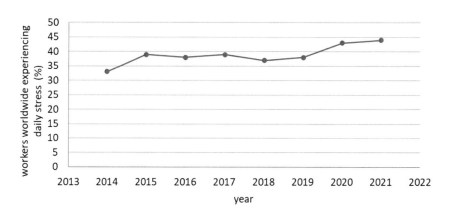

Fig. 18.1   Percentage of workers worldwide experiencing daily stress at work according to a survey conducted in 160 countries with at least 1000 respondents per country in 2021 (Gallup, 2022)

- unfair treatment at work,
- unmanageable workload,
- unclear communication from managers,
- lack of manager support, and
- unreasonable time pressure.

In a survey conducted by Microsoft (2021) among 31,092 full-time employed or self-employed workers (across 31 occupational sectors in 31 countries with at least 1000 respondents per sector), analysts examined the percentage of workers who cried in the presence of a colleague. Overall, the proportion was 17%, of which 64% referred to three professional sectors: healthcare (23%), travel and tourism (21%), and education (20%).

Figure 18.2 illustrates the distribution of stress experienced by employees in 2021 around the world by major geographic areas according to the Gallup survey (2022).

Figures 18.3 and 18.4 show the distribution of perceived daily stress at work in terms of proportion among employees surveyed by country in 2021 (Gallup, 2022).

While the European zone appears to be under little stress in Figs. 18.2, 18.3, and 18.4 show that European countries are distributed across the entire spectrum of possible values. The same is true for each of the geographic areas

Fig. 18.2 Distribution of employee's perceived daily stress at work by major areas worldwide expressed as a percentage of surveyed populations in 2021 (number of respondents: more than 160,000 employees) (Gallup, 2022)

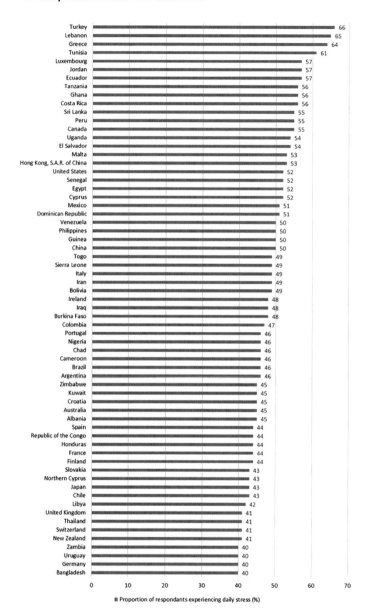

Fig. 18.3 The 65 most work-stressed countries in the world: employee's perceived daily stress at work expressed as a percentage of surveyed populations in 2021 (number of respondents: more than 160,000 employees) (Gallup, 2022)

in Fig. 18.2. For Europe, the most affected countries are Greece and Luxembourg with proportions above 55%, and the least affected are Estonia and Latvia with proportions below 30%. It should also be noted that the least

18 Stress in Different Professional Sectors 341

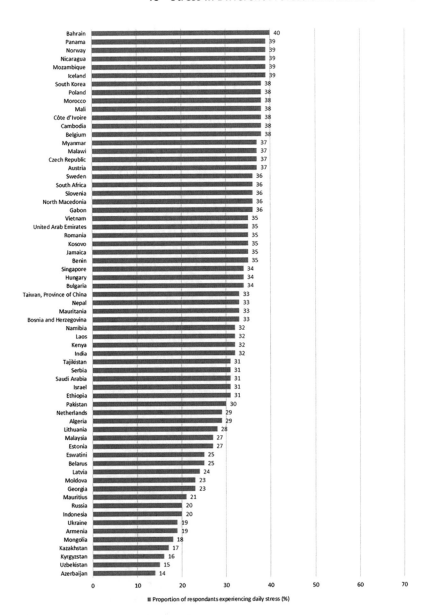

Fig. 18.4 The 65 least work-stressed countries in the world: employee's perceived daily stress at work expressed as a percentage of surveyed populations in 2021 (number of respondents: more than 160,000 employees) (Gallup, 2022)

work-stressed countries in Europe are mostly countries from the former Soviet bloc. This observation refers to the impact of the cultural dimension on the perception of stress (see Chap. 16 of the present book).

3   Occupational Stress with Time

It is difficult to obtain comparable data for specific occupational sectors over long periods. For example, Statista (2019) gives a table of workers affected by burnout globally for 2019 per professional sectors (Fig. 18.5). The survey was conducted among more than 1000 workers ranging in age from 19 to 81 years old worldwide.

This might seem high values for the Statista survey (2019) but it is coherent with research studies. For example, in the UK, Farrell et al. (2019) reported that 85% of English medical students could be classified "exhausted" using the Oldenburg Burnout Scale, Vincent et al. (2019) reported 50% among nurses and 35% among doctors felt exhausted in UK intensive care unit staff. For India, Saravanabavan et al. (2019) reported that the prevalence of high burnout in intensive care units was 80% when applying the Maslach burnout inventory.

It is highly likely that the COVID-19 pandemic led to variations in the distribution of stress in 2020 and 2021. To investigate this, the scale of a country must be considered. For example, for the UK, the Labour Force Survey (https://www.hse.gov.uk/statistics/lfs/index.htm; source: lfsillocc.xlsx) presents the evolution of the employees concerned by self-reported stress, depression, or anxiety caused or made worse by current or most recent job, by occupation over three periods from 2011 to 2021. For each of the sectors of

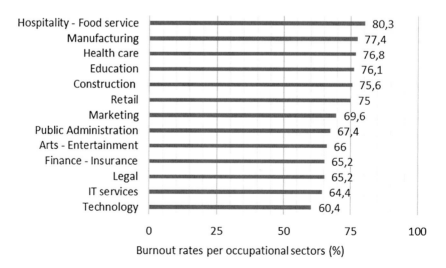

Fig. 18.5 Global professional sectors most affected by burnout in 2019: proportion per sectors (Statista, 2019)

18 Stress in Different Professional Sectors

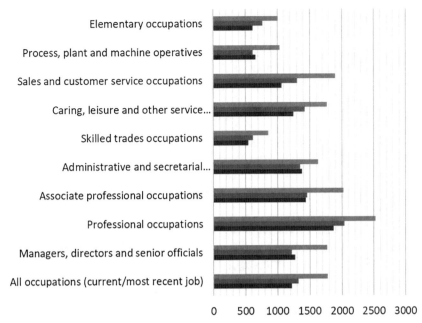

Fig. 18.6 Estimated prevalence and rates of self-reported stress, depression, or anxiety caused or made worse by current or most recent job, by occupation, for people working in the last 12 months in the UK, values being the number of persons concerned per 100,000 employees (Labour Force Survey: https://www.hse.gov.uk/statistics/lfs/index.htm: lfsillocc.xlsx)

activity identified, 500–1800 workers participated in the survey (Fig. 18.6). The data show a clear increase over the last period incorporating the pandemic, regardless of the sector of activity concerned. According to HSE (2021, p. 5), "in the recent years prior to the coronavirus pandemic, the rate of self-reported work-related stress, depression or anxiety had shown signs of increasing. In 2020/21 the rate was higher than the 2018/19 pre-coronavirus levels," and stress, depression, and anxiety were most prevalent for the education sector and the healthcare sector. Furthermore, the larger the size of the workplace the stronger the effect (HSE, 2021). Regarding the healthcare sector which has been at the forefront of managing the infection, Babore et al. (2020) found that the main protective coping strategy was a positive attitude towards the stressful situation.

Several studies and surveys show that the pandemic profoundly changed people's relationship with work. This is partly due to the fact that teleworking has assumed an important place in the world of work during the many periods of confinement. For example, Microsoft's survey (2021) carried out among 31,092 full-time workers in 31 countries concludes that hybrid work has become inevitable. Hybrid work refers to "a blended model where some employees return to the workplace and others continue to work from home" (Microsoft, 2021, p. 2). According to the results of the survey:

- 73% of employees expect flexible remote options, and
- 66% of leaders are considering redesigning the organisation for hybrid work.

To illustrate this phenomenon, between February 2020 and February 2021, Microsoft reports that time spent in Microsoft Teams meetings has multiplied by 2.5 times and continues to increase.

In the same vein, several studies warn about the associated need to reconsider work organisations and their limits with the private sphere as well as the nature of tasks at work. If not, they warn to the possible resulting professional isolation, which would be the strongest negative influence factor regarding telework (e.g. Carillo et al., 2021). Teleworking can also induce another form of stress called "techno-stress" related to the pervasive use of information and communication technologies, a phenomenon that affects both professional and private life (La Torre et al., 2019).

It is difficult to establish generalities concerning the actions to be implemented to reduce the stress due to the diversity of professional sectors considered and the fact that for each of them appears specificity related to their country and therefore to their culture. However, it appears that taking into account well-being at work is a recurrent theme in multiple studies and surveys (see Chap. 17 of the present book and also: Gallup, 2022; Fila et al., 2017; Babore et al., 2020). Therefore, taking well-being at work into account is an important action that may reduce stress at work, especially for younger workers (Microsoft, 2021).

4 Conclusion

The various surveys and studies available regarding the link between occupational stress and the professional sector show that jobs are impacted differently by stress because of the different stress factors that concern them. This is quantified both by professional sector, by country or by geographical area.

Subsequently, this necessarily involve different adjustment actions even if, at the macroscopic level, the common point in terms of action seems to be the improvement of well-being at work, whatever the occupation and whatever the country.

References

Babore, A., Lombardi, L., Viceconti, M. L., Pignataro, S., Marino, V., Crudele, M., et al. (2020). Psychological effects of the COVID-2019 pandemic: Perceived stress and coping strategies among healthcare professionals. *Psychiatry Research, 293*, 113366.

Carillo, K., Cachat-Rosset, G., Marsan, J., Saba, T., & Klarsfeld, A. (2021). Adjusting to epidemic-induced telework: Empirical insights from teleworkers in France. *European Journal of Information Systems, 30*(1), 69–88.

Farrell, S. M., Kadhum, M., Lewis, T., Singh, G., Penzenstadler, L., & Molodynski, A. (2019). Wellbeing and burnout amongst medical students in England. *International Review of Psychiatry, 31*(7–8), 579–583.

Fauquet-Alekhine, P., & Rouillac, L. (2016). The square of perceived action model as a tool for identification, prevention and treatment of factors deteriorating mental health at work. *Journal of Mental Disorder & Treatment, 2*(3), 1–13.

Fila, M. J., Purl, J., & Griffeth, R. W. (2017). Job demands, control and support: Meta-analyzing moderator effects of gender, nationality, and occupation. *Human Resource Management Review, 27*(1), 39–60.

Gallup. (2022). *State of the global workplace 2022 report—The voice of the world's employees.* Gallup Analytics. Gallup Inc.

Grant, A. M., Fried, Y., & Juillerat, T. (2011). Work matters: Job design in classic and contemporary perspectives. In S. Zedeck (Ed.), *APA handbook of industrial and organizational psychology* (Vol. 1, pp. 417–453). American Psychological Association.

HSE. (2021). *Work related stress, anxiety and depression statistics in Great Britain 2021.* Health and Safety Executive.

La Torre, G., Esposito, A., Sciarra, I., & Chiappetta, M. (2019). Definition, symptoms and risk of techno-stress: A systematic review. *International Archives of Occupational and Environmental Health, 92*(1), 13–35.

Labour Force Survey. (2021). https://www.hse.gov.uk/statistics/lfs/index.htm

Microsoft. (2021). *2021 work trend index: Annual report.*

Mohajan, H. K. (2012). The occupational stress and risk of it among the employees. *International Journal of Mainstream Social Science, 2*(2), 17–34.

Oldham, G. R., & Hackman, J. R. (2005). How job characteristics theory happened. In K. G. Smith & M. A. Hitt (Eds.), *Great minds in management: The process of theory development* (pp. 151–170). Oxford University Press.

Saravanabavan, L., Sivakumar, M. N., & Hisham, M. (2019). Stress and burnout among intensive care unit healthcare professionals in an Indian tertiary care hospital. *Indian journal of critical care medicine, 23*(10), 462–466.

Siegrist, J. (1996). Adverse health effects of high effort/low reward conditions. *Journal of Occupational Health Psychology, 1*, 27–41.

Statista. (2019). *Stress and burnout.* Statistics & Facts.

Sulsky, L. M., & Smith, C. S. (2005). *Workstress.* Thomson Wadsworth.

Theorell, T., & Karasek, R. A. (1996). Current issues relating to psychosocial job strain and cardiovascular disease research. *Journal of Occupational Health and Psychology, 1*, 9–26.

Vincent, L., Brindley, P. G., Highfield, J., Innes, R., Greig, P., & Suntharalingam, G. (2019). Burnout syndrome in UK intensive care unit staff: Data from all three burnout syndrome domains and across professional groups, genders and ages. *Journal of the Intensive Care Society, 20*(4), 363–369.

19

The Impact of Stress Among Undergraduate Students: Supporting Resilience and Wellbeing Early in Career Progression

Linda Perkins-Porras

1 Introduction

Most people look back on their life as an undergraduate student with fond memories, recalling a time of personal, social and professional development filled with fun, friendship and some study. However, the university experience can also be very stressful, and a growing number of undergraduate students are reporting anxiety, depression and stress-related illnesses and seeking counselling (Thorley, 2017; Sheldon et al., 2021). Issues related to the Covid-19 pandemic from 2020 have added a whole new dimension to this and have significantly impacted on the university experience for students in terms of their wellbeing and coping mechanisms, personal resilience and preparation for their future careers (Papapanou et al., 2022; Plakhotnik et al., 2021).

Stress can have positive attributes and may be used as a source of motivation, leading to improved performance, creativity and problem solving (Hargrove et al., 2015). This interpretation of stress is defined as eustress and incorporates the experience of academic stretch; the intellectual struggle of encountering new ideas and seeking solutions to difficult problems. This can be seen as one of the challenges that individuals are required to overcome in

---

L. Perkins-Porras (✉)

Institute of Medical & Biomedical Education, St George's University of London, London, UK

e-mail: lperkins@sgul.ac.uk

© The Author(s), under exclusive license to Springer Nature Switzerland AG 2023

P. Fauquet-Alekhine, J. Erskine (eds.), *The Palgrave Handbook of Occupational Stress*, https://doi.org/10.1007/978-3-031-27349-0_19

order to learn how to successfully navigate their undergraduate graduate degree programme. Some careers require individuals to be able to manage high levels of stress and early preparation for this may be beneficial. Exposure to intellectual, academic and emotional challenges such as uncertainty, problem solving under pressure and managing difficult situations can form part of the student's formal and informal career training, and assist in helping them to develop effective coping strategies and personal resilience. However, if students feel overwhelmed by challenges they do not feel they have adequate resources to manage, or are faced with too many challenges simultaneously, this stress can become distress. Academic challenges in combination with many of the simultaneous life changes that accompany the transition of entry into the adult world, such as leaving the family home, entering a new and unfamiliar social environment, taking on significant financial responsibilities and so on, requires multiple adjustments that can become overwhelming for some students. The disruption to normal life, education, social isolation and uncertainty caused by the Covid-19 pandemic exacerbated this and led to a re-evaluation of psychological support required to enable students to develop greater resilience and to achieve success (Appleby et al., 2022; Sauer et al., 2022; Cho & Jang, 2021; Giuntella, 2020).

This chapter will discuss the prevalence of mental health problems among undergraduates and the pressures they may experience. It will discuss the causes of stress among students and impact this may have on their studies and career preparation, including the consequences of the Covid-19 pandemic. It will also review strategies used to foster wellbeing and personal resilience within the university environment and development of innovative, more comprehensive approaches for the future.

2 Prevalence of Psychological Distress Among Undergraduates

The prevalence of some mental health problems among students, such as depression and anxiety, is higher than that found in the general population (Lim et al., 2018). This leads us to ask why this is the case? Is there something intrinsically unhealthy about higher education (HE), the student lifestyle or university environment? In 2016, a survey by the World Health Organisation found that 35% of students met the diagnostic criteria for at least one common mental health condition (Auerbach et al., 2016). A systematic review showed that rates of depression among college students across 30 different countries were higher than in the general population (12.9%) (Lim et al., 2018). Some underlying mental health conditions typically become symptomatic among young people in their late teens and early twenties, and some may be triggered by life events and experiences during this time. Indeed, around three quarters of adults with a mental illness experience the initial symptoms before the age of 25. The number of students in Higher Education disclosing a mental health problem to their institution was already rising even before the Covid-19 pandemic. For example, in England, the number of 16 to 24-year-olds reporting a mental health condition rose from 15% in 2003 to 19% in 2017, representing an increase of over 25%. In the year 2015–2016, 89% of students enrolled in undergraduate courses in higher education in the United Kingdom (UK) were aged under 25 years, and 2% of first-year students (equal to 15,395 individuals) disclosed a mental health condition, almost five times more than the number in 2006–2007 (Thorley, 2017). A pre-pandemic survey in 2018 reported that 21% of students had a current mental health diagnosis (Pereira et al., 2019). By 2020, 27.2% of applicants to higher education in the UK had declared a mental health condition of some kind. It is suggested that the stigma surrounding mental health problems has been reducing over recent years so that young people are becoming more confident in disclosing this information, and less afraid that this will impact negatively on their career plans which may account for some of this increase (UCAS, 2021). Recent research has since indicated that the Covid-19 pandemic has had a particularly negative effect on young people aged between 18 and 29 years, females, those from more socially disadvantaged backgrounds, and those with pre-existing mental health problems who are at a higher risk of developing stress-related problems (O'Connor et al., 2020).

The negative impact of stress on the mental health of students resulting in conditions such as depression, anxiety and suicidal thinking has been known for over a decade. In 2008, Dyrbye et al reported that 11% of students said they had experienced suicidal ideation over the previous year (Dyrbye et al., 2008). Male undergraduates were found to be at a higher risk for suicide while female students were more likely to experience major depression and anxiety disorders (Eisenberg et al., 2007). A survey carried out in the UK by the National Union of Students (NUS) in 2013 showed that 80% of participants reported feeling stressed, 55% felt anxious and 40% felt depressed (Kerr, 2013). While suicide rates among students are lower than in the general population, the numbers have been rising over recent years. The Office of National Statistics (ONS) showed an increase in the rate of student suicides in England and Wales from 52 in 2000 to 95 in 2017 (Office for National Statistics, 2018).

Rates of anxiety and depression among students rose during the Covd-19 pandemic, and the prevalence of stress increased due to a range of factors, including health anxiety for themselves and loved ones, problems with concentration and disturbed sleep, and anxiety about their academic performance. This has been seen across the international higher education sector, including the UK, the US, China and Europe (Cao et al., 2020; Son et al., 2020). It has been estimated that one in four students experience mental illness such as depression each year but this now appears to be increasing above the level of the general population, indicated by the significant increase in the number of students disclosing a mental health problem to their institution (Sheldon et al., 2021). There is a pressing need for universities to invest in providing support for students to enable them to increase their personal resilience and to develop effective coping strategies to manage stress as an integral part of their degree programme and career training rather than an optional add-on.

3 Student Stress and Burnout

The prevalence of stress, anxiety and depression (SAD) is known to be high among students (Lim et al., 2018). Some student groups, such as medical students, are at particularly high risk of experiencing stress related to their occupational training known as burnout. This is characterised by emotional exhaustion, depersonalisation and a sense of reduced accomplishment in day-to-day work, and can result a deterioration of the quality of care or services provided (Maslach, 1996). Meta-analyses have shown that half of junior doctors began to experience burnout even before they started their residency posts, and it is argued that burnout in qualified physicians begins in early medical training (Frajerman et al., 2019). Indeed, Shanafelt et al. (2012) reported that almost half of 7288 physicians surveyed in the US experienced burnout, and evidence confirming the high prevalence of stress and burnout amongst physicians has been growing for nearly two decades (Zhou, 2020). Studies of other professions known to be stressful show a similar pattern. Collin et al. (2019) reported high levels of stress and low levels of wellbeing among dentists, while earlier systematic reviews had been reporting high levels of stress among dental students for several years prior to this (Elani et al., 2014; Singh et al., 2016). Similar findings have been shown in undergraduate training for careers in aviation, engineering and other high pressure professional groups (Brezonakova, 2017). Early interventions to help students manage stress effectively and increase resilience during their undergraduate studies and early training may mitigate burnout, avoid the negative aspects of stress later in their careers and improve job retention (Tang et al., 2021).

4 What Are the Challenges to Mental Health Faced by Students?

4.1 Managing Finances

There is no doubt that some undergraduate students experience significant problems in managing stress. There are multiple potential causes for this. For many young people, they are moving out of their family home and becoming independent for the first time, often far from their family and previous friendship groups. As young adults, they are expected to be able to manage their financial resources however, depending on their individual life experience, they may or may not be well equipped to do this. Changes in funding for higher education in the UK, including the introduction of fees in 1998 and replacement of the maintenance grant with the student loan, have meant that many students now incur high levels of debt in order to study, undertaking large student loans in order to pay educational fees and support themselves. Indeed, the financial cost of education can be a significant stressor for all students worldwide. As a consequence, many find themselves living on a very limited budget and possibly taking on part-time employment to fund their studies (Richardson et al., 2016). Financial support from parents may alleviate some of this stress for some, but those from a low income background may find the financial strain particularly challenging and face balancing the need to spend time earning money against the need to spend time studying.

Benson-Egglenton (2019) reported a clear relationship between a student's mental wellbeing and their financial wellbeing. For example, medicine is one of the most expensive and longest undergraduate degree courses usually requiring five or six years to complete rather than the standard three years. Debt levels among medical students are negatively associated with mental wellbeing and academic outcomes. Students with high levels of debt are likely to be driven towards choosing higher paying specialties in order to pay off their accumulated debt but also potentially influencing their career choices, job satisfaction and long-term mental health (Pisaniello et al., 2019). The Covid-19 pandemic has caused additional financial hardship for students who relied on casual part-time work to support themselves as many of the common jobs undertaken by students such as shop work, bar work, catering, tutoring, cleaning and so on were untenable due to social distancing and travel restrictions imposed by governments to reduce infection rates. Many had to return to their family home which had the advantage of providing financial and social support but also led to strains in family relationships as young people sought to maintain their independence (Bolumole, 2020; Yorguner et al., 2021).

4.2 Managing Existing or Emergent Health Issues

Some students enter university with existing physical and/or mental health problems or will develop health problems during the course of their study. The emergence of a new health problem whilst studying for a degree can be very stressful due to the potential need to identify the health problem, gain a diagnosis and make the psychological and physical adjustments required to cope, alongside the academic demands of studying (Thorley, 2017). It was necessary for some students to shield during the pandemic in order to protect themselves or vulnerable family members from the virus, during which time almost all university teaching and assessment moved to online platforms. Whilst this may have been a reasonable alternative during the lock downs, as restrictions lifted they often had to make some difficult choices in managing risk for themselves and/or vulnerable others in attending onsite teaching amid fluctuating high infection rates and partial uptake of the vaccine programme: balancing the conflicting requirements of their education with the need to protect themselves or vulnerable dependents. Students may also have caring responsibilities for parents, spouses, children or siblings while they are studying. This may reduce the time available for studying and attending lectures, reduce rest time and increase to pressure to perform well. Home schooling of children during the pandemic undoubtedly increased these pressures for students with parental or childcare responsibilities, and the loss of support from outside carers and social care services significantly impacted on the ability of some students to continue their studies (Blake-Holmes, 2020).

4.3 Transition into Higher Education

For many students, entering university means entering a new environment with an unfamiliar set of social and academic expectations which requires a transitional period of adapting to the new conditions. Social pressures of living with peers in university student accommodation or in privately rented accommodation and having to navigate a new social structure can be confusing and relationship problems are common. The need to fit in with peers can be overwhelming and students may experience homesickness, social isolation and loneliness. It may be particularly stressful for students who are the first in their family to attend university, or who have no family support or may have grown up in the state care system. In addition, there are the pressures of meeting academic deadlines, passing exams and getting good grades in order to progress through the course and justify the financial investment (Thorley,

2017; Richardson et al., 2016). Mature or graduate students may also find it challenging in adjusting to their student status and working within the hierarchical structures of higher education institutions. In their final year, students also have to begin applying for jobs and making decisions about their life beyond university education, another major life change.

4.4 Substance and Alcohol Misuse

Addictive behaviours and substance misuse are often used as coping mechanisms to manage the symptoms of stress. A recent survey of 37,500 students conducted in the UK in 2018 reported that 45% of students used drugs and/or alcohol as a means of coping with difficulties in their lives and 10% did this often (Pereira et al., 2019). Sleep disturbance may accompany stress and indeed 7% of participants used drugs or alcohol in order to sleep at night. Alcohol misuse among students is not new; indeed, an earlier study by Dantzer et al. found that English female students had one of the highest rates of 'heavy drinking' when evaluated with international comparisons (Dantzer et al., 2006). The student population in the UK higher education sector has expanded considerably over recent years, and alcohol-related issues in this group have also increased despite positive attempts made by universities to address harmful drinking patterns.

The motivation for drinking alcohol among students has been associated with drinking for social reasons to fit in, drinking to cope and drinking to enhance mood. Students reported that they were most likely to drink alcohol for positive social reasons such as socialising or celebrating with friends and because it made them feel good and generally enhanced their experience. When asked what effects they expected from drinking alcohol, students most frequently reported that it increased social expressiveness and social and physical pleasure such as being more open and confident and feeling greater warmth, positivity and enjoyment when socialising with others. Dantzer et al. (2006) reported that much of student social drinking took place in university accommodation and students often pre-loaded before going out. This is supported by a recent survey undertaken by the National Union of Students (NUS) finding that 48% of students regularly do this (National Union of Students, 2018a).

Use of recreational drugs and/or alcohol, however, is also associated with harmful and risky behaviours, para/suicidal behaviours and accidental death. For example, just over 10% of students said they had been a passenger in a car when the driver was over the limit and 5% had driven when over the limit; a third had been separated from friends and 13.2% had got lost; 15.2% had had unprotected sex and 12.2% had had sexual intercourse when they 'ordinarily wouldn't have done' (Dantzer et al., 2006). According to the NUS, the prevalence of these behaviours has persisted and increased over time, and this leads to higher levels of vulnerability (National Union of Students, 2018a).

University students are more likely to use drugs than young people in the general population in the UK (National Union of Students, 2018b). Of the 2810 students who completed the survey, 56% they said they had ever used an illegal drug, with 39% saying they currently used them. This compares to 35% of 16- to 24-year-olds in the general UK population who have ever taken a recreational drug, and 19% who have taken one in the last year. Cannabis is by far the most commonly used substance often to aid relaxation or sleep, having been tried at some point by 94% of those who had used an illegal drug. Ecstasy is the second most commonly used drug for students, followed by cocaine (which is the second most used drug among 16- to 24-year-olds in the general population, ahead of ecstasy), nitrous oxide, ketamine and lysergic acid diethylamide (LSD), also known as 'acid'. Some students argue that they use alcohol and illicit drugs to manage stress and mental health conditions in the absence of medical and psychological support, but long-term alcohol and substance misuse can negatively affect mood, exacerbate symptoms of mental illness and lead to addiction. A small number of students also said they used 'smart' drugs to enhance memory and concentration (National Union of Students, 2018b).

There is an evident need to address alcohol and drug misuse among students. There is a persistent belief that alcohol is an accepted aspect of university life. The 2017–2018 NUS survey reported that 79% of students agreed that drinking and getting drunk is part of university culture (National Union of Students, 2018a). It is possible that moves towards more structural changes could reduce the risk of alcohol-related harm and simultaneously meet the requirements of non-drinkers, such as increasing provision of formal and informal social opportunities for students without undue dependence on alcohol, offering wider access to cafes, juice bars, snack bars and non-alcohol-related functions/events. First-year students seem to be at particular risk of participating in social activities involving large amounts of alcohol as they attempt to integrate into university life, and their inexperience has been shown to increase the risks attached to heavy drinking and use of recreational drugs. Although student initiation rites into certain societies involving excessive alcohol and risky behaviours are prohibited within universities, they may still take place off campus (UK Universities, 2019). Other social activities such as annual dinners, end-of-term celebrations, sports tours and alumni events may also involve students undertaking risky behaviours in their attempts to prove their allegiance to a team or to demonstrate their fearlessness. This can add additional stress to students seeking social acceptance and or increased social standing among peers. Those students living in the familial home appear to be less affected by this culture and less likely to participate in risky behaviours.

4.5 Safeguarding and Management of Behavioural Issues

University policies on safeguarding students and policing issues involving behaviour, personal safety and conduct have been called into question more often over recent years. Issues concerning sexual harassment, misconduct and assault involving students, on or off campus, have become controversial and topical. This is not a new issue in higher education institutions across the world which bring large numbers of young people together on campus, but the increasing availability and use of social media has allowed new types of abusive behaviour to emerge which can cause high levels of distress to the victim and be divisive within the student community, such as cyber bullying, trolling, sexting and revenge porn. The number of incidents reported by the general media has been increasing. There has also been public criticism of some UK university's management of such complaints and poor support of students involved. For example, Sussex University was criticised for poor management of a sexual assault case of a student by a lecturer in 2016 (Pells, 2017); Warwick University was strongly criticised for their management of complaints made by two female students in 2019 when it came to light that a group of 11 male students had set up an online group chatroom where they discussed and sent sexually explicit, violent and racist messages to each other over a long period of time referring to female students within their social group (Westmarland, 2019). These are not isolated incidents and there are numerous other similar examples of universities failing to act effectively in response to student complaints concerning harassment, racism, bullying and inappropriate behaviour across the international higher education sector. Universities have found themselves out of step at times with the tech savvy, social media oriented, "hashtag-me too" generation who are more assertive and less acquiescent in maintaining the status quo than earlier generations. Indeed, the courage and resilience of complainants such cases has fundamentally changed the way universities respond and manage issues around misconduct and student support. It can be argued that universities need to be proactive rather than reactive in their responses to such issues.

4.6 The Experience of Loneliness and Social Isolation Among Students

Loneliness is defined as perceived social isolation involving a lack of interactions with others (social loneliness) and the absence of meaningful relationships (emotional loneliness) (Weiss, 1973; Hawkley & Cacioppo, 2010). Loneliness is characterised by anxious feelings about a lack of connection or communication with other people, including friends or family. This can also happen when an individual's expectations of the character and quality of social relationships not being met; when there is discrepancy between what an individual expects from a relationship and what they actually experience. It can lead to depression and suicidal ideation.

It has long been known that young adults studying at university are vulnerable to experiencing greater loneliness due to changes in social networks, separation from home and established friendships (Weiss, 1973). This may produce a deficit in social interaction and support, and create the perception of a smaller support social network leading to feelings of loneliness and social isolation until new relationships can be established (Özdemir & Tuncay, 2008). Loneliness is prevalent among young people under the age of 25 years (Victor & Yang, 2012). In 2018, a large UK wide survey found that 40% of 16- to 24-year-old participants felt lonely (Hammond, 2018). Among first-year undergraduates, 49% reported mental health issues and 31% cited social isolation as the global cause (Storrie et al., 2010). Ironically, people with more years of education are less likely to experience loneliness in the long term. Despite this, being a young adult and living in rented accommodation, which is a common experience for students, leads to an increased likelihood of feeling lonely (Office of National Statistics, 2018). Depending on their field of study, requirement for lecture attendance, practical teaching and contact time, some students may have a significant amount of independent study time alone which may reduce their opportunities for interactions with peers. Research has shown that students studying social sciences may be particularly at risk of this (Diehl et al., 2018). Students living in the familial home or commuting long distances to save money may also be at greater risk social isolation from limited interactions with peers.

Extra-curricular activities run by the university or Student's Union can be important in encouraging a sense of belonging to the university community. This involves a subjective sense of relatedness or connectedness to the institution. As well as academic engagement, this involves social engagement with peers, including the provision of societies ranging from sports to arts to politics and so on, and volunteering to work for charities (Thomas, 2012).

Students may also use social media to stay in contact with family and friends and to build new networks. It is important that universities recognise the importance of online communication by supporting and subscribing to a range of platforms to enable this, from local course-related or subject-area discussion groups and social groups to platforms with national and global reach (Thomas, 2012). Studies of young adults have shown that feelings of loneliness can lead to a decreased perception of wellbeing (Chue, 2010). Loneliness has been described as 'social pain' which acts as a psychological mechanism that is meant to motivate an individual to seek social connections (Cacioppo et al., 2008). It is important that when students seek to make these connections, that universities provide opportunities and resources for them to find and develop them.

The Covid-19 pandemic has had a significant impact on social isolation of university students around the world. Most universities were forced to transfer their teaching into an online format, and to close their campuses either partially or completely during waves of high infection rates. Imposition and relaxation of these restrictions varied at different times across countries. Many students were left to study in their rooms in university residences or at home with their families due to travel restrictions. International students, in some instances, were unable to return to their home country prior to lockdowns and the requirements of quarantine policies and spent long months away from their families. In March 2021, the UK Office for National Statistics reported that over a quarter (26%) of students surveyed reported feeling lonely "often or always," compared with 8% of the adult population in Great Britain over a similar period. In the short-to-medium term, these conditions are likely to continue intermittently in different countries as different variants of the Covid-19 virus cause waves of infections until an effective level of vaccination and immunity had been reached. It is likely then that the resulting psychological distress will continue in varying presentations as those impacted progress through the education system and into their chosen occupations (Browning et al., 2021).

5 Response to the Changing Needs of Students from Higher Education

The Covid-19 pandemic had a significant impact on structure and delivery of higher education in 2020 necessitating a rapid transfer to online teaching at very short notice to a student group who were unprepared for this. This presented a significant challenge for university teaching staff and there were unavoidable delays while staff adapted their learning materials and adjusted to using new software to enable this new delivery format on a large scale. Lectures were pre-recorded or delivered via online platforms. Small group meetings using Zoom or Microsoft Teams became the modus operandi. Assessments and exams were redesigned and delivered in a new online format. Graduation ceremonies were postponed or cancelled. Despite the best efforts of academic staff, many students were left feeling confused, frustrated and disappointed by their university experience. Further research studies will be needed to evaluate the impact of this on psychological and professional career outcomes for the current and future generations of students whose experience of school and university during this time was forever changed.

As vaccines became available and the impact of the pandemic receded, universities across countries have worked hard to return to onsite teaching. Efforts are underway to try to understand the impact of the pandemic on students and young people in an effort to mitigate the negative effects in future, to maintain a healthy mindset and to foster resilience in the future work force (Browning et al., 2021; Yorguner, 2021; Defeyter et al., 2021). There is increasing awareness of the need to increase the availability of welfare support services and embed wellbeing into higher education, such as expanding the role of personal tutors and peer support, increasing funding for counselling and access to online psychological interventions such as cognitive behaviour therapy and mindfulness. Universities have been forced to re-think their dependence on lectures and didactic teaching. Students now expect to have access to online resources, subject focussed online chat rooms, social media platforms and online assessments (Clements, 2015; Walker et al., 2021). The virtual classroom has become a reality so the requirement for their physical attendance in a physical classroom is much reduced. This also reduces opportunities for in-person social interaction and may increase social isolation, which appears to be at odds with interventions to protect and improve wellbeing, and must be balanced with requirements for human interactions as outlined earlier if it is not to have a detrimental effect. Using online media effectively in both teaching and social networking will be integral to the development of future higher education and management of good mental health among students. Traditional lectures will still have their place in university education but it is likely that audio and visual recording of lectures, use of podcasts and increasing use of remote learning will continue.

6 Student Wellbeing, Resources and Resilience: Impact on Future Careers

In recent years, interest in student wellbeing and how students can be better supported during their university years has been growing in order to increase productivity and avoid future mental health problems such as burnout. Three components of wellbeing have been identified (Steptoe et al., 2015). Evaluative wellbeing focuses on broad cognitive judgement of achievement of career goals, health and financial status. It involves a global assessment using an individual's personal criteria in order to measure life satisfaction. Reduced wellbeing is an indicator of future mental illness and of later development of disorders such as depression (Diener et al., 1985). Hedonic wellbeing refers to the individual's experience of emotion and includes feeling of happiness and contentment as well as negative feelings such as sadness, despair, loss and so on. Eudemonic wellbeing refers to an individual's judgement regarding the purpose of their life. This indicates the sense of meaning derived from interaction with others or events, and such existential issues that are determined by a combination of internal and external factors (Steptoe et al., 2015). Various aspects of wellbeing have been found to be protective against poor health and to impact on morbidity and mortality. Wellbeing is defined as a complex multidimensional construct. Stable wellbeing is achieved when an individual has sufficient resources (psychological, social and physical) to cope with the challenges they confront, and a sense of equilibrium is reached, however this dynamic can fluctuate depending on the external and internal demands of the challenge (Dodge et al., 2012; Cummins & Cummins, 2010).

Resilience is integral to this concept of wellbeing as a protective factor. It is defined as the ability to adapt and use available resources in the face of adversity to achieve and maintain healthy functioning. It is a psychological characteristic that enables individuals to continue to thrive even after exposure to a stressful event. Dunn and colleagues argued that resilience can be learned and increased, and they suggest a conceptual model whereby increasing resilience may help prevent the development of burnout (Dunn et al., 2008).

They use the metaphor of a psychological 'coping reservoir' which can either be replenished by positive inputs such as psychological support, healthy social activities, mentorship, intellectual stimulation and so on, or be drained by negative inputs such as stress, internal conflicts and demands on time and energy. The students own personal traits, temperament and coping style are also important in forming the internal structure of the reservoir. In combination, these can lead to positive or negative outcomes, including resilience and enhanced mental health, or burnout and cynicism. This concept presents the replenishing and depleting of the reservoir as a dynamic process so it is important to students learn how to bolster their internal reservoir in order to foster resilience and wellbeing, and are provided with opportunities and resources to do this. Dunn et al argued that helping students to identify and focus on the unique strengths of the internal structure of their own reservoir (coping style, personal traits and temperament) while also helping them identify supportive inputs that help replenish the reservoir will foster greater resilience, self-esteem and competence (Dunn et al., 2008).

Resilience is associated with increased quality of life, wellbeing and functional capacity at times of adversity (Abiola & Udofia, 2011; Cassidy, 2015) (see also Chap. 13 in this present book). It is claimed that resilience is more important than intelligence in achieving success in academic attainment (Duckworth, 2017). A strategy which could successfully embed the development of resilience and wellbeing into the undergraduate curriculum could potentially help to protect students against stress and mental illness, reduce the dropout and lead to a more economically productive, healthy and creative professional workforce (Thomas, 2012; Burns et al., 2020).

7 Interventions to Increase Wellbeing, Resilience and Success

There are many opportunities that universities can provide within the educational environment to help students to develop good wellbeing and improve resilience. Wellbeing is multi-faceted and requires a multi-component approach. This may fall into four areas as discussed below: (1) the university environment and social activities; (2) teaching approaches and methods within the particular subject area studied; (3) courses specifically intended to improve wellbeing; (4) pastoral support.

(1) **University environment and social activities**

Working with the Students Union and student organisations, universities can encourage students to engage in social activities in a wide range of different areas, including sports clubs, creative arts and crafts, community projects and social action, charity and volunteer work, professional societies and so on. Membership of societies and clubs can help to increase a sense of belonging and to build social networks, reduce loneliness and social isolation. This can also provide opportunities to develop new skills and increase self-confidence, which can assist students in their future careers. Extra-curricular projects and programmes can support self-development by exposing students to new experiences and people, and by requiring them to develop skills in problem solving and leadership within an educational environment that supports wellbeing. Providing social spaces where students can meet, study, socialise helps to build a community. These might be indoor spaces such as cafes, bars, function rooms, comfortable seating areas and so on, or outdoor spaces such as nature gardens, green areas and sports facilities.

Access to good-quality career advice can help students make important and realistic early choices about their future employment and help them to develop their ambitions (Thomas, 2012). For example, they may get involved in charity/ volunteer work or apprenticeship style work experience. This can increase motivation and help them to set realistic goals. It can also broaden their outlook, help them to develop flexible ways of thinking and challenge them to undertake activities that may help them to increase their chances of success in their chosen field. Being aware of a wider range of options may enable them to review the time scale of their career progression or undertake alternative, more flexible career pathways than originally envisioned (Hizzett & Snaith, 2022; Ogunde et al., 2017).

(2) **Teaching approaches and methods in supporting wellbeing and resilience**

There are a number of teaching approaches and strategies that can support student wellbeing and build resilience, many of which can be embedded in current teaching practice. The shift to online teaching during the Covid-19 pandemic served to highlight the importance of active social contact during learning activities to promote a sense of belonging to the group and self-esteem. Developing opportunities for students to work together in small groups, online or in-person, encourages communication, team working, independent learning, problem solving, increased enjoyment and so on allows students to engage emotionally with their learning (Camacho-Morles et al., 2021). The increasing use of technology during the pandemic left some students feeling overwhelmed, so using a variety of teaching media, including in-person lectures and seminars as well as pre-recorded teaching, telephone and video calls, and online communication, is helpful in normalising the use of these media, managing fear and anxiety, and increasing resilience (Tseng et al., 2020). It may help students to make friends and manage their own emotions along with those of others. They therefore have the opportunity to practice self-regulation and develop emotional intelligence (Cleary et al.,

2018). Having opportunities to present their work to the class or tutor helps to increase self-confidence, presentation skills, verbal/technical/social skills and manage performance anxiety (Aliyu et al., 2019). It also allows information to be presented in different formats using different media and encourages students to be intellectually creative and inquisitive.

Interventions that encourage social integration, the development of strong formal and informal social support networks, and development of cognitive restructuring appear to foster resilience (Morales-Rodríguez, 2021) Creating a conducive environment in which this can happen, identifying and incorporating teaching methods designed to nurture these abilities and skills could produce a cost-efficient way of increasing student resilience and wellbeing. There are many examples of this. Use of group and paired work, presentations and projects designed for students to work together over a period of time offers opportunities for improving social and communication skills. Team based learning where students are set objectives and tasks to complete as a team has many advantages in developing knowledge, roles and leadership skills (Hamada et al., 2019). The flipped classroom approach where students are required to undertake preparatory work and planning prior to the taught session in order to participate effectively encourages a higher level of motivation, organisation and participation. This also encourages students to take a greater level of responsibility for their own learning (Mortensen & Nicholson, 2015). There are, however, several limitations, including the need for a curriculum designed to support this strategy, investment in staff to facilitate teaching, high-quality resources and technical support. Educational placements in professional, community and industry settings can help to build confidence, provide work experience and generate careers opportunities. These can also sometimes allow students to be paid an income and act as joint ventures between the business and education sectors.

Realistic feedback on academic performance and progress is essential in order for students to learn from mistakes and difficulties, to be able to struggle with challenging intellectual problems and uncertainties in a safe space and to adapt their behaviour and learn to be more flexible in their cognitions. This is known as a growth mindset and this approach seeks to normalise the struggles many students have in confronting the intellectual challenges any good academic course of study should present (McIntosh & Shaw, 2017). The inclusion of tasks that require students to reflect on their own behaviour, performance or a particular experience in a structured way can also produce valuable learning in both academic and personal spheres. This usually needs to be facilitated in small groups or pairs to be meaningful and positive modelling by staff can demonstrate the value of this.

Feedback is often a contentious issue between students and university lecturers in terms of the type of feedback, its frequency and delivery. There is long running debate among academics about the most effective ways to give feedback and meeting student's expectations (Thomas, 2012). Learning as a process can often be uncomfortable because it involves uncertainty and effort over a period of time, and the outcome may not immediately reflect the personal cost involved. Students may sometimes have unrealistic expectations of this process and so meaningful feedback from academics and pastoral staff is essential in guiding them in their progress, sustaining effort, developing their resilience and maintaining good wellbeing (Esterhazy & Damşa, 2019).

(3) Courses designed to improve wellbeing and resilience

Persistence and self-management (the ability to set goals) are two key characteristics of resilience, but others such as emotional control (the ability to self-regulate by not dwelling on negative experiences or overreacting to situations), motivation and commitment are also important. These abilities could potentially be learned and refined within the university environment by providing short courses focussing on wellbeing and resilience as part of the curriculum. Mindfulness has been shown to reduce stress and increase resilience in students and can be taught effectively as a short course (Pidgeon et al., 2015). Many students struggle with perfectionistic thinking, self-criticism and anxiety so provision of self-development courses which allow students the opportunity to explore their own psychological coping strategies and learn new ones could be beneficial. Cognitive restructuring has been shown to be particularly helpful as a way of reflecting on experiences and positively reframing them (Morales-Rodríguez, 2021; Pidgeon et al., 2015). These could be student selected components or integrated into the curriculum. Recent research suggests that the most effective courses in wellbeing and resilience incorporate multiple components.

(4) Pastoral support

Establishing consistent pastoral support may involve allocating mentors or personal tutors who support students throughout their three or four years (or more) undergraduate journey. The availability of counsellors, peer support and provision of self-development courses are important in allowing students to develop effective coping strategies, mature emotional regulation as well as their intellectual ability (McIntosh & Shaw, 2017). Allocating personal tutors to students on a long-term basis throughout the period of their undergraduate education rather than just for short, one-year periods creates the opportunity for staff to model consistent positive approaches to problem solving and cognitive restructuring, both in managing academic issues and life events over time. It also allows for early intervention when problems arise in the short term by staff who have built a rapport with the student. Personal tutors are usually not counsellors, rather their role is to offer academic and pastoral support, and possibly mentoring, and to have pastoral oversight of the students allocated to them so that they can refer to other staff specialising in counselling, accommodation advice, financial support, disability and health and so on (Earwaker, 1992 as cited in Walker 2022). They provide a consistent, stable presence and may be the only member of staff to follow a student throughout their university career, since the head of year, module leaders and course leads may change as the student progresses from one year to the next through their undergraduate studies (Walker, 2022). This provides the opportunity to build trust and for the student to feel 'known' as an individual. It can provide a sense of continuity and reassurance throughout the intellectual and emotional changes exposure to higher education brings. The presence of a trusted colleague or mentor can be an important element in building resilience.

A high-quality, professional counselling service is an essential component of student welfare services provided by universities. Funding accessible university counselling services for students with psychological problems or in distress can protect them against further deterioration and long-term illness, and support them in times of immediate distress. It can also provide early identification and referral for students with more serious mental illness. Most universities have policies to protect students against bullying, harassment and anti-social behaviour, and endeavour to provide a safe environment in which students can thrive. A clear complaints process supported by staff trained in student conduct and compliance can provide students with the sense of security and reassurance that expected standards of behaviour will be upheld and their personal safety protected.

Supporting students to develop and cultivate skills to sustain their wellbeing and resilience throughout their careers has important payoffs for whatever career path they choose to follow, including promotion and enhancement of professionalism within their field and personal fulfilment. It can reduce dropout rates and improve retention, increase student satisfaction and impact on academic and professional success.

8 Conclusion

Over the last decade there has been increasing evidence to show that students in higher education may experience levels of stress that damage their mental health in response to the challenges of modern life. The consequences of this affect may their long-term academic attainment, ability to complete their studies and sustain successful career trajectories, as well as their social and financial positions. There is interest from universities in adopting a more holistic approach to supporting the mental health of students and in equipping them to meet these challenges. A larger number of students are entering the university system and increased fees have changed student's expectations of the types of support universities should provide to enable students to be successful and lead healthy lives, including social, emotional, psychological, spiritual and physical support. The Universities UK Good Practice guide to Student Mental Wellbeing in Higher Education (2015) states that mental health

> [e]ncompasses the emotional resilience that enables us to enjoy life and to survive pain, disappointment and sadness, and an underlying belief in our own, and others' dignity and worth. It also allows us to engage productively in and contribute to society or our community. (Universities, 2015)

Convincing evidence presented here argues that stress and burnout often begins in the early years of career training, during the undergraduate years, and impacts on career development and occupational performance. Covid-19 has significantly impacted the approach to education and student experience. Higher education institutions must adapt their pedagogical approach and welfare provision to promote and maintain student wellbeing as well as academic excellence in order to attract students to their courses. Universities are centres of academic learning but pressure is mounting on them to provide the resources for students to develop effective coping strategies to manage stress and avoid burnout as well as obtain the qualifications they need to enable them to reach their potential in the workplace. This is becoming increasingly influential as a marker used by students when choosing which university to attend and later as a measure in judging how well the university has performed. The physical and mental health of students is important in enabling students to achieve their personal and intellectual potential. It will be essential for universities in future, post Covid-19, to develop a range of innovative teaching strategies and welfare support to operationalise this. Healthy, resilient students are more likely to successfully complete their studies, less likely to drop out or experience burn out later in their career, and more likely to make a positive, long-term contribution society.

References

Abiola, T., & Udofia, O. (2011). Psychometric assessment of the Wagnild and Young's resilience scale in Kano, Nigeria. *BMC Research Notes, 4*(1), 509. https://doi.org/10.1186/1756-0500-4-509

Aliyu, M. M., Korau, S. M., & Basiru, A. (2019). Reducing undergraduates speaking anxiety through class interactions and oral presentations. *Asian Journal of Contemporary Education, 3*(1), 36–43. https://doi.org/10.18488/journal.137.2019.31.36.43

Appleby, J. A., King, N., Saunders, K. E., Bast, A., Rivera, D., Byun, J., Cunningham, S., Khera, C., & Duffy, A. C. (2022). Impact of the COVID-19 pandemic on the experience and mental health of university students studying in Canada and the UK: a cross-sectional study. *BMJ*. https://doi.org/10.1136/bmjopen-2021-050187

Auerbach, R. P., Alonso, J., Axinn, W. G., Cuijpers, P., Ebert, D. D., Green, J. G., Hwang, I., Kessler, R. C., Liu, H., Mortier, P., Nock, M. K., Pinder-Amaker, S., Sampson, N. A., Aguilar-Gaxiola, S., Al-Hamzawi, A., Andrade, L. H., Benjet, C., Caldas-de-Almeida, J. M., Demyttenaere, K., et al. (2016). Mental disorders among college students in the World Health Organization World Mental Health Surveys. *Psychological Medicine, 46*(14), 2955–2970. https://doi.org/10.1017/S0033291716001665

Benson-Egglenton, J. (2019). The financial circumstances associated with high and low wellbeing in undergraduate students: A case study of an English Russell Group institution. *Journal of Further and Higher Education, 43*(7), 901–913. https://doi.org/10.1080/0309877X.2017.142162

Blake-Holmes, K. (2020). *Understanding the needs of young carers in the context of the covid-19 global pandemic.* University of East Anglia. www.uea.ac.uk/crcf

Bolumole, M. (2020). Student life in the age of COVID-19. *Higher Education Research & Development, 39*(7), 1357–1361.

Brezonakova, A. (2017). Pilot burnout as a human factor limitation. *Transportation Research Procedia 28*, 11–15. https://doi.org/10.1016/j.trpro.2017.12.163

Browning, M. H. E. M., Larson, L. R., Sharaievska, I., Rigolon, A., McAnirlin, O., Mullenbach, L., Cloutier, S., Vu, T. M., Thomsen, J., Reigner, N., Metcalf, E. C., D'Antonio, A., Helbich, M., Bratman, G. N., & Alvarez, H. O. (2021). Psychological impacts from COVID-19 among university students: Risk factors across seven states in the United States. *PLOS ONE, 16*(1), e0245327. https://doi.org/10.1371/journal.pone.0245327

Burns, D., Dagnall, N., & Holt, M. (2020). Assessing the Impact of the COVID-19 Pandemic on Student Wellbeing at Universities in the United Kingdom: A conceptual analysis. *Frontiers in Education (Lausanne), 5*. https://doi.org/10.3389/feduc.2020.582882

Camacho-Morles, J., Slemp, G. R., Pekrun, R., Loderer, K., Hou, H., & Oades, L. G. (2021). Activity achievement emotions and academic performance: A meta-analysis. *Educational Psychology Review, 33*(3), 1051–1095. https://doi.org/10.1007/s10648-020-09585-3

Cao, W., Fang, Z., Hou, G., Han, M., Xu, X., Dong, J., & Zheng, J. (2020). The psychological impact of the COVID-19 epidemic on college students in China. *Psychiatry Research, 287*, 112934. https://doi.org/10.1016/j.psychres.2020.112934

Cassidy, S. (2015). Resilience building in students: The role of academic self-efficacy. *Frontiers in Psychology, 6*, 1781. https://doi.org/10.3389/fpsyg.2015.01781

Cho, S., & Jang, S. J. (2021). Effects of an existential nursing intervention for college students in the COVID-19 pandemic situation. *International Journal of Environmental Research and Public Health, 18*(10), 5268. https://doi.org/10.3390/ijerph18105268

Cleary, M., Visentin, D., West, S., Lopez, V., & Kornhaber, R. (2018). Promoting emotional intelligence and resilience in undergraduate nursing students: An integrative review. *Nurse Education Today, 68*, 112–120. https://doi.org/10.1016/j.nedt.2018.05.018

Clements, J. C. (2015). Using Facebook to enhance independent student engagement: A case study of first-year undergraduates. *Higher Education Studies, 5*(4). https://doi.org/10.5539/hes.v5n4p131

Collin, V., Toon, M., O'Selmo, E., Reynolds, L., & Whitehead, P. (2019). A survey of stress burnout and well-being in UK dentists. *British Dental Journal, 226*(1), 40–49.

Cummins, R., & Cummins, R. (2010). Subjective wellbeing, homeostatically protected mood and depression: A synthesis. *Journal of Happiness Studies, 11*(1), 1–17. https://doi.org/10.1007/s10902-009-9167-0

Dantzer, C., Wardle, J., Fuller, R., Pampalone, S. Z., & Steptoe, A. (2006). International study of heavy drinking: Attitudes and sociodemographic factors in university students. *Journal of American College Health, 55*(2), 83–90. https://doi.org/10.3200/JACH.55.2.83-90

Defeyter, M. A., Stretesky, P. B., Long, M. A.,, Furey, S., Reynolds, C., Porteous, D., Dodd, A., Mann, E., Kemp, A., Fox, J., McAnallen, A., & Gonçalves, L. (2021). Mental well-being in UK higher education during Covid-19: Do students trust universities and the government? *Frontiers in Public Health*. https://doi.org/10.3389/fpubh.2021.646916

Diehl, K., Jansen, C., Ishchanova, K., & Hilger-Kolb, J. (2018). Loneliness at universities: Determinants of emotional and social loneliness among students. *International Journal of Environmental Research and Public Health, 15*(9). https://doi.org/10.3390/ijerph15091865. E1865 [pii].

Diener, E., Emmons, R., Larsen, R., & Griffin, S. (1985). The satisfaction with life scale. *Journal of Personality Assessment, 49*, 71–75. https://doi.org/10.1207/s15327752jpa4901_13

Dodge, R., Daly, A., Huyton, J., & Sanders, L. (2012). The challenge of defining wellbeing. *International Journal of Wellbeing, 2*(3), 222–235. https://doi.org/10.5502/ijw.v2i3.4

Duckworth, A. (2017). *Grit: The power of passion and perseverance* (1st ed.). Vermilion.

Dunn, L. B., Iglewicz, A., & Moutier, C. (2008). A conceptual model of medical student well-being: promoting resilience and preventing burnout. *Academic Psychiatry: The Journal of the American Association of Directors of Psychiatric Residency Training and the Association for Academic Psychiatry, 32*(1), 44–53. https://doi.org/10.1176/appi.ap.32.1.44

Dyrbye, L. N., Thomas, M. R., Massie, F. S., Power, D. V., Eacker, A., Harper, W., Durning, S., Moutier, C., Szydlo, D. W., Novotny, P. J., Sloan, J. A., & Shanafelt, T. D. (2008). Burnout and suicidal ideation among U.S. medical students. *Annals of Internal Medicine, 149*(5), 334–341. 149/5/334 [pii]

Earwaker, J. (1992). *Helping and supporting students.* Society for Research into Higher Education and Open University Press.

Eisenberg, D., Gollust, S. E., Golberstein, E., & Hefner, J. L. (2007). Prevalence and correlates of depression, anxiety, and suicidality among university students. *American Journal of Orthopsychiatry, 77*(4), 534–542. https://doi.org/10.1037/0002-9432.77.4.534

Elani, H. W., Allison, P. J., Kumar, R. A., Mancini, L., Lambrou, A., & Bedos, C. (2014). A systematic review of stress in dental students. *Journal of Dental Education, 78*(2), 226–242. https://doi.org/10.1002/j.0022-0337.2014.78.2.tb05673.x

Esterhazy, R., & Damşa, C. (2019). Unpacking the feedback process: An analysis of undergraduate students' interactional meaning-making of feedback comments. *Studies in Higher Education (Dorchester-on-Thames), 44*(2), 260–274. https://doi.org/10.1080/03075079.2017.1359249

Frajerman, A., Morvan, Y., Krebs, M.-O., Gorwood, P., & Chaumette, B. (2019). Burnout in medical students before residency: A systematic review and meta-analysis. *European Psychiatry, 55*, 36–42. https://doi.org/10.1016/j.eurpsy.2018.08.006

Giuntella, O. (2020). *Lifestyle and mental health disruptions during COVID-19.* SSRN. https://doi.org/10.2139/ssrn.3666985

Hamada, S., Haruta, J., Maeno, T., Maeno, T., Suzuki, H., Takayashiki, A., Inada, H., Naito, T., Tomita, M., Kanou, N., & Baba, T. (2019). Effectiveness of an interprofessional education program using team-based learning for medical students: A randomized controlled trial. *Journal of General and Family Medicine, 21*(1), 2–9. https://doi.org/10.1002/jgf2.284

Hammond, C. (2018). *Who feels lonely? The results of the world's largest loneliness study.* BBC Radio 4. https://www.bbc.co.uk/programmes/articles/2yzhfv4DvqVp5nZyxBD8G23/who-feels-lonely-the-results-of-the-world-s-largest-loneliness-study

Hargrove, M. B., Becker, W. S., & Hargrove, D. F. (2015). The HRD Eustress Model. *Human Resource Development Review, 14*(3), 279–298. https://doi.org/10.1 177/1534484315598086

Hawkley, L. C., & Cacioppo, J. T. (2010). Loneliness matters: A theoretical and empirical review of consequences and mechanisms. *Annals of Behavioral Medicine, 40*(2), 218–227. https://doi.org/10.1007/s12160-010-9210-8

Hizzett, K., & Snaith, B. (2022). Career intentions, their influences and motivational factors in diagnostic radiography: A survey of undergraduate students. *Radiography (London, England. 1995), 28*(1), 162–167. https://doi.org/10.1016/j.radi.2021.09.013

Kerr, H. (2013). *Mental distress survey overview.* National Union of Students. https://www.nus.org.uk/Global/Campaigns/20130517/Mental/Distress/Survey/Overview.pdf

Lim, G. Y., Tam, W. W., Lu, Y., Ho, C. S., Zhang, M. W., & Ho, R. C. (2018). Prevalence of depression in the community from 30 countries between 1994 and 2014. *Scientific Reports, 8*(1), 2861. https://doi.org/10.1038/s41598-018-21243-x

Maslach, C., Jackson, S. E., & Leiter, M.P. (1996). *Maslach burnout inventory manual* (3rd ed.). Consulting Psychologists Press.

McIntosh, E. A., & Shaw, J. (2017). Student resilience: Exploring the positive case for resilience. http://ubir.bolton.ac.uk/1224/

Morales-Rodríguez, F. M. (2021). Fear, stress, resilience and coping strategies during COVID-19 in Spanish University Students. *Sustainability (Basel, Switzerland), 13*(11), 5824. https://doi.org/10.3390/su13115824

Mortensen, C. J., & Nicholson, A. M. (2015). The flipped classroom stimulates greater learning and is a modern 21st century approach to teaching today's undergraduates. *Journal of Animal Science, 93*(7), 3722–3731. https://doi.org/10.2527/jas.2015-9087

National Union of Students. (2018a). *NUS alcohol impact—Students and alcohol survey.* NUS. https://www.nusconnect.org.uk/resources/students-alcohol-national-survey

National Union of Students. (2018b). *Taking the hit: Student drug use and how institutions respond.* NUS.

O'Connor, R. C., Wetherall, K., Cleare, S., Mcclelland, H., Melson, A. J., Niedzwiedz, C. L., O'carroll, R. E., O'Connor, D. B., Platt, S., Scowcroft, E., Watson, B., Zortea, T., Ferguson, E., & Robb Background, K. A. (2020). Mental-health-and-well-being-during-the-covid-19-pandemic. *The British Journal of Psychiatry, 218*(6), 326–333.

Office for National Statistics. (2018). *Estimating suicide among higher education students, England and Wales: Experimental statistics.* Office for National Statistics. https://www.ons.gov.uk/peoplepopulationandcommunity/birthsdeathsandmarriages/deaths/articles/estimatingsuicideamonghighereducationstudentsenglandan dwalesexperimentalstatistics/2018-06-25

Office of National Statistics. (2018). *Loneliness—What characteristics and circumstances are associated with feeling lonely?.* https://www.ons.gov.uk/peoplepopulationandcommunity/wellbeing/articles/lonelinesswhatcharacteristicsandcircumstancesareassociatedwithfeelinglonely/2018-04-10

Ogunde, J. C., Overton, T. L., Thompson, C. D., Mewis, R., & Boniface, S. (2017). Beyond graduation: Motivations and career aspirations of undergraduate chemistry students. *Chemistry Education Research and Practice, 18*(3), 457–471.

Özdemir, U., & Tuncay, T. (2008). Correlates of loneliness among university students. *Child and Adolescent Psychiatry and Mental Health, 2.* https://doi.org/10.1186/1753-2000-2-29

Papapanou, M., Routsi, E., Tsamakis, K., Fotis, L., Marinos, G., Lidoriki, I., Karamanou, M., Papaioannou, T. G., Tsiptsios, D., Smyrnis, N., Rizos, E., & Schizas, D. (2022). Medical education challenges and innovations during COVID-19 pandemic. *Postgraduate Medical Journal, 98*(1159), 321. https://doi.org/10.1136/postgradmedj-2021-140032

Pells, R. (2017, 18/1/). Sussex University failed duty of care to student assault victim, inquiry finds. *The Independent.* https://www.independent.co.uk/news/uk/home-news/sussex-university-student-assault-allison-smith-senior-lecturer-dr-lee-salter-beat-punch-stamp-a7533751.html

Pereira, S., Reay, K., Bottell, J., Dzikiti, C., Platt, C., & Goodrham, C. (2019). *University Student Mental Health Survey 2018.* The Insight Network. https://uploads-ssl.webflow.com/561110743bc7e45e78292140/5c7d4b5d314d163fecdc3706_Mental%20Health%20Report%202018.pdf

Pidgeon, A. M., Bales, T. S., Lo, B. C. Y., Stapleton, P., & Magyar, H. B. (2015). Cross-cultural differences in coping, connectedness and psychological distress among university students. *International Journal for Innovation Education and Research, 3*(2), 114–125. https://doi.org/10.31686/ijier.vol3.iss2.318

Pisaniello, M. S.,Asahina, A. T., Bacchi, S., Wagner, M., Perry, S. W, Wong, M.-L., & Licinio, J. (2019). Effect of medical student debt on mental health academic performance and specialty choice: A systematic review. *BMJ Open, 9*(7), e029980. https://doi.org/10.1136/bmjopen-2019-029980

Plakhotnik, M. S., Volkova, N. V., Jiang, C., Yahiaoui, D., Pheiffer, G., McKay, K., Newman, S., & Reißig-Thust, S. (2021). The perceived impact of COVID-19 on student well-being and the mediating role of the university support: Evidence from France, Germany, Russia, and the UK. *Frontiers in Psychology, 12*, 642689. https://doi.org/10.3389/fpsyg.2021.642689

Richardson, T., Elliott, P., Roberts, R., & Jansen, M. (2016). A longitudinal study of financial difficulties and mental health in a national sample of British undergraduate students. *Community Mental Health Journal, 53*(3), 344–352. https://doi.org/10.1007/s10597-016-0052-0

Sauer, N., Sałek, A., Szlasa, W., Ciecieląg, T., Obara, J., Gaweł, S., Marciniak, D., & Karłowicz-Bodalska, K. (2022). The impact of COVID-19 on the mental well-being of college students. *International Journal of Environmental Research and Public Health, 19*(9), 5089. https://doi.org/10.3390/ijerph19095089

Shanafelt, T. D., Boone, S., Tan, L., Dyrbye, L. N., Sotile, W., Satele, D., West, C. P., Sloan, J., & Oreskovich, M. R. (2012). Burnout and satisfaction with work-life balance among US physicians relative to the general US population. *Archives of Internal Medicine, 172*(18), 1377. https://doi.org/10.1001/archinternmed.2012.3199

Sheldon, E., Simmonds-Buckley, M., Bone, C., Mascarenhas, T., Chan, N., Wincott, M., Gleeson, H., Sow, K., Hind, D., & Barkham, M. (2021). Prevalence and risk factors for mental health problems in university undergraduate students: A systematic review with meta-analysis. *Journal of Affective Disorders, 287*, 282–292. https://doi.org/10.1016/j.jad.2021.03.054

Singh, P., Aulak, D. S., Mangat, S. S., & Aulak, M. S. (2016). Systematic review: Factors contributing to burnout in dentistry. *Occupational Medicine, 66*(1), 27–31. https://doi.org/10.1093/occmed/kqv119

Son, C., Hegde, S., Smith, A., Wang, X., & Sasangohar, F. (2020). Effects of COVID-19 on college students' mental health in the United States: Interview survey study. *Journal of Medical Internet Research, 22*(9), e21279. https://doi.org/10.2196/21279

Steptoe, A., Deaton, A., & Stone, A. A. (2015). Subjective wellbeing, health, and ageing. *Lancet (London, England), 385*(9968), 640–648. S0140-6736(13)61489-0 [pii].

Storrie, K., Ahern, K., & Tuckett, A. (2010). A systematic review: Students with mental health problems—A growing problem. *International Journal of Nursing Practice, 16*(1), 1–6. https://doi.org/10.1111/j.1440-172X.2009.01813.x

Tang, X., Wang, M.-T., Parada, F., & Salmela-Aro, K. (2021). Putting the goal back into grit: Academic goal commitment grit and academic achievement. *Journal of Youth and Adolescence, 50*(3), 470–484. https://doi.org/10.1007/s10964-020-01348-1

Thomas, L. (2012). *Building student engagement and belonging in Higher Education at a time of change.* https://www.heacademy.ac.uk/system/files/what_works_final_report_0.pdf

Thorley, C. (2017). *Not by degrees: Improving student mental health in the UK's Universities.* Institute for Public Policy Research. http://www.ippr.org/research/publications/not-by-degrees

Tseng, H., Kuo, Y., & Walsh, E. J. (2020). Exploring first-time online undergraduate and graduate students' growth mindsets and flexible thinking and their relations to online learning engagement. *Educational Technology Research and Development, 68*(5), 2285–2303. https://doi.org/10.1007/s11423-020-09774-5

UCAS. (2021). *Starting the conversation: UCAS report on student mental health.* Rosehill, New Barn Lane, Cheltenham, GL52 3LZ UK: UCAS. https://www.ucas.com/files/ucas-student-mental-health-report-2021

UK Universities. (2019). *Initiations at universities.* UUK. https://www.universitiesuk.ac.uk/policy-and-analysis/reports/Documents/2019/initiations-in-uk-universities.pdf

Universities UK. (2015). *Good practice guide: Student mental wellbeing in higher education*. Universities UK.

Victor, C. R., & Yang, K. (2012). The prevalence of loneliness among adults: A case study of the United Kingdom. *The Journal of Psychology, 146*(1–2), 85–104. https://doi.org/10.1080/00223980.2011.613875

Walker, B. W. (2022). Tackling the personal tutoring conundrum: A qualitative study on the impact of developmental support for tutors. *Active Learning in Higher Education, 23*(1), 65–77. https://doi.org/10.1177/1469787420926007

Walker, D. I., Navarro-Carrillo, G., Morgan, B., Volkova, N. V., Plakhotnik, M. S., Volkova, N. V., Jiang, C., Yahiaoui, D., Pheiffer, G., Mckay, K., Newman, S., & Reißig-Thust, S. (2021). *fpsyg-12-642689 (4)*. https://doi.org/10.3389/fpsyg.2021.642689

Weiss, R. S. (1973). *Loneliness: The experience of emotional and social isolation*. MIT Press.

Westmarland, N. (2019, 11/07/). The Warwick 'rape chat' case exposes universities' failings on sexual violence. *The Guardian Newspaper*. https://www.theguardian.com/education/2019/jul/11/the-warwick-chat-case-exposes-universities-failings-on-sexual-violence

Yorguner, N., Bulut, N. S., & Akvardar, Y. (2021). An analysis of the psychosocial challenges faced by the university students during COVID-19 pandemic and the students' knowledge attitudes and practices toward the disease. *Archives of Neuropsychiatry*. https://doi.org/10.29399/npa.27503

Zhou, A. Y., Panagioti, M., Esmail, A., Agius, R., Van Tongeren, M., & Bower, P. (2020). Factors associated with burnout and stress in trainee physicians. *JAMA Network Open, 3*(8), e2013761. https://doi.org/10.1001/jamanetworkopen.2020.13761

Part V

Dealing with Stress

20

Stress Prevention Measures in the Workplace

James Erskine and Philippe Fauquet-Alekhine

1   Defining Stress

Stress is defined as the perception that one's ability to cope with the present scenario has been exceeded and that relative to other situations, the individual has insufficient resources to successfully cope (Harms et al., 2017; Lazarus & Folkman, 1984).

It is important to frame this discussion of stress by recognising that some stress in life is often beneficial, providing motivational energy to tackle difficult situations. Selye (1959) originally termed this positive form of stress as eustress. However, there is general agreement in the literature that once stress grows past certain levels it quickly becomes detrimental to the individual (Fauquet-Alekhine et al., 2014; O'Connor et al., 2021; Salem, 2015).

J. Erskine (✉)
Institute for Medical and Biomedical Sciences, St George's University of London, London, UK
e-mail: jerskine@sgu.ac.uk

P. Fauquet-Alekhine
SEBE-Lab, Department of Psychological and Behavioural Science, London School of Economics and Political Science, London, UK

Laboratory for Research in Science of Energy, Montagret, France

Groupe INTRA Robotics, Avoine, France
e-mail: p.fauquet-alekhine@lse.ac.uk; philippe.fauquet-alekhine@groupe-intra.com

© The Author(s), under exclusive license to Springer Nature Switzerland AG 2023
P. Fauquet-Alekhine, J. Erskine (eds.), *The Palgrave Handbook of Occupational Stress*,
https://doi.org/10.1007/978-3-031-27349-0_20

At this juncture there are some points rarely made in the literature that need to be made. The first is that when an individual is stressed in a stressful environment, this means that the person is functioning properly. Therefore, the assumption that stress is always a manifestation of individual lack of coping ability or environmental issues is fundamentally flawed. Stress is an interactive process delineated across time with an overdetermined set of influences from genetics, biology, economics and the built environment.

Stress is a major issue in the modern workplace (Lazarus, 2020). Organisations have become interested in intervening by instigating numerous organisational programmes designed to reduce stress and promote greater well-being and health. In part this is driven by the sheer cost of not intervening, for example, impact on bottom line and the number of working days lost. Stress is the second most frequently reported health issue at work and therefore there is a move towards legislation on health and safety in the workplace (EU-OSHA, 2022). There is also evidence that work stress can spill over into life outside work (Grzywacz et al., 2002). Chirico and colleagues (2019) examined the literature on psychosocial risk prevention in an occupational context, and reported that most countries have not included mandatory risk assessment and prevention in their national legislation around health and safety. This is important, as psychosocial hazards include how work is designed, organised and managed, and its effect on individual workers in terms of causing various harms (Cox & Griffiths, 2005).

Research has consistently demonstrated that work stress is associated with risks to physical and mental health (Ganster & Rosen, 2013; Seymour & Grove, 2005; Steptoe & Kivimaki, 2013). It is also associated with negative and severe financial implications (Pieper et al., 2019). Furthermore, it is estimated the 15% of working people have mental health conditions (Hesketh et al., 2020). Thus, there is data demonstrating that mental health issues are the fastest growing cause of long-term workplace absence in developed nations (Harvey et al., 2009; OECD, 2012). Furthermore, stress is now widely acknowledged to be one of the leading causes of long-term sickness worldwide (American Psychological Association, 2022; UK Health & Safety Executive, 2021). However, there are effective methods of treatment (LaMontagne et al., 2007; van der Klink et al., 2001).

O'Connor and colleagues (2021) review the evidence linking stress and health outcomes and conclude that stress has direct effects on health through changes in autonomic and neuroendocrine systems. However, it also impacts health indirectly by increasing the likelihood of obesity, cancers and cardiovascular compromise (Hill et al., 2018; O'Connor et al., 2008; O'Connor et al., 2021). Allostatic load is the term used to denote wear and tear accruing from repeated long-term stress (McEwen, 1998). The evidence indicates that longer-term stress causes damage to multiple systems notably cardiovascular, metabolic, neural and cellular. This has led to the term allostatic overload which pertains to the detrimental stress effects on biological systems due to sustained overactivation (Fava et al., 2019; McEwen, 1998, 2000, 2007; McEwen & Seeman, 1999). The authors then demonstrate using viral challenge studies that stressful life events can increase the likelihood of developing diseases across a range of pathogens (Cohen et al., 1991, 1998; Segerstrom & Miller, 2004). The authors also examine vaccine studies concluding that response to vaccination is modified by stress. With improved responses occurring in participants with lower stress (Cohen et al., 2001; Marsland et al., 2006; Pedersen et al., 2009; Vedhara et al., 1999). Of critical importance to the present chapter the authors review some of the work on stress and early life adversity and health consequences. They note that research is demonstrating that early adverse experiences seem to convey later health issues with data indicating more physical and mental health issues in those having previous adversity (Bellis et al., 2015; Hughes et al., 2017; Waehrer et al., 2020). Stress can impact health directly thought biological and genetic changes but also indirectly through behaviour. What is clear is the potential negative effects of stress are more broad and more nuanced than perhaps realised. It is therefore much more crucial to take steps to mitigate stress.

Although mental health issues are not synonymous with stress, over long periods, stress can exacerbate and cause mental health issues (Carter et al., 2006; Moylan et al., 2013). This is important as research indicates that depression, anxiety and stress decrease productivity while increasing workplace absence and unemployment due to sickness (Birnbaum et al., 2010; Dewa et al., 2011). Furthermore, estimates suggest the annual cost to the UK economy from these issues to be between £33 and £42 billion (Stevenson & Farmer, 2017). Other estimates put the UK figure at £28.3 billion per year in 2009 (NICE, 2009). US estimates put annual healthcare costs for workplace stress at $190 billion using data from 2015 (Goh, 2016). However, other estimates put the US figure much higher at $500 billion lost each year due to workplace stress and 550 million workdays (APA, 2015). Furthermore, costs associated with poor metal health are expected to amount to more than $6 trillion by 2030 (Greenberg et al., 2015; WFMH, 2017). In addition, employer health costs for US employees rapidly outpaced inflation (Patton, 2015). Peak incidence and onset for 75% of mental health conditions is before 24, while diabetes and heart attacks onset at 53.5 years and 65 years respectively. This makes it likely that mental health costs will be higher than other issues (Arango et al., 2018; CDC, 2014; Kessler et al., 2005). Furthermore, data indicates that 50–60% of adults with mental health issues do not access effective treatment or wait years before seeking treatment (Kessler et al., 1994; MHA, 2017; SAMHSA, 2015; WFMH, 2017).

Depression affects 280 million people worldwide and is the second largest cause of disability (WHO, 2021; Ferrari et al., 2013). Self-reported depression is the most frequent cause of absenteeism (Almond & Healey, 2003). Anxiety and depression accounted for 54% of working days lost in 2018/19 (HSE, 2019). Furthermore, mental illness accounts for 32% of years lived with disability globally and strongly impacts the workforce (Vigo et al., 2016). In the US data indicates that 30–50% of all adults will have a mental health issue during their life (Kessler et al., 2005; Moffitt et al., 2010; Takayanagi et al., 2014).

Goh et al. (2016) find that more than 120,000 deaths per year in the US are associated with how companies manage their staff. This translates to 5–8% of annual healthcare costs. Goh et al. (2016) create mathematical models of the relationships between workplace stressors, mortality and health care costs. The final models suggest that workplace associated mortality would be comparable to the fourth (cerebrovascular diseases) and fifth (accidents) largest causes of death in the US. The implications are clear, there is a definite link between employer actions and health care outcomes. Goh et al. (2019) conducted further analysis examining the number of excess deaths on a country basis and how the relative wealth of the nation affects this. Results indicated that in Europe as GDP per capita rose, per capital workplace mortality and costs reduced. They then measured how the US deviated from the regression line of European nations demonstrating 17,000 preventable deaths per year and costs of $44 billion. Furthermore, the International Labour Organisation estimates there are 1.74 million work-related deaths per year and 160 million workers affected by diseases of the workplace (ILO, 2019). Therefore, it is vital to examine exactly how employers and work stress affect employee health outcomes.

McDaid et al. (2019) examine the economic case regarding prevention of mental illness, and demonstrate significant economic consequences. They show that in 2013 mental health issues cost the US $201 billion and compared this to expenditure on heart conditions of $147 billion (Roehrig, 2016). Furthermore, these costs are unlikely to represent the true cost, as mental health issues have numerous other costly consequences such as lost revenue from workers, increased mortality, informal carer costs, increased costs of criminal justice. Given the worldwide burden of mental health conditions there is an increasing focus on prevention (Collins et al., 2011, McDaid et al., 2019, Wykes et al., 2015). However, despite clear benefits of increasing prevention focus and mental health promotion these areas are consistently underfunded. Furthermore, dividing conditions into mental or physical excludes much overlap and there is a wealth of evidence indicating one frequently leads to the other (France et al., 2012; Mercer et al., 2012; Naylor et al., 2012). Critically employer physical health costs have far outweighed costs for mental health, despite mental health conditions being the costliest illnesses in the US, exceeding physical health costs (Goetzel et al., 2000; Goetzel et al., 2003; Greenberg et al., 2015; Roehrig, 2016).

One area highlighted in the McDaid et al. (2019) analysis as an area with a strong economic evidence base for acting concerns workplace stress. They highlight the findings that in OECD countries mental health issues represent 30–40% of disability benefit caseloads (OECD, 2015). Furthermore, there are multiple issues created by metal health conditions in the workplace such as lost productivity, absence due to illness and the human costs. The incentives to prevent these issues are strong, such as increased production, less absenteeism, healthier workforce. Economic data strongly supports intervention, with data indicating return on investment of between $0.81 and $13.62 for every $1 spent on intervention (Matrix, 2013) or using WHO data for every $1 spent on treatment results in a return of $4 (WHO, 201). Hampson and Jacob (2020) in a report for Deloitte put the return on intervention at £5 for every £1 spent (See also Knapp et al., 2011). Therefore, workplaces represent a vital setting for prevention that is often overlooked (Goetzel et al., 2018).

Interestingly no widely agreed upon definition of job stress exists. However, it is often seen as conditions or items in the workplace that lead to significant psychological strain or "negative psychophysiological responses" (Chirico et al., 2019, p. 2).

Reducing excessive stress in the workplace would have several downstream benevolent consequences for both the organisation and the individual employees. These would include, enhanced productivity, workplace commitment, happiness and well-being. These consequences would accrue to both the organisation and the individuals working within it. Simultaneously reducing stress would also result in decreased absenteeism, staff turnover and reduced staff sickness of all kinds (De Neve et al., 2013; Warr, 2003).

One issue exacerbated by stress is burnout which has a significant impact on modern workplaces. The next section will explore these effects.

2 Defining Burnout

Burnout occurs when the individual loses the ability to care about their work and the individuals they work, with usually as a response to cumulative stress over long periods (Maslach, 1978, 2003; Maslach et al., 2001). It is traditionally seen as being composed of three components; these are:

Emotional exhaustion—the individual feels they lack sufficient resources to cope with the situation and report feeling tired and drained.

Cynicism—the individual increasingly detaches from others and their work as their negative attitude grows, they may start to treat others more like objects than people

Reduced personal efficacy—the individuals' work-based productivity declines, and they feel incompetent and loose meaning regarding their work (Maslach, 2003; Maslach et al., 2001).

Burnout is now recognised by the World Health Organisation and included in their latest global disease classification system—ICD-11 (WHO, 2019).

Concerning burnout there is evidence that not all occupations are equal and that occupations where stress is an integral part of the role suffer burnout at higher rates, this is especially true of healthcare workers who suffer elevated stress (Koinis et al., 2015; Portoghese et al., 2014; Ruotsalainen et al., 2015). Healthcare workers report more mental ill health, burnout and stress partly as a result of workplace conditions that increase stress such as work overload, shift work and violence (Gray et al., 2019; Shanafelt et al., 2015; Williams et al., 2001). Data indicates 22% of US and 27% of physicians in Great Britain suffer burnout (Linzer et al., 2001). In addition, patients of doctors that are burned out experience more medical errors and have lower patient satisfaction (Salyers et al., 2017; Shanafelt et al., 2010). Burnout is also very prevalent in caregivers and leads to much higher suicide rates than the general public (Moss, 2019a). Furthermore, data indicates the pandemic exacerbated these issues (Kang et al., 2020; Lai et al., 2020).

Regarding the effects of burnout, high levels of employee burnout and low employee well-being are related to much greater staff turnover, reduced organisational involvement and prolonged work absence through sickness (Allen et al., 2018; Dyrbye et al., 2019; Ruitenburg et al., 2012; Swider & Zimmerman, 2010). Moss (2019a, b) argues that viewing burnout as an individual problem (and locating the genesis with the individual) may be harmful. Thus, companies without employee well-being systems have higher turnover, lower productivity and higher health care costs (APA, 2015).

Sultana et al. (2020) reviewed evidence-based interventions for managing burnout among healthcare providers during the Covid-19 pandemic. They report the following methods effective: making people aware of the risks, promoting positive mental health (e.g. mindfulness and self-care, decrease unmanageable workloads and improve schedules, ensure mental health service availability) using digital technology to help (e.g. digital health records and app-based interventions), creating healthier enabling environments (e.g. improve communication, coping skills, reduce workloads). This is important as although many have examined strategies to reduce stress, it is rare to see these in the context of high ongoing stress (Sultana et al., 2020).

A meta-analysis examining 27 studies to prevent burnout in mental health providers from 1980 to 2015, indicated that interventions (mainly directed at the organisation 70.4%, with job training and education being the most represented 44.4%) had a small positive effect on burnout $p = 0.006$. Moderator analysis demonstrated that individual directed interventions were better than organisational interventions. Job education was the most effective organisational intervention. Perhaps most importantly, baseline levels of burnout affected outcomes with lower initial burnout being associated with less intervention effect (Dreison et al., 2018).

3   Why Work Is Stressful?

That work can be stressful may seem a self-evident truth but there are several reasons work is stressful relative to other pursuits. Erskine and Georgiou (2017) outlined these reasons in a non-exhaustive list. These were:

1. The sheer amount of time spent at work relative to other life activities (e.g. sleeping, home, travel); 2. Consistent demands to perform and produce results; 3. Managing relationships with other individuals in the workplace; 4. Reduced autonomy; 5. Financial imperative to work irrespective of desire; 6. Usually a hierarchical power structure; 7. Career aspirations and wage discrepancy awareness; 8. Potential for bullying, victimisation, harassment and inequality; 9. Managing work life balance; 10. Job security; 11. Unmanageable workloads, deadlines and expectations; 12. Lack of training or support. (Erskine & Georgiou, 2017, p. 28)

Factors recognised to be significant determinants of worker stress and health include job demands, autonomy, workplace social support, workplace change, job insecurity, shift work, stress, bullying, perceived lack of reward for effort or career growth opportunities, low income, long working hours, role conflict or ambiguity, poor physical environment and inadequate resources (Burman & Goswami, 2018; Costa, 2010; Harvey et al., 2017; Theorell et al., 2015; Vaníčková, 2021).

In 2017, about 61% of 3440 American adults surveyed reported that their work was a substantial source of stress (APA, 2017). Furthermore, research has demonstrated that work is a source of stress and ill health (Quick & Henderson, 2016). Chirico et al., (2019) suggest there are many paths leading

382   J. Erskine and P. Fauquet-Alekhine

to work stress such as poor working conditions or organisation of work and management. They also cite lack of support from managers or supervisors and workplace violence as issues. One modern source of stress comes from the rapid pace of technological change as workplaces become increasingly digitalised, this is explored below.

3.1   Digitalisation and Modern Causes of Stress

A modern workplace stress concerns digital transformation, working from home, automatisation and global shifts (Bregenzer & Jimenez, 2021; Contreras et al., 2020). The pace of workplace technological adoption has led to the term fourth industrial revolution pertaining to digitalisation (Molino et al., 2020). Workplaces have become more cognitively demanding as positions are increasingly replaced with automatisation leading to increases in stress (Lee et al., 2016; Longo & Leva, 2019). Further worker stress may accrue from fears of technology replacing people's jobs (Bessen, 2019). In addition, artificial intelligence is quickening the pace of change, with a greater diversity of jobs being replicable by algorithms and machines (Jarrahi, 2018). In order to keep up with the changes employees must constantly receive updating of their skills, leading to more stress (Wang et al., 2008). González-López et al. (2021) investigated technostress defined as stress experienced by users in the workplace due to the impact of rapid adoption of new workplace digital technologies and how this affects staff well-being (Ragu-Nathan et al., 2008).

Their study investigated 337 undergraduates in Spain that had no choice but to continue their education using technology during the Covid-19 pandemic. They evaluated the relationships between technostress, individual differences and the level of effect (individual, group or professional). Technostress was shown to have negative consequences at individual, group and professional levels. There was evidence that individual differences within the students impacted the levels of anxiety produced by technology. Individuals defined as discrepancy (almost totally engaged in social media, but unrealistic when concerning time loss) and narcissist (uses social media to compete with others) were most affected by anxiety.

Similar themes were investigated by Molino et al. (2020) in 598 Italian factory workers as a result of the increased pace of innovation and its relationship to resilience, goal orientation, opportunities for information, training and work engagement. They argue there are multiple benefits of increased technological adoption such as reducing costs, maintenance, quality costs, energy, improved safety and more independence. However, these benefits are balanced by risks such as worker fears and stresses arising from the pace of change. Workers may fear losing their jobs, not having the requisite skills and how and when the changes will occur. To study this, workers were divided into 220 defined as white collar workers and 378 defined as blue collar. Results indicated that there were positive relationships between resilience, opportunities for information, training, acceptance of technology and workplace engagement in both samples. The authors argue it is therefore necessary to provide information and training opportunities to help employees transition to a more digitised and technological environments. Resilience demonstrated a positive relationship with technology acceptance among all workers (see Chap. 13 of the present work).

The relationship between technology, psychological detachment from work and work overload was examined in 313 health sector professionals (Sandoval-Reyes et al., 2019). They argue that as connection becomes more ubiquitous due to technology and workers may be contacted beyond standard hours, it is possible that workloads become excessive, and workers have problems detaching from work. Results indicated that there was a negative effect of technology use on the ability to detach psychologically from work. Furthermore, technology use was positively correlated with work overload. Work overload is linked to poor health (De Beer et al., 2016; Krause et al., 2005; Kubicek et al., 2013). The authors suggest it is important to instil practices and policies that enable psychological detachment.

Bondanini et al. (2020) conducted a critical review of research on technology stress. The authors note that use of positive technologies in psychology occurs at three levels: one hedonic or experiencing positive states and emotions, two eudemonic increasing individuals experience of personal meaning and three social improving relationships (Riva et al., 2012). The review highlights that with the speed of growth of the internet since 2003 there has been an explosion in research on technostress. The authors suggest in view of the negative associations between technostress, job satisfaction and organisational commitment it is vital that companies provide methods to help individuals to cope, while the authors argue that might be technical support it could also be methods of increasing resilience.

The growth in stress is problematic for organisations as it contributes to increases in mental health issues and absenteeism (Ganster & Rosen, 2013; Seymour & Grove, 2005; Steptoe & Kivimaki, 2013). In addition, anxiety and depression have been estimated to cost the global economy US$1 trillion per year (WHO, 2017). Importantly, in many countries worldwide employers have a legal duty to minimise employee stress and risks of harm (HSE, 2019,

2021). The Covid-19 pandemic further exacerbated mental health issues and data has indicated that younger individuals seem to have seen greatest rise in rates of psychological distress during the pandemic (Jung et al., 2020; Pierce et al., 2020; Rossell et al., 2021; Varma et al., 2021). Although not directly related to work there is evidence that rates of anxiety and depression are very high in university students and rose during the Covid-19 pandemic (Deng et al., 2021; Eisenberg et al., 2012; Lipson et al., 2019; Pinder-Amaker & Bell, 2012; Ramón-Arbués et al., 2020). Thus, data indicates roughly 31% of university students worldwide have a mental health disorder (Auerbach et al., 2018). Pascoe et al. (2020) report on 540,000 students in 72 countries and find 66% of students were stressed about poor grades with 59% anxious regarding school testing. 37% reported feeling stressed when studying with girls reporting more anxiety than boys. These issues are critical to tackle as individuals with depression are twice as likely to develop coronary artery disease and stroke, in addition after having a heart attack they are four times as likely to die in the following six months (Glassman, 2007). The lines demarking mental and physical health are not as clear as people often assume. Importantly, multiple factors seem to mediate links between stress and mental health. For instance, poor sleep, previous psychiatric diagnosis, isolation and hopelessness (Bartlett & Jackson, 2016; Killgore, Cloonan, et al., 2020; Serafini et al., 2020).

Another issue of concern is that mental health is often conceptualised as merely pathology and the presence or absence of mental illness. It could equally be defined by the presence of positive well-being and mental health (Deci & Ryan, 2008; Gray et al., 2019). Thus, new terms have come to the fore such as psychological well-being which examine variables such as subjective well-being, having positive relationships and a sense of purpose (Ryff et al., 2004). Furthermore, psychological well-being is itself associated with reduced staff turnover, absenteeism and increased employee engagement (Robertson & Cooper, 2010). Research has demonstrated that many effective actions can be taken to mitigate stress. For example, 80% of depression sufferers can be treated effectively when caught early (Finkelstein et al., 1996; Simon et al., 2000). Furthermore, Burman and Goswami (2018) distilled from their review the main stress reduction strategies listed below:

Meditation/mindfulness based, holidays, recreational activities, sports, stress management counselling, workplace restricting, plan work schedules in line with demands and responsibilities, job rotation to avoid repetitive and monotonous work, clear job descriptions, clear path to promotion, improved communication, stress management workshops, fair salaries, provision of emotional support for employees when fulfilling tasks and enhanced organisational training linked to the employee performance evaluation system to aid skill development.

Another area that is often overlooked forms the focus this chapter, which is interventions designed to prevent stress and mental health issues from arising in the first place. However, estimates suggest that only 5% of mental health funding goes towards prevention and that mental health is an area of health that is consistently underfunded (Christensen et al., 2011; Kingdon, 2006; MQ, 2015).

4 Types of Intervention

As the focus of this chapter is on examining the effects of interventions to reduce stress in the workplace it makes sense at the outset to examine various frameworks for categorising interventions at a higher level to provide structure.

Broadly stress reduction interventions have been categorised by multiple authors along two main dimensions. The first dimension pertains to the focus of the intervention itself—whether it is focused on individual employees, or the organisation. The second dimension pertains to the level of prevention it aims at altering, for example, primary, secondary or tertiary. Under this framework primary strategies are tantamount to action taken to try to eliminate stressors or prevent stress from occurring, for example, by shifting cultures or removing risk factors in the workplace. Secondary strategies are ones that target stressed individuals and aim to reduce the effects of stress by using interventions such as mindfulness, workshops, time management, therapy-based approaches, coping skills training or relaxation training. These occur once stress has occurred and aim to prevent it worsening. Finally, tertiary strategies focus on treatment for mental health conditions and recovery from stress in those employees that are experiencing mental health conditions, through counselling or employee assistance programmes. Therefore, tertiary strategies are reactive (Jacobs et al., 2018; Holman et al., 2018; Howe et al., 2022; Ivandic et al., 2017). Jacobs et al. (2018) amend this framework slightly to include three categories of focus for interventions defined as: individual focused interventions, those focusing on the interface of individuals and organisations and finally those focused on the organisation.

In line with a similar framework suggested by Erskine (2021), these levels of strategy could also be conceptualised from the individual employee perspective as strategies occurring at the following three time points: prior to stress (mapping on to primary) during stress (mapping to secondary) and post stress (mapping to tertiary prevention).

Various authors have suggested there are certain methodological difficulties when attempting to demonstrate that organisation-level stress management interventions are effective. These would include the fact that these interventions frequently fail at rates between 50% and 80%. These programmes also have very high attrition rates and the intervention itself may prove a source of stress. The difficulty of random allocation to groups or employing experimental designs in real-world contexts and the fact that participation is voluntary (Jacobs et al., 2018; Semmer, 2006). Further complications relate to the fact that many studies have also reported that individuals with mental health issues often do not seek any support. Thus, although pertaining to medical students' data indicates 21% would not seek treatment for depression (Schwenk et al., 2010) and 43% would not seek help from mental health providers even if they felt it necessary (Van Remortel et al., 2018). Furthermore, academic stress is related to reduced accomplishment and lower motivation (Liu & Lu, 2011; Walburg, 2014). Resilience and social support have been shown to offer protection against mental health issues and there is evidence that resilience can be modified (Killgore, Taylor, et al., 2020; Serafini et al., 2020). Well-being and metal health initiatives may have different targets. For example, they may target whole populations irrespective of risk, or merely individuals that are at increased risk, or individuals already showing signs of subclinical distress (WHO, 2004).

We propose that there is another focus of interventions other than individual or organisational and that these would be leadership focused interventions. If we accept this as a third intervention focus a table of effects can be constructed as below (Table 20.1):

Table 20.1 Examples of the focus of interventions by the type of strategy (non-exhaustive)

	Focus of Intervention		
	Individual	Organisational	Leadership
Strategy			
Primary	Resilience training	Removing risks	Leadership training
Secondary	Stress management	Workload reduction	Communication
	Mindfulness	Flexible working	Leader recognition
	Therapy based	Improved communication	
Tertiary	Employee assistance	Time off	Recognition
	Therapy		Understanding

For the purpose of this review strategies focused on leaders will not be examined in detail as these are covered in Chap. 4 of the present book. Furthermore, strategies designed to prevent future stress by increasing individual resilience are covered in Chap. 13 of the present book. Therefore, the focus on this chapter will be to review strategies focused on the individual or the organisation that occur mainly at the primary, secondary or tertiary levels.

Although not exhaustive some of the main types of workplace stress interventions appear below and data pertaining to their effectiveness is reviewed under each intervention type.

4.1 Cognitive Behavioural Therapy (CBT)-Based Interventions

These approaches start from the premise that maladaptive cognitions maintain psychological issues and behavioural problems. The aim of CBT is to uncover these misperceptions of the world through testing for accuracy and developing new understandings. Furthermore, individuals undergoing CBT are encouraged to explore a greater range of behavioural options especially in response to stress. The idea being that through CBT individuals come to broaden their understanding and behaviour and develop more productive responses. There is a wealth of evidence that CBT is an effective treatment for stress and depression in the workplace (Bhui et al., 2012; Butler et al., 2006; Yunus et al., 2018; Tan et al., 2014).

Richardson and Rothstein (2008) examined intervention studies using meta-analysis and concluded that cognitive behavioural approaches are the most effective for stress reduction. However, they also report employee education regarding workplace stress is useful.

Yunus et al. (2018) provided a systematic review of interventions targeting workplace depression. They report on 22 randomised controlled trials and found that CBT approaches were the most frequently used. However, it was found that interventions combining different therapeutic methods demonstrated greatest effects on lowering depression. In addition, interventions delivered to groups were most frequent and showed lowest dropout rates. The authors suggest that therapist support alongside digital interventions seemed to have good treatment outcomes and lower attrition rates.

4.2 Mindfulness-Based Interventions

Mindfulness could be defined as a form of enhanced attention to one's current experience alongside deep awareness in a non-judgmental accepting way (Brown & Ryan, 2003; Kuyken et al., 2010). The mechanisms underpinning the effects of mindfulness are currently widely debated but several hypotheses exist. Some suggest that they enable individuals to experience difficult emotions and retain awareness of these without undue stress, thus enabling better emotional regulation. Others suggests that greater self-compassion and acceptance helps with managing stress (Alberts & Hülsheger, 2015; Shapiro et al., 2006). It is also clear that mindfulness also results in the individual being able to dissociate negative emotions and thoughts from behavioural and emotional responses (Holman et al., 2018). One crucial difference between mindful approaches and alternative stress management techniques concerns the fact that in mindfulness negative experiences are never avoided or suppressed and alternative more adaptive responses result (Richards & Gross, 1999). This is crucial, as avoidance and suppression have been demonstrated to have several unintended negative consequences (Erskine et al., 2010; Erskine & Georgiou, 2011).

The most used form of mindful intervention is Mindfulness-Based Stress Reduction (Kabat-Zinn, 2003). The usual components on this intervention include:

a. Body scans—paying close attention to the body
b. Sedentary meditations—paying close attention to things such as ones breath, environmental sounds, or sensations within the body
c. Moving mediations—for example, walking and paying attention to the sensations and movement patterns of walking
d. Everyday mediation—paying close attention to everyday activities such as eating or how the seat feels beneath you as you work.

Another approach is Mindfulness-Based Cognitive Therapy—MBCT (Segal et al., 2002). This adds a cognitive component in the form of education regarding the idea that thoughts are just mental events rather than facts, the meaning of thoughts is deemphasised. Finally, acceptance and commitment therapy (Hayes, 2004) would also fall under this umbrella.

Christopher et al. (2016) investigated an eight-week mindfulness-based resilience training programme using multiple experiential exercises such as body awareness scans and mindful movement in police officers. Results demonstrated a significant increase in resilience, mindfulness, mental and physical health and decreases in fatigue, burnout, anger and stress (Christopher et al., 2016).

A systematic review of 23 studies on mindfulness-based stress reduction indicated MBSR led to reduced stress, emotional exhaustion, depression and anxiety. Importantly, alongside reduction in distress, participants demonstrated increases in mindfulness, self-compassion and relaxation (Janssen et al., 2018).

Hesketh et al. (2020) reviewed mindful interventions and report that these interventions have positive effects on distress and mental health conditions but that effects are small to moderate (Bartlett et al., 2019; Hesketh et al., 2020; Slemp et al., 2019).

4.3 Education-Based Interventions

These are designed to provide employees information regarding stress and how it can be managed effectively. These sometimes encompass initiatives designed to foster healthier lifestyles in employees on the assumption that these will improve well-being (Anger et al., 2015). These may also include interventions such as skills training, time management and goal setting. Evidence suggests these are effective although they are rarely used alone and are most likely utilised alongside other interventions (Nishiuchi et al., 2007).

4.4 Exercise-Based Interventions

These interventions use v arious forms of physical exercise in the workplace to engender changes in mental and physical health. Multiple studies have reported significant stress reduction effects of exercise (Calogiuri et al., 2016; Kettunen et al., 2015; Proper & van Oostrom, 2019; Stults-KolehMainen & Sinha, 2014; Sun et al., 2013; Van Rhenen et al., 2005). Furthermore, in the APA's 2017 study, more than half (53%) of the adult Americans surveyed stated that they used exercise to cope with their stress (APA, 2017). However, the effectiveness of workplace exercise interventions to reduce job stress was examined by Park and Jang (2019). Stress was measured before and after the interventions. Results indicated only two out of the eight studies found significant reductions in job stress as a result of the interventions. The authors argue that this represents a departure from previous evidence where studies have reported significant effects of exercise. Therefore, they suggest collecting more data is important.

One type of intervention that could fall under multiple sections concerns yoga-based interventions, although they clearly involve physical exercise. Cocchiara et al. (2019) examined 11 studies on yoga interventions in healthcare workers. They found some evidence that yoga-based interventions could reduce stress. Thus, the authors argue that yoga-based interventions can be effective stress reduction techniques in healthcare workers. However, the quality of evidence is low.

4.5 Greenspace/Nature-Based Interventions

Multiple studies have demonstrated that spending time in nature has significant health benefits mainly in the form of increased mental well-being and that it appears psychologically protective against mental health conditions (Bezold et al., 2018; Bratman et al., 2015; Gascon et al., 2018; Haluza et al., 2014; Helbich et al., 2018; Sarkar et al., 2018; Ward Thompson, 2011; van den Bosch & Ode Sang, 2017; Vujcic et al., 2017).

Nature-based interventions can be seen as activities designed to engage individuals with natural settings like forests, parks, gardens with the express aim of improving health (Moeller et al., 2018; Shanahan et al., 2019). Twohig-Bennett and Jones (2018) conducted a meta-analysis including 143 greenspace exposure studies and reported that these were effective at significantly reducing salivary cortisol levels.

In a similar paradigm Hunter et al. (2019) examined biomarkers of stress in 36 people living in urban areas before and after nature experiences. The nature experience was defined as spending time in an outdoor place bringing a sense of contact with nature at least three times a week for 10 minutes at a time or more. Saliva samples were provided before and after the nature experience. Results demonstrated a 21.3% drop in cortisol beyond the hormones 11.7% diurnal dip. Similar results were obtained with alpha-amylase where a 28.1% drop was recorded after adjustment. Spending time in nature resulted in a significant stress hormone reduction. In addition, there was evidence of a dose deponent relationship with longer durations of the nature experience further contributing to greater reductions in stress hormones. Importantly, the greatest benefits seemed to accrue between 20 and 30 minutes. Longer durations did result in greater benefits, but the rate of gain reduced.

Jones et al. (2021) conducted a study examining greenspace interventions and their relationship to stress and biological markers such as cortisol. The authors criticise the previous literature for being overly heterogeneous in its operalisation of exactly what greenspace interventions are, stating that forest bathing, gardening and visiting parks have all been grouped together in previous interventions. Therefore, the authors define greenspace interventions as a subdomain of nature-based interventions which are any activity to engage people in natural settings with the explicit goal of improving health outcomes. The authors reviewed 18 studies on greenspace interventions and found very high levels of heterogeneity with the samples, for example, not reporting participant ethnicity, having very broad age ranges, or having very skewed samples in terms of gender breakdown. The review reports that greenspace interventions could have the potential to significantly reduce stress measured by cortisol levels; however, given the heterogeneity and conceptualisation issues, they err on the side of more data being necessary to draw conclusions.

Kondo et al. (2018) examined spending time outdoors as a stress reduction technique by tracking stress response in real time. The review examined a range of biological markers. 43 studies met the inclusion criteria. Thirty-one of the studies included biological measures such as blood pressure (BP), heart rate (HR) and cortisol levels. Fourteen studies reported that blood pressure was significantly lower in green environments than condition conditions, six reported no statistical differences. With respect to heart rate results were mixed, with 14 studies out of 23 finding lower HR in green environments than control and the other studies found no difference or did not collect comparisons. In studies examining pre- and post-cortisol measures, 7 out of 18 studies found no statistical differences and 11 of the remaining 13 found a significant decrease in cortisol as a result of intervention.

The results paint a mixed picture; however, where HR and BP were reported, these provided the strongest evidence of potential benefits of green environments. Having said that, the data does suggest this area requires further investigation.

4.6   Architecture Based/Environment Based

These interventions concern building design and optimising the built environment to engender human mental and physical health. Towards that aim Hui and Aye (2018) examined workplace design to reduce occupational stress. The authors start by outlining that employees are 90% of most company expenditure (WGBC, 2014). Thus, employee costs far exceed building costs. The key point is that any increments in worker productivity will bring large organisational benefits and it possible that workplace design can enhance staff productively.

There are four levels where the design of the workplace may impact staff health (Stokols, 2011):

1. The physical organisation of the work area for employees
2. The ambient qualities of the environment in the work area
3. The physical organisation of the buildings comprising the workplace
4. The amenities and site planning regarding those buildings

The authors present the argument that green natural environments can represent a physical resource that can aid in stress reduction via promotion of connection to nature. Therefore, access to nature could be seen as a protective factor.

They present an argument from Hobfoll (1989) that there are four types of resources:

1. Physical resources aiding staff in their ability to work
2. Conditions as resources such as marital status, seniority and education
3. Personal characteristics as resources, for example, personality, skills and abilities
4. Energy as a resource such as having time or a greater levels of social support

This is important as greater resources usually translates to greater resilience (Mayerl, et al., 2016).

The main argument is that connection to nature is one resource that individuals can use. Thus, buildings that employ natural elements may act as a resource that passively enhances mental health. This is termed the biophilic design hypothesis (Ulrich et al., 1991). There are many ways this could operate—for example, increasing exposure to natural light, air, water or plants. It could also occur by indirect experiences—for example, pictures of nature, natural colours or naturalistic forms. Furthermore, it is argued that nature access will reduce stress.

Importantly, studies have indicated that biophilic workplaces do have positive benefits on well-being and job s atisfaction (Gray & Birrell, 2014; Mangone et al., 2017).

4.7 Music-Based Interventions

A range of music-based i nterventions have been developed and reviewed in the literature. Perhaps the simplest form concerns listening to music. This is usually contrasted with music therapy which "is specifically characterized by using the specific qualities of music in a therapeutic relationship with a music therapist" (De Witte et al., 2022, p. 135).

This is important as previous research indicates that music can reduce stress, and have useful physiological effects such as reduced health rate, blood pressure and improved hormone profile levels (Agres et al., 2021; Bradt et al., 2013; Chanda & Levitin, 2013; de Witte, Spruit, van Hooren, Moonen, & Stams, 2020; Juslin & Västfjäll, 2008; Koelsch, 2015).

De Witte et al. (2022) examined music therapy-based interventions to reduce stress using systematic review and meta-analysis. In their review of music therapy 47 studies were examined. Results indicated medium to strong effects of music therapy for reducing stress when compared to control groups.

4.8 Dance-Based Intervention

Although not specific to dance, Martin et al. (2018) provide a systematic review of 37 studies using creative arts for managing and preventing stress. Interventions include art, music, drama and dance. Of the included studies 73% were randomised control trials. Crucially 81.2% of studies reported significant reductions in stress across all types of intervention. The main benefits accrued from anxiety reductions. However, there were limitations—for example, effect sizes could not be compared on due to incomplete data. Further data and investigations are necessary to tease apart actual effectiveness.

4.9 Relaxation-Based Interventions

These approaches operate on the premise that states of relaxation and stress are opposites and that becoming one excludes the other (Russell, 1979, but see also Egloff, 1998). This suggests that by increasing relation, stress should automatically reduce. Multiple techniques are used to reduce stress such as progressive muscle relaxation where muscles are tensed and relaxed one by one in a particular order throughout the body (McCallie et al., 2006; Murphy, 2003). Meditation could also be considered a relaxation technique, albeit one using mental rather than physical means. Another relaxation technique often associated with mediation would be breathing techniques. Several studies demonstrate these are effective interventions for reducing stress (Allison et al., 2020; Chellew et al., 2015; Rausch et al., 2006).

4.10 Organisation-Level Interventions

Interventions in this do main aim to remove the causes of stress by adapting the workplace and organisation in terms of ethos and policies (Anger et al., 2015). Many operate by modifying the individual job characteristics such as reducing workload, allowing greater autonomy or modifying hours. This is important as several sources demonstrate that job characteristic have a large bearing on stress (Humphrey, Nahrgang & Morgeson, 2007; Demerouti, Bakker, Nachreiner & Schaufeli, 2001).

Organisation-level interventions would also encompass peer support groups and various skills training with a view to helping employees manage stress more effectively (Leiter et al., 2011; Peterson et al., 2008). These types of intervention where the focus in on changing organisational practices are difficult and therefore how they are implemented is key (Nielsen & Abildgaard, 2013). In order to increase the effectiveness of these interventions' findings suggest employee involvement in the process may be key (Sørensen & Holman, 2014).

Daniels et al. (2017) reviewed organisation-level interventions and found mixed evidence but more promising evidence around job redesign and training. Furthermore, Harvey et al. (2014) find moderate evidence for interventions around job control via promotion of increased participation in the role and allowing greater autonomy.

4.11 Digital Interventions

De Korte and colleagues (2018b) note that re search on mental health apps and digital apps are relatively rare, but they suggest the any interventions are likely to be more useful if backed by sound empirical evidence regarding behaviour change. Furthermore, the authors distil from the literature which workplace interventions are likely to be most effective and suggest that any technology developed should employ the following:

1. Engages participants through multiple modalities
2. Assesses participant needs at the outset
3. Increases engagement by higher frequency of contract
4. Is specific to participant needs
5. Seeks to intervene in multiple risk factors
6. Supports participants to self-manage
7. Uses incentives

8. Be easy to access and allow follow-ups
9. Utilises social support
10. Uses the evidence base of behavioural theory to design interventions. (De Korte et al., 2018b; Goetzel & Ozminkowski, 2008; Rongen et al., 2013; Richardson & Rothstein, 2008)

De Korte et al. (2018a) argue mobile health apps have several advantages such as being wearable or usually carried meaning behaviour can be monitored in real time. They also offer the possibility to bring behavioural interventions into a real-world context. They are also likely to be cheaper and more convenient (Armaou et al., 2020; Warmerdam et al., 2010). They also offer the possibility to share data with health professionals (European commission, 2014). One issue with the recent growth in apps targeting physical and mental health concerns the fact they are rarely evaluated scientifically are not grounded in empirical theory and have limited evidence of effectiveness (Conroy et al., 2014; Direito et al., 2014; De Korte et al., 2018b). Thus, one crucial point concerns the fact that any technology-based apps developed must have psychological input during the intervention design process. Digital health interventions demonstrate much promise for improving heath interventions and when combined with machine learning algorithms a new class of potentially effective interventions may be developed (Marques et al., 2020; Murray et al., 2016; Obermeyer & Emanuel, 2016).

With these considerations in mind, Carolan et al. (2017) conducted a systematic review and meta-analysis of 21 web-based workplace psychological interventions. They found significant positive effects of digital interventions on psychological well-being, including reduction of depression and stress and improved effectiveness at work. Importantly, no significant differences emerged when the type of intervention (cognitive behavioural versus other psychological approaches) were compared. The analysis also revealed several important insights regarding the design of future interventions. Firstly, using email or text messages in addition to the basic web intervention resulted in greater engagement with the program. Secondly, shorter (roughly six weeks) interventions proved optimal.

In a recent investigation, Howe et al. (2022) conducted a four-week longitudinal study with 86 participants testing a digital workplace stress reduction intervention. The digital intervention varied both by intensity and by difficulty (low effort—get mind off work, medium effort—stay present and feel calm, high effort—think through the stress) and had two possible schedules (prescheduled by participants or just in time interventions activated when the system identified participant stress). Results demonstrated that participants completed more interventions when JIT was employed versus prescheduled. However, there was no significant difference in stress reduction between the two. Participants preferred low effort interventions, but the high effort ones were most effective for reducing stress. The authors suggest that while digital interventions have multiplied greatly recently, much more stringent testing of their effectiveness is necessary. Furthermore, despite availability adherence remains low. The main advantage of smartphone-based apps as is their potential to offer real time support (Howe et al., 2022; Neary & Schueller, 2018).

One advantage of technology and app-based interventions are they can be very short in length enhancing engagement. Furthermore, they can be personalised in terms of preferred types of activity and adapted for just in time interventions (Nahum-Shani et al., 2018; Smyth & Heron, 2016). There is also evidence that personalising digital interventions seems to improve engagement and preference (Doherty et al., 2012; Schueller, 2010).

Howe et al. (2022) provide several useful recommendations for the design of interventions. Firstly, digital interventions should be integrated into the usual work day and can consist of micro interventions that are very short. Secondly, the system should allow users to control the timing and content of interventions. Thirdly, it was useful to be able to initiate interventions on demand. Fourthly greater variety of interventions were preferred. Fifthly, it is useful to encourage users to experiment with intervention content and effort required. Finally, user feedback regarding interventions and timing is crucial.

Ebert et al. (2018) discuss internet- and mobile-based psychological interventions and mental health in Europe. The authors argue that traditional mental health interventions are limited by several factors such as the availability of trained clinicians and that digital interventions have the potential to increase access to alternative treatments. In addition, digital interventions could be tailored to the latest evidence. They cite several arguments for digital interventions—cost effectiveness, ease of access, possibly increased treatment effects, increased use due to their anonymous nature and flexibility over where and when the interventions occur. They argue that unanticipated benefits may accrue from treatment being placed in the context of the individual's general life. They also argue that digital interventions probably require support from human interaction to engender greater adoption.

Digital interventions have most often been tested for anxiety and depression and compared to control groups the interventions mostly report positive effects (Andrews et al., 2010; Richards et al., 2015). However, these interventions also have proven efficacy for post-traumatic stress disorder (PTSD) and eating disorders (Kuester et al., 2016; Zachariae et al., 2015). Importantly, digital interventions accompanied by therapeutic input are more successful (Baumeister et al., 2014).

There are risks of digital interventions although more research is necessary to tease these apart. Potential risks concern responding adequately to risks and emergencies if interventions are being employed without therapeutic support. This would also include risk of suicide.

A meta-analytic review to investigate studies on e-health interventions conducted between 1975 and 2016 indicated that interventions differed in the short term with mindfulness-based interventions demonstrating larger effects that cognitive behavioural therapy interventions or stress management-based interventions (Stratton et al., 2017). Importantly, stress management interventions were more effective when used in targeted groups pre-identified as struggling relative to when employed in all participants. The authors suggest this is evidence that e-health interventions seem to have employee benefits such as reductions in depression, anxiety and stress. Furthermore, the effect sizes were moderate and significant. However, the authors note that there was evidence that particular interventions that work more effectively with particular cohorts and this requires further research.

In an overview of technology-related stress interventions in the workplace Giorgi et al. (2022) argue that the Covid-19 pandemic and technology-related interventions have changed modern workplaces and as a result the pace of adoption of new workplace technologies has increased. This increased rate of adoption could create employee well-being challenges. For example, more individuals working from home which can lead to unclear boundaries between the work and personal life. Workers are now much more prone to being contacted outside of working hours.

Lattie et al. (2019) evaluated 89 studies in a systematic review of digital mental health interventions for college students. Most interventions were delivered by websites (80%) and most frequently involved cognitive behavioural therapy (31%). 47% were found to be effective and a further 34% demonstrated partial effectiveness. The average length of intervention was eight weeks. The authors conclude that digital interventions can be effective for reducing depression and anxiety in college students but suggest more robust data is necessary to truly evaluate effectiveness. However, in line with the known issues concerning low engagement and completion for many digital health interventions, the review also found some evidence of high participant drop out (See also Fleming et al., 2018). Digital interventions have the potential to reach more of the university student generation as they permit accessing services in a less stigmatising way and are more cost and time effective. Furthermore, they are more in line with social trends in accessing support via more remote digital means (Lattie et al., 2019; Rai et al., 2016). Furthermore, recent meta-analytic reviews indicate that internet-based interventions are effective at treating an array of mental health conditions in university students (Harrer et al., 2019).

Importantly, Torous et al. (2018) reviewed user engagement of digital health apps and found that engagement issues developed when the programmes were not tailored to users, did not address issues important to users, did not respect privacy, were untrustworthy and not helpful in emergency situations. It is critical that interventions appeal to the end users.

Digital interventions may be of particular use to caregivers due ease of access and the ability to provide support and emotional outlets (Shin & Choi, 2020). This is important, as with an ageing population and more individuals living with long-term disabilities, the carer population is rapidly growing. In addition, caregivers are often ill prepared for caregiving and therefore suffer from depression and anxiety at high rates (Wadhwa et al., 2013). Regarding specific interventions for caregivers, self-compassion and mindfulness both demonstrated effectiveness (Shapiro et al., 2007).

One final technological development that may revolutionise the delivery of mental health interventions concerns utilising virtual reality technology and machine learning algorithms. Virtual reality is a computer generating three-dimensional environment viewed via a display mounted on the persons head. Jerdan et al. (2018) examined 82 studies using VR technology in mental health interventions. Results indicated that VR results in realistic reactions to feared stimuli when treating anxiety. It also showed promise for managing pain. However, there is a lack on VR data on treating depression and stress. The authors conclude that VR has the potential to be a useful tool for intervening in mental health. Areas that VR could potentially be useful were: phobias where the treatment involves exposure to the feared stimuli (Morina et al., 2015; Valmaggia et al., 2016), anxiety, pain management, stress, depression and addictions (Bouchard et al., 2017; Kampmann et al., 2016).

Another very new area which holds much promise yet is under researched concerns using machine learning algorithms in digital health interventions. Triantafyllidis and Tsanas (2019) examined eight intervention studies and found that six (75%) showed statistically significant improvement in health. Thus, the authors conclude that digital health using machine learning algorithms interventions show significant positive health outcomes in real-world settings.

4.12 Employee Assistance Programmes

It is important to stress that employee wellness programmes are usually seen as separate from employee assistance programmes with the distinction being that wellness programmes are preventative as opposed to EAP's instigated once issues manifest (Csiernik, 2011; Richardson, 2017). Note that individual-level interventions are much more often employed than organisation-level interventions often because they are easier to implement and less costly (Pieper et al., 2019). Another important consideration concerns data indicating that many mental health counselling centres are under-resourced and operate at capacity most of the time and this picture is based on data available, before the Covid-19 pandemic greatly exacerbated the situation (Xiao et al., 2017).

5 Why Prevention?

Having provided an overview of the breadth of possible interventions and their effectiveness it is necessary to say that as authors we favour a preventative approach rather than intervening after individuals develop issues requiring treatment. This is mainly due to the potential to prevent individual and organisational misery and lack of productivity. Once issues develop the outcome of treatment is never certain. This is important as most people with mental health issues seek no treatment (Wittchen et al., 2011). Therefore, less than half of people suffering from a mental health issue are treated (Kohn et al., 2004). Furthermore, mental health issues have an estimated lifetime prevalence between 18.1% and 36.1% depending on nation (Kessler et al., 2009). One key point concerns data indicating that mental health and employee well-being interventions seem to work best when they are multifaceted and integrate both mental and physical interventions (Murray et al., 2016; Panagioti et al., 2018; Wagner et al., 2016). It is also necessary for interventions to tackle at some level the social determinants of mental health issues such as access to employment, education, safety in terms of housing, food and crime (Alegría et al., 2018). Furthermore, data indicates one underused technique which has some of the widest evidence base concerns helping individuals to self-monitor behaviour (Michie et al., 2009).

Another conceptual issue concerns whether one views interventions as potentially reducing negative health issues or increasing potentially positive qualities such as resilience and adaptability. The following section will briefly explore this under the heading of resilience.

5.1 Resilience

Research has recently focused more on the possibility that interventions can enhance psychological well-being via developing resilience, increasing optimism and general positivity (Di Fabio, 2017; Knight et al., 2017). In general research has demonstrated that susceptibility to mental health conditions increases with exposure to risk factors such as social isolation, financial difficulties, trauma, general adversity and stress (Arango et al., 2018). In a workplace context these same general relationships persist. Thus, enhancing resilience may be one route to well-being. As resilience research continues it is now seen as being necessary at all levels: individual, organisational and increasingly national (Codreanu & Vasilescu, 2022; Eshel & Kimhi, 2016; Vinkers et al., 2020).

Ungar and Theron (2020) examined resilience and mental health and make the point that while much is known regarding the predictors of later disorder little is known regarding the factors promoting positive development in individuals and how these interact with stress. The authors argue that many approaches have focused on what the individual themselves contributes to resilience while ignoring the fact that resilience is an interaction between the individual and their physical and social ecology. Therefore, they suggest investigating which protective factors work best for which individuals and in which contexts (see also Masten, 2018). Resilience can be best understood as a process where various sources of support, some within the individual, some without (found in social systems), support development during adversity.

Therefore, nations have started to develop guidance and legislation pertaining to worker health and safety and resilience. One such example is the British Standard 65000. BSI definite resilience as an organisational ability to "anticipate, prepare for, respond and adapt" BSI 2018.

Similarly, ISO 22316 (2017) views resilience as encompassing the following qualities:

a. Shared vision purpose and values guiding all levels of decision making
b. Understanding the organisation external and internal environment in order to guide priority-based decision making
c. Leadership effectiveness demonstrated by employing diverse knowledge skills and tools to achieve objectives along with leadership adapting well to challenges
d. Organisational culture anchored in shared values promoting positive attitudes and behaviour

e. Use of accessible, adequate, understandable, timely conveyed information and knowledge as resources for learning and decision making within organisations
f. Prioritisation and allocation of resources in accordance with organisations vulnerabilities responding to challenge
g. Design, development and coordination of management disciplines contributing to achieving objectives from an uncertainty-based perspective
h. Living performance management system focused on ongoing improvement

Furthermore, Biggs et al. (2015) argue that there are seven key principles for building resilience; these are as follows:

a. Maintaining high diversity and redundancy
b. Managing connectivity by managing information sources their reliability and observing tension between too much connectivity and modularity
c. Managing slow variables and feedback
d. Encouraging the understanding of the system as complex and adaptive
e. Encouraging learning and experimentation
f. Enlarging participation
g. Promoting polycentric governance

Regarding resilience training reviews suggest positive effects on mental health and well-being and resilience in the work environment (Harvey et al., 2014; Robertson et al., 2015; Vanhove et al., 2016). Data suggests these programmes may be most beneficial for occupations known to be detrimental to health and highly stressful such as military and first responders.

5.2 What Works and What Doesn't—Overview of Large-Scale Comparative Interventions

This section will review large scale comparative interventions where different interventions are directly compared.

Pieper et al. (2019) reviewed 38 workplace intervention studies in Germany aiming to reduce worker mental health issues and the economic impact. They examined the effectiveness of the following interventions mainly targeting individuals: resilience training programmes, mindfulness training, cognitive behavioural therapy, relaxation techniques and organizational-level workplace interventions. All the interventions reduced worker stress, anxiety and depression while simultaneously improving well-being. Economic effects were less clear, while some studies reported increased return on investment and productivity others did not. The authors concluded that although the quality of evidence is low it is likely that these interventions are cost effective (see Carolan et al., 2017; Furlan et al., 2012). Several overall conclusions could be made, these were: First, that employee interventions, particularly CBT and stress management programmes, should continue, as they have positive effects on worker health. Second, programmes using multiple components demonstrated greater efficacy that single interventions. Third, interventions must be well designed, including evaluation procedures and effective longer-term monitoring to increase effectiveness. Fourth, it is vital to have support and engagement from management. Prevention and promotion interventions represent new approaches to health with increased focus on prophylaxis and organisational changes may be necessary to implement these in effective ways.

In another large-scale review Wiederhold et al. (2018) examined 13 studies on physician burnout and prevention methods. Burnout has been reported to be present in between 19% and 76% of doctors (Firth-Cohen, 2006). Even the lowest range value would represent a fifth of doctors suffering burnout. The main methods investigated were: cognitive behavioural therapy, counselling based, mindfulness, stress management, communication skills, exercise based, workload reduction and organisation leadership interventions. Overall, the interventions were effective in reducing one or more components of burnout. With only 3 out of 13 interventions reporting no effects. The authors provide the following recommendations. First, interventions considering the multidimensional causes of burnout are more successful. Therefore, merely reducing stress represents only part of the issue. Secondly, interventions need to approach the issues from both the individual and organisational perspectives simultaneously. The authors also make the argument that physicians should be provided with resilience training to develop more effective stress management and coping techniques.

Proper and van Oostrom (2019) examined 23 reviews of multiple health promotion interventions in the workplace and their effects on both physical and mental health. Results indicated that interventions targeting physical activity and diet were effective for improving health. In addition, cognitive behavioural and e-health interventions demonstrated positive effects on preventing mental health issues. Thus, in the author's own words: "In sum, based on the high-quality reviews, there is strong evidence that workplace psychological interventions, especially those that use e-health and cognitive behavior techniques yield positive effects" (Proper & van Oostrom, 2019, p 554).

In a related vein, Klein et al. (2020) examined the personal strategies employed by 854 healthcare workers to reduce stress. Results demonstrated that 94% of the sample used at least one stress management strategy. Four main themes emerged from responses. First the main category of personal stress management emerging was termed self-focused and was endorsed by 67.5% of the sample. This concerned strategies undertaken alone such as taking time away from work, having short mental breaks, going for walks, stretching, deep breathing, relaxation techniques, meditation, prayer or practising yoga. Furthermore, these were shown to be used repeatedly throughout the workday. The next largest category of personal strategy endorsed by 16.1% of the sample was termed Relational focused. This concerned seeking social support or socialising/talking to others, particularly about annoying issues at work. However, this category also included building relationships with colleagues and having a laugh to lessen stress. The third category to emerge in 11.5% of the same was termed job focused. This referred to attempts to adapt the work environment to make things easier, for example, goal setting, taking one thing at a time and scheduling work optimally. The final category represented no strategy and was endorsed by 4% of the sample. This study suggests that workers should be encouraged to use their own personal strategies alongside other preventative interventions implemented by the company.

One organisation that has been effectively employing resilience training and work stress reduction for years is the US Air Force (Hardison et al., 2020a, b). This is important as 14% of the US air force have physical symptoms of stress with 20% binge drinking and 26% reporting hazardous drinking. Their programmes operate at all levels. Thus, promotion means interventions designed to make the environment inherently less stressful or increase the individuals' resilience to stress. Prevention means delivering helpful interventions before clinical disorders begin to manifest. The treatment point on the continuum is defined as discovering the individuals that are manifesting clinical levels of distress and instigating effective treatments. The recovery phase refers to longer-term treatment enabling recovery.

Holman et al. (2018) reviewed the literature on secondary-level interventions, as these are the ones that aim to reduce stress in employees. They also examine primary organisational strategies seeking to remove the sources of stress. The authors find both approaches are viable but argue more data is needed to ascertain the effects of context on interventions and some of the long-term effects. One example of an effective primary intervention strategy rarely mentioned in the literature concerns having more rigorous employee selection procedures, choosing individuals that have the skills necessary to manage stress effectively and deselect those likely to experience undue stress (Bartone et al., 2008).

Gray et al. (2019) present a review of 60 studies on interventions promoting mental health in healthcare workers. Critical themes emerging concerned having employees engaged in any interventions at the level of development and implementation. Furthermore, it was important that any interventions had broad support from all organisational levels. The authors also report that it is critical to manage worker expectations around interventions. They also argue that it is vital research starts to investigate the long-term effects of workplace mental health interventions. Furthermore, the results indicated that there are often unique features of the healthcare environment that mean they are particularly emotionally demanding and stressful. One issue noted concerned the definition of mental health where many different measures are used in studies. This speaks to the multidimensionality of mental health.

Pijpker et al. (2020) investigated burnout and combined interventions. The authors argue that burnout develops from an interaction of multiple factors some within the employee and many present in the organisation or environment. They therefore suggest that previous reviews which focus on either employee factors alone or organisational factors provide poorer evidence. Their study investigates combined interventions operating on multiple levels simultaneously. They examined ten combined interventions on burnout and found all the interventions were effective means of rehabilitation. However, combined interventions were unsuccessful in improving personal accomplishment or professional efficacy. When examining possible mediators, job demands and job control along with social support were mediators of the effects. Thus, it is important for individuals to have control over as many aspects of their work as possible, and social support while having manageable workloads. Therefore, being sensitive to employee needs is an important aspect of rehabilitation.

Jacobs et al. (2018) conducted a review on workplace stress and prevention and found eight criteria that would facilitate interventions. First management support guarantees access to resources supporting the intervention. Second, context-specific interventions targeted towards individual circumstances should be employed, this would also involve discerning the causes of stress and intervening. Third, implemented strategies should be multidimensional on multiple levels (individual, organisational and the interface). Fourth, individual workers should be involved with the design and implementation of interventions, including buy-in and engagement from management. Fifth, the project must be managed with clear responsibilities and focus on tasks most likely to bear fruit. Sixth, buy-in from all management levels ensures interventions are fully supported. Seventh, external agents of change should be viewed and act as facilitators rather than being autocratic. Eighth, for longer-term change, a culture of responding to stress must permeates the ethos of the organisation.

Bradley et al. (2022) reviewed 41 interventions to reduce stress in UK medical students. This is important as medical students may experience mental health issues at very high rates (Honney et al., 2010; Zvauya et al., 2017). Previous meta-analysis has also reported that interventions are moderately effective (Yusoff, 2014). Most pertinently 80% of UK medical students describe well-being support available as poor (Billingsley, 2015). The following interventions were reviewed: yoga/mindfulness, stress management, behavioural, cognitive, mentorship, multifaceted and educational. The review found several effective stress reducing strategies that also improved the situation regarding mental well-being these were: mindfulness, yoga, CBT, group physical activity and stress management or relation techniques. Groups-based interventions with a social component also resulted in improvement. Importantly, making interventions part of the curriculum allowed student to undertake self-care without guilt.

Brooks et al. (2019a) examined traumatic stress management in the workplace. They note the previously reported fact that critical incident debriefing following trauma exposure can be detrimental to mental health (Wessely et al., 2000) and note the NICE guidelines on PTSD specifically do not initially recommend any debriefing (NICE, 2018). They do however recommend watchful waiting and being aware that individuals may subsequently develop issues. The authors also note that employees frequently may not seeks help due to stigma (Coleman et al., 2017). The authors distil down the evidence to three factors that seem to be optimal for prompting resilience following trauma. These are: social support, work-based emergency response training and teaching effective coping strategies such as active coping rather than avoidance or denial (Brooks et al., 2019a, b).

Milligan-Saville et al. (2017) examined mental health training in Australian fire and rescue service managers and effects on employee sick leave. Managers received 4 hours of training coving mental health, their responsibilities and effective communication regarding staff mental health issues. Results demonstrated improved manager mental health literacy, less stigmatising attitudes regarding recovery and reduced rates of employee sick leave. At six-month follow-up, managers reported improved confidence in tackling employee mental health issues. Cost benefit analysis suggested a £10 return on every £1 training spend. The authors argue this is evidence for a significant effect of management training on staff well-being.

Varma et al. (2021) investigated international vulnerability to stress, anxiety and depression during the Covid-19 pandemic. A key goal was to identify vulnerability factors that may relate to increased likelihood of mental health decline. 1653 participants completed surveys across 63 countries. Results indicated 70% of the sample reported moderate or higher levels of stress, 59% had scores indicating clinical anxiety and 39% moderate depression. Individuals with previous mental health diagnoses demonstrated greater distress. Links between stress and depression and stress and anxiety were found to be mediated by sleep disturbance, lower resilience, younger age and loneliness. Young age was related to greater vulnerability to stress, depression and anxiety. This is evidence that mental health interventions may need to become adapted to the particular group rather than a blanket interventional approach.

Arango et al. (2018) investigated preventative strategies for mental health. Several key outcomes became apparent. Firstly, there are prevention interventions that can promote well-being and prevent subsequent mental ill health. Furthermore, data indicates that interventions can lessen severity and delay onset in vulnerable individuals. The authors argue that mental health workers should focus more on prevention and integrate it into operations. While research is identifying paths to vulnerability and resilience these are not yet widely integrated into public health initiatives or clinical practice. Worldwide the focus is still firmly on treatment once conditions manifest rather than on prevention from the outset. The authors state that prevention aims to modify risk factors and individual exposure while simultaneously improving the individuals coping mechanisms (WHO, 2004). The authors make the important point that most risk factors in the environment have small effect sizes that alone could not account for the later disorders (Tsuang et al., 2004). These factors might include poor nutrition or infections, birth complications, poverty, living in urban areas, social isolation and trauma. Risk factors may have multiplicative effects acting synergistically, as an example poverty and exposure to drug use often co-occur. What challenges the identification of risk and protective factors is the fact that events are processed by the individual throught the veil of their history, environment and this modifies responses (See also Rutter et al., 1997). What seems important is cumulative risk in the face of a lack of protective factors (Sroufe, 2013). Thus, resilience concerns adapting well after or during adversity and this is a quality that many interventions try to foster. They suggest resilience promotion includes mainly enhancing competencies and social skills, adaptability and problem solving.

Soklaridis et al. (2020) examined mental health interventions during the Covid-19 pandemic. They found a need for resilience training for healthcare professionals, particularly those with a history of mental health issues, for coping with pandemics (Maunder et al., 2008; Lancee et al., 2008). They argue that resilience training will support health care workers but also that some of the effects of resilience training may not become apparent until months after training (Sijbrandij et al., 2020). They also suggest that digital interventions need to be developed as these can be provided despite distancing and quarantine and can be cost effective at the time of greatest need.

This review is not exhaustive, and several potential interventions await further research. Possibilities would include effects of fruit and vegetable intake on mental health which data indicates to be protective (Blanchflower et al., 2013; Głąbska et al., 2020; Ocean et al., 2019; White et al., 2013).

There is data indicating that increasing use of health technology can cause stress levels to worsen. Thus, 70% of doctors sampled report health information technology stress, and this is predictive of burnout (Gardner et al., 2019). Methods to lower stress-related burnout include changing organisational cultures to address health information technology-related stress and reducing overall level of information to enable patient focus. Monitoring health information technology-related stress may be necessary to address burnout in doctors more globally.

Hesketh et al. (2020) review the literature on effective workplace interventions and report that while there is evidence to support interventions the effect sizes are often small and that it is difficult to reach firm conclusions regarding which types of intervention are most effective. Furthermore, the evidence on longer-term follow-up suggests time diminishes effects. Thus, it is not yet possible to determine the optimal length, intensity or delivery mode. The authors also found that multiple factors or moderating variables can affect the outcomes—for example, the mode of delivery. The authors note digital interventions are growing in popularly and are cheaper to deliver. Regarding their effectiveness they conclude that digital interventions have an overall small positive effect on mental health even at follow-up, but that while mindful interventions show best short-term effects, stress management interventions seem to work best when targeted to specific populations (Stratton et al., 2017).

6   Conclusion: What Are the Solutions?

There are three key points at which interventions can be made, prior to experiencing stress, during and after (See Erskine, 2021), these map on to primary, secondary and tertiary interventions in alternative frameworks (Holman et al., 2018; Jacobs et al., 2018). The results of this review suggest it is important that all levels are attended to and interventions proceed on all levels simultaneously. However, it is probable that interventions designed to reduce stress before it occurs and equipping individuals with techniques and principles necessary to successfully navigate stressful periods will result in the greatest gains for individuals, organisations and society. The economic case for interventions is clear—mental health issues are projected to amount to more than \$6 trillion by 2030 (Greenberg et al., 2015; WFMH, 2017). This leaves aside the cost in terms of human misery, organisation turmoil and social upheaval. We suggest intervention in the form of preventative initiatives is the most profitable option.

Regarding how to intervene this review has shown that multiple interventions can be effective in both reducing stress and improving mental health. The following interventions have empirical support, as examined in this review:

Cognitive behavioural therapy (CBT)-based interventions—(Bhui et al., 2012; Butler et al., 2006; Richardson & Rothstein, 2008; Tan et al., 2014; Yunus et al., 2018).

Mindfulness-based interventions—(Bartlett et al., 2019; Christopher et al., 2016; Hesketh et al., 2020; Janssen et al., 2018; Slemp et al., 2019).

Exercise based interventions—(Calogiuri et al., 2016; Kettunen et al., 2015; Proper & van Oostrom, 2019; Stults-KolehMainen & Sinha, 2014; Sun et al., 2013; Van Rhenen et al., 2005).

Greenspace/nature-based interventions—(Bezold et al., 2018; Bratman et al., 2015; Gascon et al., 2018; Haluza et al., 2014; Helbich et al., 2018; Hunter et al., 2019; Jones et al., 2021; Kondo et al., 2018; Sarkar et al., 2018; Twohig-Bennett & Jones, 2018; Ward Thompson, 2011; van den Bosch & Ode Sang, 2017; Vujcic et al., 2017).

Architecture based/environment based—(Gray & Birrell, 2014; Mangone et al., 2017; Ulrich et al., 1991).

Music-based interventions—(Agres et al., 2021; Bradt et al., 2013; Chanda & Levitin, 2013; de Witte, et al., 2020, 2022; Juslin & Västfjäll, 2008; Koelsch, 2015).

Relaxation-based interventions—(Allison et al., 2020; Chellew et al., 2015; Rausch et al., 2006).

Organisation-level interventions—(Daniels et al., 2017; Harvey et al., 2014; Leiter et al., 2011; Nielsen & Abildgaard, 2013; Peterson et al., 2008; Sørensen & Holman, 2014)

Digital interventions—(Armaou et al., 2020; Carolan et al., 2017; De Korte et al., 2018b; Goetzel & Ozminkowski, 2008; Hesketh et al., 2020; Rongen et al., 2013; Richardson & Rothstein, 2008; Yunus et al., 2018; Warmerdam et al., 2010).

While all the above interventions have demonstrated empirical support studies that have directly compared their effectiveness have rarely demonstrated meaningful differences. Thus, all seem effective (Arango et al., 2018; Bradley et al., 2022; Pieper et al., 2019; Proper & van Oostrom, 2019; Wiederhold et al., 2018).

It is also worth noting that some of the interventions above are not truly interventions but more akin to platforms or methods of delivery. Thus, digital interventions will traditionally employ other specific interventions such as mindfulness or CBT or exercise just delivered in a digital format.

However, the delivery format is important as digital interventions are easy to deploy to large groups and cheaper and can track behaviour in real time and real-world contexts (De Korte et al., 2018a; Hesketh et al. 2020).

However, several issues arise with digital interventions chiefly that they are subject to very high dropout rates (Yunus et al., 2018). However, there is evidence these attrition rates can be reduced through therapist support alongside digital interventions (Yunus et al., 2018) or providing email or text messages support (Carolan et al., 2017).

The main issue of concern regarding digital interventions is that these are often developed by programmers, commercial organisations or human resource departments with limited or no psychological or scientific input (Conroy et al., 2014; Direito et al., 2014; De Korte et al., 2018b). This is tantamount to having a kidney removed by the butcher when a qualified surgeon is unavailable. Therefore, we suggest all interventions are strongly evidence based and designed and implemented by suitably qualified staff.

In terms of optimal timeframe for intervention there is evidence that shorter interventions are not effective (Ivandic et al., 2017). However, there is some evidence that shorter interventions of roughly six weeks may be suitable with digital formats (Carolan et al., 2017).

There is also evidence that the recipients of the interventions should be involved in the choice, design and implementation of said interventions (Jacobs et al., 2018). Interventions should also be available in different modalities providing autonomy and choice (De Korte et al., 2018a). Interventions should be employed in multiple ways both generally and targeted to specific populations of need (Stratton et al., 2017).

One area of future promise relates to using machine learning algorithms in the development of novel interventions but this awaits more research (Marques et al., 2020; Murray et al., 2016; Obermeyer & Emanuel, 2016).

There needs to be a concerted effort to move resources from treatment once issues develop towards greater focus on prophylactic mental health interventions (Arango et al., 2018)—particularly in younger age groups, where data indicates increased vulnerability (Varma et al., 2021). Towards this end researchers must investigate the web of interrelated sources of resilience rather than excessively focusing on individuals (Ungar & Theron, 2020). Thus, interventions altering only one system may show limited long-term advantages (Fenwick-Smith et al., 2018). Simultaneous intervention on multiple levels has the best chance of fostering long-term benevolent changes.

Intervention is extremely cost effective with multiple analyses demonstrating significant financial returns on investment (Barker & Twin, 2021; Hampson & Jacob, 2020; Matrix, 2013; McDaid et al., 2019; Milligan-Saville et al., 2017; WHO, 2017). Data also indicates workers have their own strategies for coping with stress and these should be encouraged (Klein et al., 2020).

For jobs requiring stress resilience such as medics, emergency responders and military it is vital resources are also put into selection procedures that optimise selecting stress resilient individuals in the first instance (Bartone et al., 2008).

It is also important that where prevention strategies are implemented these are not used as excuses to continue detrimental working practices such as unmanageable workloads. Thus, organisations need to work on reducing stressors in the environment alongside building capacity in staff (Gray et al., 2019).

In short it is vital interventions are employed much more broadly on multiple fronts simultaneously. It is also vital the organisation changes in line with the focus on prevention. Regarding types of intervention the key point is these need to be evidence based and employed by suitable qualified psychological specialists. If these changes were to be initiated it is highly likely individuals, organisations and society would profit from reduced mental and physical illness and sizable increments in productivity.

References

Agres, K. R., Schaefer, R. S., Volk, A., van Hooren, S., Holzapfel, A., Dalla Bella, S., ... & Magee, W. L. (2021). Music, computing, and health: a roadmap for the current and future roles of music technology for health care and well-being. *Music & Science, 4.*

Alberts, H. J., & Hülsheger, U. R. (2015). Applying mindfulness in the context of work: Mindfulness-based interventions. In J. Reb & A. PWB (Eds.), *Mindfulness in organizations. Foundations, research and applications* (pp. 100–132). Cambridge University Press.

Alegría, M., NeMoyer, A., Falgàs Bagué, I., Wang, Y., & Alvarez, K. (2018). Social determinants of mental health: Where we are and where we need to go. *Current Psychiatry Reports, 20*(11), 1–13.

20 Stress Prevention Measures in the Workplace   411

Allen, D., Hines, E. W., Pazdernik, V., Konecny, L. T., & Breitenbach, E. (2018). Four-year review of presenteeism data among employees of a large United States health care system: A retrospective prevalence study. *Human Resources for Health, 16*, 1–10.

Allison, S., Irwin Hamilton, K., Yuan, Y., & Wallis Hague, G. (2020). Assessment of progressive muscle relaxation (PMR) as a stress-reducing technique for first-year veterinary students. *Journal of Veterinary Medical Education, 47*(6), 737–744.

Almond, S., & Healey, A. (2003). Mental health and absence from work: New evidence from the UK quarterly labour force survey. *Work, Employment and Society, 17*, 731–742.

American Psychological Association. APA. (2017). Stress in America: The state of our nation. https://www.apa.org/news/press/releases/stress/2017/state-nation.pdf

American Psychological Association. APA. (2015). Stress in America: Paying with our health. https://www.apa.org/news/press/releases/stress/2014/stress-report.pdf

American Psychological Association. APA. (2022). Stress in America. Retrieved September 2022, from https://www.apa.org/news/press/releases/stress/2022/march-2022-survival-mode

Andrews, G., Cuijpers, P., Craske, M. G., McEvoy, P., & Titov, N. (2010). Computer therapy for the anxiety and depressive disorders is effective, acceptable and practical health care: a meta-analysis. *PloS One, 5*(10), e13196.

Anger, W. K., Elliot, D. L., Bodner, T., et al. (2015). Effectiveness of total worker health interventions. *Journal of Occupational Health Psychology, 20*, 226–247.

Antony, J., Brar, R., Khan, P. A., Ghassemi, M., Nincic, V., Sharpe, J. P., et al. (2020). Interventions for the prevention and management of occupational stress injury in first responders: A rapid overview of reviews. *Systematic Reviews, 9*(1), 1–20.

Arango, C., Díaz-Caneja, C. M., McGorry, P. D., Rapoport, J., Sommer, I. E., Vorstman, J. A., et al. (2018). Preventive strategies for mental health. *The Lancet Psychiatry, 5*(7), 591–604.

Armaou, M., Konstantinidis, S., & Blake, H. (2020). The effectiveness of digital interventions for psychological well-being in the workplace: A systematic review protocol. *International Journal of Environmental Research and Public Health, 17*(1), 255.

Auerbach, R. P., Mortier, P., Bruffaerts, R., Alonso, J., Benjet, C., Cuijpers, P., & Collaborators, W. H. O. W. M. H.-I. C. S. (2018). WHO world mental health surveys international college student project: Prevalence and distribution of mental disorders. *Journal of Abnormal Psychology, 127*(7), 623–638.

Barker, S., & Twin, J. (2021). 4G. 001 Improving worker mental wellness–from the office to front line workers.

Bartlett, D., & Jackson, M. L. (2016). The bidirectional nature of sleep problems and psychopathology. *Medicine Today, 17*(3), 23–28.

Bartlett, L., Martin, A., Neil, A., Memish, K., Otahal, P., Kilpatrick, M., & Sanderson, K. (2019). A systematic review and meta-analysis of workplace mindfulness training randomized controlled trials. *Journal of Occupational Health Psychology, 24*(1), 108.

Bartone, P. T., Roland, R. R., Picano, J. J., & Williams, T. J. (2008). Psychological hardiness predicts success in US Army Special Forces candidates. *International Journal of Selection and Assessment, 16*, 78–81.

Baumeister, H., Reichler, L., Munzinger, M., & Lin, J. (2014). The impact of guidance on Internet-based mental health interventions – A systematic review. *Internet Interventions, 1*(4), 205–215.

Bellis, M. A., Hughes, K., Leckenby, N., Hardcastle, K. A., Perkins, C., & Lowey, H. (2015). Measuring mortality and the burden of adult disease associated with adverse childhood experiences in England: A national survey. *Journal of Public Health, 37*(3), 445–454.

Bessen, J. (2019). Automation and jobs: When technology boosts employment. *Economic Policy, 34*, 589–626.

Bezold, C. P., Banay, R. F., Coull, B. A., Hart, J. E., James, P., et al. (2018). The association between natural environments and depressive symptoms in adolescents living in the United States. *Journal of Adolescent Health, 62*, 488–495.

Bhui, K. S., Dinos, S., Stansfeld, S. A., & White, P. D. (2012). A synthesis of the evidence for managing stress at work: A review of the reviews reporting on anxiety, depression, and absenteeism. *Journal of Environmental and Public Health, 2012*, 515874.

Biggs, R., Rhode, C., Archibald, S., Kunene, L. M., Mutanga, S. S., Nkuna, N., et al. (2015). Strategies for managing complex social-ecological systems in the face of uncertainty: Examples from South Africa and beyond. *Ecology and Society, 20*(1).

Billingsley, M. (2015). More than 80% of medical students with mental health issues feel under-supported, says Student BMJ survey. *BMJ, 351*.

Birnbaum, H. G., Kessler, R. C., Kelley, D., Ben-Hamadi, R., Joish, V. N., & Greenberg, P. E. (2010). Employer burden of mild, moderate, and severe major depressive disorder: Mental health services utilization and costs, and work performance. *Depression and Anxiety, 27*(1), 78–89.

Blanchflower, D. G., Oswald, A. J., & Stewart-Brown, S. (2013). Is psychological well-being linked to the consumption of fruit and vegetables? *Social Indicators Research, 114*, 785–801.

Bondanini, G., Giorgi, G., Ariza-Montes, A., Vega-Muñoz, A., & Andreucci-Annunziata, P. T. (2020). Technostress dark side of technology in the workplace: A scientometric analysis. *International Journal of Environmental Research and Public Health, 17*, 8013.

Bouchard, S., Dumoulin, S., Robillard, G., Guitard, T., Klinger, E., Forget, H., et al. (2017). Virtual reality compared with in vivo exposure in the treatment of social anxiety disorder: A three-arm randomised controlled trial. *The British Journal of Psychiatry, 210*(4), 276–283.

Bradley, R., Yousofi, T., & Rafey Faruqui, K. (2022). Nurturing doctors: A systematic review of interventions to reduce stress and distress. *Kent Journal of Psychiatry, 2*(1), 5–7.

Bradt, J., Dileo, C., & Potvin, N. (2013). Music for stress and anxiety reduction in coronary heart disease patients. *Cochrane Database of Systematic Reviews*, (12).

Bratman, G. N., Daily, G. C., Levy, B. J., & Gross, J. J. (2015). The benefits of nature experience: Improved affect and cognition. *Landscape and Urban Planning, 138*, 41–50.

Bregenzer, A., & Jimenez, P. (2021). Risk factors and leadership in a digitalized working world and their effects on employees' stress and resources: Web-based questionnaire study. *Journal of Medical Internet Research, 23*(3), e24906.

Brooks, S., Rubin, G. J., & Greenberg, N. (2019a). Managing traumatic stress in the workplace. *Occupational Medicine, 69*(1), 2–4.

Brooks, S. K., Rubin, G. J., & Greenberg, N. (2019b). Traumatic stress within disaster-exposed occupations: Overview of the literature and suggestions for the management of traumatic stress in the workplace. *British Medical Bulletin, 129*(1), 25–34.

Brown, K. W., & Ryan, R. M. (2003). The benefits of being present: Mindfulness and its role in psychological wellbeing. *Journal of Personality and Social Psychology, 84*(4), 822–848.

Burman, R., & Goswami, T. G. (2018). A systematic literature review of work stress. *International Journal of Management Studies, 3*(9), 112–132.

Butler, A. C., Chapman, J. E., Forman, E. M., & Beck, A. T. (2006). The empirical status of cognitive-behavioral therapy: A review of meta-analyses. *Clinical Psychology Review, 26*(1), 17–31.

Calogiuri, G., Evensen, K., Weydahl, A., Andersson, K., Patil, G., Ihlebæk, C., & Raanaas, R. K. (2016). Green exercise as a workplace intervention to reduce job stress. Results from a pilot study. *Work, 53*, 99–111. https://doi.org/10.3233/WOR-152219

Carolan, S., Harris, P. R., & Cavanagh, K. (2017). Improving employee well-being and effectiveness: Systematic review and meta-analysis of web-based psychological interventions delivered in the workplace. *Journal of Medical Internet Research, 19*(7), e7583.

Carter, J. S., Garber, J., Ciesla, J. A., & Cole, D. A. (2006). Modeling relations between hassles and internalizing and externalizing symptoms in adolescents: A four-year prospective study. *Journal of Abnormal Psychology, 1153*, 428–442.

CDC. (2014). Mean and median age at diagnosis of diabetes among adult incident cases aged 18–79 years, United States, 1997–2011.

Chanda, M. L., & Levitin, D. J. (2013). The neurochemistry of music. *Trends in Cognitive Sciences, 17*(4), 179–193. https://doi.org/10.1016/j.tics.2013.02.007

Chellew, K., Evans, P., Fornes-Vives, J., Perez, G., & Garcia-Banda, G. (2015). The effect of progressive muscle relaxation on daily cortisol secretion. *Stress, 18*(5), 538–544.

Chika, C. (2021). Occupational diseases and diseases associated with the workplace. *International Journal of Medical Evaluation and Physical Report, 5*, 1–13.

Chirico, F., Heponiemi, T., Pavlova, M., Zaffina, S., & Magnavita, N. (2019). Psychosocial risk prevention in a global occupational health perspective. A descriptive analysis. *International Journal of Environmental Research and Public Health, 16*(14), 2470.

Christensen, H., Batterham, P. J., Hickie, I. B., McGorry, P. D., Mitchell, P. B., & Kulkarni, J. (2011). Funding for mental health research: The gap remains. *Medical Journal of Australia, 195*(11–12), 681–684.

Christopher, M. S., Goerling, R. J., Rogers, B. S., Hunsinger, M., Baron, G., Bergman, A. L., et al. (2016). A pilot study evaluating the effectiveness of a mindfulness-based intervention on cortisol awakening response and health outcomes among law enforcement officers. *Journal of Police and Criminal Psychology, 31*(1), 15–28.

Cocchiara, R. A., Peruzzo, M., Mannocci, A., Ottolenghi, L., Villari, P., Polimeni, A., et al. (2019). The use of yoga to manage stress and burnout in healthcare workers: A systematic review. *Journal of Clinical Medicine, 8*(3), 284.

Codreanu, A., & Vasilescu, C. (2022). *Professional military leadership development from the perspective of national resilience.* Defence. https://en-gmr.mapn.ro/pages/1-2022

Cohen, S., Miller, G. E., & Rabin, B. S. (2001). Psychological stress and antibody response to immunization: A critical review of the human literature. *Psychosomatic Medicine, 63*, 7–18.

Cohen, S., Tyrrell, D. A., & Smith, A. P. (1991). Psychological stress and susceptibility to the common cold. *NEJM, 325*, 606–612.

Cohen, S., Frank, E., Doyle, W. J., Skoner, D. P., Rabin, B. S., & Gwaltney, J. M. Jr. (1998). Types of stressors that increase susceptibility to the common cold in healthy adults. *Health Psychology, 17*, 214–223.

Coleman, S. J., Stevelink, S. A. M., Hatch, S. L., Denny, J. A., & Greenberg, N. (2017). Stigma-related barriers and facilitators to help seeking for mental health issues in the armed forces: A systematic review and thematic synthesis of qualitative literature. *Psychological Medicine, 47*, 1880–1892.

Collins, P. Y., Patel, V., Joestl, S. S., March, D., Insel, T. R., & Daar, A. S. (2011). Grand challenges in global mental health. *Nature, 475*, 27–30.

Conroy, D. E., Yang, C., & Maher, J. P. (2014). Behavior change techniques in top-ranked mobile apps for physical activity. *American Journal of Preventive Medicine, 46*(6), 649–652.

Contreras, F., Baykal, E., & Abid, G. (2020). E-leadership and teleworking in times of COVID-19 and beyond: What we know and where do we go. *Frontiers in Psychology, 11*, 590271.

Costa, G. (2010). Shift work and health: Current problems and preventive actions. *Safety and Health at Work, 1*(2), 112–123.

Cox, T., & Griffiths, A. J. (1995). The nature and measurement of work stress: Theory and practice. In J. R. Wilson & E. N. Corlett (Eds.), *The evaluation of human work: A practical ergonomics methodology.* Taylor & Francis.

Cox, T., & Griffiths, A. (2005). The nature and measurement of work-related stress: Theory and practice. In J. R. Wilson & N. Corlett (Eds.), *Evaluation of Human Work* (3rd ed.). Routledge.

Csiernik, R. (2011). The glass is filling: An examination of employee assistance program evaluations in the first decade of the new millennium. *Journal of Workplace Behavioral Health, 26*, 334–355.

Daniels, K., Watson, D., Gedikli, C., Semkina, A., & Vaughn, O. (2017). Job design, employment practices and well-being: A systematic review of intervention studies. *Ergonomics, 60*(9), 1177–1196.

De Beer, L. T., Pienaar, J., & Rothmann, S., Jr. (2016). Work overload, burnout, and psychological ill-health symptoms: A three-wave mediation model of the employee health impairment process. *Anxiety, Stress, & Coping, 29*(4), 387–399.

De Korte, E., Wiezer, N., Roozeboom, M. B., Vink, P., & Kraaij, W. (2018a). Behavior change techniques in mhealth apps for the mental and physical health of employees: Systematic assessment. *JMIR mHealth and uHealth, 6*(10), e6363.

De Korte, E. M., Wiezer, N., Janssen, J. H., Vink, P., & Kraaij, W. (2018b). Evaluating an mHealth app for health and well-being at work: mixed-method qualitative study. *JMIR mHealth and uHealth, 6*, e6335.

De Neve, J.-E., Diener, E., Tay, L., & Xuereb, C. (2013). The objective benefits of subjective well-being. In J. Helliwell, R. Layard, & J. Sachs (Eds.), *World happiness report 2013*. UN Sustainable Development Solutions Network.

De Witte, M., Pinho, A. D. S., Stams, G. J., Moonen, X., Bos, A. E., & van Hooren, S. (2022). Music therapy for stress reduction: A systematic review and meta-analysis. *Health Psychology Review, 16*(1), 134–159.

De Witte, M., Spruit, A., van Hooren, S., Moonen, X., & Stams, G. J. (2020). Effects of music interventions on stress-related outcomes: A systematic review and two meta-analyses. *Health Psychology Review, 14*(2), 294–324. https://doi.org/10.1080/17437199.2019.1627897

Deci, E., & Ryan, R. (2008). Hedonia, eudaimonia, and well-being: An introduction. *Journal of Happiness Studies, 9*, 1–11.

Demerouti, E., Bakker, A. B., Nachreiner, F., & Schaufeli, W. B. (2001). The job demands-resources model of burnout. *Journal of Applied Psychology, 86*, 499.

Deng, J., Zhou, F., Hou, W., Silver, Z., Wong, C. Y., Chang, O., et al. (2021). The prevalence of depressive symptoms, anxiety symptoms and sleep disturbance in higher education students during the COVID-19 pandemic: A systematic review and meta-analysis. *Psychiatry Research, 301*, 113863.

Dewa, C. S., Thompson, A. H., & Jacobs, P. (2011). The association of treatment of depressive episodes and work productivity. *The Canadian Journal of Psychiatry, 56*(12), 743–750.

Di Fabio, A. (2017). Positive Healthy Organizations: Promoting well-being, meaningfulness, and sustainability in organizations. *Frontiers in Psychology, 8*, 1938.

Direito, A., Dale, L. P., Shields, E., Dobson, R., Whittaker, R., & Maddison, R. (2014). Do physical activity and dietary smartphone applications incorporate evidence-based behaviour change techniques? *BMC Public Health, 14*, 646.

Doherty, G., Coyle, D., & Sharry, J. (2012). Engagement with online mental health interventions: An exploratory clinical study of a treatment for depression. In *Proceedings of the SIGCHI conference on human factors in computing systems* (pp. 1421–1430).

Dreison, K. C., Luther, L., Bonfils, K. A., Sliter, M. T., McGrew, J. H., & Salyers, M. P. (2018). Job burnout in mental health providers: A meta-analysis of 35 years of intervention research. *Journal of Occupational Health Psychology, 23*(1), 18.

Dyrbye, L., Johnson, P., & Shanafelt, T. (2019). Efficacy of the well-being index to identify distress and stratify well-being in nurse practitioners and physician assistants. *Journal of the American Association of Nurse Practitioners, 31*(7), 403–412.

Ebert, D. D., Van Daele, T., Nordgreen, T., Karekla, M., Compare, A., Zarbo, C., et al. (2018). Erratum: Internet and mobile-based psychological interventions: Applications, efficacy and potential for improving mental health. A report of the EFPA E-Health Taskforce (European Psychologist (2018) 23 (167–187)). *European Psychologist, 23*(3), 269.

Edmunds, M. (2014). Growth in NP role satisfaction may have limits. *The Journal for Nurse Practitioners, 10*(1), A9–A10.

Egloff, B. (1998). The independence of positive and negative affect depends on the affect measure. *Personality and Individual Differences, 25*(6), 1101–1109.

Eisenberg, D., Hunt, J., & Speer, N. (2012). Help seeking for mental health on college campuses: Review of evidence and next steps for research and practice. *Harvard Review of Psychiatry, 20*(4), 222–232.

Erskine, J. (2021). Training pilots for stress resilience. In *Proceedings of the International Workshop INTRA–IWIN2021* (Vol. 13).

Erskine, J. A., Georgiou, G. J., & Kvavilashvili, L. (2010). I suppress, therefore I smoke: Effects of thought suppression on smoking behavior. *Psychological Science, 21*(9), 1225–1230.

Erskine, J. A. K., & Georgiou, G. (2011). Thoughts on suppression: How trying not to think of an action might lead you down that very path. *The Psychologist, 24*, 824–827.

Erskine, J. A. K., & Georgiou, G. J. (2017). Leadership styles: Employee stress, well-being, productivity, turnover and absenteeism. *Understanding Stress at Work*, 28–40.

Eshel, Y., & Kimhi, S. (2016). Community resilience of civilians at war: A new perspective. *Community Mental Health Journal, 52*(1), 109–117.

EU-OSHA. (2022). Foresight on new and emerging occupational safety and health risks associated with digitalisation by 2025. Retrieved August 7, 2022, from https://osha.europa.eu/en/publications/foresight-new-and-emerging-occupational-safety-and-health-risksassociated/view

European Commission. (2014). Green paper on mobile health ("mHealth"). *Shaping Europe's digital future*. https://digital-strategy.ec.europa.eu/en/library/green-paper-mobile-health-mhealth

Fauquet-Alekhine, P., Geeraerts, T., & Rouillac, L. (2014). Characterization of anesthetists' behavior during simulation training: Performance versus stress achieving medical tasks with or without physical effort. *Psychology and Social Behavior Research, 2*(2), 20–28.

Fava, G. A., McEwen, B. S., Guidi, J., Gostoli, S., Offidani, E., & Sonino, N. (2019). Clinical characterization of allostatic overload. *Psychoneuroendocrinology, 108*, 94–101.

Fenwick-Smith, A., Dahlberg, E. E., & Thompson, S. C. (2018). Systematic review of resilience-enhancing, universal, primary school-based mental health promotion programs. *BMC Psychology, 6*, 30.

Ferrari, A. J., Charlson, F. J., Norman, R. E., Patten, S. B., Freedman, G., Murray, C. J., et al. (2013). Burden of depressive disorders by country, sex, age, and year: Findings from the global burden of disease study 2010. *PLoS Medicine, 10*(11), e1001547.

Finkelstein, S. N., Berndt, E. R., Greenberg, P. E., Parsley, R. A., Russell, J. M., & Keller, M. B. (1996). Improvement in subjective work performance after treatment of chronic depression: Some preliminary results. Chronic Depression Study Group. *Psychopharmacology Bulletin, 32*(1), 33–40.

Firth-Cohen, J. (2006). New stressors, new remedies. *Occupational Magazine, 50*(3), 199–201.

Fleming, T., Bavin, L., Lucassen, M., Stasiak, K., Hopkins, S., & Merry, S. (2018). Beyond the trial: Systematic review of real-world uptake and engagement with digital self-help interventions for depression, low mood, or anxiety. *Journal of Medical Internet Research, 20*(6), e199.

Foster, J. A., Rinaman, L., & Cryan, J. F. (2017). Stress & the gut-brain axis: Regulation by the microbiome. *Neurobiology of Stress, 7*, 124–136.

France, E., France, E. F., Wyke, S., Gunn, J. M., Mair, F., & McLean, G. (2012). A systematic review of prospective cohort studies of multimorbidity in primary care. *The British Journal of General Practice, 62*, e297–e307.

Furlan, A. D., Gnam, W. H., Carnide, N., Irvin, E., Amick, B. C., DeRango, K., McMaster, R., Cullen, K., Slack, T., Brouwer, S., et al. (2012). Systematic review of intervention practices for depression in the workplace. *Journal of Occupational Rehabilitation, 22*, 312–321.

Ganster, D. C., & Rosen, C. C. (2013). Work stress and employee health: A multidisciplinary review. *Journal of Management, 39*(5), 1085–1122.

Gardner, R. L., Cooper, E., Haskell, J., Harris, D. A., Poplau, S., Kroth, P. J., & Linzer, M. (2019). Physician stress and burnout: The impact of health information technology. *Journal of the American Medical Informatics Association, 26*, 106–114.

Gascon, M., Sánchez-Benavides, G., Dadvand, P., Martínez, D., Gramunt, N., et al. (2018). Long-term exposure to residential green and blue spaces and anxiety and depression in adults: A cross-sectional study. *Environmental Research, 162*, 231–239.

Giorgi, G., Ariza-Montes, A., Mucci, N., & Leal-Rodríguez, A. L. (2022). The dark side and the light side of technology-related stress and stress related to workplace innovations: From artificial intelligence to business transformations. *International Journal of Environmental Research and Public Health, 19*(3), 1248.

Głąbska, D., Guzek, D., Groele, B., & Gutkowska, K. (2020). Fruit and vegetable intake and mental health in adults: A systematic review. *Nutrients, 12*(1), 115.

Glassman, A. H. (2007). Depression and cardiovascular comorbidity. *Dialogues in Clinical Neuroscience, 9*(1), 9.

Goetzel, R. Z., Hawkins, K., Ozminkowski, R. J., & Wang, S. (2003). The health and productivity cost burden of the "top 10" physical and mental health conditions affecting six large US employers in 1999. *Journal of Occupational and Environmental Medicine, 45*(1), 5–14.

Goetzel, R. Z., Ozminkowski, R. J., Meneades, L., Stewart, M., & Schutt, D. C. (2000). Pharmaceuticals – Cost or investment? An employer's perspective. *Journal of Occupational and Environmental Medicine, 42*(4), 338–351.

Goetzel, R. Z., Roemer, E. C., Holingue, C., Fallin, M. D., McCleary, K., Eaton, W., ... & Mattingly, C. R. (2018). Mental health in the workplace: A call to action proceedings from the mental health in the workplace: Public health summit. *Journal of Occupational and Environmental Medicine, 60*(4).

Goetzel, R. Z., & Ozminkowski, R. J. (2008). The health and cost benefits of work site health-promotion programs. *Annual Review of Public Health, 29*, 303–323.

Goh, J., Pfeffer, J., & Zenios, S. A. (2016). The relationship between workplace stressors and mortality and health costs in the United States. *Management Science, 62*, 608–628.

Goh, J., Pfeffer, J., & Zenios, S. A. (2019). Reducing the health toll from US workplace stress. *Behavioral Science & Policy, 5*(1), iv–13.

González-López, Ó. R., Buenadicha-Mateos, M., & Sánchez-Hernández, M. I. (2021). Overwhelmed by technostress? Sensitive archetypes and effects in times of forced digitalization. *International Journal of Environmental Research and Public Health, 18*, 4216.

Gray, P., Senabe, S., Naicker, N., Kgalamono, S., Yassi, A., & Spiegel, J. M. (2019). Workplace-based organizational interventions promoting mental health and happiness among healthcare workers: A realist review. *International Journal of Environmental Research and Public Health, 16*(22), 4396.

Gray, T., & Birrell, C. (2014). Are biophilic-designed site office buildings linked to health benefits and high performing occupants? *International Journal of Environmental Research and Public Health, 11*, 12204–12222.

Greenberg, P. E., Fournier, A. A., Sisitsky, T., Pike, C. T., & Kessler, R. C. (2015). The economic burden of adults with major depressive disorder in the United States (2005 and 2010). *The Journal of Clinical Psychiatry, 76*(2), 155–162.

Grzywacz, J. G., Almeida, D. M., & McDonald, D. A. (2002). Work–family spillover and daily reports of work and family stress in the adult labor force. *Family Relations, 51*(1), 28–36.

Haluza, D., Schonbauer, R., & Cervinka, R. (2014). Green perspectives for public health: A narrative review on the physiological effects of experiencing outdoor nature. *International Journal of Environmental Research and Public Health, 11,* 5445–5461.

Hampson, E., & Jacob, A. (2020). *Mental health and employers: Refreshing the case for investment.* Deloitte.

Han, H., Ariza-Montes, A., Giorgi, G., & Lee, S. (2020). Utilizing green design as workplace innovation to relieve service employee stress in the luxury hotel sector. *International Journal of Environmental Research and Public Health, 17,* 4527.

Han, H., Lho, H., & Kim, H. (2019). Airport green environment and its influence on visitors' psychological health and behaviors. *Sustainability, 11,* 7018.

Hardison, C. M., Vaughan, C. A., Meredith, L. S., Weilant, S., & Ross, R. (2020a). *Getting to outcomes (registered trademark) operations guide for US Air Force Community Action Teams: Content area module for workplace stress prevention and reduction in the air force.* RAND Corporation Santa Monica United States.

Hardison, C. M., Vaughan, C. A., Meredith, L. S., Weilant, S., & Ross, R. (2020b). *Getting to Outcomes (registered trade mark) Operations Guide for US Air Force Community Action Teams: Content Area Module for Workplace Stress Prevention and Reduction in the Air Force.* RAND Corporation Santa Monica United States.

Harms, P. D., Credé, M., Tynan, M., Leon, M., & Jeung, W. (2017). Leadership and stress: A meta-analytic review. *The Leadership Quarterly, 28,* 178–194.

Harrer, M., Adam, S. H., Baumeister, H., Cuijpers, P., Karyotaki, E., Auerbach, R. P., et al. (2019). Internet interventions for mental health in university students: A systematic review and meta-analysis. *International Journal of Methods in Psychiatric Research, 28*(2), e1759.

Harvey, S. B., Henderson, M., Lelliott, P., & Hotopf, M. (2009). Mental health and employment: Much work still to be done. *British Journal of Psychiatry, 194,* 201–203.

Harvey, S. B., Joyce, S., Tan, L., Johnson, A., Nguyen, H., Modini, M., & Groth, M. (2014). Developing a mentally healthy workplace: A review of the literature. A report for the National Mental Health Commission and the Mentally Healthy Workplace Alliance, Australia.

Harvey, S. B., Modini, M., Joyce, S., Milligan-Saville, J. S., Tan, L., Mykletun, A., ... & Mitchell, P. B. (2017). Can work make you mentally ill? A systematic meta-review of work-related risk factors for common mental health problems. *Occupational and Environmental Medicine, 74,* 301–310.

Havermans, B. M., Brouwers, E. P., Hoek, R. J., Anema, J. R., van der Beek, A. J., & Boot, C. R. (2018). Work stress prevention needs of employees and supervisors. *BMC Public Health, 18*(1), 1–11.

Hayes, S. C. (2004). Acceptance and commitment therapy, relational frame theory, and the third wave of behavioral and cognitive therapies. *Behavior Therapy, 35,* 639–665.

Health and Safety Executive. (2019). Health and safety at work: Summary statistics for Great Britain 2019.

Health and Safety Executive. (2021). *Work-related stress, anxiety or depression statistics in Great Britain 2021*. Crown Copyright. Downloaded September 2022, from https://www.hse.gov.uk/statistics/causdis/stress.pdf

Helbich, M., de Beurs, D., Kwan, M.-P., O'Connor, R. C., & Groenewegen, P. P. (2018). Natural environments and suicide mortality in the Netherlands: A cross-sectional, ecological study. *The Lancet Planetary Health, 2*, e134–e139.

Hesketh, R., Strang, L., Pollitt, A., & Wilkinson, B. (2020). What do we know about the effectiveness of workplace mental health interventions. *Literature review. The Policy at Institute King's college London.*

Hill, D. C., Moss, R. H., Sykes-Muskett, B., Conner, M., & O'Connor, D. B. (2018). Stress and eating behaviors in children and adolescents: Systematic review and meta-analysis. *Appetite, 123*, 14–22.

Hobfoll, S. E. (1989). Conservation of resources: A new attempt at conceptualizing stress. *American Psychologist, 44*, 513–524.

Holman, D., & Axtell, C. (2016). Can job redesign interventions influence a broad range of employee outcomes by changing multiple job characteristics? A quasi-experimental study. *Journal of Occupational Health Psychology, 3*, 284–295.

Holman, D., Johnson, S., & O'Connor, E. (2018). Stress management interventions: Improving subjective psychological well-being in the workplace. In *Handbook of well-being*. DEF Publishers.

Honney, K., Buszewicz, M., Coppola, W., & Griffin, M. (2010). Comparison of levels of depression in medical and non-medical students. *The Clinical Teacher, 7*(3), 180–184.

Howe, E., Suh, J., Bin Morshed, M., McDuff, D., Rowan, K., Hernandez, J., … & Czerwinski, M. P. (2022). Design of digital workplace stress-reduction intervention systems: Effects of intervention type and timing. In *CHI conference on human factors in computing systems* (pp. 1–16).

Hughes, K., Bellis, M. A., Hardcastle, K. A., Sethi, D., Butchart, A., Mikton, C., Jones, L., & Dunne, M. P. (2017). The effect of multiple adverse childhood experiences on health: A systematic review and meta-analysis. *The Lancet Public Health, 2*, e356–e366.

Hui, F. K. P., & Aye, L. (2018). Occupational stress and workplace design. *Buildings, 8*(10), 133.

Humphrey, S. E., Nahrgang, J. D., & Morgeson, F. P. (2007). Integrating motivational, social, and contextual work design features: A meta-analytic summary and theoretical extension of the work design literature. *Journal of Applied Psychology, 92*, 1332.

Hunter, M. R., Gillespie, B. W., & Chen, S. Y. P. (2019). Urban nature experiences reduce stress in the context of daily life based on salivary biomarkers. *Frontiers in Psychology, 10*, 722.

ILO. (2019). Prevention of occupational diseases in the Netherlands. *Occupational Environmental Medicine, 69*, 519–521.

Ivandic, I., Freeman, A., Birner, U., Nowak, D., & Sabariego, C. (2017). A systematic review of brief mental health and well-being interventions in organizational settings. *Scandinavian Journal of Work, Environment & Health*, 99–108.

Jacobs, S., Johnson, S., & Hassell, K. (2018). Managing workplace stress in community pharmacy organisations: Lessons from a review of the wider stress management and prevention literature. *International Journal of Pharmacy Practice, 26*(1), 28–38.

Janssen, M., Heerkens, Y., Kuijer, W., Van Der Heijden, B., & Engels, J. (2018). Effects of Mindfulness-Based Stress Reduction on employees' mental health: A systematic review. *PloS One, 13*(1), e0191332.

Jarrahi, M. H. (2018). Artificial intelligence and the future of work: Human-AI symbiosis in organizational decision making. *Business Horizons, 61*, 577–586.

Jerdan, S. W., Grindle, M., Van Woerden, H. C., & Boulos, M. N. K. (2018). Head-mounted virtual reality and mental health: Critical review of current research. *JMIR Serious Games, 6*(3), e9226.

Jones, R., Tarter, R., & Ross, A. M. (2021). Greenspace interventions, stress and cortisol: A scoping review. *International Journal of Environmental Research and Public Health, 18*(6), 2802.

Joyce, S., Modini, M., Christensen, H., Mykletun, A., Bryant, R., Mitchell, P. B., & Harvey, S. B. (2016). Workplace interventions for common mental disorders: A systematic meta-review. *Psychological Medicine, 46*(4), 683–697.

Jung, S. J., Yang, J. S., Jeon, Y. J., Kim, K., Yoon, J. H., Lori, C., … & Kim, H. C. (2020). The impact of COVID-19 on psychological health in Korea: A mental health survey in community prospective cohort data. Available at SSRN 3618193.

Juslin, P. N., & Västfjäll, D. (2008). Emotional responses to music: The need to consider underlying mechanisms. *Behavioral and Brain Sciences, 31*, 559–575. https://doi.org/10.1017/S0140525X08005293

Kabat-Zinn, J. (2003). Mindfulness-based interventions in context: Past, present and future. *Clinical Psychology: Science and Practice, 10*(2), 144–156.

Kalisch, R., Baker, D. G., Basten, U., Boks, M. P., Bonanno, G. A., Brummelman, E., et al. (2017). The resilience framework as a strategy to combat stress-related disorders. *Nature Human Behaviour, 1*(11), 784–790.

Kampmann, I. L., Emmelkamp, P. M., Hartanto, D., Brinkman, W. P., Zijlstra, B. J., & Morina, N. (2016). Exposure to virtual social interactions in the treatment of social anxiety disorder: A randomized controlled trial. *Behaviour Research and Therapy, 77*, 147–156.

Kang, L., Ma, S., Chen, M., Yang, J., Wang, Y., Li, R., et al. (2020). Impact on mental health and perceptions of psychological care among medical and nursing staff in Wuhan during the 2019 novel coronavirus disease outbreak: A cross-sectional study. *Brain, Behavior, and Immunity, 87*, 11–17.

Kass, A. E., Balantekin, K. N., Fitzsimmons-Craft, E. E., Jacobi, C., Wilfley, D. E., & Taylor, C. B. (2017). The economic case for digital interventions for eating disorders among United States college students. *International Journal of Eating Disorders, 50*(3), 250–258.

Kessler, R. C., Aguilar-Gaxiola, S., Alonso, J., Chatterji, S., Lee, S., Ormel, J., et al. (2009). The global burden of mental disorders: An update from the WHO World Mental Health (WMH) surveys. *Epidemiologia E Psichiatria Sociale, 18*(1), 23–33.

Kessler, R. C., Berglund, P., Demler, O., Jin, R., Merikangas, K. R., & Walters, E. E. (2005). Lifetime prevalence and age-of-onset distributions of DSM-IV disorders in the National Comorbidity Survey Replication. *Archives of General Psychiatry, 62*(6), 593–602.

Kessler, R. C., McGonagle, K. A., Zhao, S., et al. (1994). Lifetime and 12-month prevalence of DSM-III-R psychiatric disorders in the United States: Results from the National Comorbidity Survey. *Archives of General Psychiatry, 51*(1), 8–19.

Kettunen, O., Vuorimaa, T., & Vasankari, T. (2015). A 12-month exercise intervention decreased stress symptoms and increased mental resources among working adults – Results perceived after a 12-month follow-up. *International Journal of Occupational Medicine & Environmental Health, 28*, 157–168. https://doi.org/10.13075/ijomeh.1896.00263

Killgore, W. D., Cloonan, S. A., Taylor, E. C., & Dailey, N. S. (2020). Loneliness: A signature mental health concern in the era of COVID-19. *Psychiatry Research, 290*, 113117.

Killgore, W. D., Taylor, E. C., Cloonan, S. A., & Dailey, N. S. (2020). Psychological resilience during the COVID-19 lockdown. *Psychiatry Research, 291*, 113216.

Kingdon, D. (2006). Health research funding: Mental health research continues to be underfunded…. *BMJ: British Medical Journal, 332*(7556), 1510.

Klein, C. J., Dalstrom, M. D., Weinzimmer, L. G., Cooling, M., Pierce, L., & Lizer, S. (2020). Strategies of advanced practice providers to reduce stress at work. *Workplace Health & Safety, 68*(9), 432–442.

Knapp, M., McDaid, D., & Parsonage, M. (2011). Mental health promotion and mental illness prevention: The economic case.

Knight, C., Patterson, M., & Dawson, J. F. (2017). Building work engagement: A systematic review and meta-analysis investigating the effectiveness of work engagement interventions. *Journal of Organizational Behavior, 38*, 792–812.

Koelsch, S. (2015). Music-evoked emotions: Principles, brain correlates, and implications for therapy. *Annals of the New York Academy of Sciences, 1337*(1), 193–201.

Kohn, R., Saxena, S., Levav, I., & Saraceno, B. (2004). The treatment gap in mental health care. *Bulletin of the World Health Organization, 82*(11).

Koinis, A., Giannou, V., Drantaki, V., Angelaina, S., Stratou, E., & Saridi, M. (2015). The impact of healthcare workers job environment on their mental-emotional health. Coping strategies: The case of a local general hospital. *Health Psychology Research, 3*, 1984.

Kondo, M. C., Jacoby, S. F., & South, E. C. (2018). Does spending time outdoors reduce stress? A review of real-time stress response to outdoor environments. *Health & Place, 51*, 136–150.

20 Stress Prevention Measures in the Workplace 423

Krause, N., Scherzer, T., & Rugulies, R. (2005). Physical workload, work intensification, and prevalence of pain in low wage workers: Results from a participatory research project with hotel room cleaners in Las Vegas. *American Journal of Industrial Medicine, 48*, 326–337.

Kubicek, B., Korunka, C., & Ulferts, H. (2013). Acceleration in the care of older adults: New demands as predictors of employee burnout and engagement. *Journal of Advanced Nursing, 69*, 1525–1538.

Kuester, A., Niemeyer, H., & Knaevelsrud, C. (2016). Internet-based interventions for posttraumatic stress: A meta-analysis of randomized controlled trials. *Clinical Psychology Review, 43*, 1–16.

Kuyken, W., Watkins, E., Holden, E., et al. (2010). How does mindfulness-based cognitive therapy work? *Behaviour Research & Therapy, 48*, 1105–1112.

Lai, J., Ma, S., Wang, Y., Cai, Z., Hu, J., Wei, N., et al. (2020). Factors associated with mental health outcomes among health care workers exposed to coronavirus disease 2019. *JAMA Network Open, 3*(3), e203976–e203976.

LaMontagne, A. D., Keegel, T., & Vallance, D. (2007). Protecting and promoting mental health in the workplace: Developing a systems approach to job stress. *Health Promotion Journal of Australia, 18*, 221–228.

Lancee, W. J., Maunder, R. G., & Goldbloom, D. S. (2008). Prevalence of psychiatric disorders among Toronto hospital workers one to two years after the SARS outbreak. *Psychiatric Services, 59*(1), 91–95.

Lattie, E. G., Adkins, E. C., Winquist, N., Stiles-Shields, C., Wafford, Q. E., & Graham, A. K. (2019). Digital mental health interventions for depression, anxiety, and enhancement of psychological well-being among college students: Systematic review. *Journal of Medical Internet Research, 21*(7), e12869.

Lazarus, R. S. (2020). Psychological stress in the workplace. In *Occupational stress* (pp. 3–14). CRC Press.

Lazarus, R. S., & Folkman, S. (1984). Coping and adaptation. In W. D. Gentry (Ed.), *The handbook of behavioral medicine* (pp. 282–325). Guilford.

Lee, A. R., Son, S., & Kim, K. K. (2016). Information and communication technology overload and social networking service fatigue: A stress perspective. *Computers in Human Behavior, 55*, 51–61.

Leiter, M. P., Laschinger, H. K., Day, A., & Oore, D. G. (2011). The impact of civility interventions on employee social behavior, distress, and attitudes. *Journal of Applied Psychology, 96*, 1258–1274.

Linzer, M., Visser, M. R., Oort, F. J., Smets, E. M., McMurray, J. E., & De Haes, H. C. (2001). Predicting and preventing physician burnout: Results from the United States and the Netherlands. *The American Journal of Medicine, 111*(2), 170–175.

Lipson, S. K., Lattie, E. G., & Eisenberg, D. (2019). Increased rates of mental health service utilization by US college students: 10-year population-level trends (2007–2017). *Psychiatric Services, 70*(1), 60–63.

Liu, Y. Y., & Lu, Z. H. (2011). The Chinese high school student's stress in the school and academic achievement. *Educational Psychology, 311*, 27–35.

Longo, L., & Leva, M. C. (2019). H-workload 2019: 3rd International symposium on human mental workload: Models and applications (Works in Progress).

Mangone, G., Capaldi, C. A., van Allen, Z. M., & Luscuere, P. G. (2017). Bringing nature to work: Preferences and perceptions of constructed indoor and natural outdoor workspaces. *Urban Forestry & Urban Greening, 23*, 1–12.

Marques, H., Carvalho, H., Morgado, J., Garcia, N. M., Pires, I. M., & Zdravevski, E. (2020, December). Control and prevention of personal stress. In *2020 IEEE international conference on big data (big data)* (pp. 3783–3785). IEEE.

Marsland, A. L., Cohen, S., Rabin, B. S., & Manuck, S. B. (2006). Trait positive affect and antibody response to hepatitis B vaccination. *Brain, Behavior, and Immunity, 20*, 261–269.

Martin, A., Sanderson, K., & Cocker, F. (2009). in the workplace on depression and anxiety symptoms workplace on depression and anxiety symptoms. *Scandinavian Journal of Work, Environment & Health, 35*, 7–18. https://doi.org/10.5271/sjweh.1295

Martin, L., Oepen, R., Bauer, K., Nottensteiner, A., Mergheim, K., Gruber, H., & Koch, S. C. (2018). Creative arts interventions for stress management and prevention – A systematic review. *Behavioral Sciences, 8*(2), 28.

Maslach, C. (1978). Job burnout: How people cope. *Public Welfare, 36*, 56–58.

Maslach, C. (2003). Job burnout: New directions in research and intervention. *Current Directions in Psychological Science, 12*, 189–192.

Maslach, C., Schaufeli, W. B., & Leiter, M. P. (2001). Job burnout. *Annual Review of Psychology, 52*, 397–422.

Masten, A. S. (2018). Resilience theory and research on children and families: Past, present, and promise. *Journal of Family Theory & Review, 10*, 12–31.

Matrix, S. O. I. (2013). *Economic analysis of workplace mental health promotion and mental disorder prevention programmes and of their potential contribution to EU health, social and economic policy objectives.* Published May.

Maunder, R. G., Leszcz, M., Savage, D., Adam, M. A., Peladeau, N., Romano, D., et al. (2008). Applying the lessons of SARS to pandemic influenza. *Canadian Journal of Public Health, 99*(6), 486–488.

Mayerl, H., Stolz, E., Waxenegger, A., Rásky, É., & Freidl, W. (2016). The role of personal and job resources in the relationship between psychosocial job demands, mental strain, and health problems. *Frontiers in Psychology, 7*, 1214.

McCallie, M. S., Blum, C. M., & Hood, C. J. (2006). Progressive muscle relaxation. *Journal of Human Behavior in the Social Environment, 13*(3), 51–66.

McDaid, D., Park, A. L., & Wahlbeck, K. (2019). The economic case for the prevention of mental illness. *Annual Review of Public Health, 40*, 373–389.

McEwen, B. S. (1998). Protective and damaging effects of stress mediators. *NEJM, 338*, 171–179.

20 Stress Prevention Measures in the Workplace 425

McEwen, B. S. (2000). Allostasis and allostatic load: Implications for neuropsycho-pharmacology. *Neuropsychopharmacology, 22,* 108–124.

McEwen, B. S. (2007). Physiology and neurobiology of stress and adaptation: Central role of the brain. *Physiological Reviews, 87,* 873–904.

McEwen, B. S., & Seeman, T. (1999). Protective and damaging effects of mediators of stress: Elaborating and testing the concepts of allostasis and allostatic load. *Annals of the New York Academy of Sciences, 896*(1), 30–47.

McEwen, B. S., & Wingfield, J. C. (2010). What is in a name? Integrating homeostasis, allostasis and stress. *Hormones and Behavior, 57,* 105–111.

Mental Health America. (2017). *The State of Mental Health in America.*

Mercer, S. W., Gunn, J., Bower, P., Wyke, S., & Guthrie, B. (2012). Managing patients with mental and physical multimorbidity. *BMJ, 345.*

Michie, S., Abraham, C., Whittington, C., McAteer, J., & Gupta, S. (2009). Effective techniques in healthy eating and physical activity interventions: A meta-regression. *Health Psychology, 28*(6), 690–701.

Milligan-Saville, J. S., Tan, L., Gayed, A., et al. (2017). Workplace mental health training for managers and its effect on sick leave in employees: A cluster randomised controlled trial. *Lancet Psychiatry, 4,* 850–858.

Moeller, C., King, N., Burr, V., Gibbs, G. R., & Gomersall, T. (2018). Nature-based interventions in institutional and organisational settings: A scoping review. *International Journal of Environmental Health Research, 28,* 293–305.

Moffitt, T. E., Caspi, A., Taylor, A., Kokaua, J., Milne, B. J., Polanczyk, G., & Poulton, R. (2010). How common are common mental disorders? Evidence that lifetime prevalence rates are doubled by prospective versus retrospective ascertainment. *Psychological Medicine, 40*(6), 899–909.

Molino, M., Cortese, C. G., & Ghislieri, C. (2020). The promotion of technology acceptance and work engagement in industry 4.0: From personal resources to information and training. *International Journal of Environmental Research and Public Health, 17*(7), 2438.

Morina, N., Ijntema, H., Meyerbröker, K., & Emmelkamp, P. M. (2015). Can virtual reality exposure therapy gains be generalized to real-life? A meta-analysis of studies applying behavioral assessments. *Behaviour Research and Therapy, 74,* 18–24.

Moss, J. (2019a). Burnout is about your workplace, not your people. *Harvard Business Review, 11.*

Moss, J. (2019b). When passion leads to burnout. *Harvard Business Review, 1.*

Moylan, S., Maes, M., Wray, N. R., & Berk, M. (2013). The neuroprogressive nature of major depressive disorder: Pathways to disease evolution and resistance, and therapeutic implications. *Molecular Psychiatry, 185,* 595–606.

Mozaffarian, D., Benjamin, E. J., Go, A. S., et al. (2015). Heart disease and stroke statistics – 2015 update: A report from the American Heart Association. *Circulation, 131*(4), e29–e322.

MQ. (2015). *UK mental health research funding. MQ landscape analysis.* MQ.

Murphy, L. (2003). Stress management at work: Secondary prevention of stress. In M. J. Schabracq, J. A. M. Winnubst, & C. L. Cooper (Eds.), *Handbook of work and health psychology* (2nd ed., pp. 533–549). Wiley.

Murray, E., Hekler, E. B., Andersson, G., Collins, L. M., Doherty, A., Hollis, C., et al. (2016). Evaluating digital health interventions: Key questions and approaches. *American Journal of Preventive Medicine, 51*(5), 843–851.

Nahum-Shani, I., Smith, S. N., Spring, B. J., Collins, L. M., Witkiewitz, K., Tewari, A., & Murphy, S. A. (2018). Just-in-time adaptive interventions (JITAIs) in mobile health: Key components and design principles for ongoing health behavior support. *Annals of Behavioral Medicine, 52*(6), 446–462.

Naylor, C., Parsonage, M., McDaid, D., Knapp, M., Fossey, M., & Galea, A. (2012). *Long-term conditions and mental health: The cost of co-morbidities*. The King's Fund.

Neary, M., & Schueller, S. M. (2018). State of the field of mental health apps. *Cognitive and Behavioral Practice, 25*(4), 531–537.

NICE. (2009). Promoting mental wellbeing at work. Business case. National Institute for Health and Clinical Excellence. Retrieved August 2022, from http://guidance.nice.org.uk/PH22/BusinessCase/pdf/English

NICE. (2018). Post-traumatic stress disorder. guideline NG116. Retrieved August 2022, from https://www.nice.org.uk/guidance/ng116/resources/posttraumatic-stress-disorder-pdf-66141601777861

Nielsen, K., & Abildgaard, J. S. (2013). Organizational interventions: A research-based framework for the evaluation of both process and effects. *Work & Stress, 27*, 278–297.

Nishiuchi, K., Tsutsumi, A., Takao, S., Mineyama, S., & Kawakami, N. (2007). Effects of an education program for stress reduction on supervisor knowledge, attitudes, and behavior in the workplace: A randomized controlled trial. *Journal of Occupational Health, 49*(3), 190–198.

O'Connor, D. B., Thayer, J. F., & Vedhara, K. (2021). Stress and health: A review of psychobiological processes. *Annual Review of Psychology, 72*, 663–688.

O'Connor, D. B., Jones, F., Conner, M., McMillan, B., & Ferguson, E. (2008). Effects of daily hassles and eating style on eating behavior. *Health Psychology, 27*(1S), S20.

Obermeyer, Z., & Emanuel, E. J. (2016). Predicting the future – Big data, machine learning, and clinical medicine. *The New England Journal of Medicine, 375*(13), 1216–1219.

Obrist, B., Pfeiffer, C., & Henley, R. (2010). Multi-layered social resilience: A new approach in mitigation research. *Progress in Development Studies, 10*(4), 283–293.

Ocean, N., Howley, P., & Ensor, J. (2019). Lettuce be happy: A longitudinal UK study on the relationship between fruit and vegetable consumption and well-being. *Social Science & Medicine, 222*, 335–345.

OECD. (2012). *Sick on the job? Myths and realities about mental health and work*. Organisation for Economic Co-operation and Development Publishing.

OECD. (2015). *Fit mind, fit job: From evidence to practice in mental health and work.* Mental Health Work Series. OECD.

Organisation for Economic Co-operation and Development. (2012). Sick on the job? In *Myths and realities about mental health and work.* OECD Publishing.

Organization O'Connor DB, Jones, F., Conner, M., McMillan, B., & Ferguson, E. (2008). Effects of daily hassles and eating style on eating behavior. *Health Psychology, 27*, S20–S31.

OSH in Figures: Stress at work – Facts and figures. Retrieved August 12, 2022, from https://osha.europa.eu/en/publications/osh-figures-stress-work-facts-and-figures.

Oshri, A., Duprey, E. B., Kogan, S. M., Carlson, M. W., & Liu, S. (2018). Growth patterns of future orientation among maltreated youth: A prospective examination of the emergence of resilience. *Developmental Psychology, 54*, 1456–1471.

Panagioti, M., Geraghty, K., Johnson, J., Zhou, A., Panapgopoulou, E., Chew-Graham, C., et al. (2018). Association between physician burnout and patient safety, professionalism, and patient satisfaction: A systematic review and meta-analysis. *JAMA Internal Medicine, 178*, 1317–1331. https://doi.org/10.1001/jamainternmed.2018.3713

Park, S., & Jang, M. K. (2019). Associations between workplace exercise interventions and job stress reduction: A systematic review. *Workplace Health & Safety, 67*(12), 592–601.

Pascoe, M. C., Hetrick, S. E., & Parker, A. G. (2020). The impact of stress on students in secondary school and higher education. *International Journal of Adolescence and Youth, 25*(1), 104–112.

Patton, M. (2015). *US health care costs rise faster than inflation.* Forbes.

Pedersen, A. F., Zachariae, R., & Bovbjerg, D. H. (2009). Psychological stress and antibody response to influenza vaccination: A meta-analysis. *Brain, Behavior, and Immunity, 23*, 427–433.

Peterson, U., Bergstrom, G., Samuelsson, M., Asberg, M., & Nygren, A. (2008). Reflecting peer-support groups in the prevention of stress and burnout: Randomized controlled trial. *Journal of Advanced Nursing, 63*, 506–516.

Pieper, C., Schröer, S., & Eilerts, A. L. (2019). Evidence of workplace interventions – A systematic review of systematic reviews. *International Journal of Environmental Research and Public Health, 16*(19), 3553.

Pierce, M., Hope, H., Ford, T., Hatch, S., Hotopf, M., John, A., et al. (2020). Mental health before and during the COVID-19 pandemic: A longitudinal probability sample survey of the UK population. *The Lancet Psychiatry, 7*(10), 883–892.

Pijpker, R., Vaandrager, L., Veen, E. J., & Koelen, M. A. (2020). Combined interventions to reduce burnout complaints and promote return to work: A systematic review of effectiveness and mediators of change. *International Journal of Environmental Research and Public Health, 17*(1), 55.

Pinder-Amaker, S., & Bell, C. (2012). A bioecological systems approach for navigating the college mental health crisis. *Harvard Review of Psychiatry, 20*(4), 174–188.

Portilla, X. A., Ballard, P. J., Adler, N. E., Boyce, W. T., & Obradović, J. (2014). An integrative view of school functioning: Transactions between self-regulation, school engagement, and teacher-child relationship quality. *Child Development, 85*, 1915–1931.

Portoghese, I., Galletta, M., Coppola, R. C., Finco, G., & Campagna, M. (2014). Burnout and workload among health care workers: The moderating role of job control. *Safety and Health at Work, 5*, 152–157.

Proper, K. I., & van Oostrom, S. H. (2019). The effectiveness of workplace health promotion interventions on physical and mental health outcomes – A systematic review of reviews. *Scandinavian Journal of Work, Environment & Health, 45*(6), 546–559.

Quick, J. C., & Henderson, D. F. (2016). Occupational stress: Preventing suffering, enhancing wellbeing. *International Journal of Environmental Research and Public Health, 13*(5), 459.

Ragu-Nathan, T. S., Tarafdar, M., Ragu-Nathan, B. S., & Tu, Q. (2008). The consequences of technostress for end users in organizations: Conceptual development and empirical validation. *Information Systems Research, 19*, 417–433.

Rai, M., Vigod, S. N., & Hensel, J. M. (2016). Barriers to office-based mental health care and interest in e-communication with providers: A survey study. *JMIR Mental Health, 3*(3), e35.

Ramón-Arbués, E., Gea-Caballero, V., Granada-López, J. M., Juárez-Vela, R., Pellicer-García, B., & Antón-Solanas, I. (2020). The prevalence of depression, anxiety and stress and their associated factors in college students. *International Journal of Environmental Research and Public Health, 17*, 7001.

Rasool, S. F., Wang, M., Zhang, Y., & Samma, M. (2020). Sustainable work performance: The roles of workplace violence and occupational stress. *International Journal of Environmental Research and Public Health, 17*(3), 912.

Rausch, S. M., Gramling, S. E., & Auerbach, S. M. (2006). Effects of a single session of large-group meditation and progressive muscle relaxation training on stress reduction, reactivity, and recovery. *International Journal of Stress Management, 13*(3), 273.

Richards, D., Richardson, T., Timulak, L., & McElvaney, J. (2015). The efficacy of internet-delivered treatment for generalized anxiety disorder: A systematic review and meta-analysis. *Internet Interventions, 2*(3), 272–282.

Richards, J. M., & Gross, J. J. (1999). Composure at any cost? The cognitive consequences of emotion suppression. *Personality and Social Psychology Bulletin, 25*, 1033–1044.

Richardson, K. M. (2017). Managing employee stress and wellness in the new millennium. *Journal of Occupational Health Psychology, 22*(3), 423–428. https://doi.org/10.1037/ocp0000066

Richardson, K. M., & Rothstein, H. R. (2008). Effects of occupational stress management intervention programs: A meta-analysis. *Journal of Occupational Health Psychology, 13*(1), 69–93. https://doi.org/10.1037/1076-8998.13.1.69

Riva, G., Baños, R. M., Botella, C., Wiederhold, B. K., & Gaggioli, A. (2012). Positive technology: Using interactive technologies to promote positive functioning. *Cyberpsychology, Behavior, and Social Networking, 15*, 69–77.

Robertson, I., Cooper, C., Sarkar, M., & Curran, T. (2015). Resilience training in the workplace from 2003 to 2014: A systematic review. *Journal of Occupational and Organizational Psychology, 88*(3), 533–562.

Robertson, I. T., & Cooper, C. L. (2010). Full engagement: The integration of employee engagement and psychological well-being. *Leadership & Organization Development Journal, 31*, 324–336.

Roehrig, C. (2016). Mental disorders top the list of the most costly conditions in the United States: $201 billion. *Health Affairs, 35*, 1130–1135.

Rongen, A., Robroek, S. J. W., Van Lenthe, F. J., & Burdorf, A. (2013). Workplace health promotion: A meta-analysis of effectiveness. *American Journal of Preventive Medicine, 44*(4), 406–415.

Rossell, S. L., Neill, E., Phillipou, A., Tan, E. J., Toh, W. L., Van Rheenen, T. E., & Meyer, D. (2021). An overview of current mental health in the general population of Australia during the COVID-19 pandemic: Results from the COLLATE project. *Psychiatry Research, 296*, 113660.

Ruitenburg, M. M., Frings-Dresen, M. H., & Sluiter, J. K. (2012). The prevalence of common mental disorders among hospital physicians and their association with self-reported work ability: A cross-sectional study. *BMC Health Services Research, 12*, 292–298.

Ruotsalainen, J. H., Verbeek, J. H., Mariné, A., & Serra, C. (2015). Preventing occupational stress in healthcare workers. *The Cochrane Database of Systematic Reviews, 4*, CD002892.

Russell, J. A. (1979). Affective space is bipolar. *Journal of Personality and Social Psychology, 37*(3), 345.

Rutter, M., Dunn, J., Plomin, R., et al. (1997). Integrating nature and nurture: Implications of person environment correlations and interactions for developmental psychopathology. *Development and Psychopathology, 9*(2), 335–364.

Ryff, C. D., Singer, B. H., & Love, G. D. (2004). Positive health: Connecting well-being with biology. *Philosophical Transactions of the Royal Society, 359*, 1383–1394.

Salem, I. E. B. (2015). Transformational leadership: Relationship to job stress and job burnout in five-star hotels. *Tourism and Hospitality Research, 15*, 240–253.

Salyers, M. P., Bonfils, K. A., Luther, L., et al. (2017). The relationship between professional burnout and quality and safety in healthcare: A meta-analysis. *Journal of General Internal Medicine, 32*(4), 475–482.

Sandoval-Reyes, J., Acosta-Prado, J. C., & Sanchís-Pedregosa, C. (2019). Relationship amongst technology use, work overload, and psychological detachment from work. *International Journal of Environmental Research and Public Health, 16*, 4602.

Sarkar, C., Webster, C., & Gallacher, J. (2018). Residential greenness and prevalence of major depressive disorders: A cross-sectional, observational, associational study of 94 879 adult UK Biobank participants. *Lancet Planet Health, 2*, e162–e173.

Schueller, S. M. (2010). Preferences for positive psychology exercises. *The Journal of Positive Psychology, 5*(3), 192–203.

Schwenk, T. L., Davis, L., & Wimsatt, L. A. (2010). Depression, stigma, and suicidal ideation in medical students. *JAMA, 304*(11), 1181–1190.

Segal, Z. V., Williams, J. M. G., & Teasdale, J. D. (2002). *Mindfulness-Based Cognitive Therapy for depression; a new approach to preventing relapse.* The Guilford Press.

Segerstrom, S. C., & Miller, G. E. (2004). Psychological stress and the human immune system: a meta-analytic study of 30 years of inquiry. *Psychological Bulletin, 130*, 601–630.

Selye, H. (1959). Perspectives in stress research. *Perspectives in Biology and Medicine, 2*, 403–416.

Semmer, N. K. (2006). Job stress interventions and the organization of work. *Scandinavian Journal of Work, Environment & Health, 32*, 515–527.

Serafini, G., Parmigiani, B., Amerio, A., Aguglia, A., Sher, L., & Amore, M. (2020). The psychological impact of COVID-19 on the mental health in the general population. *QJM, 113*, 531–537.

Seymour, L., & Grove, B. (2005). *Workplace interventions for people with common mental health problems: Evidence review and recommendations.* British Occupational Health Research Foundation.

Shanafelt, T. D., Balch, C. M., Bechamps, G., et al. (2010). Burnout and medical errors among American surgeons. *Annals of Surgery, 251*(6), 995–1000.

Shanafelt, T. D., Hasan, O., Dyrbye, L. N., Sinsky, C., Satele, D., Sloan, J., & West, C. P. (2015). Changes in burnout and satisfaction with work-life balance in physicians and the general US working population between 2011 and 2014. *Mayo Clinic Proceedings, 90*, 1600–1613.

Shanahan, D. F., Astell-Burt, T., Barber, E. A., Brymer, E., Cox, D. T. C., Dean, J., Depledge, M., Fuller, R. A., Hartig, T., Irvine, K. N., et al. (2019). Nature-based interventions for improving health and wellbeing: The purpose, the people and the outcomes. *Sports, 7*, 141.

Shapiro, S. L., Brown, K. W., & Biegel, G. M. (2007). Teaching self-care to caregivers: Effects of mindfulnessbased stress reduction on the mental health of therapists in training. *Training and Education in Professional Psychology, 1*(2), 105.

Shapiro, S. L., Carlson, L. E., Astin, J. A., & Freedman, B. (2006). Mechanisms of mindfulness. *Journal of Clinical Psychology., 62*(3), 373–386.

Shepard, D. S., Gurewich, D., Lwin, A. K., Reed, G. A., Jr., & Silverman, M. M. (2016). Suicide and suicidal attempts in the United States: Costs and policy implications. *Suicide and Life-Threatening Behavior, 46*, 352–362.

Shin, J. Y., & Choi, S. W. (2020). Interventions to promote caregiver resilience. *Current Opinion in Supportive and Palliative Care, 14*(1), 60.

Shin, J. Y., Kang, T. I., Noll, R. B., & Choi, S. W. (2018). Supporting caregivers of patients with cancer: A summary of technology-mediated interventions and future directions. *American Society of Clinical Oncology Educational Book, 38*, 838–849.

Sijbrandij, M., Horn, R., Esliker, R., O'may, F., Reiffers, R., Ruttenberg, L., et al. (2020). The effect of psychological first aid training on knowledge and understanding about psychosocial support principles: A cluster-randomized controlled trial. *International Journal of Environmental Research and Public Health, 17*(2), 484.

Simon, G. E., Revicki, D., Heiligenstein, J., et al. (2000). Recovery from depression, work productivity, and health care costs among primary care patients. *General Hospital Psychiatry, 22*(3), 153–162.

Slemp, G. R., Jach, H. K., Chia, A., Loton, D. J., & Kern, M. L. (2019). Contemplative interventions and employee distress: A meta-analysis. *Stress and Health, 35*(3), 227–255.

Smyth, J. M., & Heron, K. E. (2016, October). Is providing mobile interventions "just-in-time" helpful? An experimental proof of concept study of just-in-time intervention for stress management. In *2016 IEEE Wireless Health (WH)* (pp. 1–7). IEEE.

Soklaridis, S., Lin, E., Lalani, Y., Rodak, T., & Sockalingam, S. (2020). Mental health interventions and supports during COVID-19 and other medical pandemics: A rapid systematic review of the evidence. *General Hospital Psychiatry, 66*, 133–146.

Sørensen, O. H., & Holman, D. (2014). A participative intervention to improve employee well-being in knowledge work jobs: A mixed-methods evaluation study. *Work & Stress, 28*, 67–86.

Sroufe, L. A. (2013). The promise of developmental psychopathology: Past and present. *Development and Psychopathology, 25*(4 Pt 2), 1215–1224.

Steptoe, A., & Kivimaki, M. (2013). Stress and cardiovascular disease: An update on current knowledge. *Annual Review of Public Health, 34*, 337–354.

Stevenson, D., & Farmer, P. (2017). *Thriving at work: The Stevenson/Farmer review of mental health and employers.* Department for Work and Pensions and Department of Health and Social Care. Downloaded September 2022, from https://assets.publishing.service.gov.uk/government/uploads/system/uploads/attachment_data/file/658145/thriving-at-work-stevenson-farmer-review.pdf

Stokols, D. (2011). Chapter 34: Psychosocial and organizational factors. In J. M. Stellman (Ed.), *The ILO Encyclopaedia of occupational health & safety* (Vol. 4, 4th ed.). International Labor Organization.

Stratton, E., Lampit, A., Choi, I., Calvo, R. A., Harvey, S. B., & Glozier, N. (2017). Effectiveness of eHealth interventions for reducing mental health conditions in employees: A systematic review and meta-analysis. *PloS One, 12*(12), e0189904.

Stults-KolehMainen, M. A., & Sinha, R. (2014). The effects of stress on physical activity and exercise. *Sports Medicine, 44*, 81–121. https://doi.org/10.1007/s40279-013-0090-5

Substance Abuse and Mental Health Services Administration (SAMHSA). (2015). Subst Abus Ment Heal Serv Adm Rockville MD. Results from the 2015 national survey on drug use and health (NSDUH).

Sultana, A., Sharma, R., Hossain, M. M., Bhattacharya, S., & Purohit, N. (2020). Burnout among healthcare providers during COVID-19: Challenges and evidence-based interventions. *Indian Journal of Medical Ethics, 5*(4), 308–311.

Sun, J., Buys, N., & Wang, X. (2013). Effectiveness of a workplace-based intervention program to promote mental health among employees in privately owned enterprises in China. *Population Health Management, 16*, 406–414. https://doi.org/10.1089/pop.2012.0113

Swider, B. W., & Zimmerman, R. D. (2010). Born to burnout: A meta-analytic path model of personality, job burnout, and work outcomes. *Journal of Vocational Behavior, 76*(3), 487–506.

Takayanagi, Y., Spira, A. P., Roth, K. B., Gallo, J. J., Eaton, W. W., & Mojtabai, R. (2014). Accuracy of reports of lifetime mental and physical disorders: Results from the Baltimore Epidemiological Catchment Area study. *JAMA Psychiatry, 71*(3), 273–280.

Tan, L., Wang, M. J., Modini, M., Joyce, S., Mykletun, A., Christensen, H., & Harvey, S. (2014). Preventing the development of depression at work: A systematic review and meta-analysis of universal interventions in the workplace. *BMC Medicine, 12*(1), 74.

Theorell, T., Hammarström, A., Aronsson, G., Träskman Bendz, L., Grape, T., Hogstedt, C., et al. (2015). A systematic review including meta-analysis of work environment and depressive symptoms. *BMC Public Health, 15*(1), 1–14.

Torous, J., Nicholas, J., Larsen, M. E., Firth, J., & Christensen, H. (2018). Clinical review of user engagement with mental health smartphone apps: Evidence, theory and improvements. *Evidence-Based Mental Health, 21*(3), 116–119.

Triantafyllidis, A. K., & Tsanas, A. (2019). Applications of machine learning in real-life digital health interventions: Review of the literature. *Journal of Medical Internet Research, 21*(4), e12286.

Tsuang, M. T., Bar, J. L., Stone, W. S., & Faraone, S. V. (2004). Gene-environment interactions in mental disorders. *World Psychiatry, 3*(2), 73–83.

Twohig-Bennett, C., & Jones, A. (2018). The health benefits of the great outdoors: A systematic review and meta-analysis of greenspace exposure and health outcomes. *Environmental Research, 166*, 628–637.

Ulrich, R. S., Simons, R. F., Losito, B. D., Fiorito, E., Miles, M. A., & Zelson, M. (1991). Stress recovery during exposure to natural and urban environments. *Journal of Environmental Psychology, 11*, 201–230.

Ungar, M., & Theron, L. (2020). Resilience and mental health: How multisystemic processes contribute to positive outcomes. *The Lancet Psychiatry, 7*(5), 441–448.

Valmaggia, L. R., Latif, L., Kempton, M. J., & Rus-Calafell, M. (2016). Virtual reality in the psychological treatment for mental health problems: A systematic review of recent evidence. *Psychiatry Research, 236*, 189–195.

van den Bosch, M., & Ode Sang, Å. (2017). Urban natural environments as nature-based solutions for improved public health – A systematic review of reviews. *Environmental Research, 158*(Suppl. C), 373–384.

20 Stress Prevention Measures in the Workplace 433

Van der Klink, J. J., Blonk, R. W., Schene, A. H., & van Dijk, F. J. (2001). The benefits of interventions for work-related stress. *American Journal of Public Health, 91*(2), 270–276.

Van Remortel, B., Dolan, E., Cipriano, D., & McBride, P. (2018). Medical student wellness in Wisconsin: Current trends and future directions. *WMJ: Official Publication of the State Medical Society of Wisconsin, 117*(5), 211–213.

Van Rhenen, W., Blonk, R. W., van der Klink, J. J., van Dijk, F. J., & Schaufeli, W. B. (2005). The effect of a cognitive and a physical stress-reducing programme on psychological complaints. *International Archives of Occupational and Environmental Health, 78*, 139–148. https://doi.org/10.1007/s00420-004-0566-6

Vanhove, A., Herian, M., Perez, C., Harms, P., & Lester, P. (2016). Can resilience be developed at work? A meta-analytic review of resilience-building programme effectiveness. *Journal of Occupational and Organizational Psychology, 89*(2), 278–307.

Vaníčková, R. (2021). Psychology of health and mental hygiene: Psychosocial risks, consequences, and possibilities of work stress prevention. *Problems and Perspectives in Management, 19*, 68–77.

Varma, P., Junge, M., Meaklim, H., & Jackson, M. L. (2021). Younger people are more vulnerable to stress, anxiety and depression during COVID-19 pandemic: A global cross-sectional survey. *Progress in Neuro-Psychopharmacology and Biological Psychiatry, 109*, 110236.

Vedhara, K., Cox, N. K., Wilcock, G. K., Perks, P., Hunt, M., Anderson, S., Lightman, S. L., & Shanks, N. M. (1999). Chronic stress in elderly carers of dementia patients and antibody response to influenza vaccination. *Lancet, 353*, 627–631.

Vigo, D., Thornicroft, G., & Atun, R. (2016). Estimating the true global burden of mental illness. *Lancet Psychiatry, 3*, 171–178.

Vinkers, C. H., van Amelsvoort, T., Bisson, J. I., Branchi, I., Cryan, J. F., Domschke, K., et al. (2020). Stress resilience during the coronavirus pandemic. *European Neuropsychopharmacology, 35*, 12–16.

Vujcic, M., Tomicevic-Dubljevic, J., Grbic, M., Lecic-Tosevski, D., Vukovic, O., & Toskovic, O. (2017). Nature based solution for improving mental health and wellbeing in urban areas. *Environmental Research, 158*, 385–392.

Wadhwa, D., Burman, D., Swami, N., Rodin, G., Lo, C., & Zimmermann, C. (2013). Quality of life and mental health in caregivers of outpatients with advanced cancer. *Psycho-Oncology, 22*(2), 403–410.

Waehrer, G. M., Miller, T. R., Silverio Marques, S. C., Oh, D. L., & Burke, H. N. (2020). Disease burden of adverse childhood experiences across 14 states. *PLoS One, 15*, e0226134.

Wagner, S. L., Koehn, C., White, M. I., Harder, H. G., Schultz, I. Z., Williams-Whitt, K., et al. (2016). Mental health interventions in the workplace and work outcomes: A best-evidence synthesis of systematic reviews. *The International Journal of Occupational and Environmental Medicine, 7*(1), 601–607.

Walburg, V. (2014). Burnout among high school students: A literature review. *Children and Youth Services Review, 42*, 28–33.

Wang, K., Shu, Q., & Tu, Q. (2008). Technostress under different organizational environments: An empirical investigation. *Computers in Human Behavior, 24*, 3002–3013.

Ward Thompson, C. (2011). Linking landscape and health: The recurring theme. *Landscape and Urban Planning, 99*, 187–195.

Warmerdam, L., Smit, F., van Straten, A., Riper, H., & Cuijpers, P. (2010). Cost-utility and cost-effectiveness of internet-based treatment for adults with depressive symptoms: Randomized trial. *Journal of Medical Internet Research, 12*(5), e53.

Warr, P. (2003). Well-Being and the Workplace. In D. Kahneman, E. Diener, & N. Schwartz (Eds.), *Wellbeing: Foundations of hedonic psychology* (pp. 392–412). Russell Sage Foundation.

Wessely, S., Bisson, J., & Rose, S. (2000). A systematic review of brief psychological interventions ('debriefing') for the treatment of immediate trauma related symptoms and the prevention of post traumatic stress disorder. In M. Oakley-Browne, R. Churchill, D. Gill, M. Trivedi, & S. Wessely (Eds.), *Depression, anxiety and neurosis module of the Cochrane database of systematic reviews, Issue 1*. Update Software.

WGBC. (2014). World Green Building Council. Health, Wellbeing and Productivity in Offices: The Next Chapter for Green Building; World Green Building Council, London, UK.

White, B. A., Horwath, C. C., & Conner, T. S. (2013). Many apples a day keep the blues away-daily experiences of negative and positive affect and food consumption in young adults. *British Journal of Health Psychology, 18*, 782–798.

Wiederhold, B. K., Cipresso, P., Pizzioli, D., Wiederhold, M., & Riva, G. (2018). Intervention for physician burnout: A systematic review. *Open Medicine, 13*(1), 253–263.

Williams, E. S., Konrad, T. R., Scheckler, W. E., Pathman, D. E., Linzer, M., McMurray, J. E., et al. (2001). Understanding physicians: intentions to withdraw from practice: The role of job satisfaction, job stress, mental and physical health. *Advances in Health Care Management, 5*(2), 105–115.

Wittchen, H.-U., Jacobi, F., Rehm, J., Gustavsson, A., Svensson, M., Jönsson, B., et al. (2011). The size and burden of mental disorders and other disorders of the brain in Europe 2010. *European Neuropsychopharmacology: The Journal of the European College of Neuropsychopharmacology, 21*(9), 655–679.

World Federation of Mental Health. WFMH. (2017). Mental Health in the Workplace.

World Health Organization. WHO. (2004). Prevention of mental disorders: Effective interventions and policy options: Summary report.

World Health Organization. WHO. (2016). Investing in treatment for depression and anxiety leads to fourfold return. https://www.who.int/news/item/13-04-2016-investing-in-treatment-for-depression-and-anxiety-leads-to-fourfold-return

World Health Organization. WHO. (2017). Mental health in the workplace. https:// www.who.int/teams/mental-health-and-substance-use/promotion-prevention/ mental-health-in-the-workplace

World Health Organization. WHO. (2019). Report mental health in the workplace. https://www.who.int/teams/mental-health-and-substance-use/promotion-prevention/mental-health-in-the-workplace

World Health Organization. WHO. (2021). Depression. Retrieved September 2022, from https://www.who.int/en/news-room/fact-sheets/detail/depression/

Wykes, T., Haro, J. M., Belli, S. R., Obradors-Tarragó, C., Arango, C., et al. (2015). Mental health research priorities for Europe. *Lancet Psychiatry, 2*, 1036–1042.

Xiao, H., Carney, D. M., Youn, S. J., Janis, R. A., Castonguay, L. G., Hayes, J. A., & Locke, B. D. (2017). Are we in crisis? National mental health and treatment trends in college counseling centers. *Psychological Services, 14*(4), 407.

Yu, J., Ariza-Montes, A., Hernández-Perlines, F., Vega-Muñoz, A., & Han, H. (2020). Hotels' eco-friendly physical environment as nature-based solutions for decreasing burnout and increasing job satisfaction and performance. *International Journal of Environmental Research and Public Health, 17*(17), 6357.

Yunus, W. M. A. W. M., Musiat, P., & Brown, J. S. (2018). Systematic review of universal and targeted workplace interventions for depression. *Occupational and Environmental Medicine, 75*(1), 66–75.

Yusoff, M. S. (2014). Interventions on medical students' psychological health: A meta-analysis. *Journal of Taibah University Medical Sciences, 9*(1), 1–3.

Zachariae, R., Lyby, M. S., Ritterband, L., & O'Toole, M. S. (2015). Efficacy of Internet-delivered cognitive behavioral therapy for insomnia – A systematic review and meta-analysis of randomized controlled trials. *Sleep Medicine Reviews, 30*, 1–10.

Zvauya, R., Oyebode, F., Day, E. J., Thomas, C. P., & Jones, L. A. (2017). A comparison of stress levels, coping styles and psychological morbidity between graduate-entry and traditional undergraduate medical students during the first 2 years at a UK medical school. *BMC Research Notes, 10*(1), 93.

21

Stress Management

Bruno Guion de Meritens and Philippe Fauquet-Alekhine

1 Forms and Intensity of Stress

Stress refers not only to stress-induced effects (psychological discomfort) but also to the constraint itself: aggression, threats, dangerous situations or simple exit from the individual's comfort zone (a psychological state in which individuals perceive things and the environment to be under control and feel at ease; Brown, 2008). By extension, in common language, it may also designate the adaptive reaction that occurs to adapt oneself to these constraints (see Chaps. 2 and 3 of the present book).

Reactions to stress are immediately consecutive to the subject's perception of factors of stress (or stressors) and are universal: stress touches everyone but not with the same intensity depending on the psychological experience and state of each individual and also on the social context. It is adaptive and adaptable according to the degree of intensity and is also cumulative because the

---

B. G. de Meritens
Department of DPN/FARN, EDF, Saint Denis, France
e-mail: bruno.guion-de-meritens@edf.fr

P. Fauquet-Alekhine (✉)
SEBE-Lab, Department of Psychological and Behavioural Science,
London School of Economics and Political Science, London, UK

Laboratory for Research in Science of Energy, Montagret, France

Groupe INTRA Robotics, Avoine, France
e-mail: p.fauquet-alekhine@lse.ac.uk; philippe.fauquet-alekhine@groupe-intra.com

© The Author(s), under exclusive license to Springer Nature Switzerland AG 2023   **437**
P. Fauquet-Alekhine, J. Erskine (eds.), *The Palgrave Handbook of Occupational Stress*,
https://doi.org/10.1007/978-3-031-27349-0_21

stressors add up. Moreover, stress may be predictable by an individual who is trained since it is possible to forecast and anticipate the threats in certain circumstances. Stress is usually surmountable by an individual without psychological vulnerability (see Chap. 3 of the present book).

However, individuals learn from these situations in order to adapt to their environment, to be able to anticipate by generating their own defence mechanisms and to be able to develop avoidance strategies. Individuals can also innovate and create in order to manage or even dominate the situation.

The term acute stress was first used by US physicians caring soldiers back from Europe after the First World War. Musser (1920, p. 664), for example, who addressed neurocirculatory asthenia (somatoform disorder involving heart disease symptoms without any identifiable physiological abnormalities) explained that "many soldiers were sent to France who were of this type, but in whom the manifestations of disorder remained latent until they were put in position of acute stress." At the same period, Walter B. Cannon, an American physiologist, professor at Harvard Medical School, conceptualized the notion of "fight or flight" when studying animals (1933, p. 1030): "In wildlife, where the struggle for existence is unmitigated, the emotion of fear is associated with the instinct to flee, and the aggressive feeling of rage is associated with the instinct to attack. If there is an attack, the organism attacked must either fight back or run. If there is flight, there is likely to be pursuit. In either situation the organisms involved may be engaged in a life-or-death struggle." He popularized it in his book *Wisdom of the Body* (1932). Acute stress was then adopted to designate intense stress with limited duration experienced leading to the "fight or flight" response and associated to the first stage of a "General Adaptation Syndrome" as defined by Selye (1936) (see Chap. 2 of the present book). Acute stress is thus experienced in a crisis situation, and, more broadly, when tackling any punctual event disturbing the well-being or the objectives of an individual. This notion is to be contrasted with that of chronic stress, which refers to stress experiences that take place over a longer period of time in response to long-lasting stresses on the individual (see Chap. 3 of the present book).

In the case of crisis situations occurring in process management, the distinction should be made between the "usual" stressors, related to the peculiarities of the work (e.g. disturbance of sleep-wake cycles for shift teams, presence of hazards for chemical industries, isolation or "additional" stressors that are added when nuclear power plant operators encounter unexpected situations) and "additional" stressors that are added when operators encounter situations outside the ordinary. For individuals concerned by chronic stress, these stressors generate acute stress that cumulates with chronic stress, increasing the difficulty to cope with the situation. Indeed, chronic stress reduces the ability to cope with acute stress situations.

Hans Selye (1956) presented stress as a "General Adaptation Syndrome" (GAS), a set of biological reactions that allow the organism to cope with threatening factors by temporarily increasing the overall level of activation (arousal) and capacity of response of the organism, boosting the trigger of behaviours necessary to survive through increased mobilization of physiological and muscular effectors. He distinguished three stages of the stress response: the stage of alarm (to which the reaction to acute stress is associated), the stage of resistance and the stage of exhaustion. The latter appears when the stressors are too numerous, too intense or last too long and exceed the body's resistance threshold. It is characterized by a collapse of defences and the emergence of various psychological and somatic disorders. On the contrary, the first stage, the stage of alarm, corresponds to a general elevation of the level of activation, non-pathogenic if occasional. Stress might thus be considered as an adaptive mechanism of vigilance, allowing the organism to detect threats in its environment and prepare the response.

While occasional exposure to stressors may give rise to acute stress (short-term stress), repeated exposures to acute stress may lead to chronic stress (long-term stress). When increasing stressors intensity, acute stress may lead to posttraumatic stress disorder (PTSD), a psychological state characterized by the development of specific symptoms following exposure to a traumatic event such as serious accidents, physical or sexual assault, war or torture (www. nhs.uk).

Managing stress might help individuals to reduce the impact of acute stress, to lessen the perceived intensity of stressors (thus reducing the risk of PTSD) and also to reduce the impact of repeated exposure (thus reducing the risk of chronic stress). The present chapter aims at providing methods and tools for stress management.

2   From Acute Stress to Crisis Management

The Health and Safety Executive (HSE, 2018, p. 3) reported that the main causes of stress at work in the UK were workload pressure (including tight deadlines and too much responsibility) (44%); lack of managerial support (14%); violence, threats or bullying (13%); and changes at work (8%). These factors are stressors leading to both acute and chronic stress.

However, in the world of work, other circumstances may lead to situations designated as "crisis" that generate high levels of stress. "Crisis" is defined as "low-probability, high-impact event that threatens the viability of the organization and is characterized by ambiguity of cause, effect, and means of resolution, as well as by a belief that decisions must be made swiftly" (Pearson & Clair, 1998, p. 60). Crisis is the situation preceding a disaster and crisis management aims at avoiding disaster. Such a situation may relate to natural origin (epidemic, storm, flood, earthquake etc.) or be anthropogenic (financial bankruptcy, transport accidents, collapse of structures, chemical or nuclear accidents etc.) and may result in major damage sometimes with sustainable negative effects. They pose a threat to the people and the environment, but also to the organizations and individuals expected to manage the crisis. Crises are unpredictable with more or less rapid variable kinetics that are difficult to model but characterized by the unforeseen, the unknown, the loss of benchmarks and the overcoming of existing plans. They are also marked by urgency, which requires timely and relevant decisions and actions. Weisæth et al. (2002, p. 37) list the significant stressors of crisis management as follows: (i) a severe threat to important values such as human lives, finances, ecology, (ii) a complex combination of infrequent events, (iii) reduced control, (iv) high uncertainty, (v) lack of information and (vi) time pressure.

One of the links between acute stress and crisis management is that the former may lead to the latter due to inappropriate decision making or non-adaptive behaviour. In their recent review, Gok and Astan (2016) underlined that stress impacts mainly three stages: the gathering and judgement of information, the generation of options, the judgement and comparison of options decision making and behaviour. Therefore, when combined with other technical, organizational or sociocultural factors (case of the Chernobyl nuclear catastrophe in 1986, for instance), this may lead to a crisis situation for which the stress intensity will increase again. This can make the situation more difficult to manage as such a situation is also characterized by the inadequacy or overtaking of resources and procedures usually assigned to the resolution of identified and known incidents. Under high-intensity acute stress and, a fortiori, during crisis management, the level of stress may exceed a threshold that puts the individual in a cognitive deficit state (e.g. Yerkes & Dodson, 1908; Staal, 2004; Fauquet-Alekhine et al., 2011, 2014).

Confronted with destruction of the environment, the destabilization of the organization, the impairment of reasoning and the non-applicability of procedures, the actors must create and imagine solutions to cope and allow one to exit the crisis. This is basically a paradoxical context as acute stress impairs high level (imaginative) cognitive functions (see, e.g.: Arnsten, 2009). At the same time, the characteristics of the crisis situation usually become significant stressors for crisis managers (Weisæth et al., 2002). Moreover, exit from the crisis situation may be more difficult to achieve because the hostile or extreme environment can generate complexity, uncertainty and additional risks amplifying the constraints towards individuals' cognitive resources but also impairing or hindering communication and coordination.

To summarize, an excessive level of stress leading to a cognitive deficit state has negative impacts on individuals according to three dimensions:

- physiological dimension, for which observable symptoms may be an increased heart rate, difficult breathing, excessive sweating or muscular tensions
- psychological dimension:

    - psychoemotional level, for which observable symptoms may be worry or fear
    - psychocognitive level, for which observable symptoms may be a confused speech, loss of memory, reduced analytical capacity, loss of attention or excessive attentional focus

- behavioural dimension, for which observable symptoms may be agitation, uncoordinated movements, freezing, panic, aggressiveness or relational difficulties

The best way to avoid the cognitive deficit state is to reduce the level of stress, and thus, to reduce stressor intensity or to remove stressors. When this is not possible, stress management strategies, at an individual level, may be applied to one or more of the three aforementioned dimensions, in order to reduce the effect of the stressors. Doing so, these effects being part of the context of the stressful situation and determining in part the individual's characteristics in this context, reduces the effect of the stressors, changes the context and the individual's characteristics. Consequently, the perceived stress and its effects are lessened according to a process described by the two 3-D space model for short-term occupational stress (see Fig. 21.1; Fauquet-Alekhine, 2012).

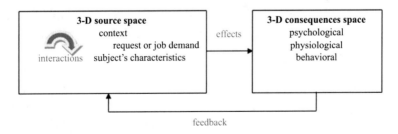

Fig. 21.1 The two 3-D space model for short-term occupational stress

The following presents, describes and discusses several stress management strategies that have been successfully applied or tested with athletes (Perraut-Pierre, 2000; Samulski et al., 2011), students (Steiler et al., 2011), physicians (Trousselard, 2016), firefighters (Obry, 2014; Trousselard et al., 2015), air force pilots (Saint-Aubin, 2009; Trousselard et al., 2009), submariners (Crosnier, 2013) and nuclear industry operators. For crisis management, this may be of great importance by helping the leader to manage stress and keep it at the appropriate level. Doing so, the leader will be able to provide a course to follow during the crisis: studies have shown that the leader is able to federate the 70% of people in such a context provided that s/he is able to give the way forward, that is, to guide people by what s/he recommends or asks.

Other strategies or techniques may be found on the web or in the literature. However, the following were chosen because they have demonstrated utility in reducing mental stress and because they are applicable at work without additional equipment or coaching: they are applicable in the moment they are needed, even though few of them need a short training beforehand in order to develop what will be mentally summoned in situations.

3 Stress Management Strategies

3.1 Emotion Regulation

Emotion regulation is a psychological process by which individuals influence, experience and express their emotions. The process may be conscious (for instance, beating the table with a pen when impatient) or unconscious (e.g. shifting attention from an unattractive gift). Emotion regulation may occur before activation of the emotion (e.g. envisaging the PhD viva voce as an opportunity to share with professors rather than as a trial): this is an antecedent-focused strategy. Or it may occur when emotion is activated (e.g. keeping one's anxiety from showing during the PhD exam): it is a response-focused strategy.

Gross (2002) suggests two kinds of voluntary emotional regulation strategies the effectiveness of which have been confirmed recently (Kelley et al., 2019):

- Re-appraisal strategy is antecedent focused: it intervenes early in the process of emotion generation, at the time when the events are interpreted (or re-interpreted in a cyclical process). The situation is voluntarily tailored in order to reduce its emotional impact. This strategy takes place in anticipation of the emotional response and contributes to regulate negative emotional reactions. For this aim, the individual must foresee the potential negative impact of a situation and reconsider this situation before experiencing it.

- Suppression strategy intervenes late, once the emotional response is activated, a response-focused strategy. It consists in inhibiting the outward signs of the emotion felt. It may be an appropriate solution when the potential negative impact of a situation could not be foreseen.

Re-appraisal strategy offers the advantage of not requiring constant supervision. Therefore, it is lower resource-consuming in the long term than suppression strategy.

3.2 Stimulating Breathing

Breathing is our first source of energy, so it is necessary to train regularly to a method that allows one to quickly mobilize this energy to get away from different physical or psychological tensions and to master the reality of a situation.

Stimulating breathing (or boosting breathing or energizing exhalation) implements the three stages of complete (or controlled) respiration: abdominal belt, chest belt and scapular belt.

Stimulating breathing is a way to mobilize in order to energize and quickly enter the action. It consists in energizing oneself by performing a series of deep inspirations ending with apnoeas through the nose, making sure that the duration of the inspiration is three to five times longer than the duration of the expiration through the mouth. A good exercise is to repeat this energizing cycle three times, making sure to inhale for over 6 seconds and to expire violently for 2 seconds.

During this exercise, one should focus on the flow of air entering the nostrils and then blow through the mouth, releasing all the air contained in the lungs. At the same time it is possible to use a positive mental image to further increase the effects of respiration and using a positive and energizing internal dialogue.

This stimulating breathing takes on the principle of complete respiration: inspiration with belly, lungs and shoulders through the nose—suspension (apnoea)—expiration with shoulders, lungs, belly through the mouth.

Inspiration (about 4 seconds): one must inspire through the nose, filling the lungs and relaxing the belly which rises, proving that the inspiration is complete.

Apnoea (about 2 seconds): one must realize full lungs apnoea. During this apnoea, the fists are clenched and the arms are stretched downward, and it is necessary to make movements more or less rapid by climbing and descending the shoulders without breathing.

Expiration (about 2 seconds): one must expire strongly through the mouth and open hands.

After a short recovery time, it is necessary to redo the exercise three times.

The body is soothed and tensions loosen to release vital energy and let emotions and thoughts pass through.

This stimulation breathing is not like "Sudarshan Kriya Yogic Breathing," which requires an inspiration/expiration every 2 seconds. According to the study of Brown and Gerbarg (2005, p. 713), persons "who tend to hyperventilate may become fearful during the rapid-cycle breathing of Sudarshan Kriya or Bhastrika because it may remind them of hyperventilation. This fear can trigger a panic attack." Instead of 30 ventilations per minute, the stimulation breathing proposed here suggests about seven ventilations per minute (see also Brown & Gerbarg, 2012).

3.3 Relaxing Breathing or Diaphragmatic Breathing

Diaphragmatic breathing is distinguished during breathing by movements of the abdomen instead of those of the chest. This voluntary slow deep breathing results in physiologic effects that contribute to relaxation, thus lessening stress effects: decreased oxygen consumption, decreased heart rate, decreased blood pressure and increased parasympathetic activity (Jerath et al., 2006; Varvogli & Darviri, 2011).

To begin with, inhale by inflating the belly.

Then exhale slowly through the mouth as if to push a deep long and ample sigh. The longer is the expiration, better is the relaxation.

In a second step, pay attention to the following three points: the chin (to relax the whole face), the shoulders (to release the neck, arms, trunk and back) and the abdomen (to help loosening the belly).

In a third time, inhale slowly, then expire as if to blow in a thin pipe, releasing the chin, shoulders and abdomen.

The expiration time can be three times longer than the inspiration time.

The beneficial effect of this breathing can be increased by the combination of positive mental images and relaxing thoughts.

3.4 Square Breathing

Square respiration is a breathing technique that allows an individual subjected to acute stress to stabilize in less than a minute through the control of the respiratory rhythm, slowing down the heart rhythm while mastering the emotional state that puts the individual out of the comfort zone.

However, in order to be able to achieve this during critical situations, it requires daily practice and repetitions in different atmospheres and environments to guarantee its success.

The virtues of the square breathing are multiple. Thanks to the voluntary control exercised over breathing, it is possible to regulate emotions and restore well-being. Breathing has a powerful action on the brain: the square respiration improves the blood oxygenation as well as the reflexes of the vegetative nervous system (involuntary). This exercise also helps to learn how to better mobilize the respiratory muscles, especially the diaphragm (see Sect. 3.3).

Square breathing (Gosling & Gosling, 2012) is a simple, natural and "easy to perform" practice. It just requires one getting to relax and focus on breathing. It takes only a few minutes to feel its benefits and to improve physiological, physical and emotional balance. Square breathing, like many breathing strategies, helps us to relax effectively while becoming aware of the respiratory needs of the body.

The square breathing exercise is performed in four phases of equal length (with a duration of 4, 6 or 8 seconds): inspiration, retention (apnoea, full lungs), expiration, retention (empty lungs). This combination is to be performed several times, until recovering a state of inner calm, well-being and appeasement. Breathing is done only through the nose. Although a quiet place is ideal, all places are good to breathe consciously: at home, in public transport, in the gym, in a queue, with friends, at work.

The duration of the four phases is to be determined according to one's desires and one's feelings. To determine the ideal rhythm, tests before bedtime are useful. The duration of 4 seconds is often recommended because it corresponds to the vast majority of people and ensures an excellent result. However, it is possible to adapt this figure according to the desires. It must be bore in mind that ease must be sought rather than performance. It is not necessarily to seek lengthening the phases. The square breathing exercise with 4-second phases is very effective.

Example: 4 seconds of inspiration + 4 seconds of apnoea + 4 seconds of expiration + 4 seconds of retention.

The number of repetitions also depends on the individual's appreciation. It is suggested to carry out this exercise three times a day to improve efficiency. It will be more effective.

The use of a positive mental image during the breathing exercise increases the benefits of square breathing.

3.5 Progressive Muscle Relaxation

This strategy was elaborated in the early twentieth century (Jacobson, 1938): it was found that alternately tensing and relaxing muscles had a positive effect on anxiety and stress. Despite the fact that it involves a priori a physical technique, it also has a psychological dimension.

Varvogli and Darviri (2011, p. 75) explain that "the physical component involves the tensing and relaxing of muscle groups over the legs, abdomen, chest, arms and face. In a sequential pattern, with eyes closed, the individual places a tension in a given muscle group purposefully for approximately 10 seconds and then releases it for 20 seconds before continuing with the next muscle group. The mental component requires that the individual focuses on the distinction between the feelings of the tension and relaxation. With practice, the patient learns how to effectively relax in a short period of time." This may be done for about 10 minutes, if possible comfortably lying down, two or three times a day.

By mentally focusing on muscles tensing and relaxing, concentration is improved and this may be put to good use blocking negative thoughts and one's inner speech if negative too. Moreover, as it relaxes breathing, this contributes to a lessening of stress effects: decreased oxygen consumption, decreased heart rate, decreased blood pressure and increased parasympathetic activity (Varvogli & Darviri, 2011). It was also found to have an effect on chronic stress by reducing the level of cortisol (Pawlow & Jones, 2002).

3.6 Internal Dialogue or Self-talk

> Also referred to as *verbal thinking, inner speaking, covert self-talk, internal monologue, and internal dialogue*, inner speech has been proposed to have an important role in the self-regulation of cognition and behavior in both childhood and adulthood. (Alderson-Day & Fernyhough, 2015, p. 931)

Internal dialogue allows us to have positive control, to interpret our own reactions and to analyse our feelings. For stress management, it is mainly used to give instructions and build positive reinforcements.

The benefits generated by this strategy are the development of self-esteem and self-confidence.

It is essential to use positive phrases, positive words, valorizing and reinforcing words. This allows both returning to the known "you've already done it, you know how to do it" and placing oneself in a perspective, even in a logic of success.

This internal dialogue also promotes attention and makes it possible to focus on the immediate actions that need to be carried out. So, it helps to reduce anxiety and reduce the probability of reaching a level of stress that may exceed a threshold that puts the individual in a cognitive deficit state.

To do so, it may be sometimes necessary to stop negative thoughts. A technique named "verbal stop" can help to end negative thoughts, to chase them away and replace them with positive ideas. It consists in deciding and forcing oneself to use sentences like "I do," "I want" instead of "I'll try" or "I can't." Another method is to apply progressive muscle relaxation (see Sect. 3.5).

During internal dialogue, the use of "I" or "you" may have a significant impact. Kross et al. (2014) showed that using non-first-person pronouns and one's own name (rather than first-person pronouns) during internal dialogue helps "to appraise future stressors in more challenging and less threatening terms" (p. 304), reduce stress and increase performance, and this is independent of personality traits.

The use of this internal dialogue combined with mental imagery contributes to further strengthening the effectiveness of respiration.

3.7 Mental Rehearsal

Mental rehearsal (or mental repetition) refers to "the cognitive rehearsal of a task in the absence of overt physical movement" (Driskell et al., 1994, p. 481).

It is the interiorized repetition of a motor pattern, on the concomitant production of the muscular activity normally required for the execution of these motor patterns. At work, for example, mental repetition is when an individual visualizes the steps of a complex movement of an action to be performed. Several authors have shown its positive impact on job performance and stress (e.g. Driskell et al., 1994; Arora et al., 2011). However, sometimes, even though performance was improved, stress was not impacted (Ignacio et al., 2016).

The practice therefore requires a scheme of actions to come (the ones that we are about to achieve after repeating it mentally) and therefore implies a minimum of knowledge about these actions (for instance, having already watched it or performed it).

For this strategy to work, it is also necessary that the occurrence of the stress is intimately linked to this scheme of actions rather than to a context, or that the context of stress is intimately linked to the scheme of actions (e.g.: the surgeon may reduce acute stress related to a surgical act by mental rehearsal before entering the operating theatre of what s/he is about to do).

It is thus a strategy of mental dynamization and immediate anticipation, practising a situation just before action.

3.8 Reflex Adjustment Signal-Sign

The reflex adjustment signal-sign was developed in sophrology and is part of the techniques for optimizing potential (Perreaut-Pierre, 2019). Reflex adjustment signal-sign is a kind of relaxation response technique focused on a single signal. It is a resource that allows the person to instantly regain the necessary means to act (necessary state of activation) in the moment. It is a technique of conditioning based on the Pavlovian-type reflex through a psychological process anchoring unconsciously an internal reaction to an external stimulus: the signal-sign positively recalls a feeling of calm, concentration, confidence, energy recovery, pleasure or security, for instance. Usually, the signal-sign is attached to only one feeling. Most often, people have only one reflex adjustment signal-sign but it is possible to have two provided that they are different; for example, one sign to energize and be put in a logic of success and victory; the second sign to relax, to calm down or to moderate.

The reflex adjustment signal-sign aimed at being used in public, must be chosen to be as discreet as possible. Especially, it must be chosen so that this cannot be interpreted by others who could use it with the aim of destabilization. The reflex adjustment signal-sign may be quite common: clenching the fist to control anger, sighing long to relieve stress. It is usually a gesture, a sign, a movement of the fingers or of the hand (tighten the fist, rub the thumb on the forefinger, a sigh). This can also be a short internal dialogue: an injunction such as "go ahead" or "calm down." And it can also be a gesture associated with such an injunction. Conversely, it should not be associated with a fetish object in order to avoid the link to an object whose loss would disrupt the recall process or even create a situation of failure or defeat or prevent one from acting. To be efficient, the signal-sign must be repeated often (several times a day) and every time the related chosen feeling is perceived: this is the reactivation process. To make the feeling of anchoring the gesture easier, it is possible to associate the recall of positive images of success or relaxing images. This sort of training is a necessity in order to be able to activate the reflex adjustment signal-sign as soon as the situation makes it necessary or indispensable.

3.9 Power Nap and Caffeine Nap

The correct psychological balance of an individual is also based on the appropriate management of sleep-wake rhythms. Sleep deprivation has become a health hazard promoted by modern cultures although many studies have demonstrated its negative effects, including one's ability decrease to cope with stress; however, many companies have now introduced workplace napping (Autumn et al., 2016). In daily life at work and a fortiori to deal correctly with situations of acute stress, it is interesting to be able to take a rest to restore the capacities of vigilance, attention and concentration. Doing so, the vulnerability to stress is lessened. Studies have shown that taking such daily naps neither reduces the quantity nor affects the quality of nighttime sleep (Pilcher et al., 2001).

The power nap (or micro-nap, refreshing nap, flash nap) is a short nap. It lasts about 5–20 minutes depending on the subjects. It is preferably taken in a seated position.

This nap has the effect of causing a transient restoration of mental and physical performance for a duration of about 1–2 hours. Effective for a driver or operator, it allows performance to be maintained in situations of sleep deprivation or crisis situations (Pilcher et al., 2001).

However, to be able to take the power nap properly, one must train in a chair in order to be sure that it can be achieved in a seated position, in a stressful environment without comfort and for a limited time. Salvador Dali always practised it, holding a small spoon in his hand: when he sank into deep sleep, this spoon fell and the noise of the falling object woke him. Limiting the nap duration avoids falling into a deep sleep and waking up experiencing negative effects such as sleep inertia, drowsiness or disorientation (Tassi & Muzet, 2000).

This micro-nap can be valorized by the use of caffeine to restore the performance of an individual for a much longer duration. In this case it is a matter of cumulating the effects of a power nap with the bioavailability (30–40 minutes after taking) of the caffeine in the organism (Reyner & Horne, 1997; Hayashi et al., 2003): a 20-minute power nap reduces the level of adenosine in the organism, a neuromodulator promoting sleep and suppressing arousal; thus, when achieving such a power nap, the level of adenosine is lessened (tiredness tends to disappear) and the effect of caffeine begins. This is another argument for limiting the duration of the power nap.

A good practice is to have coffee at the beginning of the lunch meal and then settle down after the meal to take a nap (Hayashi et al., 2003). At the time of awakening, one takes benefit from the release of the caffeine in the organism and the benefits provided by the rest. In this case it is possible to restore increased vigilance capabilities and to hold attention more easily all afternoon or perform an operation requiring vigilance at the end of the night, for example, especially during the 02:00–5:00 AM slot where it is the hardest to keep awake.

3.10 Effect of Light

Light plays three essential roles for our well-being because it influences our organism: blocking the secretion of melatonin, regulating the biological clock to facilitate the synchronization of biological rhythms (XU & Lang, 2018) and has an impact on serotonin that has an antidepressant effect (Neumeister et al., 1995; Puglisi-Allegra & Andolina, 2015).

Hadi et al.'s review (2019) concluded: "Short-term bright light exposure in the morning, up to 2 hr of moderate (3 000–10,000 lux) morning exposures, up to 4 hr of moderate evening exposure, and whole-day exposures to lower illuminance levels (<3000 lux) can improve patient sleep outcomes" (p. 1). It is therefore advisable to use the 10,000 lux phototherapy to re-match the circadian rhythms altered by the working conditions in staged hours or due to sleep deprivation. Light therapy may be used in particular for persons subject to night work before taking office or in a phase advance at about 17 hours. It is also profitable for all those who are subject to a permanent low brightness in a work area.

However, Xu and Lang (2018), in their review, emphasized the role of spectral wavelength of the light: if blue light of low irradiance increases alertness levels at night, moderate bright white light is more suitable to reduce sleepiness during the daytime.

4 Conclusion

This chapter has suggested several strategies that are easy to implement in order to manage stress. Even though some of them require a little practice to be effective, none of them need to attend training sessions and thus may be quickly implemented at the workplace. The fact that they are used by high-risk professions such as firemen or soldiers is a proof that they are worth using when one experiences a difficult stressful episode. These strategies being quite different from each other, it is advisable not to be discouraged if a first test is inconclusive and to move to another.

Furthermore, for information, it is worth mentioning other strategies requiring a coach or special training: Mental preparation (Tilman et al., 2011; Samulski et al., 2011), Mindfulness-Based Stress Reduction (Varvogli & Darviri, 2011; Sharma & Rush, 2014), Guided imagery (Joe, 2006; Varvogli & Darviri, 2011), Resilience training (see Chap. 13 of the present book).

References

Alderson-Day, B., & Fernyhough, C. (2015). Inner speech: Development, cognitive functions, phenomenology, and neurobiology. *Psychological Bulletin, 141*(5), 931–965.

Arnsten, A. F. (2009). Stress signalling pathways that impair prefrontal cortex structure and function. *Nature Reviews Neuroscience, 10*(6), 410–423.

Arora, S., Aggarwal, R., Moran, A., Sirimanna, P., Crochet, P., Darzi, A., Kneebone, R., & Sevdalis, N. (2011). Mental practice: Effective stress management training for novice surgeons. *Journal of the American College of Surgeons, 212*(2), 225–233.

Autumn, M., Monica, H., Jitendra, M., & Bharat, M. (2016). The perfect nap. *Advances in Management, 9*(4), 1–9.

Brown, M. (2008). Comfort zone: Model or metaphor? *Journal of Outdoor and Environmental Education, 12*(1), 3–12.

Brown, R., & Gerberg, P. (2012). *The healing power of the breath: Simple techniques to reduce stress and anxiety, enhance concentration, and balance your emotions*. Shambhala Publications.

Brown, R. P., & Gerberg, P. L. (2005). Sudarshan Kriya Yogic breathing in the treatment of stress, anxiety, and depression: Part II—clinical applications and guidelines. *Journal of Alternative & Complementary Medicine, 11*(4), 711–717.

Cannon, W. (1932). *Wisdom of the Body*. W.W. Norton & Company.

Cannon, W. (1933). The functional organization of the involuntary nervous system and its humoral mediators. *Annals of Internal Medicine, 6*(8), 1022–1032.

Crosnier, S. (2013). Evaluation du sommeil des sous-mariniers en situation opérationnelle sur Sous-marins Nucléaires lanceurs d'Engins: Intérêt des Techniques d'optimisation du Potentiel (TOP) (Evaluation of the submariners' sleep during a patrol: interests of the TOP program). PhD thesis, University of Medicine of Brest, France.

Driskell, J. E., Copper, C., & Moran, A. (1994). Does mental practice enhance performance? *Journal of Applied Psychology, 79*, 481–492.

Fauquet-Alekhine, P. (2012). Causes and consequences: Two dimensional spaces to fully describe short term occupational stress. *Socio-Organizational Factors for Safe Nuclear Operation, 1*, 45–52. http://hayka-kultura.org/larsen.html

Fauquet-Alekhine, Ph., Frémaux, L., & Geeraerts, Th. (2011). Cognitive disorder and professional development by training: Comparison of simulator sessions for anaesthetists and for nuclear reactor pilots. In *Proceedings of the the XVe European conference on Developmental Psychology* (pp. 83–87). Medimond Srl.

Fauquet-Alekhine, P., Geeraerts, T., & Rouillac, L. (2014). Characterization of anesthetists' behavior during simulation training: Performance versus stress achieving medical tasks with or without physical effort. *Psychology and Social Behavior Research, 2*(2), 20–28.

Gok, K., & Astan, N. (2016). Decision-making under stress and its implications for managerial decision-making: A review of literature. *International Journal of Business and Social Research, 6*(3), 38–47.

Gosling, M., & Gosling, K. (2012). *How to reduce your stress and achieve wellness.* Gosling International.

Gross, J. J. (2002). Emotion regulation: Affective, cognitive, and social consequences. *Psychophysiology, 39*(3), 281–291.

Hadi, K., Du Bose, J. R., & Choi, Y.-S. (2019). The effect of light on sleep and sleep-related physiological factors among patients in healthcare facilities: A systematic review. *HERD: Health Environments Research & Design Journal*, 1–26.

Hayashi, M., Masuda, A., & Hori, T. (2003). The alerting effects of caffeine, bright light and face washing after a short daytime nap. *Clinical Neurophysiology, 114*(12), 2268–2278.

HSE. (2018). *Work related stress depression or anxiety statistics in Great Britain.* Health and Safety Executive. http://www.hse.gov.uk

Ignacio, J., Dolmans, D., Scherpbier, A., Rethans, J. J., Lopez, V., & Liaw, S. Y. (2016). Development, implementation, and evaluation of a mental rehearsal strategy to improve clinical performance and reduce stress: A mixed methods study. *Nurse education today, 37*, 27–32.

Jacobson, E. (1938). *Progressive relaxation.* University of Chicago Press.

Jerath, R., Edry, J. W., Barnes, V. A., & Jerath, V. (2006). Physiology of long pranayamic breathing: Neural respiratory elements may provide a mechanism that explains how slow deep breathing shifts the autonomic nervous system. *Medical Hypotheses, 67*(3), 566–571.

Joe, U. (2006). Guided imagery as an effective therapeutic technique: A brief review of its history and efficacy research. *Journal of Instructional Psychology, 33*(1), 40–43.

Kelley, N. J., Glazer, J. E., Pornpattananangkul, N., & Nusslock, R. (2019). Reappraisal and suppression emotion-regulation tendencies differentially predict reward-responsivity and psychological well-being. *Biological Psychology, 140*, 35–47.

Kross, E., Bruehlman-Senecal, E., Park, J., Burson, A., Dougherty, A., Shablack, H., Bremner, R., Moser, J., & Ayduk, O. (2014). Self-talk as a regulatory mechanism: How you do it matters. *Journal of Personality and Social Psychology, 106*(2), 304–324.

Musser, J. H. (1920). Notes on gastric secretions in Neurocirculatory Asthenia. *American Journal of Medical Sciences, 159*(5), 664–668.

Neumeister, A., Rieder, N., Hesselmann, B., & Kasper, S. (1995). Short-term availability of brain serotonin is crucial for antidepressant effect of light therapy. *European Neuropsychopharmacology, 3*(5), 269.

Obry, R. (2014). *Programme de gestion du stress chez les pompiers: un essai contrôlé randomisé.* Doctoral dissertation, Paris Est University (France).

Pawlow, L. A., & Jones, G. E. (2002). The impact of abbreviated progressive muscle relaxation on salivary cortisol. *Biological Psychology, 60*(1), 1–16.

Pearson, C., & Clair, J. A. (1998). Reframing crisis management. *Academy of Management Review, 23*(1), 59–76.

Perraut-Pierre E. (2000). *La gestion mentale du stress pour la performance sportive* (mental stress management for performance in sport). Amphora.

Perreaut-Pierre, E. (2019). *Comprendre et pratiquer les Techniques d'Optimisation du Potentiel* (3rd ed.). InterEditions.

Pilcher, J. J., Michalowski, K. R., & Carrigan, R. D. (2001). The prevalence of daytime napping and its relationship to nighttime sleep. *Behavioral Medicine, 27*(2), 71–76.

Puglisi-Allegra, S., & Andolina, D. (2015). Serotonin and stress coping. *Behavioural Brain Research, 277*, 58–67.

Reyner, L. A., & Horne, J. A. (1997). Suppression of sleepiness in drivers: Combination of caffeine with a short nap. *Psychophysiology, 34*(6), 721–725.

Saint-Aubin, K. F. (2009). *Impact of positive emotions enhancement on physiological processes and psychological functioning in military pilots.* Report reference RTO-MP-HFM-181, CERPAIR Bretigny sur Orge (France).

Samulski, D. M., Noce, F., & Costa, V. T. (2011). Mental preparation. In Y. C. Vanlandewijck & W. R. Thompson (Eds.), *Handbook of sports medicine and science–The paralympic athlete* (pp. 198–213). Blackwell Publishing.

Selye, H. (1936). A syndrome produced by diverse nocuous agents. *Nature, 138*, 32.

Selye, H. (1956). *The stress of life.* McGraw Hill.

Sharma, M., & Rush, S. E. (2014). Mindfulness-based stress reduction as a stress management intervention for healthy individuals: A systematic review. *Journal of Evidence-Based Complementary & Alternative Medicine, 19*(4), 271–286.

Staal, M. (2004). Stress, cognition, and human performance: A literature review and conceptual framework. NASA report, reference: NASA/TM-2004-212824.

Steiler, D., Denis, J., & Trousselard, M. (2011). Developing positive emotions for the improvement of first year students' well-being. In *Proceedings of the International Congress of Positive Psychology*, Philadelphia, USA.

Tassi, P., & Muzet, A. (2000). Sleep inertia. *Sleep Medicine Reviews, 4*(4), 341–353.

Tilman, T. S., Ravizza, K., & Statler, T. (2011). Clear your mind to clear the way: Mental preparation. *Army Engineer, 41*(3), 32–35.

Trousselard, M. (2016). Performance, vigilance et concentration: quoi de neuf pour leur optimisation dans l'exercice de la chirurgie? Conference at the *91ᵉ réunion annuelle de la Société Française de Chirurgie Orthopédique et Traumatologique*, Bordeaux, France. https://www.sauramps-medical.com/wp-content/uploads/2016/11/nicolas-andry-fac-simile.pdf

Trousselard, M., Dutheil, F., et al. (2015). Stress management programs in Paris' firefighters: A randomized controlled trial. *Medical Acupuncture, 27*(5), 367–375.

Trousselard, M., Perraut, E., & Saint-Aubin, K. (2009) Impact of positive emotions enhancement on physiological processes and psychological functioning in military pilots. Human performance enhancement for NATO military operations (sciences, technology, and ethics). *Human factors & medicine panel symposium (HFM-181)*, Sofia, 05-08/10.

Varvogli, L., & Darviri, C. (2011). Stress management techniques: Evidence-based procedures that reduce stress and promote health. *Health Science Journal, 5*(2), 74–89.

Weisæth, L., Knudsen, Ø., Jr., & Tønnessen, A. (2002). Technological disasters, crisis management and leadership stress. *Journal of Hazardous Materials, 93*(1), 33–45.

Xu, Q., & Lang, C. P. (2018). Revisiting the alerting effect of light: A systematic review. *Sleep Medicine Reviews, 41*, 39–49.

Yerkes, R. M., & Dodson, J. D. (1908). The relation of strength of stimulus to rapidity of habit-formation. *Journal of Comparative Neurology and Psychology, 18*, 459–482.

22

Stress and Resilience in the Workplace

James Erskine and George Georgiou

1 Introduction

In the twenty-first century, work-based well-being interventions have become popular as employers realise that optimising the well-being and health of their workforce has direct and measurable benefits for both individual employees and organisations (Batt, 2009; Donaldson-Feilder & Bond, 2004; Piao & Managi, 2022; Tsai & Morissette, 2022).

Furthermore, employer legislation in many industrialised economies has made workforce health and well-being a mandatory compliance issue (MacKay et al., 2004; Schulte et al., 2015). Importantly, there is evidence that 92% of employers with over 200 workers believe workplace well-being interventions should be offered (Mattke et al., 2013). As a result, employers have implemented a range of interventions designed to enhance staff well-being. These interventions have targeted a range of possible outcomes but chief among these have been programmes designed to reduce employee stress and to

---

J. Erskine (✉)
Institute for Medical and Biomedical Sciences, St George's University of London, London, UK
e-mail: jerskine@sgu.ac.uk

G. Georgiou
University of Hertfordshire, Hatfield, UK
e-mail: g.j.georgiou@herts.ac.uk

© The Author(s), under exclusive license to Springer Nature Switzerland AG 2023
P. Fauquet-Alekhine, J. Erskine (eds.), *The Palgrave Handbook of Occupational Stress*,
https://doi.org/10.1007/978-3-031-27349-0_22

promote well-being in both physical and mental health. Modern interventions have witnessed a growth of interest in the concept of resilience and currently many organisations specifically aim to increase this characteristic in their workforce.

At the outset, the definition of stress will be examined, and then the definition of resilience. Research on well-being/resilience interventions in a work context will be reviewed and their effectiveness will be discussed. Finally, practical advice will be suggested.

2 Defining Stress

Widely accepted definitions of stress conceptualise it as occurring when an individual appraises a situation as a threat to things they value, while also believing they do not have the resources to meet these situational demands. Therefore, limiting their ability to cope. This in turn reduces their psychological and physical well-being (Frenchet al., 1982; Harms et al., 2017; Lazarus & Folkman, 1984; also see Chaps. 2, 3, 10 and 11 of the present book).

While no one is a stranger to the concept of stress it is worth reiterating that the effects of stress are not always negative. Thus, original conceptions of stress indicated that mild-to-moderate levels are motivating and encourage a person to work harder. This positive motivational aspect of stress has been defined as eustress (Gibbons et al., 2008; Hargrove et al., 2015; Kupriyanov & Zhdanov, 2014; Selye, 1936). However, the extent to which mild-to-moderate stress may be positive will differ across individuals and contexts. Given the resource-based definition of stress, once one's personal resources to deal with stress are perceived to have been reached or overstretched the individual becomes unable to cope and further stress is seen as detrimental to their well-being and health (Harms et al., 2017; Lazarus & Folkman, 1984).

Adverse events requiring individuals to adapt are common; thus, research shows that the average person at least in a Western world context has experienced one major potentially traumatic event in their lifetime (Bonanno et al., 2005; Karam et al., 2014). Examples of these traumatic events would include, losing ones' job, being born into poverty, experiencing war, abusive parents, divorce, death of friends and family, crime, bullying and harassment. Therefore, it is very unlikely an individual will escape major life stress across the lifespan. It is imperative for research to investigate ways to cope more effectively with adverse events and stress. One concept that helps individuals deal with stress concerns resilience, which is examined below.

3 What Is Resilience?

Resilience is the term used to denote one characteristic which may help people deal with adverse circumstances. Resilience has been discussed in various forms for millennia, yet concerted efforts to systematically study resilience as a discrete phenomenon only began in the twentieth century. But how does one define resilience? The word itself originates from a Latin word "resilire" meaning to leap back or rebound. The online *Oxford Dictionary* (2017) suggests that resilience can be defined as "[t]he capacity to recover quickly from difficulties; toughness" or "[t]he ability of a substance or object to spring back into shape." Important in this definition is the idea that resilience is a capacity that is not required under normal circumstances but comes into its own when faced with adversity or load.

Modern psychological definitions echo these basic ideas, and thus reliance is seen in individuals that mange to sustain normal development or functioning despite ongoing adversity or difficulties (Denckla et al., 2020; Friborg et al., 2003; Garmezy, 1981; Kalisch et al., 2017; Rutter, 1985; Tusaie & Dyer, 2004; Windle, 2011). However, some have suggested that resilience should be conceptualised more broadly as a general protective measure supporting individuals to learn and grow through challenges (Youssef & Luthans, 2007).

Some have suggested resilience is seen in very specific patterns of functioning following exposure to trauma; thus, Bonnano and colleagues have argued resilience is best represented by a stable response to trauma that demonstrates consistent healthy functioning (Bonanno, 2004; Bonanno et al., 2011). From this perspective, the individual can show a degree of destabilisation during the trauma and immediate aftermath; however, they also continue to function adequately. The important point to note is that the work of Bonanno and colleagues has consistently demonstrated that the common trajectory of resilience over time is relatively flat and is often the most frequently seen even after exposure to extreme trauma (Bonanno, 2004; Bonanno et al., 2010; Bonanno et al., 2015). This indicates that one must not underestimate the basic human capacity to continue to function through adversity. However, most of the research is based on reactions to a single traumatic event, whereas real world circumstances may not always follow this pattern, with multiple stressful life events sometimes occurring simultaneously. It is also important to note Bonanno's view is that resilience could result from multiple sources and is not unidimensional, and therefore resilient individuals cannot be described as a homogeneous group (Southwick et al., 2014).

One major debate within the literature concerns whether resilience is a quality that is inherent in certain individuals like a trait, or a process (Lepore & Revenson, 2006). While resilience has been viewed by some as a relatively stable trait (Silk et al., 2007) this requires a cautious approach as some have suggested that it implies a person that does not have this attribute may be viewed negatively (Windle, 2011). There is some debate regarding the generalisability of resilience across life domains. For example, Tusaie and Dyer (2004) suggest that while individuals may demonstrate resilience in certain life domains, they may not demonstrate it in others. An example of this may be where a person comes from a poverty-stricken war zone, yet is able to overcome these setbacks and do well in education and have a career they enjoy; however, they may still show difficulties in other life domains such as close relationships. What is clear is that resilience varies across the life span and is certainly not uniform in its distribution across different life domains, which would indicate that resilience in not generalised. Modern views of resilience show that it is a highly interactive phenomenon that varies depending on the following factors: (1) internal to the individual (both psychological and biological); (2) the immediate external environment (and subject to fluctuations); (3) background culture and nation. Therefore, the level of resilience an individual displays will depend on numerous interactions between the person and their environment across a time course and must be seen as a dynamic and temporally adaptive process (Egeland et al., 1993; Hunter, 2001; Kalisch et al., 2019; Rutter, 1985).

3.1 Risk/Protective Factors

Most definitions of resilience include reference to the concept of risk factors, which will now be examined. Resilience is traditionally seen to be needed under conditions of adversity and is demonstrated by successful engagement with adversity. This suggests adversity conveys increased risk of destabilisation to the individual. Risk factors increase the likelihood of future destabilisation, which include situational factors such as being born into poverty, experiencing childhood abuse, divorce, death of a close relative, homelessness and job loss, among many others. Furthermore, risk factors can be either discrete acute events or ongoing chronic events (Garmezy, 1991). Importantly, research has indicated that the effects of high levels of uncontrollable ongoing adversity without sufficient support can have detrimental biological effects on the body and central nervous system, resulting in future disease and behavioural disruption (Shonkoff et al., 2009).

In contrast to risk factors there are also protective factors that function to ameliorate risk which can be internal or external to the individual. Protective factors seem to operate at three basic levels which are commonly defined in the literature as (1) individual—factors such as psychological and biological makeup within the individual; (2) social—factors such as having a supportive family or network of friends and high levels of parental support; (3) community—these operate at the wider societal level and would encompass factors such as living in a region with good social security systems and general economic well-being (Windle, 2011).

Common examples of internal and external protective factors could be greater socio-economic status, the presence of multiple supportive personal relationships and having particular levels of specific personality traits, for example, low neuroticism. Regarding personality, a meta-analysis investigated the "big five" personality traits across 30 studies based on a total sample of 15,609 individuals and reported that resilience correlates significantly and negatively with neuroticism, and positively and significantly with extraversion, openness, agreeableness and conscientiousness—all correlations were above 0.30 and therefore moderate. Thus, more resilient individuals are agreeable, conscientious, high in openness and extravert, while simultaneously low on neuroticism (Oshio et al., 2018). Further to this, studies have demonstrated a significant positive relationship between resilience and self-esteem (Liu et al., 2014).

What is clear is that there is a complex set of relationships within and between risk and protective factors and therefore they should not be considered separately as the dynamic interaction of these factors will influence the overall level of functioning in the face of adversity. Psychology is only just beginning to understand the complex web of interactive factors that impinge upon the individual to convey their ultimate risk or whether they are classified as displaying resilience or not. Therefore, at present, understanding is in its infancy.

3.2   Review of Resilience Research

Studies have shown that rates of resilience vary enormously from study to study with estimates ranging from 15% to 84% being seen to be resilient. However, the population under study, the way the researchers conceptualise resilience and the measures used will strongly impact the rates found. As mentioned previously, individuals can frequently display resilient outcomes in one domain of life while simultaneously showing impoverished function in other domains. (Bernard, 1997; Haskett et al., 2006; Richardson, 2002; Rutter, 1985). Another important point regarding the rates of resilience found, is that they can only be invoked and therefore indexed in the presence of significant adversity. Thus, in the absence of significant adversity, which would be known to destabilise a majority of individuals and require serious adaptation, resilience will not be present (Roisman, 2005).

Research on resilience can be conceptualised as having occurred in successive waves, with each wave focusing on a different aspect of resilience. The literature developed out of research on children exposed to adversity in mainly Western world contexts. The critical observation being that some children exposed to adversity seemed to do well, displaying functioning at a level way beyond what might be expected given the early adversity. This led the first wave of researchers to search for characteristics that might account for the different outcomes. Initially it was thought these factors would mostly be individual characteristics that were features of the individual's makeup. Thus, much of the early work looked for stable factors within the individual that could account for the better-than-expected outcomes. As the literature then began to demonstrate that some of these factors were present in the individual's external environment it broadened to include these factors. Examples of factors reported by the early resilience researchers were: intelligence, optimism, cognitive flexibility, positive self-concept, emotional regulation, positive emotions, creativity, hardiness, humour, enhanced life meaning, internal locus of control, active coping skills, spirituality, the presence of supportive adults and social support (Barbarin et al., 2001; Herrman et al., 2011; Schweizer et al., 1999; Seligman, 1975; Werner, 1993; Werner & Smith, 1992; White et al., 1989). Importantly, evidence exists that social support is generally protective whether received or given (Brown et al., 2003). There is also evidence that the number of adverse events experienced has a cumulative effect with the general rule seeming to be that more adverse experiences convey greater risks (Holmes & Rahe, 1967; Infurna et al., 2021; Tusaie & Dyer, 2004). Although studies have also reported that moderate levels of adversity are predictive of the highest levels of adaptive functioning when compared to no adversity or high adversity (Höltge et al., 2018). What is clear is the precise conditions under which adversity is cumulative across the lifespan and those under which previous moderate adversity can convey later strength are only beginning to be delineated.

Successive waves of resilience research quickly recognised that it was not merely the presence or absence of risk or protective factors and whether these were internal or external to the individual that mattered, but the way the factors interacted. Furthermore, the process of how an individual responds to adversity and utilises the resources they have at their disposal became critical (Yates et al., 2003). Therefore, the resilience literature began to move from seeing resilience as a stable feature to an interactive process (Herrman et al., 2011; Richardson, 2002). Furthermore, this suggests that resilience is specific to the context and time period and not necessarily uniform across all life domains—one can show resilience occupationally or academically while displaying social decrements. Due to its interactive nature, paths towards resilience are multifarious and numerous (Luthar et al., 2000; Masten, 2001; Ungar & Theron, 2020).

One reason resilience represents an important target for workplace intervention is because resilience correlates negatively with multiple mental health issues such as depression and anxiety, post-traumatic stress disorder and addictions (Babić et al., 2020; Cuomo et al., 2008; Delgado et al., 2021; Fossion et al., 2013; Fossion et al., 2015; Hartley, 2011). This is supported by a meta-analysis supporting the same conclusions (Hu et al., 2015).

As a result of these findings and proposed legislative changes, organisations have started to examine ways that employee stress might be reduced, and well-being/resilience increased (Verra et al., 2019). This is important as Erskine and Georgiou (2018) highlighted that there are several characteristics of work that make it a very likely source of significant life stress. Furthermore, it is noteworthy that employee well-being interventions focus on building capacity at the individual employee level. Thus, despite a wealth of evidence that leadership styles and workplace culture have significant and enduring impacts on employee well-being (See Erskine & Georgiou, 2018; Erskine & Georgiou—see also Chap. 4 of the present book) the focus of employee well-being programmes has mainly been on increasing resilience in individual employees. Even though workplace resilience/well-being programmes show efficacy these need to be considered in line with other potential beneficial interventions such as workload reductions that may deliver similar or greater positive outcomes (Holland et al., 2019; Mejalli et al., 2019; Pace et al., 2021).

Thus, individual resilience training programmes help individuals to demonstrate enhanced well-being and health through coping better with the challenges often faced in the workplace, rather than minimising the challenges themselves (which may not always be possible given the occupational setting, e.g., military). The next section will investigate studies that have examined employee well-being/resilience-building interventions and seek to determine their efficacy and effectiveness.

4 Employee Well-being/Resilience Interventions

While this chapter will focus on workplace interventions it will also examine school and university-based interventions as these are akin to work for those studying within them.

4.1 School-Based Interventions

There is mixed evidence of effectiveness for resilience-based interventions targeted at primary or secondary school children. Thus, Caldwell et al. (2019) conducted a systematic review and a network meta-analysis of 137 studies (56,620 participants) of interventions to prevent anxiety and depression in children. The findings indicated little evidence that cognitive behavioural interventions were able to prevent or reduce anxiety in school age children. Furthermore, there was no evidence to suggest that any interventions to prevent depression were effective. There was some significant evidence for the effectiveness of relaxation and mindfulness-based interventions for reducing anxiety when compared to no interventions in secondary school settings (Caldwell et al., 2019).

Research has also been employed to examine studies designed to improve resilience more generally in children. Thus, the Penn Resilience Programme has been shown in meta-analysis to reduce anxiety and depression in younger people. Furthermore, the effects of the intervention in children seem to increase even after the intervention is discontinued, as shown at 12-month follow-up (Brunwasser et al., 2009). Meta-analysis has also been used to examine the effects of resilience programmes in children on the tendency to use tobacco, alcohol and illicit drugs. Broadly the results show resilience building interventions to be effective at reducing illicit drug use but not alcohol or tobacco (Hodder et al., 2017).

A systematic review of school-based mental health promotion programmes demonstrated that in 10 out of 11 studies improvements in resilience, coping skills and self-efficacy were in evidence during and at post assessment. However, where outcomes were examined over longer timeframes post interventions these benefits were not maintained. They key components of working interventions were using teachers to deliver the programme, and adapting the programme to the unique environment or needs of the cohort. Importantly, outcomes were not related to the length of the programme (Fenwick-Smith et al., 2018).

22 Stress and Resilience in the Workplace   463

Thus, overall, this represents a mixed pattern of results where improvement in well-being while possible is less consistent than might be expected. Even though the outcomes often seem not to demonstrate benefits over longer time periods, it may be the case that these resilience and coping skills interventions could provide benefits at a much later point in life. For example, where the individual finds themselves in periods of intense adversity.

4.2   University-Based Interventions

Flinchbaugh et al. (2012) investigated four specific stress management techniques (deep breathing, progressive muscle relaxation, guided imagery and positive self-talk) and keeping a gratitude journal on overall student stress, experienced meaningfulness and classroom engagement in 117 undergraduates. The study took place over a semester (12 weeks) and four groups were created:

1. Stress management only
2. Gratitude journaling only
3. Combined stress management and journaling
4. Control condition

Pre and post semester surveys included measures of stress, meaningfulness, engagement and general life satisfaction. Results indicated that none of the interventions had a significant effect on overall classroom stress or life satisfaction. However, the combination of stress management techniques and gratitude journaling did have a significant effect on course meaningfulness and engagement (Flinchbaugh et al., 2012).

Houpy et al. (2017) investigated resilience in 117 US medical students. Results indicated that medical student resilience was lower than a sample from the general population. This was also previously reported in a sample of Canadian medical students (Rahimi et al., 2014). Furthermore, Houpy et al. (2017) found that resilience was higher in male students, those with more years of experience and those who reported being able to cope. Importantly, medical students believed resilience training would be useful and seemed to have insight into their general level of resilience.

A review of the effectiveness of using resilience interventions to increase resilience, and reduce depression and stress was conducted using university students. They included 21 RCT's in their meta-analysis and metaregression. Results indicated small positive effects of interventions for increasing resilience. Furthermore, small positive effects were found for reducing depression and stress. However, when controlling for large levels of heterogeneity the meta-analysis showed even smaller effects. The authors argue that the meta-analysis suggests resilience-based interventions may be a useful prevention strategy in university students (Ang et al., 2022).

One large-scale review of the effects of psychological interventions in healthcare students examined 30 RCT's. Results indicated that compared to control groups, healthcare students benefited from resilience training reporting higher subsequent resilience, showing lower levels of anxiety and stress. However, effect sizes were small to moderate. Importantly, resilience training showed no evidence of effectiveness on depression, well-being or quality of life. However, the authors note that this represents "very-low certainty evidence (meaning that the true effect may differ markedly from the estimated effect) that resilience interventions might be more effective than control for improving resilience, self-reported symptoms of anxiety, and stress or stress perception at post-test" (p. 32., Kunzler et al., 2020). Furthermore, increases in resilience were not maintained post intervention in the short term or medium term. The moderate or small effects for resilience and stress or stress perception found at post-test, respectively, were no longer evident at short-term follow-up. At medium-term follow-up (more than three months to six months or less), no longer found evidence for a difference between a resilience intervention and control for resilience, while a single study still provided evidence for a decrease in stress symptoms. Anxiety, depression and well-being or quality of life were not measured at medium-term follow-up by any study. Long-term follow-up assessments (more than six months post-intervention) were not available for any primary outcome.

Once again, there is no consistent direction of findings, as the evidence appears mixed on the effectiveness of interventions targeted at university students. However, resilience will be increaseingly necessary as universtity leavers transition to employment (Ng & Kong, 2022).

4.3 Workplace Interventions

Joyce and colleagues conducted a systematic review and meta-analysis of resilience training programmes and interventions (Joyce et al., 2018). They found 11 randomised control trials suitable for meta-analysis. They examined effects of interventions of three types: (1) cognitive behavioural interventions, (2) mindfulness-based interventions and (3) a combination of both. Results indicated a significant positive effect of all the interventions.

22 Stress and Resilience in the Workplace 465

Chmitorz et al. (2018) systematically reviewed resilience training programmes and they highlight several pertinent findings. Firstly, there is no consistent definition of resilience used across studies with many not including a definition. Furthermore, outcome measures vary across studies in terms of ways to measure mental health and resilience, limiting generalisability and comparison across studies. The authors also stress that for resilience to be demonstrated, this requires the presence of significant adversity, although many studies do not include a measure of this (Chmitorz et al., 2018). Furthermore, many studies use measures of well-being as proxies for resilience. Where questionnaire-based measure of resilience are used, these tend to mostly capture trait-based levels of resilience with no corroborating behavioural evidence. No current gold standard measure of resilience is widely accepted (Windle et al., 2011).

Sood et al. (2011) investigated a resilience training intervention delivered to US academic medical clinicians. The intervention consisted of a short 90-minute training programme focusing on altering attention and interpretation. Thus, it directs participants to focus more attention on novelty in the world and to delay judgement. In conjunction the programme also encourages participants to examine prejudiced ways of understanding the world and move towards gratitude, compassion, acceptance, forgiveness and finding meaning. Measures of resilience, stress and anxiety were taken at baseline and eight-week follow-up. Results showed that participants significantly increased in resilience because of the intervention and showed decreased stress and anxiety compared to waiting list controls (Sood et al., 2011).

One study investigated a 12-week stress management and resilience training programme for healthcare workers with outcomes examining well-being, life satisfaction, gratitude, mindfulness, spiritual well-being and stress (Berkland et al., 2017). One hundred and ten healthcare workers were assessed at baseline, at the end of the intervention and three months follow-up after the intervention. Results indicated sample attrition with 98 participants at baseline and end of the study, and 85 taking part at all time points. The intervention consisted of 60- to 90-minute, weekly educational sessions for 12 weeks. These involved attentional training, and positive mindset development focusing on fostering gratitude, compassion, acceptance, meaning and forgiveness. Outcomes demonstrated that from baseline to follow-up, participants increased significantly on happiness, life satisfaction, gratitude, mindfulness and spiritual well-being, and had lower stress. The authors make the point that large-scale meta-analyses suggest that happiness is related to success in many life areas such as life expectancy, relationships, energy, engagement, performance and social success (Berkland et al., 2017; Lyubomirsky, King, & Diener, 2005; Lyubomirsky, Sheldon, & Schkade, 2005).

Unsurprisingly resilience interventions and programmes used in workplace settings have focused on occupations where heightened risk levels have been predicted or demonstrated, such as police, medical professionals, firefighters and armed forces personnel (Adriaenssens et al., 2015; Brown et al., 2009; Campbell Jr et al., 2001; Larner & Blow, 2011; Parrish Meadows et al., 2011). These occupations are sometimes termed critical occupations (Paton & Violanti, 1996). One occupation regularly exposed to traumatic experiences represents armed-forces personnel (Adler et al., 2011) with many armed forces around the world having instigated resilience programmes into their training regimes. Perhaps the most studied and largest programme represents the Master resilience training programme in the US army (Reivich et al., 2011). Reivich et al. (2011) present a review of this programme that is based on the Penn Resilience Programme, and included factors which were suggested by Masten and Reed (2002) including optimism, self-efficacy, self-regulation, emotional awareness, empathy, flexibility, effective problem solving and good quality relationships (Reivich et al., 2011). Reivich et al. (2011) found that it was rated extremely beneficial by forces personnel that had undertaken it. Furthermore, subsequent examinations of the programme have suggested that personnel undertaking it not only find it helpful but show significant changes in resilience skills, chiefly better self-awareness, optimism and increased connection to others (Griffith & West, 2013).

There is much evidence that resilience can be improved and changed in individuals (Grant et al., 2009; Joyce et al., 2018; Masten, 2001; Sood et al., 2011). One critical study examined resilience training programmes and conducted a systematic review and meta-analysis of randomised controlled trials (Leppin et al., 2014). The outcomes of interest focused on several domains:

1. Resilience, coping or hardiness
2. Well-being, quality of life
3. Self-efficacy, confidence regarding disease management
4. Depression
5. Stress and anxiety

From an original pool of 516 studies screened for inclusion, 68 trials with sufficient data were found. Of these, 22 were eligible for inclusion and a further three were added totalling 25 analysed studies. The interventions studied were very varied ranging from training sessions to coaching to self-directed and group sessions. Furthermore, interventions varied by time taken and theoretical basis. Results indicated that interventions to increase resilience demonstrated a significant overall positive effect at three-month follow-up. However, effects on quality of life and depression while indicative of effectiveness were not statistically significant. One issue reported concerned a moderate-to-high level of assessed bias within the studies. When two studies with high bias were excluded the improvement in other outcomes did reach statistical significance. Trauma-focused programmes demonstrated a significant effect on stress reduction and depression. The authors suggest that resilience programmes seem to have a small to medium effect regarding increasing resilience and mental health (Leppin et al., 2014).

Robertson et al. (2015) reviewed resilience studies completed between 2003 and 2014 and identified 14 studies examining mental health and well-being outcomes. Results indicated that resilience training had several benefits such as significant increments in resilience and simultaneously improved well-being and mental health. Furthermore, performance improvements and social and psychological improvements were seen (Robertson et al., 2015). However, the authors point out several limitations that need to be considered. Firstly, a minority of studies measured resilience as an outcome and those that did had very different definitions of resilience. The authors therefore stress: "It is essential that future interventions demonstrate consistency in terms of how resilience if defined, conceptualized, developed and assessed" (Robertson et al., 2015, p. 27). This point is a consistent theme running through the literature and meta-analyses.

A similar meta-analysis was conducted regarding resilience interventions for workplace settings (Vanhove et al., 2016). Vanhove and colleagues investigated this question in 37 studies. They make the critical point that in contrast to stress management interventions which often occur post stress exposure, resilience programmes often focus on primary prevention occurring prior to issues. These resilience programmes aim to prevent future problems due to coping and self-management skills. Prior evidence indicates these programmes may be effective in children and that effects are stronger at 12-month follow-up than immediately post intervention (Brunwasser et al., 2009). Thus, Vanhove et al. (2016) investigated the effects of workplace resilience programmes both in the immediate aftermath of delivery and over time following the interventions. Once again programmes varied widely in terms of time taken to deliver and method of delivery (one-to-one, group or via computer). Results indicated that resilience building interventions had an overall significant modest positive effect on well-being and performance. However, follow-up analysis indicated that the effectiveness diminished over time although remained statistically significant even at distal follow-up. The results also demonstrated that one-to-one-based interventions had stronger effects than group-based or computer-based.

While resilience is a desirable characteristic for company employees, it may also be developed via other routes than the training programmes reviewed so far (Bustinza et al., 2019). Thus, the authors suggest that human resource practices are well placed to facilitate the development of resilience, rather than place the focus of development on training the individual. They define resilience in this context as "the ability to dynamically reinvent an organisation when circumstances change, facilitating a firms' capacity to respond to uncertain conditions at the organizational level" (Bustinza et al., 2019, p. 1371). This was investigated in 205 manufacturers using Structural Equation Modelling (SEM) which showed that technological capabilities of an organisation could be used to enhance organisational resilience and adapt to change. Furthermore, the same was suggested to occur by enhancing resilience through human resource practices designed to foster some of the familiar factors associated with organisational well-being and resilience in staff (employee involvement, empowerment, teamwork capacity, resilience training, self-motivated learning, problem solving skills). Organisational effectiveness was a composite of various business performance measure such as commitment to continual improvement, stability of production, customer requirement knowledge, improving business models, financial results. The results of the SEM analysis supported a model where resilience capacities within the organisation mediated the positive effects of technological capacity on organisational effectiveness. Thus, having the technological capability to respond to dramatic change is mediated through the ability of the organisations resilience capacities which then feeds into organisational effectiveness (Bustinza et al., 2019). However, many human resources departments will prefer to solely outsource resilience training to external well-being providers, although they may already employ or can implement human resource practices that can facilitate both organisational and individual resilience.

4.4 Resilience in Healthcare Settings

One occupational area that has been shown to consistently involve high levels of stress is healthcare (Dall'Ora et al., 2015; McCray et al., 2008; Moss et al., 2016). Resilience building programmes often use mindfulness-based interventions. Mindfulness can be conceived as involving self-regulation of attention to immediate experiences, with openness and acceptance (Bishop et al., 2004). Burton et al. (2017) conducted a meta-analysis examining the effectiveness of these type of interventions in healthcare professionals for reducing stress. Findings from this study demonstrate an overall moderate effect of mindfulness-based approaches on reducing stress levels in healthcare professionals (Burton et al., 2017). Therefore, while mindfulness-based interventions may be effective for reducing stress in healthcare professionals the extent to which they enhance resilience is still unclear, even though resilience and stress are negatively related (Shatté et al., 2017).

A quantitative study examining resilience in medical professionals set out to examine important traits that either facilitate or impair resilience. Thus, Eley et al. (2013) examined 479 Australian doctors and measured personality, temperament and resilience. Results indicated resilience was significantly and positively related to self-directedness, persistence, cooperativeness. Furthermore, resilience was significantly and negatively related to harm avoidance. The authors suggest that resilience is a crucial attribute for doctors and should be fostered and nurtured. In addition, they suggest that it is best represented by a personality that is "mature, responsible, optimistic, persevering and cooperative" (Eley et al., 2013). A qualitative study also shows that some of the same factors are central to resilience in doctors, which included the following four factors (Jensen et al., 2008):

1. Attitudes and perspectives—valuing one's role, having self-awareness, accepting limitations
2. Balance/prioritisation—setting limits, valuing oneself
3. Practice management—using effective management principles
4. Supportive relationships—positive personal relationships and effective professional ones

In addition to the relationship between individual differences and resilience in healthcare professionals, it has been found that situational factors also play a role. Thus, Howard and colleagues systematically reviewed 33 studies regarding personal resilience in psychiatrists (Howard et al., 2019). The aim was to examine factors that impair well-being and those that promote resilience. Factors shown to impair well-being/increase stress—being a trainee, low personal accomplishment—perceived or actual, working in community or acute wards, rural working, being female, excessive workload, long hours, inadequate financial resources, poor facilities, aggressive/difficult patients, high job demands, inadequate colleague support, poor management support, career prospects, personal safety issues, illness, litigation. Factors fostering resilience/reducing stress were found to be less ward-based time by varying work activities, redistributing responsibility across staff, greater clinical experience, supportive colleagues, participation in holidays and hobbies, having a supportive partner, self-care interventions—utilising competency training and CBT principles, socialising, improving the workplace with better management and administration. The review also suggests that psychiatrists demonstrated higher levels of burnout than other physicians. This builds on a large-scale Finnish study (n = 3133) also demonstrating psychiatrists to have higher levels of burnout and mental health issues than other medical specialties (Korkeila et al., 2003).

Having considered the individual differences and situational factors related to resilience in healthcare professionals, it is important to consider which practices and skills may be amenable to enhancement through training (Middleton et al., 2022). In line with this, one direct intervention study examined implementing a resilience training programme in Australian health service staff (Van Agteren et al., 2018). The programme consisted of two days of training aimed at teaching ten skills (meaning making, event thought reaction connections, what's most important, balanced thinking, cultivating gratitude, mindfulness, interpersonal problem solving, active constructive responding, capitalising on strengths, value-based goals). The design involved screening mental health before the intervention and one month following its completion. The PERMA profiler (positive emotion, engagement, relationships, meaning, accomplishment) represented the measure of mental health (Butler & Kern, 2016). Results indicated that resilience and mental health significantly improved from baseline to follow-up.

What is interesting to note is that there is data to suggest the positive results seen in resilience training in healthcare settings are still effective when training is brief compared to longer interventions (Slatyer et al., 2018). In addition, patients have even been demonstrated to benefit from brief resilience interventions. Loprinzi et al. (2011) describe a randomised control trail of a SMART (Stress Management and Resiliency Training) intervention provided to 25 female breast cancer patients (Loprinzi et al., 2011). The SMART intervention was a developed from Attention and Interpretation Therapy. The intervention was brief and consisted of two 90-minute group sessions, one individual session and three phone calls. Results indicated that compared to a waiting list control the programme led to higher resilience and quality of life, and less stress and anxiety after 12 weeks.

Having reviewed the evidence base for resilience interventions in the workplace the overwhelming picture is that these interventions can and often do have positive effects on the individual's well-being (Andersen et al., 2021). In addition, data indicates that resilience following training may be significant factor in reducing turnover intentions (Lee & De Gagne, 2022). Finally, it seems that the length of the interventions and the specific type are less important to the outcomes.

5 Potential Consequences of Resilience Training

Despite the evidence of their effectiveness, there are potential consequences to resilience training in occupational contexts as specified above. Firstly, it firmly places the responsibility for well-being at the hands of the individual even though organisations may offer the training. The reason this chapter appears in a book on work stress is that stress and negative health consequences stemming from stress are only partially a function of the individual. Secondly, these programmes could be used by managers and leaders to enhance the resilience capacities of individuals for them to continue to function in pathogenic environments that should be moved away from and/or altered. Thus, one suggestion of this chapter is that resilience courses, where they are invoked, place an emphasis on training individuals to identify pathogenic environments and the extent to which these can be challenged and improved, if the system is resistant to change it is in the best interests of health for the individual to avoid these workplaces. Thus, employers may react to staff that have been trained to cope more effectively by increasing workloads and offering less resources representing one route via which resilience training may prove ultimately pyrrhic (Card, 2018; Taylor, 2019). Liu et al. (2019) have examined resilience and well-being from a human resource management perspective and suggest resilience has been a longstanding issue in organisational psychology (Liu et al., 2019). This is important as modern research on resilience has moved towards integrating personal resilience with management and human resources interventions designed to foster resilience more broadly (Lim et al., 2020). Therefore, the suggestions offered below will focus on three levels at which resilience may implemented—Leaders, individual employees and the organisation.

6 Practical Suggestions

6.1 For Organisations

Employee well-being programmes should not be considered add-ons, that can be cancelled at will. They are necessary to long-term organisational health and productivity. Staff are a resource that requires fostering for maximum efficiencies. Staff health is organisational health. Prophylactic programmes focusing on averting issues before sickness is evident should be seen as optimal rather than waiting until issues develop before taking expensive and costly interventions that may ultimately fail. In short, fostering resilience is fostering organisational health.

Following the implementation of resilience/well-being interventions, organisations should not see this as an opportunity to impose further demands on employees, for example, increases to workloads, as the management may perceive staff as being better able to cope following training. Furthermore, there needs to be recognition that organisations, systems, and management may still contribute towards negative individual employee outcomes. Therefore, interventions and practices conducive to staff resilience/well-being must continue simultaneously on multiple fronts.

6.2   For Leaders

Well-being and building resilience in leaders and staff will ultimately mean the organisation is more fit to tackle challenges involved in ongoing operations. Developing resilience in staff should not be a method of enabling unfeasible workloads to be imposed on followers or leaders.

Leadership endorsement of well-being interventions must not be merely cursory. There is evidence that managers that engage with these programmes themselves and show genuinely greater support for them have workforces that engage at significantly higher rates, are less stressed and show better health behaviours (Hoert et al., 2018). This is in line with the research on transformational leadership where leaders authentically model and embody the principles they are supposed to desire in followers. The study of Hoert et al. (2018) provides direct evidence of this (see also Erskine & Georgiou, 2018; see also Chap. 4 in the present book).

Finally, leaders should choose resilience building interventions that use empirical evidence-based interventions, designed and run by qualified psychologists rather than lay people.

6.3   For Followers

The evidence suggests that resilience programmes are beneficial to follower well-being, both physically and mentally, and followers should be encouraged to take part in these programmes. Resilience building will empower workers to make better choices regarding their place within the organisation, which should result in less time off sick and healthier work life balance, and will have beneficial effects beyond the workplace. Self-care is intrinsic to long-term organisational health. One approach could be to reconceptualise the concept of failure, which at times is inevitable, but offers an opportunity for growth and learning. Persistent failures or inability to meet demands, with minimal time in between these events is not a productive way to build resilience. At a minimum, followers should seek to avoid strategies known to be ineffective in dealing with stress, for example use of thought suppression and avoidant coping (Crane & Boga, 2017; Erskine, 2008; Erskine et al., 2010; Erskine & Georgiou, 2011; Hayes et al., 2004).

However, resilience interventions and individual adaptation only goes so far. Management acceptance of environmental influences on stress is also required, for example workload, scheduling, autonomy, capacity limitations and unrealistic expectations are necessary for management to address as these are systemic issues involved in the development of pathogenic work environments. Where possible, staff and management should examine co-creation of more salutogenic work environments, rather than staff feeling they are solely responsible for their resilience and well-being in the workplace. Mutually beneficial practices can benefit both individuals working for organisations and the organisations themselves.

7 Conclusion

Resilience-based interventions in the workplace have been demonstrated to bring improvements in well-being and foster greater employee resilience (Zhai et al., 2021). Furthermore, they are likely to bring significant organisational benefits such as increased productivity (Gladfelter & Haggis, 2022; Walpita & Arambepola, 2020). Where employed it is vital these interventions are not merely undertaken to comply with legislation but are viewed as valuable and authentically endorsed by supportive leaders and managers.

Research shows that the delivery (in person, computerised, group) and the length of intervention does not dramatically affect outcomes. However, our recommendation is that all resilience building interventions are evidence based and delivered by suitably qualified professionals. Furthermore, building resilience will become increasingly necessary as the pace of change in organisational and global systems continues to increase. Resilience is one quality that research suggests helps people to adapt to change and therefore should be fostered wherever possible (Malik & Garg, 2020).

Importantly, in view of the current work, research on resilience is now demonstrating that a supportive leadership team directly contributes to increased resilience in the workplace (Berger & Czakert, 2022; Cooke et al.,

2019). Therefore, when examining ways to improve employee resilience, organisations should consider the following: (1) resilience is not the sole responsibility of the employee; (2) interventions should target increasing resilience in individuals via training; (3) leadership training interventions can also significantly impact individual and organisational resilience.

References

Adler, A. B., Bliese, P. D., & Castro, C. A. E. (2011). *Deployment psychology: Evidence-based strategies to promote mental health in the military*. American Psychological Association.

Adriaenssens, J., De Gucht, V., & Maes, S. (2015). Determinants and prevalence of burnout in emergency nurses: A systematic review of 25 years of research. *International Journal of Nursing Studies, 52*, 649–661.

Andersen, S., Mintz-Binder, R., Sweatt, L., & Song, H. (2021). Building nurse resilience in the workplace. *Applied Nursing Research, 59,* 151433.

Ang, W. H. D., Lau, S. T., Cheng, L. J., Chew, H. S. J., Tan, J. H., Shorey, S., & Lau, Y. (2022). Effectiveness of resilience interventions for higher education students: A meta-analysis and metaregression. *Journal of Educational Psychology, 114*(7), 1670.

Babić, R., Babić, M., Rastović, P., Ćurlin, M., Šimić, J., Mandić, K., & Pavlović, K. (2020). Resilience in health and illness. *Psychiatria Danubina, 32*(suppl. 2), 226–232.

Barbarin, O. A., Richter, L., & DeWet, T. (2001). Exposure to violence, coping resources, and psychological adjustment of South African children. *American Journal of Orthopsychiatry, 71*, 16–25.

Batt, M. E. (2009). Physical activity interventions in the workplace: The rationale and future direction for workplace wellness. *British Journal of Sports Medicine, 43*, 47–48.

Berger, R., & Czakert, J. P. (2022). Stress management and resilience building. In *Organisational Excellence and Resilience* (pp. 63–88). Springer.

Berkland, B. E., Werneburg, B. L., Jenkins, S. M., Friend, J. L., Clark, M. M., Rosedahl, J. K., et al. (2017). A worksite wellness intervention: Improving happiness, life satisfaction, and gratitude in health care workers. *Mayo Clinic Proceedings: Innovations, Quality & Outcomes, 1*, 203–210.

Bernard, B. (1997). *Turning it all around for youth: From risk to resilience*. Resiliency Associates and Global Learning Communities.

Bishop, S. R., Lau, M., Shapiro, S., Carlson, L., Anderson, N. D., Carmody, J., Segal, Z. V., Abbey, S., Speca, M., Velting, D., & Devins, G. (2004). Mindfulness: A proposed operational definition. *Clinical Psychology: Science and Practice, 11*, 230–241.

22 Stress and Resilience in the Workplace   475

Bonanno, G. A. (2004). Loss, trauma, and human resilience: Have we underestimated the human capacity to thrive after extremely aversive events? *American Psychologist, 59*, 20–28.

Bonanno, G. A., Brewin, C. R., Kaniasty, K., & Greca, A. M. L. (2010). Weighing the costs of disaster: Consequences, risks, and resilience in individuals, families, and communities. *Psychological Science in the Public Interest, 11*, 1–49.

Bonanno, G. A., Rennicke, C., & Dekel, S. (2005). Self-enhancement among high-exposure survivors of the September 11th terrorist attack: Resilience or social maladjustment? *Journal of Personality and Social Psychology, 88*, 984.

Bonanno, G. A., Romero, S. A., & Klein, S. I. (2015). The temporal elements of psychological resilience: An integrative framework for the study of individuals, families, and communities. *Psychological Inquiry, 26*(2), 139–169.

Bonanno, G. A., Westphal, M., & Mancini, A. D. (2011). Resilience to loss and potential trauma. *Annual Review of Clinical Psychology, 7*, 511–535.

Brown, S. D., Goske, M. J., & Johnson, C. M. (2009). Beyond substance abuse: Stress, burnout, and depression as causes of physician impairment and disruptive behavior. *Journal of the American College of Radiology, 6*, 479–485.

Brown, S. L., Nesse, R. M., Vinokur, A. D., & Smith, D. M. (2003). Providing social support may be more beneficial than receiving it: Results from a prospective study of mortality. *Psychological Science, 14*, 320–327.

Brunwasser, S. M., Gillham, J. E., & Kim, E. S. (2009). A meta-analytic review of the Penn Resiliency Program's effect on depressive symptoms. *Journal of Consulting and Clinical Psychology, 77*, 1042.

Burton, A., Burgess, C., Dean, S., Koutsopoulou, G. Z., & Hugh-Jones, S. (2017). How effective are mindfulness-based interventions for reducing stress among healthcare professionals? A systematic review and meta-analysis. *Stress and Health, 33*, 3–13.

Bustinza, O. F., Vendrell-Herrero, F., Perez-Arostegui, M., & Parry, G. (2019). Technological capabilities, resilience capabilities and organizational effectiveness. *The International Journal of Human Resource Management, 30*, 1370–1392.

Butler, J., & Kern, M. L. (2016). The PERMA-Profiler: A brief multidimensional measure of flourishing. *International Journal of Wellbeing, 6*(3).

Caldwell, D. M., Davies, S. R., Hetrick, S. E., Palmer, J. C., Caro, P., Lopez-Lopez, J. A., et al. (2019). *School-based interventions to prevent anxiety and depression in children and young people: A systematic review and network meta analysis* (Vol. 6, pp. 1011–1020). *Lancet Psychiatry*.

Campbell, D. A., Jr., Sonnad, S. S., Eckhauser, F. E., Campbell, K. K., & Greenfield, L. J. (2001). Burnout among American surgeons. *Surgery, 130*, 696–705.

Card, A. J. (2018). Physician burnout: Resilience training is only part of the solution. *The Annals of Family Medicine, 16*, 267–270.

Chmitorz, A., Kunzler, A., Helmreich, I., Tüscher, O., Kalisch, R., Kubiak, T., et al. (2018). Intervention studies to foster resilience – A systematic review and proposal for a resilience framework in future intervention studies. *Clinical Psychology Review, 59*, 78–100.

Cooke, F. L., Wang, J., & Bartram, T. (2019). Can a supportive workplace impact employee resilience in a high pressure performance environment? An investigation of the Chinese banking industry. *Applied Psychology, 68*(4), 695–718.

Crane, M., & Boga, D. (2017). A commentary: Rethinking approaches to resilience and mental health training. *Journal of Military and Veterans Health, 25*, 30.

Cuomo, C., Sarchiapone, M., Di Giannantonio, M., Mancini, M., & Roy, A. (2008). Aggression, impulsivity, personality traits, and childhood trauma of prisoners with substance abuse and addiction. *The American Journal of Drug and Alcohol Abuse, 34*, 339–345.

Dall'Ora, C., Griffiths, P., Ball, J., Simon, M., & Aiken, L. H. (2015). Association of 12 hour shifts and nurses' job satisfaction, burnout and intention to leave: Findings from a cross-sectional study of 12 European countries. *BMJ Open, 5*, e008331.

Delgado, C., Roche, M., Fethney, J., & Foster, K. (2021). Mental health nurses' psychological well-being, mental distress, and workplace resilience: A cross-sectional survey. *International Journal of Mental Health Nursing, 30*(5), 1234–1247.

Denckla, C. A., Cicchetti, D., Kubzansky, L. D., Seedat, S., Teicher, M. H., Williams, D. R., & Koenen, K. C. (2020). Psychological resilience: An update on definitions, a critical appraisal, and research recommendations. *European Journal of Psychotraumatology, 11*(1), 1822064.

Donaldson-Feilder, E. J., & Bond, F. W. (2004). The relative importance of psychological acceptance and emotional intelligence to workplace well-being. *British Journal of Guidance and Counselling, 32*, 187–203.

Egeland, B., Carlson, E., & Sroufe, L. A. (1993). Resilience as process. *Development and Psychopathology, 5*, 517–528.

Eley, D. S., Cloninger, C. R., Walters, L., Laurence, C., Synnott, R., & Wilkinson, D. (2013). The relationship between resilience and personality traits in doctors: Implications for enhancing well being. *PeerJ, 1*, e216.

Erskine, J. A. (2008). Resistance can be futile: Investigating behavioural rebound. *Appetite, 50*, 415–421.

Erskine, J. A., Georgiou, G. J., & Kvavilashvili, L. (2010). I suppress, therefore I smoke: Effects of thought suppression on smoking behavior. *Psychological Science, 21*, 1225–1230.

Erskine, J. A. K., & Georgiou, G. (2011). My own worst enemy: How trying not to think of an action might lead you down that very path. *The Psychologist, 24*, 824–827.

Erskine, J. A. K., & Georgiou, G. J. (2018). Leadership styles: Employee stress, well-being, productivity, turnover and absenteeism. In *Understanding stress at work* (p. 28).

Erskine, J. A. K., & Georgiou, G. J. (Present Work) *Leadership styles: Work stress and related outcomes.*

22 Stress and Resilience in the Workplace 477

Fenwick-Smith, A., Dahlberg, E. E., & Thompson, S. C. (2018). Systematic review of resilience-enhancing, universal, primary school-based mental health promotion programs. *BMC Psychology, 6*(1), 1–17.

Flinchbaugh, C. L., Moore, E. W. G., Chang, Y. K., & May, D. R. (2012). Student well-being interventions: The effects of stress management techniques and gratitude journaling in the management education classroom. *Journal of Management Education, 36*, 191–219.

Fossion, P., Leys, C., Kempenaers, C., Braun, S., Verbanck, P., & Linkowski, P. (2013). Depression, anxiety and loss of resilience after multiple traumas: An illustration of a mediated moderation model of sensitization in a group of children who survived the Nazi Holocaust. *Journal of Affective Disorders, 151*, 973–979.

Fossion, P., Leys, C., Vandeleur, C., Kempenaers, C., Braun, S., Verbanck, P., & Linkowski, P. (2015). Transgenerational transmission of trauma in families of Holocaust survivors: The consequences of extreme family functioning on resilience, sense of coherence, anxiety and depression. *Journal of Affective Disorders, 171*, 48–53.

French, J. R., Caplan, R. D., & Van Harrison, R. (1982). *The mechanisms of job stress and strain* (Vol. 7). Chichester [Sussex]; New York: J. Wiley.

Friborg, O., Hjemdal, O., Rosenvinge, J. H., & Martinussen, M. (2003). A new rating scale for adult resilience: What are the central protective resources behind healthy adjustment? *International Journal of Methods in Psychiatric Research, 12*, 65–76.

Garmezy, N. (1981). Children under stress: Perspectives on antecedents and correlates of vulnerability and resistance to psychopathology. In A. L. Rabin, J. Arnoff, A. M. Barclay, & R. A. Zuckers (Eds.), *Further explorations in personality* (pp. 196–269). Wiley.

Garmezy, N. (1991). Resilience in children's adaptation to negative life events and stressed environments. *Pediatric Annals, 20*, 459–466.

Gibbons, C., Dempster, M., & Moutray, M. (2008). Stress and eustress in nursing students. *Journal of Advanced Nursing, 61*, 282–290.

Gladfelter, A. S., & Haggis, W. A. (2022). Burnout among probation officers: The importance of resilience. *International Journal of Offender Therapy and Comparative Criminology, 0306624X221102835*.

Grant, A. M., Curtayne, L., & Burton, G. (2009). Executive coaching enhances goal attainment, resilience and workplace well-being: A randomised controlled study. *The Journal of Positive Psychology, 4*, 396–407.

Griffith, J., & West, C. (2013). Master resilience training and its relationship to individual well-being and stress buffering among Army National Guard soldiers. *The journal of behavioral health services & research, 40*, 140–155.

Hargrove, M. B., Becker, W. S., & Hargrove, D. F. (2015). The HRD eustress model: Generating positive stress with challenging work. *Human Resource Development Review, 14*, 279–298.

Harms, P. D., Credé, M., Tynan, M., Leon, M., & Jeung, W. (2017). Leadership and stress: A meta-analytic review. *The Leadership Quarterly, 28*, 178–194.

Hartley, M. T. (2011). Examining the relationships between resilience, mental health, and academic persistence in undergraduate college students. *Journal of American College Health, 59*, 596–604.

Haskett, M. E., Nears, K., Ward, C. S., & McPherson, A. V. (2006). Diversity in adjustment of maltreated children: Factors associated with resilient functioning. *Clinical Psychology Review, 26*, 796–812.

Hayes, S. C., Strosahl, K., Wilson, K. G., Bissett, R. T., Pistorello, J., Toarmino, D., et al. (2004). Measuring experiential avoidance: A preliminary test of a working model. *The Psychological Record, 54*, 553–578.

Herrman, H., Stewart, D. E., Diaz-Granados, N., Berger, E. L., Jackson, B., & Yuen, T. (2011). What is resilience? *The Canadian Journal of Psychiatry, 56*, 258–265.

Hodder, R. K., Freund, M., Wolfenden, L., Bowman, J., Nepal, S., Dray, J., et al. (2017). Systematic review of universal school-based "resilience" interventions targeting adolescent tobacco, alcohol or illicit substance use: A meta-analysis. *Preventive Medicine, 100*, 248–268.

Hoert, J., Herd, A. M., & Hambrick, M. (2018). The role of leadership support for health promotion in employee wellness program participation, perceived job stress, and health behaviors. *American Journal of Health Promotion, 32*, 1054–1061.

Holland, P., Tham, T. L., Sheehan, C., & Cooper, B. (2019). The impact of perceived workload on nurse satisfaction with work-life balance and intention to leave the occupation. *Applied Nursing Research, 49*, 70–76.

Holmes, T. H., & Rahe, R. H. (1967). The social readjustment rating scale. *Journal of Psychosomatic Research, 11*, 213–218.

Höltge, J., McGee, S. L., Maercker, A., & Thoma, M. V. (2018). A salutogenic perspective on adverse experiences: The curvilinear relationship of adversity and well-being. *European Journal of Health Psychology, 25*, 53–69.

Houpy, J. C., Lee, W. W., Woodruff, J. N., & Pincavage, A. T. (2017). Medical student resilience and stressful clinical events during clinical training. *Medical Education Online, 22*, 1320187.

Howard, R., Kirkley, C., & Baylis, N. (2019). Personal resilience in psychiatrists: Systematic review. *BJPsych Bulletin, 43*, 209–215.

Hu, T., Zhang, D., & Wang, J. (2015). A meta-analysis of the trait resilience and mental health. *Personality and Individual Differences, 76*, 18–27.

Hunter, A. J. (2001). A cross-cultural comparison of resilience in adolescents. *Journal of Pediatric Nursing, 16*, 172–179.

Infurna, F. J., Luthar, S. S., & Grimm, K. J. (2021). Lifetime adversity in the context of monthly adversity and psychological well-being in midlife: Evidence of cumulative disadvantage, but not steeling effects of lifetime adversity. *The Journals of Gerontology: Series B, 77*, 1394–1405.

Jensen, P. M., Trollope-Kumar, K., Waters, H., & Everson, J. (2008). Building physician resilience. *Canadian Family Physician, 54*(5), 722–729.

Joyce, S., Shand, F., Tighe, J., Laurent, S. J., Bryant, R. A., & Harvey, S. B. (2018). Road to resilience: A systematic review and meta-analysis of resilience training programmes and interventions. *BMJ Open, 8*, e017858.

Kalisch, R., Baker, D. G., Basten, U., Boks, M. P., Bonanno, G. A., Brummelman, E., et al. (2017). The resilience framework as a strategy to combat stress-related disorders. *Nature Human Behaviour, 1*(11), 784–790.

Kalisch, R., Cramer, A. O., Binder, H., Fritz, J., Leertouwer, I., Lunansky, G., et al. (2019). Deconstructing and reconstructing resilience: A dynamic network approach. *Perspectives on Psychological Science, 14*(5), 765–777.

Karam, E. G., Friedman, M. J., Hill, E. D., Kessler, R. C., McLaughlin, K. A., Petukhova, M., et al. (2014). Cumulative traumas and risk thresholds: 12-month PTSD in the World Mental Health (WMH) surveys. *Depression and Anxiety, 31*, 130–142.

Korkeila, J. A., Töyry, S., Kumpulainen, K., Toivola, J. M., Räsänen, K., & Kalimo, R. (2003). Burnout and self-perceived health among Finnish psychiatrists and child psychiatrists: A national survey. *Scandinavian Journal of Public Health, 31*, 85–91.

Kunzler, A. M., Helmreich, I., König, J., Chmitorz, A., Wessa, M., Binder, H., & Lieb, K. (2020). Psychological interventions to foster resilience in healthcare students. *Cochrane Database of Systematic Reviews, 7*.

Kupriyanov, R., & Zhdanov, R. (2014). The eustress concept: Problems and outlooks. *World Journal of Medical Sciences, 11*, 179–185.

Larner, B., & Blow, A. (2011). A model of meaning-making coping and growth in combat veterans. *Review of General Psychology, 15*, 187–197.

Lazarus, R. S., & Folkman, S. (1984). Coping and adaptation. In *The handbook of behavioral medicine* (pp. 282–325). Guilford.

Lee, E., & De Gagne, J. C. (2022). The impact of resilience on turnover among newly graduated nurses: A 1-year follow-up study. *Journal of Nursing Management, 43*, 415–421.

Lepore, S. J., & Revenson, T. A. (2006). Resilience and posttraumatic growth: Recovery, resistance, and reconfiguration. In L. G. Calhoun & R. G. Tedeschi (Eds.), *Handbook of posttraumatic growth: Research and practice* (pp. 24–46). Erlbaum.

Leppin, A. L., Bora, P. R., Tilburt, J. C., Gionfriddo, M. R., Zeballos-Palacios, C., Dulohery, M. M., et al. (2014). The efficacy of resiliency training programs: A systematic review and meta-analysis of randomized trials. *PloS One, 9*, e111420.

Lim, D. H., Hur, H., Ho, Y., Yoo, S., & Yoon, S. W. (2020). Workforce resilience: Integrative review for human resource development. *Performance Improvement Quarterly, 33*, 77–101.

Liu, Y., Cooper, L., & C., & Y. Tarba, S. (2019). Resilience, wellbeing and HRM: A multidisciplinary perspective. *International Journal of Human Resource Management, 30*, 1227–1238.

Liu, Y., Wang, Z., Zhou, C., & Li, T. (2014). Affect and self-esteem as mediators between trait resilience and psychological adjustment. *Personality and Individual Differences, 66*, 92–97.

Loprinzi, C. E., Prasad, K., Schroeder, D. R., & Sood, A. (2011). Stress Management and Resilience Training (SMART) program to decrease stress and enhance resilience among breast cancer survivors: A pilot randomized clinical trial. *Clinical Breast Cancer, 11*, 364–368.

Luthar, S. S., Cicchetti, D., & Becker, B. (2000). The construct of resilience: A critical evaluation and guidelines for future work. *Child Development, 71*, 543–562.

Lyubomirsky, S., King, L., & Diener, E. (2005). The benefits of frequent positive affect: Does happiness lead to success? *Psychological Bulletin, 131*, 803–855.

Lyubomirsky, S., Sheldon, K. M., & Schkade, D. (2005). Pursuing happiness: The architecture of sustainable change. *Review of General Psychology, 9*, 111–131.

MacKay, C. J., Cousins, R., Kelly, P. J., Lee, S., & McCaig, R. H. (2004). "Management Standards" and work-related stress in the UK: Policy background and science. *Work & Stress, 18*, 91–112.

Malik, P., & Garg, P. (2020). Learning organization and work engagement: The mediating role of employee resilience. *The International Journal of Human Resource Management, 31*(8), 1071–1094.

Masten, A. S. (2001). Ordinary magic: Resilience processes in development. *American Psychologist, 56*, 227–238.

Masten, A. S., & Reed, M. G. J. (2002). Resilience in development. *Handbook of Positive Psychology, 74*, 88.

Mattke, S., Schnyer, C., & Van Busum, K. R. (2013). A review of the US workplace wellness market. *Rand Health Quarterly, 2*, 7.

McCray, L. W., Cronholm, P. F., Bogner, H. R., Gallo, J. J., & Neill, R. A. (2008). Resident physician burnout: Is there hope? *Family Medicine, 40*, 626–632.

Mejalli, A. K., Rehman, M. G., Taylor, M. E., & Eck, L. M. (2019). Reducing resident physician workload to improve well being. *Cureus, 11*(6).

Middleton, R., Kinghorn, G., Patulny, R., Sheridan, L., Andersen, P., & McKenzie, J. (2022). Qualitatively exploring the attributes of adaptability and resilience amongst recently graduated nurses. *Nurse Education in Practice, 103406*.

Moss, M., Good, V. S., Gozal, D., Kleinpell, R., & Sessler, C. N. (2016). A Critical Care Societies collaborative statement: Burnout syndrome in critical care healthcare professionals. A call for action. *American Journal of Respiratory and Critical Care Medicine, 194*, 106–113.

Ng, B., & Kong, L. C. (2022). Graduate resilience in future workplace: Mindfulness-based research on personality traits, trait affect and resilience. In *Higher education and job employability* (pp. 255–285). Springer.

Oshio, A., Taku, K., Hirano, M., & Saeed, G. (2018). Resilience and Big Five personality traits: A meta-analysis. *Personality and Individual Differences, 127*, 54–60.

22 Stress and Resilience in the Workplace 481

Pace, F., D'Urso, G., Zappulla, C., & Pace, U. (2021). The relation between workload and personal well-being among university professors. *Current Psychology, 40*(7), 3417–3424.

Parrish Meadows, M., Shreffler, K. M., & Mullins-Sweatt, S. N. (2011). Occupational stressors and resilience in critical occupations: The role of personality. In *The role of individual differences in occupational stress and well being* (pp. 39–61). Emerald Group Publishing Limited.

Paton, D. E., & Violanti, J. M. (1996). *Traumatic stress in critical occupations: Recognition, consequences and treatment.* Charles C Thomas, Publisher.

Piao, X., & Managi, S. (2022). Long-term improvement of psychological well-being in the workplace: What and how. *Social Science & Medicine, 298*, 114851.

Rahimi, B., Baetz, M., Bowen, R., & Balbuena, L. (2014). Resilience, stress, and coping among Canadian medical students. *Canadian Medical Education Journal, 5*, e5–e11.

Reivich, K. J., Seligman, M. E., & McBride, S. (2011). Master resilience training in the US Army. *American Psychologist, 66*, 25.

Richardson, G. E. (2002). The metatheory of resilience and resiliency. *Journal of Clinical Psychology, 58*, 307–321.

Robertson, I. T., Cooper, C. L., Sarkar, M., & Curran, T. (2015). Resilience training in the workplace from 2003 to 2014: A systematic review. *Journal of Occupational and Organizational Psychology, 88*, 533–562.

Roisman, G. I. (2005). Conceptual clarifications in the study of resilience. *American Psychologist, 60*, 264–265.

Rutter, M. (1985). Resilience in the face of adversity. Protective factors and resistance to psychiatric disorder. *The British Journal of Psychiatry, 147*, 598–611.

Schulte, P. A., Guerin, R. J., Schill, A. L., Bhattacharya, A., Cunningham, T. R., Pandalai, S. P., et al. (2015). Considerations for incorporating "well-being" in public policy for workers and workplaces. *American Journal of Public Health, 105*, e31–e44.

Schweizer, K., Beck-Seyffer, A., & Schneider, R. (1999). Cognitive bias of optimism and its influence on psychological well-being. *Psychological Reports, 84*, 627–636.

Seligman, M. E. (1975). *Helplessness: On depression, development, and death.* WH Freeman/Times Books/Henry Holt & Co.

Selye, H. (1936). A syndrome produced by diverse nocuous agents. *Nature, 138*, 32.

Shatté, A., Perlman, A., Smith, B., & Lynch, W. D. (2017). The positive effect of resilience on stress and business outcomes in difficult work environments. *Journal of Occupational and Environmental Medicine, 59*, 135–140.

Shonkoff, J. P., Boyce, W. T., & McEwen, B. S. (2009). Neuroscience, molecular biology, and the childhood roots of health disparities: Building a new framework for health promotion and disease prevention. *Jama, 301*, 2252–2259.

Silk, J. S., Vanderbilt-Adriance, E., Shaw, D. S., Forbes, E. E., Whalen, D. J., Ryan, N. D., & Dahl, R. E. (2007). Resilience among children and adolescents at risk for depression: Mediation and moderation across social and neurobiological contexts. *Development and Psychopathology, 19*, 841–865.

Slatyer, S., Craigie, M., Heritage, B., et al. (2018). Evaluating the effectiveness of a brief Mindful Self-Care and Resiliency (MSCR) intervention for nurses: A controlled trial. *Mindfulness, 9*, 534–546.

Sood, A., Prasad, K., Schroeder, D., & Varkey, P. (2011). Stress management and resilience training among Department of Medicine faculty: A pilot randomized clinical trial. *Journal of General Internal Medicine, 26*, 858–861.

Southwick, S. M., Bonanno, G. A., Masten, A. S., Panter-Brick, C., & Yehuda, R. (2014). Resilience definitions, theory, and challenges: Interdisciplinary perspectives. *European Journal of Psychotraumatology, 5*, 25338.

Taylor, R. A. (2019). Contemporary issues: Resilience training alone is an incomplete intervention. *Nurse Education Today, 78*, 10–13.

Tsai, J., & Morissette, S. B. (2022). Introduction to the special issue: Resilience and perseverance for human flourishing. *Psychological Trauma: Theory, Research, Practice, and Policy, 14*(S1), S1.

Tusaie, K., & Dyer, J. (2004). Resilience: A historical review of the construct. *Holistic Nursing Practice, 18*, 3–10.

Ungar, M., & Theron, L. (2020). Resilience and mental health: How multisystemic processes contribute to positive outcomes. *The Lancet Psychiatry, 7*(5), 441–448.

Van Agteren, J., Iasiello, M., & Lo, L. (2018). Improving the wellbeing and resilience of health services staff via psychological skills training. *BMC Research Notes, 11*, 924–929.

Vanhove, A. J., Herian, M. N., Perez, A. L., Harms, P. D., & Lester, P. B. (2016). Can resilience be developed at work? A meta-analytic review of resilience-building programme effectiveness. *Journal of Occupational and Organizational Psychology, 89*, 278–307.

Verra, S. E., Benzerga, A., Jiao, B., & Ruggeri, K. (2019). Health promotion at work: A comparison of policy and practice across Europe. *Safety and Health at Work, 10*(1), 21–29.

Walpita, Y. N., & Arambepola, C. (2020). High resilience leads to better work performance in nurses: Evidence from South Asia. *Journal of Nursing Management, 28*(2), 342–350.

Werner, E. E. (1993). Risk, resilience, and recovery: Perspectives from the Kauai Longitudinal Study. *Development and Psychopathology, 5*, 503–515.

Werner, E. E., & Smith, R. S. (1992). *Overcoming the odds: High risk children from birth to adulthood*. Cornell University Press.

White, J. L., Moffitt, T. E., & Silva, P. A. (1989). A prospective replication of the protective effects of IQ in subjects at high risk for juvenile delinquency. *Journal of Consulting and Clinical Psychology, 57*, 719–724.

Windle, G. (2011). What is resilience? A review and concept analysis. *Reviews in Clinical Gerontology, 21*, 152–169.

Windle, G., Bennett, K. M., & Noyes, J. (2011). A methodological review of resilience measurement scales. *Health and Quality of Life Outcomes, 9*, 8. https://doi.org/10.1186/1477-7525-9-8

Yates, T. M., Egeland, B., & Sroufe, L. A. (2003). Rethinking resilience: A developmental process perspective. In S. S. Luthar (Ed.), *Resilience and vulnerability: Adaptation in the context of childhood adversities* (pp. 243–266). Cambridge University Press.

Youssef, C. M., & Luthans, F. (2007). Positive organizational behavior in the workplace: The impact of hope, optimism, and resilience. *Journal of Management, 33*, 774–800.

Zhai, X., Ren, L. N., Liu, Y., Liu, C. J., Su, X. G., & Feng, B. E. (2021). Resilience training for nurses: A meta-analysis. *Journal of Hospice & Palliative Nursing, 23*(6), 544–550.

23

Pharmacology for Stress

Philippe Fauquet-Alekhine and Jean-Claude Granry

1 Introduction

This chapter addresses psychopharmacology, namely the pharmacology of so-called higher brain functions, with a focus on treatments for conditions associated with stress, including stress induced by work (Fig. 23.1). It is provided here for information purposes only and is not a substitute for official medical or regulatory body guidelines and documents. A full description of the pharmacological treatment of the stress response may be found in Everly and Lating (2013).

The neuro-psychological manifestations of stress are essentially of two main kinds: (see Chap. 3 of the present book):

- psychological and emotional: anxiety that can go as far as the appearance of anxiety attacks, phobias, depression and/or irritability, sometimes aggressiveness, memory problems, disruption of sleep cycles and difficulty concentrating.

P. Fauquet-Alekhine (✉)
SEBE-Lab, Department of Psychological and Behavioural Science,
London School of Economics and Political Science, London, UK

Laboratory for Research in Science of Energy, Montagret, France

Groupe INTRA Robotics, Avoine, France
e-mail: p.fauquet-alekhine@lse.ac.uk; philippe.fauquet-alekhine@groupe-intra.com

J.-C. Granry
University Hospital, Angers, France

© The Author(s), under exclusive license to Springer Nature Switzerland AG 2023
P. Fauquet-Alekhine, J. Erskine (eds.), *The Palgrave Handbook of Occupational Stress*,
https://doi.org/10.1007/978-3-031-27349-0_23

Fig. 23.1 Stress induced by work

- physiological: headache, dizziness, tremors, muscle fatigue, nausea and diffuse pain.

It is important to note that these signs vary from one individual to another and depend in part on their personal history, the causes of their stress and the treatments already undertaken.

Drug treatment for stress is generally associated with anxiolytic, antidepressant or antipsychotic drugs, which fall under the umbrella of psychotropic drugs (Fig. 23.2). However, even though the clinical signs presented by the patient are temporary and not important, it is possible to consider so-called natural treatments, but always after advice from a health professional (e.g. pharmacist) such as trace elements, homeopathic medicines, magnesium or even extracts of certain plants (hawthorn, valerian). These products have the advantage of not causing side effects at the doses used and reducing certain symptoms such as irritability, sleep disorders or fatigue.

Anxiolytics treat various acute manifestations of anxiety with immediate calming effects but present risks of dependence. Antidepressants also treat anxiety by acting on the patient's mood as a background treatment. Antipsychotics (including neuroleptics) treat certain psychiatric conditions specific to the patient such as psychoses, especially schizophrenia. They may also be offered in the treatment of certain forms of depression.

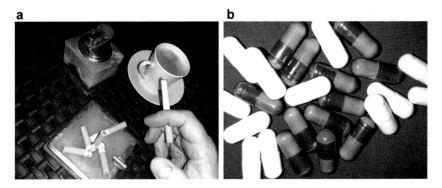

Fig. 23.2 Drugs and stress

These drugs act on brain function according to their modes of action by agonism or antagonism of receptors at synapses or membrane or vesicular transporters.

The administration of such drugs presupposes that psychiatric disorders are first and foremost clearly established. The action of each drug can be associated with dose-response curves from clinical trials, with one curve for each effect. For example, if a substance antagonises N receptors, in theory, N dose-response curves should be available. In addition, these dose-response curves may vary depending on the target organ. The problem with these curves is that they are clinically tested over periods not exceeding several weeks whereas, as presented in Chap. 3, stress-related disorders are sometimes spread over several years. There is therefore a gap between what clinical trials offer and the reality of long-term psychopharmacological treatments. In addition, some psychiatric disorders, such as post-traumatic stress, are associated with multiple symptoms that a single medication will not be able to treat. So, there is a need for a combination. This combination presupposes that it has correctly assessed the possible drug interactions as well as the adverse effects of each of the substances considered for the combination.

The initiation of psychopharmacological treatment can only be carried out as part of a psychotherapeutic accompaniment of the patient. The objective of psychotherapeutic support is to determine the reality of the need for pharmacological treatment, and if such treatment is engaged, to support the patient during treatment by promoting an accurate evaluation of possible clinical changes.

2 Psychotropic Drugs

2.1 Antidepressants

Since the mid-1980s, tricyclic antidepressants (TCA) and monoamine-oxidase inhibitors (MAOI) are no longer the only ones available for the treatment of anxiety. Selective serotonin reuptake inhibitors (SSRI), selective noradrenergic reuptake inhibitors (SNRI), serotonin-norepinephrine reuptake inhibitors (SNRI) and reversible inhibitors of monoamine-oxidase are preferred.

The effectiveness of these substances is described below, and their adverse effects are given in Table 23.1:

- Tricyclic antidepressants, TCA
- Their effectiveness is generally similar from one TCA to another with a greater or lesser sedative effect. It should be noted that associated adverse reactions are an important cause of treatment discontinuation by the patient.
- Monoamine-oxidase inhibitors, MAOI
- Their use is difficult if there is consumption of foods and drinks rich in tyramine (cheese, chocolate, beer etc.) with possible serious complications associated with a rapid and persistent rise in blood pressure, a risk that persists until more than 15 days after stopping treatment. According to Baldwin et al. (2014: 11), MAOI "has proven efficacy in panic disorder and social phobia: but side effects and the need to follow dietary restrictions limit its use, so it should generally be reserved for when patients have not responded to, or proved intolerant of, other treatment approaches."
- Selective serotonin reuptake inhibitors, SSRI
- The efficacy of SSRIs is similar to that of TCAs in major depressive episodes with some clinical superiority for TCAs in melancholic syndrome. Overall, SSRIs are well tolerated compared to TCAs.
- Selective noradrenergic reuptake inhibitors, selective NRI
- By increasing prefrontal noradrenaline and dopamine levels without significant impact on subcortical dopamine levels, they have a real added value for the treatment of negative cognitive symptoms.
- Serotonin-norepinephrine reuptake inhibitors, SNRI
- SNRIs demonstrate better efficacy than SSRIs in several studies (e.g. Papakostas et al., 2007). They reduce the disadvantages of TCAs and maintain their mode of action.
- Reversible inhibitors of monoamine-oxidase
- When they are selective, they are only really effective at doses at which they lose their selectivity.

23 Pharmacology for Stress 489

Table 23.1 Main side effects of antidepressants (HUG, 2015)

	TCA	SSRI	SNRI	SNRI
Digestive system	Dry mouth, constipation	Nausea, vomiting, dyspepsia, diarrhea, anorexia	Dry mouth, constipation, nausea	Dry mouth, nausea, constipation, diarrhea
Central nervous system	Drowsiness, sleep disturbances, tremors, convulsions, myoclonus, cognitive impairment, confusional state, lowering of epileptogenic threshold, possible serotonin syndrome	Drowsiness, dizziness, headache, nervousness, insomnia, restlessness, anxiety	Insomnia, nervousness, restlessness, dizziness	Drowsiness, dizziness, insomnia, nervousness
Cardiovascular system	Orthostatic hypotension, tachycardia, cardiac rhythm and conduction disorders			
Other	Sweating, hot flashes, accommodation problems, urinary retention, weight gain, sexual disorders	Agitation, anxiety, nausea, diarrhea	Sweating, dysuria or delayed urination	Headache, asthenia, sweating, sexual disorders

Antidepressants should only be considered as a second-line treatment in the management of the clinical consequences of stress, when anxiety disorders worsen and alter the daily life of the patient and entourage. These drugs must be prescribed for several months as their action on the symptoms is not immediate. The duration depends on the evolution of clinical signs and therefore on regular medical monitoring. Discontinuation of treatment should be gradual. The risks of interactions with alcohol and other drugs are significant justifying patient information and careful medical vigilance.

2.2 Anxiolytics

Anxiolytics include benzodiazepines and non-benzodiazepine anxiolytics (such as antihistamines, hydroxyzine, beta-blockers).

Benzodiazepines are the most prescribed anxiolytics. They rapidly reduce the physical manifestations of anxiety but should not be prescribed long-term because of the risk of addiction. Monitoring of treatment should be regular by the physician and discontinuation should be gradual due to the risks of withdrawal.

Benzodiazepines (BZD), anxiolytic GABAergic agonists, bind to the GABA-A receptor (gamma-amino-butyric acid-A) and act as positive allosteric modulators. Their effect is sedative, hypnotic, anxiolytic, anticonvulsant, muscle relaxant and amnesiac.

BZDs have good tolerability and a limited number of drug interactions.

Adverse reactions (Table 23.2) are mainly muscle weakness, fatigue, drowsiness, impaired coordination, dizziness, anterograde amnesia (more common at high doses). There are also cases of rare serious side effects such as respiratory depression or coma occurring especially when taking alcoholic substances concomitantly. As there is a dependent effect on BZDs, the discontinuation of BZDs should be gradual.

2.3 Antispychotics

The first antipsychotics, developed in the 50s, are termed "traditional" or "typical" antipsychotics, also known as neuroleptics. The second generation of antipsychotics was developed in the 70s. It is said to be "atypical" antipsychotics.

Antipsychotic adverse effects (Table 23.3) range from relatively minor tolerability issues (e.g. dry mouth, constipation) to life-threatening (e.g. myocarditis). Stroup and Gray (2018) provide a list of side effect for antipsychotic drugs.

Table 23.2 Main adverse reactions of benzodiazepines

	Benzodiazepines (BZD)
Digestive system	Constipation
Central nervous system	Fatigue, drowsiness, sedation, dizziness, loss of balance, amnesia, including anterograde; in high doses: confusion, disorientation
Cardiovascular system	Respiratory problems
Other	

23 Pharmacology for Stress 491

Table 23.3 Main adverse reactions of antispychotics

	Antispychotics
Digestive system	Dry mouth, constipation
Central nervous system	
Cardiovascular system	Hypotension, myocarditis (rare)
Other	

3 Therapeutic Drug Monitoring and Pharmacovigilance

Therapeutic drug monitoring (TDM) (https://medlineplus.gov/lab-tests/therapeutic-drug-monitoring/; Buclin et al., 2020) consists of monitoring drug concentrations in the patient's plasma or serum. These measurements make it possible to know if the dosages are actually in the value ranges for which the best effectiveness of the treatment is usually observed. Each patient reacts differently to a given substance, so TDM can adjust the dosage according to what is being measured. However, they are sensitive to many factors such as gender, age or blood collection schedule.

Plasma concentration-clinical response curves are useful for some antidepressants, but unfortunately useless for benzodiazepines, they are mainly used for the treatment of stress symptoms.

In particular, TDM can be used to monitor:

- the quality of therapeutic benefit,
- adverse effects,
- the adequacy of the dosage and
- drug interactions.

The usual plasma concentration margin values for antidepressants, antipsychotics and mood stabilisers are available in Hiemke et al. (2011).

Substances are also characterised by their elimination half-life period. This is the time after which the substance has lost half of its pharmacological or physiological activity. Almost all of the drug is usually eliminated after five half-lives.

These methods of monitoring the effect of the drug are part of a pharmacovigilance approach. Pharmacovigilance is defined by WHO (2015: 1) as "the science and activities related to the detection, assessment, understanding and prevention of adverse drug effects or any other possible drug-related problems". Adverse drug effects refer to unexpected reactions following normally recommended dosages. These effects vary between patients. A number of risk factors have been identified by Zopf et al. (2008). The classification of Adverse drug effects is available in Edwards and Aronson (2000). Other possible drug-related problems refer to medication errors (unintentional dysfunction in the therapeutic process), deviations in use, therapeutic failures, effects on sensitive patients (pregnant women, children).

4 Dependency

When treatment lasts over time and the effect of the drug substance wears off, dose escalation may become necessary. It can then set in a drug dependence with the disadvantage of associated withdrawal. Discontinuation of treatment therefore implies a transitional phase with gradual reduction of doses.

Drug dependence is therefore a drug addiction that "is defined as the enslavement of a subject to a drug of which he has contracted the habit by a more or less repeated use. This phenomenon may be the consequence of tolerance to the drug (decreased sensitivity to the drug following repeated administration, resulting in the obligation to increase the doses to produce an effect of the same intensity)" (Lapeyre-Mestre, 2013: 66).

The set of symptoms appearing with the gradual or abrupt cessation of a treatment (usually several weeks) is called "antidepressant withdrawal syndrome" or "antidepressant discontinuation syndrome". These symptoms do not necessarily involve dependence and include all symptoms associated with chemical disorders (sometimes severe) that are a normal physiological response of the patient following the cessation of treatment.

5 Rates of Use

Since everyone is affected by stress in everyday life and especially at work, it is interesting to have an overview of what usage rates are in different countries, which necessarily reflects the combination of how populations are affected by stress and how this type of difficulty is treated in the country.

Figure 23.3 shows the rate of variation in antidepressant use for OECD countries with available data between 2010 and 2020 or 2021 for some countries. The rate of variation on Fig. 23.1 is calculated using the 2010 value as a basis. With the exception of France and Denmark, the rate of variation shows a continuous upward trend for all countries over the period under review. The plot concerning the consumption of anxiolytics for the same countries and

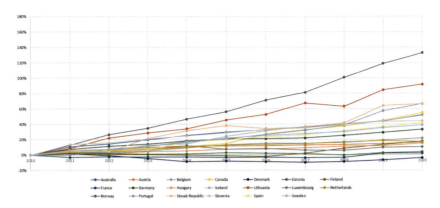

Fig. 23.3 Rate of variation of antidepressant consumption compared to 2010 based on defined daily dosage per 1000 inhabitants per day (available data for OECD countries) from 2010 to 2020. (Source: https://stats.oecd.org/; Files in: health/Pharmaceutical Market/Pharmaceutical consumption)

over the same period indicates a gradual reduction in consumption ranging from −8% (for Portugal) to −56% (for Australia and Denmark) except for the Slovak Republic and Spain whose rates are increasing. A zoom over the period 2018–2021 (the period concerned by the COVID-19 pandemic) for the countries for which data are available (Fig. 23.4) indicates a growth in antidepressant consumption only for Estonia and Portugal. The opposite is observed for the consumption of anxiolytics over this period (Fig. 23.5) since most countries for which data are available show a steady growth except for Canada, Portugal and Sweden.

However, these data must be supplemented by the consumption of antidepressants in absolute values based on defined daily dosage per 1000 inhabitants per day. Figure 23.6 shows an intercomparison for OECD countries over three periods, 2010, 2015 and 2020. Figure 23.7 does the same for anxiolytics.

Figures 23.6 and 23.7 show that the ranking of countries does not change over time: the highest consumers remain the highest consumers and vice versa. Regarding the consumption of antidepressants, the countries of the North and the Anglo-Saxon countries generally have the highest values; at the opposite, their ranking relative to the consumption of anxiolytics places them lower than the other countries on the scale (see Table 23.4). Conversely, the countries at the top of the ranking for the consumption of anxiolytics are mostly at the bottom of the ranking for the consumption of antidepressants. There are, however, exceptions such as the Netherlands and Italy which are at the bottom of both rankings.

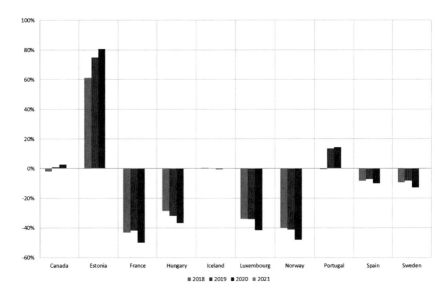

Fig. 23.4 Variation of the rate of antidepressant consumption based on defined daily dosage per 1000 inhabitants per day (available data for OECD countries) from 2018 to 2021. (Source: https://stats.oecd.org/; Files in: health/Pharmaceutical Market/Pharmaceutical consumption)

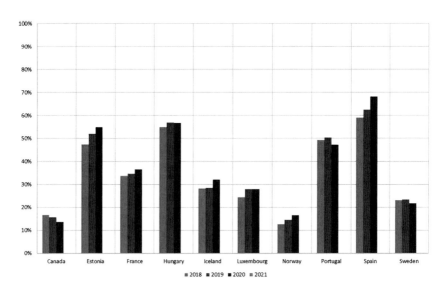

Fig. 23.5 Variation of the rate of anxiolytic consumption based on defined daily dosage per 1000 inhabitants per day (available data for OECD countries) from 2018 to 2021. (Source: https://stats.oecd.org/; Files in: health/Pharmaceutical Market/Pharmaceutical consumption)

23 Pharmacology for Stress 495

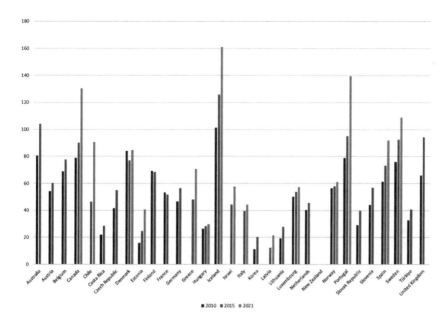

Fig. 23.6 Antidepressant consumption—defined daily dosage per 1000 inhabitants per day for OECD countries (2010–2015–2021). (Source: https://stats.oecd.org/; Files in: health/Pharmaceutical Market/Pharmaceutical consumption)

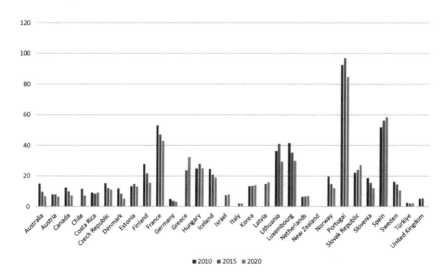

Fig. 23.7 Anxiolytic consumption—defined daily dosage per 1000 inhabitants per day for OECD countries (2010–2015–2021). (Source: https://stats.oecd.org/; Files in: health/Pharmaceutical Market/Pharmaceutical consumption)

Table 23.4 Ranking of countries regarding their consumption of antidepressants and anxiolytics, from highest to lowest values

Antidepressant consumption ranking (+ to -)	Anxiolytic consumption ranking (+ to -)
Iceland	Spain
Australia	France
United Kingdom	Lithuania
Canada	Luxembourg
Sweden	Slovak Republic
Spain	Greece
Finland	Finland
Denmark	Iceland
Greece	Slovenia
Czech Republic	Norway
Slovenia	Estonia
Austria	Latvia
Germany	Sweden
Norway	Korea
Israel	Czech Republic
Luxembourg	Canada
France	Australia
Turkey	Costa Rica
Slovak Republic	Denmark
Netherlands	Austria
Italy	Israel
Costa Rica	Netherlands
Estonia	United Kingdom
Lithuania	Germany
Korea	Türkiye
Latvia	Italy

Source: https://stats.oecd.org/; Files in: health/Pharmaceutical Market/Pharmaceutical consumption

Several factors can contribute to this significant consumption of psychotropic drugs. Estrela et al. (2020: 8) propose the following hypothesis for Portugal that can probably be generalised to other countries: "This phenomenon could be explained by several factors: the increased prevalence of common mental disorders, antidepressant prescription over non-pharmacological therapies, growing access to antidepressants or low investment in therapeutic innovation".

6   Conclusion

Psychopharmacology may be necessary depending on the circumstances but have the disadvantages of generating more or less serious adverse physiological effects and sometimes creating a dependency that can be difficult to manage.

Thus, it is above all necessary to prefer the psychological approach and, only in case of difficulties, to integrate the psychopharmacological approach while keeping the perspective of the possible need for psychological support for withdrawal. It is fundamental to keep in mind that the initiation of psychopharmacological treatment can only be achieved within the framework of psychotherapeutic accompaniment of the patient.

Website to Check
In French: https://pharmacomedicale.org/medicaments/par-specialites/category/neurologie-psychiatrie

References

Baldwin, D. S., Anderson, I. M., Nutt, D. J., Allgulander, C., Bandelow, B., den Boer, J. A., et al. (2014). Evidence-based pharmacological treatment of anxiety disorders, post-traumatic stress disorder and obsessive-compulsive disorder: A revision of the 2005 guidelines from the British Association for Psychopharmacology. *Journal of Psychopharmacology, 28*(5), 403–439.

Buclin, T., Thoma, Y., Widmer, N., André, P., Guidi, M., Csajka, C., & Decosterd, L. A. (2020). The steps to therapeutic drug monitoring: A structured approach illustrated with imatinib. *Frontiers in Pharmacology, 11*, 177.

Edwards, I. R., & Aronson, J. K. (2000). Adverse drug reactions: Definitions, diagnosis, and management. *The Lancet, 356*(9237), 1255–1259.

Estrela, M., Herdeiro, M. T., Ferreira, P. L., & Roque, F. (2020). The use of antidepressants, anxiolytics, sedatives and hypnotics in Europe: Focusing on mental health care in Portugal and prescribing in older patients. *International Journal of Environmental Research and Public Health, 17*(22), 8612.

Everly, G. S., & Lating, J. M. (2013). *A clinical guide to the treatment of the human stress response* (4th ed.). Springer.

Hiemke, C., Baumann, P., Bergemann, N., Conca, A., Dietmaier, O., Egberts, K., et al. (2011). AGNP consensus guidelines for therapeutic drug monitoring in psychiatry: Update 2011. *Pharmacopsychiatry, 21*(06), 195–235.

HUG. (2015). *Guide pour l'emploi des psychotropes d'usage courant.* Hôpitaux Universitaires.

Lapeyre-Mestre, M. (2013). Addiction médicamenteuse: quelles données pour évaluer et prévenir ? *Psychotropes, 19*, 65–80.

Papakostas, G. I., Thase, M. E., Fava, M., Nelson, J. C., & Shelton, R. C. (2007). Are antidepressant drugs that combine serotonergic and noradrenergic mechanisms of action more effective than the selective serotonin reuptake inhibitors in treating major depressive disorder? A meta-analysis of studies of newer agents. *Biological Psychiatry, 62*(11), 1217–1227.

Stroup, T. S., & Gray, N. (2018). Management of common adverse effects of antipsychotic medications. *World Psychiatry, 17*(3), 341–356.

WHO. (2015). *WHO pharmacovigilance indicators: A practical manual for the assessment of pharmacovigilance systems.* World Health Organization.

Zopf, Y., Rabe, C., Neubert, A., Hahn, E. G., & Dormann, H. (2008). Risk factors associated with adverse drug reactions following hospital admission. *Drug Safety, 31*(9), 789–798.

24

Conclusion

James Erskine and Philippe Fauquet-Alekhine

As we reach the end of this work, it is timely to synthesise the learning into a coherent overall whole. In our attempts to provide an overview, we feel a framework is needed that captures the overall value and necessity of the work, and one that demonstrates the impact of stress via a tangible sense of the pain and human misery that stress at work often leaves in its wake.

The early chapters of this work focus on conceptualising and defining stress from multiple perspectives (the physiological, psychological and behavioural). What contextualises all these approaches is that stress is routed in the human emotion of overwhelm, a feeling that one is not up to the task and that the consequences of this deficiency will be negative. What is also clear from the early chapters is that this can lead to real physical compromise in a biological sense, beyond mere psychology and behaviour. Chapters also introduce how work on animal models add to our knowledge and introduces the notion of

J. Erskine (✉)
Institute for Medical and Biomedical Sciences, St George's University of London, London, UK
e-mail: jerskine@sgul.ac.uk

P. Fauquet-Alekhine
SEBE-Lab, Department of Psychological and Behavioural Science, London School of Economics and Political Science, London, UK

Laboratory for Research in Science of Energy, Montagret, France

Groupe INTRA Robotics, Avoine, France
e-mail: p.fauquet-alekhine@lse.ac.uk; philippe.fauquet-alekhine@groupe-intra.com

© The Author(s), under exclusive license to Springer Nature Switzerland AG 2023
P. Fauquet-Alekhine, J. Erskine (eds.), *The Palgrave Handbook of Occupational Stress*,
https://doi.org/10.1007/978-3-031-27349-0_24

sex differences in response to stress, that have multiple implications for organisations and humans.

Critical chapters are presented on the measurement of stress. These chapters go beyond the usual reviewing and articulate how to conduct behavioural assessments and simulations of stress situations which have high ecological validity, and are often omitted from traditional treatments of the area. Chapters are presented on experience sampling, which again collect data on the individuals state in the context of their ongoing life rather than retrospective accounts of potentially misremembered prior experience. This discussion leads into chapters conceptualising psychosocial risks in the workplace. This treatment is crucial, as it leads directly into notions that if one can mitigate risk factors at work, one can ultimately reduce the burden of disease and pain downstream. Chapters discuss how to measure risk factors and critically how to present these graphically to management in a way that saves time and should motivate prophylactic actions.

What seems lacking is an ethos that ties these chapters together. From a clinical perspective, we would say that the latent ethos concerns care. One must care sufficiently, a priori, in order to see stress as an issue that requires intervention. Furthermore, one must develop ways of measuring and defining stress with a critical eye on care, always remembering the benefits to come if one can, through wise interventions, simultaneously increase productivity while reducing the economic and personal costs of human misery arising from stress.

Chapters also discuss how leadership and management styles, and ways of being can themselves directly and indirectly contribute to increased or decreased stress depending on the style and approach of the leader. This is a frequently omitted area of work despite a wealth of data supporting its usefulness. Once again, the missing factor appears to be a crucial attitude of care for one's staff and a motive to prevent costs (in all senses). If only from the productivity loss perspective, it seems curious that this has been slow to be enacted and, in many cases, required the prompting of government and legal legislation.

This work also covers practical ways to reduce risks and personal interventions that individuals can employ to reduce the impact of stress in their lives. Thus, chapters appear on resilience and selection of employees that are more stress resilient in the first place.

For a scientific and rigorous work, such as this book, it seems slightly ironic that the glue that cements its import is a variable as empirically vague as care. Be that as it may, it is now crucial that we find the will to care about staff and the impacts of stress. We must care as managers, as individuals, and form companies that embody an ethos of care in order to avoid a future replete with a tide of human compromise in body, mind and spirit.

It is our sincere hope that collectively we can develop this spirit and spread it with genuine and authentic dedication to a prosperous future where individuals can enjoy their work without suffering unintended consequences.

Index[1]

NUMBERS AND SYMBOLS

3-D space model, 26, 27, 40, 441
3-Level qualitative scale, 275, 276, 283, 285, 291

A

Absenteeism, v, 147, 221, 228, 229, 236–237, 239, 241, 242, 244, 257, 378, 379, 383, 384
ACTH, *see* Adreno-corticotropic hormones
Acute stress, 27, 28, 33, 35–37, 47, 52, 84–87, 103, 105–109, 125, 144, 201, 270, 271, 273–282, 284, 289, 295, 438–442, 445, 448, 449
Adaptive logic, 300
Adjustment reaction, 300
Adrenaline, 8, 30, 32, 34–37
Adrenergic axis, 30–33
Adreno-corticotropic hormones (ACTH), 34

Adverse reactions, 488, 490, 491
Aggressiveness, 231, 441, 485
Air Force, 302, 403, 442
Airplane pilot, 72, 287
Alcohol, 15, 18, 49–51, 138, 333, 353–355, 462, 489
Allostasis, 13–15, 31, 31n2, 48
Alpha-amylase, 66, 79–82, 390
Amygdala, 31, 32, 34, 35, 49, 54, 56
Analysis of the demand, 177, 178, 180, 186, 188
Analyst's posture, 152–155
Anesthesiologist, 270, 273, 282–284, 286, 296
Animal models, vi, 2, 9, 11, 47–57, 499
ANS, *see* Autonomic Nervous System
Antidepressant consumption, 493–495
Antidepressants, 450, 486, 488–489, 491–493, 496
Antipsychotics, 486, 490, 491

---

[1] Note: Page numbers followed by 'n' refer to notes.

© The Author(s), under exclusive license to Springer Nature Switzerland AG 2023
P. Fauquet-Alekhine, J. Erskine (eds.), *The Palgrave Handbook of Occupational Stress*,
https://doi.org/10.1007/978-3-031-27349-0

504   **Index**

Anxiety, v, 10, 11, 13, 15, 40, 47, 49, 51–54, 105, 124, 128, 137, 138, 146, 170, 172, 265, 306, 311, 330, 342, 343, 347, 349, 350, 361–363, 377, 378, 382–384, 389, 393, 396–398, 401, 405, 406, 442, 446, 447, 461, 462, 464–466, 470, 485, 486, 488–490
Anxiolytic consumption, 494, 495
Anxiolytics, 486, 490, 492, 493, 496
Appraisal of Life Events Scale (ALES), 106, 110, 111, 283, 284, 286
Appraisal of stress, 106, 118–119
Architecture based/environment based, 391–392
Authentic leadership, 223, 225–227, 233, 234, 242, 259
Autonomic Nervous System (ANS), 31–35, 79, 80, 117
Autonomy, 146, 153, 170, 186, 211, 214, 228, 230, 233, 239, 258, 261, 381, 394, 409, 473

B

Benzodiazepines, 490, 491
Blood pressure, 66, 72–75, 85, 391, 393, 444, 446, 488
Boosting breathing, 443
Brain, 14, 15, 17, 29, 31, 32, 35, 36, 41, 48–50, 54, 56, 445, 485, 487
Burnout, 350, 359, 379–381

C

Categorisation, 156, 164, 165, 167–174, 178, 194, 195, 202, 207, 208, 211–212, 217, 278–280
Categorisation consistency, 208, 212–215
CBRN, 291–294

Central Nervous System (CNS), 29, 48, 458
Charismatic leadership, 224, 226, 232
Chronic psychosocial stress, 13, 15–17
Chronic stress, 2, 15, 27, 28, 36, 47, 51–57, 66, 84, 118, 143, 144, 146, 438, 439, 446
CNS, see Central Nervous System
Coefficient of stress, 68
Cognitive behaviour therapy (CBT), 358, 387, 397, 402, 405, 409, 470
Cognitive Behavioural Therapy, 387
Concept of stress, 8, 10, 19, 456
Conflicts, 9, 38–40, 138, 146, 168, 171, 173, 174, 186, 211, 231, 232, 239, 243, 244, 260, 264, 280, 323, 324, 359, 381
Confucianism, 324
Consumption of antidepressants, 493, 496
Consumption of anxiolytics, 492, 493
Continuous improvement model, 162
Coping, vi, 10, 14, 27, 41, 48, 49, 118, 230, 234, 301, 306, 307, 310, 312, 323, 325, 332–334, 343, 347, 348, 350, 353, 359, 360, 363, 365, 376, 380, 385, 402, 405, 406, 410, 460–463, 466, 467, 473
COPSOQ, 111, 200
Corticosterone, 50, 51
Corticotropic axis, 30, 31, 33–35
Corticotropin-releasing hormone (CRH), 9, 34, 36, 39
Cortisol, 9, 14, 18, 33–39, 50, 66, 81–85, 123, 124, 127, 390, 391, 446
Covid-19/COVID-19, 138, 169, 261, 262, 265, 329, 342, 347–349, 351, 357, 361, 365, 380, 382, 384, 397, 399, 405, 406, 493

CRH, *see* Corticotropin-
releasing hormone
Crisis, 98, 138, 227, 261, 262, 282,
438–442, 449
Crisis management, 439–442
Cross-cultural, 3, 321–334
Culture, 48, 138, 173, 233, 235, 258,
278, 322–334, 344, 354, 355,
385, 400, 405, 407, 449,
458, 461
Cynicism, 16, 143, 237, 360, 380
Cytokine, 35, 36, 66, 84–85

D

Dance based intervention, 393
Danger, 30, 31, 291, 295, 299, 314
Demand, 10–12, 14, 25, 26, 28, 65,
97, 102, 104, 125, 129,
144–146, 160, 163, 169, 170,
172, 177, 178, 180, 181, 186,
188–190, 199, 200, 222, 230,
232, 233, 240, 242, 287, 306,
311, 313, 332, 337, 352, 359,
381, 384, 396, 404, 469,
472, 473
Dependency, 492, 496
Depression, v, 11, 14, 16, 18, 19, 28,
36, 40, 47, 51–54, 105, 125,
128, 137, 265, 306, 311, 313,
342, 343, 347–350, 356, 359,
377, 378, 383, 384, 386, 387,
389, 395–398, 401, 405, 406,
461–464, 466, 467, 485,
486, 490
Detrimental leadership, 242–244,
258, 265
Diaphragmatic breathing, 444
Digital interventions, 387, 394–398,
407, 409
Digitalisation, 259, 260, 382–385
Disability, 16, 364, 378, 379, 398
Discomfort, 26, 66, 169,
277, 437

Distress, 9, 70, 107, 108, 123, 127,
332, 348–350, 357, 364, 384,
386, 389, 403, 406
DNA, 18
Drugs, 3, 18, 47, 51, 53, 138, 353,
354, 406, 462, 486–492, 496
dependence, 492
treatment, 486

E

Education based interventions, 389
Effort-Reward Imbalance (ERI), 111,
145, 176, 199, 202
Electrodermal activity, 77
Emotional exhaustion, 16, 237, 239,
240, 350, 380, 389
Emotional loneliness, 356
Emotional regulation strategies, 234,
306, 442
Emotion regulation, 307, 311, 442–443
Employee assistance programs, 260,
385, 399
Energizing exhalation, 443
Engagement, 198, 226, 228, 232–236,
238, 239, 242–244, 258, 287,
356, 382–384, 394–398, 402,
404, 458, 463, 465, 470
Epigenetic, 17–19, 40–41
Epinephrine, 30, 32
Episodic acute stress, 27
Episodic stress, 28
Ethical considerations, 56–57, 265
Ethics, vi, 67, 85, 87, 110, 139, 154,
155, 160, 181, 183, 184, 235,
293–296, 313
Eustress, 9, 222, 347, 375, 456
Evaluation report, 2, 140, 160, 167,
168, 178, 180, 185, 186, 191
Exercise based interventions, 389–390
Experience Sampling Method (ESM),
97, 117–130
External consultant, 151, 152, 155,
163, 183

506 **Index**

F

Family, v, 39, 41, 138, 274, 275, 302, 322, 327–330, 348, 351, 352, 356, 357, 456, 459
Family sphere, 329
Feedback, 74, 157, 160, 167, 174, 179, 185, 190–192, 362, 363, 396, 401
Fighter pilot, 81, 270, 287–288, 295, 313
Fight or flight, 31, 35, 37, 117, 438
Financial issues, 327
Firefighter, 239, 272, 299, 442, 466

G

Galvanic skin response (GSR), 78
GAS, *see* General Adaptation Syndrome
General Adaptation Syndrome (GAS), 8, 25, 438, 439
Glucocorticoids, 55
Gratitude journaling, 463
Greenspace/nature-based interventions, 390–391

H

Half-life period, 491
Harassment, 148, 171, 173, 244, 264, 280, 355, 364, 381, 456
Heart rate (HR), 26, 29, 66–72, 75, 79, 85, 86, 108, 123, 281, 282, 391, 441, 444, 446
Heart rate variability (HRV), 66, 70–72, 75, 76, 79, 85, 281
Hemodynamic, 73
High-risk, 12, 299–314, 330, 350, 450
Hippocampus, 12, 31, 36, 49, 54, 55
Homeostasis, 8, 13–15, 19, 31, 31n1, 31n2, 34, 37, 41, 48, 49
HPA, *see* Hypothalamic-pituitary-adrenal
HR, *see* Heart rate
HRV, *see* Heart rate variability

Hypodynamia, 12
Hypophysis, 31, 34
Hypothalamic-pituitary-adrenal (HPA) system, 9, 10, 17, 30, 35, 36, 117
Hypothalamus, 9, 30, 31, 34, 36, 82

I

Immune system, 15–17, 36
Impact of event scale, 208
Information meeting, 152, 158, 177, 181, 182, 187, 188
Internal consultant, 151, 152, 154–155, 162
Internal dialogue, 443, 446–448
International Classification of Diseases (ICD-10), 119n1
International Classification of Diseases (ICD-11), 16, 142, 143, 380
Interview groups, 174, 175, 180–193, 197
Interviews, 38, 72, 98, 100, 106, 140, 158, 160, 167, 168, 176, 177, 179–188, 191, 193, 292, 302–308, 310–312

J

Job Content Questionnaire(JCQ), 102, 103, 111, 176, 199
Job insecurity, 102, 145, 174, 199, 200, 381
Job satisfaction, 226, 228–230, 232–237, 243, 244, 351, 383, 392
Job Stress Survey (JSS), 103, 111, 199, 201, 208–212, 214–217

L

Laissez-faire leadership, 227, 236, 242–244, 260
Leader-member exchange (LMX), 222, 224, 226, 229, 259

Leadership, 221–245, 258–265, 284, 361, 362, 386, 400, 402, 472–474, 500
Leadership styles, 221–245, 257–265, 461
Locus coeruleus, 31, 32
Loneliness, 125, 352, 356–357, 360, 406
LSD, *see* Lysergic acid diethylamide
Lysergic acid diethylamide (LSD), 354

M

Management's reluctance, 190
Maslach burnout inventory, 342
Mental health, 12, 13, 15, 16, 18, 19, 40, 120, 138, 140, 141, 231, 243, 260, 348–357, 359, 360, 365, 376–381, 383–386, 389, 390, 392, 394–402, 404–409, 456, 461, 462, 465, 467, 470
Mental rehearsal, 447–448
Mindfulness, 261, 358, 363, 380, 384–386, 388–389, 397, 398, 401, 402, 405, 409, 462, 464, 465, 468, 470
Mindfulness-Based Intervention, 388–389
Momentary stress measures, 122–126
Music based interventions, 392–393

N

NASA Task Load Index, 104, 111
National Institute for Occupational Safety and Health (NIOSH), 111, 202, 204
Negative leadership, 244
Norepinephrine, 31, 32, 55, 56
Nuclear, 49, 81, 108, 140, 151, 191, 270, 272, 284–286, 289, 295, 296, 438, 440, 442

O

Occupational training, 269–296, 350
O*NET taxonomy, 301
Optimal level of analysis, 159–160
Organisation level interventions, 394, 399

P

Pandemic, 138, 169, 261, 262, 265, 329, 330, 342–344, 347–352, 357, 358, 361, 380, 382, 384, 397, 399, 405, 406, 493
Panic, 441, 444, 488
Parasympathetic, 30, 33, 71, 79, 444, 446
Paraventericular nucleus (PVN), 49
Participatory approach, 159
Partner relationship, 327
Perceived Stress Scale (PSS), 10, 105, 106, 111, 124, 330
Performance, 3, 8, 12, 28, 37, 52, 53, 86, 87, 104, 145, 147, 148, 202, 222, 223, 225–228, 231, 233, 234, 239–242, 244, 466–468
Peritraumatic Distress Inventory (PDI), 107, 110, 111
Pharmacology, 3, 485–497
Pituitary gland, 30, 31, 34, 82
Positive leadership, 222–225, 227, 228, 230, 231, 233–235, 237, 240, 241, 244, 245, 258–260, 263, 265
Post-traumatic stress disorder (PTSD), 15, 38, 47, 51, 107, 108, 119, 119n1, 396, 405, 439, 461
Power nap, 449–450
Prevention, 147, 376, 378, 379, 385, 399–407, 410, 464, 467, 491
Prevention measures, 375–410

508 **Index**

Private sphere, 143, 344
Probability, 17, 70, 71, 73, 140, 141, 143, 447
Productivity, 7, 12, 138, 221, 228, 229, 231, 236, 238, 240–242, 244, 245, 257, 258, 260, 261, 265, 359, 377, 379, 380, 391, 399, 402, 410, 471, 473, 500
Professional sector, 337–345
Professional sphere, 138, 168, 169, 174
Progressive muscle relaxation, 393, 446, 447, 463
Protective factors, 300, 359, 392, 400, 406, 458–460
Psychiatric disorders, 16, 487
Psychological discomfort, 437
Psychopharmacology, 120, 485, 496
Psychosocial disorders (PSD), 3, 138, 140–144, 146, 156, 158
Psychosocial risks (PSR), 2, 3, 29, 42, 137–148, 151, 162, 164, 165, 167–193, 197–205, 207–218, 376, 500
Psychosocial stress, 12, 13
Psychosocial Stress Model (PSM), 26
PTSD, *see* Post-traumatic stress disorder

Q

Questionnaire, 2, 65, 85, 87, 98–112, 119–125, 140, 157, 160, 167, 168, 174–180, 188–189, 193, 197–205, 207–218, 230, 238, 284, 286, 295, 302, 325, 330

R

Recreational activities, 384
Reflex adjustment signal-sign, 448
Relaxation based interventions, 393

Relaxing breathing, 444
Resilience, 3, 19, 54, 86, 128, 261, 263, 300, 301, 313, 314, 347–366, 382, 383, 386–388, 392, 399–401, 403, 405, 406, 409, 410, 455–474, 500
Resilience training, 260, 261, 264, 388, 401–403, 406, 407, 451, 461, 463–468, 470, 471
Resistance, 8, 27, 87, 299, 302, 304, 310, 313, 439
Respiratory frequency, 66, 75–77, 85
Restitution/validation, 99, 103, 105–107, 121, 158, 160, 181–186, 190, 191, 200, 201, 334
Retrospective stress, 119, 126–127
Robot, 72, 86, 289–295
Robotics, 72, 86, 87, 151, 289, 292, 295
Rodents, 18, 48, 50–54, 57

S

Salivary alpha-amylase (sAA), 66, 79–82, 84, 85
Salivary cortisol, 81–85, 124, 390
SAS, *see* Sympatho-adrenal system
Schizophrenia, 70, 486
Self-assessment of stress, 98, 100–102, 109, 110
Self-confidence, 146, 301, 360, 362, 447
Self-efficacy, 230, 238, 240, 263, 301, 314, 324, 466
Self-esteem, 7, 124, 146, 300, 314, 360, 361, 447, 459
Shift work, 168, 169, 380, 381
Simulation, vi, 83, 270–273, 278, 280–282, 284–286, 288, 289, 291, 293–296, 500

Index **509**

Simulator, 68, 72, 81, 83, 270, 271, 273, 282, 283, 287, 288, 291, 295, 308
Skin conductance response (SCR), 77, 78
Skin resistivity or conductance, 66, 77–79, 85
Social isolation, 145, 146, 348, 352, 356–358, 360, 400
Social loneliness, 356
Social Readjustment Rating Scale (SRRS), 99, 322, 325–328, 330, 331, 334
Sociocultural, 324, 440
Sociotropic, 300
Somatoform disorder, 438
SPEAC, *see* Square of PErceived ACtion model
Square breathing, 445–446
Square of PErceived ACtion model (SPEAC), 39, 40
SRRS, *see* Social Readjustment Rating Scale
State-Trait Anxiety Inventory (STAI), 105, 111
Statistical test, 176, 178, 207, 208, 212, 213
Stimulating breathing, 443–444
Strategic leadership, 262
Stress 3-D space model, 26, 27, 40, 441
Stress adjustment, 299–314
Stress assessment, 2, 98, 99, 102, 105–107, 117–130
Stress episode, 35–37, 68, 70, 73–75, 77, 79, 81, 82, 84, 85, 104, 105
Stressful episode, 72, 450
Stress management, 144, 261, 270, 273, 281, 288, 295, 308, 384, 386, 388, 397, 402, 403, 405, 407, 437–451, 463, 465, 467

Stress-test, 26, 82, 86, 281
Students, 3, 16, 81, 109, 232, 239, 274–277, 284, 296, 323, 342, 347–366, 382, 384, 386, 397, 398, 405, 442, 463, 464
Suicide, 19, 41, 138, 146, 349, 380, 397
Supportive relationships, 469
Survey, v, 137, 157, 189, 201, 207, 241, 324, 338, 339, 342–344, 348, 349, 353, 354, 356, 406, 463
Sympathoadrenal medullary activity (SAM), 79
Sympatho-adrenal system (SAS), 9

T

Taylorism, 20
Techniques for optimizing potential, 448
Thalamus, 31, 32, 34
Therapeutic drug monitoring, 491–492
Tonometric, 73
Training, 3, 53, 138, 139, 191, 202, 260–262, 264, 269–296, 301, 310, 314, 323, 348, 350, 365, 381–383, 385, 388, 389, 394, 401–403, 405–407, 442, 448, 450, 451, 461, 463–468, 470–472, 474
Transactional model, 10, 25, 26, 65, 97, 273, 276, 306
Transformational leadership, 221, 222, 224–226, 229–233, 235, 236, 238, 240–242, 245, 259, 260, 263–265, 472
Traumatic event, 107–109, 111, 119, 439, 456, 457
Traumatic stress, 27, 35, 405

510   Index

U

UCS, *see* Unpredictable chronic stress
Unemployment, 11, 377
Unit of analysis, 159, 160, 168,
      176–190, 192, 208, 212, 215
Unpredictable chronic stress (UCS), 52

V

VAKOG, 277, 278, 284, 286
Violence, 47, 138, 146, 148, 170, 171,
      380, 382, 439
Visualizing results, 207–218

W

Wellbeing, 158, 221, 222, 228, 229,
      245, 257–259, 265, 306, 338,
      347–366, 380, 390, 392, 401,
      405, 406, 450, 455,
      456, 462–470
Workload, 8, 12, 104, 105,
      111, 118, 163, 168, 172,
      173, 175, 190, 230, 232, 239,
      261, 263, 278, 285, 288, 299,
      339, 380, 381, 383, 394, 402,
      404, 410, 439, 461,
      469, 471–473

Printed in the United States
by Baker & Taylor Publisher Services